The Kaiser

THE KAISER
and His Times

by MICHAEL BALFOUR

Professor of European History
University of East Anglia, Norwich

With an Afterword

The Norton Library
W · W · NORTON & COMPANY · INC ·
NEW YORK

Books That Live
The Norton imprint on a book means that in the publisher's
estimation it is a book not for a single season but for the years.
W. W. Norton & Company, Inc.

Library of Congress Cataloging in Publication Data

Balfour, Michael Leonard Graham, 1908–
   The Kaiser and his times.

  (The Norton library)
  Bibliography: p.
  1. Wilhelm II, German Emperor, 1859–1941. I. Title.
[DD229.B26 1972]   943.08'4'0924
[B]   72-6600
ISBN 0-393-00661-1

PRINTED IN THE UNITED STATES OF AMERICA

1 2 3 4 5 6 7 8 9 0

72-11330

Preface

'Political problems never reach tidy mathematical conclusions enabling us to draw up a balance sheet. Instead, they arise, have their day and yield place to other historical problems. This is the course of organic development.'[1]

S O SPOKE BISMARCK in 1881. There could scarcely be any more striking confirmation of his views than the contrast between the problems occupying statesmen when the present century opened and those occupying them today. But what Bismarck omitted to say (though certainly seeing) was that the political problems of the past leave consequences behind them. The whole range of circumstances leading to the war of 1914–18 and the way in which it was fought go far to explain the nature of the settlement made when it finished. Out of that settlement grew, by another process of organic development, the world of the 1930's and the war of 1939–45 which in turn did so much to shape our world today. Moreover in a wider sense the war of 1914–18 was an early symptom of a developing world process which we today can see in better perspective, the beginning of the end of the hegemony of Western Europe.

This must be the justification for a new biography of Kaiser William II, that complex and disputed character who occupied such a central position in the three decades before 1918. Nobody of course would want either to write or to read a mere chronicle of what the Kaiser said or did. There would not be much more justification for a study confined to analysing his character. The historian must rather seek to show how that character came to be what it was, how a man of such a character came to hold a key post, and what were the main consequences of his holding it. This involves setting the Kaiser in the context of German history and against his family background. Believing profoundly as I do that an individual can only be properly understood in the light of his surroundings, I make no apology whatever for the number of pages which the reader will have to cover before he comes to any effective mention of the ostensible subject!

I have hoped to interest not only scholars and students but also those who want to understand how the world they live in has come about. To this end, I have swept details of sources and their interpretation into an Appendix with which the ordinary reader need not bother; I ought however to warn him that my versions of some episodes are open to argument. I have tried to include enough background facts to make the Kaiser's actions intelligible without perpetual recourse to textbooks; on the other hand, I have occasionally omitted to explain trivial comments which may interest the informed without being essential to the novice. But it has not been my purpose to write another history of European diplomacy, or of the First World War or of German political parties. The kind of book which I had in mind would have lost much of its point if it had grown too long, yet the volume of material available, even from printed sources, meant that it could only be kept short by rigorous selection and compression. This also decided me against any attempt at tapping fresh documentary sources which in the time at my disposal (for the book has been written as a leisure occupation) could only have been fragmentary and haphazard. At the same time I have tried to avoid making the book so compressed as to be unreadable. The inevitable result has been a series of compromises; I shall be content if each of my readers thinks that some of them are justified.

I have for convenience used the word 'Kaiser' only in relation to William II. For convenience also I have sometimes (but not always) talked of 'Austria' when accuracy required 'Austria-Hungary'. I have tried to remember that the proper appellation of our islands is 'Britain' though the fact that most Europeans talk of them as 'England' has involved me in some inconsistency. I have adopted Pareto's term 'élite' as the handiest label for describing the German ruling classes or 'Establishment', and I have used the word 'culture' to denote not merely the intellectual and artistic manifestations of life in a society but the whole range of that life.

My first thanks must be to my publisher and one-time pupil, John Howard, for suggesting the subject to me, lending an ear at all times to my problems and offering me much sound advice. Sir John Wheeler-Bennett not only encouraged me to tackle a subject which should have been his, but gave me both material and counsel. Duncan Wilson and George Allen increased my already great debts to them by reading the book in typescript and making a number of valuable comments. My wife helped me in many ways, particularly in constructing the index of names and in reading proofs. I benefited not only from conversation with Dr. Eugen Rosenstock-Huessey but also from his uncanny gift of tracking down unsuspected material for other people's work. I am indebted for help on individual points to Dr. H. V. Dicks, Mr. C. Hamilton Ellis, Mrs. W. Jackson, Dr. Heinz Koeppler, Miss J. M. Maton, Mr. M. Neven du Mont, Sir Harold Nicolson, the late Sir Victor Schuster, Mrs. N. Taylor and Sir Anthony Wagner. Finally it gives me pleasure to record the interest and encouragement shown by my friends Count Helmuth von Moltke and Baron Wolfgang von Marschall.

M. L. G. B.

Contents

I   THE HISTORICAL BACKGROUND: 400 B.C.–A.D. 1880   1

II   THE BACKGROUND TO ANGLO–GERMAN RELATIONS:
     TRADE AND COLONIES   39

III   THE FAMILY BACKGROUND   56

IV   EARLY LIFE   73

V   ACCESSION TO POWER   105

VI   THE NEW MASTER   138

VII   THE NEW COURSE   167

VIII   THE CLIMACTERIC   187

IX   NIGHTMARE BECOMES REALITY   241

X   THE SHADOWS DEEPEN   303

XI   A WHIRLWIND TO BE REAPED   356

XII   OUT TO GRASS   413

XIII   THE FRONTIERS OF MORALITY   421

Family Tree of the Kaiser   436

Appendix I: A Statistical Comparison between the Economies
          of the United Kingdom and Germany, 1870–
          1914   437

Appendix II: Strength of Parties in the *Reichstag*   447

Appendix III: Notes on Sources   448

Appendix IV: Biographical Index of Persons Mentioned   487

Subject Index   519

Afterword to the Norton Library Edition   525

Illustrations

THE KAISER   *Frontispiece*
Historisches Bildarchiv Lolo Handke

Following page 260

THE KAISER AS A BOY WITH HIS MOTHER
Historisches Bildarchiv Lolo Handke. Caption: Bülow, *Memoirs
'03–'09*, p. 410

DR. GEORGE HINZPETER, 1869
Ullstein Bilderdienst. Captions: Müller, *The Kaiser and his Court*,
19–iv–18; Eulenberg, *Aus 50 Fahren*, II, p. 231

KAISERIN AUGUSTA VICTORIA ('DONA')
Radio Times Picture Library

FOUR GENERATIONS
Süddeutsche Zeitung

THE KAISER AND BISMARCK
Ullstein Bilderdienst. Caption: Schiffer, *Ein Leben für den Liberalismus*, p. 143

THE KAISER IN SCOTTISH DRESS
Süddeutsche Zeitung. Caption: Lee, *King Edward VII*, I, p. 478

ON AND OFF PARADE
*Historisches Bildarchiv Lolo Handke.*Caption:Eckardstein,*Lebenserinnerungen*, I, 240

IN FANCY DRESS AS THE GREAT ELECTOR
Historisches Bildarchiv Lolo Handke. Caption: Hegermann-Lindencrone, *The Sunny Side of Diplomatic Life*, p. 313

AT SWINEMÜNDE
Historisches Bildarchiv Lolo Handke

'THE KAISER SIMPLY CANNOT DO WITHOUT FEMININE
SYMPATHY AND UNDERSTANDING'
Ullstein Bilderdienst. Caption: *Princess Daisy of Pless*, by Herself,
p. 225

THE KAISER AND 'THE DWARF'
Süddeutsche Zeitung

EARLY MORNING ON THE *HOHENZOLLERN*
Ullstein Bilderdienst. Caption: Eulenburg, *Aus 50 Jahren*, II, p. 110

INSPECTING EXCAVATIONS AT CORFU
Ullstein Bilderdienst. Caption: Spitzemberg, *Tagebuch*, p. 528

STATUARY GROUP AT ALTONA STATION
Deutsche Presse Agentur

'PEOPLES OF EUROPE, PROTECT YOUR MOST SACRED
        POSSESSIONS'
Ullstein Bilderdienst

THE KAISER AT TANGIER
Ullstein Bilderdienst. Caption: *Grosse Politik*, XIX, 6237

THE KAISER IN RUSSIAN UNIFORM
Ullstein Bilderdienst. Caption: Hegermann-Lindencrone, p. 302

PRINCE VON BÜLOW
Ullstein Bilderdienst. Caption: Rogge, *Holstein und Herden*, p. 12

AT WINDSOR WITH KING EDWARD AND THE DUKE OF
        CONNAUGHT
Ullstein Bilderdienst. Caption: Remark made by the Kaiser to Sir
John Wheeler-Bennett in 1939

LEAVING ENGLAND AFTER KING EDWARD'S FUNERAL
Ullstein Bilderdienst

THE KAISER WITH ADMIRALS VON TIRPITZ AND VON
        HOLTZENDORFF
Süddeutsche Zeitung

THE KAISER WITH BETHMANN HOLLWEG
Ullstein Bilderdienst

THE SUPREME WAR LORD
Caption: Hegermann-Lindencrone, p. 397

THE KAISER WITH HINDENBURG
Historisches Bildarchiv Lolo Handke

THE KAISER WITH HINDENBURG AND LUDENDORFF
Ullstein Bilderdienst. Caption: Wheeler-Bennett, *Hindenburg*, p. 137

THE SQUIRE OF DOORN
Ullstein Bilderdienst

'Not dry reports only, please, but now
and then a funny story.'

The Kaiser to Baron von Lyncker, 1908

CHAPTER I

The Historical Background: 400 B.C.–A.D. 1880

a. *The Earliest Times*

THAT THE HISTORIES of countries differ according to their circumstances is a truth which will be as readily acknowledged as it is repeatedly forgotten. The story of Germany's Second *Reich* under its third Emperor may only be a phase in the secular process by which human development, after 'taking off' on the western coasts of Europe, is winging its way to the ends of the earth. But Germany is neither on the western coasts of Europe nor in Central Africa and the manifold implications of this fact need to be outlined before the consequences can be appreciated.

An initial question is why their character as Germans should have been the crucial distinguishing badge on which in the nineteenth century a number of frustrated people living in Central Europe found it natural to base their claim for closer political association. How did it come about that they possessed the common badge, yet lacked a common government?

When history dawns in the Iron Age, almost all the area now described as Germany seems to have been inhabited by Celts, and it was only east of the River Weser and towards the base of the peninsula now called Denmark that tribes of a different culture were to be found, one of which called itself German and another Teuton. The shifting circumstances of supply and demand forced upon these groups, as upon most primitive peoples, the character of intermittent excursionists, and it was one such trip which in 102 B.C. brought a party of Teutons to Aix-en-Provence and to defeat at the hands of the Roman general, Marius. Gradually, about the second century B.C., the whole group shifted southwards and westwards; there were more frequent forays down to and across the Rhine. The victims of these raids rewarded the prominent part which the Germans must have assumed in them by applying the name indiscriminately to anyone east of the river— the first of many occasions on which the destiny of the Germans was shaped without their consent by the opinion of others!

Tacitus defined 'Germania' as the area between, on the one hand, Gaul and Rhaetia (Switzerland), from which it was separated by the Rhine and the Danube, and, on the other, the Sarmatians and Dacians, from whom it was separated by mountains and mutual terror. But the two Roman provinces of Germania lay outside this area and were hardly inhabited by 'Germans' at all. Much of modern Germany and most of the people who were to settle there never came under Roman law or absorbed Roman culture. That this made them different from other West Europeans is easy to see; how great that difference was is harder to say. The general difficulties of distinguishing one group of the area's inhabitants from another has not been assisted by the enthusiasms of later historians and their consequent tendency to describe any tribe defeated by the Romans as 'Celtic' and any victorious tribe as 'Germanic'. The necessary effort to trace the origins of later nomenclatures can have devastating effects upon our ability to understand past ages if it leads us to assume that terms which only became distinguished afterwards had a separate significance from the outset. The chieftain Arminius (not to beg the issue by calling him Hermann) defeated the Roman Varus in A.D. 9 at the battle of the 'Teutonic Wood' (*Teutoburgerwald*). But he himself belonged to the Cherusci, as did Charlemagne to the Franks; both would have been highly unlikely to admit without protest to being called either 'Teuton' or 'German'!

As the Roman Empire was declining, a further ethnic explosion occurred, and in the fourth and fifth centuries A.D. Germanic tribes (i.e. the Germani or tribes akin to them) swarmed out of Scandinavia, Germany, and the regions beyond the Elbe into central and western Europe, the Balkans, Italy and the Iberian Peninsula. The Franks (or 'free men'), a name which had come into use in the third century A.D. for a group of Rhenish tribes, went to France, the Lombards to Italy, the Visigoths to Spain. In the new surroundings their characteristics gradually altered. Today's 'Germany' was peopled by the Bavarians, Swabians (or Alemanni), Thuringians, Franconians, Frisians, Saxons, and

Lorrainers, loose groupings without any effective political link or sense of cohesion between one another. With language, the story seems to have been somewhat the same, though in the absence of written records, much has to be conjecture. The various tribes all appear to have spoken dialects of a single basic tongue (which suggests a common origin even further back). But where the invaders settled in Roman provinces, Latinized variants developed. Then in about the sixth century an adjective derived from the root 'thiod' or 'people' began to be applied to the vernacular speech of the groups remaining between the Rhine and Elbe. The Latin form of this adjective was *theodisca*, the old High German *diutisk*, whence it gradually developed into *diutsch* and so into the term by which the people we call 'Germans' actually describe themselves.

In about the eighth century, this vernacular language began to be written, and it was at the same time that the seven tribal duchies began to have cohesion imposed upon them by coming under the Emperor of the Franks. When after Charlemagne's death in 814 this Empire fell apart, the eastern section remained united under the Frankish King Louis, who actually described himself as 'Germanicus'. It is with the Treaty of Verdun in 843 which established his kingdom and which (to remedy the fact that Franks and Theodisci could no longer understand one another) had to be drafted in both languages, that what we can now recognize to have been 'German' history properly begins. The habit of cohesion so developed that in 911 the seven tribes, to avoid being ruled by any more Franks, agreed to elect Duke Conrad of Franconia as their King, and within a decade we find his realm being described as *regnum teutonicorum*—the Kingdom of the Teutons. In the course of the next century the name Teutonici rapidly became used as the collective noun describing the inhabitants.

b. *The Middle Ages*

Up to this point, and indeed for another century, the history of 'Germany' did not differ radically from that of areas further west. It was the story of the consolidation of loose tribal groupings under the central domination of strong and predatory kings. Not for the last time did blood and iron forge unity. Indeed, the process was so successful that the consciousness of common destiny with which

the government imbued its population never became quite effaced
and so proved a historical factor of decisive importance. 'By 1075
Germany had far outstripped France and England . . . and was
already on the path leading to more modern forms of government. . . . Had this success proved durable, it is scarcely doubtful
that Henry IV (1056–1106) would have created a great German
state coeval with Norman England and Philip Augustus.'[1]

One of the causes of this success proved its undoing. For the
election of Otto, King of the Germans, as King also of the Romans
in 942, and thus as successor to the Emperors (though the actual
title Roman Emperor is not found till later), not only added to his
prestige but gave him the valuable support of the Church. Many
bishops and abbots in Germany and Northern Italy were virtually
officials of the royal household, and it was the Emperor's attempt to
dictate who should become Archbishop of Milan that precipitated
the conflict with the Papacy. The challenge which Pope Hildebrand offered to Henry IV may in the long run have served the
cause of liberty and pure religion, but it quickly disrupted the
development of Germany. The imperial energies which might
have gone to consolidating the central government were diverted
to undermining the Papal opposition, while the Church turned
from a reinforcement into an ubiquitous focus of disaffection.
Moreover, by challenging the principle of hereditary succession to
the imperial throne, and giving the right of election to a number of
subordinate princes (Electors), the Popes not only decentralized
ultimate authority *de jure*, but opened the door *de facto* to a long
and debilitating process of bartering and disputed successions.
One—though only one—of the reasons drawing the Emperors into
the south became the need to get help against their northern vassals.
Great Emperors like Frederick Barbarossa (1152–90) may have
temporarily restored the position and thereby aroused among their
subjects a loyalty which, by lingering long in memory, acted as a
further unifying factor. But henceforward an uninhibited co-
operation between Empire and Papacy was out of the question,
while the task of ruling Germany was recurrently interrupted by
plunges into the complexities of Mediterranean politics. As the
Kaiser once said, the later medieval Emperors were drawn south
in order to maintain intact their world-wide title and forgot about
Germany's existence.[2]

Meanwhile in another direction there began in the thirteenth century a process which was to prove equally significant. When, a thousand years earlier, the German tribes had moved west and south, the gap left behind east of the Elbe had been filled by Slavonic groups. These peoples, who in one or two places even infiltrated west of the Elbe, remained little affected in religion, society and farming methods by Mediterranean culture. As Central Germany developed, the Christian duty of converting the heathen on the east combined with a desire to get the land put to better use. It is interesting to speculate on what changes might have resulted if the vigour devoted to this work had been applied to consolidating a central German government. But as that vigour was equally likely to have been employed on rebellion against that government, there is no adequate reason to regret that the colonists succeeded.

In Bohemia and Silesia the operation of conversion and colonization went ahead with relative ease. In many parts of eastern Europe, German-speaking settlers were welcome for their skills as traders and craftsmen; by the nineteenth century it was only a small exaggeration to say that one could travel by ox-cart from the Baltic to the Black Sea and stop each night in a German village. But further north the Prussians, a Slavonic people akin to the Latvians and Lithuanians, offered the fiercest resistance. A prominent part in subduing them was played by the Teutonic Knights, an order originally formed to free the Holy Land from the infidel, which after the Fourth Crusade decided to seek other areas for applying the techniques of the Church Militant. Their first start, Transylvania, proved abortive but they then moved on, in 1225, to North East Germany and, by fifty years of bitter struggle, succeeded in imposing on the Prussians not merely German habits but even German names. Nor was it only in Prussia that original inhabitants became Germanized. A parallel assimilation was achieved widely in the conquered territories, thereby complicating the task of anyone who seeks to judge to which race the lands should properly belong. It was in the course of this process that the Emperor Conrad III bestowed upon an Ascanian called Albert the Bear (1100–70) a new fortress area in Brandenburg and that as a result peasants from the west were encouraged to settle in the swamps surrounding the village of Berlin.

Further west, the resources which were needed to sustain the Emperor's title steadily passed from its holders to their nominal vassals until the only hope of getting its responsibilities discharged lay in assigning it to someone who already possessed in his own right—or his wife's—the money and lands needed for the task. Such a man would assume the title to further the interests of his dynasty and their possessions—though whether the influence brought by being Emperor outweighed the concessions needed in order to become it must often have been a nice calculation. This is the explanation of the links between the Habsburgs and the Empire which grew steadily closer until in 1438 the family succeeded in appropriating the post as an heirloom. Yet many of the lands from which they drew their strength were not inhabited by Germans at all (a state of affairs to be aggravated by the seventeenth-century victories of Prince Eugen). Though in their hands the Empire regained a good part of its strength and dignity, the dignity was not an exclusively German symbol and the strength was often exerted for non-German ends. Moreover, the degree of Habsburg control over the princes ruling in Germany remained limited.

In the two centuries after the relations between the Emperor and his Electors had been formalized by the Golden Bull of 1356, the princes consolidated their position and did much to re-establish order in Germany. All strove to introduce primogeniture and the indivisibility of their lands; to replace local assemblies by Estates-General representative of the whole people and meeting only when summoned (usually to authorize taxation); and to create orderly finances based upon the taxes thus obtained. Especially prominent in this respect was the Hohenzollern family who had for generations held an imperial post in Nuremberg until, in 1415, the Emperor Sigismund made his friend, Frederick of Hohenzollern, Elector of Brandenburg; fifty-eight years later Frederick's son Albrecht Achilles promulgated a law regulating the family inheritances and estates.*

At the end of the Middle Ages Germany, the land of the *Deutsch*, was an idea rather than a political reality. Possibly it was a dawning awareness of this and the resulting sense of frustration which produced in the fifteenth century the first wave of interest in the distinctive features of German culture. Historical studies flourished as never before; several of the first books to be printed were

* For dates of these and other persons mentioned in the book, see Appendix IV.

concerned with the German past. This was the century which created the myth of Barbarossa sleeping in his cave on the way to Berchtesgaden, a common-enough form of folk legend but significant in that it projected its believers forward from an unsatisfactory present to a future revival of greatness. This was also the time that the words 'of the German nation' were added to the title of 'Holy Roman Emperor'. A new form of language began to spread from beyond the Elbe where settlers from varied parts of the country had been forced by circumstances to fuse their dialects. This new form of German found its way into Luther's Bible which thereby assumed the function, performed elsewhere by the central administration, of establishing a standard speech—like the King's English—familiar to (though not necessarily practised by) the whole country.

c. *The Reformation and Religious Wars*

The Reformation itself was a symptom of malaise, projecting on to the venal and decadent leaders of the Catholic Church responsibility for the weakness and misgovernment of which Germans were so conscious. It has been described as 'Germany's belated revenge for the continuous thwarting of her destinies by the Papacy from the eleventh century onwards'.[3] Luther, who appealed to the 'Christian nobility of the German nation', seems first to have thought in terms of an independent German Church. But the Reformation, though sparked off by dissatisfaction with Germany's troubles, ended by aggravating them. For the absence of a dominating political authority meant that, once religious controversy was introduced, there was no effective way of settling it. Differences of view on topics which men considered vital to their souls' salvation fanned the flames of ordinary rivalry between states. Questions of abstruse theology, such as the relations between the various persons of the Trinity, were discussed with an intensity of passion reminiscent of the early Christian Church. A Professor of Divinity on one occasion asked to be relieved of his post since its duties involved the writing of so many controversial pamphlets that his eyesight was failing.[4] As the ideals which had originated the Reformation proved impossible of attainment and lost force, men began to concentrate more and more upon achieving salvation by adherence to the pure message of orthodox doctrine. In a country where religion could vary with the local

ruler, fanaticism bred of disillusion spelt a peculiarly virulent form
of civil war. It was no accident that in Germany the Wars of
Religion lasted as long as they did, reduced the population from
sixteen to six million and when they ended in 1648 left the country
divided into 234 territorial units.

The subsequent history of Germany has been dominated by the
fact that during the Middle Ages the process of political consolidation was not carried through. Consequently, whereas in
western Europe the process of secularization known as the Reformation strengthened the power of the central royal governments, in
the lands inhabited by Germans it had a disintegrating effect.
Britain and France anyhow possessed certain inherent natural
advantages which Germany lacked—a more equable climate, more
clearly defined boundaries, a position athwart the new trade routes.
But the factors which gave Britain her dominating advantage, and
made her the scene of that technological break-through known as
the 'Industrial Revolution', derived from the achievements of the
Normans, Plantagenets and early Tudors. The three main spurs
underlying that 'Revolution' are accumulation of capital (with
institutions for transferring it from savers to worth-while spend-
ers), technical invention (which presupposes the accumulation of
knowledge and is particularly important in its application of
power to communications) and population pressure. The vital
precondition for these three developments is stable and effective
government with all that this can bestow in the way of security,
peace, and a clear, reliable legal system. The accidents, or if one
prefers, the destiny of history placed Britain in a specially favourable position for establishing such government and its accom-
paniments. Their progressively accelerating development involved
an early swelling in the numbers of town-dwelling merchants and
technicians, a class of men well above subsistence level with their
own individualistic culture. This in turn meant that the crucial
conflict between a monarchy tending to absolutism and a bourgeoisie bearing within it the seeds of the popular State was in
Britain fought at a relatively early stage and settled decisively in
favour of the popular side. This shift of power intensified the
awareness of common involvement which had been growing under
a relatively enlightened royal government since medieval days;
the resulting social cohesion (or to use a simpler term, patriotism)
considerably increased the international effectiveness of the State.

True, the power of the King was for a time replaced by that of an oligarchy. But the oligarchy was never a closed one, owed much of its resources to its connection with commerce, and never wholly lost the spark of the liberal creed. When the social transformation wrought by the Industrial Revolution began to gather way, there were within the ruling élite enough believers in the principle of liberty to provide a focus for the dissatisfied and to offer what proved to be a justified hope that the necessary adjustments could be made by reform from within rather than by revolution from without.

In Germany, by contrast, the preconditions for these developments were lacking. The development of the new trade routes, which brought so much stimulus to Britain, had turned Germany into an economic backwater just at the moment when the middle classes 'might have been expected to become the dominating political force, as they were already the dominating economic force, in central Europe'.[5] Lives and property were notoriously insecure, justice was hard to be had, the population fell instead of rising, trade languished and with it the trading classes. Awareness of common interest, a sense of being master of one's own fate, belief in ability to control one's environment were all absent. While Britain was entering on the most exciting period in its history and expanding all over the world, Germany was at best stagnating. The consequences have been far-reaching.

d. *The Eighteenth Century*

Germany took over a century to recover from the Thirty Years War (1618–48). During this period foreign, and particularly French, interference was endemic in politics and Italian influence dominant in culture. It was the period of the despotic ruler, supported by a mercenary standing army, a necessary episode in the rebuilding of the social fabric but hardly an inspiring one. Prominent among the matters decided by a ruler were the religious views of his subjects. The strife which had resulted from allowing religion to influence politics was stilled by leaving belief to depend on the accident of State membership. But this solution increased the difference between the various parts of Germany. In the north and east where the Protestants dominated, religion was restricted to the individual's personal relationship with his God and discouraged from influencing men's relations with one another. The

result was personal piety rather than Christian action, an atmosphere more stimulating to musicians than to social reformers.
In the south and west, Catholicism re-established its hold, aided
by the fidelity of the Habsburgs to the Roman faith and by the
anxiety of the trading cities, fighting for life against the shift of
traffic to the North Sea and Atlantic, to maintain at all costs
their links with the Mediterranean. These parts of Germany
were thereby brought within the orbit of the Counter-Reformation
as this movement spread from Spain and Italy through Catholic
Europe, with 'baroque' as its distinctive art form.

With the major exception of Prussia, none of the German states
had a sufficient record of success to inspire its subjects (most of
whom were, anyhow, excluded from any share in the government)
with any strong feelings of pride or loyalty. The middle classes
remained weak and were composed more of officials, teachers and
clergy than of merchants, still less manufacturers. These were,
however, the circles in which the first signs of a national revival
appeared, taking the form of an academic protest against French
cosmopolitanism, a reassertion of the values of German learning
and the German cultural heritage. The common language and the
memory of a common history, the two great legacies of the
medieval Empire to modern Germany, began to be recognized
as the essential links uniting the inhabitants of the many political
pieces into which the area had been splintered. Looking round
the outside world, those inhabitants of the area who had attained
the level of self-consciousness needed for effective reflection saw
that elsewhere links of language and culture had become the
keystones of the most successful political societies yet evolved.
In France and Britain (and to a lesser extent in Spain, Holland
and Scandinavia) national feeling had grown spontaneously as a
loyalty to a homogeneous social structure evolved under a settled
central government, and enjoying the highest level of prosperity
which the world had yet seen. The Germans gradually came to feel
that, since they had a common language and culture, nature had
intended them also to have a common government and that the
lack of it was a major cause of their disadvantages. German
national spirit was thus a much more self-conscious growth,
based on a deliberate imitation of what had happened unintentionally elsewhere, and drawing its emotional drive from dissatisfaction with the contrast. In France and Britain the facts

preceded and formed the basis for theory; in Germany the theory was taken over ready made by the intellectuals in the population, and adopted as an ideal to which the facts must be altered to fit. It was only a step from this position to the feeling that, somehow, destiny had treated Germany badly and that destiny must therefore be coerced. Treitschke was to lament the absence of 'sunshine' in German history and the way in which the German Imperial splendour of the Middle Ages had passed away 'like a Midsummer Night's Dream'.[6]

Meanwhile Prussia had been evolving in a different and in many ways opposite direction from the rest of Germany. The Grand Master of the Teutonic Knights at the time of the Reformation had been a man belonging to a junior branch of the Hohenzollerns. Luther advised him to renounce his vows, abolish the Order, marry and found a dynasty; this comprehensive programme he executed in full. But early in the seventeenth century his line died out and the Prussian Dukedom was merged with the Electorate of Brandenburg. And whereas the peasants needed to colonize the Slav lands had had to be tempted by offers of exceptional freedom from manorial duties, a variety of forces operated as the Middle Ages ended to turn them back into serfs bound to the land. The towns also decayed except for a few ports through which the surplus corn, grown by large-scale farming on the noble estates, was for lack of local demand shipped to the West. The middle classes were conspicuously absent, and for about two centuries the Junker nobility reigned supreme.

With the reign of the Great Elector (1640–88) the Hohenzollerns gradually began to gain the upper hand: in 1701 his son, Frederick, became 'King in Prussia'. The family based themselves upon the principle that a state like theirs, of moderate size, could prosper only if it was strong enough to exploit the divisions between its bigger neighbours. In view of Prussia's limited resources, the essential minimum of strength which this policy implied could be achieved only by the strictest care and control in the use of those resources. The situation was in many ways parallel to that of Soviet Russia in the 1930's and 40's and to the other developing countries in Asia and Africa today. But the basic industry to which the fruits of economy were devoted was war, and since mercenaries were on the whole too expensive, Prussia anticipated revolutionary France by producing a national army. On this Frederick the Great

(1712–86) spent two-thirds of his revenue and in it one-sixth of the adult male population was required to serve; by his death it was practically as big as the French. Its officer corps was imbued with a high sense of duty—'a moral compulsion which forced them, out of respect for themselves and their calling, to bear hardship, danger and death without flinching and without expectation of reward. This feeling of honour, the King believed, could be found only in the feudal nobility, not in other classes and certainly not in the bourgeoisie which was driven by material rather than moral considerations and was too rational in moments of disaster to regard sacrifice as either necessary or commendable'.[7] The civil administration was virtually a branch of the army. The chief officials were drawn from the same noble class and were required to show the same unflinching obedience to their King.

This absolutism was tempered in three ways. First, the government was among the most up-to-date in Europe, inspired by the latest ideas of eighteenth-century rationalism and tolerating almost any religious view. True, the individual was allowed no say in it, but rationalists are always apt to prefer good government to self-government. Secondly, the King accepted the same code as he imposed and regarded himself as the first servant of his people. When the ruler at the top was mediocre, the system worked badly —but the Hohenzollerns managed to produce more above-average rulers than mediocre ones. Finally, Prussia was successful, growing rapidly in size and international standing. The human reluctance to jump off band-wagons is in itself enough to explain why the most autocratic state in Germany was also the only one to succeed in evoking among its subjects a loyalty and sense of national independence.

This was the environment in which was formulated the philosophy of Kant (1724–1804) whom the Kaiser once rightly described as 'our greatest thinker' (though there may be argument as to whether he was justified in going on to add the further epithet, 'clearest').[8] Kant, who had his troubles with the authorities, struggled to reconcile in the circumstances of eighteenth-century Prussia the twin values of freedom and order, just as in the field of knowledge he sought to reconcile freedom with the universal causality which he found in nature. He held that the factor most distinguishing men from animal creation was their intuitive awareness of an inner moral law embodying the spirit of reason.

Human conduct was to be judged not by the nature and consequences of acts but by their underlying motives. An act was moral in proportion as it was motivated by reason; the test of such motivation lay in whether the principle involved in the act could be applied universally. For unless the underlying principle could be so applied, the act itself would not be absolutely disinterested, and this all truly moral acts were required to be. The 'categorical imperative' incumbent on man was always so to act that the action could be taken as the basis of a universal law. Sympathy and compassion were to be excluded as motives of moral action since they confused the application of reason. The starting-point of Kant's own thought may have been his hatred of tyranny. But in the effort to render external tyrants unnecessary, the individual was required to impose on himself an even more rigorous code than the King of Prussia imposed on his subjects. A man could be allowed to be free only if he was completely subjected to an inner control.

With Kant, resistance to the State could still be justified if the state's own principles could be shown to lack universal application. It only remained for the seat of reason to be transferred from the individual conscience to the community, as was done by Hegel (1770–1831), and the world was faced with the paradox that only in obedience to the State could the individual be truly free. It may be that, because in western Europe government was on the whole strong and well-established, political theorists tended to emphasize freedom and individual rights; in central and eastern Europe where the need for strong government was easy to see, they gave priority to order and the rights of the State.

Now the exaltation of individual rights at the expense of government authority clearly leads to selfishness and anarchy, while the exaltation of government authority without regard to the rights of the individual leads to despotism and injustice. The idea of holding the two in balance is more easy to state than to execute. Equilibrium can be achieved verbally by saying that the highest freedom consists in obedience to law as the embodiment of reason, and that social liberty is a constituent of, rather than a check on, the power of the State. But the formula is treacherous (especially when it is expressed in language difficult for the ordinary man to understand) and tends in practical implementation to be given one of two slants. Either existing law is attacked in the name of freedom as a palpably inadequate embodiment of reason. Or else obedience is demanded, in the name of reason, to law equated with the current demands of the government, even where this appears to be at the expense of the individual. Both deviations were to be met in Germany during the nineteenth century. The main stream of thought continually slipped into an uncritical assertion of the rightness of whatever happened to be; the assailants of the *status quo*, handicapped by lack of political experience, carried the demand for liberty to excessive lengths.

e. *The French Revolution and its Consequences*

The Kaiser once spoke of the humiliations which the 'Corsican parvenu'[9] had inflicted on Germany and his complaint illustrates a resentment against France which was widespread in his country throughout the nineteenth century. The French Revolution provided Germany—and indeed the world—with an unprecedented demonstration of what could be achieved by a resolute and fanatical government able to fire its people with enthusiasm and so to mobilize the full resources of the country. In face of this whirlwind, the cosmopolitan rationalism of Goethe's Weimar and the Spartan discipline of Frederick's Potsdam alike proved futile. The result was a wave of romantic dissatisfaction with 'enlightenment' and a widespread (though by no means universal) desire to emulate France in exploiting the national idea for political purposes and securing, if necessary by political concessions, popular support for a war to liberate and even to unify Germany. The revolution must be fought by its own weapons. The problem with which the patriots concerned themselves was how to rouse the population to enthusiasm and evoke a determination which would triumph over all obstacles. The views of Clausewitz, formed at this time, take as starting point the question 'how a community which has rested on a merely cultural basis could be turned into a community with a political will—a self-conscious national state capable of defending itself and keenly concerned about its freedom and external prestige'.[10]

It was as a step towards this end that in the years following defeat at Jena (1806) a thorough overhaul of the Prussian system was put in hand—principally by non-Prussians in the King's service. Outmoded economic restrictions were removed, the towns were given a certain amount of self-government and the serfs were emancipated. The professional standing army, on whose size Napoleon had set a limit, was reorganized and supplemented by a popular short-service 'Home Guard' (*Landwehr*). The beginnings of a General Staff were created. The reformers sought to sacrifice all other values to the re-establishment of Prussia as an independent European Power.

The same atmosphere favoured the development of that emphasis on the individuality of peoples which distinguishes German political thought for the following century. The academic interest in national characteristics was given a political application. This occurred as a reaction against the universalism of the enlightenment, against the domination of France over German affairs and against the Napoleonic attempt to unify Europe. Such a view came more easily to Germans, since the doctrines of natural law with their emphasis on universalism, the intellect and the individual had never enjoyed the same ascendancy in central as in Western Europe.[11] Each people was thought of as a separate entity with distinct characteristics and capacities; the differences were more important than the similarities. Moreover, the State rather than the individual was the embodiment of the national identity and as such the repository of ultimate values. There could be no higher, more universal authority, and the final arbiter between States must therefore be force (though the road to this conclusion was often smoothed by a facile optimism which suggested that States in which the national will rather than the whim of a ruler was sovereign would have the same view of world politics and so live in peace with one another). In this development it was Hegel who was again the key figure.

> 'His political philosophy is the most decisive expression of the intellectual movement which replaced the old connections and ideals of a European universalism with a ruthless individualization of the international scene.'[12]

Hegel, though by birth a Swabian, was a Professor at the University of Berlin, founded in 1812 by William von Humboldt as an integral part of the Prussian revival. In a country where nationalism began as an intellectual exercise, universities have an obvious political role. But Berlin thoroughly deserved its name of the 'First Guards Regiment of Learning'. For this was the intellectual power-house where thinkers such as Hegel, Ranke,

Droysen and Treitschke generated the distinctive and character-istic view of the world which Germany was to offer as its gospel, a coherent and comprehensive alternative to the rational individual-ism stemming from the Graeco-Roman tradition. 'The revival of the German nation did not begin at the altar but in the lecture-room.'[13]

To take the German Humpty-Dumpty completely to pieces again was beyond the power of the Congress of Vienna. The number of individual political units remained reduced to some thirty, and the rulers of Bavaria, Saxony and Wurtemburg were allowed to keep their title of King (Hanover being raised to the same rank). At the last moment Prussia, as a compensation for losing some of her Polish conquests to Russia, was given con-siderable areas of the Rhineland which she did not much want and in which her restrictive methods proved a highly unwelcome contrast to the previous twenty years of French rule. (One result was to bring within her frontiers six million Roman Catholics, one million of whom were Poles.) But the popular movements which had contributed so much to the victory were allowed small share in its fruits. In Prussia the work of the patriots was left half done. The poorer peasants remained economically dependent on the Junkers (landowners) and as the Junkers were still masters of the countryside, the municipal reforms had the effect of widen-ing the gap between town and country. The *Landwehr* remained but was looked at askance by the professional soldiers who were elevated into a closed officer caste with special privileges and its own courts of honour. Nobody could obtain a commission, even from the King, unless he had been educated in a cadet school or, having enlisted as a volunteer, was nominated by his commanding officer. The enthusiasm which had been generated was baulked of fulfilment and a sense of frustration was the inevitable result.

The problem for German nationalists in the years prior to March 1848 was to find a rallying-point. The most obvious step towards providing the German peoples with their own State was to revive the Empire. But even if this had not been formally abolished by Napoleon, it rested in the hands of a dynasty whose interests were only partly German and who had signally failed to rouse a consolidating spirit of loyalty among the miscellaneous peoples inhabiting their domains. Less than a third of the Habsburg

Empire was included in the German Confederation, set up as a loose association in 1815, and of the twelve millions which were so included, almost half were Slavs.[14] Yet the rulers of Austria, though unwilling to risk losing their extra-German interests by taking the lead in unifying the Germans, sensed on the other hand that a united Germany would throw their own power into shadow. Moreover, a true unification of the German people would involve dividing the Habsburgs' German subjects from the non-German ones, and bringing the former alone into the new state. The Habsburgs were therefore as opposed to allowing anyone else to unite Germany as to doing so themselves, a position which they could only hope to maintain as long as German nationalism continued to lack support. The other German princes, except the King of Prussia, were in much the same position. Some, as in Bavaria, had managed to rouse a limited local loyalty but it was not strong enough and their lands were not big enough to provide the basis for a national State. Yet a united Germany must spell the end of their own independence. The most to be hoped for was that their élites would be sufficiently conscious of their own German attributes not to offer intransigent opposition to unity. Prussia was a different matter.

Prussia proper (as distinct from Brandenburg) had lain outside the confines of the Holy Roman Empire. But by 1815 the King of Prussia had acquired so many territories in Germany that German unity was unthinkable without at least his acquiescence. Moreover, in Silesia and the Ruhr those territories happened to include two of the chief sources of Europe's coal. But the leaders of the German national movement, basing themselves on the English and French examples (the only ones available), took it for granted that a national State must have a liberal constitution and therefore associated unification with the establishment of responsible representative government. The demand for this constituted in fact the beginning of pressure to adapt the German political structure not only to the French but also to the Industrial Revolution. The *Zollverein* or Customs Union set up between 1828 and 1835 under Prussian leadership (but excluding Austria) helped to hasten the pace of technological change. But the last parts of Germany to be affected were the core provinces of Prussia east of the Elbe. Here middle-class influence was weak, the ruling elite was formed of landowners and of officers and bureaucrats recruited from the landowning class, and as has been seen the culture which was developing had other roots besides the liberal individualist tradition. Liberalism, so far from attracting the Prussian élite, was anathema to most of them and rather than pay the price of recasting their society in order to become leaders of Germany, they preferred to remain as they were. In any case they were bound to have misgivings about a course which carried a grave risk of collisions with Austria, still the nominal leader of the Germans, and with France, whose place in Europe was bound to be weakened by the rise of a strong, united Germany.

The biggest mistake of the Liberals in the years before 1848 was their failure to realize the importance of having organized force at their command. This was not simply due to lack of practical experience—though they certainly suffered from that. Doctrinaire theories borrowed from England and elsewhere fostered a fear that any army beyond a national militia would menace the liberties of the individual. Accordingly, they not only failed to organize a citizen force which could stand up to the King's army (though this began to happen in Berlin in 1848) but they also failed to provide either Germany or Prussia with resources enabling Austria to be defied. The result was that the democrats were humiliated by the princes at Frankfurt in 1849 and that Prussia was humiliated by Austria in the Olmütz Agreement of 1850. Thereafter, the Liberal cause might well have foundered altogether had not the economic tide been steadily strengthening the middle classes; its adherents were at all events too few to prevail. The historian Sybel wrote in 1863 that

'(the Prussian Ministers) have money and soldiers and an old administrative system with abundant reactionary powers. As for us, we have no material power at all, and thus are nowhere and in no way able to achieve a quick success. . . . You would not find anyone in Prussia who would not consider any thought of violence stupid and criminal since it would be suppressed immediately.'[15]

The groups opposed to the Liberals were neither effete nor incompetent nor half-hearted. They considered themselves to have saved Germany from chaos by their firm stand in 1848–50 and saw no reason why they should not repeat the process on future occasions. Moreover, the middle classes were beginning to doubt their ability to keep a revolution within bounds. For the struggle to break the political power of the landowners had been postponed in Germany to an epoch in which working-class consciousness was beginning to stir. Marx was teaching the proletariat to exploit the bourgeois revolution as a stepping-stone to their own dictatorship. Not for the last time those Germans who wished to put their fellow-countrymen in control of their own destiny shrank from the action needed to do so for fear that, once the impetus was created, it might hurtle beyond the goal. And indeed if the Liberals had been strong enough to put up a fight, the only result might have been a major civil war into which most of Europe would gradually have been drawn with disastrous effects on economic and social development.

Yet a widespread desire for German unity persisted and was reinforced by the example of Italy in 1859. The failure to achieve unity in 1848–50 deepened the sense of frustration among Germans and produced a reaction against what were regarded as the unpractical policies responsible for failure. Many of those reaching manhood between 1850 and 1870 were not only obsessed with the problem of unification but convinced that policies of realism (*Realpolitik*) could alone be expected to overcome the obstacles. Realism entails a hard-headed assessment of values and a readiness to sacrifice to the top priority all those subordinate to it. And whereas after 1806 it had been to liberalism that concessions were called for in the name of nationalism, now they were to be made to conservatism. The primacy which these men and women gave to the advancement of the national cause at the expense, if necessary, of freedom is one of the dominating facts of the next seventy years since this was the generation which was to provide Germany's leaders between 1880 and 1914. The world had to pay a considerable price for the obstinacy which had resisted and thus delayed German unity.

After 1848 all the indications pointed to Prussia as the focus of German unity and to lack of international influence as the price of remaining disunited. But the Prussian élite still feared that a united Germany would mean the ruin of all the things which they valued, while the other states of Germany were too proud of their own identities to accept a merger reducing them to the level of Prussian provinces. Moreover an all-German government, to deserve the name, had to be responsible for the defence and foreign policy of its territories. Yet these two prerogatives and the control thereby ensured over the Kingdom's destinies were precisely what the Prussian élite felt least inclined to surrender. Although a more liberal Ministry was called to power in Prussia in 1858, the history of the next two years showed clearly how deeply rooted the opposition was. The crucial clash came on the question of what form the army was to take and where control of it was to rest. The élite regarded the army as the personal affair of its commander-in-chief, the King, and for that reason resisted the efforts of the Prussian Parliament to regulate expenditure on it or determine the terms of service. Behind the question whether recruits should serve for two years or three, which was the occasion of the showdown, lay the efforts of the King's private advisers, led by the War Minister von Roon, to complete the reversal of the 1806–14 reforms and turn the *Landwehr* into nothing more than the regular army's reserve. 'Previously the military authorities had sought to adapt their organization to the civilian outlook; now they not merely flew in the face of civilian prepossessions but set out to extirpate these by giving the nation systematic military education.'[16] The person least prepared to compromise was King William; he would sooner have abdicated. He dissolved Parliament; the opposition were returned in greater strength, yet still he would not give way. His obstinacy showed signs of shaking the country to its foundation and might well have made his name a stock example of the social damage done by misplaced pertinacity.

From this predicament King William was not only saved but in the short space of eight years raised to the position of German Emperor. The man chiefly responsible for this transformation was, of course, a neurotic genius with a red moustache, called Otto von Bismarck. 'He was the highly educated sophisticated son of a highly educated middle-class mother, masquerading as his slow-witted Junker father and living down his maternal origins by an exaggerated emphasis on the privileges of his paternal class'.[17] He had the insight to recognize that German unity in one form or another was inevitable and that the question facing Prussia was not therefore 'whether' but 'how'. Bent on avoiding the acceptance of someone else's terms, he engineered by a series of improvisations what was in effect the conquest of Germany by Prussia. In the war of 1866, with the help of Moltke's strategic gifts and the remodelled Prussian army, he overcame Austria's opposition to

German unity under Prussian leadership and in the war of 1870 overcame that of France. He further kept these two wars isolated and prevented them from starting a European conflagration. But in addition he led Prussia to a position in which she could no longer refuse to assume the leadership of Germany and in which neither the other princes nor the Liberals could refuse to accept Prussian predominance. The exclusion of the Germans of Austria from the united German State in any case increased the chances of that State being dominated by the Protestant north rather than the Catholic south and this helped to allay Prussian fears. Finally, in the 1866 constitution of the North German Confederation, adapted in 1871 to become that of the German Empire, he evolved a compromise which gave all groups enough of what they wanted to be acceptable to most of them. Yet it is hard to contemplate this epoch-making result without pondering on the turn of chance or fate which provided that, when the man of genius appeared, he did so on the conservative side. If the Liberals had possessed a Bismarck or a Lenin in 1848, how differently the world might have developed! But was the absence of such a man due merely to the accidents of heredity or was there something in the German cultural climate which made it impossible for realists to be Liberals?

f. *The Bismarckian Settlement*

The most obvious of the changes in 1871 was the proclamation of the King of Prussia as German Emperor. This promotion, however, made him only the senior and not the superior of the other German Princes. 'The Emperor is not my Monarch,' said a Wurtemburg politician. 'He is only the Commanding Officer of my Federation. My Monarch is in Stuttgart.'[18] There were indeed those who maintained, with a considerable degree of legal accuracy, that the princes were subordinated to Empire rather than to Emperor, and in particular to the Federal Council or *Bundesrat*. To this body, which deliberated in private, each member government sent a delegation proportionate to its importance. Though all the votes of each delegation counted, each voted as a block (as in the College of Electors for a U.S. President). Of the fifty-eight members, seventeen came from Prussia, six from Bavaria and four each from Saxony and Wurtemburg. As no proposal to change the constitution could go forward if fourteen votes were cast against it, this effectively gave either Prussia or the South German states acting together a guarantee against reforms of which they disapproved. The agreement of the *Bundesrat* was required before legislation could be submitted to the *Reichstag* and it was to be consulted on all important questions of foreign policy including declarations of war.

The intention appears to have been that the *Bundesrat* would become the ruling body of the Empire. If this was so, the intention remained unrealized and the Council steadily lost influence; in 1914 it was not consulted until after war had been declared. Instead the power passed progressively into the hands of its Chairman the Imperial Chancellor who was also, as Minister President of Prussia, the head of the Prussian delegation. There was no Imperial Cabinet in the English sense of the word. The State-Secretaries for Foreign Affairs, the Interior, Finance, Justice, Post Office and (later) the Navy were regarded as mere officials, responsible to the Chancellor. There was no Federal Secretary of War; the Prussian Minister of War acted as chairman of the *Bundesrat* committee on the Armed Forces and appeared in the Federal Parliament to speak on its behalf. This was because the Prussian army remained directly responsible to its King though the troops of certain other areas were embodied in it. The armies of Bavaria, Saxony and Wurtemburg retained varying degrees of independence, though the Emperor could transfer an officer from any of them to the Prussian army regardless of the victim's wishes. The Prussian Houses of Peers and Parliament (*Landtag*) remained unaltered; votes in elections for the latter were given one of three varying weights according to the wealth of the voter, which virtually assured the possessing classes of a majority. The Prussian Ministers sometimes doubled their job with that of the corresponding Imperial State-Secretary (the Chancellor was always Foreign Minister of Prussia, Prussia's 'foreign policy' being confined to her relations with the other states in the Empire).

of Prussia, Prussia's 'foreign policy' being confined to her relations with the other states in the Empire).

On this complex and conservative structure, however, Bismarck, borrowing from the constitutional ideas of 1848, added a lower house (*Reichstag*) elected by universal (male) suffrage. This was something which in 1870 no other State in Europe possessed, and its radicalism alarmed the conservatives, as did the failure to make any distinction between the States in organizing the membership. The *Reichstag*, however, went far to justify the description given to it by the Socialist, William Liebknecht, as 'the fig-leaf of absolutism'. Apart from the fact that throughout virtually the whole of its existence it provided a majority ready to vote for the existing régime, its powers had three fatal flaws. It could not initiate legislation, it did not appoint the Chancellor and at an early date it was compelled to curtail drastically its powers over the financing of defence. The *Reichstag* reflected public opinion and could stop the Government proposals, including those for taxation, from becoming law. But it could not enforce its own wishes. The parties were left free to criticize but given no chance of putting their policies into action. Deputies never became Ministers and indeed membership of the *Reichstag* was by law incompatible with the holding of office; this must have stopped many ambitious, and some able men from seeking election. The *Reichstag* was convened by the Emperor; it had to meet every year and face re-election every third year. The Emperor could dissolve it at any time he chose, provided the *Bundesrat* agreed.*

By these arrangements, Bismarck squared the circle and produced a constitution which managed to present the appearance of being at one and the same time liberal and autocratic, German and Prussian, federal and centralized. But great as Bismarck's genius was, it lay beyond even his power to efface the conflicting forces which had blocked progress. His function was rather the diplomatic one of devising a solution in which they could be induced to work together. But Bismarck had not only to produce a compromise for the moment; he had to provide each interest with some assurance that the situation could not be transformed to its detriment. As with all Federations, his institutions tended to freeze the balance of forces at a particular instant. But political forces spring from human beings and do not admit of being frozen for long. The problem for the future lay in how far the new arrangements were susceptible of being adapted to the growth which was bound to come, especially in a country embarking on the traumatic process of economic 'take-off'.[19] Meanwhile, there were certain aspects which promised trouble.

* The constitution seems to have been partly modelled on that of the Dutch Republic, owing to Bismarck's lifelong friendship with the American historian John Motley who wrote its history.

According to the constitution, 'the Emperor appointed the Imperial officials', including the Chancellor. Their tenure of office therefore depended not upon the confidence of the majority in the *Reichstag* but upon the will—one might almost say, the whim—of the Emperor. *'N'oubliez pas'*, said a shrewd observer, *'que Bismarck est une rose dont l'Empereur est la tige* (stalk)'.[20] Or, as Bismarck himself once said in the *Reichstag*; 'The part of the Minister is merely to execute, to formulate. The royal will is and remains alone decisive.' It is true that another clause in the Constitution required the Chancellor to countersign and take responsibility for all royal decrees and orders which were to be invalid without such confirmation. But, to quote Bismarck again, 'If the Emperor has a Chancellor who feels unable to countersign whatever represents Imperial policy, he can dismiss him any day. The Emperor has a much freer hand than the Chancellor who can take no step without the Imperial sanction'.[21] There was seldom to be any lack of candidates willing to step into a Chancellor's shoes, particularly if it were a question of disagreement with the *Reichstag*. In practice, the principal limitation on the Emperor's freedom proved to be what the public would say if the Chancellor was changed too often. In theory, of course, the *Reichstag* could have forced the hand of the Emperor by refusing to vote for the measures of any Chancellor who was not their own nominee. But the Prussian Parliament had come off worst when it tried in 1863 to withhold taxation until Bismarck cancelled the Army reforms of which it disapproved. Most deputies would anyhow have recoiled from the idea of forcing upon the Emperor a Chancellor of their choosing rather than his own. In this respect German politics were much closer to the Britain of 1760 than to that of 1870. It was regarded as the duty of every loyal subject to lend a respectful ear, if not actually to give his vote, to the man whom the Emperor chose as chief official. To decide who should govern the country was not part of a politician's business.

Dependence on the Emperor was by no means the only problem facing the man who combined the offices of Chancellor and Prussian Minister-President. He had to work at one and the same time with two parliamentary bodies, the Imperial *Reichstag* and the Prussian *Landtag*, each chosen on a very different basis. How could he hope to do this if their political complexions began seriously to diverge? Moreover, although a large part of the

Chancellor's duties related to foreign policy (defined for obvious reasons in the constitution as a federal matter), he had no right of control over the armed forces which reported direct to the Emperor. Orders relating to the army and navy were exempt from the need of bearing the Chancellor's countersignature. In 1859 the then King of Prussia (later to become first Emperor) had said: 'In a monarchy like ours, the military point of view must not be subordinated to the financial and economic, for the European position of the State depends on it.' Von Roon said that his 'Prussian soldier's heart cannot bear the thought of my King and master subordinating his will to that of another'.[22] During the wars of 1866 and 1870 Bismarck, in spite of his readiness to wear a cuirassier's uniform, had experienced great difficulty in gaining access to the plans of the soldiers and ensuring that they were in accord with the requirements of the diplomatic situation. He nevertheless defended the exclusion of the Chancellor from the control of the army and navy on the ground that this might lead to interference by the *Reichstag* in matters of strategy which would be extremely dangerous for national security.[23] Yet if the Chancellor was denied the powers needed to keep military and political policies in tune, the only constitutional possibility of co-ordinating them rested with the Emperor.

Secondly, in external affairs there seemed little prospect of France ever forgiving or forgetting the defeat of 1870 and the loss of Alsace and Lorraine. Even if, in Gambetta's words, they spoke of it never, they thought of it always. The Socialist leaders, Liebknecht and Bebel, with Karl Marx in London, condemned the annexation as a portentous mistake. Bismarck had not wanted to take the French-speaking part of Lorraine but had had his hand forced by the military. He later said it had been his constant endeavour to induce the French to forgive Sedan as after 1815 they had forgiven Waterloo.[24] But the very war which had appeared to him an acceptable, if not indeed a welcome solution to one set of difficulties proved when it was over to have created another set equally intractable. From 1870 onwards Germany had to keep France isolated, and therefore to remain on good terms with everyone else; the alternative was a risk of war on two fronts. Success in this policy was clearly bound up with the interrelations of the remaining Powers; if two were to quarrel, and each to demand Germany's support, the one which considered itself to have been denied that support became at once a potential ally for France. The situation was further complicated by a less obvious result of 1870. The unification of the German people in a single State contained one glaring gap: Prussian and Habsburg opposition to the process had made it impossible to include those Germans living in Austria-Hungary. But the German example inevitably gave a great impetus to the rise of national feeling in eastern Europe. The Habsburgs had failed to rouse in their peoples a specifically Austrian loyalty or obliterate their previous loyalties as Germans, Magyars, Czechs, Poles, Serbs and the like. Any widespread demand for self-government on a national basis was therefore, in the long run, incompatible with the effective functioning and even the very existence of the Austro-Hungarian state. In 1867 the Magyars had secured self-government for Hungary: the prospects of the Austrian Germans being able to keep the upper hand over the Slavs were doubtful. Habsburg weakness and the French desire for revenge were in the long run to prove fatal to the international aspects of the Bismarckian settlement.

Few Germans, however, regarded the foreign threat as the main danger facing the new Empire. This would have been found in the fact that though most of the Germans had been collected together they were still far from being an integrated community. The Empire owed its existence to Prussia and the Prussian army, not to the pressure of public opinion. In the past, centrifugal forces had often proved too strong. Could they be now held in check? Could Prussians and South Germans be induced to work together? Still more, could the loyalty of the workers be won for the existing order of society? The Marxist gospel of a proletarian revolution made this seem improbable. In reality, the danger of any such development occurring was exaggerated. But the words of the popular leaders were more ferocious than their behaviour; Bebel, in 1871, pointed to the Commune as a weak prelude to what would happen some time in Germany. The ruling and possessing classes were thoroughly frightened, especially as industrialization began to gather speed, drawing the population into the towns and adding annually to the workers' numbers. The situation was one which called for flexible institutions and the possibility of growth—yet the circumstances in which the Empire had come about had involved putting the élite in a position where they could veto formal change. It called for a leader who could win the loyalty of the masses by propounding ideas that would catch their imagination. '*Pour chasser les démons,*' said Louis Philippe to Guizot, '*il faudrait un prophète.*'[25] But Bismarck was no prophet, he was a genius at manipulating, with an un-rivalled power of assessing the possible. His contempt for public opinion was shown by his habitual bribery of the press, for which money confiscated from Hanover in 1866 came in very useful. To tell the truth, he was not much interested in thought—his light reading was sentimental French romances and German roman-tics.[26] Bagehot fairly said of him in 1875 that he had 'real inability to measure moral influences as he measures material forces'.[27] The sayings by which he is remembered were apothegms rather than seminal ideas; they illuminated the present rather than the future. This may explain why in his twenty years of rule after 1870 he did little towards solving Germany's internal problems.

g. *German political developments 1870–80*

Just before the Franco-Prussian War broke out, the Vatican Council promulgated the doctrine of Papal infallibility. Rigidly interpreted, this was taken to offer the Pope considerable powers of interference in German internal affairs. Attempts to publish it in south Germany led to a long controversy over the general relations between Church and State in the course of which laws were passed giving the Imperial and Prussian governments wide powers over education, enforcing civil marriage and banning the Jesuits. Bismarck saw in the Catholics, represented in the *Reichstag* by the Centre Party, the allies of those European elements of whom he was most suspicious—the South German opponents of Prussian leadership, the Austrian clericals who resented a German Empire from which Austria was excluded, the French right wing who longed to avenge Sedan, the Poles who threatened Prussian security in the East. Catholic and Papal interference had wrecked German unity in past centuries; was the process to be repeated? The 'campaign for cultural freedom' (*Kulturkampf*), as the anti-Catholic movement was called, was thus a logical continuation of the campaign for a unified and liberal Germany. But many of the staunchest Protestants in Prussia were also conservatives and to them the fact that the *Kulturkampf* was liberal mattered more than that it was anti-Catholic. Their suspicions, which were shared by the Emperor himself, combined with the passive resistance of the Catholics to make the campaign an almost total failure.

By the end of the 70's Bismarck was subject to Conservative pressure from another direction. For many years the bulk of the corn grown on the large landed estates east of the Elbe had been shipped abroad, notably to Britain. But better communications, capital investment outside Europe, steamships made of iron and the opening in 1869 of the Suez Canal were all combining to bring on to European markets, both from other continents and from Russia, grain at prices considerably below the Prussian ones. On the other hand, Germany was now beginning to experience the upward surge of population which accompanied the first wave of industrialization. Consequently, the German home market looked like absorbing all the grain which Germany could grow, provided competitive supplies were kept out. The constitution empowered the Imperial Government to raise revenue only by indirect taxa-tion. Bismarck wanted more money for military and other pur-poses, so that the imposition of a revenue tariff suited his book. Heavy industry was also anxious for protection by tariffs. Imme-diately after 1870 Europe had seen a big wave of investment in productive equipment which had overreached itself; capacity had been installed on a scale which temporarily exceeded demand and this (the basic cause of most nineteenth-century depressions) led to idle resources and price cutting. Given a few more years, accumulating wealth and increasing population would have matched demand once again with supply. But such an analysis of the situation was beyond the vision of contemporary employers; the slack in the economy lent strength to the argument that a country which begins to industrialize after others cannot hope to produce on competitive terms, even in the home market, until enough of the capital cost has been recovered to let prices fall. Free trade was, however, still part of the Liberal creed and since 1870 Bismarck had depended on the Liberals for his majority in the *Reichstag*. A change to protection would involve a political revolution.

Then, in May 1878, a young workman tried to kill the Emperor. Bismarck, who refused to contemplate a preventive war against France, had no parallel inhibitions in home affairs. He introduced into the *Reichstag* a bill placing severe restrictions on the Social Democrats and other left-wing parties. Hardly had the first clause been rejected when a second attempt was made on the Emperor's life. This time Bismarck reacted by holding elections on a programme of tariff reform and repression of socialism. The voting showed a considerable rightwards swing and the laws were passed without much difficulty. How much help the tariffs gave to German industry is a moot point. It certainly flourished in the next few years but the circumstances were such that it would have flourished anyhow. What tariffs did do was to facilitate the price-fixing and market-sharing cartels which began to develop. It was, however, in agriculture that the main effect was felt. The landowners, particularly east of the Elbe, had added to the three-tier franchise another dyke to protect them from the natural course of events. Not only did the German worker have to pay more for his food than he needed to do but the food-producing countries overseas earned less than they might have done, and so had less to spend on the products of German industry. The drift to the towns was reduced and more men were kept employed on the land, where a Prussian ordinance of 1851 forbade them to combine or strike. In fact, the best way of advance for a farmworker was to serve twelve years in the army and then seek employment as a minor official. As most of the officers were drawn from the landowning class and lived on their peasants as well as on their pay, the German military subconscious was inevitably dominated by a farmer-figure.

The end of the 70's also marked a turning point in German foreign policy. Bismarck's fundamental aim being to keep France isolated, he was anxious to avoid friction between the other European powers, and notably between Russia and Austria, for fear that rivalry would lead one of those involved to seek French support. When events likely to cause a clash occurred, as they did in the Balkans after 1875, he did his utmost to mediate in finding a settlement without himself becoming committed. It was for this reason that he allowed the Congress to be held at Berlin in 1878 and there described himself as playing the 'honest broker'. Some Germans, including the Emperor William and his grandson, the Kaiser, considered the Congress a costly mistake and thought that Bismarck should have kept out of the whole business; his fear was that, if he did so, Russia and Austria would go to war, and he would then either have to intervene, or watch Austria be beaten. But the Russians resented Bismarck's refusal to support them against the Austrians and in 1879 the Tsar demanded assurances that this support would not be lacking again. When the demand was backed by a vague threat, Bismarck took alarm. Andrassy, the pro-German Magyar who had for nearly ten years been the Foreign Minister of Austria-Hungary, was on the point of retiring. Before he left Bismarck persuaded him to negotiate a secret treaty by which Germany and Austria-Hungary promised one another mutual aid if either were attacked by Russia, and neutrality if the attack came from any other country. The old Emperor disliked intensely the idea of naming as a possible aggressor the country alongside which he had in his youth defeated Napoleon. Only the insistence of Bismarck induced him to sign the treaty.

Whether Bismarck acted too hastily is a question which can never be finally answered. That Russia seriously contemplated an attack seems hard to believe, yet by committing Germany to one of the two antagonists, he created a permanent possibility of Russia joining with France. From 1879 until his dismissal, Bismarck's main aim abroad was to prevent the possibility becoming a reality, to keep, as he put it, the telegraph wire to St. Petersburg open—an aim in which he was successful. That he should have decided to back Austria against Russia is understandable given the Teuton contempt for the Slav—a contempt with its roots deep in history—and the number of people in Austria who spoke German. But, for all that, Bismarck by this Alliance linked Germany with a Power to which any extension of the principles of national independence would be fatal. Twenty-five years earlier, he had himself said that it would distress him 'if Prussia should seek protection from a possible storm by tying our trim and seaworthy frigate to the worm-eaten and old-fashioned Austrian man-of-war'.[28] Yet this was precisely what he had now done. There was always the danger that Russia, by crossing Austria's path in the Balkans, might incite the latter to attack her. Bismarck said that such a quarrel was of no interest to Germany—'would not be worth the bones of a Pomeranian grenadier'. But the need to prevent Austria from being beaten would arise no matter which country began the war. This dilemma could only be prevented from arising by a close control over Austrian policy. Eternal vigilance by the German Foreign Office was henceforward the insurance premium for grenadiers.

h. *The German Political Scene in 1880*

In the German political spectrum of 1880, the right-hand end was occupied by the *Conservatives*. These were the men who had opposed Bismarck's policy of unification and Prussia's entry into the Empire. Thereafter they had regarded the *Kulturkampf* with the deepest suspicion and been partly responsible for its enforced abandonment. From their own point of view they were perfectly right; whatever chances there may have been of maintaining Prussia's old traditions unchanged in the modern world, they were removed by the absorption into Germany. General Manteuffel, a leading figure in this camp, was gravely disturbed when he heard that the commander of the Cologne garrison was on friendly terms with several local merchants. He called in one of the officer's colleagues who assured him that although the man might go around with civilians, he was not for that reason disloyal. 'Very well,' said Manteuffel. 'Then we can count on him when the shooting begins.'[29] Loyalty to the old order was the keynote of their thinking, and their support for any particular person or organization depended on how far in their view it contributed to this end. Even where the Crown was concerned their attitude is illustrated by the jingle,

> *We put our fate in our monarch's hand*
> *As long as he does what we demand.*

Events were to prove that the implied reservation was no idle threat.

Like the English Tories after 1832, or the French Royalists after 1870, these people were out of step with the way the world was going. Unlike their foreign counterparts, they did not dwindle into political nonentities but found allies. They saw that all the tendencies of the century were likely to reduce their power, but their reaction was to resist rather than to compromise. They realized that the battle they were fighting was a losing one; their minds were therefore dominated by fear and closed to rational argument in case its pursuit should weaken their case. Instead they tended to seek rationalizations of their own prejudices, and in particular decried the values of urban and democratic society. Some of the more efficient had overcapitalized their land to modernize their farming methods and were as a result heavily in debt, vulnerable to economic depressions. The arrival of cheap corn from overseas made all increasingly dependent on State action, and it was natural to wonder how long a class in such a position could hope to dominate society. There were plenty of people ready to argue that the Empire must not be allowed to become a 'benevolent institute for indigent agrarians'. The landowners position was further weakened by the tendency of the German peasants to drift to the towns and be replaced by Poles. All these factors made the Conservatives anxious, and nagging fears made them vehement. Yet they were strongly entrenched not only at court and in the army but also in the higher ranks of the bureaucracy; until 1914 every Prussian Minister of the Interior but one was a Junker and the sole exception belonged to this Party. Wholly Prussian in origin, the Party was reconstituted in 1876 with a view to attracting recruits from elsewhere in Germany. This met with some success but for obvious reasons the focus remained east of the Elbe and there a number of small farmers, peasants and craftsmen were induced to consider their interests best served by voting Conservative.

The *Free Conservatives*, a party formed in 1866, were distinguished primarily by the fact that they accepted the inevitability of industrialization but sought to maintain the old German (or Prussian) principles in the new conditions. Their leaders included von Kardorff, who in 1875 founded the Central Committee of German Industrialists, and von Stumm-Halberg, an industrialist from the Saar who was prepared to rain benefits on his workers provided they did as they were told. The Free Conservatives owed their influence to the standing of their leaders rather than to numbers. Their outlook approached most closely to that of Bismarck himself and they were his steady supporters. In their view the basic Prussian principle of *suum cuique* involved giving to each what he was entitled to and no more; consequently the State alone could have a monopoly of power over the individual. The idea of giving any rights (e.g. of interference with blacklegs) to unions of the workers was abhorrent to them, though they conveniently overlooked the fact that their own associations possessed (and used) such powers. 'The German employers', said the Secretary of one association in 1889, 'will never negotiate with the workers on a basis of equal rights.'[30] While by no means uninterested in the workers' welfare, they were not prepared to encourage self-reliance. This was the spirit in which, in 1881, Bismarck introduced his projects for compulsory insurance (without workers' contributions) against accident and sickness—a piece of legislation which set a European precedent.

The weakness of the outlook was that it expected the workers to be loyal to something in which they had no say and made acceptance of the *status quo* into a test of loyalty. The essence of the popular demand was, however, for a say in national affairs, in other words, responsible government. The grant of this would have led straight to the introduction of equal rights. Realizing that the two went together, the industrial élite were not prepared to grant either. They claimed that government by parties would mean government by material interests and a degree of internal strife which a country like Germany, surrounded by external enemies, could not afford. They failed to see, or at least to admit openly, that the essence of politics is the achievement of compromise between conflicting material interests and that, if the introduction of responsible government was in fact likely to lead to civil war, that was only because they themselves were not ready to let their own material interests take second place. As long as groups in a key position in the State stuck rigidly to this attitude, there was no peaceful way of solving Germany's internal problem, and the adaptation of Germany to the social consequences of industrialization could only be tinkered with, not tackled.

The *National Liberals*, formed in 1866 of Liberals who wanted to support Bismarck in uniting the nation, were the party chiefly favoured by heavy industry, though many of their votes and most of their leaders came from the intellectual and professional classes. The events of 1870–1 satisfied their immediate national aims, but not their liberal ones. The question for the following decades was how far they would remain content with what had been achieved and how far they would insist on pressing ahead. Which of the two adjectives in their title was to be the one that really counted? There were, of course, a number of Germans whose interest in Liberalism had been primarily due to the belief that only in a liberal State could the Germans be united. When Bismarck demonstrated the contrary, they yielded to an uncritical admiration of his achievement and ceased to look for further reform. This tendency was reinforced by that of the possessing classes, especially as their possessions multiplied, to rally to the established order in face of the growing demands of the workers. Just as in England the people who had been Liberal in the 40's and 50's began to shift their allegiance to Disraeli's reformed Conservative Party, so in Germany the rich bourgeoisie began to align themselves with the ruling classes. This process was justified ideologically by the theory that individual personal liberties and local self-government really mattered more than parliamentary and ministerial arrangements. The existence of laws to secure these gave Germany its own form of liberalism. The authoritarian State (*Obrigkeitsstaat*) had been replaced by the State in which law reigned supreme (*Rechtsstaat*), assigning to each citizen his obligations and rights. The truth of this theory was limited: the local self-government accorded by the Prussian laws of 1872 and 1875 did not do much to limit the power of the nobility and bureaucracy. But it all went to build up the thesis of a specifically German solution to the problems presented to Central Europe by the innovations from the West. Other liberals justified inaction by saying that a pause was needed to let the middle classes gain in local government the experience which they so sadly lacked.

The acid test of the National Liberal outlook came in 1878 when Bismarck proposed to introduce tariffs and deprive the Socialists of the right of assembly. In the end this split the party, in accordance with Bismarck's declared intention of squeezing them against the wall until they squealed.[31] In 1880 twenty-eight members of the left wing broke away to form the core of the Progressive Party. The remainder accepted tariffs (which were indeed welcome to the heavy-industrialists in their ranks) and continued to support Bismarck. The differences between themselves and the Free Conservatives faded and they became the two 'Establishment' parties of the Second *Reich*, though occasionally an issue would arise to throw into evidence their differences of origin. The National in the label having triumphed over the Liberal, they became the party of national aggrandizement abroad, the people who talked most about the need for Germany to break through as a world Power. In the years ahead, their ranks were to produce most of the steam behind the Germany navy. The professors and journalists who were so strongly represented among them, instead of realizing how much the victories of 1866 and 1870 owed to superior political dexterity and better military organization, not only invented an erroneous legend that Prussian hegemony had been inevitable all along, but also engaged in a dangerous perversion of logic. They treated the fact of Germany's success as proof that German culture and morals were superior to all others and deduced not merely the possession of a right to dominate but also an assurance that Germany could be confident about victory in future.

As successive generations and social groups among the German middle classes reached maturity, they tended to assimilate themselves to the standards which they found dominant instead of rejecting those standards and creating their own. The institutions of society, notably the student corps and the system of reserve officers, powerfully fostered the tendency. For this, the obsession with national unity and the nervousness with regard to the workers were largely responsible. But the middle classes, in their anxiety to conform, carried their code of conduct to the point of distortion and set up an ideal which asked too much of human nature. The society held up to admiration was essentially masculine, laying exaggerated emphasis on toughness, self-sacrifice and discipline.[32] These qualities, of course, have their place in all realistic philosophies of life. But unless they are balanced by other considerations, they make demands which the majority of individuals are incapable of satisfying. Any society in which they are dominant is likely to be full of tensions, basically due to the fact that a number of its members are aiming at a rigour of conduct which they fear they cannot maintain. This in turn produces frantic attempts to repress the lack of confidence. People force themselves into the attitudes which they believe to be expected of them, and inevitably overact in the process.

Thus, in Germany, tenderness became taboo; charity and tolerance were too easily condemned along with it. Violence was exalted and little awareness shown of its effects on other people. Courage turned into contempt for modesty and common-sense, self-reliance into a disdain for all who did not belong to the warrior caste, discipline into a demand for unquestioning obedience, patriotism into a blazing lust for domination. The law that material resources are useless without the will to use them (enunciated in theory between 1807 and 1813 and exemplified in practice between 1864 and 1870) became a faith that all things are possible to the obstinate. There had, of course, always been a tendency in Prussia to over-emphasize this approach to life, but in the earlier Prussian conditions it had not been inappropriate to landowners still largely feudal in their manner of life. When copied by middle-class businessmen and intellectuals in the middle of ninetenth-century Europe, it not only became a menace to others but completely misled its practitioners about the realities of the world surrounding them. And since tenderness is a natural sentiment, a by-product of its repression was lapses into the other extreme of excessive sentimentality. Moreover, the individual's need to insure against a fear that he would prove inadequate in the moment of crisis helped to reinforce the Prussian dogma about unquestioning obedience to the State. By doing what the government told him, he hoped to reduce the risk that he would let the Fatherland down. Of course this tendency to assimilate and exaggerate was not universal; many Germans approached in varying degrees to a more balanced view of life, while others had enough character to challenge the prevailing standards (though it is significant how many of these went to live abroad). But in contrast to some other countries, they were not numerous or influential enough to affect the mental climate. The easy way out was to look intransigent and of the Germans who took it, probably most voted National Liberal.

The *Progressives* were the reverse side of the medal, the people who refused to sacrifice liberal principles to national interest. From Britain they had derived the principle that the individual should be left to go his own way, free from the interference of State or Church in his private life or business affairs. For the most part their ranks were drawn from intellectuals and small business men, though their leaders were to include the banker George Siemens. Being essentially individualists and men of principle, they were prone to internal dissensions which reduced their political effectiveness. Like the agrarians, though in a different sense, they were people who wanted to put the clock back, overthrow the Empire as Bismarck had created it, and set up instead a constitutional State on the British model. Had they ever obtained a chance to do this, they would have at once come into conflict with all the parties to the right of them who would have been unlikely to confine their opposition to constitutional means. It is most unlikely therefore that they could have succeeded, any more than they were able to succeed between 1848 and 1870. But one of Bismarck's chief bugbears was the thought of an alternative government centring round a Progressive Chancellor which he sought to ridicule by describing as 'The German Gladstone Ministry'.[33] For long they were more inclined to sigh for what was not than to work for aims which were practicable in the context of the Second *Reich*. Only gradually as the century came to a close did this state of affairs begin to change.

The *Centre Party* was that unusual phenomenon for the nineteenth century, a party based on religious principles, being the political organization of the Catholic Church. Though there were considerable numbers of Catholics in Silesia and Posen, the main strength of German Catholicism has always lain in the south and west. The Centre was therefore anti-Prussian and opposed to any further extension of federal power. Believing that a ministry responsible to the *Reichstag* would tend to strengthen that body at the expense of the states, they were suspicious of left-wing proposals for reform. Their Catholic principles made them opposed to Liberalism and individualism but sympathetic to corporate ideas. Bismarck could not bring himself to trust an organization which looked up to an authority outside Germany and even after 1880, as the anti-Catholic laws were allowed gradually to fall out of use, was reluctant to depend for his majority on Centre votes. There was, however, little real difference between the Catholic landowners from Silesia and South Germany who at that time dominated the party, and the groups explicitly labelled Conservative. The Church has always tended to support authority against revolution. To get its way the Centre had to sell its votes to the Government, a process in which the bargaining power of the leaders depended on the loyalty of the rank and file; this made it the best disciplined of the German parties. In proportion as the Socialists and Progressives gained votes at the expense of the Conservatives and Liberals, the temptation to regard the Centre as a Government party grew. Yet Bismarck's instinct was sound. For many of the Catholics in South Germany were small men and many of the workers in the Rhineland and Silesia were Catholic. Moreover, Catholicism did not exclude the exercise of a lively social conscience. The Centre was therefore bound to be affected as the social foundations of Germany were transformed. In due course a left wing was to develop which, if unlikely to man revolutionary barricades, was equally unlikely to die in the last ditch for the established order.

There remained the *Social Democrats*—with nine deputies in the *Reichstag* of 1878 a cloud no bigger than a man's hand on the horizon, yet a cloud which portended a hurricane. The party came into being at the Gotha Conference of 1875 by the amalgamation of the followers of Lassalle with those of Marx; of the two, only the second explicitly looked to revolution as a means of achieving its aims. The unknown factor about the Social Democrats remained the extent to which they really believed in revolution. Events were to show that few people were in fact more orderly and law-abiding than the average German worker. Of course, it suited the book of the Right to regard him as a dangerous anarchist. Yet the Right are not wholly to be blamed for believing that the Socialists meant what they said. For one thing, most Socialists believed it themselves. The impression was reinforced by the venom expended on anyone challenging the view that revolution was both necessary and bound to come. Of course such a view, with its implication that those voting Socialist merely accelerated the inevitable, was too good a vote-catcher to be lightly discarded. Even the immediate aims of the party in 1891—things like universal suffrage, proportional representation, a graduated income tax, an eight-hour day, and unrestricted rights of combination— must have seemed as drastic to the élite of those days as they seem jejune to us. One is tempted to wonder how history would have gone if they had been granted outright. But the reader will by now appreciate how academic any such speculation would be.

CHAPTER II

The Background to Anglo-German Relations: Trade and Colonies*

THE DISTORTIONS OF German internal politics caused by the country's previous history were all the more unfortunate because the social fabric had to be adjusted not simply to one revolution but to two, the Industrial as well as the French. By 1870 Germany was just beginning to feel the full effects of that peculiarly intense phase which each country experiences at the outset of its industrialization and which an American writer has called 'take-off'.[1] To appreciate what was happening, it is necessary to go back nearly a century.

Soon after the War of American Independence ended, the rate of increase in British production began noticeably to outstrip the rate of increase in population. This deceptively simple statement contains the key to the history of the world during the last two hundred years. What happened in Britain had never happened before, but once it occurred it was 'irreversible, like the loss of innocence'.[2] The fact that this development occurred in Britain was due to the convergence of numerous interacting chains of historical causation, some of which have been already mentioned.

(a) An essential accompaniment to increase in the rate of output is an increase in the rate at which machinery is installed and so (since machinery has to be paid for) in the rate of investment. But this in turn requires that:

(i) capital should have been accumulated by people who have more money than they require for their immediate needs and so can afford to save

* The reader's attention is particularly directed to the statistical evidence underlying this chapter which is contained in Appendix I.

(ii) the machinery of banking should have been developed to a stage at which the capital accumulated by some can be put at the disposal of others in a position to devote it to productive use

(iii) some should be prepared to take risks in lending their capital on the strength of a reasonable expectation of private profits, while others should be prepared to take the lead in introducing innovations.

The development of all these factors in Britain owed much to a century or more of stable government with a legal system that was reliable and undiscriminating, so that people could feel confidence in the future.

(*b*) Thanks largely to Britain's favourable position on the world trading routes opened by the navigators of the sixteenth century; thanks also to the enterprise with which those routes were exploited, Britain had developed the habit of overseas trade, with the greater variety in material resources which it made possible and the credit and commercial institutions which it demanded. The British grew accustomed to devising new solutions to unprecedented situations. The spirit of innovation and the spirit of risk-bearing became more widely diffused than in any previous century.

(*c*) The capture of the government by the middle classes and small squirearchy in the seventeenth century led to the removal of official impediments to trade, risk-bearing and innovation. A commercial outlook permeated political policy just as the successful merchants permeated the aristocracy.

(*d*) The raw materials most needed in the early stages of in-dustrialization—coal, iron, wool and cotton—were either at hand in Britain or could be imported easily.

(*e*) Scientific discovery developed to the stage at which it could be effectively applied to the productive processes. In particular, the invention of the steam cylinder revolutionized the situation regarding supplies of energy. Underlying this practical development, however, was a fundamental change of mental attitude. Whereas for centuries most men had conceived of the physical world as something outside their control, mysterious and there-fore unpredictable, they now looked on it as subject to knowable laws and therefore capable of controlled manipulation. Here again much was due to the stimulus which internal peace and regular government gave to education and research. Two particularly important applications of this principle were:

(i) Communications, which vastly increased the size of potential markets. (Sir Robert Peel, travelling at top speed from Rome to London in 1834, took thirteen days on the journey, about as long as he would have needed sixteen centuries earlier; twenty years later, he could have done it in three.)

(ii) Medicine, where clearer ideas about the causes of disease led to quick progress in its prevention, and so to a rapid increase in population.

(*f*) This is the final factor calling for mention and one of the most important; the sudden swelling in the numbers of human beings constituted both a problem, owing to the resulting pressure on resources, and at the same time an opportunity, thanks to the increase in the available labour force and in the size of the potential market.

Mechanical production in quantity became not merely technically possible but also, in view of the economies of scale which it involved, financially attractive. But the full effect of this would not have been felt if there had not been at the same time an absolute increase in the number of consumers and an extension of the area over which effective distribution became possible. Finally, the machines for the productive process could only be installed because the spare financial resources existed and could be made available.

The industrial changes brought in their train a transformation of society, of which the main signs have been a steady growth in standards of living and leisure and a widespread diffusion of literacy, partly in answer to the demand of the workers for what they regarded as the key to advancement and partly to meet industry's need for trained operatives and technicians. The application of machinery to the media of intellectual communication fostered this diffusion. But behind this lay the deeper shift in outlook involved in the transition from a static and largely customary society to one in which change, popularly regarded as 'progress', is accepted as the normal order of life. This brought in its train an expansion of men's conception of what is possible, fostered by an awareness of alternative societies either in time or space, and so a questioning of all accepted values. This in turn found expression in a transformation of ideas about the aims to be achieved by common action in communal life, in other words, politics. But thanks to the improvement in communications, these widening interests and awareness of possibilities were matched by growth in the possibilities of control from a single centre, and therefore of what could be achieved by communal action. There were more things which men wanted to do, and as facilities increased, so did the amount which one man could accomplish; life began to be lived at a greater intensity. Above all, advance consisted in a steady extension of the fields in which problems were brought to the level of consciousness where they could be analysed—the essential first step towards their solution.

These changes of outlook produced what can be conveniently, if repulsively, labelled 'the modern mind'. The outstanding internal and international problem of the last hundred years has been to adjust the social framework to accommodate that mind. Not surprisingly, the process has been hampered by misconceptions. One of the most pregnant and one which was particularly prevalent in Germany concerned the relationship between liberal democracy, with responsible Parliamentary government, and industrialization. In those western European States which pioneered the process of industrial innovation, the political adjustment to that process took the form of liberal democracy and it was therefore assumed that this, instead of being the form appropriate to a particular area and time, was an inevitable accompaniment. An industrial country would always have a liberal parliamentary constitution. The opposite was also accepted; the social consequences of industrialization could be escaped if the introduction of liberal democracy could be prevented. A narrow and closed élite could then enjoy the benefits of industrialization without losing its social privileges. But this was the reverse of the truth. For longer experience has shown that there are other political forms equally compatible with 'the modern mind', but that one thing which is not compatible is the unimpaired retention of privileges by an élite whose position rests on birth and tradition. Had they been astute, the German élite might have done well to bow to the inevitable, sacrifice a number of their privileges in the hope of salvaging the rest, and set out to devise a new political order in which they could retain the maximum influence. Their preoccupation with resisting liberal democracy ruled out such a policy and doomed them to ultimate defeat.

But there were other and more sinister consequences of industrialization. The purposes to which machinery was applied were not solely those of peace. Its application to war transformed the speed and scale on which hostilities were conducted, the efficiency with which the enemy could be slaughtered and the percentage of the population whose whole-hearted co-operation in the war effort became important. It was Moltke who familiarized the concept of 'strategic railways' and turned mobilization into a matter of timetables. The increasing use of novel raw materials and the accidental way in which these were distributed throughout the world made the economies of the various nations interdependent. The growth of industrial areas with populations too great to be fed from the local farms made Europe dependent on supplies from overseas. Naturally, this enhanced the importance of blockade as a weapon of war. But at the same time as they became more dependent on one another, and perhaps partly as a result, societies differentiated from one another by language, culture and traditions became more conscious of one another. The process of widening self-consciousness on the part of the individual was matched by a growing awareness of distinctive identity on the part of peoples possessing prominent distinguishing marks in common, in other words, nations. The advocates of national self-advancement by joint endeavour, at the expense of other parallel but clearly distinct societies, became articulate on a scale hitherto unknown. With this went an anxiety about national security, an almost instinctive desire to counter the effects of international interdependence by getting control over sources of supply and transport routes. Most of the new supplies came in by water from across the seas (though whether there were alternative sources and routes is another matter). No army, however strong, could ensure their delivery. The significance of navies and sea-power became plain to all and attention was naturally focused on the country which claimed to rule the waves and which insisted on maintaining a fleet bigger than those of the next two powers put together. And this was the country which had pioneered the new social order and which, though her share of world trade was already on the decline, still held a larger one than anybody else. Once the Germans were able to regard their problem of unity as solved and began to look outside Europe, the question of their relationship to Britain assumed a new importance.

In Britain, it was the textile industry which led the way in mechanization. The demand for improved means of power to drive the new spindles and looms led to the development of the steam engine which, when applied to railways (initially, to shift the coal needed to produce steam in the mills) revolutionized transport. The demand for machines, for locomotives and above all for iron rails, necessitated a transformation of the iron industry. Thus the key industries of the first stage of development were coal, iron, textiles, railways and shipbuilding. In these industries, the main work of providing Britain with her basic productive equipment was over by 1870. By that year, for example, two-thirds of Britain's present railway mileage had been built. But the output produced by British machines did not go to Britain alone; other western European countries rapidly followed her example. Before they could do so they needed both capital, with the institutions for raising it, and basic plant. In the provision of both, as well as of finished products, Britain played a considerable part. By 1840 the firm of Robert Stephenson, for example, was already shipping locomotives to France, Belgium, Austria, Germany, Italy and Russia.[3] The years of the mid-century were the years of the British heyday on the Continent. But in due course the countries which approximated most closely to Britain in social conditions acquired their own railroads, their own textile mills, their own locomotive factories. All this could not be done in a day and though they profited by British experience, it was some time before they were to reach the level already achieved across the Channel. Germany, for example, had to build roads as well as railways and it was not until about 1860 that she reached the same stage of development which Britain had reached in 1830. But western Europe could no longer serve as an adequate outlet for Britain's surplus capacity.

In these circumstances Britain's attention from 1870 onwards turned to the opening-up of new countries overseas. Railways remained the favourite investment but the railways that were financed were increasingly remote from London. The attraction of these countries as homes for surplus population and as sources of raw materials had been enormously increased by the greater accessibility which the steamship and later the electric telegraph gave them. But there followed a demand for additional capital to provide 'not the marginal additions which the emigrants would have needed in their own country but the whole stock of a newly founded community'.[4] During the years 1870–74, 36·4 per cent. of British investment was going abroad and though the figure fell in bad years, the average for the years till 1914 was to remain well above a quarter. No other country approximated to anything like this figure and for a long time no other country was as well off as Britain.

The capital which Britain invested mostly came back again for spending in the form of orders to keep British factories busy. Where the overseas areas were colonized by people of British origin, the placing of orders in Britain was natural. This was one of the advantages of colonization and could be enjoyed even where, as in South America, the government did not actually pass into British hands. Indeed, the chief advantage of actually governing, in a more or less free-trade world, was the extra security and stability which resulted. But the biggest benefit which Britain secured for herself by sending so high a proportion of her resources overseas was the reduction which she thus brought about in the cost of procuring raw materials and foodstuffs. From 1873 the British price index fell more or less steadily until 1896 and as a result real wages improved by 77 per cent. between 1860 and 1900. To do this, resources were diverted from the development and modernization of Britain's industrial equipment—in other words, we preferred to bring down costs by getting cheaper raw materials rather than by improving the efficiency of our production methods. The prevailing view of competent judges is that the marginal advantage produced by putting the resources to use at home would have been lower, so that the price was one worth paying. Certainly the test of interest rates points in the same direction, since the chief reason why money went abroad was the prospect—not always justified—that it could thereby earn more than in Britain.* The choice between the two alternatives was not one made deliberately; it followed from accepting the economic theory that money should be allowed freedom to go where the greatest gain offered. And the more capital that went abroad, the less there was left for investment at home; once the competition of the other countries became severe, Britain's best hope of meeting it was to keep one step ahead of her competitors, which called for new processes to be developed and new plant to be installed, and thus for fresh capital to be invested. German industry by

---

* Assuming that investment in either form of activity was equally easy, which may not have been the case.

contrast must have benefited from the fact that so much capital and trained manpower were available at home instead of going overseas to develop an Empire.

For reasons which have been described, German economic development began some fifty years behind British. The four main German banks, for example, were founded between 1853 and 1872. But, as always, the imitator moved faster than the pioneer. The achievement of unification gave a great impetus and in the ensuing three decades the German economy, and with it German society, was to be transformed. In the decade 1860–70 British production was still growing faster than German (32 per cent. as against 24 per cent.) but thereafter the positions were strikingly reversed (1870–80, 23–43 per cent.; 1880–90, 16–64 per cent.; 1890–1900, 22–60 per cent.). When Germany appeared on the world economic scene, the second phase of industrialization was beginning. The key industries were no longer to be textiles and iron, but steel, electricity, chemicals and optical goods. In these Britain had no pronounced advantage over Germany. Practically none of the important inventions in this phase were British; Germany's share is illustrated by the familiarity of the names Daimler, Diesel and Siemens. Throughout the period 1870–1914, however, exports absorbed a higher proportion of the British national product than of the German. Until about 1910 Germany remained a poorer country than Britain and even after that date the average British income was higher (since the population of Germany was about half as great again). Moreover, British efficiency of production was greater, although her workers had shorter hours. In all aspects, however, Germany was catching up fast. This is not a matter for surprise or congratulation; it follows automatically from the fact that the pace of growth in the earlier stages of industrialization is greater than that which can be maintained once the main 'infrastructure' has been built. Germany's principal handicap was probably the proportion of her population which continued to work on the land. Her armed forces also absorbed a higher proportion of manpower, although in terms of finance the burden of defence in the two countries was not dissimilar. (A navy costs more than an army but absorbs fewer men.) On the other hand, German economic life must have gained valuable recruits from the inability of politicians to become Ministers.

But the most striking difference between the two economies

lay in the matter of investment because although, as far as can be ascertained, the German rate of investment cannot have been much behind the British (and subsequently exceeded it), a significantly higher proportion was spent at home. This reflects not only the greater need due to the later start. German domestic rates of interest seem to have been nearly twice as high as British,[5] thus reducing the attraction of overseas loans. In addition the German banks, which provided a higher proportion of the investable funds than their British counterparts, placed their money in close concert with industry and preferred ventures near at hand on which they could keep watch. Indeed, Germany probably owed more than she recognized to the international exchange facilities provided by the various London markets and to the part which they played in making it easier for her to expand her sales abroad.

There had been some suspicion in Britain about German development. In 1833 the Secretary to the Committee of the Privy Council for Trade described the *Zollverein* as 'an alliance conceived in a spirit of hostility to British industry and British commerce'. And in 1841 the Foreign Secretary was warned about 'the extent and perfection that has for some years been progressing in the manufactures of Germany' which had 'greatly reduced the demand and estimation for British fabrics in the great markets of Europe'.[6] There was considerable hostility, on theoretical grounds, to Prussia among liberal circles, which led *The Times* in 1860 to jeer that 'She has a large army but notoriously one in no condition for fighting. . . . No one counts on her as a friend; no one dreads her as an enemy. How she became a great Power history tells us; why she remains so nobody can tell.'[7] But as Lord Palmerston had pointed out in 1847: 'Both England and Germany are threatened by the same danger . . . an attack from Russia or from France separately, or . . . united. England and Germany . . . have mutually a direct interest in assisting each other to become rich, united and strong.'[8] Fear of France, the fact that Prussia was not strong enough to be a menace, and ethnic and dynastic ties all combined to produce in mid-Victorian Britain a general predisposition to favour things German. In 1844, Jowett met Erdmann, Hegel's chief disciple, at Dresden and thereafter began the introduction of Hegelian philosophy to Oxford where by the 70's it was to achieve a dominating position. Germanophilia lasted into the opening weeks of the Franco-Prussian War but began to change into doubt when Germany was seen to emerge as the strongest military power in the world.

In Germany, opinions about Britain were more varied. British material achievement was widely admired and widely envied. Many patriots wished Germany to follow suit. For long the Liberals took British practices as their model in constitutional as well as economic affairs. Lasker, one of the earlier Liberal leaders, had spent much time in England, as had the Socialist, Edward Bernstein. But admiration was by no means universal. Since the Liberal principles of Britain were the direct antithesis of the traditional Prussian view, it suited those upholding that view to scorn Britain as being sunk in materialism; Treitschke, among many other attacks, said that a German could not live long in the English 'atmosphere of sham, prudery, conventionality and hollowness'.[9] In the fashionable terms of Hegelian logic, they looked to Germany to provide the antithesis to Britain's thesis and act as model for the second half of the nineteenth century as Britain had done for the first half. The Hegelian challenge to the Utilitarians was matched by List's challenge to Adam Smith. Britain thus became an issue in German internal politics, though even the most conservative were ready to believe that Britain might be valuable as an ally. British self-assurance was also widely resented. In 1860 a Captain Macdonald had a row with a German ticket-collector which resulted in his being imprisoned at Bonn. When his case came for trial, the public prosecutor said that 'the English residing and travelling abroad are notorious for the rudeness, impudence and boorish arrogance of their behaviour.' This provoked *The Times* to assume a 'tone of virulence' which, according to Queen Victoria, 'could not fail to produce the deepest indignation among the people of Germany.'[10]

* * *

During the years between 1880 and 1913 British exports were roughly going to double, even allowing for changes in the value of money. The result was an impression of prosperous expansion. While correct in absolute terms, the impression was misleading because during the same period world trade nearly trebled. That the British share of it should drop from 38·2 per cent. to 27·2 per cent. is in no way surprising, because for a number of reasons Britain could never have hoped to hold for long the advantage which she gained by pioneering the process of industrialization. This explains the paradox that while the British people felt that they were going from strength to strength, the rest of the world considered Britain's power to be on the wane. In particular Germany's exports rose by 240 per cent. and her share of the world total from 17·2 per cent. to 21·7 per cent.: her people could justifiably consider that they were catching up an older, less enterprising and less efficient rival.

In the second half of the 1880's general over-investment caused productive capacity temporarily to exceed consumer demand. The expansion of world trade was checked, and British exports were hit more seriously than German. In 1885 German exports to Holland for the first time exceeded British ones, and the same thing occurred in Sweden and Roumania.[11] This led British manufacturers to start worrying about competition and, not for the first or last time, to assume that any advantage which other countries were gaining must be the result of sinister influence rather than of greater efficiency in production or selling. What was happening, of course, was that, as a result of development elsewhere, certain British producers were ceasing to be economic and the country was faced with the need to shift their resources into other activities. The trend was, anyhow, in this direction in the normal course of growth. Though, for example, British exports of cotton and wool multiplied four times between 1840 and 1880, total exports multiplied by five times so that the share of cotton and wool dropped from 56 per cent. to 43 per cent. Between 1880 and 1900, following a 20 per cent. fall in prices, the value of cotton and wool exports dropped by 6 per cent., whereas those of iron, steel and machinery rose by 40 per cent.[12] There was no intrinsic reason why Germany could only expand her exports at the expense of Britain. The productive capacities of both countries have, after all, grown vastly since those early days, yet they are still both able to find outlets for their products. As the figures for the exports of the two countries show, there was plenty of room for both prior to 1914 provided—and it is a big proviso—that the problems of finance and organization involved in matching demand with supply could have been first recognized and then resolved. But secular trends are seldom appreciated by the individuals whose fate it is to provide the basis for the generalizations, and, rather than make their own painful adjustments, the firms concerned will look keenly for alternative solutions, of which the most obvious is government regulation of economic forces.

When the effects of German competition began to be noticed in Britain, a great deal was made of Germany's refusal to sign the Convention of the Industrial Property Union set up in 1883. Rumours were rife of cheap German goods masquerading under false labels as British and damaging the national reputation for quality. Cases of this kind undoubtedly did occur. Official hints that Germany ought to sign the Convention met with no response and in 1887 Parliament passed a Merchandise Marks Acts forbidding misrepresentation of place or country of origin and requiring all goods made abroad but sold by U.K. merchants to be marked to that effect. This stipulation quickly revealed that much of the trouble had been due to British dealers buying cheap foreign goods for resale and putting U.K. labels on them to give the impression that they came from Britain. As soon as the labels disclosed the true origin, purchasers cut out the English middleman and bought direct from the manufacturer—which hardly suggests that the goods themselves were shoddy.[13]

An official enquiry into the inadequacy of British exports led to much correspondence between the Government and the Chambers of Commerce, and the collection of much evidence from British officials abroad. Some of this sounds curiously familiar:

'The British manufacturer does not move with the times or sufficiently consult the tastes and wishes of foreign customers.'

'The British do not study the market closely enough.'

'The millowners of Britain . . . rather despise a small trade and will not alter their production to suit a demand that does not offer a certainty of extensive future business.'

'The reasons for successful foreign competition would seem to be a higher standard of technical education, greater activity in the employment of commercial travellers speaking the local language, greater attention paid to the wants of the market, greater facilities for delivery and payment.'

'The frequent strikes which have occurred of late years in Great Britain have been the means of encouraging competition.'[14]

'There is no denying that the youths who go from Belgium or Germany to push their fortunes abroad in trade go better equipped than do our own in knowledge of languages and of the methods of business. They are willing to live more plainly than Englishmen will do, to work for smaller profits, to allow themselves fewer amusements. . . . They are more alive to the results attainable by attention to minutiae, and perhaps more keenly watchful of all such new facilities as the progress of science affords.'[15]

Not only were the reasons for German progress shown to be relatively innocent; an official report in 1888 cut down to size the very extent of that progress. 'Germany has not been gaining in common markets in late years at the expense of English trade. Its gains have been special and in certain directions. Our preponderance remains substantially what it was ten years ago'.[16] (This, as will be seen from Appendix I Table VIII d, was not altogether true.) Whether these official assurances would by themselves have stilled the clamour for protection is hard to tell. But at this point trade picked up and once expansion was again in the air, suggestions that Germany might be stealing Britain's livelihood found fewer listeners. The chief legacies were a substantial improvement in the overseas commercial services of the British Government and a feeling of suspicion and misunderstanding in both countries. The Germans liked to believe that they had been unjustly traduced and made much of the fact that the compulsory label 'Made in Germany' turned out a recommendation rather than a stigma. In Britain, some circles harboured a belief that behind so much smoke there must have been some fire.

When a few years later General Caprivi was discussing the question of trade competition, he said that the growing need for imports faced Germany with a choice between exporting goods and exporting men. Between 1689 and 1914, six million persons, more than the entire population of medieval Germany, left the country;[17] 800,000 of these went in the first decade after unity, 1871–81. Most went to established countries like the United States and Brazil and so were irrevocably lost to the Fatherland. This loss of manpower disturbed patriots as well as generals and it was the hope of finding places to which both men and goods could go with advantage that led to German interest in colonies. While Britain had been acquiring control over miscellaneous parts of America, Africa, Asia and Australasia 'in a fit of absence of mind', German attention had been absorbed elsewhere and various possibilities which did present themselves were neglected or turned down. In 1842 Mexico offered to sell California to Frederick William IV, while two years later a German company sent out an advance party of seven thousand settlers to Texas, still at that time an independent state. But the Mexican offer was refused and in 1845 Texas was annexed by the Union.[18] Between 1833 and 1871 various German traders established factories in S.W. Africa, Zanzibar, Liberia, Gabun, the Cameroons, Samoa and New Britain, but none of these received official protection or absorbed any significant numbers of settlers. List in 1841 said that 'colonies are the best means of developing manufactures, import and export trade and finally a respectable navy'.[19] But the ambitions latent in this sentence were frustrated by the fact that settlers from Europe preferred temperate climates, that all countries with such climates had by then acquired established governments and that the tropical areas which remained unappropriated could only be made to produce trade after considerable capital expenditure. Treitschke may have been giving ammunition to Germanophobes when he wrote that 'the outcome of our next successful war must be the acquisition of colonies'[20] but he at least seemed to be facing the facts.

Most Germans who ventilated the subject wanted colonies primarily as status symbols and as the result of arguing that because countries with colonies were wealthy, colonies caused wealth. Bismarck, who was not merely a realist but averse to antagonizing additional neighbours, gave the idea of acquiring territory overseas little encouragement, though he favoured German merchants establishing themselves. In 1871 he refused a suggestion that France surrender Cochin China instead of Lorraine; in 1876 he rejected a proposal to set up a colony in South Africa; in 1880 he ignored a plan for the colonization of New Guinea; in 1881 he asserted that, as long as he was Chancellor, Germany would carry on no colonial activities; in 1882 he announced that the political situation prevented the government from taking any part in the work of the Colonial Society; in 1884 he proclaimed German sovereignty over five colonial areas in rapid succession.

A variety of reasons has been given for this *volte-face*. Dr. Taylor once attributed it to a desire to draw closer to the Conservative Ferry cabinet in France by a demonstration bound to antagonize England.[21] It may well have been devised on account of its nuisance value to Britain and as a means of getting concessions in other directions. (In 1882 Britain had occupied Egypt although by international law her right to do so was questionable.) Herbert Bismarck later said that the policy was 'conveniently adapted to bring us into conflict with England at any given moment' in case the Crown Prince, on coming to the throne, tried to carry out his intention of working closely with that country.[22] The American historian of the German colonial empire believes that it represented the seizing of the first convenient political opportunity to carry out a policy for which Bismarck had always had more sympathy than he let on and which his change of attitude on tariffs made a more natural activity for the government. It certainly represented a concession to the Right which was likely to ease the difficult task of managing the *Reichstag*. It even pleased the Emperor who said he could now look the statue of the Great Elector in the face when he crossed the long bridge in Berlin.[23] But Bismarck seldom did anything exclusively for one reason and this episode is unlikely to have been an exception to that rule. By long practice and the sacrifice of all other considerations, he had acquired such an ability to appreciate situations that he could manipulate any given event so as to make it serve a number of his purposes at the same time. Herein lies one of his chief titles to historical fame.

Anglo-German discussions on colonial questions had their sharp edges. When the German Ambassador in London first asked Lord Granville, Gladstone's Foreign Secretary, for recognition of the German protectorate just proclaimed over S.W. Africa, adding on instruction the suggestion that Heligoland might be ceded as well, Granville replied that the British Government (which had underrated the significance of S.W. Africa and as a result got itself into a weak position) did not intend to recognize the protectorate. As regards Heligoland, Granville supposed that the cession of Gibraltar might improve British relations with Spain. Might not people, however, suspect that if Britain made such a bargain, she really wished to buy German assistance on another matter (Gordon was at that moment besieged in Khartoum)? Although the Ambassador hastily disclaimed any such idea, there can be little doubt that this was precisely what Bismarck had in mind.[24] When London suggested to the Australian government that Germans in the Pacific would not be very near and therefore not very dangerous neighbours, the answer came back that the Australians preferred not to have any neighbours at all! Such reactions were met by German press articles (probably inspired) to the effect that, 'if John Bull thinks he can block German colonial policy with all kinds of funny nonsense, he is wasting his efforts, for Germany is determined to hold on to what she has and will pay him back in his own coin'.[25] On another occasion the Germans published a blue-book on colonial policy containing a letter putting the British Cabinet quite in the wrong; what was omitted was the subsequent telegram telling the Ambassador not to deliver the letter.[26] Bismarck had long ago found a peremptory tone effective in dealing with Lord John Russell, and his acolytes seem to have concluded that it was the right way to handle all Foreign Secretaries. When Lord Rosebery assumed that post in 1886, he had to give the German Ambassador 'a strong hint that they must take care at Berlin of the style of their communications, which is apt to savour distantly of menace'.[27] In spite of such civilities, the German colonial empire was established (for the additions to it in subsequent years were insignificant) without a major crisis with England. For this Bismarck had his *bête noire*, Gladstone, largely to thank. The Liberal Government was not much interested in colonies and reluctant to pick a quarrel. German sovereignty in S.W. Africa was in the end recognized in 1884 and further German agitation led to an agreement early in 1885 by which Germany got Togoland, the Cameroons, part of New Guinea, the Solomon and Marshall Islands and an indefinite stake in Tanganyika. The northern part of East Africa went to Britain, as did the island of Zanzibar, though Germany retained some rights in the latter.

Bismarck's interest in colonies disappeared almost as rapidly as it had arisen, and by 1889 he was declaring that he was 'fundamentally non-colony-minded'. The nationalist revival in France had again made the chance of a reconciliation faint and, in face of a menacing France, English co-operation had once more become important. Herbert Bismarck wrote to the German Ambassador in London that 'Salisbury's friendship is worth more to us than the whole of East Africa; my father is of the same opinion'.[28] This did not prevent his father from putting in claims to bits of East Africa when they were inconvenient, but he did refuse to support the grandiose plans of explorers like Emin Pasha.

In the interlude, however, Germany had acquired colonial

territories some four times as large as herself. Parts of them, and notably S.W. Africa, were capable of white settlement. But they were arid and undeveloped areas; had they not been, someone else would have acquired them earlier. All in all, they proved a sad disappointment, absorbing relatively few men, providing relatively few imports and requiring relatively heavy expenditure. By 1914 there were less than 25,000 Germans in all the colonies taken together, including the armed forces. Hemp and phosphates were the only commodities of which they met anything like Germany's full requirements (though by 1914 they were producing one-fifth of her rubber and of her cocoa) and there is no reason why these could not have been obtained equally cheaply and with considerably less effort from areas not in German possession. Admittedly the colonies were until 1906 mismanaged, but this was not the root of the trouble. In colonial matters the Germans were the victims of much fallacious thinking, but the fallacies did not originate with them. We are now becoming able to see how relatively transient Europe's colonial episode was in the nature of things bound to be. But it would be idle to deny that Britain, thanks to her luck and enterprise in leading the way and to the effort and expenditure which she put in, found in her colonies useful markets and sources of cheap supplies to an extent which Germany never did. On the other hand the Germans as persistently underestimated the importance of investment for gaining overseas trade as they over-estimated the importance of possessing territory. Had they invested overseas the same proportion of their national income as Britain, they would soon have come to enjoy much the same advantages, although the consequential reduction in home investment might have reduced their competitive power.

When the German colonies did not come up to German expectations, the disillusionment created a suspicion that once again Germany had started too late. And when Germans went on to ask why the process of parcelling out the world should be halted at a moment more favourable to others than to them, it would have required more insight than men then possessed to answer that of course the process would never halt, since history abhors a full-stop as much as nature a vacuum. Certainly only a visionary could have seen in those days that, although the course on which events were moving was destined to weaken Britain, it was not to any State in Europe that the benefit would accrue.

CHAPTER III

The Family Background

'IF I AND MY BROTHERS had been born the sons of a petty official,' said King Frederick William IV of Prussia (b. 1795, succeeded 1840), 'I would have been an architect, William a sergeant-major, Charles would have gone to prison and Albert turned out a ne'er-do-well.'[1] However accurately he may have delineated his brothers, he underestimated his own talents. Numerous castles and churches in a bogus medieval or early Renaissance style testify to his passion for building, just as innumerable sketchbooks do to his talent as a draughtsman. But he had also inherited from his mother, the graceful and spirited Queen Louise, charm of manner and fluency of expression. Treitschke said that he was never happy except when emitting a flood of thoughts and sentiments. 'I could not rest until I had spoken.' Here was a Hohenzollern who could make jokes, who could sway audiences by his intelligence and eloquence. Here too was a Hohenzollern who could not sit a horse and whose chief title to military fame lay in designing a helmet. One of his main interests was the establishment of a Protestant bishopric in Jerusalem. Unfortunately his gifts, like those of his great-nephew, were not matched by stability of character or staying power. The liberal sprinkling of exclamation marks and underlinings which cover his letters indicate a volatile and enthusiastic temperament. Tense, introspective, romantic, he used the world of ideas as an escape route from the preoccupations of ordinary men. 'The King,' said one of his friends, 'has the gift of discerning the practical side of a problem and for that very reason despising it.'[2] Always a prey to the impressions of the moment he did not, all the same, allow those impressions to affect his fundamental views. This led not only to indecision but to accusations of treachery.

At heart a kindly man, he wished to look after his subjects and began his reign by a series of concessions. But his youthful experiences during the Napoleonic Wars had given him a horror of everything remotely connected with the French Revolution. This led to a view of monarchy and of Germany which lacked relevance to the facts of the day and likelihood of application. As the Prince Consort once told him, he expected his nation 'to preserve a slow and gradual development as if it still found itself in the Middle Ages'.[3] The idea of becoming a constitutional monarch seemed akin to blasphemy. In 1847 he said that he would 'never allow a written piece of paper to come between the purposes of Almighty God and this country, to rule us with its paragraphs and make them a substitute for the ancient sacred loyalty'.[4] When, in 1849, the Frankfurt Parliament offered him the German Imperial Crown, he told them that he could not accept at the hands of revolutionaries an authority which rested on divine right. In 1850, when things were quiet again, he said that the Liberals 'had wanted to put a dog's collar round the neck of the Prussian King and chain him to the sovereignty of the people', besides reflecting that 'only soldiers are any help against democrats'.[5] But during the revolution he had made his officers feel like 'drenched poodles' by asseverating his faith in his 'loyal Berliners', while he gave away his whole standpoint of principle by telling one of the Parliamentary delegation in an unguarded moment that, whereas Frederick the Great might have accepted their offer, he himself was not a sufficiently great ruler. Yet the middle course which he followed between the democrats and the soldiers, only to be abused first by one side and then by the other, may well have had the effect, by omissions rather than decisions, of saving the country from outright civil war.

From that time onwards he was 'like a man who had failed in an examination' and in 1857 his mind finally succumbed to its internal tensions. His brother William who then became regent, succeeding as King in 1861, was a much simpler character. He once told how at the Tsar's banquet after the battle of Leipzig in 1814, he, as a youth of sixteen, refused lobster because he had never encountered it before and did not know how to tackle it. Even when he was King, his household lacked egg-cups and used liqueur glasses instead, while at the end of each meal he would take a pencil and mark the level of wine left in the bottle. Until late in his life he had no bathroom in the palace in Berlin so that when he wanted to immerse himself a suitable receptacle had to be brought across from a neighbouring hotel.[6] When he went by train, he used a single small coach, halted at midday and ate in the station restaurant, putting a limit *per capita* on the amount allowed to his household. His main interest was the army, his chief relaxation the music-hall to which he resorted on most evenings. He attended the first complete performance of 'The Ring' at Bayreuth but left in the middle to go on manœuvres.[7] On one occasion his Chamberlain needed to see him immediately after dinner and was asked by the valet to wait while the Emperor changed his trousers. When surprise was expressed at such an action occurring at such a time, the valet replied, 'Do you imagine that he would go to the theatre in his new dinner trousers? It would not be like our old gentleman to be so extravagant!'[8] Whereas Frederick William had been the pupil of Humboldt and Niebuhr and the friend of Ranke, William was said in 1881 never to have heard of Mommsen;[9] on the other hand, he had met Talleyrand.

For some time he was known as the 'Grape Shot Prince' because of his insistence that, once troops were called into the streets to deal with political rioters, they must use their weapons to show the masses the futility of trying to oppose the military. As a result he became highly unpopular and in 1848 had to be smuggled out of Berlin to escape the mob, spending several days in hiding on an island near Potsdam, an experience which he never forgot. He disguised himself with the help of his small son by cutting off his beard and was then sent on an invented mission to London to keep him out of harm's way. There he was made much of by Victoria and Albert who tried, without very lasting effect, to broaden his outlook. On getting back he took two Prussian army corps to put down democracy in Baden with appreciable loss of life.

In his youth he had been deeply in love with Princess Elisa Radziwill. But her family did not rank high enough to satisfy the requirements of court protocol and (in the words of his grandson) he 'remained true to the Hohenzollern-Prussian categorical imperative of duty'[10] by giving her up. Instead he married Augusta of Saxe-Weimar, a small, vivacious brunette whose grandfather was Tsar Paul I. As a girl at her father's court, she had absorbed the enlightening influence of Goethe. Her father had been under his wife's thumb and her own ambition had been to repeat the relationship. In this she was frustrated, first by the masculine traditions of the Prussian Court and then even more decisively after 1862 by Bismarck whose domination over her husband left less and less room for her liberalizing influence. She and the Chancellor became 'intimate enemies'. Even in the 80's he is said to have told her not to agitate the Emperor by pressing her views upon him; she broke off the interview in fury with the words, 'Our most gracious Chancellor is very ungracious today.'[11] A vivid picture of her in 1868 is given in a letter of her daughter-in-law (who did not find relations smooth):

'The Queen can stand more fatigue, excitement and knocking about than anyone I know. She has more physical power and stronger reserves than anybody. She wears out everybody who belongs to her Household, gentlemen and all. She never sits down indoors, for fourteen or fifteen consecutive hours—she is never without talking, loud and long, on exciting topics to dozens of different persons. She walks, eats, dresses and writes in the most tremendous hurry, she has parties every night, she is never alone—she never takes up a book or paper because she never has time, she reads the newspapers aloud at breakfast, she pays visits innumerable, she gives audiences unceasing—in fact, the mere thought of what she does all day long makes me quite giddy. And while she does all this, she complains of her health the whole time. . . . But this sort of existence is a bane, it has taken all peace away, it makes her excited and irritable, and being of a violent disposition by nature, it works up her temper to a pitch which makes it difficult for all who surround her and yet it cannot satisfy or content. When one has her to herself, you know she is quite different, she is so kind and quiet then and so easy to get on with that it is quite a pleasure to be with her.'[12]

*　　　　*　　　　*

The Kaiser's other grandparents require less introduction. It is clear that Queen Victoria's was an extremely emotional character, always seeking some image on to which to project itself. Her first fixation was on Melbourne, the apotheosis of detachment; her second on Albert, the apotheosis of involvement, and it was this which had the most lasting influence on her character. The surprising thing is that, in these circumstances, she so seldom allowed her common-sense to be swept away. 'The Queen's opinion', said Lord Clarendon, 'is always worth hearing, even if you don't agree with it.' She was neither clever nor an intellectual nor particularly devout, though under the influence of the Prince Consort she made a considerable effort to cultivate intellectual and artistic tastes. 'You are quite your dear beloved Papa's child,' she once told her eldest daughter. 'You are so learned and so fond of deep philosophical books that you are quite beyond me and certainly have not inherited that taste from me, for to say the honest truth the sight of a Professor or learned man alarms me and is not *sympathique* to me.'[13] Her sense of humour, like that of her age, was crude; she laughed uproariously when a deaf admiral, failing to appreciate that the conversation had switched from his ship to his sister, announced his intention of having the latter's bottom scraped. Her views on conduct may have been strict but she was capable of surprising generosity to those who transgressed them; while reacting against her uncles, she remained their niece. Once she had made up her mind, she was apt to display great obstinacy, no doubt the joint product of feeling and principle. In these and other ways, she not only set a pattern which many of her subjects followed but embodied their salient characteristics. Lord Salisbury once said that when he knew what the Queen thought, he knew pretty certainly what view her subjects would take, and especially the middle class of her subjects.

Albert is a figure whom it is harder to make come alive. Statesman, composer, artist and scientist, the man who inspired the Great Exhibition, who raised the revenues of the Duchy of Cornwall fourfold in twenty years, the patron whose taste included Duccio and *Così Fan Tutte*—it all seems too good to be true. That he was unpopular in England during his lifetime is not necessarily to his discredit, because he set out deliberately to remould a society whose credit left something to be desired. Lord Granville, who knew a good deal more about the world and a good deal less about Europe, said he was unloved because he possessed all the virtues which tend to be lacking in Englishmen. He was serious-minded to a fault and did not easily relax. Thus, though he could certainly laugh at a joke, he was probably unable to laugh at himself. That he was over-strung was shown by a childish irritability over trifles and a nervous hesitation in making up his mind. The tension may have been aggravated by over-work, but that itself was a sign of the inner conscientiousness which provided the mainspring of his actions.

'If the world be overruled by a God, as I believe it is, vile and wicked actions must bear evil fruits which frequently do not show themselves at once but long years afterwards, as the Bible tells us in the words "The sins of the father shall be visited on the children to the third and fourth generation". This being so, I ask myself what are the duties of those who are to come after in reference to the sowing of such dragons' teeth? And I am constrained to answer to myself that they are enjoined by morality, conscience and patriotism.'[14]

Albert's desire to reform the world extended as much to his native country as to his adopted one. When he came to England in 1840 he vowed to remain 'a loyal German, Coburger and Gothaner'. His dearest wish was to see both pursuing parallel policies of enlightened Liberalism so that in alliance with each other they could exert an influence on world events which would be decisive. His heart warmed with sympathy to the cause of German national unity, believing that it was a sacred duty to respect 'the popular feeling, the national feeling'. He wished to see Prussia leading Germany to unity, but he was one of those who thought that, for this to happen, Prussia must itself become liberalized. As he wrote to his friend, King William, 'The internal weakness *vis-à-vis* the liberal system of government, the demonstrated, unfortunately well-known antipathy of the higher classes and government to popular rights and representative government, etc., make it *impossible* for Prussia to be the champion of popular rights.'[15] He denounced the 'great Junker and bureaucratic party which comes together in the Army and particularly the Guards, which is determined not to allow the constitution and constitutional government to develop and which for this purpose does not shrink from cunning, fraud and violence for the provocation of a revolution or of a *coup d'état*'.[16] He realized that by sympathy and tradition the King belonged to this group and for that reason exerted all his persuasiveness in the opposite direction. Yet when, at the time of William's coronation, *The Times* engaged in 'persevering efforts to attack, vilify and abuse everything German and particularly everything Prussian', it was presumably the Prince Consort who prompted Victoria's request to Palmerston for help in curbing such bias. Delane, when taken to task, replied that he would have been 'very glad to give the Prussians a respite from that most cruel of all inflictions—good advice' had not William uttered 'surprising anachronisms upon Divine Right'.[17]

'Family happiness', Albert earlier told William, 'is the only real one that we enjoy here below; we must create it for ourselves and find in it a sure foundation for love, friendship and trust.'[18] On his own children he lavished attention, instruction and affection, while he encouraged his friends to do the same. So it was natural that in 1851 William and Augusta should bring over their two children Fritz and Louisa to see the Great Exhibition (although King Frederick William had taken so much to heart the tales propagated against Paxton's glass palace that he almost refused his permission). Fritz, frail, blond and dutiful, not only saw the sights but met his host's eldest daughter Victoria, then a girl of eleven. Five years later he came to Balmoral (accompanied as adjutant by a taciturn colonel called Von Moltke who had once transferred from the Danish to the Prussian army) and on the slopes of Lochnagar professed his love. The match seemed an ideal one; the parents were friends, the young couple genuinely in love, and there was every prospect of the seal being set upon the Prince Consort's dreams. Fritz's father was already nearly sixty and it was therefore reasonable to expect that before many years had passed, he would himself come to the Prussian throne. With an English wife and an admiration for English ways, under the benevolent guidance of his father-in-law, he would exert the considerable powers of the Prussian crown in favour of Liberal Ministers and an English alliance. With Prussia reformed, the objections to German unity under her leadership would vanish and the peace of Europe would be assured.

As we all know, this prospect was frustrated by the arbitrary way in which Death deals and withholds his blows. If William I and the Prince Consort had both lived for the threescore years and ten allotted by the Psalmist—and no more, if Fritz had lived as long as his father, much would certainly have been changed. But just how much? Can the course of history really depend on such a limited number of heart-beats? Were not forces at work in Germany strong enough to have frustrated Fritz even if he could have met them in his full vigour? When all the possibilities are weighed up, it is hard to avoid concluding that, however desirable may have been the Prince Consort's aims, he was visionary in thinking them capable of achievement in the circumstances of nineteenth-century Germany. True, the only thing needed to permit their realization was a wide enough change of outlook; what were lacking were the conditions and forces needed to bring such a change about. Nor does it necessarily follow that a Germany united under a Liberal, responsible government would have worked hand-in-hand with Britain.

The Crown Prince modelled himself on his father-in-law, recording in 1870 how much he was thinking of the plans which Albert had laid for Germany, and how much would have gone differently if he had lived. Fritz was subject to fits of depression and sudden anger, said to have been inherited from his Russian forebears, from whom also came a frailty of physique which is probably the clue to his character. Honourable, sensible and considerate, he had neither the inclination nor the stamina to dominate. Yet in war he proved well-qualified for high command. Although no great strategist, he took pains over organization, got people to work well together, kept his head in crises, stuck to decisions once made, and succeeded in conveying to his troops his genuine concern for their welfare. He is said to have assumed when being photographed a special pose of severity and vigour which did not come naturally to him, but which he conceived necessary for the effective holding of his office. A sense of duty could thus drive him to display qualities which he was too modest to exert on his own behalf.

He was devoted to his wife and greatly respected her abilities; he consequently deferred to her more vigorous opinions with a frequency which many people, including his son, despised. In 1874, Queen Victoria described her son-in-law as 'straightforward and honest and kind-hearted but rather weak and to a certain extent obstinate, not *conceited* but absurdly proud, as all his family are, thinking *no* family greater or *higher* than the Hohenzollerns.'[19] But when he died, she wrote that 'none of my own sons could be a greater loss. He was so good, so wise and so fond of me.'[20] Perhaps the most remarkable tribute came from his brother-in-law Edward who on his death wrote to the future King George, 'Try . . . never to forget Uncle Fritz. He was one of the finest and noblest characters ever known; if he had a fault, he was too good for this world.'[21]

The Princess Royal inherited from her father his seriousness of purpose and a conscientious concern for the things of the mind. The Imperial Chamberlain described her desire 'to educate everybody round her' as 'truly touching', while her son said she was 'wrapped in an aura of poetry'.[22] From her mother she derived emotion and obstinacy. Once, as a child, she found the Queen talking to Ministers; when her attempts to get them to go away failed, she stamped her foot in anger, and said, 'Queen, queen, make them obey me.'[23] The American Minister in London described her at the age of sixteen as having 'an excellent head, and a heart as big as a mountain'.[24] 'Pussy' was her father's favourite both as child and pupil; and his affection was returned. We find him setting her, when still quite young, to write 'a short Compendium of Roman History' and translate into English Droysen's *Duke of Saxe-Weimar and German Politics*.[25] The tutor employed to teach her and the Prince of Wales the Principles of Political Economy noted the superior quickness of the girl who 'found a literary curriculum thoroughly congenial'.[26] The habits inculcated in youth persisted. She told Sir Henry Ponsonby that she 'regularly read the *Quarterly* and *Fortnightly* Reviews and the *Journal of Mining and Metallurgy*'. She spent most of her time at the Paris Exhibition in examining surgical instruments.[27] She must have been the first royal student of *Das Kapital* which she read about 1879, shortly afterwards sending an emissary to inspect the author.*[28] There was practically nothing human in which she did not interest herself; politics, art, science, medicine, music, religion and gardening were all fields in which she was active and on which she had views. Her tastes were pronounced; she much disliked Wagner, thought Schiller's 'Ode to Joy' 'terribly exaggerated' and regretted that 'the horrid *Marseillaise* should now be the French anthem, associated as it is with the horrors of the Revolution and used by the Socialists as the symbol of violence and all their mad Labour principles'.[29] She spoke three languages besides English but is said to have done so in all cases with a foreign accent. She once expressed her regret at her inability to read Marcus Aurelius in the original Latin; when it was delicately hinted that the imperial philosopher had actually written in Greek, she replied that, of course, the original text was in Greek which she could

* The emissary reported that 'it will not be he who, whether he wishes it or not, will turn the world upside down'.

never have expected to understand, whereas she might have hoped to read a contemporary Latin translation.[30]

For all her great abilities, she had equally great defects. Her intellect was hopelessly at the mercy of her emotions. She reached her conclusions by feeling and then convinced herself that she had done so because they were rational. She took rapid and violent likes and dislikes, which led to frequent disillusionment and lost her helpful allies. Secondly she was deficient in empathy, neither realizing the varying outlooks of other people nor stopping to consider why they were held. She was in consequence a bad judge of character, as her own mother admitted,[31] and signally lacked tact. Lord Clarendon said that she threw everything away by her neglect of the common courtesies of life. One of her husband's A.D.C.s said that she had 'talent but no common-sense' while Lord Granville described her as 'very clever but not wise'.[32] In these circumstances her extreme energy became a positive danger. The British Ambassador in Berlin said 'she would write her head off'.[33]

Unfortunately, the position to which she came at the age of eighteen called for just those qualities which she did not possess. Her father designed her to be an instrument for converting Prussia to Liberal ways; the Prussians strongly suspected such designs of being held. Bismarck, on being asked what he thought of the marriage, replied that if the Princess could leave the Englishwoman at home and become a Prussian, then she might be a blessing to her adopted country. But this was just what the Princess could not do without surrendering the principles on which she had been brought up and, despite good intentions, all that she succeeded in doing was to become a Prussian in England while remaining an Englishwoman in Prussia. As her son wrote seventy years afterwards:

'She came from a country which had had little to do with the Continent, which had for centuries led a life of its own, and developed on its own lines, quite different from the traditions and growth of the country which she was to join. The Prussians were not Englishmen. They had a different history, a different past, and different traditions. Their state had developed on different lines to the English; they were Europeans. They had a different concept of monarchy and of class; the class

distinctions were different from England. . . . My Mother set out
with burning zeal to create in her new home everything which
according to her English education, convictions and outlook
was necessary for the creation of national happiness.'[34]

The wedding, which took place on 25 January 1858 in a
'pea-souper', was itself an affront to Prussian pride, since no
Crown Prince had ever before been married abroad. But Queen
Victoria made short work of the suggestion that it should be held
in Berlin. On reaching her new home with a magnificent trousseau
which included such things as twenty pairs of indiarubber clogs
and two drawers of sponges, the Crown Princess found a great deal
to criticize in the traditional frugality of the Prussian court.
Although she and her husband had been engaged for over two
years, no steps had been taken to find them a palace. They had to
spend the first winter months in the old Berlin castle which,
although a magnificent piece of Baroque architecture, had scarcely
been lived in or altered since Frederick William III had died there
eighteen years before. His death chamber, left undisturbed in
keeping with German tradition, formed the only way by which the
Princess could get from her bedroom to her boudoir! No changes
could be made without the permission of Frederick William IV
who was becoming more and more eccentric. The Princess complained bitterly about German boots, the want of baths, the thin-
ness of the silver plate, and the boring etiquette. On one occasion
she told Bismarck there was more silver plate in Birmingham than
in the whole of Prussia.[35] The habit of invidious comparison died
hard. Many years later she said to a British diplomat, who had lost
his hat on his way to visit her, 'Poor Sir Edward! And you couldn't
so much as buy another in such a country!'[36] About the same time
she told her son to speak more quietly, 'Germans have such a
habit of speaking too loud.'[37] 'She delivered judgment on everything and found everything wrong with us and better in England'
which she habitually called 'home'.[38] The fact that her preferences
may have been justified did not make them popular.

Only a few months elapsed after the wedding before the Prince
Consort came to visit his daughter; two months later he re-
appeared, accompanied by the Queen, three Ministers and Baron
Stockmar. The impression that England was trying to run Prussia
roused almost as much resentment as would have been provoked

by the impression that Prussia was trying to run England. It is perhaps as well that no German should have known of 'a long memorandum upon the advantages of a law of ministerial responsibility, drafted so as to remove apprehensions in the Prussian court as to the expediency of such a measure'[39] which the Crown Princess sent to her father in December 1860. The view that her sex should have no say in politics, though firmly established in Prussia, she, of course, brushed aside as mistaken. She wrote to her husband that:

'to govern a country is not a business that only a King and a few privileged men are entitled to do and that does not concern others. . . . It is on the contrary the right and sacred duty of the individual as well as of the whole nation to participate in it. The usual education which a Prince in Prussia has hitherto received is not capable of satisfying present-day requirements, although yours, thanks to your Mama's loving care, was far better than that of the others. . . . You were not, however, sure of, nor versed in, the old liberal and constitutional conceptions and this was still the case when we married. What enormous strides you have made during these years!'[40]

Her encouragement of her husband in liberal attitudes was widely known; no doubt after the Prince Consort's death in December 1861 it became a trust sacred to his memory. At the height of the Prussian army crisis in 1862, just before Bismarck's appointment as Minister President, Fritz made a final effort at persuading his father to compromise with Parliament. The King, finding himself unable to refute his son's arguments but determined not to act on them, offered to abdicate. The Crown Princess favoured acceptance but her husband could not reconcile this with his duties as son and subject. He understood his father to have promised in return never to call in Bismarck; when three days later Bismarck was appointed, the Crown Prince began to think that his wife had been right. When in 1863 Bismarck relied on the revenues of the Cologne-Minden railway to defy Parliament and muzzle the press, the Crown Prince in a speech at Danzig openly declared his disagreement. In doing so he was acting, as he presumably knew, on the advice which his father had received eight years before from the Prince Consort in case Frederick William IV should use unconstitutional methods. But now the

King demanded a recantation. Fritz, supported by his wife, offered to lay down all his offices but refused to retract anything. He only escaped imprisonment in a fortress because Bismarck advised the King to 'spare the young Absalom', and was told never to express his views in public again, an order which he dutifully obeyed. He wrote, however, to Bismarck in words which Prince Albert would have approved:

'A loyal administration of the Laws and of the Constitution, respect and goodwill towards an easily-led, intelligent and capable people, these are the principles which, in my opinion, should guide every Government in the treatment of the country. I think that the Government needs a stronger basis than very dubious interpretations which do not appeal to the sound commonsense of the people.'[41]

* * *

The struggle with Bismarck lasted long. In 1865 and 1866, the Crown Prince was the only member of the Prussian Crown Council to uphold the rights of the Duke of Augustenburg and oppose the idea of a war with Austria which he described as 'fratricide'.[42] Bismarck replied that if a war in alliance with France against Austria was ruled out, a Prussian policy was no longer possible. But if war were waged against Austria, it had to bring about not only the annexation of the Schleswig-Holstein Duchies but a new arrangement in the relations between Prussia and the smaller German states. Fritz could not accept that war was the right way to unite Germany. Queen Victoria, on her own initiative, sent a personal letter warning King William against being misled by Bismarck and adjuring him to pause 'if you have any regard for my affection and friendship'.[43] Privately she was describing the Prussians as 'odious people'.[44] The Crown Princess, contrary to gossip, showed herself a vigorous defender of German interests. 'English policy distresses me very much indeed!' she wrote in 1864. 'In addition it makes me angry that they always interfere in matters which don't concern them in the least. Children who always poke their fingers into everything end up by getting hurt. This stupid English foreign policy will receive a good slap in the face which the country will have to put up with.'[45] Her attitude led to a distinct if temporary coolness with her brother Edward and his Danish wife. Yet she got the worst of both worlds, since Bismarck later said that she could 'hardly bear the sight of him'[46] after the annexations of Schleswig and Hanover in 1866.

The Crown Prince was not only a Liberal, however, but also a convinced Nationalist. He used to show his son, as a special treat, a book with coloured illustrations of the medieval imperial insignia, and descriptions of the coronation ceremony in Aachen. He always ended by saying 'We have got to bring this back. The power of the Empire must be restored and the Imperial Crown must regain its glamour. Barbarossa must be brought down again out of his mountain cave.'[47] He was also an out-and-out centralist who considered the minor German princes the chief obstacle to unity after 1866; he is alleged once to have said that they were 'like wasps with one wing pulled out—as long as they could crawl they would sting'.[48] Accordingly, after the victory at Königgratz (to which he made no small contribution) and Bismarck's magnanimity in insisting on an immediate peace with Austria, Fritz's opposition began to moderate. The arrangement by which the military budget was settled in the North German Confederation (and the army crisis of 1862 thereby liquidated) was largely due to his mediation. In 1870 he was appointed to lead the South German armies, which he did with distinction, although after the war he rejected a money grant on the ground that he had had no real responsibility. There were clashes between him and Bismarck over the way the war was to be conducted and over the way the Empire was to be brought into being. In this latter process, however, he played a leading part, particularly in overcoming the reluctance of his father who said that being offered the title of 'German Emperor' was like a major being told to call himself 'acting lieutenant-colonel'. Yet the Crown Prince still had doubts about the means which had been chosen, noting in his diary that 'Bismarck has made us great and powerful but has robbed us of our friends, of the sympathies of the world—and of our clear conscience'. 'I still hold fast to the conviction that Germany could make moral conquests, not by blood and iron but by her just cause.'[49] He described the Imperial Constitution as 'ingeniously contrived chaos'. In common with his brother-in-law, the Grand Duke of Baden, he opposed the annexation of French-speaking areas.

The Crown Princess was indignant with England for not giving Prussia active support, and had another brush with her brother who made no secret about sympathizing with France. She busied herself organizing hospital services but, in the true Nightingale tradition, soon clashed with the medical authorities and won less credit than she deserved. At a time when she was rumoured to be trying to postpone the entry of the victorious troops into Berlin, Bismarck said that, since the marriage and the kingdom together were an absurdity and since Germany needed the kingdom, the marriage would have to go.[50] He did not, in practice, try to carry matters so far, but the enmity between the two was implacable. The Crown Prince and Princess shared the outlook of the Progressive Party, and Bismarck was haunted by the fear that should the old Emperor die—and he was now in his seventies—they would call on one of the Progressive leaders to become Chancellor. He sought to guard against such a turn by keeping the Crown Prince from a position of any influence and by using foul means as well as fair to make him widely unpopular. The Crown Princess, according to her Mother, was 'quite Renan' in her religious views[51] and must have sympathized with the *Kulturkampf*, but this did not suffice to get the hatchet buried. Her letters to her mother remained full of frustrated tirades against the system and complaints about the intrigues and accusations to which she and her husband were subjected. 'I wonder', she wrote in 1881 'why [Bismarck] does not say straight out, "As long as I live both the constitution and the crown are suspended" because that is the exact state of the matter'—which would only have been true if the constitution had taken the form which the Princess would have liked to give it. The real situation was summed up in two further remarks, 'I do not like this state of things, but most Prussians and Conservatives do' and 'our rich bourgeoisie are cowardly'.[52] She and her husband found themselves in the unenviable predicament, typical of opposition leaders in prosperous times, of almost having to hope that things would go wrong.

Yet, during the troubles which led to the Congress of Berlin, they were warm supporters of Bismarck's policy and the Crown Prince once more helped the Chancellor to talk his father round, this time into signing the Austrian Treaty. There was even an odd episode in 1877 when the Crown Princess lent herself to Bismarck's policy of encouraging England to take Egypt and thereby get embroiled with Russia and France. This was a good example of Bismarck's favourite technique of trying to provide that any power attempting to move in any direction would be met by a strong coalition of third parties, and so saving Germany from the need to provide the opposition herself. Third parties did not, however, choose on all occasions to walk into the trap, and this was one of the exceptions. Queen Victoria tartly replied that 'it is not *our* custom to *annex countries* (as it is in *some others*) unless we are obliged and forced to do so,' while Disraeli commented that 'if the Queen of England wishes to undertake the government of Egypt, Her Majesty does not require the suggestion or permission of Prince Bismarck'.[53] The upshot of this attempt to serve the Chancellor's purposes can hardly have endeared him to the Princess, and she did not repeat the experiment.

Her views on Russia continued to be expressed trenchantly:

'The more I hear, and the more time passes, the more I regret the English fleet and troops not being at Constantinople.'

'I trust there may be *energy* and *decision* enough at the Foreign Office to *take* the right step and *not* to wait or hesitate; in a fortnight it would be too late. The Russians will be into Constantinople like a shot on the first opportunity. . . . [Their interests] are purely selfish and not humane or civilizatory or for the honour and glory of liberty and progress.'[54]

The tone is, in the strictest sense of the word, familiar:

'There is not a moment to be lost or the whole of our policy of centuries, of our honour as a great European Power, will have received an irreparable blow!'

'Oh! if the Queen were a man, she would like to go and give those Russians, whose word one cannot believe, such a beating!'[55]

So her mother. And much the same views were to be echoed by her son:

'These lazy mendacious Russians put on an idiot boy act, perjure themselves black in the face, and then invent a few more fables to save themselves from being shown up.'[56]
'I hate the Slavs. I know it is a sin to do so—we ought not to hate anyone. But I can't help hating them.'[57]

Some reflections of Bismarck provide instructive comment:

'Sympathies and antipathies with respect to foreign Powers and persons I cannot justify to my sense of duty to the foreign service of my country, either in myself or in others. Therein lies the embryo of disloyalty towards one's master or the land one serves. When in particular one undertakes to arrange one's current diplomatic connections and the maintenance of friendly relations in peacetime in accordance with such things, one ceases in my opinion to conduct politics and begins to act according to personal caprice. In my view, not even the King has the right to subordinate the interests of the fatherland to personal feelings of love and hate towards the foreigner.'[58]

CHAPTER IV

Early Life

PRINCE FRIEDRICH WILHELM Viktor Albrecht von Hohenzollern was born in the Royal Palace in the Unter den Linden, Berlin on 27 January 1859. The same day a hundred and three years earlier had seen the birth of another restless spirit; Mozart, however, was able to escape into the world of music and there find integration. The Prince's one hundred and twenty-eight ancestors at the seventh generation consisted in practice of only eighty separate individuals, which indicates a fair amount of inter-breeding. Of these eighty, seventy-six would seem to have spoken German as their native language, one Swedish, one Polish, and one Russian, while one was a Lithuanian peasant who ended up as Tsaritsa of Russia.[1] In 1859, Marx was forty-one, Clémenceau eighteen, Foch eight, Woodrow Wilson and Freud three. Bergson was born in the same year, which also saw the publication of the *Origin of Species*. Lloyd George was not to be born for four more years, George the Fifth for six, and Lenin for eleven. With some of these, the Hohenzollern princeling was to be more intimately connected than with others.

William's career was heralded with a gesture which foreshadowed his diplomacy at its worst. Old Marshal Wrangel, inside the palace, would not wait for the window to be opened so pushed his fist through it instead. 'Children,' he shouted to the crowd below, 'it's a braw recruit.' William's grandfather, the Prince Regent, had given the artillery exact orders as to how the happy event should be greeted, methodically anticipating all eventualities, including twins. But the first salvo so excited him that, rather than wait for his carriage, he rushed out of the building where he happened to be and, regardless of the expense, hailed a cab to get home. On arriving, he found that the Marshal had spoken too soon. The strains accompanying the Crown Princess's arrival in Germany had not eased her pregnancy and the birth was a difficult one. For some time the whole attention of the English doctor sent over by Queen Victoria for the event was concentrated on the mother and only some time later was it noticed that the baby's left arm had been almost pulled from its socket.[2] Despite many exercises and painful treatment, the arm and hand never recovered; though perfectly formed and healthy, they did not grow to full size. The left sleeves of jackets were cut the same width as the right but had to be shorter; the little hand could just go into the pocket and there it was usually kept. William could not use an ordinary knife and fork but had a special combined one always carried by his bodyguard and with this he managed quite well. But his next-door neighbour at table often cut up his food for him without his appearing to mind.[3] The handicap and the lack of bodily balance in which it resulted made life difficult. But by practice and determination he made himself a good horseman, though mounting was a problem. King George V (who knew what he was talking about) once recorded that 'William shot remarkably well considering he has only one arm'. He also played the piano and tennis (which he learnt from the daughters of a British Ambassador at the Hague), rowed and swam.[4]

Some historians have sought to find the key to William's character in his physical disability, and no doubt the desire to prove that he was really no different from other men helped to make him different. Moreover the trouble was not confined to the arm but to some extent affected the whole left side, and in particular his ear. The extent of this may have been exaggerated but it probably caused a certain amount of nervous irritability and, by coming on suddenly, quick changes of mind.[5] But other men who have had deformities have not had their characters warped by the fact—the late Lord Halifax, for example, had a withered arm. The physical handicaps were one element, but one element only, in the complex causes of the Kaiser's personality. All the same, it is tempting to wonder what would have happened if a German doctor had concentrated on the baby and allowed the mother to die.

The child soon showed itself father of the man. At one month, his mother wrote that he would not be satisfied unless kept dancing about continually, while at his christening 'he seemed very much taken up with the Prince Regent's orders and kept moving his hands as if he wanted to play with them'. When he was twenty months old, he was taken to Coburg to see for the first time his maternal grandmother; she thought him 'a dear little boy, so intelligent and pretty, so good and affectionate'.[6] A year later he was brought on his first visit to England when he was dandled in a napkin by the Prince Consort, an incident which he did not allow his English relations to forget (though if he himself really remembered its occurrence, his precociousness must have been pronounced). In 1863, he returned for the marriage of his Uncle Bertie, at which his chief impressions were the drum fastened on one man's back for another to beat and the beauty of Mendelssohn's Wedding March.* He had been dressed for the occasion in a kilt complete with sporran and toy dirk and when his Uncle Leopold tried to stop him fidgeting, he broke the cairngorm off this and threw it across the aisle, after which he proceeded to bite the avuncular leg—an incident which his family did not allow him to forget. Frith was commissioned to paint the ceremony and his efforts to get the 'royal imp's' likeness led to the comment that 'of all the little Turks, he is the worst'.[7] In later years the 'Imp' associated Buckingham Palace with the natural consequences of eating too much pudding.[8] There is a persistent story, which seems, however, to rest only on hearsay, that on one occasion he crawled under the table during lunch and removed all his clothes; his grandmother, to everybody's surprise, thereupon covered him with kisses.

His first nurse was an Englishwoman, his first governess a Fräulein von Doberneck later described by him as 'a great gaunt dame of firm character whose method by no means excluded the use of the palm'. His father used to take him on sight-seeing expeditions in Brandenburg and on picnics in the woods and lakes round Potsdam—a family custom started by Frederick William IV.[9] According to his mother, however, the Crown Prince never had much time to spare for his children while she claimed to have neglected them herself until the death of her third son Sigismund in 1866. Shocked by this, she sought to remedy previous neglect by watching 'over every detail, even the minutest, of his education'. Queen Victoria's comment was shrewd. 'I am

---

* His mother's wedding appears to have been the first public occasion on which this item from the incidental music to the *Midsummer Night's Dream* was put to its now familiar use.

sure you watch over your dear boy with the greatest care but I often think too great care, too much constant watching, leads to the very dangers hereafter which one wishes to avoid.' The Queen wanted him to mix with all classes of the population, 'going amongst them, as we always did and do and as every respectable lady and gentleman does here, is of such immense benefit to the character of those who have to reign hereafter'. The daughter in reply expressed 'horror of low company' and her mother had to explain (maybe with a sidelong glance at the Prince of Wales) that actors, actresses, musicians and 'barkers' were the very reverse of what she had in mind. 'Mere contact with soldiers *never* can do that or rather the reverse, for they are bound to obey and *no independence of character* can be expected in the ranks.'[10] 'Bring him up simply, plainly,' she said in 1865, 'not with that terrible Prussian pride and ambition which grieved dear Papa so much and which he always said would stand in the way of Prussia taking that lead in Germany which he ever wished her to do. Pride and ambition are not only very wrong in themselves but they alienate affection and are in every way unworthy for great Princes—and great Nations.'[11]

A major influence on the handsome young prince was exercised by George Hinzpeter, the son of a Bielefeld professor who at the age of thirty-nine was in 1866 appointed as tutor on the advice of Sir Robert Morier. Hinzpeter was one of nature's headmasters, a benevolent despot who believed that the best way of inculcating tolerance and compassion was to dictate. For this reason Ernst von Stockmar (son of the Prince Consort's adviser who had been installed as secretary to the Crown Princess by their respective fathers) disapproved of the choice.[12] Hinzpeter was instructed by the Crown Prince to give his pupil 'the mental equipment of the intellectual cream'. Looking back over thirty years later, he explained that, regardless of all other considerations, he had chosen

'the curriculum which gave the greatest assurance of a harmonious development of the lad's intellectual powers. There could be no doubt that only a classical education could be chosen for such a purpose. He would derive from it the rigorous intellectual discipline which only a Grammar School course in the dead languages seemed capable of supplying; he would also get practice in solving intellectual problems and in making the efforts needed to acquire genuine scholarship and knowledge.'[13]

The recollections of the pupil disclosed a somewhat familiar gap between intention and effect:

'We tortured ourselves over thousands of pages of grammar, we applied its magnifying glass and scalpel to everything from Phidias to Demosthenes, from Pericles to Alexander, and even to dear old Homer. And all through the innumerable dissecting-operations which I had to perform on Hellenic remains in the name of classical education, my heart rose up within me and every instinct of proportion which I possess cried out "This isn't, can't be the genuine legacy of Greece to Germany!"'[14]

Hinzpeter also expected his curriculum to develop a sense of world history. Such a sense William certainly acquired, though how far he did so in the schoolroom may be questioned since there history seems to have ended in 1648. Mathematics he never mastered. A Mademoiselle D'Arcourt was employed to teach French, and a Mr. Dealtry, English. In this language the Prince read widely, Shakespeare, Dickens, Scott, Byron, Macaulay, Tennyson, Marryat, *Robinson Crusoe* and Bishop Heber's *Palestine* being specially mentioned. He knew his Fenimore Cooper by heart and games of Indians with the son of an American Ambassador led to a lifelong friendship.[15] He was subsequently said to be able to speak English and German with equal facility and often to be unaware which language he was using; however that may be, our elusive tongue sometimes tripped him up.* He also at some stage acquired a smattering of Italian and Russian.

Hinzpeter, who stayed with the Prince till he was twenty, sought as a devout Calvinist to instil in his pupil a strong sense of duty and of the need to seek redemption from original sin by unceasing hard work without hope of reward or recognition. The lesson was absorbed, if not always acted on. 'Life', he said on another occasion, 'means labour, labour means creation, creation means

* A few examples: 'I too had to remain in bed for a few days and am indoors nearly since a week.' 'The *Caesar* is the most fighting ship I know.' 'I have just passed successfully the new Canal.' 'Try always to be good and obedient to your parents, then you will once deserve to their account.' 'I venture to express my gratification at the event of being able to spend some hours with so many charming brother officers.' 'I shall count the hours till I can again sight dear Osborne rising out of the blue waters of the Solent.' Readers will find other examples on subsequent pages.

working for others.'[16] In practice, the theory meant that lessons started at six in the summer and seven in winter and were liable to go on for twelve hours. To inculcate self-control Hinzpeter once let William hand round to his playmates a 'fine fruit' sent by a fond aunt, but took it away before he could have any himself.[17] In his memoirs, William also described how Hinzpeter taught him to ride by placing him on a stirrupless pony and replacing him there as often as he fell off, until he acquired the sense of balance which his physical defect prevented him from having by nature. Such handling might well have stimulated a revulsion but William retained a respect and liking for his tutor, seeking not very successfully to bring him into public life and attending his funeral in 1907. All the same this sunless, austere upbringing was hardly calculated to produce a relaxed and balanced character. On the other hand Queen Victoria in 1874 complained to Empress Augusta that Willy was getting spoilt by too much kindness.

Hinzpeter's supervision was not confined to academic subjects. On Wednesday and Saturday afternoons they went off to see museums and galleries, factories and mines; at the end of each visit, William had to go up to the man in charge, take off his hat and make a suitable speech of thanks. Hinzpeter would take the Prince for walks and call for an expression of opinion about everyone they met. He further insisted that a monarch should never allow himself to be dominated by anyone else, even his responsible advisers.[18] As the pupil grew up much given to snap judgments and at the mercy of anyone who could talk plausibly, the tutor can hardly be said to have been fortunate in either precept.

These were, of course, the years when the German Empire was coming into existence. One of the prince's earliest memories was seeing the Hungarian Regiment of which the King of Prussia was colonel parade in their white uniforms on their way to the Danish war in 1864. He remembered, too, the return of his father and the victorious army from the war of 1866. In 1869 he was commissioned as a lieutenant by his grandfather; wearing the uniform of the 2nd Pomeranian Regiment, he took part in the last Corps Review before the French war.[19] In 1871 when the newly created Emperor came back to ride in triumph with all the princes of Germany through the Brandenburg Gate, Prince William trotted on his pony as the junior member of the company. It must have been an exciting moment for someone at an impressionable age who no doubt found it hard to understand why his parents had misgivings about the future. Meanwhile, in 1869 his mother had taken him with her other children on a trip to Villefranche and Cannes to meet their father who was coming back from the opening of the Suez Canal.

In 1874 he was confirmed—a more exacting occasion in Germany than in England. His parents had wanted to entrust his preparation to a Protestant Association but his grandfather had insisted that, in accordance with precedent, a Court chaplain should be employed.[20] His uncle Bertie came over for the ceremony, bringing a large portrait of the Prince Consort as a present from the Queen. In the following year he and his brother Henry were sent as pupils to the Lyceum at Kassel, where, amongst other activities, he wrote a tragedy on the subject of Hermione.[21] To go to such a school was an innovation in the education of Prussian princes, who would normally at this stage have done some military training, and it aroused comments. People said that his parents were trying to frustrate his grandfather's desire for him to appear in public as much as possible, a policy which was certainly vigorously opposed by the Queen.[22] After he became Emperor, William once told an educational conference that he could speak with first-hand knowledge as one who had been to a Grammar School (*Gymnasium*) and knew what happened there. The experience led him to believe that too much emphasis was laid on the classics and on learning, too little on the formation of character and on the needs of practical life. That this view was hardly novel does not necessarily make it wrong, but one wonders whether his position as tenth in a class of seventeen should be regarded as the cause or effect of holding it.[23] There were those who said that the Prince was incapable of concentrating on anything, and Hinzpeter himself admitted that this was his greatest difficulty; others thought that his mother and tutor worked him too hard. Perhaps the effort needed to overcome his natural handicaps left him without the energy needed to master other things.

In 1877, when he was eighteen, he came of age. His grandmother, realizing that he was now too grown-up for portraits, offered him the G.C.B. By comparison with the treatment which he was receiving from the Emperors of Russia and Austria and that which his uncles had received from his grandfather, he considered he was being meanly done by and got his mother to say that 'while Willy would be satisfied with the Bath, the nation expects the Garter'. The Queen, whether or not realizing that the true position was the reverse, took the hint. It was about this time that Jowett, through Morier, tried to get the Prince to Balliol, where he would have been the pupil of Toynbee and T. H. Green, the contemporary of Milner and Curzon.[24] But even Balliol would have been unlikely to resolve the complexities of William's character and might indeed have intensified them. In any event the fascinating possibility never came near realization, for in 1877 the Prince went for four terms to Bonn, as his father had done before him.

Here he attended lectures in history, philosophy, law, art, politics, economics, government and science. (What would be interesting to know is whether anyone called his attention to the works of the 'academic socialists' Wagner, Brentano and Schmoller, who just at this time began to challenge the doctrine that the national economy was the field of unchangeable natural laws which it was senseless to tamper with.) The range was in any event wide for anyone bad at concentration and throughout his life William suffered from a superficial knowledge of too wide a field. Rudolf Gneist, the German expert on England who taught him constitutional law, said that, like all royalty who had been over-flattered in youth, the Prince believed he knew everything without having learnt anything.[25] No sooner was he supplied with information than he forgot it like superfluous ballast. His mother also complained that 'he does not care to look at anything, took no interest whatever in works of art, did not in the least admire beautiful scenery and would not look at a Guide Book or any other book which would give him information about the places to be seen'.[26] On the other hand he was made a member of the most swagger students' club, Borussia, though excused the obligation to duel. He also made his first public speech, devoted to praising a bogus General during the Cologne carnival.[27] In the spring of 1878 he went to Paris for the World Exhibition. He was never to return to the city in which his uncle was so much at home; the omission may, however, have owed more to the refusal of the French to invite their conqueror's ruler than to that ruler's indifference to their capital's attractions.[28] England, however, he visited on several occasions, going in 1877 to Cowes and Osborne and in 1878 on a tour which included Ilfracombe. He then went on to Balmoral where he again assumed a kilt and was taken stalking, an operation of which he does not seem to have quite grasped the intricacies, judging by his report that it took him and the ghillie three hours to pick up the scent of the stag. (He also appears to have been under the impression that foxhunting goes on through the summer.)[29]

*   *   *

Up to this point, comment on his character had been mostly favourable. When he was eight, his mother wrote:

'Willy is a dear, interesting charming boy—clever, amusing, engaging—it is impossible not to spoil him a little—he is growing so handsome and his large eyes have now and then a pensive, dreamy expression, and then again they sparkle with fun and delight.'[30]

At twelve it was much the same story:

'I am sure you would be pleased with Willy if you saw him. He has Bertie's pleasant, amiable ways—and can be very winning. He is not possessed of brilliant abilities, nor any strength of character or talents, but he is a dear boy and I hope and trust will grow up a useful man. . . . He is already an universal favourite, as he is so lively and generally intelligent. He is a mixture of all our brothers—there is very little of his Papa or the family of Prussia about him.'[31]

In the same year, his grandmother found him 'not only loving and pleasant but sensible and ready to take hints'. In 1874 the wife of the British Ambassador wrote, 'Everyone who has the gratification of speaking to Prince William is struck by his naturally charming and amiable qualities, his great intelligence and his admirable education.'[32]

Some defects, admittedly, were noticed as well. His mother said he was 'inclined to be selfish, domineering and proud', while Hinzpeter referred to him as 'my dearly beloved problem child'.[33] And about the time of his departure from Bonn, signs of revolt from authority began to cause trouble. His criticism of Bismarck over the Congress of Berlin has already been mentioned. He disagreed with his father's opposition to tariffs. All these tendencies were intensified when in 1879 he came to Potsdam and took up the life of a Guards subaltern. By his 22nd birthday in 1881 his mother had discovered that 'This son has never really been mine'.[34]

Something has been said (p. 35) about the circumstances which caused an unnaturally rigorous code of masculine conduct to become established in German society and about the tensions which resulted. In such a society, the pressure on the heir to the throne will clearly be much greater than that on ordinary individuals and therefore the risk of inner tensions being created in him will also be greater. One of William's sons said that, to avoid the appearance or accusation of being 'soft', his father forced himself to a kind of hearty toughness which was quite out of keeping with his real character.[35] William's American dentist said that he had complete control over his features and could relax his muscles at will. In the street and in public, he assumed the fiercest and most imperious expression which he could command; the moment he got out of general view, he eased up.[36] In this he resembled his father, whose practice of assuming an unnaturally severe attitude has already been mentioned (p. 63) while the Kaiser's great-grandfather, the Duke of Kent, was apt to be converted by 'a mistaken sense of duty' from a kindly, affectionate man into a 'violent sadistic lunatic'.[37]

> 'On State occasions the Kaiser is in the habit of assuming a very rigid attitude and a severe, if not forbidding expression of countenance. M. Jules Cambon [the French Ambassador] . . . was struck by this attitude which the Kaiser assumed during the official part of the audience at which he presented his credentials and he came away with the impression that H.M. had to make a great effort, and a very great effort, to maintain the severe and dignified attitude befitting a sovereign and that it was a great relief to him, when the official part of the audience was over, to relax and indulge in agreeable and even jocose conversation which he believed to be much more in consonance with H.M.'s real nature.'[38]

A member of his staff referred to a kind of self-consciousness which he had to overcome, often by a brusque jocularity apt to be misunderstood or resented.[39] He once nearly unleashed an international incident by pinching the King of Bulgaria's behind.[40] In William's case, of course, the situation was accentuated by the handicap of the stunted arm. He had a stiffer standard to achieve than others and was worse equipped for the attempt.

But this was by no means the end of the problem. William was the product of two cultures, not of one. He had two ideals held out in front of him, that of the Prussian Junker and that of the Liberal English gentleman. Each sprang from its own peculiar environment and since the two environments co-existed in the same continent and the same century, it was not generally appreciated that they represented different phases of social growth. While each ideal had qualities that the other would respect, the conviction of each that it embodied a materially higher proportion of truth impeded mutual comprehension. Britain's achievement in the mid-nineteenth century was so spectacular as to foster belief that a solution had been found, not to the social problems of a particular epoch and area but for good and all. The tendency to talk as though God had taken English nationality and treat everyone else as 'lesser breeds without the law' aroused as much resentment as emulation. William once wrote bitterly of 'the same old arrogance, the same old overestimation.'[41] In Germany, as has been seen, the attitude to England had become an issue of internal politics. It was fought in the household of Prince William's parents. It was the focus of the contest of will between himself and his mother. It was the cause of a deep-rooted split in his own personality.

Crown Princess Frederick was like Queen Victoria in being a determined and domineering woman who, as often happens, did as much to mould her son's character by repulsion as by influence. She disliked Wagner; he promptly assumed a fondness for that composer, although later on he asked: 'Why do people make such a fuss of this fellow? He was after all only a simple conductor.'[42] Her attempt to impose upon him, as self-evidently the best, her own outlook and standards produced, as it would on most young men of spirit, a reaction in the opposite direction, a reaction all the easier because there was the alternative Prussian viewpoint at hand to adopt and plenty of people ready to urge it upon him. The stories that his mother openly expressed aversion from his crippled condition are none too well authenticated; but its origin and the painful treatment imposed in the search for remedy must have contributed to their mutual unease.

And yet the Crown Princess left her deep and lasting mark.

From her William inherited, almost without noticing it, a host of minor tastes and characteristics—a passion for fresh air and exercise, for cleanliness, for early rising, for dabbling in the arts, even a tendency to be seasick.[43] To someone who remarked that prevention of illness was better than cure, William rejoined 'What matters most is soap'.[44] But he inherited more substantial qualities as well—a strong constitution without which he could hardly have stood up to his daily round; a quick enquiring mind; an intelligence which was continually at the mercy of his emotions; a preoccupation with himself which left him insensitive to the views of other people; an inability to judge character—his closest friend, Prince Eulenburg, said that his complete lack of any insight in this direction was his vulnerable spot. He said to the British Ambassador soon after his accession: 'My Mother and I have the same characters. I have inherited hers. That good stubborn English* blood which will not give way runs in both our veins. The consequence is that, if we do not happen to agree, the situation becomes difficult.'[45]

Just as his heredity conditioned him in spite of his efforts at liberation, so William could never shake off the respect instilled into him in the nursery for English ideals and habits of life. As late as 1911 he could say to Theodore Roosevelt 'I ADORE England'.[46] He wanted to be accepted by the English on their own terms and keenly resented his failure to achieve this—though the resentment often took the form of ridiculing the terms.

'The Kaiser often criticized England; he always did so impatiently or petulantly as one does when criticizing relations whom one sincerely likes and admires but who, one feels, are at times lacking in understanding or appreciation. That was the real grievance. The Kaiser felt that he was never properly understood or appreciated by Queen Victoria, King Edward, King George or the British people. Feeling his own sincerity and believing in himself, he sought to force his personality on us. As an actor of ability in a favourite part will sometimes endeavour to win, by overacting, the applause and admiration of an audience which he has failed to win by charm and subtlety so the Kaiser tried to dominate British public opinion by acts which antagonized or—worse still—merely bored or amused us.'[47]

* He should have said Guelph-Coburg.

But the desire to be the English gentleman was alternating all the time with the desire to be the Prussian prince—and each conspiring to frustrate the other. The tension between the two, superimposed on his physical disability and upon the tensions already endemic in Prussian society, is the ultimate key to his character, taut, restless, lacking the self-confidence which comes with integration, the living embodiment of Dryden's *Zimri*. His sense of duty, instilled by his upbringing and never lost to sight, was another bar to relaxing. Not that placidity, or a readiness to leave well alone, ran in the family; we have noticed the opposite in the Prince Consort and in Queen Augusta, while in a great-uncle, Frederick William, and in two great-great-grandfathers, George III and the Tsar Paul, restlessness ended in mental disintegration.

A common product of tension is escapism, and there can be no doubt that William lived largely in a world of his own creation. In his case, however, the escape was not into a dream world of thought or imagination but into a version of the actual world which bore only a limited relation to the reality. 'He was such a good actor', said Princess Daisy of Pless, 'he could make himself do anything'.[48] Sarah Bernhardt, when asked how she had got on with him, replied: 'Splendidly, for aren't the two of us both troupers.'[49] He was in fact always acting a part. In a large repertoire three roles were particular favourites, those of Frederick the Great, of an English milord and of Bismarck. For a private person, the weakness might have been engaging. For a man occupying a key position in a key European state when Europe was the centre of the world, it had its inconveniences. And, of course, there came moments when the illusion was rudely shattered, when the lime-light and the proscenium arch, so industriously propped up by a bevy of diligent courtiers, collapsed and the imperial poseur found himself in broad daylight, surrounded by no applauding audience but by the coldly critical men and women whose lives he had been playing with. The greater part of his life (as of many people's) was an illusion, a sort of perpetual sleight-of-hand to bolster his ego (or even his id) and conceal the true state of affairs. He could easily bring himself to believe anything he wanted to, without being conscious that hypocrisy was involved. On the few occasions when he got to the point of seeing through the situation, he hovered on the verge of mental collapse. Fortunately for himself—perhaps not unfortunately for others—the determination to look at the world through his own set of spectacles reasserted itself and he died in the not uncommon conviction that he was an unjustly maligned man. Once in the middle of a fervent complaint that he was always misunderstood and never had the truth told to him, he contrived to let a large tear fall upon his cigar![50] The incident, with its mixture of sincerity and art, of unhappiness and luxury, is one of those which epitomize a character. But though the situation can easily be made fun of, the question for the historian is how far, given the total background, any other result could have been expected. As an Alsatian deputy once said, he was a 'product of his milieu'.[51]

A good deal depends on what kind of woman such a man marries and in this respect William played for safety. In February 1880 he became engaged to Augusta Victoria of Schleswig-Holstein-Sonderburg-Augustenburg, commonly known as Dona. Her father was the Duke of Augustenburg whom Bismarck had manœuvred out of his claim to Schleswig-Holstein in 1864–5 and whom the Crown Prince and Princess had then supported. Her grandmother was a half-sister of Queen Victoria by the Duchess of Kent's first marriage, while her uncle, Prince Christian, was married to the Queen's daughter, Helena, and was thus William's uncle by marriage. William married young to get more freedom—Dona was the elder of the two. His mother wrote afterwards as though she had arranged the match, and William in his memoirs spoke as though this had been so.[52] But at the time she wished that Willy would see a little of the world first. Moreover, eyebrows were raised because the bride was not of the inner court circle—'the poor Holsteins are *mal vu* and there is a widespread though false idea that they are not of equal rank (*ebenbürtig*)'.[53] Even at the outset, however, the young couple appear to have been genuinely fond of one another, and when they came over to England in the summer for a visit to their common uncle and aunt at Cumberland Lodge, and for Dona to be inspected, Queen Victoria thought well of her.

Dona was a plain, unimaginative person with few intellectual interests and few talents. Princess Radziwill described her as a good and amiable woman who never read a paper and had no idea of what was happening in politics.[54] Princess Daisy of Pless considered her 'nice but silly'.

'Clothes and children are her chief conversation and the only things she thoroughly understands. Just herself and one lady-in-waiting and I and the children; she had on a chiffon dress with a long train and a large ugly hat covered with feathers. The same sort of dress she wears for lunch on the *Hohenzollern* at Kiel instead of a smart plain yachting frock. . . . For a woman in that position I have never met *anyone* so devoid of any individual thought or agility of brain and understanding. She is just like a good, quiet, soft cow that has calves and eats grass slowly and ruminates. I looked right into her eyes to see if I could see anything behind them, even pleasure or sadness, but they might have been glass.'[55]

Smarter sisters are seldom, however, unprejudiced witnesses, and in Berlin's conservative circles Dona was considered 'an excellent woman'.[56] One of the Crown Princess's staff said that 'she lived among the rural nobility and so knew the real roots of our strength'; the implied comparison was not lost on her mother-in-law.[57] She bored William, who found her exclusive company irksome. Determined not to be dominated by a woman in the way his father was, he 'displayed a regrettable lack of consideration to her in minor matters'.[58] But she remained devoted to him and reluctant to let him out of her sight. She represented a point of stability in his restless life and, besides presenting him with six sons and a daughter between 1882 and 1892, did what she could to keep him calm. She even placed on his desk a lampshade on which she had painted in blue letters 'He who prevails over himself, conquers'.[59] Hinzpeter on meeting her expressed relief that William was 'going to be united with someone who understands him and sympathizes with him in his weaknesses'. Dona herself wrote to Hohenlohe: 'Despite [the Kaiser's] exceptional gifts—and I as his wife may say this with pride there probably is at present no other monarch in Europe as gifted as he—he is still young and in youth one is apt to act spontaneously.'[60]

Moreover, Dona's hold over William was increased by her ability to satisfy his sexual appetites. There is no reason to doubt Bismarck's assertion that these were strong; he certainly had a pronounced emotional strain in his make-up. 'There was a great deal of the woman in the Kaiser.' 'He simply could not do without feminine sympathy and understanding.'[61] He was over-harsh with his sons but spoilt his only daughter. His relationship with some of his male friends, such as Count Eulenburg, had an emotional element and he was given to pinching young men on the cheeks and slapping his pals on the behind.[62] But regrettable as such habits may be in a ruler, they hardly amount to proof of perversion. And the complete lack of worthwhile evidence of his ever having been unfaithful is certainly remarkable when one considers how many people would have liked to catch him erring. Aberrations of any kind would certainly have upset Dona severely, for she was deeply pious, a great builder of churches and strait-laced to a degree. When she went to visit the Pope she insisted on wearing a hat rather than the usual mantilla.[63] She had the Intendant of the Berlin theatres sacked for allowing an actress to appear 'scantily clad' and insisted on Strauss' *Salome* being taken out of the repertory as blasphemous.[64] Although to begin with she did not much meddle in politics, her outlook was conventional and her influence against innovation. She regarded Liberalism as a betrayal, tariffs as a necessity and Britain as a baneful menace. Her husband had frequent cause to realize that she had been brought up at Primkenau rather than Windsor. As time passed and other advisers disappeared, he became increasingly dependent on her company; he could rely on her advice being available, even if he could not rely on its wisdom. This was unfortunate both for him and for Germany, but he would have been the last to admit as much.

Dona arrived in Berlin for her wedding on Friday, 25th February 1881, and next day entered the city in state, flocks of white doves greeting her at the Brandenburg Gate. The only jarring incident resulted from the enterprise of an advertising agent who managed to insert in the procession a float extolling the virtues of Singer Sewing machines.[65] The wedding ceremony took place on the Sunday evening and was followed by the traditional torch-light procession in the White Hall, where thirty-three years later William was to tell the *Reichstag* deputies that Germany had gone to war. First of all the bridegroom, preceded by pages with candelabra in their hands, had to lead each princess round the room, bowing as they passed the Emperor and Empress. Next, the best man had to lead round the bride and all the other royalties followed. By the time a hundred such circuits had been made, most guests must have been as bored as they were sleepy. The bride then retired and sent her 'garter' to be distributed among the company; this picaresque survival now took the genteel form of pieces of white satin ribbon, rather like bookmarkers, embroidered with initials, crown and date.[66] Next day there was a banquet and a performance of Gluck's *Armida*. Only on the Wednesday were the bride and bridegroom allowed away and even then they did not go further than Potsdam.

Here, the Marble Palace to the north of the town had been assigned as their residence but it required alteration and, as with William's parents, much of the first year of married life had to be spent in lodgings—which took the form of a disused castle. In the autumn of 1881 the Prince was promoted major and a year later transferred from the foot-guards to the hussars. During the winter of 1882–3 he worked on most weekday mornings for two hours with the Governor of Brandenburg. This and his legal studies at Bonn were almost the only training he received in the arts and processes of civil government. He is said to have written several military memoranda, including one on the uselessness of ceremonial parades. He also lived a gay social life, including such entertainments as beer evenings at the house of General Von Versen; the company on such occasions was mixed and once included Mark Twain, by whom William was not amused[67] (though Bret Harte was a favourite of his). But two more influential acquaintances made at this time were Count Philip zu Eulenburg and General Count von Waldersee.

He first met Eulenburg at a shooting-party in 1885. Twelve years the Prince's senior, Eulenburg was a man of many talents and many enemies who combined personal charm with a high level of general competence. Nobleman, diplomat and creative artist, he stood for many years closer to William and exercised a more continuous influence on him than anyone else.

'His poetic imagination was capable of anything. How often have I read sonnets in which he described and went into rhapsodies about affairs of the heart with women with such feeling that I thought, "Heavens, what has this man not endured!" On making enquiries later, I found it was quite a casual matter without any tragic overtones. But he himself firmly believed it to have been the kind of experience he described. When he told stories, they gradually changed out of recognition, but if you called his attention to the fact, he would get furious, convinced that he had been telling the truth.'[68]

The friendship, founded initially on a common love of Nordic balladry and Bavarian art, extended to involve an exchange of views on the whole contemporary scene from spiritualism to Zionism. Eulenburg, who was by no means blind to William's failings, was one of the few people who both dared to speak when he saw mistakes being made and succeeded in criticizing without losing William's affection. As he was too intelligent to be a reactionary, this made him unpopular among those of whom he got the better. Stories came to be circulated of the improper influence of a clandestine camarilla, centred on Eulenburg's castle of Liebenberg where William was a frequent guest. Uglier rumours were whispered about homosexuality. As to this, there seems little doubt that Eulenburg, though a happily married man and father, had had his homosexual moments and there was certainly an effeminate streak in his character. Nobody, however, has ever demonstrated conclusively that this failing damaged the advice which William received. If, on occasion, he used his influence to put his friends in office, he was not alone in thinking them qualified for their jobs. Eulenburg was too facile to be a great artist and lacked the resolve needed in a major statesman. But on the whole he served William faithfully and wisely, and got remarkably little out of it.

General Count von Waldersee, nicknamed 'the Badger' through his fondness for nosing underground, was both an older acquaintance and a more sinister figure.[69] His inclination to political intrigue distinguished him from most of his military colleagues. Appointed in 1882 as quartermaster-general, or in effect Deputy Chief of the General Staff, he showed himself an active and ambitious protagonist of military influence in general and his own office in particular. He sought not only to impress his views on William but angled to win the succession when Field Marshal von Moltke retired. He played a leading part in forcing the Minister of War out of office in 1883 for being too accommodating to the *Reichstag*, and in insisting that the successor should before appointment agree to allow the Chief of the General Staff direct access to the Emperor and surrender to the Chief of the Emperor's Military Secretariat responsibility for all appointments in the army. These two changes not only succeeded in their object of elbowing the *Reichstag* still further out of a say in military affairs but, as a less deliberate by-product, gave the army three heads instead of one. Waldersee had previously said that 'unless the General Staff is freed from dependence on the War Ministry, we shall doubtless end up with the French state of affairs where the Minister commands the army'.[70] Waldersee was aided and abetted by an energetic American wife who had already seen into the grave a great-uncle of Dona's, and who combined hot-gospelling with self-promotion. William, having never met anything quite of the kind before, fell heavily under her spell. She exerted a beneficial influence on his habits, being against cigars, filthy pictures and bad language, and a more varied one on his political opinions. She provided the two things which he needed most, a sympathetic audience and a sense of protection. The friendship was understandably an emotional one—given the characters of the two persons concerned, it could not have been anything else—but the fact that Dona throughout remained on the warmest terms with the Countess makes it hard to believe that the bounds of propriety were exceeded.[71] Though William came in time to see through both the Waldersees, and they through him, the General was at the outset delighted with his protégé. 'Prince William is more than ordinarily vigorous and goes into everything he takes up thoroughly and conscientiously. . . . If his parents have aimed at training him to be a Constitutional Monarch ready to bow to the rule of a parliamentary majority, they have failed. The very opposite would seem to be the case.' 'Prince William is a singular young man but is giving proof of a resolute character and that is the essential thing. . . .'[72]

The Waldersees maintained a salon in their flat in the General Staff Headquarters near the Brandenburg Gate at which William (and Dona in the intervals of child-bearing) were frequent visitors. The range of interest was by no means confined to this world; every Wednesday evening a group of the great and good gathered for a prayer meeting led by the Director of the Berlin City Mission, Dr. Adolph Stöcker. The Mission represented the early stirrings of the German Protestant conscience in face of the social events of the Industrial Revolution. It challenged the Lutheran tradition that religion was a concern of the individual and should not meddle in matters of State. It further challenged the convenient Liberalism of the manufacturers according to which the

State should not intervene in economic affairs; indeed, in party terms the group sought to detach the Conservatives from any form of alliance with Liberals. It refused to regard the allegiance of the workers to Socialism as irremediable. Not that it was in any sense revolutionary. Its leading figure, Stöcker, now a court chaplain, never recovered from serving early in his ministry as an army padre. Well-meaning rather than clear-thinking, he was more concerned with inducing the upper classes to treat the workers humanely than with influencing the workers themselves. If he talked vaguely about Christian Socialism (a term which seems to have been borrowed from England), his emphasis was on the adjective rather than the noun. All the same, his ideas caused alarm among those who did not appreciate their limitations—an alarm possibly justified by the more radical approach which they were capable of suggesting to others. When Stöcker's friend Weber founded evangelical trade unions in the hope of detaching Christian workers from the Socialist ones, the industrialist Stumm-Halberg called him a dangerous agitator. And the potential effect of Stöcker's views on the Conservative–Liberal alliance caused Bismarck to view him with an animosity which extended to his patrons the Waldersees.

On the subject of William and his parents, however, Bismarck and the Waldersees saw eye to eye. Waldersee once said: 'If ever there is any question of a *coup d'état* against the Crown Princess, you can count on me.'[73] Bismarck assigned to his son, Herbert, the task of cultivating the future ruler. An onlooker remembered the Prince at a stag party of Herbert's standing censoriously just outside the door when the repertoire of the music-hall entertainer became too suggestive.[74] But there is no doubt about the effect on the Prince of the flattery and blandishments of those who thought it their duty, as conscientious upholders of the Prussian tradition, to encourage William in his opposition to his father and mother. Another factor telling in the same direction was the friendship which now developed between the Prince and his grandfather, on whom, rather than on his parents, the young man was financially dependent. The old Emperor had been fond of him as a boy but had viewed him hesitantly, expecting him to turn out a pro-English Liberal. When he discovered the reverse to be the case, he was correspondingly gratified.[75] With his own son he found difficulty in coming to terms. The Crown Prince was allowed little authority and kept uninformed about matters of

State; in return he was not always discreet in his criticisms of Imperial policy and the Imperial entourage.

One of the Crown Princess's letters to her mother illustrates the resulting situation:

'Willy has more brains than Ernst Günther and can be very nice and amiable when he likes. Vain and selfish they both are, and they both hold the most superficial rubbishy political views— rank retrograde and chauvinist nonsense in which they, in their childish ignorance, are quite fanatical and which makes them act as they do, each in his way. It pleases the Emperor, Bismarck and his clique and the Court, so they feel very tall and grand. Bismarck is a great man and you know that I am always ready to give him his due in all things and try my best to get on with him in every way but his system is a pernicious one, which can only do young people harm in every way—to admire his blind followers and admirers and the many who wish to rise by a servile and abject pandering to his every wish and whim. These are all W's friends now and he is on a footing of the greatest intimacy with them. It is easy to see how bad and dangerous this is for him and for us. . . . W's judgement is being warped, his mind poisoned by this. He is not sharp or experienced enough to see through the system, nor through the people, and they do with him what they like. He is so headstrong, so impatient of any control except the Emperor's, and so suspicious of everyone who might be only a halfhearted admirer of Bismarck's that it is quite useless to attempt to enlighten him, discuss with him, or persuade him to listen to other people's opinions. The malady must take its course, and we must trust to later years and changed circumstances to cure him. Fritz takes it profoundly *au tragique* whilst I try to be patient and do not lose courage.'[76]

The lot of the Crown Prince and Crown Princess was hard, even if its full tragedy had still to be revealed. It was more than the not infrequent spectacle of the active man kept waiting. Born heir to a hereditary office which still conferred great political powers, firmly convinced that he could by the exercise of those powers bring permanent benefit to his countrymen and to mankind, he was not merely condemned to wait until long after the age at which he might reasonably have expected succession, but also to watch the powers being exercised in a manner of which he disapproved. Moreover, German society was developing along lines which would make it increasingly difficult to introduce the changes which he desired. 'He intended to rule with and for the bourgeoisie and is thrown into perplexity by the more and more rapid emergence of the workers; his formulae do not cover this situation.'[77] That he had increasing fits of gloom is hardly surprising. In such a situation his patent failure to imbue his eldest son and heir with his own sense of values must have seemed particularly irksome. Not only did the Crown Prince's own chance of exercising influence appear to be dwindling; if he could not manage to make a mark in his own lifetime, there was clearly little chance of his outlook being put into practice after his death.

William was often impulsive and inconsiderate, but the faults were by no means wholly on one side. The father showed equally little readiness to understand an alien outlook, and went out of his way to complain publicly about the son's immaturity, lack of tact and foolish views. 'See how life treats me,' he once said. 'Just look at my son, the complete Guards officer.' The most serious clash came a year or two later, in 1886, when Bismarck induced the old Emperor to let William gain insight into Germany's external relations by working for some months in the Foreign Office. The father, bitterly hurt by the grant to one whom he despised of an opportunity never extended to himself, made the mistake of complaining in writing that his son was too immature, inexperienced, overbearing and conceited for it to be safe for him to have anything to do with foreign affairs. Though subsequent events may be thought to vindicate this judgement, it constituted, in view of the laws of succession, an attempt to avoid the inevitable while the charge of immaturity was hardly a valid objection to an attempt at providing experience. Moreover, the letters of the Crown Princess leave little doubt that the real objection was the extent to which the attachment would increase Bismarck's ability to sway the Prince. As the protest was overridden, its only result was to leave soreness all round. Yet to William's credit it must be said that he put up with a number of affronts in public and did not lose his respect or concern for either parent. At one point, when relations had become particularly strained, the Crown Prince complained that William avoided his parents and told them nothing of what passed between him and the Emperor. William replied that the Crown Princess merely got angry when he expressed opinions contrary to her own. The Crown Prince described the answer as 'impossible'—but plenty of evidence shows that it was only too true.[78] On one occasion the Princess is said to have left the house as soon as she saw her son coming in at the front door. They were both assertive characters who wanted their own way; her Chamberlain once said that what she needed was powerful contradiction. Since mutual charity was lacking, antagonism was almost inevitable. When such antagonism develops in a family circle, almost every act by either party is liable to be misinterpreted and so to intensify the situation. Even attempts at reconciliation are apt to do more harm than good because the conciliatory moods seldom coincide on the two sides, and the rejection of an olive branch is doubly wounding when the decision to hold it out has taken a lot of making.

The same Chamberlain already quoted also said that the Princess responded to rough treatment, and resigned herself when she saw she was up against a brick wall. 'But she refuses to be passed over entirely. She can endure being told she is an Englishwoman with no enthusiasm for Germany, provided it is conceded that she has political talent and was reared in the classical school of politics. But any hint of doubt as to her political sagacity would infuriate her.'[79] The Princess's career had been an uphill struggle and life had brought to reality few of the bright hopes which at one time seemed to stretch before her. Being a more passionate character than her husband, she felt the deprivation more keenly, and the suppressed desires inevitably found expression in ill-considered actions and futile words. Her fate calls to mind the words of von Hofmannsthal:

> *Leicht muss man sein,*
> *mit leichtem Herz und leichten Händen*
> *halten und nehmen, halten und lassen. . . .*
> *Die nicht so sind, die straft das Leben und*
> *   Gott erbarmt sich ihrer nicht.*

> (*Life must be taken easily, as it comes,*
> *With easy heart and easy hands*
> *Holding and taking, holding and giving. . . .*
> *Those who do otherwise have a hard time and*
> *   God shows little mercy to them.*)

*   *   *

Anglophobia was a natural by-product of Prince William's tension with the 'English Princess'. How far this was based on genuine conviction and how far an affectation, was probably more than he himself knew. It was the inevitable consequence of an attempt to hold up England and English ways as a model. In his teens he had underlined in a book about Bismarck all the Chancellor's anti-English statements, and in moments of irritation was known to describe his English relatives as 'the damned family'.[80] Herbert Bismarck, however, who had done his full share to inflame William against England, said that although the Prince could never hear too much ill spoken about that country, the hatred concealed a powerful and unconscious attraction.[81] A further facet of this love–hate relationship which began to emerge during the eighties was William's attitude towards his Uncle Bertie. Here again the antagonism was nourished by many similarities. It is on the whole remarkable that, except for the cloud caused by Prussian policy between 1864 and 1870, the relationships between the Prince of Wales and his elder sister should have been so close. The girl had been her father's favourite child and best pupil; the boy had been a disappointment and by loose conduct contributed directly to the Prince Consort's death. 'Bertie', wrote his mother, 'is my caricature, that is the misfortune and in a man this is so much worse.' The girl was an intellectual with a sense of mission; the young man seldom opened a book and gave a high priority to his own pleasure. When he went to stay with his sister in Berlin soon after her marriage, the Prince Consort told her:

'You will find Bertie grown up and improved. Do not miss any opportunity of urging him to work hard. Our united efforts must be directed to this end. Unfortunately, he takes no interest in anything but clothes and again clothes. Even when out shooting he is more occupied with his trousers than with the game. . . . [Bertie] has remarkable social talent. He is lively, quick and sharp when his mind is set on anything, which is seldom . . . usually his intellect is of no more use than a pistol packed at the bottom of a trunk if one were attacked in the robber-infested Appenines.'[82]

The affection and regard which brother and sister felt for one another, coupled with William's deep regard for his grandmother, prevented uncle and nephew from being drawn together by the fact that both were at loggerheads with their mothers. Yet Edward and William had many other things in common. 'Both had a remarkable power of perception; both of them could be extraordinarily genial and could combine graciousness with charm. Neither of them could be reckoned as well-read for neither had acquired the habit of deep-reading; but both of them had vast stores of information that had been rapidly picked up in conversation or from the perusal of diplomatic or other documents. Both had that supreme gift of quickly grasping the inward aspects of many things.'[83] Neither could maintain interest for any length of time; the staffs of each complained about having to catch snap answers as their master was preparing to do something else.[84] Both were at bottom kindly and conscientious, anxious to benefit their peoples and the world in general. But for all that they found it extremely difficult to get on.

William was undoubtedly the abler of the pair. He too might have committed the solecism of handing to the man he was negotiating with the confidential brief telling him what and what not to say, but the cause in his case would have been a fit of enthusiasm, not muddle-headedness. It was said of Edward that, while he could play a good hand at bridge if his partner was dummy and all his cards therefore on the table, he was quite incapable of working out what cards other players held; William on the other hand once said that a good whist player should know where all the cards are after playing his fifth.[85] William was also the more moral of the two. He must have felt, for both these reasons, entitled to be the more successful—yet found himself continually frustrated, whereas his uncle appeared to carry everything easily before him.* The basic difference was undoubtedly one of temperament. The German was more self-centred, though not necessarily more selfish; he had a higher estimation of his own capacities and a higher expectation of other people. He had always to be doing and could not leave well alone. The Englishman, along with more worldly wisdom, had that streak of laziness without which nobody can be effective in a high position. When booed on his first State visit to Paris, he met the comment 'They

---

* 'When he (the Duke of Kent) saw his elder brothers roystering through life, generally in a state of tipsy infatuation but far more successful than himself, with his sober ways and his old French lady, he was stricken by the injustice of it all and instead of facing misfortunes, comforted himself in querulous tartufery.'[86]

do not seem to like us' with the question 'Why should they?'*
He once insisted, despite the fears of French Ministers, on being
in Paris on May Day. 'It will interest me to see a revolution.'[87]
The nephew's charm of manner had something calculated about it
and betrayed too great a desire to please; his involvement and
tension were the signs of an underlying lack of self-confidence.
The uncle's detachment came spontaneously as the reflection of
an integrated personality—though a personality which seems to
have been achieved rather than inherited. Behind the difference
lurked the fact that one represented an established Great Power
which had succeeded in imposing her outlook and standards of
value on the age, while the other stood for a newly arrived country
which was seeking to get both her political position and habits of
thought recognized.

There is no evidence in these early years of any unkindness or
underhand criticism by the uncle towards the nephew. The
Prince of Wales had thought well of Prince William at the latter's
confirmation. During William's first visit to England with Dona,
he caused offence by leaving Sandringham prematurely the day
before the Prince of Wales's birthday and going back to Cumberland Lodge;[88] this incident must have had a cause but what it was
is not recorded. The gift in 1883 of a complete costume in Royal
Stewart tartan seems to have had a queer reception; William
distributed photographs of himself in the unlikely guise of a
Highlander with the enigmatic inscription 'I bide my time'.[89]
The root of the trouble was undoubtedly the refusal of the older
man to accept the younger's valuation of himself. William felt
patronized by someone whom he secretly wanted to emulate. The
feeling instigated a determination to qualify for admiration by
England's own standards, alternating (especially after any particular attempt had been unsuccessful) with a fierce rejection of
those standards in favour of Prussian ones. Such a relationship
was bound to result in mutual misunderstanding and the taking of
offence even when (and this was by no means always) no offence
was intended. Wives exacerbated the antagonism instead of
reducing it. The chief exception to Alexandra's lovable nature was
her fierce hatred of Prussia which she could not forgive for humiliating her native country in 1864—an episode to which the Duke

* Many years later a head of the German State, on a visit to London,
is said to have displayed the same breadth of view.

of Augustenburg had in his own way contributed. The Duke's daughter, Dona, shared the Junker dislike of England and disapproved of Edward's worldly ways.

*   *   *

In 1884, William was sent on a visit to England's bugbear—Russia. Bismarck had had considerable success with his efforts to prevent the Austro-German Alliance from creating a gulf between Russia and Germany, and in 1881 the German, Russian and Austrian Emperors had concluded a treaty of neutrality to last three years. The chances of getting it renewed were jeopardized, however, by Austro-Russian antagonism over Bulgaria; when this State had been given independence in 1878, it had been expected to become a Russian satellite, but five years later it sought to make its status a reality by throwing out its Russian advisers. The principality of Bulgaria had been given to Alexander of Battenberg, a son of the Grand Duke of Hesse, and nephew of the Dowager Tsaritsa. There were many in Germany who expected Bismarck, as a good patriot, to back up a German prince. But the Chancellor was wisely above such considerations and concerned first and foremost to strengthen Russian confidence in German good intentions. In March 1884 he got the Three Emperors' League renewed for a further three years but he still felt a need to consolidate this success. These were the circumstances in which Prince William was chosen to represent his grandfather at the coming-of-age celebrations of the Russian Crown Prince Nicholas. The very choice caused umbrage because William's father considered that this should have been a Crown Prince's occasion; others, however, decided that similarity of age was more important than equality of rank. William was to all appearances a great success. He made, as he thought, a lifelong friend of the Russian heir who when patronized was always too diffident to show the resentment which he was sensitive enough to feel. He won high praise from the Tsar who invited him to be on second person singular terms and wrote to his grandfather that 'everything the Prince said pleased me enormously'. As the Prince had been carefully coached by Bismarck to say the right thing, he must have stuck to his brief—an aptitude not invariably apparent. He told the Tsar that the three Empires should stand together as a three-sided bastion against the furious onslaught of liberty and democracy. 'Yes', said the Tsar afterwards to his foreign minister Giers. 'We clearly need a triple alliance as a dyke against the flood-tide of anarchy.' As Giers had been trying for more than six months to make his master think on such lines, he regarded the German visitor's achievement as prodigious, and this was duly reported to Bismarck.[90]

Once home again, the Prince thought to improve the shining hour by establishing a regular correspondence with his new-found friends. If Soviet sources are to be trusted, he believed that this could most effectively be done at the expense of other people:

'The visit of the Prince of Wales has yielded and is still bringing extraordinary fruit which will continue to multiply under the hands of my mother and the Queen of England. But these English have accidentally forgotten that *I* exist.'[91]

'I only beg of you on no account trust my English uncle. Do not be alarmed at anything you may hear from my father. You know him, he loves being contrary and is under my mother's thumb and she, in turn, is guided by the Queen of England and makes him see everything through English eyes.'

'Today . . . there was a sudden outburst from my father who expressed himself in the most unbelievable terms about the Russian Government and the infamous way in which this "excellent"(!) Prince (Alexander) was being treated. He (Papa) poured out a stream of words such as lies, treason, etc., about the Government, in fact there was no spiteful word or epithet he did not use to disparage it. I tried in vain to parry these blows. . . . Thereupon he called me Russophile and Russianized and said my head had been turned and God knows what else. . . . Altogether, my dear cousin, the Prince of Bulgaria—by fair means or foul—has got my mother in his pocket and consequently my father too . . . but these English have not taken me into account. . . . We shall see the Prince of Wales here in a few days; we are not at all pleased at this appearance—pardon, he is your brother-in-law—with his duplicity and love of intrigue he will doubtless try either to encourage the Bulgarian—may Allah banish him to Hell—or discuss politics with the ladies behind the scenes. I shall do my best to keep an eye on them but it is impossible to be everywhere.'[92]

To disagree with the views of one's family is perfectly lawful but some ways of expressing such disagreement are more expedient than others, while it is always as well to be sure that the recipient of confidences can be relied on to treat them as such. These letters do not make pretty reading; their significance proved not lost on the Tsar.

The English relation who showed William most affection and for whom he usually showed respect was his grandmother. But in 1885 he managed to exhaust even her patience. Her youngest daughter, Beatrice, became engaged to Henry of Battenberg, Alexander's brother. The political complications which this match involved were by no means the only objection seen in Germany to the marriage. For the two princes were born on the wrong side of the Almanach de Gotha, since their father had married a mere Polish countess whose mother was even rumoured to have been a French governess. For a man who had thus disregarded quarterings to have a sister married to the Tsar and a son on the throne of Bulgaria pained the correct, and the prospect of Henry becoming son-in-law to the Queen of England did nothing in their eyes to atone. Although William's marriage had come under similar criticism (or perhaps for that very reason), he and Dona adopted a supercilious attitude, which his mother was tactless enough to report to the Queen, adding that her own husband sympathized with it. The Queen had no use for snobbery:

> 'The extraordinary impertinence and insolence and, I must add, great unkindness of Willie and the foolish Dona force me to say I shall not write to either. As for Dona, poor little insignificant princess, raised entirely by your kindness to the position she is in —I have no words. . . . As for Willie, that very foolish, un-dutiful and, I must add, unfeeling boy, I have no patience with and I wish he could get a good "skelping" as the Scotch say.'[93]

The Queen further let it be known that, in view of what had happened, William would not be welcome as a visitor at Windsor, to which the Prince of Wales added that, as one could not properly visit Sandringham and omit Windsor, he would have to forego the pleasure of seeing his nephew in Norfolk. William was very angry, referred to the Queen as 'the old hag' and tried without success to enlist his mother's help in his favour:

> 'William is always much surprised', she wrote, 'when he is thought unkind or rude, . . . fancies that his opinions are quite

infallible and that his conduct is always perfect—and cannot stand the smallest remark, though he criticizes and abuses his elders and his relations. . . . This only finds encouragement from Dona and all around him. I trust the faults which make him so difficult to get on with will wear off as he gets older and wiser and associates more with people who are superior to him and can laugh at many of his foolish ideas.'[94]

To complicate the situation still further, William's sister, Victoria, now developed a violent passion for Prince Alexander. Court gossip said that William was the first to let this particularly awkward cat out of the bag, having learnt about his sister's feelings indirectly from a disappointed suitor.[95] The Crown Princess, however, may well have instigated the whole affair; she certainly spared no pains to foster it once it got going. William was quite right in saying that Alexander was a favourite of hers as indeed he was of Queen Victoria, who had made Beatrice bring her husband (Alexander's brother) to live in Buckingham Palace. Bismarck was furious. Not only would such a marriage make it extremely difficult to convince the Russians that Alexander meant nothing to Germany. He had further taken it into his head (without, so far as is known, any justification whatever) that the Crown Prince had Alexander in mind as head of the Liberal Government which he intended to appoint on succeeding to the throne. Where possible supplanters were concerned, Bismarck's suspicions were pathological.[96] Moreover, he had plans to marry off the Princess to a Russian or a Portuguese—or even to his own son, Herbert. In fact negotiations with Portugal had been in train for some time but had broken down on the score of religion; the Crown Princess, learning about them at second-hand, erupted with anger at what she considered unwarranted meddling in her family's affairs.[97] Indeed, her anxiety to push through the marriage with Alexander may have owed much of its fervour to a wish to be even with Bismarck. The disproportionate flood of passion and controversy which the whole affair called forth can only be understood in the light of the previous relations between the parties concerned, but when seen against that background, reveals only too clearly the resentments which had been accumulating.

Meanwhile, Bulgaria was living up to a Balkan reputation for incident. In the autumn of 1885 Eastern Roumelia, set up in 1878 as a semi-independent province of Turkey, revolted and Prince Alexander gave the revolt armed support. Russia, who would not have minded a bigger Bulgaria if she could have been sure of keeping it under her control but objected to any reinforcement of Alexander's position, recalled all her officers from the Bulgarian army. Serbia, on Austrian prompting, invaded Roumelia but got badly beaten by Alexander's troops. In 1886 the Sultan was induced to make the 'Prince of Bulgaria' governor-general of Roumelia for five years. The reason for not saying who the 'Prince of Bulgaria' might be became clear soon afterwards when Alexander was kidnapped and removed from the country by a Russian-instigated army coup. A counter-revolution had no sooner procured his return than a Russian ultimatum demanded his withdrawal; he acquiesced without much reluctance and retired to Germany. What strains this series of events placed on the relations between Russians, Austrians and British (strangely prone at this epoch to let Bulgaria go to their heads) can easily be imagined. Queen Victoria shared her people's views and could hardly find words strong enough to express her indignation at the 'barbaric semi-Asiatic tyrannical' Tsar.[98] The Pan-Slav faction in Russia bitterly attacked Germany for not giving more whole-hearted support. The task of keeping the peace grew far from easy and Bismarck's concern for maintaining good relations with Russia became almost an obsession.

The Crown Prince saw the dangers involved in his daughter's proposed marriage and, though under great pressure from his wife, gave it no more than lukewarm support. His son's attitude lacked nothing in definiteness but owed this only in part to considerations of foreign policy. He was still smarting at the way his views on the Battenbergs had been received and everything combined to make the task of opposing the match as much a pleasure as a duty. At the height of the squabble, an invitation arrived for a German prince to attend Russian manœuvres. Bismarck could not trust the Crown Prince to convince the Tsar that Germany had no interest in Bulgaria and suggested that the mission be again entrusted to William. The Crown Prince begged his father to refuse—'my son possesses too little experience and is too immature to make decisions in such important political questions'. Bismarck, however, argued that the Liberal views of the Crown Prince would make him suspect at St. Petersburg, and

the Emperor decided in favour of William. Thereupon William
(who at this period was having trouble with his ear) said that his
father's attitude would make the trip too much of an embarrassment and was only induced to go by being told that he had no
choice but to obey an imperial command.[99] The visit was less
successful than its predecessor. William had no difficulty in
communicating his views about Prince Alexander but when, on
Bismarck's behalf, he offered Russia a free hand in the Straits of
Constantinople, the Tsar commented (much as Disraeli had done
about Egypt) that he was not aware of Bismarck's consent being
an indispensable preliminary to their seizure.

Such were the circumstances in which the year 1887 opened.
Although Alexander was out of the way, the provisional Bulgarian
government proved unexpectedly deaf to Russian advice, a mood
which both Austria and Britain were disposed to encourage. In
France, the national excitement associated with General Boulanger
was working to its climax, and revenge for 1870 seemed almost to
have become an article of official policy. In Germany, the elections
of 1884 had resulted in a *Reichstag* with a majority unsympathetic
towards Bismarck's policy and manageable only with considerable
contrivance. The old Emperor was about to celebrate his nine-
tieth birthday and at last showed signs of failing. A decisive period
lay ahead of Germany, and not of Germany alone. As events
proved, the next six years were to transform the situation.

CHAPTER V

Accession to Power

THE FIRST SIGNIFICANT event in 1887 was a German election, precipitated by a fresh dispute between the Government and *Reichstag* over the army. In 1874 Bismarck had submitted to the *Reichstag* a bill which would not only have granted the Government the right to go on indefinitely raising funds to pay an army of a stated size but would also have left the Government free to alter that size without consultation. The *Reichstag*, however, refused to accept so wide a delegation of their powers, and only with difficulty was a compromise reached by which the size was fixed and the funds granted for seven years (hence the name *Septennat*). In 1880 this arrangement was renewed without much difficulty although the size of the army was to be increased. In November 1886 Bismarck introduced a further bill designed to repeat the arrangement, but found himself unable to prevent a clause being added which reduced the seven-year period to three. As this was the frequency with which the *Reichstag* itself was re-elected, the stipulation may not appear unreasonable. But the Emperor and generals, who objected on principle to Parliamentary control in any form, were indignant, and without waiting for the final vote to be taken, Bismarck produced an imperial decree of dissolution. In his election campaign, he accused the anti-government parties in the *Reichstag* of playing politics with national security. How far he seriously believed this may be questioned; some writers have accused him of deliberately exaggerating the dangers and forcing an early election in order to get a *Reichstag* subservient to him, and so weaken the Progressive Liberals before the Crown Prince succeeded to the throne. But Bismarck, as has been said, seldom did anything for one reason alone. That shrewd old contriver with the squeaky voice and the inordinate thirst once defined the function of a statesman as being to wait 'until he hears the step of God sounding through events and then spring forward and seize the hem of his garment'.[1] Without doubt his internal difficulties made him welcome the chance to exploit the situation as he did. But there is no need to suppose that he exaggerated his fears of attack, since the situation unquestionably looked ugly.

In the election the Liberal and Conservative parties supporting the Government reached a working alliance, and the resulting 'cartel' came back much strengthened. Bismarck said that the new *Reichstag* was an accurate expression of contemporary Germany— the Junkers and the Catholic Church who were quite clear as to what they wanted, and a bourgeoisie with a childlike innocence and political naïvety which desired neither justice nor freedom.[2] But the vote of 227 to 31 by which the new *Reichstag* passed Bismarck's Army Law was due not so much to the polls as to the Pope. Since the relaxation of the *Kulturkampf*, Bismarck had been cultivating good relations with the Vatican, and even before the dissolution had offered to barter the abandonment of anti-Catholic legislation for Centre support over the Army Law; the deal had then been wrecked by the refusal of the party leaders to do as the Pope advised. During the election campaign, Bismarck published the Pope's letter to him and the Centre leaders no doubt heard the step of God sounding through the polling booths; they therefore decided, when the law was resubmitted, to refrain from voting. When fighting the Catholics, Bismarck made it one of his chief reproaches that the Centre obeyed the orders of an authority outside Germany; when he needed their support, he did not hesitate to bring in the external authority on his own side. The incident was a good illustration of Bismarck's political methods; it also showed how valuable the support of the Centre could be.

While the election was being fought, two significant events had occurred in diplomacy. On 20 February 1887 the Triple Alliance between Germany, Austria-Hungary and Italy had been renewed, though only after Germany had agreed in long negotiations to promise more help for Italian aspirations. Secondly, on Bismarck's initiative, the British, Italian and Austrian governments exchanged letters by which they mutually agreed to oppose all changes in the Mediterranean and Black Sea except such as they might themselves favour. By this device Bismarck had built up a coalition strong enough to block French adventures in the Mediterranean and Russian adventures in the Balkans, without involving Germany in quarrels of no intrinsic importance to her. These agreements (though they were secret) came in the nick of time, for in April a French intelligence officer was wrongfully arrested in Alsace; Bismarck disowned the action but the French Cabinet wanted to send an ultimatum. At the same moment, anti-German agitation in Russia reached a new peak. The French President, however, induced the Chamber of Deputies to install a new and less bellicose cabinet. The corner was safely turned, but for some months the situation remained tense.

These were the circumstances in which Bismarck took his hotly debated action of secretly concluding the Reinsurance Treaty (*Rückversicherungsvertrag*, lit. Treaty providing security for one's rear). This secret Russo-German agreement replaced the Three Emperors' Agreement which, though due for renewal in 1887, had been made a dead letter by Austro-Russian hostility over Bulgaria. Bismarck's object, then as always, was to keep Russia out of the arms of France, and this he realized he could only do if he was prepared to show some sympathy for Russian aims. If those aims included a direct attack on Austria, Bismarck could not support them and would have to back Austria. But the Russians realized and accepted this limitation, though they did so with a bad grace; their main ambitions lay elsewhere, in the Balkans and the Bosphorus. But Bismarck had once said that Germany 'must not encourage the tendencies to which the Austrians are prone by pledging the armed force of Germany for the sake of Hungarian and Catholic ambitions in the Balkans. . . . For us no Balkan question can constitute a motive for war.'[3] He was prepared to defend Austria against direct Russian attack and he believed that the knowledge of this would make such an attack unlikely. But he was not prepared to support Austria in the Balkans. The Reinsurance Treaty demonstrated this by providing for Russia and Germany to remain neutral if either were involved in war with a third country, except for an Austro-Russian war begun by Russia or a Franco-German war begun by Germany. The Treaty was to last three years. For Bismarck believed that the only things which it was wise to make long-term were objectives; long-term treaties made for a rigidity undesirable in a situation constantly changing.[4]

In this way Bismarck secured his much-desired promise that Russia would not take Germany in the back in the event of a

French attack. He had secured this without betraying Austria because he remained free to help her against a direct Russian attack and had always made clear that he would not help her to attack Russia. It was, of course, true that, if Russian action in the Balkans led to an Austrian attack and if in the ensuing war Austria were to be in danger of defeat, Germany might feel compelled to rescue her in spite of the Reinsurance Treaty. But Bismarck considered that he had safeguarded himself against this contingency by the Anglo-Austro-Italian Mediterranean agreements, which provided a coalition strong enough to block a Russian advance in the Balkans without Germany becoming involved. He may be said to have encouraged the Russians by the Reinsurance Treaty to think that they had an open road in the Balkans although he knew (as they did not) that in fact the road was blocked to them. But Bismarck's diplomacy must not be judged simply by concentrating on the embarrassment which might have arisen in certain eventualities; he must at the same time be given credit for the extent to which his arrangements rendered these eventualities unlikely. He said in another context that it was not a question of being stronger in the event of war but of stopping war from eventuating. A Prussian diplomat had once spoken of Bismarck's faculty for 'keeping a lie within a hair's breadth of the truth'[5] but in this case his apparent contradictions have to be justified by the value of his dominating aim. That aim was to safeguard peace—not because he saw any special virtue in peace but because he did not think war in Germany's interest. The concept underlying his network of treaties was to leave any country likely to contemplate offensive action in little doubt of finding itself up against an uncomfortably strong coalition. His ideal was a political situation in which all the Powers except France would need Germany and be deprived of the possibility of coalition against her by their relations to each other. Lord Salisbury less kindly called it 'employing his neighbours to pull out each other's teeth'.[6]

*   *   *

While the Treaty was being signed, William and Dona were in London for his grandmother's Golden Jubilee. They were little pleased by their reception, being treated 'with exquisite coolness, with bare courtesy—he only saw his grandmother a couple of times, at court functions; *she* was always placed behind the black

Queen of Hawaii!'[7] His father, by contrast, rode in the procession in a white cuirassiers uniform which evoked from the crowd whispers of 'Lohengrin'. But in reality it was a terrible shadow rather than a flashing plume which lay over him. During the spring increasing hoarseness had led the German doctors, believing the trouble to be cancer, to contemplate, without obtaining the patient's consent, a dangerous operation which would have left him permanently speechless. Before taking a final decision, however, they decided, on their own initiative, to call in an outside authority, a step in which they were supported by Bismarck; he refused to let the heir to the throne be treated in the way contemplated and got the Emperor to order the operation's postponement. Of the four names canvassed, they chose an Englishman, Morell Mackenzie, probably with an eye on the Crown Princess. What they do not appear to have known was that Mackenzie was a convinced opponent of treatment by operation. On arrival, he refused to accept the diagnosis without a pathologist's confirmation and the outstanding German specialist called in for this was unable to give it.* Through the summer, under Mackenzie's care, the patient seemed better and was able to lead a normal life. After a two months' visit to Britain, he went in October to San Remo. There trouble recurred, though in a different part of the throat; Mackenzie called in an Austrian and two German doctors who made a definite diagnosis of cancer and said it must have been going on for at least six months. Though cancer was undoubtedly the cause of Frederick's death, the whole course of his illness has been described as far from typical and Mackenzie is said to have 'felt sure the Emperor had syphilis of the larynx before the cancer appeared'. The Crown Prince's reputation was hardly such as to bear out this suggestion, but there are stories of overgenerous Oriental hospitality at the opening of the Suez Canal.[7a] If they are true, de Lesseps' work becomes even more significant in the history of the nineteenth century than has been supposed. But could one say of Fritz, as Amonasro did of Aida in Verdi's contribution to the celebration:

'*No, tu non sei colpevole, era voler del fato*'?[8]

The Crown Prince accepted the verdict with 'unaffected heroism' and a composure that was only outward, but still refused to

* He was also the man who named the *Kulturkampf*.

undergo the operation; even if he had survived it, his life is unlikely to have been thereby prolonged much beyond the two years which were the most the doctors would hope for. The official bulletin announcing the news transformed the political situation. It documented both a historical turning-point and a personal tragedy. The possibility of Germany being given responsible parliamentary government by royal action, the only method of introducing it short of revolutionary pressure, virtually disappeared. The test of the Crown Prince was not to consist, as had been hoped and expected, in his ability to match ideals with action but in reconciling himself to a life which would have been almost wholly sterile. From this test he emerged with a nobility which can only increase regret that such should have been his fate. For his ambitious and tenacious wife the cup was filled to overflowing. As her son wrote of her long afterwards:

> 'Her acute agony contained an element of exasperation. She was sensitive. Everything hurt her. She had always been prone to speak hastily and put down words on paper without thinking. She now saw everything in the worst possible light and read coldness and indifference into a silence really caused by inability to help. Such was her temperament that she had to lash out in all directions. She surpassed most of her contemporaries in intelligence and good intentions, yet was the most wretched and unfortunate woman ever to wear a crown.'[9]

To the failure of her hopes and the loss of her husband was added the cruelty of her neighbours and of her son. The facts about the Crown Prince's illness were imperfectly known and rumours to supply the vacuum were plentiful. The Crown Princess was supposed to have suppressed the truth in her determination that nothing should be allowed to interfere with his and her accession to power. The responsibility for calling in Morell Mackenzie was attributed to her and he was accused of having given biased advice at her instigation. Bismarck, who could have put the picture right, did not choose to do so, while the German doctors were primarily concerned with vindicating their professional credit at the expense of the English specialist who had taken over from them; any inclination to admit that they had called him in was extinguished by Mackenzie's unwillingness to take accusations lying down. All the Germans whose patriotic feelings had been affronted by the employment of an Englishman were only too eager to believe him wrong. The unfortunate man at the centre of the picture spent his last days in an atmosphere of charge and counter-charge, suspicion and intrigue.

His eldest son did nothing to alleviate the position, but said it would have been better if Fritz had fallen in 1870. To do William justice, he had affection for his father and accepted a little too easily the popular view that the case was being mishandled. He came to believe that the German doctors had not been allowed a free hand, and that if they had had their way over the operation, his father's life might have been saved. Excited at the sudden prospect of power, he tried to exert his influence in what he considered to be the right direction and promptly came into collision with his mother, who was never one to take kindly to interference and was by this time considerably distraught. He arrived at San Remo at the time of the crucial consultation, and was present at it—while she was not. Her letter to the Queen illustrated the resulting atmosphere:

'You ask how Willy was when he was here. He was as rude, as disagreeable and as impertinent to me as possible when he arrived, but I pitched into him with, I am afraid, considerable violence, and he became quite nice and gentle and amiable (for him)—at least quite natural, and we got on very well. He began with saying he would not go out walking with me "because he was too busy—he had to speak to the doctors". I said the doctors had to report to me and not to him, upon which he said he had the "Emperor's orders" to insist upon the right thing, to see that the doctors were not interfered with and to report to the Emperor about his Papa. I said it was not necessary, as we always reported to the Emperor ourselves. He spoke before others and half turning his back to me, so I said I would go and tell his father how he behaved and ask that he should be for-bidden the house—and walked away. Upon which he sent Count Radolinsky flying after me, to say he had not meant to be rude and begged me to say nothing to Fritz, "but that it was his duty to see that the Emperor's commands were carried out". I instantly said I had no malice, but I would suffer no interference. So it all went off quite smoothly and we had many a pleasant little walk and chat together. . . . W is of course much too young and inexperienced to understand all this. He was merely put up to it at Berlin. He thought he was to save his Papa from my mismanagement. When he has not his head stuffed with rubbish at Berlin, he is quite nice and *traitable* and then we are pleased to have him; but I will not have him dictate to me—the head on my shoulders is every bit as good as his.'[10]

Trouble, however, did not stop at disputes over treatment. The old Emperor was reaching a condition in which arrangements for papers to be signed by a deputy became essential. The responsibility was not unreasonably given to Prince William, who was on the spot, rather than to his father who was not. The Crown Princess was warned of what was intended but saw fit not to pass on the information; as a result her husband learnt of the *fait accompli* from a printed document and was much upset.[11] There was also a movement to declare the Crown Prince incapable of reigning and to have William succeed his grandfather directly. There is no conclusive evidence that he himself abetted this, but he was reported by his friend Eulenburg to have said that 'it is very questionable if a man who cannot speak has any right whatever to become King of Prussia'.[12] If he did use such words, a heartless remark has seldom been more devastatingly rewarded. For the people of Prussia were in due course to wish that, of all the faculties, speech had been the one of which the author, before becoming their King, had been deprived.

*   *   *

The European situation continued to cause Bismarck anxiety. The Bulgarians had chosen another German prince, Ferdinand of Coburg, to succeed Alexander and, in spite of Russian disapproval, he took up the position in August 1887. For some time Russian intervention seemed touch and go, and this might well have sparked off a European war. Bismarck's solution was to build up the Anglo-Austro-Italian coalition and to do so, he had to counter Lord Salisbury's fears that William, on becoming Emperor, might give German policy an anti-English bias. Bismarck replied that William could no more do that than his father could have given it a pro-English one. Popular support was essential for any policy which might involve mobilizing the full strength of the German nation, and that would only be forthcoming for a war of defence, which might extend to a war in defence of Austria but not to one in defence of Turkey. 'German policy follows a course dictated to it by the European political situation from which neither the likes nor dislikes of a Monarch or of a Minister can deflect it.'[13] In the light of this, Salisbury agreed to sign a strengthened version of the earlier Treaty; though its text remained secret, the fact of the three countries having agreed on common resistance became known.

At about the same time Tsar Alexander III visited Berlin, and Bismarck, who was spending more and more time on his estates, did the same. At the railway station the train anticipated the invention of film comedy by stopping at the wrong point and the Chancellor was reduced to charging along the platform, shouting, '*Je suis le prince Bismarck*'. The comment of a Russian courtier who had been displaced was, '*Ça explique mais ça n'excuse pas.*'[14] But the only person to whom the Tsar talked seriously was the French Ambassador, and in the same month Bismarck forbade the *Reichsbank* to discount Russian bills (the '*Lombardverbot*') for fear of 'people making war on us with our own money'. The chief result of this was that the Russians took their bills to Paris instead and the foundation was laid for a financial connection of no small importance in the development of European politics. In February 1888 Bismarck, without asking the Austrians, published the text of the 1879 Austro-German Alliance, so as to leave no doubt about the German attitude in the event of a Russian attack. He gave a long explanation of his policy in the *Reichstag*, of which the peroration was 'We Germans fear God and no one else in the world'. The words are more famous than accurate, since Bismarck's fear of God was much more open to question than his fear of coalitions, Empresses, Socialists, Alexander of Battenberg and a host of other dangers, real or imaginary. Five days later he introduced a bill providing for an increase in the wartime strength of the German armed forces to seven hundred thousand men. But he gave no encouragement whatever to Waldersee's advocacy of a preventive war with Russia. Gradually the Tsar and his ministers began to realize that the cost of having their own way would be too great and that they would do better to limit their ambitions.

The gist of Salisbury's question to Bismarck evidently reached William's ears for, through his friend the British Military Attaché in Berlin, he sought in December 1887 to counter the impression that he was anti-English. Not for the first or last time, he assumed the role of a much misunderstood man. His English relatives did not take the trouble to discover his real views, which were no more Russophil than Anglophobe. 'I am personally attached to the Tsar because he has always treated me most kindly and when I am with him he always makes me feel as if I were talking with a Prince of my own nationality' (which was clearly not what Uncle Bertie did). But, echoing the Prince Consort, he thought that Britain and Germany should go hand-in-hand in all political questions and, being strong and powerful, should uphold the peace of Europe. 'You with a good fleet and we with our great army can do this.' The Queen's comments on this approach were fair but uncompromising. The Prince's English relations had not intended to be hostile but had been pained at the way he behaved to his parents, especially at San Remo. To be treated on the old terms of affection, he had only to behave as a dutiful son. 'As regards his anti-English feeling, this comes to the Queen's ear from many quarters.'[15]

His English relations were not the only people who refused to understand him in the way he wished. In November 1887 he and Dona had attended a meeting of some thirty people in the Waldersee flat to launch the extension of the Stöcker Mission to other cities outside Berlin. William had for the moment formed an undeservedly high opinion of Stöcker whom he described as 'having something of Luther about him'.[16] In the course of the proceedings, he said:

> 'The most effective protection for throne and altar in face of the nihilistic tendencies of an anarchistic and godless party should be in bringing back to Christianity and the church those who have lost their faith, and getting them to recognize the authority of their legal superiors and the need for loyalty to the Monarchy. For this reason the ideas behind Christian Socialism deserve to receive more emphasis than hitherto.'[17]

This was described by his mother as 'a very foolish speech'.[18] But it also annoyed Bismarck, who disapproved of the Church having ideas of its own about social matters and feared that Stöcker's group (which he had nicknamed 'the Protestant Centre')[19] would get out of hand. He may also have realized that since Stöcker's proposals were far too mild to win round the workers, the only effect his agitation could have would be to weaken the unity of the possessing classes. An obviously inspired article in the *Norddeutsche Rundschau* took William briskly to task for meddling in party politics. (Bismarck once said that he believed in politeness in diplomacy but rudeness in the press.)[20] Coming from where it did, the criticism went home and was resented because the Mission's object of rescuing the masses from Marxism might have been expected to be one after Bismarck's own heart. William told Hinzpeter he did not consider he deserved such treatment from a man for whom he had, so to speak, locked himself out of his parents' house.[21] He sent Bismarck a long letter of justification; the reply recalled the elaborate courtesy displayed by Wotan towards Mime, but yielded no ground. He also fell foul of Bismarck for drafting a proclamation to be communicated to all the German princes in the event of his accession.[22] To regard them, in the way his father had tended to do, as troublesome vassals was, he argued, a mistake; they were virtually colleagues whose views deserved to be listened to, especially by an Emperor who would be younger than most of them. Of course, 'the old uncles' must be held in their place but this was much better done by affability than by issuing orders. The underlying attitude did William more credit than the naïvety with which he expressed it, and Bismarck's advice to burn the letter in which it was set out once more cut deep. Hitherto William had been able to attribute disagreement with his views to influences alien to the true German spirit; he now had to revise this belief and the process virtually amounted to making a fresh approach to life.* He began to talk about the need to make the Chancellor realize that in Germany the Emperor was the master. He also lent himself to the anti-Semitism which Stöcker was increasingly showing and tried to explain away the public criticism by attributing it to the influence exerted over the press by Jews who disapproved of any interference with their freedom to make money. When he announced his intention of stopping this on

---

* In 1894 William took Prince Ludwig of Bavaria severely to task for denying that the German princes were 'vassals' of the Emperor, and in 1896 he told von Stumm-Halberg that a political parson was a monstrosity and Christian-Socialism a nonsense. Thus within ten years of challenging Bismarck, he characteristically changed his mind about both points at issue.[23]

coming to the throne, the Minister of the Interior, although a noted reactionary, felt compelled to point out that any such regulation would violate the constitution. 'Then we must get rid of the constitution.'[24]

Meanwhile, at San Remo, the Crown Prince's growing inability to breathe had made a secondary operation necessary. A month later, on 9th March, William I at last died, preoccupied to the end by the need for good relations with Russia. Earlier obsessions about the Tsar arriving in Berlin without anyone being at the station to greet him changed into more coherent advice to his son (for whom he mistook his grandson) to nurse and keep the Russian friendship.[25] The death of the man who had fought in the Napoleonic Wars, gone through the revolution of 1848 and finally become the first German Emperor marked the end of an age. When Lord Salisbury heard of it, he wrote that the ship was leaving harbour. 'This is the crossing of the bar. I can see the sea covered with white horses.'[26]

*   *   *

The Crown Prince (who took the title of Frederick III) issued a dignified message to the German people and a warm one to his mother-in-law.[27] He left San Remo and travelled to the cold north. He made it clear that Bismarck was to remain Chancellor and during his reign of ninety days no real attempt was made to liberalize the court entourage. To defeat the espionage network surrounding him the steps to secure the advice of an Independent politician were so carefully concealed that they have only recently come to light. The most significant result of this contact was the enforced resignation of the Minister of the Interior in circumstances which suggested that, had the Emperor been a fit man, a constitutional crisis would not have been long in arising.[28]

The crisis which did arise was precipitated by the Empress, who insisted on reviving the proposal that her daughter should marry Alexander of Battenberg. Alexander's father opposed the match, Alexander himself had formed what was delicately described as 'a *zärtliches Verhältnis* (tender relationship) with a member of the histrionic profession' (whom he afterwards married) and the role of the Princess appears to have become that of dutiful daughter.[29] There can accordingly be little doubt that the Empress (who was, of course, verging on fifty and in a highly emotional condition) was primarily concerned with asserting her power while its basis still existed. But that was a game at which two could play. Alexander no longer had any official position and had been replaced on the Bulgarian throne. Yet Bismarck continued to claim that his marriage into the Imperial family would poison Russo-German relations and threatened to resign if the engagement were announced. As the Russian Foreign Minister, on being invited to confirm this claim, signally refrained from doing so, there can be little doubt that Bismarck was deliberately exaggerating the issue so as to provide himself with an opportunity for worsting the Empress.[30] That he succeeded was largely due to the prompt support of William who told Alexander he would regard anyone who worked for the marriage as an enemy not only of his house but also of his country, and would deal with him accordingly.[31] The implications of William's statement were not lost on his mother and passions rose high round the sick-bed. On Bismarck's birthday, William made a speech in which he compared the *Reich* to a regiment whose general had been killed and whose second-in-command lay badly wounded, thus opening the way for an appeal to rally round the junior lieutenant. The Emperor thought that this reflected unmistakably on his own capacity to govern and remonstrated with his son, who later sought to make up for the offence by arranging for a Guards Brigade to take a route back from manœuvres which would bring them under their monarch's eye.

Such was the environment in which Queen Victoria found herself when, after a holiday in Italy, she decided in April 1888 to return home via Berlin and see her favourite son-in-law once again. As Bismarck had been representing her as the real instigator of the marriage, and in view of the anti-British feeling provoked by Mackenzie (whom she had knighted at her daughter's request) Lord Salisbury took fright and advised her to keep away. But the Queen was not to be deflected:

'Perhaps [Sir Henry Ponsonby] would write to Lord Salisbury about the outrageous conduct of Prince William and of the terrible *cercle vicieux* which surrounds the unfortunate Emperor and Empress and which makes Bismarck's conduct really disloyal, wicked and really unwise in the extreme. . . . How Bismarck and still more William *can* play such a double game it

is impossible for us honest straightforward English to understand. Thank God! we *are* English.'[32]

On arrival she gave a remarkable demonstration of how to keep
one's head when other people are losing theirs. She comforted her
daughter, to whom she gave the wise advice only to pursue the
marriage project if William consented fully to it, and sought to
reconcile mother and son. (She can also be assumed to have heard
something of William's side of the story.) More remarkably, two
of the outstanding figures of the nineteenth century met and
talked for the only time in their lives (though he had seen her at a
distance in 1855 at Versailles). Charles Francis Adams, when U.S.
Minister in London during the Civil War, may have regarded the
Queen as 'nothing more than a slightly inconvenient person', but
Bismarck was put into a highly nervous state at the prospect of an
audience. All his charm was exerted and, to his relief, 'Grandmama
behaved very sensibly'. Afterwards he said, 'What a woman!
One could do business with her', and even went so far as to
describe her as 'a jolly little body'.[33] She then left Berlin, never to
return. Her daughter, instead of taking her advice, persuaded the
Emperor to include in his will a clause charging William 'as a
filial duty' to accomplish the betrothal of the Princess to Alexander. 'I count upon your fulfilling your duty as a son by precise
attention to my wishes and as a brother by not withdrawing your
co-operation from your sister.'[34]

The better relations established by the Queen did not last and
within a month the Empress was writing:

> 'What I said about William is in no way exaggerated. I do not tell
> you one-third of what passes so that you, who are at a distance,
> should not fancy that I complain. He is in a "ring" a *coterie*
> whose main endeavour is as it were to paralyse Fritz in every
> way. William is not conscious of this. This state of things must
> be borne until Fritz perhaps gets strong enough to put a stop to
> it. You have no idea of the vexations and anxieties, the trouble
> and difficulties I have to endure.'[35]

But Fritz got weaker, not stronger and on 15 June, after
putting his wife's hand into that of Bismarck, died. The previous
day the Empress had sent for the Berlin correspondent of the *New
York Herald* to whom in her presence Sir Morell Mackenzie gave

a parcel said to contain the Emperor's diary for the last ten years; this he was told to take to the British Embassy for forwarding by the Military Attaché to Windsor.[36]* The Emperor's will, which made his widow financially independent, was also put beyond reach. These determined moves to evade censorship, coupled with the fact that nobody outside the Emperor's few intimates knew what claims or statements his papers might contain, have to be borne in mind in judging the first action of William on his father's death. This was to surround the Palace with troops and forbid anyone, especially his mother, to leave until it had been searched. Since nothing of significance was found, the operation must have left both parties with an almost equal sense of grievance.

*   *   *

One of the first duties of a German Emperor was to take the oath of allegiance from the armed forces and it was in an anticipatory message to them that William made his first public utterance as Kaiser:

'We belong to each other—I and the army—we were born for each other and will cleave indissolubly to each other, whether it be the will of God to send us calm or storm. You will soon swear fealty and submission to me and I promise ever to bear in mind that from the world above the eyes of my forefathers look down on me and that I shall one day have to stand account-able to them for the glory and honour of the army.'[38]

Another duty of a Hohenzollern on ascending the throne was to read a secret document left to his successors by Frederick William IV and reported to recommend that the constitution wrung from him in 1848 be torn up. William preferred to tear up the docu-ment instead.[39] The Kaiser's message to his people, unlike his father's, came later but it did contain a filial tribute of admiration. His contrasting disregard of his father's instructions about the Battenberg marriage, which he promptly forbade, is more pardon-able than his attribution of the ban to the 'profound conviction

---

* During the previous autumn the Emperor's diaries for the years 1870–1 had in a similar way been smuggled from San Remo to Windsor. The Kaiser insisted on his grandmother allowing some of the papers to be brought back to Germany and examined, while at the end of her life, the Empress arranged for her godson Sir Frederick Ponsonby to take clan-destinely to England her own correspondence with her mother.[37]

previously held by my late deceased father and grandfather'. Soon afterwards, in the course of a meal with Bismarck and other Ministers, he heard of Alexander's decision to marry his opera singer. 'My mother', he commented, 'will have enjoyed her lunch.'[40]

The son believed that he had been deliberately kept away from the father during the last hours and in particular prevented from seeing him alone. The belief was probably well justified. So, for that matter, would have been the mother's defence that the son had only been treated as his conduct towards his father deserved. Understanding was virtually impossible because the two started from different premises. Unfortunately, although the mother rapidly ceased to be a figure of any political importance, this discrepancy of outlook was to be steadily extended from the personal to the family and then to the national scale. An inauspicious start was made by the arrival of Uncle Bertie for the funeral, which was conducted in a hole-and-corner way without any widespread evidence of grief. In the words of the Prince's own equerry:

'The first twenty-four hours, all was smooth but the Empress Frederick so succeeded in inflaming him with her own personal animosity that very likely the P of W said more to Herbert Bismarck and to the Chancellor than was prudent. We must make every allowance for the Empress Frederick's state of mind, considering what she has lost all round. But the Germans make no allowance for the P of W's brotherly feeling for his sister's sake. He not only made the pot boil over there but stayed on longer than was desirable and it went on boiling over. *All* his personal remarks went to the Chancellor's private ear.' (One of them was that the behaviour of the Germans to the Empress was 'a scandal to a civilized nation'.[41])

'Bismarck is great but *very* vindictive. His son is a caricature of the father. He had too the additional misfortune of having once been the petted friend of the P of W. . . . Every mistake the Empress Frederick made—she probably made about two big ones every day—was credited to the English influence of her brother's late visit. . . .

'On H.R.H.'s return he avoided Talleyrand's proverb—that "the tongue was given one to conceal one's thoughts"—and he was very open-mouthed. All this went back to Berlin and the Chancellor's private ear. Old Bismarck was helpless against the P of W but, like Mary, "he *pondered*" and retaliated through the nephew, the new master, like fresh wax in his hands. The system of espionage, which is one of the pillars of continental government, gave him handles to turn. Lies, no doubt—but here and there an imprudent remark true.'[42]

One particular source of trouble arose from a story that the Emperor Frederick had contemplated making frontier concessions to France and Denmark and restoring to the Duke of Cumberland the private property in Hanover which Prussia had sequestered in 1866 (and which Bismarck used to bribe the press). The Prince of Wales heard this story and asked Herbert Bismarck if there was any truth in it. Herbert turned the question into a suggestion and in next to no time the story was round Berlin that the Prince thought Germany ought to return Alsace. It was even suggested that the Empress Frederick had incited her brother 'to offend German pride in this manner'.[43] The Kaiser took eagerly to the idea that his father's memory was being insulted and in a speech at Frankfurt, 'as a reply to my Uncle Bertie', attacked, without explicitly naming, people who were saying that Germany should give away anything she had won in the Wars of Unification. Shortly after this the Kaiser discovered that, at the time when he proposed to pay a State visit to Vienna, his uncle would be staying there privately. He let it be understood that the two of them could not conveniently be there together and the Prince of Wales had to move on to Bucarest, which he did with a bad grace. Involved in this episode was the difficulty that William now expected, as a crowned head, to be treated with deference by a mere heir-apparent, forgetting that dignity, like a top hat, cannot be stood on for long; the uncle saw little need to change his treatment of his nephew:

> 'No English gentleman would behave like either the Emperor W to his uncle or like Bismarck father and son. But we must not forget that none of them happen to be *English Gentlemen*, and we must take them as we find them—pure Prussians.
>
> 'A little judicious lying all round will probably heal the outer surface, but the under matter will still fester. All cordiality, real friendship in Berlin is gone for ever. The real beginning

and cause *is the Empress Frederick*—whose champion in Berlin
the P of W is regarded to be.'[44]

To convey the formal announcement of his accession to his
grandmother, the Kaiser chose, in General von Winterfeldt, a
man who made no effort to conceal his satisfaction that the Emperor
Frederick's liberal principles had had such a short run. The cold
reception which the general not surprisingly received aroused
surprise in Berlin and the Military Attaché wrote that the Kaiser
was much hurt. 'The Queen intended it to be cold', was her
minute on the letter. 'She saw (the General) last as her son's
A.D.C. He came to her and never uttered one word of sorrow for
his death and rejoiced in the accession of his new master.'[45]
William had scarcely been on the throne two months when he went
off on a State visit to St. Petersburg, the first of a long series. The
Queen was offended by such a hasty disregard of mourning and
wrote to say so. When Bismarck offered to draft a reply, William
said that he thought he could find for himself the middle course
between sovereign and grandson. He did not do too badly,
though perhaps at some cost to sincerity:

> 'At the end of this month I shall inspect the fleet and take a trip
> in the Baltic where I shall hope to meet the Emperor of Russia
> which will be good for the peace of Europe and for the rest and
> quiet of my Allies. I would have gone later if possible but State
> interest goes before personal feelings and the fate which some-
> times hangs over nations does not wait till the etiquette of court
> mourning has been fulfilled. I deem it necessary that monarchs
> should meet often and confer together to look out for dangers
> which threaten the monarchical principle from democratic
> and republican parties in all parts of the world.'[46]

But the Queen was not easily placated. 'I trust we shall be *very cool*,
though civil, in our communications with my grandson and Prince
Bismarck, who are bent on a return to the oldest times of government.'[47] Salisbury, however, needed no prompting. 'To his few
intimates and colleagues who asked him why he was so unwilling
to respond to the German government's advances, the old statesman would reply in a low dejected voice "He's false".'[48]

William's attitude towards his uncle was another source of
offence to the Queen:

'As regards the Prince not treating his nephew as Emperor, this is really too *vulgar* and too absurd, as well as untrue, almost to be believed.

'We have always been very intimate with our grandson and nephew, and to pretend that he is to be treated *in private* as in public as "His Imperial Majesty" is *perfect madness*! He has been treated just as we should have treated his beloved father and even grandfather and as the Queen *herself* was always treated by her dear uncle King Leopold. *If* he has *such* notions, he (had) better *never* come *here*.

'The Queen will not swallow this affront. . . .

'He also said to the Crown Prince (of Austria) that, if his uncle wrote him a very kind letter, he *might perhaps answer it*! All this shows a very unhealthy and unnatural state of mind; and he *must* be made to feel that his grandmother and uncle will not stand such insolence. The Prince of Wales must *not* submit to such treatment.

'As regards the political relations of the two countries, the Queen quite agrees that these should not be affected (if possible) by these miserable personal quarrels; but the Queen much *fears* that, with such a hot-headed conceited and wrong-headed young man, this may at ANY moment become *impossible*.'[49]

Salisbury echoed his mistress in calling William Britain's most dangerous enemy in Europe and saying to a French Minister: '*There* is the dark cloud.'[50]

Meanwhile the August number of the *Deutsche Rundschau* had published, without any indication of source, twenty pages of extracts from the Emperor Frederick's War Diary which had the general effect of giving to the Emperor a good deal of the credit previously assumed to be Bismarck's. The Chancellor turned accusing eyes at the widow but this time without cause; her denial of any knowledge happened to be wholly genuine. Bismarck's first tactics were to declare the Diary a forgery, although knowing perfectly well that it was not. Further enquiry revealed the article to be the work of a lawyer called Geffcken, who had copied down extracts from the book when shown it in 1873. Bismarck thereupon had Geffcken's house broken into, his papers confiscated and a prosecution for breach of official secrecy instituted. The sequel confirmed that jealousy is a bad counsellor, for the court refused to convict and, though Geffcken was ruined, the public reputation of William and his advisers was not proportionately improved.

This was the atmosphere in which the Empress Frederick came on a visit to her mother in November 1888. Both Lord Salisbury and the Prince of Wales feared that her presence would only add fuel to the flames. But again the Queen showed how obstinate she could be:

> 'Intention doubtless well meant but it would be impossible, heartless and cruel to stop my poor broken-hearted daughter from coming to her mother for peace, protection and comfort. . . . It would be no use and only encourage the Emperor and the Bismarcks still more against us. You all seem frightened of them which is not the way to make them better.'[51]

Indeed, she hoped for some public demonstration of sympathy but perhaps fortunately this was not taken up. Her mood was maintained into 1889. 'William must *not* come this year,' she wrote to the Prince of Wales. 'You could not meet him and I could *not* after all he has said and done.'[52] Yet in August come he did, like an inverted cuckoo, and although attempts to get an apology for the Vienna incident produced no more than a statement that it was to be regarded as over, and in spite of the fact that he was $2\frac{1}{2}$ hours late, his uncle (who was particular about punctuality) went out to meet the imperial yacht. He stayed for several days at Osborne, and was made an Admiral of the Fleet. 'Fancy wearing the same uniform as St. Vincent and Nelson! It is enough to make me quite giddy.'[53] Far from regarding the rank as honorary, he pressed his views about naval gunnery on his uncle with fervour and only the sudden discovery of a bad knee which made attendance at an Aldershot review impracticable saved the latter from a similar lecture on military matters. (It is fair to add that William was at this time raising German military eyebrows by his readiness to tell the War Minister what to do.)[54] Two months later, after a visit to Athens, he wrote that the Mediterranean fleet ought to have twelve first-class battleships instead of five and in the following year announced that the fleet should be trebled to deal with the French and American navies. Lord Salisbury, in forwarding a message of this kind to the First Lord of the Admiralty, added:

> 'You will probably have a tendency to imprecate when you read the Emperor's kind solicitude for the good conduct of yr

Department. But it is wise to return a soft answer. Please send me a civil, argumentative reply. . . .

'It rather looks to me as if he was not "all there".'[55]

In 1890, a memorial to the Emperor Frederick was unveiled at Windsor; nobody told his son, who was left to read about the ceremony in the newspapers. With some dignity he made no open complaint but sent an adjutant to lay a wreath. In spite of these and other irritations, however, the personal contact which had occurred would seem to have eased the situation and for the next year or so relations with England became relatively smooth.

Meanwhile, he was infusing new energy into his court and laying about him with a lavish hand. His grandfather, in the truest tradition of the Prussian monarchy, had by careful housekeeping saved twenty-two million marks. But there was no longer any need for the King of Prussia, let alone the Emperor of Germany, to live like a needy squire. Though Bismarck grumbled and the old-fashioned criticized, the Kaiser's reforms were not out of keeping with the new age. Five months after his accession he demanded an extra six million marks a year. When the trip to St. Petersburg was followed by others to Stockholm, Copenhagen, Vienna and Rome, he took with him eighty diamond rings, one hundred and fifty silver orders, fifty breastpins, three gold photograph frames, thirty gold watches and chains, a hundred caskets and twenty diamond-set Orders of the Eagle.[56] A new imperial train of twelve blue, cream and gold coaches was ordered and a new yacht. Personal diplomacy was to be the order of the day even if in the cabarets they talked of '*der greise Kaiser, der weise Kaiser und der reise Kaiser*', as well as suggesting that the imperial anthem had become '*Heil dir in Sonderzug*'.*

One of these journeys had consequences of some importance. In 1889, William's sister Sophie became engaged to the Duke of Sparta. This involved her reception into the Orthodox Church and Dona, shocked by what she regarded as trifling with serious matters, induced William to make difficulties and even to say that, if she ceased to be a Protestant, he would never allow her in Germany again. The Princess rounded on the Kaiserin and accused

---

* These jokes are untranslatable. William I was the grey (i.e. old) Kaiser, Frederick the wise Kaiser and William II the travelling Kaiser. The imperial anthem really began '*Heil dir in Siegerkranz*', 'Hail to thee in conqueror's crown'. *Sonderzug* = special train.

her brother of hypocrisy, but the situation was smoothed over and William with Dona not only sanctioned the marriage but attended it. From Athens they went on for four days sightseeing at Constantinople. Bismarck feared that the Tsar would suspect more in the visit than met the eye and indeed he would have been justified in doing so for though no political conversations took place, this was not for want of effort on the part of the Sultan. The imperial pair were lavishly received and given a fascinating glimpse of Asiatic luxury, though it was on a later visit that Dona was taken inside a harem where she was repelled by the sight of 'a crowd of very fat women in Paris clothes which did not suit them, eating chocolates, and looking frightfully bored'.[57] The trip left with William a friendly feeling towards Turkey and a lasting interest in Near Eastern affairs which did nothing to ease Russo-German relations. One excursion which William did not, however, make was to the funeral of the Austrian Crown Prince Rudolph. He had been shocked profoundly by the latter's melodramatic suicide at Mayerling and could not resist the reflection that Rudolph had been seeing a good deal of the Prince of Wales.[58] What would he have said if he had known of the letter which Rudolph had recently written about him?

'The Kaiser is likely to cause great confusion in Europe before long. He is just the man for it; energetic and capricious, firmly convinced of his own genius, he will in the course of a few years bring the Germany of the Hohenzollerns to the position it deserves.'[59]

*   *   *

'The Kaiser', said Bismarck in 1888, 'is like a balloon, if you don't keep fast hold of the string, you never know where he'll be off to.'[60] But the Chancellor failed to act on his own diagnosis, for in July 1888 he retired to his country estate and remained there until the end of the year, when he said it was essential for him to have a talk with William twice a week.[61] But although he returned to Berlin in January 1889, he only stayed there until May, when he went back to the country (except for a few days in August and October) until January 1890. He later said William made it clear that he was not wanted in Berlin,[62] but a more probable explanation is that he saw there were too many possibilities of collision, and did not trust his own temper. During one interview William is said to have made Bismarck so angry that the Chancellor picked up his inkstand and replaced it on his desk with such force as to splash the contents all over his master.[63] He may well have thought that his son, being nearer to William in age, stood a better chance of coping successfully with the problem. But 'hateful Herbert', as Salisbury called him,[64] had inherited his father's brusqueness without his father's charm, his contempt for ideas without his power of grasping the essentials in a situation and, when it came to the point, was unable to dominate William. Bismarck had found plenty of people willing to help in turning the young man against his parents; he had not in those days allowed for the possibility of the same influences being exerted against himself. In August 1888 Stöcker wrote to the editor of the conservative *Kreuzzeitung* urging the strategy of the indirect approach. If attempts to cause bad blood between the Kaiser and Bismarck were made too obvious, they would have the opposite of the intended effect. Nothing should therefore be said about personalities but policies calculated to provoke collisions should be pressed upon William, who was reported to have said that he would give the old man six months breathing space and then take over himself. The *Kreuzzeitung* was diligent in stoking the fires of discontent and though in April 1889 Bismarck induced the Kaiser to make Stöcker withdraw from active politics, he had thereby merely bruised one head of the hydra confronting him. The outlook of the Christian Socialists was all the time being pressed by Hinzpeter and a number of other theorists. Waldersee, who had achieved his ambition of becoming Chief of the General Staff, professed to be terrified of an imminent Russian attack and contested Bismarck's refusal to contemplate a preventive war; he coined the quip that 'if Frederick the Great had had this sort of Chancellor, he would not have been great'.[65] His wife was itching to see her husband made Chancellor. Holstein, the official in the Foreign Office who was the power behind the scenes there, had equally little patience with a Russian policy which was beyond his comprehension. The Kaiser's uncle-by-marriage, Grand Duke Frederick of Baden, through his Berlin representative Baron Marschall von Bieberstein, attacked Bismarck as a reactionary. Miquel, the leader of the National Liberals, hailed in the young and gifted ruler the rallying point of those who hoped to avoid revolution by moderate reform. With such influences at work, a show-down was only to be expected.

The sight of these clouds on the horizon must have been one of the motives which led Bismarck, in January 1889, to write to Lord Salisbury suggesting an Anglo-German defensive alliance against France. 'Throughout my life,' he once wrote, 'I have had sympathy for England and her inhabitants' (was he thinking of the Miss Russell whom he had long ago nearly married?) 'and I am at certain times not yet free from it.'[66] One of those times had occurred in 1879 when he had flashed the ace of an alliance before the eyes of Disraeli only to restore it to his sleeve as soon as he had taken that particular trick with the Austrian Treaty. Since then, the fear of English Liberalism in German politics had made him keep his distance but, with Salisbury in the place of Gladstone and William in that of his father, the idea regained allure. An agreement with England, isolating France, would have been the coping-stone to his structure. But Salisbury described British foreign policy as drifting lazily downstream pushing out a diplomatic boat-hook from time to time to avoid collisions.[67] So pronounced an understatement at least indicated an indisposition to hurry and Salisbury on this occasion was not in the market. He pointed out that an alliance, to have force, must have Parliamentary sanction which in the situation of the time was unlikely to be forthcoming. So, while professing to welcome the idea personally, he declared himself unable to do more than leave it on the table without saying 'Yes' or 'No'.[68] The excuse concealed a doubt about the need for German help against France. An alliance against Russia might have been a different matter but that Bismarck was unable to offer.

That autumn the Tsar came to Berlin and Bismarck not only returned to the city for the occasion but appeared at a gala performance of *Rheingold*. The Tsar for his part invited the Chancellor to sit down while himself remaining on his feet, but also asked if Bismarck was sure of being able to stay in office. The first months of the New Year brought the answer; the basic clash of personality and method between Kaiser and Chancellor then found expression in no less than six issues at the same time.[69]

When thirty-five years later the Kaiser came to write his Memoirs, he attributed the dispute almost exclusively to differences of view over social legislation, and there is no doubt that this was the first item to arise and one of the most fundamental. William, who in the previous year had achieved a considerable personal success in settling a strike by taking a high line with the Ruhr coalowners while talking to the miners like a Dutch uncle, was anxious to see German labour legislation reformed. Bismarck felt that this was where he had come in. The apparent failure of his schemes of social insurance to reconcile the workers to the régime had left him sceptical about achieving results by kindness. He had always been allergic to regulating conditions of work by law, and the backwardness of German legislation in this direction was in marked contrast to its pioneering character where insurance was concerned. Contemptuous of people whom he described as 'dizzy with humanitarianism', he resorted to the old excuse that limiting the length of time men and women could work was interfering with their personal liberty. He at first refused to produce the decree which William wanted and when William insisted, drafted it in such a way that it raised considerably higher hopes than anyone intended to satisfy; he then refused his counter-signature so that it had to be published on the imperial authority alone. He intrigued with foreign diplomats to block the Kaiser's wish for an International Labour Congress, a piece of subversion which inevitably reached his master's ears. When the Congress met in spite of him, he vented his chagrin by keeping it short of accommodation, secretaries and even stationery. The Kaiser, in reply, argued that most revolutions had been due to failure to make reforms in good time. Maternal influences asserting themselves, he quoted the English example to prove Germany wrong, though the arguments he used in doing so were clever rather than correct. Yet there can be no doubt that on the whole issue William's attitude offered more possibility of progress than Bismarck's blunt refusal to consider concessions. The workers, with their standards of living rising, *were* reaching a point at which they would be ready to exchange dogma for practice, as the Revisionist movement in the Socialist party showed. The social insurance laws had duly made their mark but it was one which took time to become evident. If the government had been able to demonstrate that it was not tied wholly to the interests of the possessing classes, it could have won increasing working-class support and a great deal of subsequent trouble would have been avoided. The pity was that William, after fighting Bismarck on this very point, then adopted Bismarck's own attitude and wearied of well-doing.

Closely related to this question was that of anti-socialist legislation, which was due for renewal. Bismarck could probably have secured its indefinite extension if he had been prepared to compromise. An unpopular clause gave the police power to move agitators away from their chosen field of operations, which had the unintended effect of spreading their subversive views still more widely round Germany. Bismarck insisted on retaining this clause although, by doing so, he drove a wedge between the Conservatives who supported it and the Liberals and Centre who opposed it. 'If the law is not passed,' he argued, 'we shall have to get along without it and let the waves get higher. That may lead to an armed clash.'[70] He was back at his old tactics of provoking a crisis in order to prove himself indispensable; their failure to come off made their underlying cynicism more obvious.

The issue which could usually be relied upon to produce a political conflagration was army legislation and Bismarck duly proposed that, although only three out of the seven years had passed, an additional eighty thousand men should be demanded. William, however, side-stepped by asking only for an easily obtainable increase in the artillery and leaving the rest to be discussed another year.

In the middle of the controversy, the *Reichstag* elections took place. Thanks partly to Bismarck's own behaviour over the socialist law, the Cartel parties which had triumphed in 1887 went into them anything but united and lost heavily. The shape of things to come was shown by the success of the Social Democrats in winning more votes than any other party (though, owing to the way in which the constituencies were arranged, they did not get a proportionate number of seats). Close behind them came the Centre, so that in all four and a half million out of a total of seven million votes went to groups hostile to Bismarck. This added point to the arguments over the socialist law but it also put the Centre in a key position and Bismarck invited their leader, Windthorst, to call on him. The visit had no direct results; Windthorst returned saying that he had come from the political deathbed of a great man. But it produced from the Kaiser an angry demand that the Chancellor obtain his permission before negotiating with any party leaders. The demand was as angrily refused; Bismarck is said to have remarked that the authority behind an imperial command stopped at the threshold of his wife's drawing-room (though this was not, so far as is known, where the interview had taken place).[71] The demand was one which could not possibly have been put to a Prime Minister responsible to Parliament; to a Chancellor responsible to the man making it, the propriety was a more open question.

A bigger constitutional issue and the one which proved decisive was occasioned by Bismarck circulating to his subordinates a Prussian decree made by Frederick William IV in 1852. According to this, Prussian Ministers were required to consult the Minister-President before communicating with the King either orally or in writing (though not necessarily to obtain his consent). In the absence of such an order and of collective Cabinet responsibility, and in the presence of a King who chose to play off one of his advisers against the others, the position of Minister-President would clearly be impossible. Although Bismarck's successor issued what purported to be a revised text, the principle of the decree was, in fact, maintained more or less unaltered. But in 1882 Bismarck had said that 'the real effective Minister-President in Prussia is and remains the King'.[72] William had already complained of the Ministers 'deserting the colours' because at a crucial meeting they backed Bismarck rather than himself, thereby implying that their first loyalty was to him rather than to their chief. He also not unreasonably asked how the proposed restriction could work with a Chancellor who was away from Berlin for over half the year. He ordered a fresh decree to be drafted revoking the authority which his great-uncle had given and on 18th March Bismarck, rather than comply, sent in a six-page letter of resignation, drafted with more attention to effect than to accuracy.

In all these disputes, foreign policy had hardly figured. Bismarck's letter of resignation certainly made out that the two major issues had been the 1852 order and the question of policy towards Russia. But in fact it was not until after Bismarck had already been presented with the choice between repealing the 1852 order and resigning that the Russian issue cropped up at all and then only in a squabble over some despatches from Kiev in which neither side got their facts right.[73] The biggest immediate consequence of Bismarck's fall, namely the decision against renewing the Reinsurance Treaty, was not mentioned in the events leading up to it.

But, of course, none of the things which were argued about mattered by comparison with the characters of the men who were arguing. Indeed one may suspect Bismarck, as so often before, of choosing a particular line not so much because he believed in it but because he considered it good terrain for a fight. The question at stake was who was to run the country. All Bismarck's resources were deployed; he even asked the Empress Frederick to use her influence with her son on his behalf. But the wizard had lost his magic; his spells were powerless because they were exerted on people who did not respect them, and he who had so signally disregarded Kant's command to use people as ends in themselves had too small a stock of loyalty to draw on. As Lord Salisbury told Queen Victoria: 'The very qualities which Bismarck fostered in the Emperor in order to strengthen himself when the Emperor Frederick should come to the throne have been the qualities by which he has been overthrown.'[74] The Empress, with what must have been a mixture of pity and triumph, told him that her influence with her son could not save him for he himself had destroyed it.[75] The German people had expressed their views clearly at the polls; Bismarck's fall from power may have saved him from defeat at the hands of the new *Reichstag*. The loyalty of the army was, as always, to the Emperor rather than to the politician. And among the things which the Kaiser had learnt from Bismarck was the proverb '*A gentilhomme, gentilhomme! A corsaire, corsaire et demi!*'[76] This he now put into practice by suppressing Bismarck's letter of resignation while publishing his own reply so drafted as to suggest that the old man had forced his departure on a highly reluctant master for reasons of health. He showered honours, involving a change of name, on the supposed invalid. He even sent a telegram to Hinzpeter in which he said he felt as miserable as if he had again lost his grandfather:

> 'This is, however, the fate which God has decided for me and I must bear it even if it proves my downfall. It has fallen to me to be officer-of-the-watch on the ship-of-state. The course remains the same and now full steam ahead!'[77]

As Bismarck said when they saw him off at the station, 'It was a first-class funeral.' He quitted the 'public waiting-room (First Class)', as the Chancellor's Palace during his tenancy was once described, and retired to the converted hotel which served him as a country house, trailing a cellar of thirteen thousand bottles behind him.[78]

*   *   *

Bismarck's departure was a major historical event but it did not gain its significance from the time or manner of its occurrence. Another five years and the excuse of ill-health would have become a reality, while he was unlikely to have had anything fresh to contribute in the extra time. Indeed at seventy-five the old man was already losing his skill and allowing his animosities to get the better of his judgement. In the autumn of 1889 Holstein said to Herbert: 'If your father had never got to know Schweninger (his doctor), he would by now have been dead but would have vanished like a vast shining sun. As it is, he is still alive but is getting old as other people do.'[79] Having himself lost his capacity for sustained hard work, he disliked handing over jobs to other people for fear they would get too much credit as a result.[80] His handling of a number of matters, such as the *Lombardverbot*, the Stöcker meeting and the Geffcken prosecution, had been inept. On the various questions at issue with William, he was as often wrong as right. One of the most celebrated incidents in the final scenes occurred when, through a muddle, the Kaiser called at nine in the morning and Bismarck had to be fetched out of bed. But though in a hurry, he had time to find a letter from London which he then so contrived to handle during the interview as to incite William into commanding him to read it out. It proved to report that William's much-vaunted visits to St. Petersburg as Prince had led the Tsar to call him *'un garçon mal élevé et de mauvaise foi'*. Admiration of the skill by which the revelation was stage-managed has to be balanced by wonder that he should have thought it effective at that particular juncture to wound his master's vanity.

Six weeks before Bismarck resigned, the Kaiser had already been warning his next Chancellor of what was in store. To give a politician an appointment which was considered as official as that of Chief of the General Staff was out of the question; this made the search for a suitable candidate much more reminiscent of the process of finding a new Chairman for the Prison Commissioners than of filling a Ministerial appointment in the sense to which we in Britain are accustomed. The Chancellor was in fact the Emperor's chief civilian staff officer. The choice for the post lay between a courtier, a civil servant and a soldier, and, to the acute disappointment of both the Waldersees, fell in fact on General Leo von Caprivi. Caprivi had already had experience of government as head of the navy from 1883 to 1888. In this capacity, he had once asked: 'Whatever will happen if Prince William becomes Kaiser now? He thinks he understands *everything*, even shipbuilding.'[81] Soon after Prince William did become Kaiser, he summoned the chief of the shipbuilding section to see him without consulting Caprivi, who promptly resigned and went to command an army corps in Hanover.[82] When Bismarck, a few weeks earlier, had considered giving up his Prussian posts and keeping only his imperial ones, it was Caprivi whom he had designated to take over the former; Caprivi had also been thought of as a possible successor to von Moltke on the General Staff.[83] His qualifications for high office were therefore more real than apparent and consisted principally in integrity and common-sense. What was not clear was how he would run in harness with a superior who wanted the privilege of taking decisions without being prepared to shoulder the routine work which this must involve.

The technical problems of the relationship were not slow to reveal themselves. William had naïvely imagined that getting rid of the senior member of the Bismarck family would not affect his relationship with the junior and that Herbert Bismarck would remain Foreign Secretary. He was the only person to whom his father had talked with any freedom; this constituted a unique qualification for handling German foreign policy.[84] But Herbert stood and fell by his father and was not to be influenced even by William's suggestion that he ought to stand and fall by his King. Asked to suggest someone else, the Bismarcks named Count von Alvensleben, Minister to Belgium. Alvensleben was sent for but refused to consider the job. Someone (Eulenburg, Waldersee and Holstein each afterwards claimed the credit) suggested Baron Marschall von Bieberstein, the tall and amusing Baden lawyer who represented his Grand Duke in Berlin. Caprivi would have preferred a Prussian and still more a man with some experience in foreign affairs, but he allowed himself to be overborne and on the Kaiser's authority offered the job to Marschall. But when next morning he came back to report Marschall's acceptance, he found that in the interval the Kaiser's adjutant and Herbert Bismarck had been emphasizing the dangers of inexperience, and that under their influence William had called von Alvensleben back. A potentially embarrassing situation was resolved only by von Alvensleben's continued refusal. In this way the conduct of Germany's foreign policy passed into the charge of two men who knew nothing about it under a monarch who only concerned himself by fits and starts.

By the time Marschall took over, however, the die had been cast as far as the Reinsurance Treaty was concerned. At about the moment when Bismarck was drafting his letter of resignation, Shuvalov, the Russian Ambassador, had arrived back in Berlin with the Tsar's authority to renew the Treaty. Bismarck, on hearing this, told Shuvalov that he was being driven from office for being too pro-Russian, while Herbert reported Shuvalov to the Kaiser as thinking that the change of Chancellors would be bound to change the Tsar's attitude. But the Kaiser called Shuvalov to him and it quickly emerged that both sides had been misrepresented. Shuvalov explained that all he had done was to ask for fresh instructions: the Kaiser explained that Bismarck was only leaving for reasons of health and that nothing had occurred to alter Germany's relations with Russia. Shuvalov at once reported this back.

Unfortunately, it did not occur to anyone to tell Caprivi of this interview and when, on settling down at his desk, he found the renewal of the Treaty as the most urgent business to be dealt with, he had only the advice of Foreign Office officials and of the German Ambassador in St. Petersburg to go by. None of these properly understood Bismarck's objectives, which he had never taken the trouble to explain to them; part of the secret of his power was a monopoly knowledge of all the facts.[85] He had set out his views on foreign policy in two long memoranda to the Kaiser in 1888 but William does not seem to have thought of showing these to Caprivi. The army was deeply suspicious of Russia and Caprivi, as an honest unsubtle man, felt that the intricacies of Bismarck's policies were beyond him. The Foreign Office stressed the incompatibility of the Treaty with Germany's other obligations and the damage which could be done to German relations with other nations if the Russians were to publish the text; this overlooked the fact that it was the Russians who had held back when Bismarck suggested publication. But the arguments of the Foreign Office were superficially convincing to anyone coming fresh to the subject, even though their advocates were not uninfluenced by the thought that, if the Bismarckian policy were continued, the Bismarcks might soon be back to conduct it. Caprivi explained his conclusion to the Kaiser at the same time as he reported Marschall's readiness to be Foreign Secretary. William is said to have replied, 'Well then, it can't be done, whether I like it or not'.[86] He, however, insisted on further steps being taken to assure the Russians that the decision did not imply any change of policy.

By this time, however, Shuvalov had heard from the Tsar, who welcomed the Kaiser's assurances of continuity and remained anxious to extend the Treaty. The news that this was not to be done came as a slap in the face and looked like a deliberate decision by the 'new men' in defiance of the Kaiser. Small wonder that the official detailed to tell Shuvalov should have written in his diary: 'Very painful discussion; direct to Caprivi; serious situation; the noble and courageous man very distressed . . . restless sleep due to politics'.[87] The Kaiser would apparently have liked to reverse engines once again, but Caprivi was not to be persuaded and could hardly be dismissed a week after appointment. So the Treaty lapsed.

Later in the same year the Russians came back with suggestions for a revised and looser form of agreement but the German objection was to anything which would be both written and secret. Caprivi even went so far as to refuse formally to confirm the Russian record of talks during William's visit to St. Petersburg in August 1890. The fact was that the Treaty had been the work of small groups in each capital who knew that general public sentiment did not support them, a situation which as a basis for foreign policy is sometimes necessary but never satisfactory. There was considerable, if superficial, attraction in the argument that Germany must henceforward conduct a 'peaceful, clear and loyal policy' which could not create an impression of leaving her formal allies in the lurch. There was also much in the argument that only Bismarck could conduct a Bismarckian policy; to this the subsequent attempts of William, Holstein and Bülow to be as subtle as Bismarck certainly lend colour. If the conclusion might appear to be that in such circumstances Bismarck should not have been driven to resign, it is also necessary to remember that even Bismarcks are not immortal. Yet the fact remains that one of Bismarck's dominating aims had been to keep Russia out of the arms of France and that, within seventeen months of the non-renewal, a French naval squadron had visited Kronstadt, the Tsar had stood to attention while the band played the revolutionary

Marseillaise, and a Treaty had been signed pledging France and Russia to act in concert in the event of a threat to peace. It may be that sustained co-operation between Germany and Russia, between Teuton and Slav, is impracticable. But if that were so, certain consequences followed for the foreign policy of a Germany which had estranged France and therefore lived under the continual threat of a war on two fronts. These consequences particularly related to German relations with England. Much of the rest of this book will be concerned with examining the care which the men who came to rule Germany devoted to this aspect of their affairs.

The German Emperor was fully entitled by the constitution to dismiss the Imperial Chancellor and was not even obliged to explain why; nobody had contributed more to this than Bismarck who, as Lord Rosebery told him, was 'hoist with his own petard'.[88] Nor is the internal development of Germany likely to have been prejudiced by Bismarck's disappearing when he did. For he had survived into an age which he did not understand and to which he could no longer contribute much; indeed the real question is whether he could not with advantage have gone earlier. Foreign affairs are a different matter and as regards the Reinsurance Treaty in particular, the balance of advantage is hard to assess. But responsibility for the decision not to renew lay, as has been seen, with Caprivi and the Foreign Office rather than with the Kaiser, who in this allowed himself to be guided by his constitutional advisers. Even supposing that decision to have been right, however, there can be no doubt about its having been reached in the wrong way. Had William been wiser or more experienced, he would have insisted on postponing what might obviously be a crucial decision until his new team had found their feet, and would somehow have secured that, before the decision was taken, the reasons why Bismarck had made the Treaty were properly considered. The case for criticizing William proves on examination not to lie in the high and disputable fields of policy but on what at first sight seems a minor detail. Yet this in turn was part of the price Germany paid for Bismarck. As long as ultimate decisions were all taken by him, methods of procedure hardly mattered so that, when he disappeared, his successors were necessarily at a loss. Nothing which Caprivi did enraged Bismarck so much as the cutting down of the fine old trees in the Chancellery garden.[89] But no seedlings could have flourished under their shade.

CHAPTER VI

The New Master*

T HE WORLD WAS quick to seize on the young Kaiser's moustaches as his most prominent characteristic, but failed to recognize that they were a put-up job. For their aggressive upward thrust, reminiscent of a portrait by Velazquez (his father's favourite artist), did not come naturally to human hair; Herr Haby, the court barber, had to be at the Palace at seven every morning, besides going on all State visits, so as to fix the artefact into position. Let us hope he was compensated for this chore by the excellent sales of his beard-lotion 'Achievement'.[1] As was intended, the truculent front distracted attention from a sensitive, intelligent face; William reminded Prince Hohenlohe of his grandfather, Albert, in his voice and earnest manner.[2] His speech was clear and staccato with the hint of a snarl; it was left flat and lifeless by the operation to his throat in 1903.[3] His gestures were abrupt and vigorous, his laughter loud

'If he laughs, which he is sure to do a good many times, he will laugh with absolute abandonment, throwing back his head, opening his mouth to the fullest possible extent, shaking his whole body, and often stamping with one foot to show his excessive enjoyment of any joke. . . . He illustrates in his features to an unusual extent all the varied emotions that possess him and has many quaint mannerisms as for example he will continually shake the forefinger of his right hand into the face of anyone whom he wishes to convince, or will rock slowly on his toes backwards and forwards. At other times, he will "jiggle" violently on one leg.'[4]

* For other material relevant to this chapter, see pp. 74, 82-6, 96-9, 175, 291-2, 297 and note, 358, 433-5.

He had fair curly hair which began to go grey in his fifties, and fair complexion, said to have been inherited from his Russian great-grandmother, with a thick nose and thick red lips; his teeth were fine, yellow and, thanks in part to his American dentists, well-preserved. But the features which most struck people who talked to him were his eyes, cold and grey in repose yet lighting up continually with amusement or interest until they appeared almost sea-blue.[5]

In his youth he had been thought handsome in spite of the withered arm and the lack of bodily balance which it produced (see above, p. 74). He stood 5 foot 9 inches high and weighed just over eleven stone.[6] A tendency to put on weight during the early years of his reign was checked and he never acquired the traditional German thickness.[7] This was due partly to his passion for exercise (he had a rowing machine in his bedroom)[8] but chiefly to his restless, worrying character and the metabolism associated with it; he had no great appetite and eating did not make him fat. Queen Alexandra, noticing that he let the dishes at a State banquet go by untouched, said 'You ride, you work, you take a lot of trouble; why don't you eat? Eating is good for the brain.'[9] The guests at the Palace and on the imperial yacht used to grumble at the meagreness of the fare.[10] His one gastronomic passion, according to Princess Marie Louise, was mince pies with 'flaming brandy sauce', but as her evidence is unsupported, one wonders whether gallantry may not have been more involved than gluttony.[11] In earlier years, he occasionally drank more than was good for him; in the society of those days it would have been remarkable had he not.[12] But on the whole he was as abstemious in drink as in food, often contenting himself with soda water or lemon squash; he had a liking for sparkling red wine,[13] claiming that he had been prevented from drinking it as a boy. He made some attempt to reduce the amount of drinking in the army as well as other forms of expensive living. He smoked a little, principally cigarettes.

Thanks to his deformity, his right arm was extraordinarily developed and a shake of his hand was like the grip of a vice. He sadistically exploited this by wearing rings, turned so that the jewels came on the inside.[14] As a rule, he went about in uniform and insisted on all officers doing so, a ruling unpopular because of the obstacles which it created to clandestine misbehaviour. When the news leaked through that the members of a mess had gone to a slightly doubtful party in civilian suits, he put them under house arrest (and their regiment thereby out of action) for a fortnight.[15] But he returned from his grandmother's funeral in such a state of Anglophile euphoria that for a time he adopted the English practice of wearing plain clothes and continued it at intervals down to the war. He had, however, his own interpretation of plainness which did not stop at bracelets and jewelled tiepins. He was capable of coming to an informal tea party in an evening shirt under a green coat covered with gold braid,[16] or to dinner in a similar coat with knee-breeches, the underlying object of the costume apparently being to facilitate simultaneous wearing of the insignia of the Black Eagle, the Garter and the Golden Fleece.[17] He was not for nothing the great-grand-nephew of a man who arrived late at the Battle of Leipzig owing to inability to decide whether he should appear in Prussian or Russian uniform,[18] or the great-great-grandson of one who frequently dined in his crown.[19] Nor did he escape that occupational disease of royalty, fussiness about correct attire. In the first sixteen years of his reign, he altered army uniforms thirty-seven times.[20] The story that he dressed as an Admiral of the Fleet for a performance of *The Flying Dutchman* may be a cabaret joke but he certainly put on the uniform of a general of Engineers for a dinner of the Berlin Motor Club.[21] No wonder Holstein said that the Kaiser had 'dramatic rather than political instincts'.[22]

Just before his accession, Eulenburg said that 'his artlessness and disinterested friendliness give him a quite peculiarly fascinating charm, and he is one of those people who by their very nature arouse spontaneous sympathy.'[23] Many people spoke of his ability to please, perhaps the most remarkable being Queen Mary[24] (though Queen Alexandra thought him a fool).[25] He was said to have the gift of making the person he was talking to appear at their best and of giving the impression that they commanded his exclusive attention—though this was only if he found them sympathetic.[26] Slow, stiff or unduly serious people got on his nerves.[27] His conversation was described as having 'extreme plausibility and a certain magnetic power of convincing men against the dictates of their reason.'[28] A. J. Balfour said that William and George the Fifth were the only princes to whom he found he could talk as 'man to man'.[29] Holstein, after their unique meeting, called him a great artist in conversation.[30]

The domestic circle showed him to advantage. Dona disapproved of her ladies having views on public affairs—'disputes and arguments were painfully frequent necessities of existence, why introduce them unnecessarily?' Consequently, conversation round her table was apt to flag and dwindle into commonplaces unless the master of the house kept it going—as he usually did.[31] The life at Potsdam was 'home-like and cozy'[32] (which may be one reason why William spent so much time in travel). After dinner the Kaiserin and her ladies sat round with embroidery and knitting; the monotony was relieved by the Kaiser reading aloud.

'The last thing the Kaiser did last night was to read us from an English magazine an article on a new theory of the origin of the world. It lasted till twelve o'clock. . . . His interest in these things is astonishing and while he was reading it out and when he was making his own commentaries on it, it seemed as if he were living for nothing but this new idea.'[33]

'In the evenings we talked—or rather the Kaiser did. I have never met a man who can remember such millions of things at the same time, even Irish stories which I suppose he heard in England—he repeated them in German. And then he half acts while he tells the stories; one evening he went on from eleven till a quarter to one.'[34]

He had a strong but original sense of humour and much misunderstanding was caused through the slower members of his entourage failing to realize when they were being slyly teased.[35] On one occasion when three of them were talking together, William noticed some cigar ash on the carpet. 'Of course,' he said, 'this is the kind of thing I have to put up with from my Controllers. Instead of looking after my property, they do more to spoil it than anyone else. I'll teach you', he went on, shaking his finger in their faces, 'to behave yourselves, in a way that you won't forget in a hurry.' When one of them on the following day tried to explain that he had not been responsible for the ash, William replied, 'I've not the least idea what you are talking about.'[36] On being told by an American woman that he could count on a good reception in Paris if he gave back Alsace-Lorraine, he replied 'Heavens! That never occurred to me!'[37] The younger von Moltke used to describe himself as 'the lesser thinker' (*Denker*) in distinction from his uncle. One of the court came across a cigar-manufacturer called Julius Denker and William thenceforward worried the general by always addressing him as 'Julius'.[38] Once, when the Kaiser had been shooting all day and the Foreign Office insisted on his seeing a telegram, the liaison officer had to catch him between bath and tea-table; William read the message but said 'It's not etiquette to lie in wait for the German Emperor.'[39] Late in the war, travelling to the Balkans with his staff, he would retire to bed early leaving them sitting in the dining-car drinking champagne. About half an hour later, he would open the door and say, with every appearance of astonishment, 'What? Are you all still there?' This was the cue for his adjutant to reply, 'Yes, Your Majesty, we found it so pleasant that we sat on a little.' 'And what are you drinking?' was the next question. 'Sea water, Your Majesty. It's very good for the constitution.' 'Well, if it's only sea water, I can but hope it does you good.'[40] Just after the German army's 'Black Day' in August 1918, he spent an evening reading out an article on the deciphering of the Hittite language. When someone ventured to suggest that there were perhaps more important things to talk about, he declared that if only the world had busied itself more with the Hittites, France and England would have recognized that danger always came from the east, would never have become allied with Russia and so would never have got into the situation which caused the war.[41] When his doctor told him that all he had was a little cold, he replied: 'No, it is a big cold. Everything about me must be big.'[42]

The truth was that, having a retentive memory and a very quick mind, he could make rings round most of the people he associated with. He excelled at summing up the results of a long and complicated meeting. He could speak fluently without preparation or notes.[43] His interests and knowledge ranged far and wide. He was on gracious terms with classical scholars like Mommsen and Wilamowitz, theologians like Harnack, scientists like Koch and Röntgen. He founded the Kaiser William Society to encourage scientific research and promoted sensible reforms in education. As befitted the son of the man responsible for unearthing the Hermes of Praxiteles, archaeology was a passion. He lectured to members of the *Reichstag* on naval development in various lands and published articles on naval strategy under a pseudonym.[44] A keen yachtsman, he gave the Admiralty instructions about the way to build ships and was described by a qualified judge as 'probably the best cavalry leader in the German army'.[45] He gave Bertie and Nicky advice on how to win their wars. Under Eulenburg's guidance, he became a composer. He found fault with the tempo at which a cavalry band played 'Funiculi, funicula' and took over the baton to show how it was done in Italy; this so pleased him that, like Hippocleides, he went on conducting most of the evening.[46] At a musical festival, he laid down the law about how to compose for choirs of male voices. He astonished his Naval Secretary by the range of his knowledge about the Nibelungs (no doubt the Intendant of his theatres was equally astonished by his knowledge of naval matters).[47] He sketched and gave detailed instructions to artists about the pictures he wanted painted, even if he did not actually complete the work himself; the most famous of these was the allegorical portrayal of the Yellow Peril, 'Peoples of Europe, protect your most sacred possessions', of which copies were bestowed on all and sundry. He designed a chapel for one of his castles[48] and revised the architect's plans for the Central Railway station at Altona and the Central Post Office at Memel.[49] He chose the statues of Prussian princes and great men which, according to Bülow, led to the Berlin Tiergarten making an 'overwhelming impression on visitors'.[50] The sight of plaster casts for these or some other statues launched him on a ninety-minute lecture on the origin, development and decline of armour, based on some book which he had just read. He was nothing loath to mount the pulpit at Sunday services on his yacht. He even told the Cologne Council to spell their city's name with a C rather than a K.[51] Whatever he did, in the *New Yorker's* phrase, he thought he could do and threw himself into the doing with an enthusiasm which his court had to share. 'We were off by car to Frankfurt at cockcrow', wrote Valentini, 'to attend the competition of innumerable choirs, a frightful ordeal for anyone unmusical but one which the Kaiser undertook with unflagging interest from ten in the morning till six at night.'[52] 'We heard one song no less than thirty-five times,' sighed the exhausted Kaiserin.[53]

Yet William's quickness of apprehension, when combined with his energy and impatience, was more of a liability than an asset.

'One must know how to wait. This is something H.M. doesn't know how to do at all.'

'H.M.'s autocratic tendencies . . . (are) not accompanied by any serious scrutiny of the facts; he just talks himself into an opinion. Anyone in favour of it is then quoted as an authority, anyone who differs from it is "being fooled".'[54]

'The Kaiser still [1903] shows the same youthful freshness, the same power of rapidly grasping a problem, the same personal courage and the same confidence in his judgement and capacity. These qualities, valuable though they might be in a monarch, are still unfortunately outweighed by his refusal to concentrate and go into things thoroughly as well as by his almost pathological desire to take immediate decisions on everything without waiting to consult his advisers, and by his lack of any sense of proportion or of genuine political insight.'[55]

'William II wants to shine and to do and decide everything for himself. But what he wants to do unfortunately often goes wrong.'[56]

The naval staff had the unenviable task of explaining that the ship he had designed would do everything but float. When he took the helm of his yacht, he was apt to foul the buoy marking the winning line and thus get disqualified.[57] The results of his bright ideas about winning the Boer War were painful in the extreme. He had to admit to Haldane, when they started to discuss military organization, that he had never gone very deeply into the subject.[58]

'The Kaiser's custom of a critique after a military review, when he made a speech to the assembled generals telling them what was right and wrong . . . was much ridiculed in military circles.'[59]

'There is a disturbing element of dilettantism in his handling of the army and navy. He is less of a soldier than his grandfather because he lacks the steadiness of view which only down-to-earth hard work can give. But he is not only convinced that he possesses such a view but that he is a born leader.'[60]

The architecture of his age is a byword for tasteless extravagance (though, to be fair, not in Germany alone) and the statuary in the Tiergarten is one of the pieces of war damage which nobody has sought to restore. He told King Edward that motor cars ran best on potato spirit and had some sent over to England for a demonstration.[61] Even when he played 'Skat' he tended to lose. In 1891, he was with difficulty prevented from replacing his Ambassador in Paris by a general as a result of listening to cock-

and-bull stories of French war preparations cooked up by a former military attaché who wanted to get his job back and emanating from two Yankee munitions salesmen and an Italian speculator on the Paris bourse.[62]

William's fluency in speaking meant that he approached all questions with an open mouth. Caprivi once received a Captain Natzmer who said that at an imperial reception the previous evening, he had been appointed Governor of the Cameroons; thought at first to be a victim of delusions, the Captain proved on enquiry to be all too sane.[63] During a Mediterranean cruise, one of the suite, from his cabin, heard the Kaiser talking in a most confidential way to an unidentified third party. Half fearful that he might have been improperly eavesdropping, the courtier asked a sailor who the man was. 'Oh, the pilot whom we took on board at Bari.'[64] A casual word of William's during a wartime audience allowed the Bulgarians to claim that they had been promised the entire Dobrudja, thereby depriving German diplomacy of a valuable bargaining counter.[65]

> 'One would wish', wrote a British ambassador, 'to have a chance of finishing an answer or developing an argument sometimes—but that I never have—a volcanic remark or two— a momentary cyclone of words—and before one has time for anything but the *beginning* of an answer, H.M. is talking to someone else.'[66]

He was constitutionally incapable of preventing himself from saying whatever came into his head, provided he imagined it would contribute to the effect which he was trying to make at that moment, whether of benevolent despot, versatile thinker, skilful diplomat or ruthless leader. 'Once the play began, the actor in him was roused and he took the edge off his nervousness by talking.'[67] As a result, his career became a series of what one of his subjects described as 'oratorical derailments' (*rednerische Entgleisungen*).[68]

> 'The Kaiser,' wrote Holstein, 'has the unfortunate habit of talking all the more rapidly and incautiously the more a matter interests him. Hence it happens that he generally has committed himself, or at least that the entourage persuades him that he has committed himself, even before the responsible advisers or the experts have been able to submit their opinion.'[69]

Things became even worse when a passing mood became incorporated in a letter or telegram which then became public property. It was not as though he stuck to the judgements which he tossed off. 'When the same question is again submitted from a different point of view he very probably may pronounce a very different opinion.' 'Here we have the third foreign policy programme within six months.'[70]

This inconsistency was one of the chief factors undermining the confidence of responsible Germans in his leadership. They saw Bismarck's verdict—'No sense of proportion'[71]—steadily vindicated as the years passed. The other main cause of alarm was William's lack of tact. Holstein wrote to Eulenburg that 'the chief danger in the life of William II is that he remains absolutely unconscious of the effect which his speeches and actions have upon Princes, public men and the masses'. And again: 'We are dealing with a sensitive character who gives vent to *personal* displeasure in *practical* affairs.'[72] The Kaiser was continually jeopardizing good relations with people whose friendship could have been valuable to him by failure to consider their feelings. 'He does a thousand and one things which hurt and pain [his mother]. But I really think he does them out of thoughtlessness and certainly *not* from premeditation.'[73] He astonished the British Ambassador by the way he talked about the diminutive King of Italy whom he always referred to as 'the Dwarf' while calling the Queen (whose father was the Prince of Montenegro) 'a peasant girl' and 'the daughter of a cattle thief'.[74] William's liking to be surrounded by tall men on the ground that it increased his resemblance to King Frederick William I was a pardonable foible—but he need not have taken a special selection with him to Rome where they, of course, threw into emphasis Victor Emmanuel's lack of height.[75] He was capable, when in the middle of a reception for Prince Ferdinand of Bulgaria, of calling him 'the cleverest and most unscrupulous ruler in Europe'. He later made fun of Ferdinand for being 'festooned with decorations like a Christmas tree'—oblivious of the quantity which he wore himself.[76] On Russo-German occasions William delighted to display his talent for impromptu speech-making, to the acute embarrassment of the Tsar who could only read laboriously from a prepared text.[77]

With German princes his relations were rather better and

improved on those of his father. But in 1890, while Bavarian suspicion of Prussia was still lively, he announced a wish to inspect troops in Munich. The Prince Regent Luitpold was 'strongly averse to horseback' and the prospect of having to ride—perhaps even gallop—beside William so unnerved him that for a moment he contemplated resignation.[78] In 1894 William made the Bavarian Prince Ludwig come and apologize for his speech in Moscow (cf. p. 115). In 1902 came the Swinemünde telegram (cf. p. 243). The Saxons were so badly treated in 1896 that Prince George left the imperial manœuvres early and stayed away from Berlin on the Kaiser's birthday. When a princely confusion had to be un- tangled in Lippe-Detmold in 1898 and the Regent put forward some dubious claims, William acknowledged his letter so curtly as to spoil a good case and turn the other German princes against him.[79] He was once heard to say at a dinner that, if the South Germans proved too obstinate, he would declare war on them. 'The Catholics', he explained on another occasion 'are the purest pagans! They pray to their Saints.'[80] 'Initiative without tact', to quote Holstein again, 'is like a flood without dykes.'[81] The Kaiser was so absorbed in his own ideas and objectives as to be incapable of appreciating the outlook of other people. In this he resembled many of his subjects to whom a French Ambassador in Berlin applied the adjective *'inconscients'*.[82]

Conclusions were not the only things to which William rushed. In August 1894 a Berlin newspaper calculated that he had spent 199 of the previous 365 days in travelling.[83] He was a precursor of the modern habit of cruising, and indeed his journey to the Near East in 1898 was organized by Messrs. Cook. Every July he took a select party in his yacht up the coast of Norway, with physical exercises on deck before breakfast and lectures in the smoking room on wet days; a spring trip to the Mediterranean later became routine. In June he went to Kiel for the regatta and often cruised in the Baltic afterwards, in August to Wilhelmshöhe near Kassel, in September to Romintern on the Russian frontier, in November to Donaueschingen to stay with Prince Fürstenberg. It was a Berlin joke that he 'had no time to rule'. He would, however, have vigorously disputed any suggestion that these activities were pure relaxation; papers and telegrams followed him wherever he went and he once told the Tsar that 'we poor rulers are not entitled to a holiday like other mortals'.[84] The restlessness which lay behind this perpetual desire for travel and novelty no doubt had both physical and psychological causes. The nature of the tensions underlying his character have already been discussed. (Cf. p. 85). To the strain of overcoming his physical handicaps was added that of keeping up with the ghost of Frederick the Great. Moreover, William's possibilities of expending his energies were limited by his moral ways; intellectual curiosity had to take the place of mistresses. The inability of the uncomplicated King Edward to appreciate such problems contributed materially to the antagonism between them.

His unease and the shyness which accompanied it are also likely to have been responsible for his addiction to dirty stories and crude practical jokes. Some people might think that 'all men enjoy for once in their lives to be slapped on the back by an Emperor' especially if they are not aware that it is 'the usual Imperial manner'. But one Englishman who was 'smitten from behind with a tennis racket' found his 'gratification qualified by the fact that the blow could not be returned'.[85] When at a loss what to do the Kaiser acted in a forced way. His continual ridicule of 'foxy Ferdinand' was undoubtedly due to fear of being out-witted. His jokes, as has been said, often misfired. The Archduke Franz Ferdinand was anything but amused on being met at the station and told: 'Don't imagine that I've come to meet *your* train—I'm expecting the Crown Prince of Italy.'[86] Elderly gentle-men, forced to make unwonted physical movements on a cold deck before breakfast, found that being pushed over from behind when in a vulnerable posture did not add as much to their gaiety as it did to William's. Kiderlen-Wächter on one such trip wrote:

'Count Goertz had to go through his repertory of animal imitations every night. The evenings were partly musical, partly devoted to conjuring tricks. . . . I have done the Dwarf and turned out the lights to the Kaiser's vast delectation. In an improvised sing-song, I did the Chinese twins with C; we were connected by an enormous sausage.'[87]

It is only fair to remember that King Edward was also addicted to practical jokes of a type which Mr. Asquith did not consider his 'idea of family fun'; in the Englishman there was less underlying excuse.

Behind William's favourite pose of iron resolve, there was an acute lack of self-confidence, combined with an obstinate desire to have his own way. He would avoid the eyes of people who embarrassed or antagonized him. 'If he was bent on doing something and aware that his advisers would try to head him off, he made a practice of never telling them beforehand.'[88] 'What did the Kaiser say [in 1917] when you suggested Bülow for Chancellor?' 'He said nothing.' 'Then we had better look for someone else for that is a sure sign that H.M. will not accept him.'[89] To use his own words about the Tsar, he was not so much false as feeble.[90] When evasion became impossible, he was likely to give way—or rather to take the line of least resistance which might involve saying 'yes' to proposals for violent action. The strain of forcing himself to act as he thought he should do had physical consequences in bouts of acute neuralgia. At critical moments, as in 1907, 1908 and 1918, this lack of confidence and staying power became a complete loss of nerve, accompanied by such physical symptoms as giddiness and shivering. Some people went so far as to assert that the Kaiser was mentally deranged, but his later life is a fairly clear proof that no organic damage was caused by his experiences.

Continual bolstering by others was essential to William's mental equilibrium. As Eulenburg wrote to Bülow,

'Never forget that H.M. needs praise every now and again. He is one of those people who get out of sorts if they do not, from time to time, hear words of appreciation from the lips of some important person or other. You will always obtain his consent to your wishes so long as you do not neglect to express appreciation of H.M. whenever he deserves it.'[91]

When others failed, he had to do the bolstering himself. 'On the way back H.M. went through it all again with me. As always on such occasions, he set too high a value on anything that had any value at all.' Like an actress answering a curtain call, he invariably declared that the reception he had just been given was the most wonderful one in his life. No doubt some of his boasting went to keep up his own spirits.

Given the numerous occasions on which his impetuosity and lack of empathy led him into mistakes, this need to have his morale sustained made him a difficult person to handle. How could he be kept on the right path if any criticism was liable to produce a nervous crisis? Moreover, he has often been described as hypersensitive to criticism and apt to vent his displeasure on the critic.

He who took so little trouble to consider the standpoint of others, took strong exception to people who criticized him without regard for his own standpoint or in a way which lowered his dignity in public. When Waldersee conducted a post mortem on manœuvres in such a way as to call general attention to the Kaiser's mistakes, it proved the last straw in a deteriorating relationship and led to his replacement by Schlieffen as Chief of Staff.[92] Hindenburg was prematurely retired in 1911 for a similar lack of tact.[93] But this was very largely a question of how the criticism was expressed. Eulenburg said that William took everything personally and that only personal argument made any impression on him.[94] He took great offence over criticism at third hand, especially if it was expressed on paper; this explains his violent reactions to press attacks—notably those in the English press. But there are plenty of examples, of whom Eulenburg and Queen Victoria are the most conspicuous, to show that if criticism was expressed sympathetic- ally and respectfully in private, William was perfectly ready to listen and take it to heart. 'I shall be very content,' he once said, 'if people will only understand what I am trying to do and support me in it.'[95] In fact, he appreciated people who had the self- reliance to speak their minds instead of bandying polite phrases. Princess Feodora of Schleswig-Holstein, his sister-in-law, was a great favourite in spite of the fact that on almost all subjects their views clashed.[96] Count Reischach said that opposition had to be 'reasonable and in proper form'.[97] Tirpitz said that it was necessary to talk *tête-à-tête* with William since the presence of more than two parties to the conversation was easily calculated to divert his true personal judgement by playing upon his urge to show off.[98] One of Eulenburg's merits was that, by observing these principles, he was able to get plans and outlooks changed. He once suggested that William's frequent success in manœuvres was pre-arranged and when the Kaiser insisted that this was a grave affront to his generals who simply regarded him as one of themselves, replied: 'I should be very glad to learn some day that Your Majesty had been defeated.'[99] Von Moltke, on becoming Chief of Staff in 1906, ventured to criticize the pre-arranged way in which man- œuvres were conducted; William at once accepted his arguments and agreed to change. The Jewish shipowner, Ballin, was another critic who could usually count on a hearing.

This situation placed a great responsibility on the Kaiser's entourage, a responsibility made all the more difficult to discharge by the fact that, while William was easily influenced, he was seldom influenced by the same person for long. It cannot, on the whole, be said that this responsibility was well discharged. There were of course exceptions, like Lucanus and Valentini the successive heads of the Civil Secretariat, whose contacts with Ministers and deputies gave them a greater sense of realities. But the majority, while complaining bitterly that their Master was incalculable, encouraged his worst tendencies. In saying this, one has to avoid being misled by the frequent criticisms of the 'Hydra' (as the Secretariats were called) emanating from people who found attempts at personal axe-grinding foiled by the machine. The condemnation must rest primarily on the reactionary nature of the views which were disseminated at court and on the attitude of fawning adulation which was allowed to prevail. That the general outlook of the court should have been more reactionary than that of the *Reichstag* is hardly surprising. But it was also more reactionary than the majority of Ministers, principally because the need to get a majority in the *Reichstag* brought Ministers down to earth, whereas the court officials lived in the clouds. Von Plessen, the chief A.D.C. throughout the reign, insisted that the army must be kept insulated from civil life and was described by Eulenburg as talking of 'nothing but gunfire'.[100] The extreme example was Admiral von Senden-Bibran, Head of the Naval Secretariat from 1890 till 1911 and a *bête noire* of both King Edward and Eulenburg. Von Senden, who owed his position to his ability to put the Kaiser's naval desires into practicable form, is said to have assigned to 'a properly directed foreign policy' the task of acquiring an island in the Gulf of Mexico without straining relations between Germany and America! In 1896 he said openly that the German navy had to be made ready for a war with England. His ideal was 'a strong government which can manage without the *Reichstag*'. He said repeatedly in the Berlin clubs that the *Reichstag* must grant 300 million marks for the building of a fleet, and go on being dissolved until it did so.[101] It may be that William did not take all von Senden's remarks at their face value. Nevertheless, the fact that he was surrounded by such people encouraged him to talk in ways that they applauded.

When as a great concession, an audience was given in 1915 to Erzberger (who as the leader of the Centre at the time was a key

political figure), von Plessen said to him beforehand: 'I trust you
will bring only good news to His Majesty.'[102] Critics were more
likely to be discouraged than assisted to present their case in an
acceptable form. The Austrian Foreign Minister, Czernin, on
visiting the Imperial Court during the war, was shocked to find it
usual for a man to kiss the Kaiser's hands on leaving his presence
which, despite the addiction of the Habsburg court to ceremonial,
would never have occurred with Franz Joseph; the practice is said
to have been started by General von Mackensen in 1904.[103]
The man appointed as German Ambassador to China in 1897 told
Tirpitz that he had advised William to annex a base at Amoy; on
Tirpitz asking how he could talk about a place he had never
visited, the Ambassador replied: 'I could not leave His Majesty
without a positive answer.'[104] When William talked loosely about
coming to lunch on an island in the lake at Hamburg, the city
fathers, instead of reminding him that their guest house was
actually on a peninsula, built a new pavilion complete with
flower-beds on an artificial island in the middle of the lake.[105]
William had only to say to Bülow that 'your light trousers are
enough to upset the best weather forecast' and an obsequious
Chancellor hurried off to change.[106] During the visits to Donaueschingen, Prince Fürstenberg laid on a telegraphic service of Stock
Exchange jokes so as to ensure imperial good temper at breakfast[107]
(much as the Marquis de Soveral scoured the London clubs for
stories before going to Sandringham). No wonder that one of
William's officials should have written in 1912 to one of his
Ministers:

> 'We are only too conscious of having to put up with many
> idiosyncrasies of His Majesty from which we would gladly see
> our ruler free. But the responsibility for their existence does not
> rest solely with him but much more with the pusillanimity of
> his entourage who failed to check such bad habits when he was
> still young.'[108]

Germany, instead of going to Canossa, went to Byzantium.

It was not as though William mixed widely with his subjects.
The range of those admitted to the court was strictly limited.
Most of the Ministers spoke to their sovereign only once a year,
the occasion, strangely enough, being the Kiel Regatta.[109] As a
rule they had to submit projects or petitions in writing through the

Kaiser's Civil Secretariat. The Foreign Secretary and Naval and War Ministers saw the Kaiser personally from time to time; the Chancellor normally, though by no means invariably, had an audience with him once a week (Bülow, however, when in favour saw him almost daily). The Chiefs of the Army and Naval Staffs were also admitted weekly, with greater regularity. The Chief of the Military Secretariat normally had three audiences a week, the Chief of the Naval and Civil Secretariats two.[110] These three Secretariats formed the normal channel for all approaches on matters of politics and administration; if anyone else had an audience the Chief of the appropriate Secretariat had a right to be present and stayed behind afterwards to settle the follow-up action.[111] The Military and Naval Secretariats were responsible for making all the senior appointments in the armed forces.

This machinery was not devised to serve a constitutional monarch, many of whose acts are formal. The German system, by placing the army and navy outside the control of the *Reichstag* and of civilian ministers (except for limited questions of finance and administration), made the Emperor the only authority controlling (and therefore in theory co-ordinating) not merely the civil administration and the two services but even the chief commands within those services. Had William attempted to take his duties seriously, the burden could have been crushing. But in practice he had little conception of what he was supposed to do, let alone attempt to do it. Bismarck said that William wanted every day to be a Sunday.[112] His usual timetable (which was always liable to be upset by travel) allowed only about two hours for audiences and little more for work on documents.[113] Lucanus, who was Chief of the Civil Secretariat from 1888 to 1908 and was nicknamed 'the apothecary' because of the alleged occupation of his father, once at the outset of his career told William that all the supporting evidence needed about a particular case could be found in the files (which made a pretty thick bundle). The Kaiser threw them on the table, went to the window, drummed on the panes and said: 'If you attach importance to going on working with me, you will never submit appendices like that to me again. I have no time for that kind of thing.'[114] He never read newspapers but only press summaries prepared for him by the Foreign Office and a tendentious commercial précis of foreign and home news written in telegraphese.[115] When one of the first imperial motor cars had broken down, the Master of the Horse sought to mollify his master by explaining that, in the then stage of the motor industry, breakdowns were inevitable and the only remedy was to disregard expense and have more cars. William replied: 'What anything I want costs is a matter of supreme indifference. All I ask is that everything should go smoothly and you are responsible.'[116] The result of this well-meant attempt to avoid being drowned in detail was waste in the household and pre-judice, amounting at times to deception, in politics. He berated the Foreign Office for not showing despatches to him promptly, but does not seem to have realized that sometimes, as in 1905, 1909, 1911 and 1914, important ones were not shown to him at all.[117] A court official said to the Chief of the Military Secretariat 'It is extraordinary that in every department the Kaiser should have someone about him who deceives him.'[118] The day-to-day running of the country was, in fact, left to officials, but no attempt was made to delimit their functions or list the subjects reserved for the ruler's personal decision. 'The Kaiser hates to be asked questions but at the same time can be seriously annoyed if he has not been consulted about this or that.'[119] He interfered by fits and starts, often intelligently but seldom with full information and by no means always in a consistent direction. How far the Chancellor or the responsible Minister was consulted might depend on accident. If they were not, they had to choose between acquies-cence, resignation and an attempt to talk their master round. The Germans had then (as they retain today) a reputation for extreme efficiency. But a complex of out-of-date attitudes towards monarchy and politics had saddled them with an almost incredible state of inefficiency in a vital sector of their system.

William gave no sign of realizing that as far as he was concerned, there was anything wrong. An early assertion foreshadowed a lasting attitude:

'Democratic principles can only create weak and often corrupt pillars of society. A society is only strong if it recognizes the fact of natural superiorities, in particular that of birth.'[120]

In spite of all that the Kaiser did to excite ridicule and criticism, he had the highest conception of his office. 'We Hohenzollerns', he once said, 'derive our crowns from Heaven alone and are answerable only to Heaven for the responsibilities which they imply.'[121] When Leopold II of Belgium dismissed a proposal to revive the Duchy of Burgundy (and thereby draw his country into the German camp) by saying that neither his Cabinet nor his Parliament would consider it for a moment, the Kaiser burst out that he could not respect a Monarch who felt responsible to Ministers and Deputies instead of to God in Heaven.[122] In 1915 it was suggested to him that, however reluctant Victor Emmanuel might be to ally Italy with the Entente, his hand was being forced by his politicians. William replied that when it came to the Day of Judgement, the King would not be able to evade his responsibilities in this way. God would say to him, 'No, no, my little man, that won't wash with me. Who made you a King? Your Ministers? Your Parliament? No, I placed you in that exalted position and you are responsible to me alone. Go to Hell, or at least to Purgatory.'[123] In 1917, when there was some question of finding a German prince for the throne of Roumania, the Kaiser 'after some discussion with his ladies' proposed his own youngest son, Joachim. To someone who suggested that Joachim did not perhaps possess all the right qualities, he replied: 'Qualities are not really necessary.'[124] He told the Tsar that while the French President and Prime Minister might be experienced statesmen, they were not Princes or Emperors 'and I am unable to place them on the same footing as you, my equal, my cousin and my friend'.[125]

His mystical belief in the Divine Guidance available to crowned heads was in no way diminished by the fact that he himself had never been crowned.

'I am helped to press forward on the road which Heaven has marked out for me by my feeling of responsibility to the Ruler of all and by my firm conviction that God, our old ally of Rossbach and Dannewitz,* who has taken so much trouble over our homeland and our dynasty, will not desert us now.'[126]

'I approach my task in such a way that when I am finally called before the Judgement Seat, I can answer to God and to my old Emperor with a clear conscience. I draw my strength from the same source as my grandfather did for his deeds and achievements, as my father did for his triumphs and sorrows. I intend to go on my way and pursue the end which I have set for myself in the conviction which I would ask you all to take to

* Two famous Prussian victories.

your hearts, which ought to be decisive for all mankind: *Ein' feste Burg ist unser Gott, In hoc signo vinces*.'*[127]

'There is not the smallest doubt in my mind that God constantly reveals himself to the human race created by Him. He has "breathed his breath into mankind" or given it a part of himself—a soul. He follows the development of the human race with a father's love and interest; for the purpose of leading it forward and benefiting it, he "reveals" Himself in some great savant or priest or king, be they heathens, Jews or Christians. Hammurabi was one of these, likewise Moses, Abraham, Charlemagne, Luther, Shakespeare, Goethe, Kant, Emperor William the Great.† These men he has sought out and enabled by his grace to make wonderful and enduring contributions to the physical and spiritual well-being of their peoples. How often did my grandfather emphasize that he was but an instrument in the hand of the Lord. The works of great men are God's gift to mankind to enable it to develop and find the way along a confused and unexplored path.'[128]

In a speech on the centenary of his grandfather's birth, the Kaiser expressed the conviction that the former Emperor was with them in spirit, adding with some emphasis 'and he certainly paid a visit last night to the colours' which had been deposited by his successor in his former palace on the previous day. The story even went that William appointed himself extraordinary A.D.C. to his grandfather for the occasion.[129]

The line dividing a sense of responsibility from a conviction of inspiration is apt to be tenuous and William was not particular about overstepping it. Policy then tended to be a matter which was not open to discussion, since it had been settled directly between him and his creator through the mediation of his ancestors. As though oblivious of his susceptibility to influence, he liked to portray himself as the strong man, and would have agreed

---

* 'A sure stronghold our God is still, conquer in the name of this sign' i.e. the cross. The first quotation is the opening line of Luther's hymn, the second the words spoken to the Emperor Constantine in a dream before the Battle of the Milvian Bridge, A.D. 312.

† The veneration which William always accorded to his grandfather, though based on genuine affection, was also inspired by a wish to take some of the gilt off the Bismarck image. But William I's only real claim to greatness was that he had allowed great men a free hand!

with Captain Wentworth that those who would be happy must be firm.

> 'The will of the King is the supreme law' (written in the City of Munich Visitors' Book).[130]
> 'There is only one person who is master in this Empire and I am not going to tolerate any other.'[131]
> 'I am the sole master of German policy and my country must follow me wherever I go.'[132]
> 'I look on myself as an instrument of the Almighty and go on my way regardless of transient opinions and views.'[133]
> 'Once I have discerned a goal to be right, I will pursue it with an inflexible resolution from which no opposition can deflect me.'[134]
> 'What the public says is a matter of entire indifference to me. I make decisions according to my convictions and expect my officials to reply to the mistaken ideas of my people in a suitable manner.'[135]
> 'As Sovereigns who are responsible to God for the wellfare [*sic*] of the Nations entrusted to our care, it is our duty therefore to closely study the genesis and development of "public opinion" before we allow it to influence our actions.'[136]
> 'I have never read the constitution and know nothing about it.'[137]

Theodore Roosevelt explained this posturing as follows:

> 'Down at the bottom of his heart, [the Kaiser] knew perfectly well that he himself was not an absolute sovereign. He had never had a chance to try . . . on the contrary, when Germany made up its mind to go in a given direction, he could only stay at the head of affairs by scampering to take the lead in going in that direction. Down at the bottom he realized this and he also knew that even this rather shorn power which he possessed was not shared by the great majority of his fellow-sovereigns. But together with this underlying consciousness of the real facts of the situation went a curious make-believe to himself that each sovereign did represent his country in the sense that would have been true two or three centuries ago.'[138]

And Winston Churchill has imagined what his entourage would have said if he had behaved differently:

'We have a weakling on the throne. Our War Lord is a pacifist. Is the new-arrived, late-arrived German Empire with all its tremendous and expanding forces to be led by a president of the Young Men's Christian Association? Was it for this that the immortal Frederick and the great Bismarck schemed and conquered?'[139]

Indeed, in 1911, remarks very like these were actually uttered.

In fidelity to his traditions, William carried his doctrine of firmness and discipline into home politics, exaggerating 'blood and iron' to the verge of absurdity:

'The soldier and the army, not Parliamentary majorities and decisions, have welded the German Empire together. I put my trust in the army.'[140]

'You [recruits] have sworn loyalty to me. You have only one enemy and that is my enemy. In the present social confusion it may come about that I order you to shoot down your own relatives, brothers or parents but even then you must follow my orders without a murmur.'[141]

When, in 1900, the Army was called out to deal with a tramway strike, the Kaiser wired his hopes that 'at least five hundred will have been snuffed out by the time the troops return to barracks'. Sentries who, in the course of their duty, shot and killed members of the public were singled out for praise.[142] When, in 1904, Russia was called on to submit the Dogger Bank incident to arbitration and punish her officers if they were found guilty, William wrote: 'How intolerable! One cannot possibly allow foreigners to pass judgement on the action taken by one's own officers in the course of their duty.' (Though he congratulated the Tsar on the 'masterful political instinct which caused you to refer the North Sea incident to the Hague Tribunal.')[143] In 1914 he said: 'One does not confer with others on a vital question of honour.'

In international affairs it was the same story:

'I am not a man who believes that we Germans bled and conquered thirty years ago . . . in order to be pushed to one side when great international decisions call to be made. If that were to happen, the place of Germany as a world power would be gone for ever, and I am not prepared to let that happen. It is my duty and privilege to employ to this end without hesitation the most appropriate and, if need be, the sharpest methods.'[144]

'The tasks for us Germans have immensely increased and involve for me and for my government unusual and heavy efforts which can only be crowned with success if the German people, regardless of party, stand firmly united behind us.'[145]

'The only nations which have progressed and become great have been warring nations. Those which have not been ambitious and gone to war have been nothing.'[146]

'We are destined to great things and I am leading you to marvellous times.'[147]

The refusal of the Progressives and Social Democrats to accept such an approach to society was the reason why the Kaiser attacked them so bitterly.

'I regard every Social Democrat as an enemy of the Empire and Fatherland.'

'There is a breed of men who do not deserve the name of Germans. I trust that the entire nation will find the strength to beat back their outrageous attacks. If that does not occur, I shall have to call on you, my Guards, for protection against the gang of traitors and for leading the battle which will free us from such elements.'[148]

'The Party which dares to attack the foundations of our State, which sets itself against religion and does not stop at attacking the person of the All-Highest Ruler must be rooted out to the very last stump.'[149]

On being shown the house of a negro king at a colonial exhibition, with the skulls of enemies stuck on poles outside it, William suddenly burst out, 'If only I could see the *Reichstag* strung up like that!'[150]

The same basic attitudes pervade the innumerable notes which William (who once declared himself averse to writing!)[151] scribbled in the margins of despatches, in imitation of Frederick the Great and Bismarck. The context often makes clear that he put down his views without reading beyond the sentence to which they applied. Many of his remarks were simply abusive: 'Nonsense', 'Nonsense with sauce,' 'Lies,' 'Rascal,' 'Stale fish,' 'Unbelievable,' 'Typical oriental procrastinating tactics,' '*Donnerwetter*, that is cheek,' 'False as a Frenchman usually is,' 'England's fault, not ours.' Nobody (other than himself) was ever given the credit for honest motives: ulterior ones were read into the most straightforward proposal. He was determined not to let anyone pull wool over his eyes or catch him unawares; nothing on the other hand which could mislead, frighten or divide foreign nations was to be neglected. 'Above all,' he once instructed Bülow, 'foster American distrust of France and Russia.' When he was told that the American Ambassador to Russia thought the differences between Japan and China too deep to be bridged, William commented, 'I hope he is right.' On another occasion he wrote that 'friction is increasing between Japs and Yankees and that is good.'[152] Human nature being what it is, there were occasions when such remarks were well conceived and gave an impression of realism, but on the whole they constitute a deplorable display of mean-mindedness, short sight and crude humour. Trying to act the discerning diplomat, he only succeeded in being the overgrown schoolboy. The result was not merely that his distrust of others got him distrusted by everybody, but that he contributed materially to the false picture of their own position which the German élite were steadily building up.

The Kaiser was justified in holding up to admiration the qualities of responsibility and determination, of unselfishness and loyalty. But unlike respect for truth and love of one's fellow-men, these are secondary virtues and all depends on the ends for which they are exerted. William arrogated to himself the choice of those ends and, although his selection was in tune with the ideas prevailing in German society, one cannot help endorsing the poet Fontane's accusation that he was trying to look contemporary with clothes resuscitated from the attic.[153] The society on whose behalf sacrifices were demanded was the society of his ancestors. Institutions and social relations were to continue much as they had been, regardless of the transformation that had come over Germany and the world; the only changes were to extend German practices on an indefinite scale overseas and give a new grandeur to the imperial position. Traditions are valuable things and William did right to make much of history. But an appreciation of the values of past society is only one part of the historian's equipment. Equally important is awareness of the transience of all human arrangements, and the need to prepare for inevitable and continuing changes. To expect that all changes will be personally welcome is to expect the impossible and selfish; here common-sense, if not Christian charity, indicates the need to consider the views of others. If fresh classes are becoming articulate, their views have to be taken into account; an attempt to resist indefinitely the wind of change is to ask for one's house to be blown down. Bismarck, reactionary though he was, had realized this, as for example in his reply to Salisbury about the causes for which Germany would fight (see above, p. 112). But William, though anxious to be a modern ruler, wanted to confine new ideas to the field of science and industry; in the field of politics his ideas looked backwards because looking forwards called for adjustments which would have brought him into painful conflict with his immediate surroundings.

His limitations were also obvious in his literary and artistic tastes. His favourite poem was said to be Kipling's 'If' and when the author was ill, he signed himself in a telegram, 'an enthusiastic admirer of your incomparable works.' (One wonders how many of the anti-German pieces he had read!) Other favourite English authors were Dickens, Scott, Marryat, Longfellow, Bernard Shaw, Kenneth Grahame, Warwick Deeping and (later) P. G. Wodehouse.[154] But Liliencron, Dehmel and Thomas Mann found no applause at court. He took it almost as a personal insult when the Berlin High Court reversed a police ban on Gerhard Hauptmann's *Weber* while he cancelled the award of the Schiller prize to the same author's *Versunkenen Glocke* and gave it instead to an indifferent historical drama.[155] His quickness of apprehension led him to prefer the superficial to the profound—Houston Stewart Chamberlain, for example, to Max Weber. He disapproved so strongly of modern art that he tried to get the Director of his National Gallery sacked for patronizing Liebermann;[156] perhaps it is as well that he never seems to have heard of Kandinsky or Klee. Wilhelminian architecture owes its vulgarity partly to the number of Germans who during his reign acquired wealth before they had acquired taste but it also partly reflects his endeavours to make the imperial office as pompous as possible. His operatic enthusiasm centred on such composers as Lortzing and Meyerbeer; he personally supervised a lavish production of *Les Huguenots* and in the middle started thundering against the Catholics for having killed his ancestor, Admiral Coligny.[157] Another favourite piece was *Sardanapalus*, which ended with a conflagration so realistic that King Edward, who had dozed off, thought the theatre genuinely on fire. But after the first Berlin performance of *Salome*, William remarked of Richard Strauss: 'That's a nice snake I've reared in my bosom.'[158]

His interference in matters of taste made him highly unpopular in artistic circles. This he came to realize and on one occasion at least sought to excuse himself on the ground that he had derived all his knowledge of artistic matters in youth from his mother, and since he came to the throne had been too busy to keep up-to-date.[159] Though the explanation may have had a grain of truth, William was given to putting the blame on other people, and his real deficiencies were more fundamental. He looked at art not as a means of communicating feeling but as a source of moral uplift, as a weapon in the fight against materialism. At the unveiling of the Tiergarten statues he said:

> 'If art contents itself with making misery more repulsive than the reality, it is committing treason against the German people. The outstanding task of culture is to foster the ideal.'[160]

On another occasion he said that the much abused word 'freedom' was too often used as an excuse for self-indulgence and for throwing off reticence and restraint.[161] He had no understanding of what modern writers and artists were trying to do, which at a crucial stage in cultural development was a fatal handicap in one who set up as an authority in such matters. A critic has written:

> 'The final section of *Das Lied von der Erde* is not merely one of the most profoundly moving pieces of music that the art can show in its long history; it is a landmark in the history of civilization. It is the swan song of a dying world; this *Abschied* is the farewell not merely of an artist but of a culture. The first sad notes of that swan song of civilization as the world had known it since the Renaissance were sounded in *Parsifal*. . . . But it is in the *Abschied* that sorrow for the death of the civilization of the nineteenth century finds its most exquisite, its final expression.'[162]

The world of art was undergoing a revolution parallel to and closely connected with that in the world of production and communication. As has been seen in Chapter II, the growth of self-consciousness which is one of the chief clues through human history received a great impetus from the growth of knowledge and from the growing awareness of the distinctive habits and thoughts of other peoples separated from nineteenth-century Europe by time or space. This growth of self-consciousness, and particularly the discovery of the sub-conscious, enormously increased the scope of literature and art just at a moment when the traditional subjects were becoming worked out. Thanks to travel, research and exploration, thanks above all to photography and the mechanical reproduction of sound, it was becoming possible to assemble together the cultural achievements of all countries and all centuries at single points like Paris or Berlin. But this *embarras de richesses* had an inhibiting effect on the creative artist; everything worth doing seemed to have been done before. Originality could only be maintained by fundamental changes in intention and subject-matter. Fiction became internalized and self-conscious, concerned with thought and outlook rather than with narrative. Poetry turned to symbolism and allusion with highly personal associations; the fine arts deserted strict representation for impressions and the study of abstract form. Music began to explore the frontiers of rhythm and tonality. Such experiments may be difficult and disturbing to those accustomed to the old approaches but they are the essential means by which the imagination remains creative. Anyone who wishes to be a leader of taste must try to understand them. William was perfectly entitled to 'know what he liked'. How royal encouragement should be given to the arts is a far from simple matter; Ludwig of Bavaria, one of the most discerning patrons of modern times, was after all mad. What cannot be lightly excused, even by the frequency of their occurrence, are attempts to exercise influence without any effort being made to understand.

Yet when all the criticisms have been passed, one has a feeling that this was only half the man and that there was another half, and one as alive to his own deficiencies as any of the critics. His moustaches were typical of him not simply because they looked arrogant but because they were forced into position, and they were not the only part to which this happened. He was once described as 'not generous by nature and yet at times considerate of others'.[163] There are plenty of stories of minor kindnesses; he would go to considerable trouble to give other people pleasure, though woe betide those who failed to be pleased! The tyranny exercised over Frederick the Great by his father cast its shadow over William's relationship to his own sons, but his daughter could twist him round her little finger and after the abdication his grandsons had happy memories of a genial old man. He was devoted to his dogs, whom he spoilt flagrantly. He had a number of Jewish friends and only indulged in anti-Semitic remarks under the passing influence of people like Stöcker or Berg or when provoked by the Harden case. He was one of the first European monarchs to visit the Pope after 1870 and as a rule showed consideration for his Catholic subjects (though becoming anti-Catholic as a wartime reaction against the Austrian Emperor, Karl). He was quite ready to accept modern Biblical criticism and raised no protest when Houston Stewart Chamberlain told him that Abraham, so far from being a historical figure, was 'a distant memory of the moon-worship of Harar'.[164] But religion to him was not so much the outcome of knowledge as the product of man's intercourse with God.[165] 'Self reliance is good,' he once said, 'but it must be accompanied by fear of God and true religion.'[166] 'I am only a miserable human being who tries to be a useful instrument of the Lord God above.'[167] He once described himself to Queen Victoria as her 'queer and impetuous' colleague. He was, therefore, capable of humility, though his sense of election prevented him from expressing it in the form of humility towards his fellow-men.

There are other utterances to be set beside the more bombastic ones which have been quoted:

'Never forget that though the people you may meet in S.W. Africa have skins of a different colour, they for all that possess hearts susceptible to feelings of honour. Handle such people gently.'[168]

'My study of history has given me no encouragement to seek an empty world rule. . . . The world empire I have dreamt of consists above all in the enjoyment by the newly created German Empire of complete trust as a quiet, honourable and peaceful neighbour.'[169]

'Anyone who has stood on a ship's bridge at sea with only God's starry heaven overhead and has looked into his own heart will never question the value of such a journey. I hope that many of my fellow-countrymen will at some time or other in their lives have such an experience, giving a man the chance to draw up a balance-sheet of what he has attempted and what he has achieved. This is enough to cure anyone of over-estimating himself and that is something we all need to do.'[170]

'I have often at night been kept from sleep for hours by the knowledge that in a speech delivered the previous day I had failed to observe the limitations on content and expression which I set myself in advance.'[171]

'You must not bind me to my marginal notes.'[172]

Count Lerchenfeld who was Bavarian envoy in Berlin all through William's reign said that 'in spite of the volatility of his temperament one cannot deny that the Kaiser has a certain amount of cleverness, and when things are serious this will induce H.M. to take the advice of his chosen counsellors in good time'.[173] It is noteworthy that, in spite of all his apparent sympathy for strong views, he never appointed either Waldersee or Tirpitz Chancellor and none of the men whom he did appoint (except Michaelis who was not his choice) were patently unfitted for the job. Nor did he yield to the seductions of the Pan-Germans; when someone referred to what even the most rabid Pan-German would do if he stopped to think, William commented: 'They are quite incapable of thinking. That is the whole trouble.'[174] Moreover, some of the Kaiser's political speculations are not wholly devoid of foresight:

'All this while America is getting bigger, will go on gathering strength and will gradually absorb the power of England until she founds an English-speaking world empire of which England will be merely an outpost off the European continent.'[175]

'The Russians will go on amusing themselves with fictions (about their historic mission in the Balkans) until one day the Mongols stand on the Urals. Then they will realize too late where Russia's historic mission has really lain, namely in protecting Europe against the Yellow Peril.'[176]

'I prophesied in 1908 that in the event of an attack on Europe by the Yellow Peril, the Slavs will not only fail to offer opposition but will take sides against Europe.'[177]

Count Lerchenfeld said that there could be no doubt whatever about William's good intentions.[178] He himself was sincere when he said, as he frequently did, that he had the interests of his subjects, and even of the workers, at heart. One of his staff said that the Kaiser's bark was always worse than his bite.[179] He said rather pathetically to one Ambassador, 'I am not really a wicked man',[180] and puzzled another by remarking, with equal truth, '*I* am not the strong man—you must look elsewhere for him.'[181] But the remark which goes most to the root of the matter was made to Bülow after the Chancellor had criticized him for a tactless speech, 'I know you wish me well, but *I am what I am and I cannot change.*'[182]

William's main characteristics were undoubtedly determined by his parentage, his upbringing and his surroundings. Radical changes in his intensely complex personality were hardly to be looked for, particularly after he ascended the throne. But that is not to accept what actually occurred as beyond human prevention. How far the blame rests with William for not making a greater effort to overcome his weaknesses (or for not being more honest with himself in recognizing for weaknesses some of the attitudes described in this chapter), how far it rests on his companions for encouraging him in the wrong directions, is hard to say. The sad fact remains that the two tendencies encouraged one another and that taken in combination they resulted in untold damage to William, to Germany and to the world. For the Kaiser may reasonably be supposed to have had three main causes at heart: to make his country prosperous, to build good relations with Britain (for which he was uniquely equipped) and to strengthen Europe in comparison with the other continents. In practice he did much (though not exactly of set purpose) to produce a war in which Britain was the mainspring of the anti-German coalition, a war which brought on Germany catastrophe and hastened the relative decline of Europe.

CHAPTER VII

The New Course

STAFF OFFICERS ARE trained to be methodical, definite and industrious. They know how to get the best out of a team and realize the importance of identifying and securing decisions on fundamental issues. These merits Caprivi possessed, along with a good mind, the highest standards of personal integrity and a keen desire for the common welfare. He was also alive to the need for carrying the public with him; whereas Bismarck had fed stories to his favourite correspondents and paid them with money confiscated from the King of Hanover in 1866, Caprivi gave information to all respectable papers without regard for their political opinions. Sad to relate, this correct treatment and the suspension of corruption made his press bad rather than good.[1] He held the balance between the civil and military administration with scrupulous fairness. Indeed it was he who, to Waldersee's intense indignation, issued an order forbidding German military attachés to report on political matters except through and with the approval of the Ambassadors to whom they were subordinate.[2] But along with these qualities went defects which were also characteristic of the good soldier. The inbred military urge to precision hardly facilitates those ambiguities, that deliberate fluffing of the issue which are often the essence of politics. The instinct to obey makes it hard to conceive of politics as a power process in which the interests of the community may in the last resort be better served by non-co-operation than by acquiescence. Holstein told him that he was a historical philosopher but no politician.[3] He was too honest to be a flatterer or diplomat. Moreover, he was a reserved and isolated figure, a bachelor, who did not make friends easily and had never shone as a leader of troops.[4] The Kaiser used to say 'Caprivi, you get on my nerves dreadfully', to which the Chancellor replied, 'Your Majesty, I have always been an uncomfortable subordinate.'[5] While he realized the importance of establishing good imperial relations, he had not the personality to convert William's respect into friendship. As if aware of his inability, he kept himself at a distance from his master and operated largely through intermediaries such as Philip Eulenburg and Kiderlen-Wächter. As the influence of such men was disproportionate to the position which they held, a tendency resulted towards government by crony.

Another person who thereby benefited was Friedrich von Holstein. This bearded and myopic bachelor had made the Washington Embassy too hot to hold him by compromising the wife of the chairman of the Senate Foreign Relations Committee,[6] and the Paris Embassy too hot to hold him by relaying the Ambassador's machinations to Bismarck. He then in the 1870's returned to Berlin, where the happy idea of superimposing a fried egg on a veal cutlet ensured that his name, like that of Baron Nesselrode, would be enshrined in restaurants as well as registries. By sitting for long hours at his desk and supplementing his official papers through an extensive private correspondence, he gained a unique familiarity with the minutiae of German foreign policy and with the manners of its executants. Both the assiduity of his work and the acerbity of his comments brought him Bismarck's favour but, finding the master's attitude to Russia beyond his grasp, he decided to bite the hand at whose table he had frequently fed. The apostasy was rewarded on Bismarck's side by dark hints about the darker uses to which the 'man with hyena eyes' had let himself be put, and on Holstein's by a desperate anxiety to keep out of the Chancery the one potential occupant who no longer had any use for him.[7] For the *régime des apprentis sorciers* which had supplanted the old wizard would have required Holstein's diligence to supply their improvizations with a *continuo*, even if his store of inconvenient knowledge had not made his removal an operation fraught with risk.[8] Moreover, his readiness to imagine an insult was only equalled by his determination to avenge it and nobody could accuse a recluse of cowardice when his favourite relaxation was practising on pistol ranges.

For the next sixteen years, William and Holstein were to be the enduring sources of influence in German foreign policy. Chancellors and Foreign Secretaries came and went, but these two remained. Yet during the whole period they only met once, though the legend that their conversation on that occasion was confined to Pomeranian duck-shooting is an unfounded embellishment to a story already extraordinary enough. Nor was it exclusively the lack of a tail-coat which kept Holstein from court; he must have shrewdly suspected that close contact with William would soon lead him to a position from which the only escape would be resignation. Yet the attempt to control policy from a safe distance meant in practice that policy was uncontrolled. William's vagaries would in themselves have made consistency difficult. Yet when William's attention was elsewhere, it became almost a matter of chance whose influence was uppermost. Appalled by the resulting confusion, Holstein came in time to place the main blame for it on the Kaiser and to aim at excluding him from practical power. Eulenburg's refusal to lend himself to this scheme caused a feud, and the ensuing animosities spread wide devastation.[9]

Trouble was not slow in coming. The fall of Bismarck led Salisbury to revive interest in colonial negotiations which he had been playing very long; William and Caprivi, anxious for a quick achievement to embellish the New Course, agreed to accept a package deal. In this, Heligoland was bartered for an abandonment of German claims in Zanzibar and a tidying-up, to Britain's advantage, of various disputed obscurities in East Africa.[10] As neither side could possibly have held in war the territory which they renounced, the exchange was probably sensible, but it infuriated those Germans who demanded that their country should be acquiring African colonies from Britain rather than surrendering them. The critics were probably justified in accusing William and Caprivi of being uninterested in colonies[11] but did not stop to consider whether that disinterest might not itself be justified by the effort required for colonial development and the risk involved to Anglo-German relations. Indignation at the Zanzibar Treaty led to the foundation of the organization which four years later was to acquire the name of Pan-German League. The League was formed from professional and business men and above all from teachers, smallish men with incomes as limited as their outlooks, patriotic theorists who sought to compensate by their country's aggrandizement for the inadequacies of their own lives. Their aims were to arouse national self-consciousness at home, to foster the sense of racial and cultural kinship among all sections of the German people and above all to carry forward the German colonial movement to tangible results. The sinister word Master nation (*Herrenvolk*) rings like a tocsin through their utterances; this was how they regarded their nation, how they insisted that other powers must be made to regard it. Inherent in their outlook was a demand for effort in the face of inadequacy. Not only did the hope of Germany reversing the 'unfair verdict of history' seem to rest upon discipline, determination and readiness for sacrifice; the League itself could only hope to overcome its numerical insignificance (at its apogee it had less than 22,000 members) by the display of similar qualities. Vigour was the key to success, sweet reasonableness a betrayal of the German cause. The people who took the decisions may have disdained the Pan-Germans as a lunatic fringe but few remained entirely unaffected by their rabid outpourings and few were ready to disregard them in deciding what would pay in politics.[12]

A similar reaction was aroused by Caprivi's trade policy. He came into office at a time when demand had temporarily outrun supply; bread was extremely dear in Germany and most of her neighbours were putting up tariffs against her exports. The Bismarckian tariff of 1879 had undoubtedly assisted German industry at a difficult time, but in 1890 a number of important sections were becoming competitive on world markets. Germany was in fact beginning to follow the path of Britain and could only hope to keep her growing population employed and fed by increased industrialization, by higher imports of cheap foodstuffs from abroad and by extra exports to pay for them. In a time of mounting protection, easier access to foreign markets could only be secured by concessions in return. Caprivi was pursuing a rational policy in line with his belief that Germany's strategic position required her to retain as much as possible of her growing manpower at home and prevent it from emigrating or going to colonies. The political weakness of this policy was, however, that his concessions had to be made at the expense of the agrarians whose social and military influence was still sufficient to make them awkward enemies.

Caprivi began by signing 'most-favoured nation' treaties with Austria-Hungary, Italy and Belgium. There was little opposition and similar treaties extending the concessions to thirty-five other countries followed. Trouble arose when, as in the case of

Roumania and Russia, the country concerned had significant quantities of grain to put on the market and so benefited markedly by the reduction of duty on that commodity. With Russia, all sorts of nationalist and military prejudices reinforced the landowners' fears for their pockets; William himself was at this time deeply distrustful of Russian intentions. Yet he threw himself into the contest, telling the Conservatives that 'he had no desire to go to war with Russia because of a hundred stupid Junkers' and threatening their leader, Count Kanitz, that an adverse vote would cost him his position at court.[13] For Social-Democrats to refuse their support to the government was bad enough, but for Prussian noblemen to oppose their King was in his eyes an absurdity.[14] In March 1894 the *Reichstag* approved the Treaty by a substantial majority. But the victory was a costly one. The landowners east of the Elbe founded the Farmers League (*Landbund*) to organize agitation against any further sacrifice of their interests. They had a score to settle with Caprivi who, as a Prussian aristocrat and a German general, was considered to have betrayed his class. Here was a second sphere of public life in which self-advantage was to be consistently propagated under the guise of national interest.

The effect of Caprivi's trade treaties, as of all economic measures, is hard to assess because nobody can say what would have happened without them. In the following decade German production and exports certainly expanded at a great rate while emigration fell; it may, however, be that, at the stage of industrial expansion which Germany had then reached, they would have done so in any case. The treaties may at any rate be held to have accelerated an expansion which would otherwise have occurred more slowly. Nor was German agriculture in fact ruined; though some bad farmers went bankrupt, competition stimulated the introduction of better techniques and output rose. But Caprivi, in negotiating the treaties and particularly that with Russia, was not inspired by economic motives alone. Though the Triple Alliance had been renewed in 1891, Italy's signature was only obtained by a wider German commitment to support in North Africa; Caprivi sensibly hoped that, if the economic advantages of membership could be increased, there might be less need in future to bid up the political price. With Russia he was seeking nothing less than a more straightforward substitute to the Re-insurance Treaty, a means of loosening Russian dependence on

France which entailed no risks for German friendship with Austria. At the time of the French visit to Kronstadt and the signature of the Franco-Russian Alliance in 1891, this had seemed difficult to achieve. When two months later the Tsar twice passed through Germany and failed to propose a meeting, he was taken to be intending a deliberate insult; the more probable cause was fear of a conversation which might prove embarrassing. In 1892 he met William at Kiel without ill results and in 1893 hopes rose that the Panama scandal in Paris would make empires appear more respectable friends than republics. When the Tsarevitch, Nicholas, came to a family wedding William treated him to a serious talk which almost seemed to bring the Three Emperors' League back into practical politics. Admittedly the Russians showed a noticeable reluctance to follow up the hints which had been showered out and they cannot have helped noticing during the debates on the Army Bill that German military planning was obviously expecting to have to fight on two fronts. Russia, for her part, sent a squadron to Toulon in October 1893 which was fêted on all sides. But this was regarded by the Germans as a greater threat to the English than to themselves. The Kaiser and General Staff were slowly modifying their view that nothing could prevent Russia from attacking Germany and had begun to realize that by holding her at arm's length, they only increased the attractions of France. As Holstein elegantly put it, 'We desire good relations with Russia but without committing political adultery.'[15]

*   *   *

The taxation policy of the Caprivi government and his trade treaties undoubtedly made life less expensive for the workers. On the initiative of Berlepsch, the Prussian Minister of Trade, a start was made with establishing the arbitration courts which were to become so notable a feature of the German industrial scene.[16] The passage of a Workers Protection Act in May 1891 suggested that the government was concerned for the workers' welfare, even if not to the extent of giving them a position in which they could protect themselves. A conciliatory policy of this kind was essential for any government in Germany which tried to keep to the middle of the road, and the reforms which were introduced helped in due course to give the proletariat some sense of a stake in the country. Had the Kaiser been prepared to put the great influence of the crown consistently behind such a policy and make a reality of the equal rights which Bismarck had manœuvred him into promising in 1890, he could have done much to unify the country and rally his people round him. His tragedy, however, was that the steady pursuit of that or indeed any other policy was beyond his capacity. Though he could see the need to stand by his Chancellor and to benefit all sections of his people, he had a heart in too many camps and lent an ear to too many advisers for any role to be played for long. That of benevolent moderate was particularly apt to be abandoned because it was so unwelcome to his entourage.

Caprivi once said that:

'The government can hold down and strike down but that achieves little or nothing. The ills facing us can only be done away with by a change of heart and that is the justification for the Government's anxiety to spread more widely the sense of public service, pride in citizenship and readiness to devote head and heart to the tasks of the state.'[17]

The Prussian Conservatives, however, considered that such an attitude ought to be forthcoming from all citizens as a matter of course, without there being any need to arouse it by special measures. They delighted to describe the army as 'the people in arms', but any idea of allowing the people's representatives a say in the army appalled them. They exerted their influence to ridicule the ideas behind 'the New Course' and to dissuade the Kaiser from treating it seriously. The standard instruction book for the army might forbid any German officer, whether on the active list or the reserve, to join a party which was in opposition to the Emperor's government; anyone who felt compelled by his conscience to act in a contrary sense must first ask to be discharged.[18] But that by no means ensured their support for whatever proposal the Kaiser and his government chose to make. In much the same way, they would talk in general terms about the Slav menace. Yet they encouraged the influx of Polish workers into East Germany, regardless of the security risk in the event of a Russo-German war, because they thereby obtained cheap labour. And when Caprivi sought to secure the loyalty of such Poles by linguistic concessions, he was bitterly attacked for lack of patriotic feeling. The German élite were remarkable, even among possessing classes, for the firmness of their conviction that what was good for them was good for their country. But they were also remarkably pertinacious. Any policy which set them aside in the interest of wider unity would have had to be capable of withstanding sustained pressure from many directions. To such pressure William was only capable of succumbing. Little by little he discarded the views which he had asserted against Bismarck in favour of those being expressed continually around him.

Yet it was not as though the élite were able to have their way in the *Reichstag*; on the contrary, their inability to do so was the reason for their dissatisfaction with that institution. More and more the government found itself in need of support from the Centre, and such support had to be paid for. The repeal of the last anti-clerical laws was followed by the introduction of a School Bill designed to give the clergy control over religious instruction in Prussia. These concessions to clericalism, however, aroused the traditional animosities of the National Liberals whose leader, Miquel, had, by a rare exception, become Minister of Finance (though after his party had lost a majority in the *Reichstag*, not because it had gained one). Miquel tried to quit, but with Caprivi's approval, was prevented from doing so; he accordingly remained to intrigue against Caprivi in the Ministry, which became increasingly disunited. William veered from side to side, sanctioning the project before it was introduced but wavering as the opposition grew stronger. He may well have been justified in doubting whether the measure, desirable in itself, would be worth the disruption it seemed likely to cause. Such a situation called for an attitude of judicious reserve, but instead of adopting one, William showed his ability to appreciate the arguments on both sides by wholeheartedly embracing each in succession. In a speech in February 1892, delivered without the knowledge of his Ministers, he nailed his colours to the mast: the mast, however, did not prove stormproof and three weeks later he gave instructions that the bill must be amended in such a way as to satisfy its opponents. The fact that the Chancellor, Zedlitz the Minister of Education and Miquel thereupon resigned was not allowed to interfere with his hunting plans. He annotated Caprivi's resignation:

'Wouldn't dream of doing this. First to drive the cart into the mud and then to leave the Kaiser sitting there is not nice.

Caprivi made a mistake, everybody sees that. His leaving now would be a national misfortune and is impossible.'[19]

As he said on another occasion: 'It is I who dismiss my Ministers, not they me.'[20] Here he was following his grandfather who, when Ministers tried to resign because they disliked some political responsibility with which they were being saddled, 'regarded it as "Infidelity" and "Disobedience", considered that he was being left in the lurch and refused to let them go, while simultaneously threatening to abdicate himself unless he was obeyed.'[21]

The incident throws light on William's theory of government and on the German constitution. The Emperor regarded himself as being in the position of a landowner who had complete freedom in the choice of a bailiff to run his estates for him. To be chosen as bailiff was both a privilege and a duty, so that any attempt to escape from the task indicated a lack both of respect and of conscience. The bailiff's job was to manage the estate to the general satisfaction, some people's views (and particularly the owner's) being entitled to more consideration than others. The Emperor, being an enlightened ruler anxious to benefit his subjects, would pay attention to public opinion—or rather, to his views of what public opinion was or ought to be—but was in no way bound by it. The *Reichstag* should chiefly be guided in its ideas of what was desirable by the indications which the Emperor gave of what he wanted. Should the Chancellor miscalculate, and alienate an important section of the people who were considered to matter, it was his job to put things right, if necessary at the expense of a consistent policy; there was no question of calling in the man who had been urging a different policy and entrusting him with its execution.

The immediate crisis was solved by accepting one Minister's resignation, half of another's and none of the third's. Zedlitz went, Miquel remained and Caprivi, while remaining Chancellor, handed over the Premiership of Prussia to Botho Eulenburg, a reactionary cousin of Philip. As Caprivi remained President of the Federal Council and therefore head of the Prussian delegation, this led to anomalies. For the man who decided how Prussia was to vote in the Federal Council was no longer the man who decided Prussian policy. Although William expected the expedient to be temporary,[22] it lasted for two uneasy years—long enough to prevent it ever being repeated.

The School Bill sank without trace, to the displeasure of its clerical supporters. This did not matter in Prussia, where the lack of Catholics weakened the Centre and the three-tier suffrage the Social Democrats. But in the Empire as a whole where neither limitation applied, it considerably complicated Caprivi's task. This was vividly illustrated by the course of the Army Bill in 1892–3. Although secrecy enveloped the terms of the Alliance concluded between France and Russia in August 1891, its existence was openly proclaimed and attracted attention to the fact that France, with a smaller population than Germany, was training thirty thousand more conscripts every year. Caprivi's reply was a proposal to increase the peacetime strength of the German army by ninety thousand men. To make palatable the largest increase since the Empire was founded, Caprivi proposed to reduce the length of service from three years to two and the duration of the *Reichstag*'s blank cheque on army finance (the *Septennat*) from seven years to five.* As most recruits already went home after two years, and as the financial basis nearly always called for revision before the seven years were up, these concessions were more apparent than real. But the German Conservatives, like those of other countries, attached importance to appearances, while Bismarck had defeated the *Reichstag* over the three-year period in 1862–6 and over the seven-year duration in 1887. William therefore regarded any modification as treachery to his grandfather, and eighteen months of argument were needed before he could be reconciled to choosing between an increase on these conditions and no increase at all. He was unwilling to appear weak in the eyes of those who expected him to be strong, regardless of Caprivi's arguments that they were mistaking the shadow of strength for substance, and hankered after some way of securing both. He even talked about a *coup d'état* to abolish universal suffrage and give him a pliable *Reichstag* but was deterred by the reminder that any such step would bring him into conflict with the other Princes and strike at the roots of the Empire. In the end, however, after an election in June 1893 where both extremes were strengthened at the expense of the progressives and Centre, his obstinacy bore a certain amount of fruit. The *Reichstag* accepted a compromise which, without formally repealing three-year service, planned and provided only for two. William, however, did not feel

* See Chapter V, p. 105.

himself called upon to postpone the start of his Norwegian cruise in order to wait for the final vote.

Controversies of this kind did not contribute to the prestige of the administration and a number of other things helped to discredit it. First and foremost was the stream of vituperation emanating from the neighbourhood of Hamburg. Bismarck had always been a good hater and his chagrin at proving expendable, along with the unaccustomed sensation of finding himself unoccupied, found vent in a series of articles and speeches directed against Caprivi's Ministers (Marschall was described as 'the incompetent limpet from the Breisgau'), against Caprivi himself and (more discreetly) against the Kaiser. He was far more successful in organizing sympathy in retirement than he had ever been while in office (though in 1895 a *Reichstag* proposal to send a message on his eightieth birthday was rejected by 163 to 146) and his dismissal gave him a chance to found his own legend. He also proved that one of the marks of greatness is ability to win acclaim for actions—such as the disclosure of official secrets—which in others would be roundly condemned. His views on the need for a strong *Reichstag* and on the importance of the smaller German States commanded widespread assent, though when he had been in a position to advance those causes, he had not been outstanding for doing so. At first William made the mistake of trying to counter in kind:

'A spirit of insubordination is abroad in the land; veiled in iridescent and alluring garb it seeks to confuse the minds of My people and of those who are devoted to Me; it presses into its service oceans of printers' ink and paper to conceal the path which does and must lie clearly manifested to everyone who knows Me and My principles.'[23]

To the relief of the Kaiser's associates, his plan for throwing Germany's elder statesman into Spandau prison on a charge of high treason remained a mere threat. But when in July 1892 Bismarck went to Vienna for Herbert's wedding, not only was the German Ambassador told by Caprivi to 'avoid' being invited, but William on his own initiative wrote privately to Franz Joseph, with whom Bismarck had requested an audience, begging him 'as a true friend not to make my situation more difficult by receiving the rebellious servant before he has approached me and said his *peccavi*'.[24] The reception Bismarck received in all quarters was so cold as to make it plain that strings had been pulled. His reply was a burst of press vituperation and veiled references to a 'Uriah' letter. The sympathies of the public, and particularly of the right wing, were all on his side and to save William from the consequences of his meanness, Caprivi published his own instructions to the Ambassador and so took on himself the weight of popular resentment.

Twelve months later, however, Bismarck fell ill and caused the government to realize how much they would be criticized if he were to die unreconciled. As successive olive branches, the Kaiser despatched a telegram of good wishes, a bottle of old wine and an invitation to Berlin. Not only did he do this without consulting his Ministers but he brushed aside their attempts to conceal the fact. On the other hand those—and they were many—who expected Bismarck's reappointment as Chancellor reckoned without their William, and without the old man's years. In January 1894, Bismarck came to Berlin for a day and was treated royally by Kaiser and people alike, but after conversations more remarkable for their geniality than for their depth, took the evening train home to the country which by that stage he loved much more dearly than the court. 'Now they can erect triumphal arches for him in Vienna and Munich,' said William, 'I am always a horse's length ahead of him.'[25] Such a lead, however, proved inadequate insulation against shock when two years later Bismarck suddenly saw fit to divulge the text of the Reinsurance Treaty![26] Once again, William contemplated arrest for high treason and once again thought better of it. And this was the final challenge, for more and more the old man was condemned to a wheel-chair existence, and died in August 1898. Tirpitz, who visited him in 1897, found him tortured with neuralgia and holding hot water-bottles to his cheeks: he could only eat grated meat and spoke with difficulty. After drinking one and a half bottles of champagne, however, he became more lively and suddenly said: 'I am no tom-cat which gives off sparks when it is stroked.'[27] It was in the same year that William paid his final visit and plunged into a series of anecdotes to head off more serious conversation. The other, frustrated, suddenly assumed the mantle of John of Gaunt, 'Your Majesty, as long as you have the officer corps, you can do what you like. Should that ever cease to be the case, the position would be completely changed.'[28]

When William's reconciliation with Bismarck was impending but before its limitations were evident, the comic paper 'Bang' (*Kladderadatsch*) launched a series of attacks on Holstein, Kiderlen-Wächter and Philip Eulenburg, thinly disguised as 'Oysterfriend', 'Dumpling' and 'Troubadour'. The instigators are now known to have been two disappointed diplomats who had been favoured by Bismarck and therefore sidetracked by Holstein.[29] Their accusations of intrigue and backstairs influence cut uncomfortably close to the bone but William forbade the taking of legal proceedings for fear too many of the government's doings might get revealed to the public gaze. Holstein never penetrated the anonymity of the assailants, but challenged three fancied authors to duels, only to find them deny complicity. Kiderlen, however, was given to understand that his journeys with William would be over unless he found someone to fight; he therefore severely wounded the paper's editor when the latter refused to disclose his sources. When William heard how honour was being vindicated, he wrote: 'Bravo! That is my old Holstein! Plucky and won't stand any nonsense. If everyone was like him, the affairs of state would be in better shape.'[30] But though the incident did not achieve its author's object of getting Holstein removed, it left him suspicious and suspected. He had lost Caprivi's confidence and begun to distrust Eulenburg. He was at daggers drawn with von Plessen, the Kaiser's Adjutant-General, whom he considered to have let the side down by making Kiderlen treat a journalist as a man worth fighting. Holstein's appointment as Privy Councillor, by which Eulenburg hoped to restore his morale, did not succeed in dissipating his resentment against William, whom he had already accused of 'playing with the nation as though it were a big toy'.[31]

Nor was this the only rift in the lute. In June 1894 William agreed to Kotze, a Master of Ceremonies, being arrested on the charge of writing to other courtiers a series of anonymous letters which were as embarrassing as they were well informed. When, however, the trial took place, the suspect was acquitted, a result due less to the evidence of a hand-writing expert than to the fact that the letters went on arriving; the real author would seem to have been a relation of William himself. The ex-Master of Ceremonies challenged one of his bitterest opponents to a duel and killed him but was never reinstated at court; an imperial present in the shape of a floral Easter egg did not prevent wide-spread criticism of the way he had been treated.[32] Another sensation was caused by a certain Professor Quidde who at Easter 1894 published a pamphlet called *Caligula, a study in Roman Megalomania*; this unlikely subject proved a best seller since everyone recognized in a supposed Roman setting imperial characteristics which were familiar much nearer home. But the idea of prosecution was given up after a comic paper had forecast a dialogue in court:

Q: Whom had you in mind in writing this book, Professor?
A: Caligula, of course! Whom have you in mind, Mr. Prosecutor?

Soon afterwards Lord Lonsdale came to stay at the palace and was to be presented with a bust of his host. But the particular specimen selected had nothing to stand on and the courtier commissioned to deliver it pressed into service the pedestal of a classical statue in the corridor. William noticed the sudden accretion and laughed heartily on hearing how a Roman Emperor had been despoiled. 'No doubt it was Caligula!'[33]

*   *   *

Meanwhile, German relations with Britain had again struck choppy water, due largely to the passion which William had developed for yachting at Cowes. He first visited the Week in 1889 and returned every year until 1895. In 1891 he came to London on a State visit in July and went on with a considerable suite to stay at Osborne; there he sailed his new yacht, the *Meteor*, for the first time and enjoyed himself vastly. His grandmother was less pleased by the invasion and had distinct hints thrown out that 'these regular annual visits are not quite desirable'.[34] Uncle Bertie (who had just been giving evidence in the Tranby Croft case) took an equally poor view of being told that a man of his age and position ought not to gamble for substantial stakes with subalterns.[35] Indeed the constant need to keep his temper with his nephew quite spoilt the fun of the regatta for the Prince, and he began to talk of giving it a miss. Caprivi, foreseeing such possibilities, had tried to keep William away, but without success. 'The Hohenzollerns have never been popular in England. I am going to Cowes for the races and that is all there is to it.' 'Then, Your

Majesty, I have done my duty and must decline further responsibility.'[36]

Next spring the Queen visited her son-in-law at Darmstadt on her way back from Italy and the Kaiser did his best to get her to visit him in Berlin. The hint was gently but firmly rebuffed. 'I appreciate William's wish to see me. However, in my opinion it would be more fitting if the grandson were to travel to see his aged grandmother than that she should undertake a long and tiring journey to visit him.'[37] But she was equally firm with Lord Salisbury who thought that a few hours' conversation with her might rid William of some of his wilder ideas. 'No, no, I really cannot go about keeping everybody in order.'[38] The subsequent visit to Cowes passed off reasonably well; William stayed on his yacht, while court mourning for the Duke of Clarence provided an excuse for refusing his offer to bring a band.

The 1893 visit, however, was more eventful. Not only did he offend both Queen and Prince by refusing to break off a race when the yachts got becalmed, with the result that he was extremely late for dinner. One Sunday evening, when uncle and nephew were dining together, the Queen's private secretary, apparently on her instructions, brought William a telegram which she had just received; Lord Rosebery, the Liberal Foreign Secretary, alone in the Sabbath calm of his office, had instructed the captain of a British gunboat off Bangkok to reject a French ultimatum. There appeared to be some danger of war; what would Germany do? The Kaiser, back on his own yacht, was overcome by a nervous crisis.

'England's fleet was weaker than the Russian and French fleets in combination. Even with the aid of our little fleet, England would still be the weaker. The French wanted to drive Russia to some action which, considering the Tsar's hostile attitude to Germany, they might succeed in doing. Our army was not strong enough to fight simultaneously against France and Russia. It was impossible to sit still and let the tempest break. All Germany's prestige was gone if she could not take a prominent part; and not to be a world power was to cut a deplorable figure.'

His own inclination, on the spur of the moment, was to take the part of the English and assume the leadership in the whole affair.

But this was allowing imagination to run a long way ahead of facts. The estimate of British naval strength was presumably based on current Conservative criticism of the Liberal Government and had little real basis. A good deal would have had to happen before a Siamese incident produced a European war, while, as far as military preparations went, the official German appreciation was that a war with Russia would be 'as good now as later'. The impulsive Kaiser was exciting himself with a bogey of his own creation. Characteristically, next morning he had put it all behind him, going off for the day in the *Meteor* and leaving Eulenburg to exchange barbed pleasantries with Uncle Bertie 'breakfasting steadily from ten to four'. By the time he got back, the whole affair had proved a false alarm and little more was heard of it. But the Germans insisted on reading a deep-laid purpose into what was almost certainly an overhasty scare such as they themselves often indulged in. William deduced that overtures had been intended towards an alliance and that the subsequent explanations were meant to conceal a change of plan and climb-down before the French. No doubt he needed to explain the episode in a way which discredited someone else and thus covered up, even in his own consciousness, the memory of his panic.[39]

The foundation was being laid for the thesis which was to dominate German diplomatic thinking over the next decade—that Britain needed Germany more than Germany Britain and sooner or later would implore German aid. There was more than one view in Berlin as to how this point should best be brought home. William told the British Ambassador that while he did all he safely could to encourage mutual friendliness, he would defeat his own aims if he were to shove England down the throats of his people. 'The firm friendship which he desired could only be the work of time and the consequence of a continued mutual exchange of good offices in small things.'[40] In a toast to the Duke of Edinburgh, he looked forward to the day when the English and German fleet would fight together and promised that Nelson's Trafalgar signal would then 'find an echo in the patriotic heart of the German fleet'.[41] To hasten on that day he called the Military Attaché's attention to the consequences for England of the Tsar's visit to a French warship at Copenhagen and told the Ambassador that Russia had her eye on Alexandretta as a base for a Mediterranean fleet while France was trying to organize a Triple Alliance (including Spain) to recover Gibraltar.[42]

Others seemed to think rougher methods more appropriate. In January 1893 the British Ambassador in Constantinople called on the Sultan to abandon negotiations with German interests over the Baghdad railway. Marschall (on Holstein's instigation and without William's knowledge) replied by withdrawing German support from Britain in Egypt. This was a better way of securing short-term compliance than long-term collaboration. As Rosebery said: 'The game of cutting off noses to spite faces is easily continued when once begun and goes on crescendo.'[43] In the following year Rosebery concluded with the Congo Free State an exchange of territory which conflicted with promises made at the time of the Zanzibar Treaty, about which he later professed to be ignorant. He was forced to modify the deal, but not before he had complained of being addressed in a tone which might properly be used to Monaco.[44] Caprivi had been aware of the danger and minuted on one of the drafts, 'I should like the note to be in a somewhat more polite form and have marked a few places to be toned down.' He had earlier begged the German Ambassador to avoid arousing Lord Salisbury's suspicion that 'it is not the natural development of world events but the policy of Germany which is forcing on Anglo-French rivalry in the Mediterranean'.[45] But Caprivi himself could write that 'for us the best beginning for the next great war would be for the first shot to be fired from an English ship. Then we are sure of being able to convert the Triple Alliance into a Quadruple one'.[46] The Germans had read in their history books that Britain always found someone to do her fighting for her on the Continent and were determined not to allow themselves to be used, in Bismarck's words, as 'Britain's dagger pointed at Europe's heart'.[47] Superficially there was much sense in this attitude, at any rate from a German point of view. But the underlying assumption that in any alliance it would be Britain which was exploiting Germany diverted attention from the fundamental fact that France was allied to Russia.

*   *   *

In the early summer of 1894 William said to a friend, 'I get along with Caprivi but he is not congenial. The man has no imagination and does not understand me when I tell him of my wider thoughts.'[48] Caprivi, who is said to have offered his resignation

ten times in four and a half years, himself realized that things
could not go on as they were for much longer. His enemies claimed
that the Chancellor's only *Reichstag* support was the thirteen votes
of one of the splinters into which the Progressives had broken as a
result of disputes over the Army Law. Caprivi was disliked by the
soldiers for having abandoned three-year service, by the agrarians
for having lowered the tariffs, by the liberals for having offered
concessions to the clericals, by the clericals for having failed to
carry those concessions through, by the Bismarckians for having
replaced Bismarck, by the nationalists for having been weak about
Poles and inactive about colonies, by Holstein for allowing the
Kaiser too free a hand. He was becoming increasingly at cross-
purposes with Botho Eulenburg in the Prussian Ministry. Yet
such was the nature of the German constitution that he might in
spite of all these drawbacks have stayed in office provided only
that he had kept his master's confidence. William might not
unreasonably have felt it wrong to keep a Minister who had lost
public confidence—but Caprivi had succeeded in finding a
majority in the *Reichstag* for each of his major measures (except
the School Bill which had never been put to the test). The trouble
was that on each occasion the majority had been differently
composed, but that was hardly surprising when the deputies had
such limited influence over the government's policy.

Ironically enough, Caprivi went out, as he came in, on the issue
of social reform. In the summer of 1894, a wave of bomb-throwing
throughout Europe gave William a fright and the reactionaries
their opening. Typically forgetting his attitude of four years earlier,
the Kaiser was induced by von Stumm-Halberg and others to
demand action though, beyond a vague feeling that people capable
of voting Socialist ought not to be allowed to vote at all, nobody
was clear as to what should be done. Typically true to his earlier
position, Caprivi replied that violence would not change opinions
and that a *Reichstag* majority for reaction was not to be had. The
reply of the right was that the mere possibility of failure should not
deter a government which understood its real responsibilities
from doing what it believed to be right and necessary—or in other
words that if the desired end could not be reached constitutionally, it was the constitution and not the end which must be discarded. The King of Wurtemburg told William that, as none of the
Princes had sworn to uphold the constitution, there was nothing

to prevent them from subverting it. William scolded an East Prussian audience for opposing their King and then called on them to battle for morality and order against the forces of revolution, a euphemism to indicate that, since they must not act against his wishes, he was going to act in accordance with theirs.

This clear indication that his views were not acceptable led Caprivi yet again to offer his resignation, but he was told instead to resolve his differences with Botho Eulenburg. His chances of doing so might seem to have been improved by the fact that, when in October 1894 a bill repealing universal suffrage was laid before the Prussian Ministry, all Eulenburg's allies deserted him. But Eulenburg made it clear that his inability to carry through his own policy did not mean he was prepared to accept Caprivi's, and at the critical moment William saw fit to go on record as sympathizing with the agrarians and the soldiers. In again went Caprivi's resignation; back again came the telegram: 'Message received. Refuse approval. Rest orally'[49]—and orally William talked the Chancellor into agreeing to stay, after which he went off to shoot, imagining that the crisis was over.

But the Kaiser could not indefinitely continue to drive two horses, Caprivi and Eulenburg, each going in different directions, especially when the vehicles which each was drawing, the Empire and Prussia, were inseparably bound together. Even Botho Eulenburg realized that he could not logically continue in office after his master had declared confidence in Caprivi; he burst in among the butts with a resignation in his hand. William was seriously put out. 'He came up to me', said Philip Eulenburg, 'with that pale pinched look so familiar to me from all the innumerable bad hours we have been through together.' The problem of choosing between the two First Ministers was solved by the simple expedient of dispensing with both. But whom to appoint instead? The reactionary choice would have been Waldersee, but William was not prepared to make an appointment which would have entailed a resort to unconstitutional action, perhaps because his nerve failed him, perhaps because of a fundamental wish to respect that constitution which he claimed never to have read. Instead he asked for suggestions. Philip Eulenburg's reply was to list the qualifications, mostly negative, required of a Chancellor. 'A man who is neither conservative, nor liberal, neither ultramontane nor progressive, neither ritualist nor atheist, is hard to find.'[50] The only person who obviously matched the specifications was Prince Hohenlohe, the Governor of Alsace-Lorraine; his age was that at which Bismarck had been dismissed but nobody seems to have considered this an objection. All the same, he might not have been appointed, for William was still casting round for some way of giving both Caprivi and Botho Eulenburg sufficient evidence of confidence to induce them each to remain. But Holstein, in the hope that Hohenlohe would be able to educate William, leaked to the press the assurances which had been given to Caprivi and this public revelation of having been overruled made Eulenburg's position impossible.[51] Caprivi, though glad to deny his responsibility for the article, refused to deny its accuracy and at last got himself to the point of making the departure of both Eulenburg and Miquel a condition of his own stay. Within a matter of hours his resignation had been accepted and with greater dignity than Bismarck, he disappeared for good from the German stage. Five years afterwards he died of a broken heart, convinced that he failed his master in a time of need.[52]

William afterwards referred to Caprivi as 'that ill-starred man' complaining that 'he tried to teach me my business' and 'never did me a single favour'. But Caprivi's misfortune consisted in trying, without much adroitness or imagination, to do the honest thing by everyone, and if there really was to be any novelty about the 'New Course', it had to consist in some middle-of-the-road policy such as his. But William, without clearly realizing it, was seeking to live up to different ideals at the same time. Holstein accused him of treating *Reichstag* and people as negligible quantities. But this was not entirely fair. He genuinely desired to be a modern monarch, to stand above politics, to unite his people and to do them good. But he had also allowed himself to become the captive of an obsolescent élite; so far from having the strength of mind to defy the code which they shackled upon him, he showed his fidelity to it by exaggerating its tenets. Thus at the end of four years of uneasy experiment, he was not prepared to affront the views of his entourage by getting rid of Botho Eulenburg who was a member of their set and keeping Caprivi whom they hated. On the other hand, nobody could pretend that Caprivi had been an unqualified success or that Hohenlohe was an embodiment of the Prussian outlook.

CHAPTER VIII

The Climacteric

IN 'UNCLE CHLODWIG' William had acquired a Chancellor who was not merely a relative of Dona's but a sort of German Cecil, able to talk on equal terms with most of the princes of Europe. His bear-hunting wife, with whom he normally spoke French,[1] brought him big estates in Russia. One brother was an official at the Austrian court, another a cardinal; only with Britain were links lacking. A convinced Catholic who had nearly been excommunicated on the issue of Papal infallibility, he attributed to the Jesuits such of Germany's misfortunes as were not due to the Junkers. As Ambassador to France after 1870 he had joined so enthusiastically in the pleasures of *La Vie Parisienne* as to necessitate his being shadowed by the police.[2] Although he had said in the 1870's that his health was not up to the job of Chancellor, he was certainly a 'young seventy-five'. 'His melancholy aspect shocks people who do not know him; for many years he has looked worn out and broken but mentally he is as fresh as paint.'[3] A Liberal who disliked tariffs and a Bavarian who disliked Prussians, he had little sympathy for the agrarian conservatives while his appointment on top of that of Marschall meant that the two chief civil posts in the Empire were in South German hands. An exception to the rule that small men are self-assertive, he had the magnanimity of one who had never had to worry about status. He regarded his task as being to make people work in harmony rather than to pursue a policy which would provoke conflict. He was in fact well qualified to preside over an efficient government machine, or lead an integrated team. He handled William with some skill, seldom opposing projects outright but playing for time until the arrival of a fresh interest gave him a chance of discussing the previous one on its merits.[4] Though generally a pliable man, he could be stung into firmness; to one of William's more outrageous attempts at remote control, he replied: 'I am Imperial Chancellor, not an office boy, and may be presumed to know what I am talking about.'[5] But an Elder Statesman was hardly what the German situation called for, except on the assumption that, reform being impossible, there was nothing to do but wait for revolution. Certainly Hohenlohe was the last person from whom to expect vigorous initiatives in policy or a methodical overhaul of machinery—indeed if he had been, he would not have got the job.

Though Bismarck professed to welcome the new choice, it was not popular with those who had hoped for a strong man with strong (or in other words, undemocratic) measures, and sniping against the régime continued. Hohenlohe's internal policy was based on the principle that 'one cannot rule with the Conservatives alone unless one is prepared to overthrow the constitution. And that in the German Empire is out of the question.'[6] Consequently when a bill against sedition, much on the lines proposed by Caprivi, was rejected by the *Reichstag* in May 1895, the project was allowed to drop. William's reaction to the news was that 'we are left with fire hoses for everyday use and cartridges as a last resort'.[7] But Eulenburg pointed out to him that, if the government tried to get its way by tampering with the franchise, the Ministers in some of the more democratic federal States would risk being impeached by their parliaments for violating the imperial constitution. Their support could not in consequence be expected, while, when it came to the point, the Kings of Saxony and Wurtemburg would eat any fiery words that they might have uttered (partly because of their conviction that William would do so too!). The federal government, by embarking on strong action, might well get itself into a predicament out of which only the intervention of Bismarck could rescue it and from that humiliation worse than death, William not surprisingly shrank.[8] Consequently, though he continued to call for action, he never overrode Hohenlohe's opposition to it, or brought himself to the point of installing a Chancellor who would be more compliant.

The Tsar Alexander III had hardly been an unqualified admirer of William but the succession of his son, Nicholas II, in 1894 brought to the throne a young and weak man whom the Kaiser counted on charming into a supporter. In fact 'Willy's' stream of letters (all in English) which were intended to serve this end bored rather than impressed 'Nicky';[9] attempts to discourage them proved, however, unavailing. Their aim of detaching Russia from France was palpable rather than ulterior.

> 'The Republicans are revolutionists *de natura*. The blood of their Majesties is still on that country. Look at it, has it since then ever been happy or quiet again? Has it not staggered from bloodshed to bloodshed? Nicky, take my word for it, the curse of God has stricken that people for ever. We Christian Kings and Emperors have one holy duty, imposed on us by Heaven, that is to uphold the principle of "By the grace of God". We can have good relations with the R.F. but never be *intime* with her.'[10]

Meanwhile, Russo-German co-operation was assuming more practical forms. In April 1895 a Japanese attack on China, arising out of disagreement over Korea, led to the Treaty of Shimonoseki by which Japan gained notable advantages. Russia saw her ambitions in the Far East threatened and decided to press for modification of the Treaty's terms; she invited France and Germany to join in making representations, from which Britain had already decided to abstain. The French were not going to desert their ally nor the Germans to allow the French a monopoly of friendship. Moreover, William was becoming excited over an impending break-up of the Chinese Empire and a long-term Asiatic threat to Europe. He told the Tsar that:

> 'the great task of the future for Russia [is] to cultivate the Asian continent and to defend Europe from the inroads of the Great Yellow race. In this you will always find me on your side.'

He revealed rather more of his thinking to one of his officials:

> 'We must try to tie Russia down in East Asia so that she pays less attention to Europe and the Near East.'[11]

The Russian, French and German Ambassadors all called on the Japanese Foreign Office but whereas the first two took the edge off their written messages by polite explanations, the German, well-known for his dislike of the people to whom he was accredited, repeated in detail the instructions which he had received from Holstein without any attempt to cloak them in diplomatic language.

'My remarks', he said, 'made an obvious impression.' Their subsequent reproduction by the Japanese, when giving the Germans a
choice between war and evacuating Kiao-Chou, showed that the
impression lasted for nineteen years.[12]

The next scene of dispute was Armenia where heavy-handed
Turkish action to suppress a revolt created violent Western
indignation. Lord Salisbury suggested an international agreement
about the way to divide Turkey up supposing she were to collapse.
Holstein saw in this a deep-laid plan to set Austria at odds with
Italy, already restive with the Triple Alliance as being directed
more at maintenance than gain. William, just off to Cowes with
four battleships and a despatch boat, was warned against giving
the idea encouragement; he was nettled on arrival by a newspaper
article which joined issue with his Chinese policy. His first talk
with Salisbury was twice broken into by the character whom his
suite described as 'fat old Wales'. The Prime Minister could do no
more than broach the subject of partition and William deny that
Turkey was on the verge of collapse. Hatzfeldt, the German
Ambassador, read Salisbury's intentions differently; he saw in the
proposal a scheme to give Russia satisfaction in the Near East and
so detach her from France. Such an approach had obvious attractions for Germany and William asked Salisbury to see him again.

His suite, however, thought to save time by telephoning the
summons. The only instrument for receiving it at Osborne was
located in the billiard-room and guarded by a footman. As the
Prime Minister was with the Queen, the menial took the message.
But Salisbury considered a verbal request conveyed in such a
way as too casual to merit attention and left early next morning
without seeing the Kaiser who had hung about on his yacht for
two hours in vain.

'Willy', wrote the Queen 'is a little sore.'[13] 'The Kaiser', wrote
Salisbury, 'has not recovered from the intoxication of his accession
to power; it is rather growing stronger.'[14]

*   *   *

China and Turkey both combined size and independence with
weakness and inefficiency. To divide up the weak seemed for an
expanding power the only alternative—now that colonial areas had
been parcelled out—to fighting the strong. While industrialization was making war highly destructive and in consequence

slightly reprehensible, expansion was still regarded as a natural corollary of power; to assess whether, in the world as it is, great possessions are more a liability or an asset is a distinctly sophisticated pursuit. Another not dissimilar area was the Boer Republic of the Transvaal. Since the gold mines were opened in 1886, some fifteen thousand Germans had settled on the Rand and considerable quantities of German capital had been invested there, both directly and (as a result of a German ban on dealings in gold shares) through the London Stock market. An energetic German consul in Pretoria lost no opportunity of encouraging closer relations. But the independence of the Transvaal was limited by a clause in the London Convention of 1884 which deprived the Republic of the right to make agreements with other countries; London interpreted this as depriving third parties of any right to interfere in Anglo-Boer relations, a view which Berlin disputed. Whereas Britain considered that she was dealing with a turbulent vassal, the Germans thought they were helping David against Goliath. As difficulties multiplied between the Boers and business interests in Johannesburg, the British became increasingly determined to allow no outside interference and the Germans to prevent the situation being altered at their cost. The tension was increased by the opening in July 1895 of a railway, largely built with German capital, from Delagoa Bay to Pretoria, since this not only deprived Cape Colony of its monopoly of traffic to the Rand but enabled Germans to reach the Republic without crossing British territory.[15] William, who seems to have been harbouring ideas of taking the Transvaal under German protection, celebrated the opening by a telegram of congratulation which was met in London with raised eyebrows and in Germany with warm applause.

In October 1895 Sir Edward Malet, for over ten years British Ambassador in Berlin, was leaving. He used a final talk with Marschall to give a personal warning about the sympathy and encouragement which Germany was showing to the Boers. He did not think that Germans realized how strongly the British felt on this subject; Britain's patience was not unlimited so that German persistence might have serious consequences. Marschall not unfairly replied that Germany could not be held responsible for the Boers' dislike of England and that if German Ministers were to let the *status quo* be changed, they would incur the wrath of their entire nation. William took grave offence at Malet's remarks. 'And that on top of everything else! To threaten us when they need us so badly in Europe!'[16] He complained about the 'tone of undisguised menace' and told all and sundry that Malet had gone so far as to use the word 'war'—of which there is no evidence whatever.[17] When Salisbury confirmed that Malet had spoken without instructions, William minuted again 'That is all very well, we must take care to make full use of this incident, among other things eventually for naval demands to protect our growing trade.'[18] No sooner was Malet out of the way than he employed the more sympathetic but less orthodox channel of Colonel Swaine, the Military Attaché, to tell England that, if she had any spirit left and wished to escape from the isolation to which her policy of selfishness and bullying had led, she must choose between openly joining the Triple Alliance and coming out against it. With Germany and Austria behind her, she could safely counter any Russian designs on Constantinople by forcing the Dardanelles.[19]

British Ministers cannot be blamed if they began to suspect that the Boers had received more official encouragement from Germany than in fact seems to have been the case. But they were not the only people to be worried by William's behaviour. Holstein pointed out to Eulenburg that the remarks about the Dardanelles had only to be repeated in St. Petersburg to produce a Russian attack on Germany. He had forecast this kind of incident a year earlier.

> 'Now I advise you again to take care lest you go down to history as the black knight who was at the side of the Imperial wanderer when he went astray. . . . Who is to advise the Kaiser at such a serious time? The old gentleman [Hohenlohe] is behaving as though he were merely the under-butler. Do you still think that we have got to leave our Master to decide everything auto-cratically on his own in the light of his finer intuition? For H.M. to act on the impulses of the smoke room can have consequences which will astonish him as well as you. You will be in a much better position to see what has got to be done once you have discarded that misleading saying "The King can do no wrong" which was invented in a country where the King has no power.'[20]

William was in a highly nervous state, due partly to a recurrence of trouble with his ear. A crisis inside the Prussian Ministry aggravated his condition. For a number of years the *Reichstag* had been pressing for Prussian courts martial to be held, like Bavarian ones, in public. This trivial issue had become a symbol for the relationship between soldiers and civilians; while the generals were indignant at political interference, the politicians felt bound to assert their authority. William, under the influence of his Military Secretariat, sided unhesitatingly with the soldiers. The Minister of War, himself a soldier, thought it worth while giving way on this issue so as to get *Reichstag* support for a separate measure increasing the strength of the army. The Chancellor could hardly oppose a proposal which he himself had helped to introduce in Bavaria. Köller, Minister of the Interior, who had already won William's favour by showing himself more reactionary than his colleagues, was tactless enough to disclose to the imperial entourage the course of discussions in the Ministerial council. His colleagues, led by Marschall, thereupon declared that, unless he resigned, they would do so in a body. William complained that such behaviour infringed the unfettered liberty of the King of Prussia to choose as Ministers whomever he fancied. Hohenlohe persuaded him to give way but he did so with a bad grace and much muttering about things not being taken as precedents.[21]

Such was the atmosphere in which at the end of December the news broke of Dr. Jameson's raid into the Transvaal. At first sight Britain must have appeared to be playing straight into German hands. She was in the middle of a dispute with the United States over Venezuela and had managed to offend the Italians by taking too lightly their defeat in Abyssinia. Though the British Government quickly disowned Jameson, the Colonial Secretary, Chamberlain, was widely believed to have encouraged his backers and at the very least seems to have avoided having any responsibility for stopping him by taking pains not to know what he was doing. Marschall was anxious to unite Europe against Britain with the ultimate object of bringing home Britain's need for German friendship. But Salisbury's disavowal of Jameson cut the ground from under Marschall's move to break off diplomatic relations, while Jameson's defeat rendered otiose the preparations to send fifty German marines from Delagoa Bay to Pretoria, and so show that Germany was not going to let Britain annex the Transvaal.

William, who assured the Tsar that 'come what may, I shall never allow the British to stamp out the Transvaal', was becoming impatient. In talking to the War Minister about courts martial, he used language which with anyone else would have led to a duel, and on New Year's Day told his generals that under no circumstances would he agree to the measure, while his Ambassador at St. Petersburg, who saw him on the same evening, described him as 'absolutely blazing and ready to fight England'. He had already drafted a telegram of which both the recipient and precise contents are obscure but it would seem to have declared the Transvaal under German protection. The pretext for its despatch was, however, removed by the Boer victory and on the morning of 3 January, accompanied by three admirals, the Kaiser descended on Hohenlohe to settle how the new situation should be handled. A number of alternatives were discussed—an international conference, the despatch of reinforcements to Delagoa Bay, and a mission to discover what help Krüger needed. The first was discarded on the ground that it would offend the Boers, the second because it might involve war with England (though William seems to have discounted the likelihood of troops being stopped on the high seas). In the middle of the meeting a subordinate was sent out of the room to draft a congratulatory telegram to Krüger; on the way he met Holstein who, learning what was afoot, expressed doubts. 'Oh! don't you interfere,' said Marschall, 'you've no idea of the suggestions being made in there. Everything else is far worse.' This story and other evidence have long led historians to believe that the telegram was proposed by Ministers as a desperate expedient to dissuade William from more violent action. William, however, writing twenty-five years later, claimed that the telegram was forced on him by Ministers against his better judgement and evidence has just come to light which indicates that his claim has something in it. But however instigated, the telegram read as follows:

> 'I would like to express my sincere congratulations that you and your peoples have succeeded, without having to invoke the help of friendly powers, in restoring peace with your own resources in face of armed bands which have broken into your country as disturbers of the peace and have been able to preserve the independence of your country against attacks from outside.'[22]

The Kaiser's fears that the telegram might cause a stir in Britain proved as justified as his Ministers' insistence that nothing less would satisfy Germany. The widely divergent reaction of the two publics is the most sinister aspect of the business. The British resented it as an uncalled-for interference in their private vexations by someone from whom, as the Queen's grandson, they had expected support; it was taken as a sign that the hostility to England widely manifest among the German people might be shared by their leaders. It was also treated as an expression of petulance by someone who was powerless to affect the situation. President Cleveland's message about Venezuela, though hardly less offensive than the telegram, excited far less notice. 'Public opinion', said Hatzfeldt, 'changed overnight and to our disadvantage.' For several days the Kaiser received forty to fifty abusive letters, mostly anonymous. The 1st Royal Dragoons, of which William had recently been made Colonel as a result of what the Queen called 'a regrettable fishing for uniforms', cut his portrait in pieces and threw it into the fire.[23] The Prince of Wales looked upon the message as a 'most gratuitous act of unfriendliness' and thought his nephew had shown the worst possible taste. 'Independently of all this, the Prince would like to know what business the Emperor had to send any message at all. The South African Republic is not an independent state in the proper sense of the word and it is under the Queen's suzerainty.* What the Emperor has done therefore is doubly unnecessary and unfriendly. H.R.H. hopes he will not come to Cowes this year.' He also urged his Mother to give Willy 'a good snubbing'.[24]

Eighteen years later the then British Ambassador in Berlin said to his Belgian colleague that the misunderstanding between Britain and Germany dated from the Krüger telegram.[25] At the time of its despatch the Ambassador in Rome told his German colleague that the British people would never forget the box on the ear which the Kaiser had given them. This goes too far. The telegram surprised the British public much more than it did British Ministers and even so the indignation was not so deep that it could not have been outbalanced by skilful handling later. The Jameson Raid was not one of the most creditable episodes in our history, and in retrospect the indignation seems overdone. Bismarck, though he thought the reference to friendly powers a mistake, said with some justice that the telegram could perfectly

* In fact the word suzerainty, though included in the Pretoria Convention of 1881, was not repeated in the London Convention of 1884.

well have been sent to Krüger by Lord Salisbury.[26] The Queen showed a sure grasp of the position. She told her son that 'those sharp cutting answers and remarks only irritate and do harm, and in sovereigns and princes should be carefully guarded against. William's faults come from impetuousness as well as conceit, and calmness and firmness are the most powerful weapons in such cases.' The letter which she wrote to William was a masterly example of both qualities; in a way which he could neither resent nor brush aside, she told him clearly that she considered his action in every way a grave mistake and was grieved by it. The letter 'pleased' William who excused himself on the score that he had never intended to offend Britain by expressing his satisfaction that a disobedient servant of the Queen had been defeated. This argument was also used by Marschall but the Queen found it 'lame and illogical'.[27] The Prince of Wales's hopes were realized, as the Kaiser did not come to Cowes that year or indeed for several years afterwards; instead, the Tsar came to Balmoral where Lord Salisbury was heard to say with satisfaction, 'He is very different from the other Emperor'.[28]

Three years later Cecil Rhodes was received by the Kaiser (in spite of being dressed in a lounge-suit) and the talk turned to the Jameson Raid.

'You see,' said Rhodes, 'I was a naughty boy, and you tried to whip me. Now my people were quite ready to whip me for being a naughty boy, but directly *you* did it, they said, "No, if this is anybody's business, it is *ours*." The result was that Your Majesty got yourself very much disliked by the English people, and I never got whipped at all!'[29]

This comment picturesquely sums up one of the chief criticisms of German policy in the episode. The other was its palpable failure to affect the course of events in South Africa. When Britain was at her most vulnerable, the Germans still seemed to have made no headway with the aim of impressing on her the need to seek their friendship. Britain's organization of a 'flying squadron' to cruise in the North Sea, though planned before the telegram with Venezuela as much in mind as South Africa, underlined their impotence. It was no accident that three days after the despatch of the telegram, William held two conferences about enlarging the German fleet.

William's sea-fever had more behind it than his insatiable itch for a finger in every pie. Youthful memories of Kiel and Plymouth, studies of naval history, memories of the British Naval Review in 1889, Admiral Mahan's book on the influence of sea power on history (which he read in 1894) and the fascination of Cowes all played their part. But at bottom his attitude to the fleet was part of his love-hate relationship with his mother's country. He wanted a navy because the English had one, because it was a sign of being a world Power, because it was a means of forcing the English to pay him attention, of making Germany an attractive ally. And undeniably in the early years of his reign the German navy was far from being a source of satisfaction. In 1864 it had been outnumbered by the Danes.[30] For long it was regarded as a subordinate branch of the army and run by generals. In 1888 great difficulty had been experienced in collecting a squadron to accompany William on his State visit to Russia. The heavy armour-plate had all to be imported from England. In 1895 the need to provide contingents simultaneously for international squadrons in the Far East and the Aegean had strained resources to the limit.[31]

William had done what he could. On coming to the throne he had created his own Naval Secretariat parallel to the Military and Civil ones. A year later, he had taken responsibility for the navy away from the War Office and set up an Imperial Naval Office under a State Secretary with five commands all reporting directly to him.[32] To the lasting benefit of the Krupp family, Germany acquired her own facilities for making armour-plate. But much still needed to be done, and two main obstacles impeded progress. The first lay in the accepted strategic theory, which saw the tasks of the German navy as being coast defence and the maintenance of order in overseas possessions. For these purposes cruisers and other small vessels were enough; a battle fleet would be an unnecessary luxury. The second obstacle was the lack of public interest. Most of the German States were without any naval tradition. The soldiers looked down upon the sailors and did not want any competitor making claims on the public purse; they had understandable doubts as to whether any country could afford a first-class fleet as well as a first-class army. The *Reichstag* saw no reason for spending money on ships; William's hankering after a *coup d'état* was partly inspired by a desire to do for the navy what his grandfather, in totally different circumstances and at the instigation of Bismarck, had in 1862–6 done for the army. After the Krüger telegram he talked of vast appropriations for the fleet and when Hohenlohe and the Naval State Secretary replied that he would be lucky if he got his annual estimates accepted without cuts, swore that, were he to dissolve the *Reichstag*, he could easily find people who could arrange it.[33] A year later the *Reichstag* did cut the higher estimates by twelve million marks, partly because William at the crucial moment offended the Centre by describing his grandfather as the kind of person whom the Middle Ages would have canonized. William thereupon wrote a letter to his brother Henry in which he described the deputies as 'unpatriotic louts and scoundrels'; this Henry saw fit to read out to the crew of his ship. The Kaiser vowed to get the decision reversed even if it meant abolishing the constitution and replacing the *Reichstag* by a body composed of delegates from the various state parliaments.[34]

*   *   *

Meanwhile, William had by his obstinacy succeeded in getting various modifications inserted into the proposals for courts martial. When Hohenlohe questioned whether Ministers would be prepared to answer for the proposal in this form, the Kaiser minuted:

> 'The army and its internal affairs are no concern of the Ministry but are reserved under the constitution to the King as his personal affair. Consequently the Ministry is in no position to assume constitutional responsibility for the army which I command.'[35]

Such an outlook corresponded closely with that of the chief aide-de-camp von Plessen who said that the army 'must remain an insulated body into which no one dare peer with critical eyes.' The Military Secretariat transferred to the retired list five of the generals who had supported the original courts martial proposal and in the autumn of 1896 the War Minister himself was replaced. But the army was still not without worries. Waldersee and other generals had begun to fear that, if Social Democracy spread much further, conscription would fill the ranks with disaffected young men who could not be relied on in civil emergencies.[36] Yet if conscription were abandoned as too dangerous, how could

Germany hope to meet the numerically stronger forces of the Dual Alliance? They therefore pressed for action to check the Socialists before it was too late. This attitude was shared by the Agrarians who called on the government to fight socialism as a battle of ideas and not as a mere question of power politics. Such an approach was diametrically opposed to that of Berlepsch who had committed himself to a policy of conciliating the workers by legislation to protect their interests, while admitting that patience would be needed before results could be expected. When he not merely found most of his proposals blocked but was even ordered to introduce into them retrograde concessions to the right, he resigned, thereby incurring imperial displeasure.

'He seems to set great store by his reputation in Parliament and the country. He has got the constitution a bit wrong. If I am satisfied with him, that is enough and nothing else matters.'[37]

But even more important Ministers were in trouble. Bötticher, the Secretary for the Interior, got into William's bad books for making no protest when on an occasion in Hamburg attended both by him and a number of Socialists, the Mayor thought it best to omit the customary cheers for the Emperor. Soon afterwards the Kaiser made a speech in which he described the counsellors of his grandfather as 'instruments of his sublime will'. The Progressive leader Richter fell foul of this expression in the *Reichstag*, attacking William for his impetuousness and inconsistency and his Ministers for being no more than obsequious instruments. Bötticher's failure to take a strong line with such opposition was the last nail in his coffin. Meanwhile, Marschall had felt compelled to bring a libel action against a Berlin newspaper and so to uncover the curious fact that a leading police official had regularly caused the press to be supplied with defamatory material, some of which was directed against Ministers. The policeman, who was more likely to have been acting on Bismarck's initiative than his own, also included in his responsibilities the personal security of the Kaiser. The plaintiff therefore found himself more successful than popular—and this was not his only cause of offence.[38]

In February 1897 a revolt broke out in Crete, whose leaders proclaimed its transfer from Turkey to Greece, and so at once revived the controversy as to whether Turkey was to be propped up or broken up. The various Powers were both suspicious of one another and preoccupied in other directions; they were therefore able to agree on a masterly compromise by which Crete was to remain a Turkish province but be given autonomy under a Greek prince. Turkey had had a fascination for William ever since his trip to Constantinople in 1889, and although his sister was married to the Greek Crown Prince, he took a leading part in organizing an international naval demonstration which forced Greece to withdraw her troops. In Britain, however, the days of the Jingoes were over and the new generation had little sympathy for Turkey. Feeling therefore tended to be pro-Greek, an attitude which William criticized on the ground that it set Britain at odds with Austria and might even, by encouraging the partition of Turkey, lead to a European war. The result was a sharp conflict of view between himself and his grandmother.

> 'I wish you would desire Sir F. Lascelles to tell the German Emperor from me that I was astonished and shocked at his violent language against the country where his sister lives.'
>
> 'Received a rude answer from William sent *en clair* whilst my telegram was in cypher.' (A favourite trick of his.)
>
> 'Received another grandiloquent telegram, also *en clair*, from William.'
>
> 'There is hope that the Greeks may be able to pay part of the indemnity . . . but the other Powers seem averse, and Germany wishes to *force* and not to *ask* Greece. It is all due to William's shameful behaviour.'[39]

Marschall was questioned in the *Reichstag* on German policy and was rash enough to answer, a course which William found quite inappropriate:

> 'The decisive step to the solution of this problem was taken personally and directly by me and I am therefore the only person who can give the *Reichstag* information. . . . When I get back to Berlin I shall summon them to the Castle and give them a complete account of the attitude of my government to this question.'

This produced from Eulenburg the comment that 'William's studies of constitutional law had obviously not been completed when he was called to the throne' and from Hohenlohe the reminder that accounts of the government's position were open to criticism from which the Emperor should be screened.[40] But it also led in June 1897 to a group of Ministerial changes behind which lay discrepant motives. William and some of his entourage wanted to get rid of Ministers who had proved unsuccessful or obdurate and replace them by others more heedful of imperial whims, even to the extent of overriding the *Reichstag*. Eulenburg and Holstein, however, saw a need to find someone more capable of managing the Kaiser and of acting as an intermediary between him and the parties. They thought to have done so in the person of the Ambassador in Rome, Bernhard von Bülow, who became Foreign Secretary, Marschall going as Ambassador to Constantinople. Bötticher and Hollmann, the Naval Secretary, also retired, and were replaced by Count von Posadowsky and Admiral von Tirpitz. All the three newcomers were to play a leading part in the years ahead.

Bülow, who in 1900 was to become the third of William's Chancellors, indeed seemed ideally qualified to resolve the difficult relationship between Kaiser, Ministers and *Reichstag*. Combining as he did excellent wits with scanty scruples, urbane and cosmopolitan, he was always able to turn a situation to momentary advantage by a joke, an apt quotation or a ready repartee. 'He is tall and slender but not starchy; a friendly face with rather gentle eyes, a small blond-grey moustache but otherwise clean-shaven; the aspect, in general, of an old ex-lieutenant who had resigned his commission early because his gaiters bored him.'[41] Younger by some thirty-seven years than Hohenlohe, with more adaptability and political flair than Caprivi, he quickly installed himself in his master's graces, at the cost of his friend Eulenburg, and was hailed as the Bismarck of the new era. As an acute observer forecast, he was to catch many mice by his ability to have ready for each its favourite kind of cheese.[42] He attached great importance to having a good press and neglected no means of getting one. Yet in the end he was to merit the devastating comment passed by Tacitus on Galba: '*Consensu omnium capax imperii nisi imperasset.**' For, to quote a more domestic chronicler: 'Underneath the shiny paint there was nothing but plaster.' Ambition and vanity led

---

* This phrase defies translation since much of the effect comes from the compression into six words. Perhaps it is best to paraphrase 'He took office with a brilliant future behind him.'

him to rest content with short-term effects and superficial solutions. Though he probably handled William more dexterously than those who went before or came after, he too often achieved his ends by flattery and therefore his success was transient; he left the fundamental problems untackled, he allowed the opportunities to escape and even so ended by giving mortal offence. His range of vision and his courage were alike inadequate; his wide culture, which should have enabled him to transcend the conventions of his time, was used for purely decorative purposes. He had read, according to Holstein, more Machiavelli than he could digest. Tirpitz once said that an oiled eel was a leech compared to him.[43] He despised detail and left subordinates to find their own way; those who succeeded in getting an interview found him ready enough to chat but regardless of whom he was keeping waiting.[44] He had neither force of personality nor moral fibre and the rule which began in such roseate auspices did great damage to William and to Germany.

Posadowsky came of a family of ennobled bureaucrats and had the reputation of being a reactionary. He was in fact an individualist who believed legislation to be a necessary evil and was afraid of the State trying to take upon itself too much. He regretted that Germany had become industrialized and regarded the workers as irretrievably lost to the national cause. Rather inconsistently he favoured a strengthening of the Federal Government at the expense of the States and as part of this policy, got responsibility for social policy transferred from the Prussian Ministry of Trade to the Federal Ministry of the Interior. Here he found himself able to do good by stealth. Hohenlohe and Bülow were preoccupied with foreign affairs and the Kaiser was not concerned with what appeared to be mere administration. Posadowsky was a prodigious worker, unrivalled in his capacity to absorb detail and expound it lucidly. Practical contact with social questions did much to liberalize his outlook and in his ten years of office he put through a number of unobtrusive measures with the gradual effect of making the régime more congenial to the workers. That he did not do more was no doubt due to his limitations as a politician. His manner was cold and reserved, his judgement poor. 'He plays the man of firm character and principles, but the moment that difficulties crop up, firmness is regularly forgotten.'[45]

Winston Churchill once described Alfred von Tirpitz as a

'sincere, wrong-headed, purblind old Prussian'[46] but this approach somewhat evades the problem which he presents to the historian. Haldane is said to have considered him abler than Bethmann Hollweg. There can be no doubt about his energy, his skill in organization and his political dexterity. Such qualities call for a considerable degree of intelligence. But an intelligent man might have been expected to see that the naval policies which he initiated would lead sooner or later to a clash with Britain. Was such a clash his real aim? His frequent denials are hardly decisive, because 'ambitious designs against one's neighbours are not as a rule openly proclaimed'.[47] A certain amount of evidence suggests that this was in fact his aim. Yet if so, how did he suppose Germany, in face of British naval predominance, to stand a chance of success? People who want to do something keenly enough, however, can always find reasons to excuse their course and, as will be seen, a succession of theories, plausible rather than convincing, were available to conceal the fundamental weakness of German naval policy. Tirpitz, moreover, took for granted that German foreign policy would be conducted with the naval building programme always in mind. Had this not unreasonable supposition been realized, Germany might perhaps have acquired a fleet without thereby incurring the loss of a war. But to assume that in the Wilhelminian Empire any two aspects of government would be co-ordinated, let alone that foreign policy would be consistent, was optimism of a high order. And perhaps the key to the riddle is given in a description of Tirpitz written by a senior officer shortly before he took office:

'An honourable, energetic, independent and ambitious character, adroit and rather optimistic, capable of keen resourceful thinking of a speculative and abstract kind. His otherwise successful performance in responsible posts has shown a tendency to look at matters one-sidedly, and devote his whole energies to the achievement of some particular end without paying enough attention to the general requirements of the service, with the result that his success has been achieved at the expense of other objectives.'[48]

Tirpitz (whose hobby was English philology and whose wife and daughter were educated at Cheltenham) gave the German navy strategy, organization and public support. The underlying drive

was no doubt the familiar desire to aggrandize the institution with
which one is connected and in whose value one believes. He wanted
a bigger fleet for Germany and he wanted the fleet to count for
more in Germany. To justify this, he started from Caprivi's statement that Germany must export men or goods. If she chose to
export goods, she put herself at the mercy of any power which was
dominant at sea; as William put it, great colonial possessions were
an Achilles heel for a Germany hitherto out of England's reach.
Certainly Germany was no exception to the rule that, by industrial-
izing, a country makes itself dependent on supplies like rubber, oil
and cotton from distant parts of the world. Britain had acquired a
merchant marine to bring these back and warships to secure
their safe carriage as well as to maintain order in the places from
which they came. Yet it is hard to see how one country can interfere with another country's supply lines in time of peace, and in
the light of British reactions in 1914 it is difficult to believe that
Britain would have made war on Germany for trade reasons alone.
As Hatzfeldt said in 1901: 'If people in Germany would only sit
still, the time would soon come when we can all have oysters and
champagne for dinner.'[49] But not only were many people in
Germany convinced that without a fleet foreign competitors led
by Britain would drive their trade out of existence; people could
be found in Britain who accepted without question much the same
view.[50] Moreover, the German army, though still dominant, could
no longer be sure of durable victory on two fronts if the German
economy could be halted by the pressure of sea power. The
Valhalla from which German patriots thought to sway the world in
security was not itself impregnable. Instinctively, rather than
explicitly, the framers of German policy began to grope after a
means of making it so. Clearly this could not be done simply by
increasing the number of squadrons operating overseas; no war
with a Power of any size would be just a 'cruiser war'. Isolated
squadrons could be finished off one by one unless there was a
central force strong enough to force the enemy to concentrate;
true to Mahan, Tirpitz continually insisted that a country which
wished to make its power felt at sea must possess a battle fleet.

But the British Navy in 1896 possessed 33 battleships as compared with Germany's 6 and 130 cruisers as compared with 4.
Was not the prospect of catching up hopeless and was not Germany therefore doomed to remain at Britain's mercy? Tirpitz got

over the difficulty by formulating his 'risk' theory. According to this, Germany could have security without having to equal the fleet of the strongest naval power. All that was necessary was to have a fleet strong enough to inflict serious damage on any enemy that attacked it. No enemy would then attack for fear that, even if the damage inflicted brought victory, the damage suffered would be such as to put the victor at the mercy of third Powers with strong navies. Viewed as a logical exercise this theory has obvious flaws, notably in assuming that the strongest naval Power would be friendless. But it corresponded with the circumstances of the time; William's frequent claim that he was Britain's only friend on the Continent was not as ridiculous as his interpretation of friendship makes it appear. Moreover, the current British doctrine of the 'Two-Power Standard', by which the British fleet had to be stronger than the next two navies put together, was based on very much the same calculations. The Two-Power Standard of course implied that, as other countries built up their navies, Britain would follow suit. But Britain's capacity to do so had never been put to the test and, in the last resort, the scale of a country's armaments must depend on the size of its own resources and not on the behaviour of its rivals. During the whole period 1870–1914 Britain's expenditure on defence was higher than Germany's and over the years 1895–1914 Germany was still devoting a significantly smaller proportion of her national income to armaments than Britain did.* The German Admiralty believed that, if they forced the pace in naval building, the British would not be able to keep up.[51] The main danger, in Tirpitz' view, consisted of a preventive attack before the German fleet was strong enough to make Britain think twice. Had Admiral Fisher and Colonel Grierson had their way, such an attack might well have occurred.[52] But as Tirpitz may have realized, his British opposite numbers were under more effective civilian control than himself. And if Germany was to have more influence outside Europe—in other words, act as a 'World Power'—she must have a stronger navy. The only alternative to passing through the 'danger zone' was to remain without influence outside Europe.[53]

Tirpitz' final contribution to the German Navy lay in the skill with which he handled the *Reichstag*. Whereas his predecessor had met rebuff after rebuff, and had backed up Hohenlohe in arguing

* See Appendix I, Table X.

that the price of any marked increase would be a constitutional show-down of the first order, Tirpitz and Bülow, within ten months of their appointment, secured acceptance for a programme stretching forward to 1904 and involving the building of seven new battleships, two heavy and seven light cruisers. They thereby earned their master's semi-permanent gratitude and consolidated their own positions. The decision of the Centre to vote for the Bill was only the immediate cause of its success; Tirpitz refused to accept the hostility of public opinion as an unalterable fact but, spurred on by William, launched a campaign to alter it:

'We organized meetings and lectures and made special efforts to get in touch with the press on a large scale. We instituted tours to the waterside and exhibited the ships and the wharves; we turned our attention to the schools and called upon authors to write for us; stacks of novels and pamphlets were the result. Prizes were to be given by the Ministry of Education to the schools.'[54]

A month after the first Navy Law was passed, the German Navy League was formed by circles close to von Stumm and Krupp; Tirpitz at first regarded its enthusiasm with some misgiving but scandals in the management enabled the Navy Office to get it under control (undesirably so, in the opinion of the Pan-Germans) and it came to play a central role in the work of propaganda, being amply supplied with funds by the armament-manufacturers.[55] In assessing responsibility for what happened, we should always remember that William, Bülow and Tirpitz deliberately set out to implant dreams of naval power in the minds of the German people although, and indeed because, those people left to themselves might not have given their leaders the support needed to carry the project out. 'We do not wish to put anyone in the shadow', said Bülow in his first *Reichstag* speech, 'but we demand our place in the sun.' 'The trident', said William about the same time, 'belongs in our hands' and a little later: 'Our future lies on the water.'[56]

The success of the new brooms had two results on German internal politics. Firstly William's impatience with the *Reichstag* grew less once it had allowed him his ships. He continued to talk of abolishing universal suffrage and of calling in the army to discipline 'those who dared to attack the very foundations of the

State and did not spare the person of the All-Highest'.[57] But the chief spur to action had vanished, while the difficulties of taking it grew steadily more obvious. But secondly the love of the Fatherland, which among the Prussian élite had been associated with things military, began to acquire a second element. To the middle-classes of the second *Reich*, the German Navy was not only the symbol of unity in the field of defence (since there was strictly speaking no 'German Army' but only Prussian, Bavarian, Saxon and Wurtemburg ones) but also the instrument by which their nation's rise to greatness was to be carried forward from the European to the world plane. The younger generation were tired of being told what the army had done to bring the Empire into existence; the new fields in which they seemed most likely to make their distinctive contribution lay across the sea.[58] Talk of Germany's 'Break Through to World Power' became frequent. Max Weber in 1895 said that: 'The unification of Germany was a youthful indiscretion which the nation would have done better to omit if it was to be the end and not the start of a policy of German world power.' Friedrich Naumann who was translating the ideas of Stöcker into more popular terms, published in 1897 his 'National Socialist Catechism' which answered the question 'What is Nationalism?' by saying: 'The effort of the German people to spread their influence over the globe.'[59] The aristocracy might claim for themselves a privileged relationship to the Kaiser but it was among the middle classes that his enthusiasms found their readiest echo.

The only fully-fledged world Power which was out of reach of the German army was Britain and there the growth of Germany's world-wide ambitions were inevitably watched with suspicion. Britain's ability to impose her will on the world of the nineteenth century occurred as an accident of history, the combined result of the defeat of all other naval powers in the Napoleonic Wars, of her temporary lead over other countries in economic development and of the extension of politics from a European to a world stage as a by-product of the application of steam and electricity to communications. But the *Pax Britannica* was bound to be challenged at some stage; not even the assurance of peace will induce States to submit to the lasting superiority of one of their number. Yet judging the relative durability of the various elements in the contemporary scene is never easy, and many Britons at the turn of the century would have said that the predominance of their nation was as lasting a feature of the modern world as the steam engine—in which, of course, they would have been right though not quite in the way they imagined. No leading power will voluntarily yield its position until circumstances have shown this to be inevitable—and many will not do so even then. Those people who said that the world was big enough to hold both Britain and Germany, that Germany could get all she wanted without war, were probably right. But to have acted on such a belief called for a vision, a faith in reason and the prevalence of reasonableness which does not come easily to human nature. Instead a fresh economic depression produced a fresh wave of agitation in Britain between 1894 and 1898 calling attention to German competition, fanned particularly by the first popular paper, Alfred Harmsworth's *Daily Mail*. In 1897 the Norddeutsche Lloyd liner *Kaiser Wilhelm der Grosse* won the Blue Riband of the Atlantic which Cunard were not to recover for ten years. Writers were not lacking to point out the implications behind the Krüger Telegram and the First Navy Law until finally in 1897 the *Saturday Review* ended a famous article with a call for preventive war '*Carthago delenda est*'. This may have been written by an American, and certainly did not represent the views of the Cabinet.[60] But the feeling was becoming widespread that relations with Germany constituted a major problem.

June 1897, the month of the Diamond Jubilee, was perhaps Britain's high-water mark. William had fully expected to be asked to this occasion and let as much be known through his mother. The Prince of Wales was worried at the idea. 'Although the German Emperor is the Queen's grandson, it would be a great mistake if he were the only sovereign invited. He would also arrive with an enormous suite and would try and arrange things himself and endless trouble would arise. H.R.H. is certain the Queen will regret it if she gives way.' 'There is not the slightest fear of the Queen giving way. The Emperor's coming here in June would *never* do for many reasons.'[61] So it was given out that no heads of State were being invited since the Queen would not have time to entertain them in the way she would wish.

The Colonial Conference which met at the Jubilee voted among other things in favour of denouncing the Commercial Treaty which Britain had signed in 1865 with the *Zollverein* and which still regulated trade relations with Germany. As it bound both parties to give one another most-favoured nation treatment throughout their customs areas and had been negotiated two years before the British North America Act made Canada independent, the German Government was within its rights in complaining that Canadian preferential duties on British goods violated the Agreement. But William's reaction to the denunciation was that it 'would never have happened if our fleet had been strong enough to command respect'.[62] Henceforward Britain's continued enjoyment of m.f.n. rights in Germany depended on an annual resolution of the Federal Council and a clear hint was given that, if other parts of the Empire followed Canada's example, such a resolution would no longer be proposed. This was described by *The Times* as 'threatened interference with the internal affairs of the Empire which extends beyond the commercial sphere'.[63] But just at this time, with Chamberlain's encouragement, the general introduction of an Imperial preference system began to be discussed, and Germans were quick to foresee a threat to their exports. 'Now that Albion has discovered the superiority of German industry,' wrote William, 'her next endeavour will be to annihilate it, in which she will undoubtedly succeed unless we forestall her by the quickness and energy with which we build a strong fleet.'[64]

*   *   *

In August 1897, sporting among the fountains of the *Peterhof*, Willy browbeat Nicky into saying that Russia would not mind if Germany took Kiao-Chou, a Chinese port which the Kaiser had long coveted as a naval base. Two months afterwards the murder of two German missionaries in the hinterland provided a God-given pretext for implementing the bargain. William brushed aside the suggestions of his advisers that a policy of grab might precipitate conflict.

'Thousands of German Christians will breathe again when they see the ships of the German Navy in their vicinity, hundreds of German merchants will shout with joy in the knowledge that the German Empire has at long last set foot firmly in Asia, hundreds of thousands of Chinese will shiver if they feel the iron fist of the German Empire lying firmly on their neck, and the entire German people will rejoice at the firm action which their Government has taken. I am determined to show once and for all that the German Emperor is a bad person with whom to take liberties or have as an enemy.'[65]

He sent the German Far Eastern Squadron to the spot and reinforced it with a task force commanded by his brother Henry. 'Should anyone try to do us damage,' he said in a farewell speech, 'go for them with mailed fist.'[66] Nobody in the family rated Henry very high, but he knew what was expected of him. 'My sole wish is to preach Your Majesty's gospel to everyone abroad, no matter whether they want to hear it or not.' The other Powers were slightly amused by these proceedings but felt obliged to follow suit. Russia at once took Port Arthur and Dairen, which prompted a letter to St. Petersburg suggesting that 'Russia and Germany at the entrance of the Yellow Sea may be taken as represented by [*sic*] St. George and St. Michael shielding the Holy Cross in the Far East and guarding the Gates to the continent of Asia'.[67] William's reactions to Britain's acquisition of Wei-hai-Wei were, however, less enthusiastic.

A lack of enthusiasm was also evident in Britain. At the time of the Jameson Raid, Chamberlain had written to Salisbury that the British public did not much mind which of their numerous foes they defied provided that they defied somebody.[68] As Colonial Secretary, however, he was more acutely conscious of the inconveniences of isolation. He saw Russia's acquisition of Port Arthur as the start of an attempt to get North China under her control, a process which Britain would be bound to oppose. He was already wrangling over French claims in West Africa. In South Africa events were working to a climax. The Cretan affair was still unsettled. In Egypt Kitchener was starting south to avenge Gordon. All over the world Britain seemed to have trouble on her hands and no friends to help her. Applying the business principle of 'what you can't crush, join', Chamberlain decided that the time had come to abandon an isolation no longer splendid, and look for allies. He must have spoken in some such terms to Baron Eckardstein, Anglophile Counsellor at the German Embassy in London and husband (at that moment) of a rich English wife. For Eckardstein encouraged him to approach the Ambassador Hatzfeldt.[69] Lord Salisbury was away ill, and had left his nephew, Arthur Balfour, in charge. In March and April 1898 Hatzfeldt had two talks with Balfour and three with Chamberlain who, between the second and the third, gave public expression to his ideas in a speech at Birmingham. (It is evidence of the limited effect of the Krüger telegram that such a speech did not cause a public outcry.) Chamberlain's thesis was that Britain needed allies and must choose between Germany and the Franco-Russian bloc. Of the two alternatives, Germany was the more natural because German and British interests largely coincided. Once Britain could rely on German support generally, she could afford to be accommodating on colonial questions, which were the principal subjects of dispute. Chamberlain was, however, averse from the idea of bargaining about colonies by themselves. In this he differed from his colleagues, who preferred the more empirical approach of clearing up minor difficulties before tackling questions of principle.

The moment for which William had long been waiting might seem to have arrived. Britain had been reduced to seeking German assistance. But instead of the gesture being eagerly applauded, it met with an extremely reserved reception.[70] There were several good reasons for this course, which owed as much to the advice of Hatzfeldt, one of Bismarck's best pupils, as to Bülow and Holstein. William himself was fully alive to the advantage which an English alliance could offer in the field of trade and colonial concessions. But, to begin with, he and his advisers doubted whether 'Brummagem Joe' (as William knowingly described Chamberlain) could carry his colleagues with him. In this they were not far wrong, since Salisbury wrote to Balfour:

'The one object of the German Emperor since he has been on the throne has been to drive us into a war with France. I can never make up my mind whether this is part of Chamberlain's object or not. . . . France certainly acts as if she intended to drive us into a German alliance; which I look to with some dismay, for Germany will blackmail us heavily.'[71]

Balfour in reply referred to 'this amateur negotiation'. More fundamentally, the Germans distrusted the sincerity of British intentions, especially when they remembered how in 1889 Salisbury had excused himself from following up Bismarck's alliance feeler by explaining that no British Government could bind its successors. (Chamberlain discounted this difficulty, saying that an Alliance once ratified by Parliament would be honoured in all circumstances.) They were afraid of bringing down upon themselves the lasting enmity of Russia. 'The good Chamberlain must not forget that in East Prussia I have three Russian armies and nine cavalry divisions standing on the frontier opposite to one Prussian army corps, with no Chinese wall to keep them apart and no British battleships to help in holding them off.'[72] Though Bülow assumed too easily that Britain could not come to terms with France, William allowed for this possibility but reckoned that it would entail the end of the Franco-Russian Alliance, leaving Germany free to throw her whole force westwards. Hatzfeldt said he had 'no fear of our falling between two stools for no matter what happens, both sides will want us'. Bülow thought that 'the other Powers need us more than we need them'. William also rightly saw disadvantages in backing Britain outside Europe since France and Russia, faced by a decisive superiority in Asia and Africa, would abandon their hopes in those continents where their common enemy was England and turn closer home where their common enemy was Germany. Moreover, the fleet which Germany was now starting to acquire might be expected in a year or two to put up the price which Britain would pay for her friendship. William and his advisers therefore took advantage of the fact that no precise proposals had been put forward and encouraged Hatzfeldt in his policy of 'playing it long' (*freundlich aber dilatorisch zu behandeln*). One result was of course that any precise proposals which might have been made remained unuttered and the possibility of getting an Alliance which extended to Europe remained unexplored.

In the middle of the discussions, William allowed his itch to be clever to outrun his integrity and told the Tsar about them, asking in effect what counter-bid for German friendship Russia would make. Cleverness again outran honesty in the reply, a sign that it was not drafted by Nicholas himself.

'Three months ago . . . England handed us over a memorandum . . . trying to induce us to come to a full agreement with her upon all the points in which our interests collided with hers. These proposals were of such a new character, that I must say, we were quite amazed and yet—their very nature seemed suspicious to us, never before had England made such offers to Russia. . . . Without thinking twice over it, their proposals were refused. . . . It is very difficult for me, if not quite impossible, to answer your question whether it is useful or not for Germany to accept these often repeated English proposals, as I have not got the slightest knowledge of their value.'[73]

And all that Britain had done was to make some feelers about a general agreement over China, in accordance with the policy of direct negotiation on the subject which William had always recommended! But the adroit twist given to these was enough to convince the Kaiser that he had been right to think Britain insincere. 'Through his Majesty's marginal notes runs like a red thread the basic concept that England wishes us no good but is only trying to compromise us by vague suggestions, at the most will end by throwing us a few meagre crusts.' He did not seem to notice the failure of his attempt to elicit a counterbid.*

Meanwhile, Kitchener had been advancing up the Nile and at Omdurman on 2 September 1898 gave the Dervishes 'a good dusting' (as he described the engagement in which ten thousand of them were killed).[75] William was reviewing troops on the Waterloo Place at Hanover just after the news arrived and called for three cheers for the Queen. But on entering Khartoum Kitchener was ordered to push on up the river to meet a new threat. At Fashoda he found Captain Marchand installed with eight French officers, 120 Senegalese troops, a steamer which had been carted in pieces across darkest Africa, and considerable supplies of champagne. They had marched for over a year and three thousand miles to claim the Upper Nile for France. 'If we ever get to Fashoda', Lord Salisbury had said in 1897, 'the diplomatic crisis will be something to remember and "what next?" will be a very interesting question.'[76] Kitchener, wisely, did not use his overwhelming military superiority but left the French force undisturbed while the diplomats argued it out at home. There were some tense weeks in

---

* William's letter to the Tsar contained a good example of the way in which jealousy and suspicion distorted his approach to England. The letter began by explaining that, shortly before Chamberlain's first approach, he had noticed a sudden halt in what he elsewhere described as 'British press expectorations' against Germany. He had also heard, correctly, that this was his grandmother's doing. Unable to believe that this had been done out of general benevolence, he misread it as a planned setting of the stage for Chamberlain's overtures. But this did not prevent him from sneering 'This is the land of the free Press!' A month earlier he had minuted that one of the first steps towards Anglo-German understanding would be to stop inspired attacks on Germany in the British press.[74]

which both Britain and France got ready for action. The Kaiser cabled to the Tsar asking what view he took of the situation. Nicky replied that he knew nothing of an impending conflict and was averse to overhasty action; interfering without invitation in other people's business was always awkward. In France the Dreyfus case was at its height; it largely turned on the question who had spied for Germany, nobody attempting to deny that someone had done so. The case not only set the army at loggerheads with the politicians and within itself and so made it ill-prepared for war; the issue at stake was gradually seen to be the relative priorities given to national security and individual freedom and as this happened, the protagonists of freedom, whose sympathies were pro-British, gained ground politically. Delcassé, who became Foreign Minister at the crucial moment, disappointed William's confident predictions by proving less Anglophobe than his predecessor Hanotaux. France was in no position to fight and to her considerable chagrin had to give way. William was equally chagrined. He wrote to Nicky that many people were coming to look upon the French after their most ignominious retreat as a dying nation; if the Russian Foreign Office had recommended this insane step, they had been singularly and exceptionally ill-advised. William also criticized the French for failing to study Mahan and being without a fleet when they needed one.[77] He went on trying to get the Tsar to work with him but the Russians, having markedly failed to offer the French any support, felt that least said would be soonest mended. Thereupon the Kaiser told the British Ambassador that he doubted whether England would ever get a better opportunity to dispose of France without interference. But Britain did not need to act on this gratuitous advice. French concessions did not stop at Fashoda; in March 1899 an agreement was reached settling all outstanding issues in Central Africa.

William would have done better to be alarmed than indignant at France's refusal to play the role assigned to her. For expectations to be disappointed is often a sign that assumptions have been unwarranted. Fashoda did in fact mark a decisive turn in French policy. Delcassé had been a friend of the nationalist leader, Deroulède—but he had also been a disciple of Gambetta, the apostle of French resistance in 1870. For him, as for most Frenchmen, Alsace remained more important than Africa. Not only did the 1899 agreement foreshadow the group which five years later constituted the Anglo-French Entente, but in 1899 Delcassé went to St. Petersburg and there got the Russian Treaty secretly changed so as to acquire a more offensive slant. And on the majority of his countrymen the Fashoda experience had forced the realization that they could not afford two enemies. True, the hostile tone of French public comment towards Britain over the next few years hardly suggested this, which may be thought to excuse the German leaders for their failure to notice the development. But they had been warned by both Malet and Chamberlain that, if Germany continued to make difficulties, Britain could and would come to terms with France, and William himself recognized that this might happen. He made a great show of not allowing dust to be thrown in his eyes, while to Bülow and Holstein coalitions were almost as much a nightmare as to Bismarck. Yet so set were their beliefs that they failed to consider adequately what the situation of Germany would be if by any chance Britain did come to terms with France and still more with Russia.

Willy's relations with Nicky were complicated at this time by the latter's proposal, made in August 1898, for a disarmament conference. This novel idea embarrassed the leaders of Europe who at once advanced a variety of objections with which in the ensuing sixty years the world has become sadly familiar. The Kaiser was not behindhand in scouting the scheme as Utopian; he could not decide whether its author was best described as a 'youthful dreamer' or as a 'dreamy youth'.[78] As often, he attributed the worst motives to everyone except himself and said that the proposal had only been launched to give Russia protection on the cheap (in which there was unfortunately an element of truth!). He made great and legitimate fun of a French suggestion that the conference should be restricted to discussing technical military matters and attended only by Ministers of War. When in spite of his cold water, the conference actually met at The Hague in June 1899, the German delegation needed little encouragement from their master in bringing 'healthy realism to bear on the mass of Russian hypocrisy, bunk and lies'.[79] Largely owing to German efforts, the proposal for disarmament was referred back to governments without discussion, and that for a compulsory arbitration tribunal emasculated into the provision of a voluntary facility. Such a policy was more honest than prudent since it led to the main blame for the meagreness of the results being placed on the healthy realists. Since most other statesmen from Lord Salisbury to the Sultan of Turkey had treated the idea as a quaint conceit, this result was perhaps unfair. Yet Germany was after all the protagonist of the view that the sovereign nation state provided the ultimate answer to mankind's problems. William, on hearing that Americans were praying regularly for the conference to succeed, asked God to forgive 'these pharisaical Pharisees' while he threatened to box the ears of anyone who suggested to him a limitation on conscription. When it came to describing what he would like to do with the conference's conclusions, he resorted to four-letter words.[80] That disarmament was difficult he rightly saw; that it might none the less be desirable quite eluded him.

*   *   *

One reason making it difficult for William to appreciate the significance of Fashoda was that other impressions absorbed his mind. Accompanied by Dona, Bülow, Eulenburg and a picked party of German Protestant clergy, he set out for Palestine in October 1898 on a mixture of conducted tour and pilgrimage, travelling out via Constantinople and coming back via Damascus, Beirut, Rhodes and Malta. He was indignant with those who read political motives into the trip. 'It is most discouraging to note that the sentiment of real faith which propels a Christian to visit the country in which our Saviour lived and suffered, is nearly quite extinct in the so-called better classes of the nineteenth century.'[81] The nominal object of the trip was to dedicate the Church of the Redeemer in Jerusalem, built by the German Protestants. To show impartiality between the creeds of his subjects, William simultaneously presented to the German Catholics the traditional resting-place of the Virgin which he had coaxed out of the Sultan. He was not, however, impressed by what he saw of the Christians in the Holy City; Dona thought the only drawback was having to see so many Jews. Yet the Kaiser's most remarkable encounter was with Theodor Herzl and four other Zionists who had travelled specially from Vienna to seek German protection for the idea of a large Jewish colony in Palestine. William was attracted to the idea. 'Your movement, with which I am thoroughly familiar, is based on a sound, healthy idea. There is room here for everyone. My personal observations convince me that the land is arable. Only provide water and trees.' (The Imperial party had found Palestine extremely hot.) This, however, was the last that was heard of William's interest, possibly because the Sultan reacted unfavourably.[82]

The Moslems received almost as much attention as the Christians. William told the German Protestant community that they must impress the infidel by their lives and characters rather than by preaching sermons. In Damascus[83] it was Saladin whom he thought of rather than Saul. He assured the Sultan of Turkey and the three hundred million Mohammedans of whom he was Khalif that the German Emperor would at all times be their friend.[84] He considered that by this speech he had permanently won the sympathies of the Muslim world for Germany and its ruler. The chief results of the journey were to increase the interest which William took in Turkey, to extend this to the whole Middle East, and materially to foster the nervousness of the French, the Russians and particularly the British, among whose subjects a considerable proportion of the three hundred million were included. They were in no way reassured when two months later the Turks gave the Germans an extensive concession for building on the east shore of the Bosphorus a harbour and a railway terminal.

In one of his conversations with British Ministers, Hatzfeldt had as instructed advocated 'those small concessions which . . . soften international prejudices and prepare the way for stricter and more formal union'. Balfour, while 'much entertained', took care to express no dissent with this conclusion 'as, although I am inclined to favour an Anglo-German agreement, it must be made at worst on equal terms'.[85] In pursuit of this course Hatzfeldt was sent a highly confidential list of the areas on which German eyes were focused. They included five parts of Africa, three of Asia (including 'at least one' of the Philippines) and in the South Seas the Carolines and Samoa.[86] In so far as the areas concerned were not British possessions, they belonged to Spain and Portugal and it was over the Portuguese colonies that the first negotiations took place. Portugal's penurious condition, complicated by international litigation over the Delagoa Bay Railway, had led to the expectation that she might have to pawn her colonies; if there was to be a distribution, Germany did not intend to be left out. The British Government showed its chronic dislike of deciding in advance what it would do in a hypothetical situation. But with the Krüger telegram in mind and more trouble with the Boers in sight, Balfour felt it would be rash to risk Delagoa Bay falling into German hands and in August 1898 agreed to a provisional partition of Portugal's colonies which, on the assumption that these ever came into the market, gave Britain among other things all Mozambique south of the Zambesi. The deal was attacked by the Pan-Germans, who alleged that a vital bargaining counter had been given up at the instigation of German-Jewish banking interests on the Rand. William, however, told Balfour in 1899 that he regarded the treaty as settling the relations of the two countries in South Africa for all time. The French and Russians 'do not even know what is in it. Sometimes I lift the lid of the box just a little and let them have a peep; then I shut it down again. They do not like it.'[87] Such a valuation of the treaty had been fanned by Bülow who on its conclusion remarked that William could now attend his grandmother's eightieth birthday (May 1899) as '*Arbiter mundi*'.[88] The sense of achievement was somewhat overdone; Germany's mistake was to assume in spite of the Franco-Russian and Triple Alliances that she was in an intermediate position between two rival groups. But dislike of the deal was not confined to the French, Russians and Pan-Germans. Lord Salisbury, who had been ill when it was made, denounced it as treachery to an old ally. To prevent the situation which it envisaged from arising, he insisted on concluding a second secret treaty safeguarding Portugal against bankruptcy.[89] The second treaty did not involve any explicit breach of the obligations undertaken in the first but the intentions of the two were palpably in contradiction. When the Germans learnt of the second 'about the turn of the century', the fact that they might in similar circumstances have behaved in a similar way did not prevent them from harbouring an intelligible grievance.[90]

Nor did William go to his grandmother's birthday. Quixotically, he had set his heart on bringing over all his children and presenting them to her as the highlight of the celebrations. But the Queen decided it would be too much, and firmly turned the proposal down. William, whom Bülow described as 'extraordinarily sensitive to anything which he could regard as a slight either from the Royal Family or from Her Majesty's Government', took the refusal badly.[91] It coincided with a dispute over the Coburg succession in which the Queen proposed the Duke of Connaught

as the new Duke without first getting William's approval as
Emperor; he retaliated by threatening to have the Duke's election
vetoed by the *Reichstag*. William had right on his side and got the
best of the argument. In common with his countrymen, he was
also in a state of high impatience over the refusal of the British to
attach their own order of importance to the situation in Samoa
where the tribal feud between the Malietoa and Tamasese families
had once again reached a situation involving intervention by the
three protecting powers—Britain, Germany and America. All
these episodes combined to put William at his wildest and most
inconsequential. He told the Queen:

> 'How extraordinary the fact must seem to you that the teeny
> weeny brat you often had in your arms and dear Grandpapa
> swung about in his napkin has reached the forties, just the
> half of your prosperous and successful life.'

The strain on him, he went on to complain, was 'often too heavy
to bear' but he trusted to her good and genial heart to view with
compassion the failures of her 'queer and impetuous' colleague.[92]
At the same time he indulged in long tirades to Colonel Grierson,
the British Military Attaché, to the effect that for years he had
been the one true friend to Britain in Europe, had done everything he could to assist her policy and had received nothing but
ingratitude in return. Lord Salisbury agreed with the Queen that,
'while William appeared to wish to be on good terms with us, he
did not wish that we should be so with other countries and in
particular Russia whom he was always trying to set against us'.[93]
Knowing her grandson's ways, the Queen took the precaution of
writing to the Tsar:

> 'William takes every opportunity of impressing upon Sir F.
> Lascelles that Russia is doing all in her power to work against
> us. . . . I need not say that I do not believe a word of this. . . .
> But I am afraid William may go and tell things against us to
> you, just as he does about you to us. If so, pray tell me openly
> and confidentially. It is so important that we should understand
> each other, and that such mischievous and unstraightforward
> proceedings should be put a stop to.'[94]

Salisbury had once complained that the German diplomats
summoned him to conduct negotiations 'with his watch in his

hand', and his reaction to such pressure was to stonewall. This display of aristocratic indifference was more justified than wise because the impression that he was not listened to reduced the impatient William to a frenzy. Indeed Salisbury had by this time assumed for the Kaiser and Holstein the role of villain which Gladstone played for Bismarck. William described him to Grierson as 'my consistent enemy throughout' and in May 1899 wrote to the Queen:

'Lord Salisbury cares for us no more than for Portugal, Chile or the Patagonians and out of this impression the feeling has arisen that Germany was being despised by his Government. [He has treated Germany over Samoa] in a way which was utterly at variance with the manners which regulate the relations between great Powers according to European rules of chivalry. . . . I can assure you there is no man more deeply grieved and unhappy than me! and all that on behalf of a stupid island which is a hairpin to England compared to the thousands of square miles she is annexing right and left unopposed every year.'[95]

Salisbury's answer, though effective, also illustrated the attitude which had prompted the outburst. 'The only proposal he [the Kaiser] made in the autumn of last year was that Samoa should be partitioned among the three Powers. He was not left for a week without an answer; for we replied at once that the proposal was impracticable . . . because there were only *two* islands worth having in the group; and it was impossible to divide these among *three* Powers.'[96]* The Queen told William that she was 'greatly astonished':

'The tone in which you write of Lord Salisbury I can only ascribe to a temporary irritation. . . . I doubt whether any sovereign ever wrote in such terms to another, and that sovereign his own grandmother, about their Prime Minister. I never should do such a thing and I never personally attacked or complained of Prince Bismarck though I knew well what a bitter enemy he was to England.'[97]

To calm William down, he was invited to Cowes for the first

* No trace of any such reply has been found in the German archives. Salisbury was in any case misinformed: there are three islands in Samoa, of which the smallest has the finest harbour, Pago-Pago.

time since the Krüger telegram. But, still smarting from the rejection of his plans for the birthday, he said that German opinion about Britain made a pleasure trip out of the question. However, he sent over his yacht *Meteor* which won its race; to this his uncle made graceful references in a speech the same evening. Next morning the Royal Yacht Squadron received an Imperial telegram: 'Your handicaps are appalling!' 'He really drives me to despair,' said the Prince to Eckardstein. 'Here am I taking the greatest trouble to rehabilitate the Emperor after all these incidents . . . and the first thing he does is to throw mud at us.'[98]

As a further *douceur* he was invited to come on a State visit that autumn. But he was still playing hard to get and indicated that he would like to see the complicated negotiations over Samoa brought to a head first. The British Government had more serious things to think about, for in October 1899 fighting started in South Africa, and Ministers agreed to a bargain by which Britain renounced her interest in the islands while getting ample compensation elsewhere.[99] (The Germans at the outset thought of arranging things the other way round but were stopped by Tirpitz.) Bülow, who won high praise for the result, predicted that in fifteen years Samoa would be one of the brightest jewels in the German colonial crown. In fact, of the sixty-five ships which called there thirteen years later, fifty-three were British![100] Samoa was not Germany's only acquisition in the Pacific, for as a by-product of the war in which, to William's great surprise,[101] the Americans thrashed the Spaniards, she bought the Carolines for $4 million. At one stage in the negotiations Bülow had wished to hasten them on by the despatch of a gunboat, but William refused on the ground that 'it is the task of diplomacy to avoid difficulties and misunderstandings with the U.S. as long as that is compatible with the dignity of the Empire'.[102] He had already, in 1897, rejected the offer of a naval base from the President of the Dominican Republic, saying that he would not set himself at variance with the U.S. If only he had been able to approach negotiations with Britain in a similar spirit!

The visit to England was a relative success in spite of the fact that the Boer War had broken out and the German public were making no secret about the side their sympathies lay on. Dona, who came with him, was in this as in many other things thoroughly German:

'The English must realize that the poor Boers have a right to live on their own soil and property. I am afraid that otherwise we shall again be forced to take sides with England. The Kaiser has been talking a good deal in favour of the English recently.'[103]

In fact a quarrel had occurred shortly after the Krüger telegram between the German dynamite trust on the Rand and German banking interests there; the bankers became convinced that they would be better off if Britain took over from the Boers. The result was a marked decrease in the amount of sympathy and help forth-coming for the Boers from German official quarters, while the German newspapers with business connections were relatively Anglophil during the war.[104] The Pan-Germans and Agrarians, however, remained faithful to the Boers, and bitterly criticized not only the British but also the Kaiser and his government for their lack of sympathy.

The Windsor boat was pushed out to some purpose. At the banquet in St. George's Hall

'the entire service of the table was gold, all the candelabra and decorations of gold and three huge screens of velvet were covered with platters and every imaginable kind of piece in gold. In fact, all that the Queen possesses, which rumour says is valued at £3m.'[105]

William impressed Chamberlain with 'his versatile ability in ranging over matters large and small'; he also outlined his views 'with extraordinary verve and on a large variety of topics' to Balfour (who would not seem to have been quite so impressed.)[106] He and Bülow went over with Balfour, Chamberlain and Lansdowne the ground which had been covered in the previous year without reaching any very fresh conclusions. By mutual consent much of the blame for bad relations was conveniently placed on the dead Bismarck. But Bülow, who had the reputation of being prejudiced against England, wrote revealingly to Hohenlohe that the feeling in Britain was unquestionably much less anti-German than the feeling in Germany was anti-British.

'For that reason those Englishmen who . . . know . . . the acuteness and depth of Germany's unfortunate dislike of Britain are most dangerous to us. If the British public clearly realized the anti-British feeling which dominates Germany just now, a great revulsion would occur in its conception of the relations between Britain and Germany.'[107]

This anti-British feeling burst out unmistakably when Chamberlain acted on a hint of Bülow's and made a speech not only re-emphasizing Britain's need for allies but singling out Germany as the first nation to approach. Hot on the speech came news of Britain's 'Black Week' in South Africa and many people on the Continent leapt to the conclusion that Britain was beaten. Bülow, who had promised to make welcoming noises, replied in fact with an arrogant speech about 'the days of Germany's political and economic humility' being over and Chamberlain felt let down.

William behaved with surprising restraint during the South African War and took less advantage of Britain's difficulties than might have been expected. If he claimed his full share of credit for doing so, he also brought on himself a good deal of unpopularity at home. He was for example much criticized for not receiving President Krüger when the latter came to Europe in the autumn of 1900 to enlist help and for subsequently giving Lord Roberts the Order of the Black Eagle. William's critics would have been even more vocal had they known that his passion for running other people's affairs had led him to send to his uncle a couple of documents which he described as 'mental particles' (*Gedankensplitter*). They were in fact copies of appreciations by the German General Staff, embellished by personal observations on William's part and the suggestion that a compromise peace would be sensible. At the moment they served little purpose beyond annoying the Prince of Wales, who took particular exception to some sporting metaphors:

> 'The allusion to cricket and football matches', replied William, 'was meant to show that I do not belong to those people who, when the British Army suffers a reverse or is unable at a given time to master the enemy, then immediately cry out that British prestige is in danger or lost! . . . As long as you keep your fleet in good fighting trim and as long as it is looked upon as the first and feared as invincible, I don't care a fiddlestick for a few lost fights in Africa. But the fleet must be up to date in guns and officers and on the "qui vive" and should it ever be necessary to fall back on it, may a second Trafalgar be awarded to it!'[108]

It was widely believed in Britain that German regular officers were

fighting with the Boers and the Kaiser wrote to the Queen denying the rumour, which may well have been put around by the
Boers themselves. The same source seems to have been responsible
for planting false stories that German steamers were carrying
contraband; two were searched and a third held up for several
days without anything incriminating being found. William also
offered his services as mediator, declaring that the Boers had
asked him to assume this function. He further let out that he had
received and rejected Russian overtures for joint Russo-Franco-
German representations to end the war; the British Ambassador
at St. Petersburg simultaneously reported a story (which may have
been apocryphal) that William had said now was the time for the
Powers to fall on England and he was astonished that they did not
take the opportunity.[109] In any case his feelers were firmly
rebuffed.

> 'My whole nation', wrote the Queen, 'is with me in a fixed
> determination to see the war through without intervention. The
> time for, and the terms of, peace must be left to our decision. . . .
> The Emperor has proved himself such a kind friend to England
> and so affectionate to me that I wish him to know the true
> position of things.'[110]

The Prince of Wales's reply was subtly different:

> 'You have no idea, my dear William, how all of us in England
> appreciate the loyal friendship which you manifest towards us on
> every possible occasion.'[111]

When taxed in Germany for his failure to exploit Britain's
difficulties, William excused himself on the ground that, before
trying conclusions with a naval power, it is essential to have a
fleet. 'I am not in a position to go beyond the strictest neutrality
and I must first get for myself a fleet. In twenty years time, when
the fleet is ready, I can use another language.'[112] The interception
of the German steamers was grist to the mill of the Navy League.
And in January 1900 Tirpitz, on William's instigation, introduced
a new and more ambitious Navy Bill. This not only provided for a
considerable increase to the German fleet. It looked twenty years
into the future, took into account the dates at which existing ships
would become obsolete, and proposed an average building
programme of three battleships a year. At the end of the time

Germany was to have a fleet equal to its most difficult task, a naval battle in the North Sea against England (assuming that, on the risk theory, a part of the British Fleet was pinned down elsewhere, watching the French or Russian Fleets). Germany's existing facilities for building ships were inadequate to meet the programme and its fulfilment therefore involved the creation of new capacity. But the shipbuilders would look for a steady return on the money which they were being asked to lay out so that the Bill constituted —and was intended by its authors to constitute—a point of no return. The navy was not getting exactly the same form of blank cheque from the *Reichstag* which the army possessed, but once the end had been willed by the passing of the main bill, refusal to will the means in the shape of the annual naval budget would be increasingly difficult. With this in mind both advocates and opponents of the proposal girded themselves for the fray. In the previous autumn William had begged the question by speaking of 'Germany's bitter need for a fleet', and called on the deputies to stand solidly behind him. This produced from Richter the retort that he was confusing the functions of the *Reichstag* with those of the Brigade of Guards.[113] The main argument of the bill's opponents was that Germany could not afford it; the speed of German economic development blunted the argument's edge. Much as the agrarians disliked Germany's transformation into a naval power and an industrial State, they were too committed to the Establishment to oppose the bill, but their reservations made the Government inclined to give free rein to abuse of England. The bill won a majority of nearly two-thirds, though the Centre secured some minor cuts in return for their support. The advocates of the bill made no secret of its being intended as an instrument of pressure on Britain, but the inhabitants of that country took a very long time to understand the implications of the programme contained in it.

*   *   *

Before the bill had become law, a new excitement seized the Kaiser. The Boxer Rebellion, a nationalist movement largely provoked by the way in which the European Powers had been annexing territory, broke out in China. Europeans in Peking were cut off from the coast and in June 1900 the German Minister was murdered. William at once sought to put into practice the caption of his allegorical picture 'Peoples of Europe! Defend your holiest possessions'. He proposed to Nicky that Waldersee, recently promoted Field-Marshal, should be appointed commander of an allied expeditionary force and translated the Tsar's agreement into an initiative in order to secure French aquiescence. He inspected the German relief force assembling at Bremerhaven and on 27 July made such an impassioned speech that Bülow, not for the first time, found an extensive blue pencil necessary before the text was given to the press. Unfortunately he overlooked the fact that a local journalist, sitting on a roof, had taken the original down in shorthand, and as a result it was a somewhat sensational version which flashed round the world.

'The tasks which the newly established German Empire has to undertake overseas are onerous, more ·onerous indeed than many of my countrymen have expected. The German Empire has a natural duty to protect its citizens in so far as they get into difficulties abroad. . . . Its means of doing this is our army. . . . Your comrades in the navy have already stood the test; they have demonstrated to you that our training is based on sound foundations. . . . A great task awaits you. You have to remedy the serious wrong which has been done. There has been no precedent in world history for the presumptious action of the Chinese in disregarding international rights of a thousand years standing and showing their contempt in such a shocking way for the sanctity of the envoy and the rights of the guest. It is all the more disgraceful that the offence should have been committed by a nation which prides itself upon its ancient culture. This shows you, however, what comes of cultures which are not founded on Christianity. All heathen cultures, no matter how attractive and excellent they may be, collapse at the first catastrophe. Live up to Prussia's traditional steadfastness! Show yourselves Christians, happily enduring in the face of the heathens! May Honour and Fame attend your colours and arms! Give the world an example of virility and discipline! You are well aware that you have to face a brave, well-armed and savage foe. [When you make contact with him, you know that] no pardon will be given, and prisoners will not be made. *Anyone who falls into your hands falls to your sword!* Just as the Huns under their King Etzel created for themselves a thousand years ago a name which men still respect, you should give the name of German such cause to be remembered in China for a thousand years that no Chinaman, no matter whether his eyes be slit or not, will dare to look a German in the face. Carry yourselves like men and may the blessing of God go with you; each one of you bears with him the prayers of an entire people and my good wishes. Open the road for culture once and for all.'[114]

In fact the excitement caused by the speech was not as great as might have been expected. The *Daily Telegraph* for instance said that the order to give no pardon (if that in fact was the order which William gave) was perhaps the only formula which Asiatics understood and one to which the British had had recourse during the Indian Mutiny.[115] But the episode added to the uneasiness of those who had doubts about the Kaiser's rule and years afterwards the sentence about the Huns, torn from its context, was to give excellent ammunition to his enemies. It fostered the widespread—but quite unfounded—belief that the Germans are descended from the Huns.

The effect of the project was rather impaired by the news that an allied force under a Russian commander, and without any German contingent, had already relieved Peking. Although Waldersee went round the country 'getting laurels on tick' (as the Social Democrats put it), William was sadly disappointed and furious with the Tsar for wanting to make peace. Waldersee did, however, get to China, where he met with almost as much trouble from his colleagues as from his enemies. Moreover, the slit eyes of at least one Chinese looked straight in his face when he resumed a *zärtliches Verhältnis* with a wife of a former Chinese envoy to Berlin; this romantic episode, with its beneficial effects on the Marshal's readiness to give pardon, seems well on the way to cause the name of Sai-Chin-Hua to be remembered in China for a thousand years.[116] After five months he wrote recommending that, if disputes were to be avoided between the Powers providing the troops, peace negotiations must be hurried to a stage at which he could honourably go home. The process was complicated by the inability of any Chinese diplomat to accept the terms propounded to him without thereby incurring an unthinkable loss of face, but in June 1901 Waldersee finally managed to extricate himself. The concept of joint action in China was carried further by an Anglo-German agreement binding the two countries to maintain the open door 'so far as they can exercise influence'. To this the other Powers reluctantly consented. 'I regard the [China] agreement', said Holstein, 'as the second step along the road of the Portuguese Treaty. This road we must follow if we do not wish to give up our idea of extra-European acquisitions.'[117]

There was much to be said for William's idea of meeting the Boxer emergency by common action and thereby reducing the international suspicion which individual attempts at remedy might have aroused. He was also not unmoved by the fear that some other country such as Russia or Japan might win credit at Germany's expense for dealing with the Chinese. Nor could he restrain himself from investing his plan with a scale, a theatricality and thus an expense a good deal greater than were strictly necessary. The *Reichstag* was presented with a bill for an enterprise about which it had never been consulted. But its members were by no means alone in this. 'The whole Chinese business', wrote the Chancellor, 'has been organized without my being brought in. I had no advance notice of the military measures, nor of the despatch of troops nor of Waldersee's appointment. Everything connected with foreign policy is discussed and decided by the Kaiser and Bülow between themselves. Home affairs are settled by the Departmental heads on their own. All appointments are made without my advice being taken or even asked.'[118] About this time, a cartoon showed Ministers meeting in Hohenlohe's absence and one of them asking: 'Is any gentleman by chance sitting on the Chancellor?'[119] He had long been accustomed to endure humiliations in the hope of being thereby enabled to nip nonsense in the bud. Now he was reluctantly brought to see that it was time to go, and Bülow stepped with alacrity into his shoes.

Economically Germany had made great strides under Hohenlohe's rule. In production this was the time of the fastest increase, and after 1890 there was a radical change in the rate of growth of *per capita* income.[120] Exports, after being almost stationary in the first half of the 90's, began to leap ahead.[121] But this progress, with the accompanying growth of the urban and working classes in numbers and prosperity, only served to bring out more clearly the deadlock in the political field. Kaiser and élite saw no reason for any fundamental change in the legal framework of society and expected the loyalty of all citizens to that framework. The real crime of the workers in their eyes was to be anti-militarist at a time when the middle classes were showing more and more enthusiasm for the national traditions. The loyalty of the workers, as became clear in 1914, could have been captured for the national cause. But to win their whole-hearted co-operation, concessions were necessary, in particular the reduction of aristocratic privileges and the establishment of equal status for employers and employed. A government capable of enforcing such a policy might have forged a united community and so reduced many later weaknesses. Naumann said in 1895 that 'the best way of protecting ourselves in future wars is a thorough social reform'. But such an idea was beyond the grasp of the ruling classes. Thanks to the form of the constitution, only the *Reichstag* was representative of the public at large; the government reflected the views of the privileged élite and the legislation which it introduced sought to restrict rather than to speed social progress. Thus a bill on freedom of association had inserted into it drastic penalties against the use of violence in industrial disputes; a bill to protect public morals contained clauses which could be invoked to suppress free speech. The *Reichstag* in consequence rejected both bills and only finally passed them in much modified forms. In November 1898 the Kaiser was finally compelled to climb down about courts martial. Not that opposition always came from the left. A project for building a canal between the Ruhr and northern Germany on which the Kaiser rightly set store came to grief on agrarian opposition to anything likely to spread industry.

The result was a legislative stalemate; the executive was not prepared to introduce the measures which the legislature desired while the legislature, debarred from initiating bills itself, refused to accept those introduced by the executive. Any serious attempt to alter the constitution in either direction might have precipitated civil war. The *Reichstag* possessed weapons such as systematic opposition to Government proposals and a refusal to vote credits (including those for the army and navy) which legally enabled it to enforce its will. But these the leaders of the more popular parties hesitated to use for fear of provoking counter-measures which would then have confronted them with a choice between surrender and resort to force. As long as the army remained loyal to the Emperor, the verdict of force was highly doubtful and in any case a civil war would have put Germany at the mercy of her external enemies. The administration had therefore to live with the *Reichstag* and yet avoid outraging the élite. The natural supporters for such a middle course were the Centre, and during these years the Government came more and more to rely on their votes. This trend was reinforced by the Chancellor being both a Catholic and a South German, by the antagonism of the party to any strengthening of the Berlin government (which they realized would be a probable consequence of further democratization) and by their readiness to vote for the Navy Bills. But the Centre was a party based on religious rather than class or economic interests and its political outlook was bound to reflect the social occupations of German Catholics. As these got caught up in the general drift from country to town, the party leaders were bound to pay more attention to the desires of workers, and less to those of landlords or peasants. In 1899 the Bavarian branch of the party joined for the first time with the Socialists against the Liberals in an election. The significance of this alliance lay in the fact that these were the two parties destined to gain most ground in the two following decades. If they were to combine at the national level, the Government would have to rely for its majority on Conservatives and National Liberals, groups whose strength was on the wane.

*   *   *

At the beginning of 1901 an event occurred which shook William deeply. The 200th anniversary of Prussia's elevation into a Kingdom was about to be celebrated when he heard that his grandmother was dying.[122] Cancelling all arrangements, he hurried to Osborne and insisted that '*no notice* whatever is taken of me as Emperor and that I come as grandson. I suppose the petticoats . . . will kick up a row when they hear of my coming; but I don't care, for what I do is my duty, the more so as it is this "unparalleled" grandmama as none ever existed before. So should you feel counter-currents, please cut them short at once.'[123] In spite of all that had occurred, the emotional link between them had never been broken. She was one of the few people who commanded his lasting loyalty, probably because she always showed affection and understanding for his feelings and even when she scolded, did so with scrupulous fairness. Both had at bottom strongly emotional natures but the Queen had succeeded in disciplining hers in a way

which William never did. Should this be ascribed to a difference
of character or of environment? He may also have felt something
of Napoleon's attitude to Madame Mère. 'If you should die, I
should only have inferiors in the world' (except of course for the
timeless Franz Joseph).

Pushing other people aside with his usual impetuosity, William
made his way to the sick-bed and there remained. The occasion
was one which he never forgot. Asked long afterwards if it was
true that he had held the Queen in his arms as she died, he replied:
'Yes—she was so little—and so light.' It is said that she did not
recognize him but took him for his father. He surprised everyone
by his tenderness and firmness; turning the menials out of the
room, he and his uncle together lifted the body into its coffin and,
while the new king had to go ahead to London, William, to the
displeasure of his wife and people, stayed on until the funeral a
fortnight later.[124] This historic event came close to being more
historic still. The royal train left Portsmouth nine minutes behind
time, and the driver was told: 'See what you can do to make it
up as the King cannot stand people being late.' If it is true that
ninety miles an hour was reached on the bank beyond Holmwood,
the train can barely have escaped derailment on the reverse curves
near Dorking. 'Certain of those railway officers who travelled on
the train were of opinion that a maximum speed of some 92 m.p.h.
was attained on the Holmwood bank and as the Dorking reverse
curve with its speed restriction of 30 m.p.h. lies at the foot of the
bank, they had their moments of anxiety.' A fatal accident might
have altered much in European history, though the Crown
Prince's character discourages belief that the changes would have
been for the better. As it was, the old Queen, who had disliked
both speed and the London, Brighton and South Coast Railway,
kept her last appointment with two minutes in hand and the
Kaiser, accustomed to the deliberate rocking of his own royal
train, sent an equerry to express to the driver his astonishment that
so small an engine could go so fast.[125]

The British public, unlike the German, were surprised and
pleased by William's behaviour. One of the new King's first acts
was to make him a Field-Marshal and the Crown Prince a Knight
of the Garter. The Duke of York got measles in the next room and
William always had a phobia about infection but nevertheless all was
sweetness and light.[126] This had important political consequences.

Even before the Queen was known to be dying, Eckardstein and Chamberlain had had another conversation about an Anglo-German Alliance, in which Chamberlain had suggested starting with an agreement over Morocco. When on reaching London William was told of this, he wired to Bülow: 'So they would seem to be coming, in the way we have long expected.' Bülow hastily warned him against appearing over-eager and in talking to Lansdowne (who had become Foreign Secretary the previous autumn) it was on the shortcomings of Russia that the Kaiser expanded.

> 'Don't talk of the Continent of Europe! Russia is really Asiatic. The Tsar is only fit to live in a country house and grow turnips. The way to deal with him is to be the last to leave the room. The French are utterly disappointed with Russia and with the Tsar. Of course the Russian Grand Dukes like Paris and a girl on each knee but there is no love between the two countries. Russia is bankrupt but will get all the money she wants on Wall Street since America will go in with Russia out of hatred for Germany while Russia is anxious to direct American enterprise towards the Yangtse valley.'[127]

The stress laid on the need for England, Germany and France to stand together against America and Russia was no doubt designed to discourage the British from thinking there was any other ally so suitable as Germany. But, becoming excited at his own new ideas, William astonished Paul Cambon, the French Ambassador in London, by the remark that he wanted France to be strong and could be relied on for help in case of difficulty. Moreover, he told Jules Cambon, French Ambassador in Berlin, that the struggle of Europe, represented by Germany, France and Britain, with Asia, represented by Russia, Japan and the U.S., was imminent.[128] But he said to Count Metternich, his companion in London, that he could not hesitate indefinitely between Britain and Russia or he would run a risk of falling between two stools. Reversing this concept, he told Lansdowne that Britain's traditional policy of maintaining the balance of power in Europe was 'exploded'. 'I am the balance of power in Europe since the German constitution leaves decisions about foreign policy to me. The result of this is that there is no need to worry if pro-Boer sympathies occasionally become evident in Germany. It is I who make policy.'[129] Such egomania was not, of course, new. Its repetition at this moment was probably the Kaiser's way of conveying to British statesmen that they need not regard anti-British feeling in Germany as an obstacle to an alliance since it was without practical significance.

In the following weeks, Russian designs on Manchuria excited considerable alarm and Britain sought German aid in opposing them on the basis of the 1900 agreement to maintain the open door. But at the time of its conclusion Hatzfeldt had written that: 'If [the English] want us to do more, particularly if we are to draw Russian enmity upon us, they must grant us far more in return.' And Bülow now denied that it had ever applied to Manchuria. Russia was in the end induced to hold her hand by threats from Japan, whereupon William described British Ministers as 'unmitigated noodles' for having let slip the best opportunity they were ever likely to get of settling accounts with Russia. The words got back to King Edward who found it difficult to be amused. 'What would the Kaiser say if I called his Ministers such nice names?'[130]

In the course of discussing Manchuria, Eckardstein said to Lansdowne that, in the event of a Russo-Japanese war, an Anglo-German defensive alliance would help to localize it. As any reference to an alliance cut clean across his instructions, he represented the initiative as having come from the other side. His superior, Hatzfeldt, was told, on reporting this, to reply that any treaty must be with the Triple Alliance as a whole.[131] There then occurred some serious consideration of a defensive treaty between that Alliance and the British Empire, with Japan possibly included as well. The treaty was to be made public and would take effect as soon as any signatory was attacked by two or more Powers. After a pause due to Salisbury's illness, the subject was again raised, again at Eckardstein's suggestion, between Lansdowne and Hatzfeldt, each of whom tried to get the other to put proposals into writing. Soon afterwards, Hatzfeldt fell ill and returned to Germany.

In August the Empress Frederick died and King Edward went to Germany for her funeral. During a call on the Kaiser, the question of an alliance was raised and William, from whom the recent negotiations would seem to have been concealed, expressed dissatisfaction that no progress had been made since his visit in the spring but warned the King that nothing less than a formal treaty with the Triple Alliance would be acceptable.[132]* This, however, was not followed up because Bülow and the German Foreign Office gave instructions that no initiative was to be taken on the German side. The subject was, however, discussed at some length by British Ministers and just before Christmas Lansdowne, unwilling to be thought discourteous for never returning an answer to what he regarded as a German suggestion, told Metternich (who had succeeded Hatzfeldt) that Her Majesty's Government did not think the time favourable for taking up the German proposal as it stood, but suggested that the two countries might be able to arrive at a common policy about particular questions or particular parts of the world. Metternich, however, said unhesitatingly that no such proposal would find favour with the German Government. It must be 'the whole or none'. The King felt some alarm at this conclusion and in a Christmas letter to William expressed the hope that the two countries might work together to maintain the welfare of the world. William replied:

'I gladly reciprocate all you say about the relations of our two countries and our personal ones; they are of the same blood and they have the same creed and they belong to the great Teutonic race which Heaven has entrusted with the culture of the world; for—apart from the Eastern Races, there is no other Race left for God to work his will in and upon the world except ours; that I think is grounds enough to keep Peace and to foster mutual recognition and reciprocity in all what [*sic*] draws us together and to sink everything which could part us! The Press is dreadful on both sides, but here it has nothing to say, for I am the sole arbiter and master. German Foreign Policy and the Government and Country must follow me, even if I have to face the musik! [*sic*].'[134]

There were two significant tail-pieces to this discussion. Early in January Holstein sent a letter purporting to describe the negotiations to his old friend Chirol, the Foreign Editor of *The Times*. To reveal to a journalist, without authorization, discussions which had been both highly secret and abortive was in any case

* This was the occasion on which the King handed the Kaiser the confidential brief supplied to him for the discussions. In this the proposed railway to Kuwait was described as 'Transcaspian' instead of 'Anatolian' thereby occasioning heavy Imperial sarcasm about the Foreign Office's ignorance of geography.[133]

odd, but to do so to the correspondent of the paper which had been most determinedly anti-German, a man whom Bülow had described as specially dangerous because he knew too much about Germany, was odder still. Moreover, the description of the negotiations departed so far from the truth, in ways of which the author must have been aware, that the intention was clearly mischievous, even though the precise mischief intended may be obscure. Holstein wished Chirol to believe that only on one occasion in the previous year had the subject of an alliance been raised and that was in May 'when poor Hatzfeldt in an access of nervous overexcitement resulting from his fatal illness appears to have summoned Lord Lansdowne to come to terms with Germany there and then'. It had been a work of supererogation for Lansdowne ever to have returned to the subject with Metternich. 'The British Government have taken advantage of the feverish restlessness of an invalid—although he had been instantly disavowed—to send us the mittens in all form.' This was followed by the innuendo that Lord Salisbury had 'in all probability determined to stick to isolation and to await the great continental war which he thinks must come some day and which perhaps would have come already if all parties concerned were not by this time aware that Lord Salisbury is waiting for it'. Chirol naturally checked the facts with the British authorities, and the only person who may have been damaged by the letter was its writer. Holstein's knowledge of the world was as good as his familiarity with English slang.

In October 1901 Chamberlain, in defending the conduct of British troops in South Africa by comparison with that of other armies, made a not wholly felicitous reference to the war of 1870 and thereby aroused great indignation in Germany. In spite of profuse explanations that no offence had been intended, in spite of having recently told Chirol 'on his word of honour' that he would never countenance the hostile attacks on Britain of which he knew that a large section of the German press was guilty, in spite above all of clear warnings that a public rejoinder would touch the British on the raw, Bülow seized the chance to win popularity by saying in the *Reichstag* in January, immediately after the negotiations were known to be over, that anyone who made reflections on the German army would find he was 'biting on granite'. This phrase, borrowed from Frederick the Great, so pleased the Germans that they thereafter applied it to any unwelcome suggestions from Britain. In London, however, the words were taken as a sign that German Ministers shared the outlook of their public. Chamberlain in particular felt that his efforts at friendship had been poorly repaid. 'I have had enough of such treatment,' he said to Eckardstein. 'There can be no further question of association between England and Germany.' German relations were hardly a field in which the Chamberlain touch proved happy.

And so the negotiations, if such they can be called, came to an end. Three years before, in spite of such provocations as the Krüger telegram, Britain had been uncommitted, standing on the whole nearer to the Triple than to the Dual Alliance. Now there was not a single politician left on the British side inclined to start any further attempt at drawing the links closer. On 20 November 1901 *The Times* had written that 'these daily manifestations of German hatred, which at first caused surprise rather than indignation, are gradually sinking into the heart of the British people'—and much the same could be said of Ministers. With nobody in a responsible position prepared to argue the case for friendship, popular animosity had free rein and any act of either side which was capable of arousing suspicion did so. Although they may as yet only have half-realized it, the two countries were steering on collision courses. An underlying conflict of will was becoming steadily more obvious and neither side was prepared to make the compromises which would have been the pre-essential to co-operation. If this owed more to German than to British initiative, and would indeed have been welcomed by many Germans, one has to remember that Britain was the established and Germany the expanding Power. A judgement as to how far each side was justified must vary according to the premises on which it is based and so depend less on views of history or politics than on views about morality and about the circumstances under which force should be openly made the arbiter. These are difficult matters. But the page should not be turned without a thought of what might have been the consequences for humanity if a little more insight, breadth of vision and generosity had been brought to bear. At the end of the 1898 conversations Chamberlain had quoted to Hatzfeldt a proverb about *'le bonheur qui passe'*. But the hint was not taken, the opportunities went unexplored and a major link was forged in a chain of causation which brought unhappiness to countless people all over the world.

Yet there was, throughout, a curious parallelism between the negotiating parties which makes belief in the possibility of a successful outcome hard to hold. To begin with, the well-meant duplicity of Eckardstein led each side to suppose that the initiative rested with the other. While this did no good, the extent of its harm can be exaggerated; neither party was seriously misinformed about the attitudes within the other. In both camps alike there were enthusiasts and sceptics. Lord Salisbury asking when isolation had ever been dangerous and Sir Francis Bertie arguing that it had advantages were matched by a group of younger Ministers, Chamberlain, Lansdowne and Devonshire, who regarded isolation as out of date and knew all too well what lack of allies involved. So on the German side those who had long dreamt of uniting the strongest military to the strongest naval power had to contend with Bülow, Holstein and Hatzfeldt who saw only dangers without corresponding benefits. Each side distrusted the other. Bertie recalled what he considered to be Bismarck's duplicity over the Reinsurance Treaty, even Chamberlain talked uncomfortably about blackmail. 'Of this loving couple,' wrote Balfour, 'I should wish to be the one that lent the cheek, not that imprinted the kiss. This, I take it, is not the German view; and they prefer I imagine reserving their offers until they are sure of being well paid for them.'[135] On the German side the Tsar's letter of 1898 was not forgotten and much play was made with the Chestnuts Theory, according to which Britain wished to use Germany as a catspaw. In spite of the Kaiser's claims that he dictated policy, Salisbury is likely to have remembered Bismarck's 1889 denial that any German Emperor could impose a policy against the wishes of his people and this, in view of the popular animosity towards England, hardly augured well for an alliance. Salisbury was also emphatic that no British Government could make pledges regardless of the causes which public opinion might in future support. Here, though events proved him over-cautious, he found a ready echo in Berlin. No reliance could be put on a secret agreement and if an open one, after being negotiated between the governments, failed to win Parliamentary endorsement, Germany would have incurred the hostility of France and Russia for nothing.

Fundamentally, however, the difference of approach rested on a difference of appreciation. Holstein wrote to Eckardstein that 'hardly any general treaty with England is conceivable for Germany that would not involve a certain danger of war. And Germany could only exact compensation comparable to the immense risks it was taking if England had a more accurate, that is a more modest opinion of its performances.'[136] But Salisbury told the Queen that 'isolation is a lesser danger than being dragged into wars which do not concern us'. 'If once we bind ourselves to a formal Alliance', wrote Bertie, 'we shall never have decent terms with France and Russia.'[137] According to Bülow, England could not indefinitely postpone her fight for existence; when it came, Germany would be her surest ally. Hatzfeldt said that Germany could wait until the English saw for themselves the value of a closer association with the Triple Alliance and offered acceptable conditions for it.[138] Time was therefore on the German side. Bülow regarded the British threats to reach agreement with the Dual Alliance as nothing more than a bogey invented to frighten the Germans. Holstein described them as 'complete nonsense'; Britain had nothing to offer which would induce France to surrender Morocco.[139] Richthofen, the Foreign Secretary, said that an Anglo-French Alliance was in itself unthinkable and Russian and British interests too widely divergent to make even a temporary agreement between the two countries probable.[140] Bertie, on the other hand, considered it was Germany which was in the dangerous situation, surrounded by governments and peoples who disliked her. So it was essential for her to be sure of armed English support in the case of a war with France and Russia. If there were ever any danger of Britain's destruction by France and Russia, 'Germany would have to come to her aid to avoid a like fate later. . . . In our present position we hold the balance between Dual and Triple Alliances.' Yet William imagined the *Arbiter Mundi* to be himself!

Salisbury more than once told the Germans that they were asking too much for their friendship. It was this difference of appreciation which prevented the agreements on the Portuguese colonies and China from paving the way to a wider understanding, as the Anglo-French agreements of 1904 were to do, and which caused a deaf British ear to be turned to German hints of a deal over Morocco—the very area destined to be the starting point of the association with France.

The episode is one which deserves to be judged both with and without hindsight. The German position was not, on the face of it, unreasonable. Britain was still widely disliked in France. Though Bülow and Holstein might ridicule the idea of a Franco-British agreement, the Kaiser certainly treated it as a possibility but thought it would end the Dual Alliance.[141] In the Far East, Britain was on the point of allying herself with Russia's main enemy and indeed as long as Russia's attention was focused on Asia, she was much more likely to conflict with Britain than with Austria or Germany. The Entente of 1907 would have been unthinkable without Russia's defeat by Japan and indeed was only made to work by common fear of Germany. When the practical difficulties of concluding an Anglo-German Alliance, admitted on both sides, are taken into account, the German appreciation of the situation becomes intelligible enough. Such experienced diplomats as Hatzfeldt, Münster and Radolin seem to have agreed with it.[142] Yet it turned out to be disastrously wrong. The British proved to have judged the situation better and the French to handle the British with greater skill. They knew where they wanted to go and made events work in their favour instead of against them. 'Destiny', as Chamberlain's biographer said, 'always comes at one sideways.'[143] Those who wait for the ideal conjunction are in danger of finding that they have missed the most favourable one. When the last volume of Bismarck's *Thoughts and Reminiscences* was published in 1919 he was found to define on the last page the task of the policy-maker as 'foreseeing as accurately as possible the way in which other people are going to react in given circumstances'.[144] By this criterion his successors signally failed where his own record was at its most brilliant.

Moreover, the misjudgement was not simply the result of bad luck. It was a natural product of the atmosphere of swagger and confusion prevailing in high German circles, an attitude which went beyond pride in one's own country to jealous contempt for others. The British were seen as untrustworthy opponents who had to be outwitted rather than as potential colleagues whose trust had to be won. It may seem strange to accuse of over-confidence a group of men so perpetually afraid of being caught at a disadvantage. Yet the mixture of oversubtle suspicion and overweening arrogance was what led them astray. There was in fact little prospect of an agreement being reached between Britain and Germany at the turn of the century because the essential precondition for it would have been an attitude on the German side which, so far from existing, was quite out of key with the tone prevailing there. For the German leaders to have been as adroit as the French, they would have had to possess an imaginative ability to understand other people's outlooks which could not be expected to flourish in Wilhelminian Germany. Moreover, the atmosphere of intrigue and of feverish activity which surrounded the Kaiser was far from conducive to the formulation of calm judgements.

This is where the main criticism of William must be. Responsibility for the detailed decisions lay much less with him than with Bülow and Holstein. He was more alive to the real dangers; he was on the whole keener to follow up the overtures and in 1901 at any rate important papers were deliberately kept from him for fear he would insist on grasping the hand supposedly outstretched.[145] He reckoned with the possibility of an Anglo-French agreement; he saw that if he postponed too long the choice between Britain and Russia, he might end by falling between two stools.[146] But the man who so grandiloquently claimed to make policy had himself no clear idea of where he wanted to go and instead dashed after one objective or another according to how his impulses dictated. This not merely in itself made continuity of policy difficult but created a relationship between himself and his advisers which forced them to devote as much time to wheedling the captain as to steering the ship. By accepting and even encouraging the atmosphere which his less perspicacious servants and subjects created round him, he impeded a sober assessment of Germany's position in the world and a tactful handling of other nations. He did as much to exacerbate the atmosphere in which negotiations were conducted as to smooth the way for their success.

An American writer has said that 'arrogance is the inevitable result of the relation of power to weakness'.[147] To prevent strength from encompassing its own destruction, it needs to be tempered by humanity and respect for individual rights on the part of its possessor. Can it be claimed that the exercise of these qualities is the key to such success as Britain has enjoyed in wielding power? At the time of the Boer War, the unhesitating European verdict would have been that any such claim was typical of insular hypocrisy.

CHAPTER IX

Nightmare becomes Reality

'WHEN...I MADE [the] communication to the Kaiser...,
His Majesty replied in such a way that I was constrained to ask him whether he wished me to convey
such a messsage to His Majesty's Government. "No," said His
Majesty. "You surely know me well enough to translate what I
say into diplomatic language." "In that case," I said, "I propose
to report that Your Majesty has received the communication with
satisfaction." "Yes," replied His Majesty, "you may say, with
great interest and great satisfaction," a meaning which even
those intimately acquainted with His Majesty might easily have
failed to gather from his original remark, which was: "The
noodles seem to have had a lucid interval." '[1]

So, in January 1902, did the Kaiser greet the advance intimation
that Britain had ended her isolation by allying herself with Japan.
For her to choose such a partner might have been expected to
shock one who held pronounced views on the 'Yellow Peril'.
Moreover, William knew how desirable it was for Germany that
Russia should be absorbed in the Far East. Except when his
nerves got the better of his self-confidence, he had no great faith
in Russia's military capacities; any reinforcement of her enemies
might therefore have suggested danger. In the event, the British
action proved the first step in a process which transformed the
European situation to Germany's disadvantage. But these were
not the aspects which first occurred to William. Britain, instead of
taking as ally a member of the Dual Alliance, had chosen an enemy
of that Alliance. The chances of a clash between herself and Russia
seemed to be increased; her ability to reach her threatened
agreement with France appeared reduced. The German horizon
could still be considered unclouded.

Meanwhile life remained full of minor irritations, not all of William's own making. The Prince of Wales (later King George V) was to have come to Berlin in January 1902 on a good-will mission. But such was the indignation aroused in Britain by Bülow's reply to Chamberlain (see Chapter VIII) that the King wished an official protest to be made. Salisbury thought it more dignified and effective to cancel the Prince's visit and Edward accordingly wrote saying that 'it would be better for him not to go where he is liable to be insulted or to be treated by the public in a manner which I am sure no one would regret more than yourself'. William, refusing to be disconcerted, made out that the letter had never reached him. The King was induced to think again and in due course the Prince went to Berlin. This visit was by all accounts a success; the Prince, a younger man than the Kaiser, was free from his father's complexes and from 'Motherdear's' view that for him to 'become a real live filthy bluecoated *Pickelhaube* German soldier' was his 'misfortune rather than his fault'. Both then and later he and his wife were able to establish reasonable relations with their German cousins. 'Georgy left . . . all safe and sound,' wrote William, 'and we were very sorry to have to part with such a merry and genial guest. I think he has amused himself well here.'² Some years later he described the Prince to President Roosevelt as 'a very nice boy [and] a thorough Englishman who hates all foreigners but I do not mind that as long as he does not hate Germans worse than other foreigners'.³

A delegation of Boer generals caused the next awkwardness. They had come to England in the hope of getting the peace terms modified, after which in July 1902 they went over to the Continent and were much fêted. As they had had an audience of the King in London, Bülow thought that William should receive them and this he agreed to do provided that the British Ambassador was present. Then, however, the Boers upset British opinion by a tactless speech and a strong hint was given that their reception would not be well regarded. Indeed, as they were British subjects (albeit involuntarily), they could only be received if the Ambassador applied on their behalf which he showed no signs of doing. They therefore left Berlin without an audience and the Kaiser was widely criticized for undue deference to British feelings.⁴

Edward's postponed coronation caused further trouble. He himself had wished Germany to be represented by the Crown

Prince. But Dona had been unnerved by what she heard of her son's last visit to London. There appeared to have been 'unseemly romping in unlighted corridors'; an American girl 'had absolutely gone the length of taking off her slipper!'[5] William substituted his brother Henry, who, instead of landing at Sheerness, upset the Admiralty by insistence on bringing his ship to Spithead, interrupting preparations for the naval review.[6] Moreover, William had forgotten that European etiquette gave the eldest sons of sovereigns precedence over all other royalties. Consequently, Henry was pushed out of the front row and this was at once taken as a slight to Germany.

By this time William was cruising in Norway and the Baltic. He met the Tsar at Reval and next day signed a 'thank you' telegram: 'from the Admiral of the Atlantic to the Admiral of the Pacific'. On his way home, he read that the Bavarian Parliament had, in a stingy moment, refused to vote a purchasing fund for the State picture galleries. Such petty philistinism was the sort of thing which made him see red. As soon as he landed at Swinemünde he indulged in what an observer called 'one of his undergraduate impetuosities' (*studentenhaften Plötzlichkeiten*)[7] by telegraphing to the Prince Regent an outspoken expression of sympathy combined with an offer to provide the money himself. The feelings of the Regent towards William were such that a year or two later he insisted on Dona accompanying her husband on a visit so that he could turn all his attentions to her, 'which he did in a very marked manner' and save himself from having to engage for forty-eight hours in the exchange of civilities with the Kaiser alone.[8] Neither he nor his people took kindly to the idea of being helped out by the King of Prussia and criticism was almost equally divided between the man who had made the suggestion and the Parliamentary majority whose meanness had given him his opportunity. As so often, William had spoilt a generous intention by tactless execution. The Chancellor had not been at hand when the telegram went off and the diplomat in attendance, von Tschirschky, had preferred to look the other way. 'Once you are in the Kaiser's bad books, no Chancellor can be of any help.'[9] (He got himself so thoroughly into the Kaiser's good books that when in January 1906 the post of Foreign Minister fell vacant, William overrode Bülow's objections and had von Tschirschky put into it.)

In November 1902 the British suggested to the German

Government joint action to stop the Venezuelans from interfering with their ships and failing to pay their traders. The Germans not only agreed but persuaded the British to institute a joint blockade; President Roosevelt thereupon stepped in and demanded that the two nations go to arbitration. The King, in common with his Ministers, was anxious to agree, which led the Kaiser to remark: 'His Serene Highness is losing his nerve. Grandmama would never have talked like this.'[10] But Roosevelt told the German Ambassador in Washington that unless Germany behaved like Britain, an American squadron would be despatched to prevent any seizure of Venezuelan territory. The Ambassador replied that his master, having publicly refused to arbitrate, could not be expected to change his mind. Roosevelt replied that he was not arguing but merely transmitting information. A week later the Ambassador called again but made no mention of the matter; on being asked about it, he said he had no instructions from Berlin. Roosevelt said that in that case the American fleet would leave a day earlier; he met the Ambassador's protests by pointing out that nothing had been put on paper. If Germany agreed to arbitrate, he would praise the decision and treat it as a German initiative; if Germany continued to refuse, the fleet would sail. Twelve hours before the time limit expired, the Germans came to heel.[11] Curiously enough, the episode left little ill-will between Germany and America but much between Germany and Britain; three years later William could write to Roosevelt in the style used by 'an infatuated fifth-former to a housemaid', whereas Kipling spoke of 'a secret vow . . . made with an open foe'.[12]

In May 1903 the Kaiser, having told his uncle that he was not well enough to receive him in Berlin, paid a State visit to Rome with a suite of eighty including twelve horses. Not content with putting the customary wreaths on the tombs of kings, he plucked roses from the wreaths and distributed them to the Committee of Welcome. In the Forum he presented the chief excavator with a sprig as a sign that he was worthy of his laurels. He went in great state to visit the Pope, with twelve carriages, outriders in State liveries and four members of his personal bodyguard. The effect upon the irreverent inhabitants of the city was not that which had been intended.[13] At almost the same time his uncle was winning over the Parisians in the course of a State visit to President Loubet. As early as 1901 the French had suggested a discussion about the future of Morocco but the British were slow to react. On 22 February 1902, however, the evening when Chamberlain pronounced his epitaph on Anglo-German association (see Chapter VIII), Eckardstein saw him and Paul Cambon move together into the billiard room at Marlborough House and talk with great animation for twenty-eight minutes; the only words which could be caught were 'Morocco' and 'Egypt'.[14] His warning to Berlin led Bülow to seek the opinions of his Ambassadors who confirmed the view that the unlikelihood of Anglo-French agreement was only exceeded by that of Anglo-Russian.[15] Nor was this unreasonable, for negotiations moved slowly. The King's contribution was to keep the possibility in front of his Minister's eyes, to lessen by his personal tact the prejudices which had kept the two publics estranged and to create an atmosphere in which the negotiators could feel at ease. The contrast with his nephew's conduct in 1898–1901 could hardly have been more patent. But agreement was still some way off, there were such ticklish questions to be settled as whether a lobster counted as a fish[16] and Bülow in a characteristic phrase assured his colleagues that 'in face of these little local difficulties we can't be unflappable enough' (*Wir können die Dinge meo voto gar nicht pomadig genug nehmen*).[17]

Equanimity, however, was more than William could manage. He tried to sow suspicion by reminding the French naval attaché of Fashoda and prophesying (correctly) the political extinction of Chamberlain. 'The day will come when Napoleon's idea will have to be taken up again—the continental blockade. He sought to impose it by force; with us it will have to be based on common interests which we have to defend.'[18] He wrote to the Tsar that the Crimean combination was reforming again, in opposition to the interests of Russia in the East—'the democratic countries governed by a parliamentary majority against the imperial monarchies'.[19] In reviewing troops at Hanover he recalled how the Germans had saved the British from defeat at Waterloo. Such attempts to act the part of Bismarck, since pursued without any consistent plan, certainly sowed distrust among other nations, but distrust of the author rather than (as intended) of one another. To do William justice, he was far from well. His ear had given him trouble in the spring and in the autumn he developed a growth in the throat which in view of his father's fate must have been very frightening. He kept the whole matter quiet and did not allow even Dona to be told about the necessary operation until it was over. He also gave orders that if the growth proved malignant (which it did not), the fact was to be announced without delay.[20]

*   *   *

In February 1904 war broke out between Russia and Japan. As France was the ally of one belligerent and Britain of the other, the Germans were full of hope that this would prevent the Entente from being concluded. But the danger was such an obvious one that precautions had been taken against it and in April the signature of three agreements was announced. Besides dealing with the New-foundland fisheries, West Africa, Siam, Madagascar and the New Hebrides, they involved a promise that France would help Britain to maintain the *status quo* in Egypt and that Britain would do the same for France in Morocco. Secret clauses, of which the existence certainly became known in Berlin and probably the general sense, assured mutual support in case it became necessary to make political changes in either African state.[21] The agreements were the fruit of a genuine desire on the part of both nations to remove the causes of friction between them and involved no commitments other than those mentioned in their texts. But as a British State paper later pointed out: 'Wherever the Government of a country is confronted with external difficulties by the opposi-tion of another on a question of national rights or claims . . . it is impossible to overestimate the importance of the existence of a firmly established and broadly based system of friendly intercourse with those Powers whose position would enable them to throw a heavy weight into the balance of strength on either side.'[22] The Entente may not have been directed offensively against Germany but the possibility that difficulties might arise with Germany was certainly not absent from the minds of those who negotiated it. In the autumn of 1902 the First Lord of the Admiralty had told his Cabinet colleagues:

'The more the composition of the new German fleet is examined, the clearer it becomes that it is designed for a possible conflict with the British fleet. It cannot be designed for the purpose of playing a leading part in a future war between Germany and France and Russia. The issue of such a war can only be decided by armies and on land and the great naval expenditure on which Germany has embarked involves a deliberate diminution of the military strength which Germany might otherwise have attained in relation to France and Russia.'[23]

1902 was the year in which the British naval and military leaders made up their minds that the most likely foe in a future war was Germany. The discussions which led to the establishment in May 1904 of that characteristically British organization, the Committee of Imperial Defence, originated as an inquest on the Boer War, but were given emphasis by the thought that before long a stand might have to be made against German ambitions.[24]

William was cruising in the Mediterranean when he heard that the Entente had been signed; it provoked him to some deservedly scathing comments about the foresight of his advisers.

'The Treaty makes me think in a number of respects. The French have exploited their temporary political advantage very skilfully. They have made England pay heavily for their friendship without loosening their links with Russia.'[25]

Publicly he told his people 'to clear their eyes and toughen their resolution in case it becomes necessary to intervene in international affairs'.[26] Privately he expressed himself 'against any unilateral action for the time being'.[27] When Metternich, the London ambassador, said that anti-German feeling in England could be removed just as easily as anti-French had been, William minuted: 'No! We are too like [the English] and are going to become stronger than the French.'[28] Bülow, by contrast, said in the *Reichstag* that he could see nothing prejudicial to Germany's interests in the agreement but discussed with Metternich what could be done to discover exactly how far Britain was committed to France. Holstein thought that the British wanted to see France tied up in a war with Germany so as to get a free hand for themselves somewhere else, but refused to believe that in case of war the English Government would come to the aid of France, arms in hand.[29]

Paul Cambon told King Edward that he thought the Kaiser's nervousness was due to his having regarded the Entente as impossible and to feeling that it showed up his claim to be arbiter of Europe. 'Certainly,' said the King, 'he much likes to hear everyone talking about him. He is desolated because we have reached agreement without his permission and help. He feels himself isolated.'[30] To counter the feeling the King went in June

1904 to the Kiel Regatta, taking in his party a couple of French aristocrats as a bromide to Gallic suspicions. The Kaiser took immense pains to impress. He interfered with the smallest details of decoration on the royal yacht, having a large canopy built over the promenade deck, with banks of flowers and little fountains and waterfalls designed to please eye and ear. He mustered all the ships of his new navy and lined them up ready for inspection. In his eagerness he put on his parade uniform too early and had to pace the deck for forty-five minutes before his uncle arrived. But somehow it all fell flat. True, he saw the King and Lord Selborne (the First Lord) exchange 'many meaningful looks' while the naval review was in progress. At its end, however, his uncle was heard to say: 'Yes, yes, I know.... You've always been fond of yachting.' Perhaps it was in revenge that William, on hearing later that the King was at Windsor, remarked: 'I thought he was boating with his grocer.'[31]*

Before the Russo-Japanese War broke out William carefully avoided giving any promise that he would cover the Tsar's rear, but once hostilities began, was carried away by the issues which he felt to be involved. 'Papa', said the Crown Prince, 'spoke to the Guards as though we would be entraining to-morrow.'[32] It was not as though he had any illusions about the Tsar. 'Seldom has a moment of greater historical importance found two such insignificant characters at the head of two great nations.' But 'what is at stake is not simply the open door in Manchuria or a condominium in Korea but whether Russia is up to its mission of protecting the white race and indeed Christian civilization against the yellow races'. He told Bülow that his aim was to induce the Tsar to strain every nerve against Japan. When Bülow objected that if Germany gave Russia too much encouragement to fight, she might find it difficult to remain aloof, William replied: 'From the point of view of the statesman you may be right. But I feel as a sovereign and as a sovereign I am sickened by the way Nicholas lets himself down through his flabby behaviour. This sort of thing compromises all major sovereigns.'[33] It was now that William made his already-quoted comment of disdain (see above, p. 158) on hearing that Russia was submitting the Dogger Bank incident to international arbitration. When Bülow tried to redraft his master's letters he was told that no interference would be allowed in a private correspondence between monarchs. William certainly offered Nicky all aid

---

* Sir Thomas Lipton whose *Shamrock* raced so often at Cowes.

short of help; there is no evidence to support a charge that he went further. Bülow for his part told the British Ambassador: 'Depend upon it, we shall remain neutral, even if the Kaiser has said something quite different to the Tsar.'[34]

In the autumn the Tsar suggested that William draft a treaty by which Germany, Russia and France would unite to abolish Anglo-Japanese arrogance and insolence. William replied with a dissertation upon affairs in France:

> 'We both know that the Radicals and antichristian parties, which for the moment are the stronger ones, incline towards England, old Crimean traditions, but are opposed to war, because a victorious General would mean certain destruction to this Republic of miserable civilians. The nationalist or clerical party dislikes England and has sympathies for Russia, but does not dream of throwing in its lot with Russia in the present war. Between these two parties the Republican Government will remain neutral and do nothing. England counts upon this neutrality and upon the consequent isolation of Russia. . . .
>
> To make these Republicans doubly sure, England has handed Morocco over to France. The absolute certainty that France intends to remain neutral and even to lend her diplomatic support to *England* is the motive which gives English policy its present unwonted brutal assurance. This unheard of state of things will change for the better as soon as France finds herself face to face with the necessity of choosing sides and openly declaring herself for Petersburg or London. . . . If you and I stand shoulder to shoulder the main result will be that *France must openly and formally join us both* thereby at last fulfilling her treaty obligations towards Russia. . . . This consummation once reached I expect to be able to maintain Peace and you will be left a free and undisturbed hand to deal with Japan.'[35]

The implication of this somewhat involved exposé would appear to be that Germany rather than France was Russia's most reliable friend. William was thereby hoping to achieve the delicate feat of detaching Russia from France in exchange for the minimum of German commitments, and calculating into the bargain that, rather than lose Russia, France would abandon England in favour of the Russo-German block. With this end in view he proposed a draft treaty by which each Power would bind itself to

help the other (with all its ground and naval forces) in the event of
an attack by a third European Power. 'In case of necessity, the
Allies will also act in concert to recall to France the obligations
she has assumed under the terms of the Franco-Russian Alliance.'
The obligations were also to apply where one party, as the result
of actions taken during the war, received after the conclusion of
peace a protest by a third State against a supposed violation of
neutrality. In a later letter he admitted that the proposed treaty
would be unwelcome to the French but argued that, as soon as it
was signed, France would realize that she could not remain neutral
in a Russo-British war, and would therefore start bringing strong
pressure to bear on British policy. 'An excellent expedient to cool
British insolence and overbearing would be to make some military
demonstration on the Persio-Afghan [*sic*] frontier.'[36]

Unfortunately for William, Nicky refused to consider signing
the treaty without showing it previously to the French. William
was quick to see that this involved all the objections which had
been raised to the open announcement of Anglo-German negotiations. 'The result of such news would undoubtedly be a new
offensive by the two allies England and Japan against Germany in
Europe as well as in Asia. Thanks to their formidable naval
superiority my little fleet would be immediately destroyed. . . .
If you think it impossible for you to make a treaty without the
prior consent of France, it would be less dangerous to give up the
idea of any treaty at all.'[37] William told Bülow that the Tsar's
answer involved a clear refusal to consider any agreement of which
France did not have previous knowledge. 'A completely negative
result after two months of conscientious hard work and negotiation. The first failure which I have personally experienced!'[38]
For the time being he had to put aside his high hopes that this was
the way in which to rescue Germany from her growing isolation.

While allies were not forthcoming, enemies were making themselves more formidable. In October 1904 Sir John Fisher became
First Sea Lord and principal naval A.D.C. to the King to whom he
suggested 'Copenhagening' the German fleet. 'Good God, Fisher,'
was the reply. 'You must be mad!'[39] The same suggestion was
openly made in an article 'A Navy without excuse' in the November number of *Vanity Fair* which the German naval attaché sent
home saying that it was only one of several.[40] The navy was briskly
reorganized, obsolete ships were scrapped and the remainder

put on a footing of instant readiness for war. Fisher's view was that, unless reforms were 'ruthless and remorseless', Britain might as well pack up and hand over to Germany.[41] In December Lord Selborne issued a memorandum on the distribution and mobilization of the fleet, which made clear that additional ships were to be stationed in home waters. In March 1905 the Civil Lord of the Admiralty, in one of those casual constituency speeches which embarrass their authors by attracting national attention, said that as a result of the changes all the reserve ships were now ready to go to sea at a few hours' notice. 'If war should unhappily be declared, under existing conditions, the British Navy would get its blow in first, before the other side had time to read in the papers that war had been declared.' The King already thought that the publicity given to the reforms was a mistake. 'The leakage which occurs in the public offices is much to be deplored; Admiralty evidently on good terms with *Daily Express*.'[42] Certainly the impression created in Germany was considerable; during the autumn of 1904 fears of a British naval attack were widespread. William set out to convince the *Reichstag* and public that the British measures made necessary an increase in the German building programme. He sent a message expressing the hope that the desires of the Navy League for a strengthening of the forces might ripen to fulfilment and that its 'laudable endeavours' might be crowned with success. He described the Civil Lord's speech as an 'open threat of war' and told Tirpitz that he had threatened the British Ambassador with a 'colossal' programme of construction unless 'this corsair' were immediately disavowed. He invited a party of six hundred, including the Chancellor and foreign ambassadors, to see a film called 'Life in the German Navy'. He telegraphed to the Berlin Secretary of the League his thanks for 'the cheerful promise to co-operate in achieving the aims placed before the League'.[43]

The Anglo-Japanese Treaty and the Entente with France had knocked the bottom out of the 'Risk Theory'. But besides refusing to believe that either liaison would endure, the Germans continued to look for the day when British attention would be distracted by such events as a war between America and Japan or a Turkish attack on Egypt.[44] Tirpitz (unsupported by the naval staff) comforted himself with the fallacious idea that the disruption which Germany could cause to London's seaborne trade would make Britain ready to treat on equal terms.[45] The truth was that the psychological and material machine set up to provide Germany with a navy was hardly susceptible of being reversed. Any such action would have been an open confession of failure—besides bankrupting Krupps. Indeed, there is no sign that the strategic basis and purpose of the German fleet was ever seriously reconsidered in the new circumstances. To have halted or slowed down naval building would have been to abandon the instrument which had so long been relied on to make Britain listen sympathetically to German claims for a say in world affairs. It would have been tantamount to abandoning those claims and putting German interests overseas at Britain's mercy. It would have excited much criticism from the public, carefully schooled to think the fleet important. A few years later an Englishman, travelling by train to Germany, was called on to pay duty on cigarettes; when he said that he had never previously had to do so on the quantity involved, the customs officer replied: 'Ah, but in those days we didn't have a fleet!'[46] Tirpitz and Bülow did, however, agree after consultation with the Embassy in London that for at any rate the time being it would be unwise to act on the more extreme demands of the Kaiser and the Navy League. A supplementary Naval Law in the following autumn merely provided for an increase in the size and cost of the battleships to be built under the 1900 Law, along with additional cruisers, destroyers and submarines. Bülow wrote to William that:

'if we believe in the possibility of an English attack, many Englishmen are in the opposite way convinced that we are only building our fleet in order to descend on England the moment we are strong enough'.

To which William minuted: 'That is the one thing for which we shall never be strong enough.' Bülow went on:

'As Your Majesty has rightly said on many occasions, everything in our relations with England depends on our being able to get through the next few years with patience and stamina without provoking incidents or giving obvious grounds for suspicion.'[47]

*   *   *

An incident was, however, precisely what Bülow, Holstein and von Schlieffen, the Chief of the General Staff, were planning to provoke. For the increasingly patent defeat of Russia by Japan and the revolutionary movement inside Russia to which this led in January 1905 suggested to them that the favourable moment had arrived for shattering the still fragile bond between France and England. With Russia temporarily eliminated as a military factor and Britain unable to provide any help on land, France might seem to be at Germany's mercy. The scene chosen for demonstrating this was Morocco where Germany had the advantage of a plausible legal case. For if France were to take advantage of the opportunities offered to her in the British Agreement, it was more than likely that she would infringe the Madrid Convention of 1880 which assured to all signatories (Germany included) equal rights in the area. By an omission which was far from accidental (and which the British Government knew to be deliberate), the French Foreign Office, in clearing the way for action by formal communications to the various interested governments, had left out Germany, the country most likely to make trouble.[48] William had ample justification for thinking that Delcassé had wanted to pick a quarrel and bring England into it.[49] There were the usual voices in Germany, inspired by commercial motives, who saw in Morocco a valuable source of supply and would have been highly critical if France had been allowed to gain advantages without giving compensation:

> 'Morocco is a German concern owing to our increasing population and need of naval bases. If Germany does not peg out claims, she will retire empty-handed from the partition of the world. Is the German man-in-the-street to get nothing? The time has come when Germany must secure Morocco from the Atlas to the sea.'[50]

For Germany to secure Morocco exclusively for herself would probably have been out of the question. But there were at least three other policies open to her. The first was to maintain intact the principle of equal rights and the open door; that was the aim professed and on the whole believed in by William with the support and encouragement of Eulenburg.[51] The second was to barter the acquisition of advantages for Germany elsewhere against the concession of advantages to France in Morocco; this was the policy advocated by Von Kühlmann, the able young German chargé d'affaires in Tangier.[52] The third was to exploit the Moroccan affair as an occasion for demonstrating to the French how dangerous it was to disregard Germany; this was undoubtedly the object of Holstein to whom Bülow allowed a free hand.[53] Though the Kaiser was said to appreciate the need for standing firm, he certainly did not intend to let firmness lead to war; when shown in May an article in an English magazine saying that the moment was almost ideal for him to make a preventive war, he replied: 'No, I will never be capable of such an action.'[54] Not that Holstein and von Schlieffen actually wished to force war on France; what they were engaging in was brinkmanship of a high order and would have been satisfied by securing their political aims. At first sight and on the assumption that drastic action was essential to recover from the miscalculations which had allowed the Franco-Russian Alliance and the Anglo-French Entente, they may appear to have been right in their choice of moment. The probable result of a war in 1905 would have been more satisfactory to Germany than at any later date. Yet if Germany had thus established her supremacy on the Continent, she would almost inevitably have provoked a coalition against her which would in the long run have led to war on a world scale. German ambitions were not so clearly limited by respect for human rights that other peoples could have risked allowing scope to them. In practice, however, all Germany managed to do was to oscillate between the three policies which have been described, with the result that she achieved the opposite of what the advocates of any of them intended.

As he had done in the two previous years, William was in 1905 going on a spring cruise in the Mediterranean, having chartered the liner *Hamburg* and invited a number of guests, including nine retired Admirals. Von Kühlmann suggested a good-will call at Tangier, regardless of the fact that the *Hamburg* was too big to dock in the harbour. The idea was adopted in Berlin but the emphasis shifted to assuring the Moroccans of German support for their efforts to remain independent. William seems instinctively to have scented danger but allowed himself to be talked round, mainly by the argument that his visit had been announced and that the French would take the credit for any change. Before embarking, however, he gave public expression to views which, had they been consistently followed, would have altered many things:

'My study of history has given me no encouragement to seek an empty world rule. For what has become of the so-called great empires? Alexander the Great and Napoleon the First and all the great commanders swam in blood and left behind them subjugated peoples who at the first opportunity rose again and brought the empire to ruin.

'The world empire I have dreamt of consists above all in the enjoyment by the newly created German Empire of complete trust as a quiet, honourable and peaceful neighbour and if one should perhaps talk occasionally about a German world empire or of the Hohenzollerns as world leaders, this is not to be based on conquest in battle but on reciprocal trust between nations working for a common aim—to put it shortly "bounded abroad but not at home." '[55]

On 30 March the *Hamburg* arrived off Tangier; a heavy sea was running and von Kühlmann in full cavalry uniform (including spurs) had some difficulty in climbing on board. The Kaiser, who was much amused by the spectacle, had during the voyage received five telegrams from Bülow to stiffen his resolution, but further exhortation by von Schoen, the diplomat in attendance, was required before he could be induced to risk landing in an open boat through the breakers.[56] As he later impressed on Bülow:

'For your sake and because the Fatherland called, I landed, and, in spite of the incapacity caused by my crippled left arm, mounted an unknown horse, which came within a hair's breadth of costing me my life. I rode into the town between all the Spanish anarchists [who had been heavily bribed by Kühlmann to give no trouble!] because you wanted me to do so and your policy stood to benefit.'[57]

He told the French Minister that his visit signified a German demand for free trade and equal rights and that he intended to deal with the Sultan as the ruler of an independent country. 'When the Minister tried to argue with me, I said "Good morning" and left him standing.' To the Sultan he said much the same, adding the advice to see that any reforms introduced conformed with the tenets of the Koran. 'European customs and practices should not be introduced without good reason.' He then retraced his path to the *Hamburg* which left for Gibraltar 'laden in accordance with local habit with costly gifts in kind'.[58] On arrival, one of the escort vessels in the process of mooring managed to ram an English cruiser; the reception which the imperial guests received compared unfavourably in warmth with that on the African shore.[59] Next day William sailed on into the Mediterranean where at one of Frederick II's castles he reflectively observed, 'It is wonderful to think what this great Emperor achieved. If I were able to have people beheaded as easily as he could, I could do more.'[60] He also visited Corfu where he failed to find the King of Greece but saw for the first time the palace which had belonged to the Empress Elisabeth of Austria.

Meanwhile Europe waited to see what Germany's gesture at Tangier foreshadowed. King Edward was outspoken in his views of the incident, attributing a far greater initiative to his nephew than the facts as now known warrant. He called it 'the most mischievous and uncalled-for event which the German Emperor has ever been engaged in since he came to the throne. He is no more nor less than a political *enfant terrible*. His own pleasure seems to wish to set every country by the ears'. 'People can talk if they like of perfidious Albion but can there be anything more perfidious and stupid than the present policy of the Kaiser? . . .'[61] Bülow laid down that 'our attitude . . . should be that of the sphinx which, though surrounded by curious tourists, betrays nothing'.[62] The French complained that the members of the Paris Embassy were poker-faced. This led to the belief that what Germany wanted was a port on the Atlantic coast of Morocco. Sir John Fisher told Lord Lansdowne that 'this seems a golden opportunity for fighting the Germans in alliance with the French so I hope you will be able to bring this about. . . . We could have the German fleet, the Kiel Canal and Schleswig-Holstein within a fortnight.'[63] Lansdowne was more circumspect but he did tell the French that the British Government was ready to join them in offering strong opposition to any proposal of the kind anticipated. Instead, the Germans induced the Moroccans to invite all the States interested in their affairs to a conference, and let it be known in Paris that a French refusal to attend might have serious consequences. Delcassé, believing that the British message was equivalent to a promise of armed support, wanted to refuse. But the other members of the French cabinet, with whom he was notoriously at loggerheads, were not so confident; Rouvier, the Prime Minister, was warned by the Germans that negotiations over Morocco were out of the question so long as Delcassé remained in office. Despite cabled encouragement from King Edward, Delcassé was forced to resign, being replaced by Rouvier himself.[64] If Bülow and Holstein were playing their hand with the object of showing France that Britain was valueless as an ally, whereas Delcassé was playing his with the object of showing Britain the need for joint defence against German menaces, the Germans certainly seemed to have won the first game; on the day of Delcassé's fall, William made Bülow a Prince. The first game, however, was not the whole rubber and it was precisely at this point that the Germans' confusion of purpose led them astray. Rouvier had been given reason to suppose that, if he sacrificed Delcassé, Germany would cease to insist on a conference and agree to direct negotiations in which he would have been quite ready to trade compensation elsewhere for a free hand in Morocco. To his surprise he found that the German position was unchanged. The demand for a conference was maintained, a course of which William approved.[65] But Holstein apparently wished to go further and use a threat of war to secure not merely colonial concessions but French signature of a long-term alliance with Germany, thereby preventing any repetition of what was believed in Berlin to have been the British offer of a defensive alliance. Whether William was privy to this idea is highly doubtful; his attention had in any case shifted elsewhere.

For in July he met the Tsar at the Finnish island of Björkoe. Nicholas was in a worse position than usual for resisting the Kaiser's overbearing ways. The revolution had compelled him to grant a considerable measure of responsible government inside Russia and afforded William an opportunity for delivering a lecture on the best way of handling popular assemblies, on the principle that the best way of boring is to 'discourse upon the proper way of doing something which you are notorious for doing badly yourself'.[66] The Japanese annihilation of his Baltic fleet at Tshushima in May had then left the Tsar with no alternative but to accept William's advice and ask the Americans to mediate for peace.[67] The result of the meeting bore out Eulenburg's comment: 'One should never forget that a discussion between two princes is propitious only when it confines itself to the weather'.[68] Indeed that would seem to have been all they were intended to talk about since neither monarch had any of his ministers with him. William, however, saw fit to disregard Bülow's advice and have another shot at detaching Russia from France. He proposed to Nicky that they should make a treaty committing each country to help the other in Europe if either was attacked by a third European Power. The treaty was to come into force as soon as peace was signed with Japan and the contents were only to be communicated to France on signature. William could hardly contain himself in reporting to Bülow:

'[The Tsar] read [the text] once, twice and a third time. I offered a fervent prayer to God that he should be with us and guide the young ruler. It was deathly quiet; the only sound was that of the waves and the sun shone bright and clear in the cosy cabin. I could see the *Hohenzollern* glistening white with its imperial standard fluttering in the breeze. I was just reading on the black cross the letters "GOD WITH US" when I heard the Tsar's voice saying beside me *"That is quite excellent. I agree"* I pulled myself together and said with every appearance of casualness: *"Should you like to sign it? It would be a very nice souvenir of our entrevue!"* He skimmed over the sheet once more, and then said *"Yes, I will"*. I opened the inkstand, then he handed me the pen, I signed and as I stood up, he gave me a placid embrace and said *"I thank God and I thank you, it will be of the most beneficial consequences for My country and Yours. You are Russia's only real friend in the whole world. I have felt that through the whole war and I know it."* Tears of pure joy filled my eyes and I thought "Frederick William III, Queen Louise, Grandpapa and Nicholas I have certainly been with us at this moment. At least they will have looked down on what we have been doing and rejoiced." For by God's grace the morning of 24 July 1905 at Björkoe has witnessed the turning point in the history of Europe; a great load has been lifted from my dear Fatherland which has finally escaped from the terrible Gallo-Russian pincers.

'How is a thing like this possible? For me the answer is perfectly clear. God has ordained and willed it. In spite of all human thinking and in scorn of all human efforts he has brought together what belongs together. Now his ways are not our ways and his thoughts are higher than our thoughts. What Russia last winter haughtily declined and tried by intrigues to rule out to our disadvantage she has now after being brought low by the terrible harsh demoralizing hand of the Lord joyfully accepted as a welcome present. Finally I lifted up my hands to God above, committed everything to him and prayed him to lead and guide me as he wished. I am only a humble instrument in his hands and will do whatever he puts before me, no matter how hard the task may be.'[69]*

The actual task which Providence had in store for William proved, however, less congenial. So flagrant was the way in which he had preferred his own ideas to his minister's advice that the Foreign Secretary, von Richthofen, insisted on his being taught a lesson. Accordingly, Bülow fell upon the clause confining the treaty to Europe and pointed out that one of the chief places where Germany would find Russian help valuable was Asia. William, however, had changed his views about the value of demonstrations on the Persio-Afghan frontier:

> 'As far as pressure upon India is concerned, this favourite catchword of diplomatic conversation . . . is a complete illusion. . . . It is as good as impossible for a large army to undertake the invasion of India without enormous and year-long preparation and expense. . . . England would have ample time to have her counter-measures ready. Even so, it is questionable whether the invading army would reach the frontier in a condition fit to attack.'[70]

He further said that he had put in the words 'in Europe' deliberately to save Germany from having to help Russia in the Far East. But Bülow was not for the moment to be shaken; rather than take responsibility for the treaty, he proposed to resign. William was flabbergasted:

> 'For the best and most intimate friend I have to treat me in this way without offering any adequate reason has given me such a terrible blow that I am quite broken down. You say that the treaty containing the words "in Europe" has made the situation so serious that you can no longer accept responsibility. To whom? And do you think you can in the same breath accept responsibility to God for leaving your Emperor and Master to whom you have sworn allegiance and by whom you have been loaded with confidence and decorations, your Fatherland and, as I believe, your truest friend to deal with a position which you regard as particularly intensified and serious? No, my dear

* Words in italics are in English in original.

Bülow, you cannot treat us both like that! We are both called by God and created for one another to work and to labour for our beloved German Fatherland.

'Your Person is worth a hundred thousand times more than all Treaties in the world to me and our country. I have taken immediate steps to induce Nicholas to get these two words weakened or left out.

PS. I appeal to your friendship for me. Do not let us hear any more about resigning. Wire "all right" when you get this letter and I shall know you are going to stay. For the day after your request for release arrived there would no longer be a Kaiser alive! Think of my poor wife and children!'[71]

Bülow, of course, agreed to stay. But William was not alone in having trouble with his advisers. When the time arrived for the treaty to come into force, the Tsar wrote to say that it might as it stood conflict with Russia's obligations to France and that, unless France was prepared to join, would have to include a declaration releasing Russia from any obligation to back Germany against France. William vainly tried to argue that the Björkoe Treaty would only contradict the Franco-Russian one if the latter went so far as to apply to an offensive war which he was sure it did not. The Russians were not to be shifted, and the Kaiser wrote to Bülow:

'Since France will never attack us alone but only in conjunction with England and egged on by the latter, the Tsar will shelter behind the Declaration in the event of a war between us and England in which we are driven to attack France: he will also take the side of these two powers since he must remain true to his ally. The coalition is already in *de facto* existence. King Edward has been working very skilfully.'[72]

William had already been warned by Bülow about the negotiations which were ultimately to produce the Anglo-Russian Entente of 1907 and had replied: 'Sooner or later they will be successful. We must answer this grouping by a German-Japanese Alliance supported by America.'[73] Yet only six months earlier he had written:

'[Japanese hostility to Germany] will increase rather than diminish. It shows the sound instinct of the growing future leader of the yellow race that she discerns the future bonds

THE KAISER AS A BOY WITH HIS MOTHER

'*If you could persuade the Kaiser to read a serious book for two hours every day, you would have done a great deal.*'

DR. GEORGE HINZPETER, 1869

'*At least I learnt from him how to work*' (Pupil)
'*He never learnt the first duty of a ruler, hard work*' (Tutor)

KAISERIN AUGUSTA VICTORIA
('DONA')

FOUR GENERATIONS
Emperor William I, Emperor Frederick, the Kaiser, Crown Prince William

THE KAISER AND BISMARCK AT FRIEDRICHSRUH

'*The Prince forced himself into an unnatural pose of semi-respect very ill-suited to his massive body and eyes and met with an indulgent smile the stream of words which passed over him. The Kaiser's attitude and expression, still dominated by fervent enthusiasm for the great man, nevertheless strove to convey the impression that he was more distinguished and more determined than his grandfather's servant. He raised himself on tip-toe, his withered hand on his sword.*'

THE KAISER IN SCOTTISH DRESS
'*I bide my time*'

As he felt he should be.
'*That is not a portrait, it is a declaration of war*' (General Gallifet)

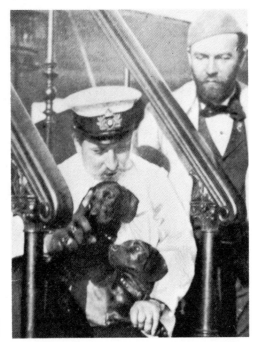

As he was naturally.
On the *Hohenzollern* with Philip Eulenburg (notice the left hand)

'No one except the Kaiser would ever have had the persistency to stay booted and spurred during the whole evening without a murmur, though he must have . . . been uncomfortable to a great degree.'

AT SWINEMÜNDE IN 1912
(WITH VALENTINI)

'*The Kaiser simply cannot do without feminine sympathy and understanding*'
(The lady in the middle is the Duchess of Hohenberg, wife of Archduke Franz Ferdinand)

THE KAISER AND 'THE DWARF'
Greeting the King of Italy at Venice

EARLY MORNING ON THE *Hohenzollern*

'It amused him to make members of his suite . . . do open air exercises and gymnastics on deck'
(The Kaiser is marked with a cross)

INSPECTING EXCAVATIONS AT CORFU

'It would be much worse if the Kaiser showed the same interest in Morocco as he does in the Gorgon'

The Kaiser is thought to have
'revised' the sculptor's first sketch

' Peoples of Europe, protect your most sacred possessions'
Allegorical picture of the Yellow Peril, drawn to the Kaiser's instructions

THE KAISER AT TANGIER

'I rode into the town between all the Spanish anarchists'

PRINCE VON BÜLOW
'Minister of Fine Appearances'

The Kaiser at Windsor with King Edward and the Duke of Connaught—
'*The nicest of my uncles, so unlike Uncle Bertie*' (said by the Kaiser of the Duke of Connaught)

Leaving England after King Edward's Funeral. Port Victoria, 23 May 1910

The Kaiser with Bethmann
Hollweg

THE SUPREME WAR LORD

Kaiser: 'This one looks like a Parsifal-de-Passage!'
Countess: 'I did not say Parsifal, your Majesty, I said Lohengrin.'
Kaiser: 'All the same thing.'
Countess: 'Not at all, the one was a knight and the other was a fool.'
Kaiser: 'Well, I look like both.'

THE KAISER WITH HINDENBURG

THE KAISER WITH HINDENBURG AND LUDENDORFF

'It will be an immense struggle—but it will be successful'

THE SQUIRE OF DOORN

which will hold together the forces of the white race when the final great fight breaks out between the yellow and white races in which Japan will lead the Chinese invasion of Europe. It will also be the final fight between the Christian and Buddhist religions: the culture of the west and the half-culture of the east. . . . Our fleet will give the Japanese an additional opponent. . . . I know for certain that some time we shall have to engage in a life-and-death struggle with Japan.'[74]

Both attitudes were to recur in his comments during later years![75]

Meanwhile, the Moroccan question remained unresolved. Holstein still wished to stake Germany's future on the belief that 'the French will only consider approaching Germany when they see that English friendship . . . is not enough to obtain Germany's consent to the French seizure of Morocco and that Germany wants to be loved for her own sake'.[76] During the autumn agents of Rouvier again conveyed hints of his readiness to offer compensation in direct negotiations.[77] But a deaf ear was firmly turned to such overtures which were into the bargain concealed from the Kaiser, who later had the hindsight to claim that he had intended the Algeçiras Conference to be 'the stepping-stone of the beginning of an agreement between France and Germany.'[78] At the turn of the year and on the verge of his retirement, von Schlieffen gave definitive form to his plan for an attack on France through Belgium and Holland. Pressure on France was increased after the British change of government in December 1905, since the Liberals were expected to favour peace at almost any price. An immediate result was that in January 1906 the new Foreign Secretary, Sir Edward Grey, with the knowledge of the Prime Minister, Asquith and Haldane, authorized General Grierson (the former military attaché in Berlin) to plan secretly with the French army the despatch of an expeditionary force to fight beside them in the event of a German attack; the reforms introduced by Haldane, the new Minister at the War Office, centred round the provision of such a force. These conversations were so secret that the German Intelligence Service learnt about them before four-fifths of the British Cabinet. Had they been public, the outcry might well have been such as to halt them; Grey felt bound to warn the French that Britain's freedom of action in a crisis remained complete. This, of course, was a delusion.[79] What was created was an implicit and moral commitment, dangerous because more imprecise than the explicit literal one which Ministers felt to be politically out of the question. The lesson of the episode was that, though the need to carry public opinion along in major questions of foreign policy may endanger a democracy's security, matters are in the long run only aggravated if the rulers think they know better than the ruled and try to evade the problem by what are inevitably compromises.

In the German camp, however, there was still disagreement over the line to be pursued. Metternich spoke up against an appeal to arms and in two letters to Bülow at the turn of the year William made it clear that in no circumstances would he consider Morocco worth a war. All he asked was to be spared a Fashoda. The moment was an impossible one for taking troops out of Germany since the Socialists were calling for open disorder and the possessions and lives of the middle classes required armed protection. 'Against a combination of France and the English navy, we are helpless. . . . First cow the Socialists, behead them and make them harmless, with a blood bath if necessary and then make war abroad. But not before and not both together.'[80] He spoke in much the same terms to his own generals on New Year's Day, to a French general on manœuvres, and to a French diplomat whom he met when staying with Eulenburg.[81]

The conference on which the Germans had insisted met finally at Algeçiras in January 1906. The French and British were in anything but a conciliatory mood; the Russians were in dire need of a French loan (William refusing to consider a German one);[82] the Italians and Spanish were determined to avoid facing the British fleet. The German delegation on 3 March carried a generally intransigent attitude to the length of elevating a question of procedure into an issue of principle. Procedure, however, was the one matter on which the conference could vote, and the Germans found themselves with Austria and Morocco in a minority of seven to three.[83] At this Bülow took matters out of the hands of Holstein, who still considered that persistence in a tough line would lead the neutrals to propose compromises.[84] With the Kaiser's full approval, a much more conciliatory attitude was adopted and the conference ended soon afterwards, having given France the leading place in Morocco and Germany the consolation of a nominal international control there. As part of the process of putting a good face on it William sent Franz Joseph a telegram thanking him for the brilliant way in which his delegation had acted as seconds to Germany on the duelling ground, and promising that if similar circumstances arose the debt would be repaid. Franz Joseph contented himself with sending the King of Italy an unusually friendly telegram about an eruption of Vesuvius.[85]

The German Government achieved in the Moroccan episode the exact opposite of what it intended for, instead of disrupting the Entente, it drew France and Britain closer together and, as Metternich had prophesied, the ultimate climb-down was too obviously the result of firm opposition to earn any gratitude. Whereas the Germans had sought to intimidate, the French had sought to involve; the pursuit of the former policy played into the hands of those who were pursuing the latter. The German Government was naturally much criticized in the *Reichstag* and just as the conference was ending, Bülow had to answer a hostile debate. In the middle of his speech, he collapsed in a dead faint which kept him away from the office for several weeks. Not only did he thereby miss the final dispiriting obsequies but, by a remarkable coincidence, it fell to von Tschirschky as Foreign Secretary and not to him to receive and accept the resignation which Holstein, in fury at the turn events had taken, sent in on the same morning. Not till long afterwards did it emerge that Bülow had sent a message from his sickbed instructing Tschirschky to submit the resignation to William and advise its acceptance.[86] Holstein was sixty-nine and had had two operations for cataract. But he was too concerned about Germany's predicament to welcome his discharge, and in retirement he nursed indignation over being taken at his word, curiosity as to who could have brought this about, and contempt for the cold feet which he considered William to have developed at the critical moment. He left a big gap in the Foreign Office. Von Tschirschky soon proved his inadequacy for the post of Foreign Secretary in which William had installed him, and von Schoen whom William chose as his successor, once more against Bülow's advice, did no better. Another mistaken choice for which William was responsible was von Moltke, the nephew of the old Field Marshal, as successor to von Schlieffen. Moltke had no faith in his own capacity and was reluctant to serve. He is supposed to have said that he was 'too reflective, too scrupulous or if you like too conscientious for such a post. I lack the capacity for staking all on a single throw.' He was out of sympathy with the current fashion in strategic thinking which assumed that armies of fifty thousand men could be enveloped after a few days. He doubted whether single decisive battles or a uniform command of million-strong armies were any more possible. 'The modern People's War will turn out to be a long and arduous struggle with a country which will not admit defeat until its strength is broken.'[87] That William should have continued to insist on appointing a man who could think for himself is more creditable than their joint failure in the ensuing eight years to make German preparations fit the form which the designated commander expected the war to take.

*   *   *

The result of the Algeçiras Conference plunged William into gloom. He minuted on one despatch that:

'for my generation good relations with France can never be hoped for. . . . England and France have been insulted together by the German press and now they have come together and France is under England's influence . . . Italy joins them—Crimean coalition—and we have let it happen.'[88]

On another he remarked that:

'all the miserable decadent Latin peoples will be mere instruments in England's hands to fight German trade in the Mediterranean. We have no friends any longer whereas these unsexed relics of the ethnic chaos left behind by Rome hate us cordially. It is just as it was in the times of the Hohenstaufens and the Anjous. All this Romance catsmeat betrays us left and right and throws itself into England's open arms for her to use against us. A fight between Germans and Latins all along the line! And unfortunately the former are divided among themselves.'[89]

He was inclined to attribute a great part of the responsibility to his Uncle. At the time of Björkoe he had written to the Tsar, as one man to another:

'Marianne (France) must remember that she is wedded to you and that she is obliged to lie in bed with you and eventually to give a hug or a kiss now and then to me but not to sneak into the bed of the bedroom of that ever-intriguing *touche-à-tout* on the island.'[90]

The feud was not by any means one-sided:

'The King talks and writes about his Royal Brother in terms which make one's flesh creep, and the official papers which go to him whenever they refer to H.I.M. come back with all sorts of annotations of an incendiary character.'[91]

William was described as 'the most brilliant failure in history'. Nor did Edward stop at remarks. When he went to Marienbad in the summer of 1905, he disregarded strong hints that he should visit William at Homburg (thereby causing a Berlin paper to picture him saying: 'How can I get to Marienbad without meeting my dear nephew? Flushing, Antwerp, Calais, Rouen, Madrid, Lisbon, Nice, Monaco—all extremely unsafe! Ha! I simply go via Berlin: then I am sure not to meet him!'). In March 1906 the King when visiting Paris invited Delcassé, although no longer a Minister, to lunch with him at the Embassy, much as in 1890 he had called on Bismarck immediately after the latter's dismissal.[92]

William's attitude was more complex. He left on Theodore Roosevelt the impression of having 'a real affection and respect for King Edward and also a very active and jealous dislike for him, first one feeling and then the other coming uppermost in his mind and therefore in his conversation'.[93] In the less kindly moments, William indulged in such remarks as: 'He is an old peacock.' 'He is a Satan; you can hardly believe what a Satan he is.' 'Every morning at breakfast the King of England, jealous of his nephew, reads of the Kaiser's doings in the newspapers and seeks how he can get even with him.' 'The arch-intriguer and mischief-maker in Europe as you [the Tsar] rightly called the King of England.' When Metternich said that the great mass of the English people desired peace and that such was King Edward's policy, the Kaiser commented: 'Untrue. He aims at war. I must begin, so that I get the odium.' He claimed to be scandalized at his uncle's debts; he spoke critically to American guests about the 'looseness of English society' and in particular the King's relations with Mrs. Keppel. To a suggestion that a meeting would clear the air, he replied: 'Meetings with Edward have no lasting value, because he is jealous.' Eulenburg complained to the British Ambassador of British coolness towards Germany and was told that if everything the Kaiser had said had been reported to London, war would have broken out between England and Germany on at least twenty occasions.[94] William, however, thought differently. He told Haldane, whom he invited to Berlin in 1906, that 'the best testimony to my earnest desire for peace is that I have had no war though I should have if I had not striven to avoid it'. He also said that what he wanted was not territory but trade expansion, quoting Goethe to the effect that if a nation wanted anything it must concentrate and act from within the sphere of its concentration. When Haldane said that the Germans had taken fifty millions of chemical trade a year from Britain by better science and organization, the Kaiser replied that it delighted him 'because it is legitimate and to the credit of my people'. But Haldane spoke German fluently and earned William's surprised respect by having read, although a mere civilian, 'the things that only German and Japanese soldiers read'.[95]

The British and German peoples as a whole lacked such an acquaintance with one another's backgrounds and their mutual relations bore an unfortunately close resemblance to those between uncle and nephew. Erskine Childers's thriller *The Riddle of the Sands* had appeared in 1903, describing in detail imaginary German plans for invading England. The *National Review* was devoting its main efforts to what its editor, Leo Maxse, regarded as 'the German menace'. Max von Schinckel, a German banker, wrote articles in 1902, 1906 and 1908 to say that Germany with her 'obligatory' drive for power must necessarily come into armed collision with Britain.[96] Lord Esher who occupied a considerably more influential position in England, had no doubt in 1906 that 'within measurable distance there looms a titanic struggle between Germany and Europe for mastery'. Britain's commercial and naval superiority was threatened, not by the Kaiser or by any individual, but by natural forces which required the expansion of Germany to sea frontiers.[97] In 1904 one August Niemann published a novel about a Franco-Russian-German combination against England which, after proving a best seller at home, was translated under the title *The Coming Conquest of England*.[98] In 1906 the *Daily Mail* serialized an account by William Le Queux of a German invasion of England in 1910. In 1907 a senior German civil servant (who, it is only fair to add, got sacked for his pains) published a description of how his nation would defeat England by landing a vast aerial armada. In fact the Germans never made official plans for an invasion, probably because very little consideration of the technical difficulties was needed to convince an expert that success was out of the question. This was indeed the conclusion come to by British official committees in 1902 and 1907 out of which the 'Blue Water' school emerged as clear victors over the 'Bolt from the Blue' school. But as Esher reminded Fisher, 'an invasion scare is the mill of God which grinds you out a navy of Dreadnoughts and keeps the British people war-like in spirit'.[99] It was the same scare which led Lord Roberts to campaign for the introduction of conscription, and to back it with a detailed study of the facilities possessed by Germany for overseas action, secret preparations and surprise attacks. Scares were not, however, altogether one-sided. Early in 1907 a rumour that 'Fisher was coming' caused a panic at Kiel and on the Berlin Bourse.[100]

At the end of 1906 Sir Eyre Crowe drafted his famous Memorandum on Britain's Relations with France and Germany, which came to the conclusion that, although Germany was not necessarily aiming at a 'general political hegemony and maritime ascendancy', she would undoubtedly take such opportunities of extending her legitimate influence as would in the long run make her as formidable a menace as if she had any such explicit design. Britain should meet her approaches 'with unvarying courtesy and consideration in all matters of common concern but also with a prompt and firm refusal to enter into any one-sided bargains or arrangements'. No risks should be taken and no concessions made purely for the sake of improving the atmosphere. Though this document did not go without challenge in the Foreign Office, it undoubtedly exercised a stiffening influence on British policy in the following years.

Trade rivalry with Germany attracted considerable public attention in Britain during these years. German imports of manufactured goods were rising more slowly than her imports of raw materials and she was increasing her sales abroad, particularly in Europe and South America. But outside Europe Britain still held a dominating position; her exports to the main Empire markets were ten times Germany's and even in South America they were in 1912 half as large again. British exports of manufactures nearly doubled between the period 1901–5 and 1914, which took the sting out of the facts that German exports more than doubled during the same period and that, as world trade grew, the British share of it steadily sank. Britain regained the Blue Riband of the

Atlantic with the *Mauretania* in 1907 and in 1914 still owned as much as 47 per cent. of the world's steamers.

On the other hand British real wages hardly rose at all between 1900 and 1914. British manufacturers who found themselves losing established markets and British workmen who found themselves getting no better off saw a simple explanation of their troubles in German competition. Britain's loss of her exceptional position, instead of being recognized as a largely inevitable trend, was naturally blamed on the nation gaining most ground, namely, Germany. The resulting agitation led many Germans, inclined as they were to envy British advantages, into fearing that Britain might try to restore the ratio by war. Complaints were made in Britain that German firms were taking out British patents, not to work them but to prevent other people doing so; in 1907 this led to a minor change in the patent laws. There is, however, little other evidence that the policy of the British Government was positively affected by the agitation, although its existence may well have acted as an inhibiting factor. The two countries were into the bargain good customers of each other. Britain took advantage of the German practice of selling abroad more cheaply than at home to import from Germany steel and other semi-finished products; the goods which Britain made from these products sold at lower prices than their German equivalents in third markets.[101]

Nor was there any major issue between the two countries in the colonial field. When in 1903 Germany repressed a rising in South-West Africa with a ferocity which certainly equalled and in the British view exceeded anything in the Boer War, the initial inclination to support the rebels was on further thought abandoned for an attitude of benevolent neutrality. The German initiators of the Baghdad Railway had sought to associate British interests with them in its financing but, although the idea of strengthening Turkey against Russia made the project at first seem attractive, what Lansdowne described as 'an insensate outcry' in Parliament and press forced him to drop the idea and in 1903 the concession was granted to Germany alone. Since, however, construction stopped in 1904 when the line reached the west side of the Taurus mountains, the question of what happened below Baghdad, in spite of arousing some excitement in London and a great deal more in Delhi, remained for the time being academic. When William was told that the British Government laid weight on having the final section under its control, he minuted: 'Impossible. It must remain a German railway. If the most important end is left out, there is no point in the whole thing at all.' During the Kaiser's visit to Windsor in 1907, however, Haldane persuaded him without much difficulty to give Britain what was described as a 'gate' to protect India from troops coming down the railway. Objections by Bülow made this concession stillborn but the subject was hardly a burning one.[102]

All this while Germany's conversion into a modern industrialized State of the first rank was making steady progress. The percentage of the population living in towns rose from forty-seven in 1890 to sixty in 1910. Trade union membership, which had actually gone down between 1890 and 1893, began to swell rapidly about 1895 and passed the million mark in 1904. Christian Trade Unions, started in 1899 to counteract the pull of the social ones, proved a two-edged weapon.[103] The reply of the industrialists was to form the German Employers Association. The Social Democrats, who had held fifty-six seats in the 1898–1903 *Reichstag*, gained another twenty-five at the 1903 elections. The number of strikes increased and in 1905 there was a particularly serious miners' strike in the Ruhr, occasioned partly by the example of Russia but partly by the Prussian *Landtag* having rejected proposals for close supervision of mining conditions. Without coal, the railways were paralysed and the war plans of the General Staff thus rendered incapable of execution; Posadowsky therefore, with William's support, insisted on a bill to meet most of the demands of the strikers being introduced and passed. In re-negotiating Caprivi's trade treaties Bülow had increased the tariffs on imported corn, thus gratifying the landowners but putting up the cost of living for the workers. Certain states such as Saxony, Hamburg and Lübeck during these years revised their suffrages in a restrictive direction, but in 1904 Baden and in 1906 Bavaria introduced universal male suffrage (as did Austria in 1906).

If, by directing attention to expansion abroad, William and Bülow had hoped to rouse an enthusiasm which would consolidate the nation, they had misconstrued the gravity of German social tensions. The attitude of the workers mellowed as social legislation edged out to bring more and more of them under the State's shelter. It was fortunate for the right that the left were not as deaf to the claims of loyalty as those who lectured them were pleased to suppose. The organization of opposition in the teeth of the established order was uphill work. As a Socialist writer explained:

'[The small bourgeoisie and workers] are not the strongest elements of the population. Practically all of them must have due regard for themselves, their families and their business. If the state throws its full power against them . . . they don't stand up. They bear up equally little if fanatic individuals use their social superiority against them. Our friends in the countryside have already to reckon with such dangers even if they only come forward as liberal individuals. If they are then branded as allies of the most radical, and the red feather is stuck in their hats, then the personal disadvantages and economic damage become endless. . . . It is easy for intellectuals in the metropolis to hand out bold suggestions. The man in the provinces who follows them can pay with his whole civic existence.'[104]

The famous hoax of the 'Captain of Köpenick' in 1906 illustrated the reverence felt by civilians for a uniform. Yet neither palliatives nor obstacles were going to do more than postpone the day of reckoning. To unify the country and 'turn the underlings of industry into true citizens',[105] more fundamental concessions were needed. Some of the ruling class were intelligent enough to realize this but not prepared to act on it. A Prussian Conservative leader said to a left-wing deputy:

'The future belongs to you. The masses are going to make themselves felt and rob us aristocrats of our influence. Only a strong statesman could hold up this development for long. Certainly we will never surrender our position voluntarily. But once you use force you will get what you choose.'[106]

On an autumn evening in 1906 Bülow and Posadowsky stood watching the sunset from the Castle in Berlin. 'If', said Posadowsky, 'the Kaiser goes on being so overbearing and in particular so indiscreet, this palace will sooner or later be menaced and perhaps even stormed by the masses.' Count Monts, one of Germany's acutest ambassadors, wrote in the same year that

'In the long run a country cannot be ruled without the working men, or against them, for, whether we like it or not, Germany has already become an industrial State. The principles of the old Prussian class State are no longer applicable particularly when the ruling classes show so little political judgement. By a timely recognition of the signs of the times, much could have been saved that was good and vital. But why should a proletarian feel any sympathy for Crown and Altar when he sees daily that under these banners the most despicable egoism is simply seizing special advantages for itself.'[107]

But even those who could read the writing on the wall were either unprepared or unable to act on their diagnosis. The Russian Revolution of 1905, instead of suggesting the need to forestall trouble by concessions, was interpreted as proof that popular rule would mean ruin. Fear of risking their country's security may have been the chief motive inhibiting the Right from attempting the changes which they would have liked to put through. Yet their patriotism lacked the vision to see that social reform would strengthen rather than subvert the Fatherland. They preferred to live on their social capital, which though large was not infinite, in the hope that their own right arms and other people's loyalty would delay if not divert the deluge. They were gambling on Germany being held together by love of Germany.

*   *   *

The rebellions in South-West Africa had led to sharp criticism of colonial policy in the *Reichstag*. The Centre in particular claimed that the colonial government had brusquely rejected the requests of the Catholic missionaries for a gentler handling of the natives. Matthias Erzberger, a Swabian of relatively humble origins who was steadily gaining influence in the Party, complained that the *Reichstag* was completely ineffective in this field. There was, however, no other body to formulate colonial policy, and no system of training for the officials sent out as administrators. Large monopolies had been given to individual companies which organized their affairs without any consideration for the welfare of the natives, and made big profits in spite of the considerable deficit which the colonies involved for the imperial treasury. Erzberger attributed the risings to lack of competence and imagination; he demanded that Christian ethics be applied to the problem. His attacks, though highly unwelcome to the Government, were difficult to answer and in the spring of 1906 William induced Bülow to put Prince Ernst zu Hohenlohe in charge of the colonies. In the autumn, however, the Prince, under fire from Erzberger, resigned; the colonial office, hitherto part of the Foreign Office, was made into a separate Ministry and a Jewish businessman, Dernburg, put in charge.[108] In the course of time this led to substantial improvements but for the moment the criticism continued and in December 1906 the Centre joined with the left-wing parties in the *Reichstag* to reject the financial appropriation for South-West Africa. Bülow promptly dissolved the *Reichstag* and held the 'Hottentot' election.

The Algeçiras episode had damaged Bülow's reputation and he had been seeking a chance of restoring it. Having a Catholic wife, he was under criticism from the Conservative party for being too conciliatory to the Centre.[109] William himself looked with suspicion at the influence which the party was gaining, seeing in it a threat to the dominating position in the Empire of Protestant Prussia. He had already been considering a change of Chancellors and for Bülow to have given way over the colonies might have been fatal to his chances of survival. For all these reasons Erzberger, on a short-term view, had played his cards clumsily. In an election manifesto sent to the general at the head of the 'Imperial League against Social Democracy', Bülow explained that he had long regarded with concern the dependence of his Government on the Centre for its majority. As long as the Centre did not abuse its power, he had thought it wise to accept the position. He felt, however, that time might have brought changes in the attitude of the various Progressive groups, making them more ready to work with the Government. He hoped, therefore, that after the elections a block could be formed from all deputies prepared to stand by the national cause which would be strong enough to give him a majority independent of the Centre. A lively campaign followed in which Bülow portrayed the Centre as selfish politicians who put party advantage above the needs of German soldiers fighting for their country in the desert. The German Navy League (nominally a 'non-political' body) distributed thousands of pamphlets with such titles as *The Lies of Mr. Erzberger* and *The Manufacturing of Colonial Lies*. The Progressives, mindful of their anti-clerical traditions and anxious to win concessions in return for their support, lent themselves to the manœuvre.[110] At the polls, the Conservatives, Liberals and Progressives obtained 221 seats as against 176 of the Centre, Social Democrats and Poles (although they largely owed this result to the fact that the constituency boundaries had remained unaltered since 1867, for in terms of votes cast, the losers had a majority of three million).[111]

Bülow, though apparently triumphant, then had to pay the bill. A Stock Exchange Amendment Act (reversing concessions made to the Agrarians in the 90's) and a revised definition of sedition did not present great difficulties. A new Law of Association, valid for the Empire as a whole and therefore replacing the separate laws of the various states, was another matter. In some of the more progressive states, its effect was actually retrograde and it stopped short of allowing associations of workers to make membership compulsory. But as it went some way towards giving them legal immunity, it was a matter of much suspicion to the employers. Posadowsky had been removed for disagreeing with Bülow's new policy and his successor Bethmann Hollweg could not induce the *Reichstag* to accept the bill. To get his way, Bülow had to threaten the Conservative and Liberal leaders that an adverse vote would lead to his resignation, a concession to parliamentary methods which was deplored by the traditionalists. Yet the Progressives were still not satisfied. In January 1908 they introduced into the Prussian Lower House a proposal to substitute universal suffrage for the three-tier franchise. The prevailing view among the élite was that, although Bismarck's adoption of universal suffrage for the Empire had been a disastrous mistake, there was no longer any chance of altering it. The Prussian suffrage, the open voting which went with it and the advantages which resulted for the upper classes were therefore the essential safeguards for maintaining the system of a government of officials responsible to the monarch and preventing it from being changed into a government of politicians responsible to Parliament. There could therefore be no question of the Kaiser or his immediate advisers allowing the wishes of the Progressives to be met. If Bülow had considered any such concession, he would immediately have been replaced. He did go so far as to suggest that the Prussian suffrage might be slightly out-of-date and in October 1908 William was induced to say: 'I intend that the regulations over the suffrage should undergo an organic development which will correspond to the economic progress, the spread of culture and of political understanding, as well as the strengthening of the feelings of national responsibility.'[112] But even these cryptic phrases, which remained without concrete application, made the Conservatives begin to wonder whether at such a price the Block was worth while. Yet if they withdrew their support, or by intransigence provoked the Progressives into withdrawing theirs, the Government would stand in immediate danger of defeat. Bülow's scheme for showing the Centre that he had no need of them was proving a sad disappointment.

Prominent among Berlin journalists at this time was a Jew called Witkowski who in 1892 founded a weekly paper called *The Future* (*Die Zukunft*). Under the name of Maximilian Harden, he wrote a good deal of the paper's contents himself, in a style as courtly as Junius and as judicious as Crossbencher. Soon after the Kaiser's accession, Harden had offered to put a pen at his disposal but William had clumsily directed him to the door rather than to the press office. Harden in pique turned to Bismarck who lost no time in signing him on. He was considerably involved in the *Kladderadatsch* affair (see Chapter VII, p. 179); other criticisms of the Kaiser led to a prosecution for *lèse-majesté* in 1893 and condemnation on the same count in 1898 and 1900 to prison sentences totalling a year. He saw in William's claim to take vital decisions himself the chief source of Germany's evils and came to the conclusion that undue and unconstitutional influence was being exercised by the group of friends and courtiers surrounding the Kaiser, in particular Eulenburg. These men may, as Harden claimed, have constituted a camarilla; he undeniably retaliated with a vendetta.[113] About 1902 he appears to have called on Eulenburg to retire from public life under threat of publicity being given to his private morals.[114] Eulenburg thereupon gave up his post as Ambassador in Vienna, but continued to associate with the Kaiser. During the Morocco crisis Harden shared Holstein's view that the best way of obtaining a Franco-German Alliance was to force humiliation on France; the part which Eulenburg played in encouraging William to be conciliatory did not escape notice, any more than the fact that the French Attaché to whom William spoke when staying with Eulenburg was an undoubted homosexual. When Holstein resigned, Harden commented in a Vienna paper that the spies and agents which he had established everywhere had not enabled him to tell what really mattered. Whereas on Bismarck's dismissal it had been France which was isolated, now it was Germany. But Holstein had come to the conclusion that the person really responsible for his resignation being accepted, as well as for William's weakness over Morocco, was Eulenburg. He read Harden's article (correctly) as a hand outstretched in disguise and wrote a letter which *Die Zukunft* published; the two rapidly became inseparable.[115]

By this time Harden had collected, from sources which remain obscure but probably included Bülow, a certain amount of compromising evidence about Eulenburg, Count Kuno Moltke (City Commandant of Berlin) and other intimate friends of William, though there is room for doubt as to whether the material was altogether as incriminating as Harden in a series of articles suggested it to be. In May 1907 the Crown Prince on the advice of a number of courtiers including Bülow showed the attacks to his father. William, who is said to have disregarded earlier warnings, remarked: 'Harden is a damned scoundrel but he would not have risked attacks like these if he did not have adequate evidence on his hands.'[116] Eulenburg and Moltke were dismissed and ordered to clear themselves by bringing libel actions. Moltke's first action against Harden resulted in the latter's acquittal but the public prosecutor then ordered a fresh trial which led to Harden being condemned to four months' imprisonment; this in turn was cancelled on appeal. Meanwhile, Harden had sued a Munich journalist on account of an article which he himself had caused to be published; the object of this involved manœuvre was to get evidence under oath as to homosexual activities by Eulenburg in Bavaria twenty years previously, since such evidence, if true, would prove Eulenburg to have been lying when he denied on oath ever having engaged in such practices. An action for perjury was brought against Eulenburg but never taken to judgement because the health of the accused broke down; before proceedings were stopped, all but one of the prosecution witnesses had been discredited. Eulenburg's enemies maintained that his illness was faked; his friends that the case against him would have been dismissed if Bülow had not stepped in to keep it going.[117] Bülow certainly arranged secretly for Harden to be handsomely compensated from public funds when he was condemned after a fresh trial in 1909 to pay heavy damages to Moltke. Yet the epithets which Harden had in the past used to describe Bülow included such compliments as: 'Foreign Office Feuilletonist', 'Good-Weather Chancellor', 'Minister of Fine

Appearances', 'Laughing Philosopher for a Façade-culture', and 'Imperial Charmer'.[118]

The episode reflects little credit on anyone, and the evidence given in public did great damage to the reputation of the ruling classes. Bülow found it necessary to say in the *Reichstag* that 'it is false and foolish to suppose that because some members of society have failings' (a fact incidentally which had not at that stage been proved) 'the nobility as a whole is corrupt or the army depraved'. Bülow's own conduct in the affair is thoroughly suspicious. Eulenburg had been frequently thought of as a possible Chancellor so that his disgrace could not have occurred more conveniently than at the moment when Bülow felt in danger. The removal of Posadowsky and von Tschirschky disposed of two further rivals.[119] Harden and Holstein may have had their revenge but secured no improvement in the system of government and did as much damage to the whole social system as to their bugbear, William. The Kaiser showed an ungenerous alacrity in abandoning his closest and oldest friend who had done him faithful service and got into trouble more for giving good advice than for the moral failings of which he was accused. To have championed Eulenburg in public was clearly out of the question, but many opportunities were missed of securing him just and even humane treatment. William's behaviour in this case contrasts markedly with that he adopted a few years earlier when similar and better substantiated accusations led the head of the Krupp family to commit suicide; the Kaiser attended his funeral and bitterly attacked the Socialists for spreading what he described as slander. Yet there is a good deal of evidence that William was stirred to the core by the Eulenburg case.[120] By the autumn he was on the verge of a nervous breakdown and at one moment said he could not go through with his visit to Windsor.[121] At Christmas he wrote to Houston Stewart Chamberlain:

'It has been a very difficult year which has caused me an infinite amount of acute worry. A trusted group of friends was suddenly broken up through Jewish insolence, slander and lying. To have to see the names of one's friends dragged through all the gutters of Europe without being able or entitled to help is terrible. It upset me so much that I had to have a holiday and rest. The first after nineteen years of hard uphill work.'[122]

No other man was ever admitted to the intimacy which the Prince had enjoyed. With Eulenburg vanished and Bülow estranged, William became a more solitary figure and turned increasingly for companionship to his wife.

*   *   *

William's 'holiday' followed on a State visit to England which itself was the result of a call on him at Kassel paid by King Edward in August on the way to Marienbad. Beyond joining to deplore the unpractical and dangerous ideas behind the Second Hague Peace Conference (June–October 1907), the two monarchs kept off politics. But even so trouble was not avoided. Without giving any warning, the Kaiser turned out an entire Army Corps to march past his uncle, who must have been more than usually aware of how uncomfortable he found German uniforms! Moreover, the King was caught at a disadvantage when William made an impromptu speech of welcome because, although he hated reading a text, he equally hated speaking without previous thought. William emphasized that no reply was necessary but Edward was not to be behind in politeness; he stood up, only to get stuck for a word in the middle and was inclined afterwards to accuse his nephew of having done it on purpose to show off (whereas William was almost certainly carried away by a sudden access of goodwill).[123]

The invitation to Windsor in November was by way of an olive-branch, and William accepted it in the hope 'that we might have good sport in the dear old park I know so well' (though the story that in fact he shot 700 pheasants must be exaggerated!).[124] William must have given evident signs of being under strain. Lord Esher wrote of the stay at the Castle:

'Our King makes a better show than William. He has more graciousness and dignity. William is ungrateful, nervous and plain. There is no "atmosphere" about him. He has not impressed Grey or Morley. Grey had two long talks with him. At the first he declaimed vehemently against Jews. "There are far too many of them in my country. They want stamping out. If I did not restrain my people, there would be a Jew-baiting." On the second occasion, he talked of the Baghdad Railway but showed no real grasp of facts. . . . The Empress is a delightful figure, admirable *tournure* and well-dressed.'[125]

Grey, whom he now met for the first time, was considered by William 'a capable sort of country gentleman', and in return thought the Kaiser 'not quite sane and very superficial'. (A year previously he had remarked that 'the other sovereigns are so much quieter.')[126] Conversations with Haldane were considerably more cordial. At the Guildhall William put history under a somewhat serious remit, requiring her to do him the justice of confirming that since his previous visit in 1891 he had pursued unswervingly the maintenance of peace! 'The main prop and base for the peace of the world is the maintenance of good relations between our two countries and I shall still further strengthen them as far as lies in my power.'[127] The visit as a whole passed off without mishap but when it ended the King was 'in excellent humour and spirits—glad to be emancipated'.[128]

On leaving Windsor William went on to stay for several weeks with Colonel Stuart-Wortley at Highcliffe Castle in Hampshire. Here, in his own words:

> 'I was in the position of guest among the great British people who received me with warmth and open arms. During my stay I sampled, as I had long wanted to do, all the delights and comforts of *English home and country life*. Comfortable affluence, excellent people in all walks of life, with all classes giving clear evidence of culture in their elegance and cleanliness. Pleasant intercourse between gentlemen and gentlemen on an equal footing without all the ceremonial of royalty. I found it immensely refreshing and soothing. . . . The way these British refrained from discussing our affairs made me ashamed. *Such a matter in our Parliament would be an utter impossibility*.'[129]*

As was later to be evident in Doorn, it was in an atmosphere of this kind that William was best able to relax, and become almost a different character. For a little while he played the part of a country gentleman, distributing sweets to the children and gossip to the neighbours. Some of the gossip, however, was in due course to have consequences.

William had treated the second Hague Peace Conference with as much scorn as the first. 'If the disarmament question comes up in any shape or form, Germany will stay away. For neither I nor my people would for a moment allow foreigners to make rules

* Italicized words in English in original.

affecting our military and naval arrangements.' He got the British Ambassador to agree that the Conference was likely to be 'a most dangerous source of vexation and discord'.[130] But the Liberal Government in Britain, under pressure from its left wing, insisted on disarmament being raised and Bülow was alert enough to see the undesirability of acting on the Kaiser's threat. William, however, was convinced that it was all a ruse to prevent Germany strengthening her fleet, and so played into the hands of those who wanted Britain to strengthen her fleet. The British and Americans got their way by having the question of a limit to arms expenditure discussed; the other Powers got theirs by making the discussion superficial. A little more of the odium for this result than was perhaps fair fell on Germany. It is interesting to think what might have happened and whose reputation suffered most if Germany had used the Conference to press the question of what imports could legitimately be stopped by blockade in time of war.

Anglo-German arguments on naval matters were beginning to grow heated. While William was in England an official proposal was published by which the life of existing German battleships was to be reduced from twenty-five to twenty years. This step, promptly condemned by the Navy League as inadequate, was a consequence of the action of the British Admiralty in building the *Dreadnought*, commissioned at the end of 1906. This battleship was both faster than any predecessor in any navy and considerably more powerful, carrying ten heavy guns instead of four. By making all existing capital ships obsolete, it forced the sailors everywhere to re-equip themselves. Incidentally it involved the end of the British 'Two-Power Standard' because it made the accumulated British superiority in battleships out of date. For Britain to have initiated the new fashion, therefore, may seem paradoxical and the Kaiser once described the British policy as insane.[131] But the thinking behind the *Dreadnought* was not confined to British heads. During his Rome visit in 1903 William had seen a ship on similar lines begun four years earlier for the Italian navy and on his return had pressed his naval designers to follow suit. The sea battles in the Russo-Japanese War had emphasized the advantage of ships which could move faster and fire a heavier salvo than their opponents. Something like the *Dreadnought* was bound to come and in fact Sir John Fisher stole a march on all other navies by getting the first specimen built in an abnormally short time. First drawings for a German version were begun at William's instigation in 1904 but took three years to get approval, by which time the *Dreadnought* itself was in service. Moreover, the new pattern, being larger than any predecessor, created greater problems for Germany since it was too big to go through the Kiel Canal while the only two naval harbours on the North Sea, Wilhelmshaven and Brunsbüttel, could only hold twelve capital ships. Until the canal was widened and the docks enlarged (a process only completed in 1914), a considerable part of the German Navy had to be kept in the Baltic. The British had therefore turned a difficult situation to the best possible advantage.[132] The Germans made no complaint about this except to emphasize that they had become more open to attack than ever. In this they were not wholly wide of the mark since an Admiralty war plan of 1907 centred round an overwhelming naval offensive off the German coast.[133] Lord Esher, who although holding no official position beyond membership of the Committee of Imperial Defence, was perhaps the chief British authority on defence matters, had written in 1906:

'There is no chance of the German Emperor being beforehand with us. There is far more risk of Jacky Fisher taking the initiative and precipitating war.

'I don't think he will do so but the chances are that he will take the fatal step too soon rather than too late'.[134]

The policy of William and Tirpitz did not go unchallenged in the German Navy. A Vice-Admiral Galster published in 1907 an essay, 'What naval armament does Germany need for war?', in which he argued that in fighting England the emphasis would have to be on small-scale actions in which torpedo-boats and submarines would be more useful than battleships.[135] Galster's thinking carried some weight with Bülow who, however, wrote:

'The idea that we could ever have even begun to compete on equal terms with the English fleet, and now with the combined fleets of the Western Powers, is naturally sheer madness. That will never be the case. But there can be no denying that most people in the *Reichstag* and the country want the gradual building of a fleet which is strong enough to protect our coasts and our seatowns, and in the event of an attack our fleet at least does not represent a *Quantité absolument négligeable*.'[136]

William too was in some moods prepared to admit that the German fleet could never hope to meet the entire British fleet single-handed with any prospect of victory; at other times he maintained that the Germans had good chances, and that a war would mean for England the loss of India and of her world position.[137] In any case neither he nor Tirpitz was prepared to accept any limitation on Germany's freedom to build or any reduction in the programme of construction authorized by the *Reichstag*. Whenever such possibilities were raised, they harped on the twin themes that the German navy had no offensive intention against anyone and that its programme was unaffected by the actions of any other Power.[138] What is not clear is how far more realistic calculations underlay these arguments of sentiment and prestige. How much was Tirpitz relying on his belief that armour (in which the German ships were undoubtedly superior) matters more in battle than speed, how much on a belief that the need to institute a close blockade would force the British ships near to the German coast where they could be sunk one by one? Did he cherish a hope that, in spite of Germany's late start, the change-over to Dreadnoughts would give her a chance of drawing level with Britain? At what stage did policy begin to be affected by the idea of using the fleet's nuisance value as a bargaining counter to coerce Britain into an alliance?

Although the *Dreadnought* itself was not much more expensive than its predecessors, its arrival did mark a further stage in the steady rise in the cost of fleets. To have to increase expenditure on armaments was unwelcome to the British Liberal Government, which wanted the money to spend on its domestic programme. But it had no intention of sacrificing external to social security. Yet the crux of the repeated naval negotiations over the next few years was that the Germans refused to believe this. They were slow to stop hoping that the left wing of the party would get its way over defence cuts, and they regarded any suggestions for agreed limitation of building as a sign that Britain was finding the pace too hot. To British Ministers who knew themselves to mean what they said, the German attitude seemed to condemn both countries to heavy expenditure which would leave neither side relatively any better off.

In February 1908 Tirpitz denied German criticisms that the new German proposals were causing alarm in Britain. *The Times* attacked this denial and said that the proposals had not so much caused alarm as made an impression. The interests of Anglo-German relations made it desirable that there should be no illusions on this subject in Berlin. Soon afterwards the same paper published a letter from Lord Esher defending the Admiralty from the criticisms of the British equivalent of the Navy League and ending: 'There is not a man in Germany from the Emperor downwards who would not welcome the fall of Sir John Fisher.' This prompted William, in his capacity as British Admiral of the Fleet, to send a private letter to Lord Tweedmouth the First Lord of the Admiralty. The avowed object of the letter was to give the First Lord authoritative material to use against those who said that the German naval increases made essential a big rise in British construction:

'It is absolutely nonsensical and untrue that the German Naval Bill is to provide a Navy meant as a "challenge to British naval supremacy". The German Fleet is built against nobody at all. It is solely built for Germany's needs in relation with that country's rapidly growing trade. . . . It is fair to suppose that each nation builds and commissions its Navy according to its needs and not only with regard to the programme of other countries. Therefore it would be the simplest thing for England to say: I have a world-wide Empire, the greatest trade in the world and to protect them I must have so-and-so many battle-ships, cruisers, etc. . . . That is the absolute right of your country and nobody anywhere would lose a word about it. Be it 60 or 90 or 100 battleships, that would make no difference and certainly no change in the German Naval Bill.

'The numbers may be whatever you think fit. Everybody over here would understand it but people over here would be very thankful if at least Germany was left out of the discussion. . . . This perpetual quoting of the "German danger" is utterly unworthy of the great British nation with its world-wide Empire and its mighty Navy which is about five times the size of the German Navy. There is something ludicrous about it. . . . Foreigners . . . might easily conclude that the Germans must be an exceptionally strong lot as they seem to be able to strike terror into the hearts of the British who are five times their superiors.

'[As regards Lord Esher's letter] I am at a loss to tell whether the supervision of the foundations and drains of the Royal Palaces is apt to qualify somebody for the judgement of Naval affairs in general.* As far as regards German affairs Naval the phrase is a piece of unmitigated balderdash, and has created immense merriment in the circles of those "who know" here. But I venture to think that such things ought not to be written by people who are highly placed, as they are liable to hurt public feelings over here.'[139]

This effusion was sent with the knowledge of the Foreign Secretary, von Schön, but without that of Bülow who was reduced to asking the British Ambassador whether the report of it was true. When told that it was, he 'fell back into his armchair with his head thrown back and his face so red that Lascelles thought he was going to have a fit on the spot'; he then asked William for a copy of the letter so as to be 'armed for all eventualities'.[140] Lord Tweed-mouth, who 'seemed rather flattered at getting a letter from so Imperial a source', talked about it so widely that it only remained 'private in the sense that the Royal Academy private view is private'.[141] A reference to its existence and character was made in *The Times* and questions were asked in Parliament. When Metternich suggested that, to silence the rumours, the full text should be published, William minuted '*The Times*'s attack comes from the King who is anxious lest the letter should produce too tranquillizing an impression.'[142] Metternich then produced evidence that the King had urged restraint, whereupon William commented 'Only now! After five weeks! He never did the slightest thing four or five weeks ago when the attack of his friend and official [Esher] on me took place, to make known his displeasure and regret! Why did not the King give him a good blowing up then?'[143] In fact the King did tell Esher he had used 'imprudent expressions', but was so angry that he wanted to write 'very tartly' to William.[144] The reply which he actually sent was drafted by Grey:

'I have received your letter in which you have informed me that you have written to Lord Tweedmouth. . . . Your writing to the

---

* Apparently written under the impression that Lord Esher was still Secretary of the Office of Works, a post which he gave up in 1902. The whole passage betrays obvious ignorance of Esher's real significance.

First Lord of the Admiralty is a "new departure" and I do not
see how he can prevent our press from calling attention to the
great increase in building of German ships of war, which
necessitates our increasing our navy also. Believe me, your
affectionate Uncle.'[145]

When about this time Fisher again proposed a preventive attack
on the German Fleet, the King seems to have been more receptive
than in 1904, but for all that the Admiral was left regretting that
'Britain possessed neither a Pitt nor a Bismarck to give the
order'.[146] Meanwhile William commented that the British
'will just have to get used to our fleet. And from time to time we
must assure them that it is not directed against them.'[147]

In the spring William went to the Mediterranean where he had
bought from Franz Joseph the former Empress Elisabeth's palace
on Corfu; this henceforward became the regular scene of his
southern holiday. He can scarcely have failed to remember that,
as Corcyra, Corfu had provided Thucydides with the classic
example of the way in which internecine feuds can undermine a
society. When he had been in England the previous autumn he had
invited his uncle to return the visit with Queen Alexandra early in
1908 and Edward had agreed. Instead, however, the King went in
June to Reval to visit the Tsar, taking with him no Ministers but
Admiral Fisher and General French. *The Merry Widow* was the
rage that summer and as the Admiral danced with the Grand
Duchess Olga to the strains of its waltz, the Tsaritsa was seen to
laugh for the first time for two years.[148] From the satisfaction
expressed on both sides at the meeting, the Germans concluded
that a military agreement must have been signed extending the
previous year's Entente; indeed some German historians still
appear unable to accept the official explanation that nothing more
occurred than a harmonious exchange of views. Unfortunately
general enthusiasm, when expressed in a language only imperfectly
understood by the other party and not translated into concrete
stipulations, is apt to create more false expectations and so be
more dangerous than the majority of secret commitments. Isvolsky,
the Russian Foreign Minister, would seem in particular to have
carried away the impression that Britain would withdraw her
objection to Russian warships passing through the Bosphorus.[149]

A few days later William, reviewing his troops at Döberitz,

used for the first time the term 'encirclement' which, representing as it did the realized version of Bismarck's nightmare of coalitions, was henceforward to be taken into the German official vocabulary as a dirty word. Furthermore, William referred to the way in which Frederick the Great, when surrounded by enemies, had polished them off one by one and announced his intention of doing the same:

> 'The "Grand Emperor", wrote one of his subjects, "had of course to make a speech at Döberitz—I suppose because it was so hot! At least, I try to excuse all the nonsense he talked by the awful heat. Why always talk? I don't think it means strength if one always has to talk about it. . . . Reval was in fact a bluff, meant to make Germany uneasy, especially 'William the Great' feel uneasy—and that just that happened so quickly was the great success. It would have been so much wiser to keep quiet and smiling—*comme si de rien n'était et comme si—ce qui est du reste vrai*—neither England without an army nor Russia without army, navy and money, nor France in its complete disorganization could seriously think of hurting Germany in any possible way." '[150]

Admiration at the shrewdness of the assessment combines with wonder that anyone capable of making it should suppose William to be capable of keeping his mouth shut!

In such circumstances, however, it is not surprising that further attempts by British Ministers, through the German Ambassador in London, to persuade the Germans to accept a mutual slowing down led to no result, except to get the unfortunate Metternich into trouble with his master. He was told that the Kaiser did not wish for good relations with England at the expense of the German fleet. 'If they want war, let them go ahead, we are not afraid. . . . If England only intends to do us the favour of holding out her hand on condition that we limit the size of our fleet, the suggestion is a gratuitous piece of impertinence involving a gross insult to the German people and their Emperor which the Ambassador should have rejected *a limine*.'[151] After a second similar incident, the Kaiser peppered the despatch with no less than fifty-one comments. He considered the Metternich should '*ab ovo*' have refused to discuss the matter on the ground that 'no State allows another to prescribe or suggest the scale and character of its armaments. . . . He should tell muddle-headed people of this kind to go to Hell. He is too flabby.'[152] When shortly afterwards Edward met William at Cronberg on his way to Marienbad, both by mutual agreement avoided the subject of fleets. Sir Charles Hardinge felt it incumbent to step into the breach and warned the Kaiser in restrained terms that unless the German Government was willing to cut down its building programme, the British Government would have to increase theirs. William told him brusquely that he had got all his figures wrong and said that as the Navy Laws had been passed by the *Reichstag*, there could be no question of departing from them. According to William's own account, the accuracy of which Hardinge then and subsequently denied, the Englishman said, 'You must stop or build slower' and received the answer: 'Then we shall fight for it. It is a question of honour and dignity.' Within a little while the Kaiser was telling people that Britain had issued an ultimatum to Germany that naval building should stop. 'The frank conversation with me in which I had shown my teeth did not fail to have its effect. That is always the way to deal with Englishmen.'[153] King Edward came back saying that his nephew was impossible, that when a limitation of armaments was suggested, he at once said that *by law* the fleet had to be completed up to a certain strength and there was no power to draw back. 'As if the law could not be altered by those who made it!'[154]

*   *   *

After leaving the Kaiser, the King went on to a meeting with the Austrian Emperor. For some time there had been signs that co-operation between Russia and Austria-Hungary, which had maintained peace in the Balkans for over ten years, was breaking down. In July a democratic revolution in Turkey had added a further question-mark to the future of the area. But Franz Joseph, who had not appreciated the *bonhomie* shown at Reval, gave no hint to his guest of any Austrian plans. In fact Aehrenthal, the Austrian Foreign Minister, had been negotiating for almost a year with Izvolsky about modifications to the ban which prevented Russian warships passing through the Bosphorus.[155] Russia in return was to agree to the annexation of the two Turkish provinces of Bosnia and Herzogovina which Austria-Hungary had been occupying ever since the Treaty of Berlin in 1878. The two men met at Buchlau in Galicia on 16 September 1908; what exactly passed between them is uncertain because the account which each man gave afterwards was principally intended to put the blame on the other. Izvolsky appears to have thought that, once he had Austrian agreement to a change in the 'Straits Formula', the consent of the remaining Powers would be a foregone conclusion. He therefore agreed—possibly in writing—to some Austrian action about the provinces at a date which he knew would be early.[156] He then went on a further journey in Europe which disclosed to him that the opening of the Straits would call for much more negotiation than he had imagined. But before he could take back his commitment to Aehrenthal, the latter faced him with a *fait accompli*. To save his position in Russia, he denied having made any commitments and thereby put himself at Aehrenthal's mercy. Franz Joseph had written to the various heads of States informing them of the Annexation but his Ambassadors were instructed not to deliver the letters till 5 October. The Ambassador in Paris, who seldom paid much attention to instructions, delivered his two days ahead of time. He told the French that arrangements had been made for Bulgaria simultaneously to declare herself independent of Turkey. While he was doing so, the British Ambassador in Vienna asked Aehrenthal if there was any truth in rumours of such a Bulgarian declaration. 'No truth at all. There is not a word about it in our reports from Sofia!'[157]

The German authorities were more than a little embarrassed by the Austrian action. Though they had known more about it in advance than they afterwards let on, they had not been formally consulted. Besides the obvious danger that it might provoke an Austro-Russian clash, it jeopardized the laborious and successful attempts which Germany had been making, largely on William's initiative, to gain influence in Turkey. When Metternich reported that Britain would only recognize the changes if all the signatories of the Berlin Treaty agreed to them, William commented. 'Very reasonable'. When Hardinge was reported as saying that 'Aehrenthal plays the fool', his comment was, 'Very harsh but not incorrect'.[158] He had the sensible idea that Germany's object in handling the crisis should be to set Russia at loggerheads with Britain over the question of opening the Bosphorus to

Russian warships. But his advisers thought that they knew better.

At the turn of the century, relations between Germany and Austria-Hungary had grown relatively distant. Bülow had taken the view that, though their Alliance was still valuable, it was no longer indispensable; Austria needed Germany more than vice versa. (Eulenburg, then Ambassador in Vienna, thought that the growing Slav influence made such an attitude highly dangerous.) Schlieffen had been unwilling to tell the Austrian General Staff much about German military plans. Holstein fancied himself to have been slighted in the past by the Austrian Foreign Minister and wished to work off the grudge. But this attitude had only been made possible by the fluid state of European relations and by Russia's absorption in the Far East. The signing of the Ententes and the Japanese victory had revolutionized the situation. Austria was now the only ally on whom Germany could rely and had to be supported. From the military point of view, the German generals counted upon the Austrians to keep the Russians occupied during the initial weeks of a war so that the German army could throw its whole weight against France. Worse still, it was no longer easy to insist, as Bismarck had always done, that German support should be confined to helping Austria against a Russian attack and should not be extended to support of a forward Austrian policy in the Balkans. Over the centuries the Habsburgs had failed to evoke a common loyalty among their miscellaneous subjects and so weld them into a nation. Consequently the growth of national consciousness threatened the Habsburg Empire with dissolution. Nowhere was this danger more acute than in relation to the Serbs, who from their independent kingdom were inciting their brothers inside the Empire to break away and form a United South Slav state. For Germany to refuse help to the Austrians in the event of an attack on Serbia becoming necessary might result in civil war inside their only substantial ally, a development which would be most unlikely to remain isolated. Holstein, to whom in spite of all that had happened Bülow still turned regularly for advice, argued that a show-down over the Balkans would mean that Austria in her own interests could be relied on to stand firm. Bülow therefore overrode William's inclination to give the Austrians only tepid support, and insisted that they be backed to the hilt. He wrote to Aehrenthal: 'I know you doubt whether the present nasty state of affairs in Serbia is permanently tenable. I trust your judgement and will accept any decision you may come to as appropriate to the circumstances.'[159] That Germany would feel compelled to offer unqualified support of this kind had been counted on by the Austrians ever since they had heard how Hardinge had been treated at Cronberg.[160]

While he was in the middle of dealing with the Bosnian crisis Bülow, on holiday on the German coast, one morning received from the Foreign Office official attending the Kaiser a somewhat bulky envelope. It contained a typescript article based on remarks which William had made to his host at Highcliffe the previous autumn; this it was proposed to publish in the *Daily Telegraph* as a contribution to better Anglo-German relations. Bülow was asked to read it through and comment, without showing it to anyone else. That Bülow should have failed to realize the sort of things which William would have said in the article is unbelievable, especially as many of them had been repeated to him on William's return home. But an attempt to prevent their publication would only have made him more unpopular with his master than he was already, whereas publication, provided the main responsibility could be shown to have rested with the Kaiser, might have results which would strengthen the Chancellor's authority. Bülow did not look at the article himself as he was told to do but sent it to the Foreign Office to be checked for accuracy against the official records. The Deputy Secretary who received it passed the hot potato hastily to a subordinate, who made one or two minor corrections. The article then returned to the Kaiser as it had come, Bülow again refraining from looking at it.[161]

On 28 October the article appeared in the *Daily Telegraph*. William was reported as having said that while he and his Ministers wished for nothing better than to live on good terms with England, he was losing patience at being misrepresented. His task was not easy, since large sections of the German people were anti-English. During the Boer War he had taken England's side, refusing French and Russian suggestions for joint intervention, and had sent to the Queen advice prepared on his instructions by the German General Staff as to how the war could best be won; this advice had been adopted with the results predicted. The German fleet was not intended for use against England but for the protection

of German trade and colonies and for potential use in the Far
East. The day would come, in the light of Japanese development
and China's national awakening, when Britain would be only too
glad of the German fleet. Like the scholar criticized by Housman,
William had an unfortunate habit of saying things which he
believed to be true, and he could hardly have given wider or
graver offence if he had been trying deliberately to do so. The place
where the article aroused least indignation was probably Britain,
where *The Times* merely observed that the chances of a war in the
Pacific seemed a surprising reason for accumulating a large naval
force in the North Sea, many units of which notoriously lacked the
coal-capacity to make lengthy cruises of any kind. In Germany,
however, the left-wing groups who wished to see the Kaiser
brought under control found themselves for once in agreement
with the right-wing groups who criticized him for being pro-
British.

Bülow was ready to admit that he had not looked at the article
but was not ready to pretend that it was a good one. He offered to
atone for his omission by resigning but this William, on account
of the Bosnian crisis, refused. The Chancellor thus slid out of any
obligation to defend the Kaiser against the attacks which were
being made from all sides (including even the Conservatives) on
his 'personal rule'. Bülow merely explained to the *Reichstag* that
William had meant well, and expressed confidence that in the
light of the experience the Kaiser would 'even in his private
conversation henceforward maintain the reserve which is as
essential in the interests of a coherent policy as in those of the
royal authority. If this were not so, neither I nor my successors
could accept the responsibility.'

While these words were being spoken William was attending
airship trials where he described Count Zeppelin as 'the greatest
German of the twentieth century', an expression which, made as
it was before a twelfth of that century had elapsed, caused widespread hilarity. He then continued his travels and on 13 November
arrived at Donaueschingen for his regular autumn shoot with
Prince Max Fürstenberg. To amuse the dinner guests on the
following evening, the Chief of the Military Secretariat, Count
Hülsen-Häseler, assumed, by no means for the first time, the
costume of a ballerina and was giving a *pas seul* when he fell dead
on the floor. The incident with all that it implied was hushed up,

and William made his way back to Berlin more shaken than ever.
There he had a further interview with Bülow who explained that
his statement had failed to satisfy the *Reichstag* and extracted
with some difficulty a further written declaration. This said
that:

> 'Unperturbed by the excesses of public criticism which he
> considers unjustified, His Majesty considers it his primary duty
> as Emperor to ensure the success of the policy of the Empire
> and maintain in full the pattern of responsibility established by
> the constitution. Accordingly the Kaiser has approved the
> statements made by the Chancellor in the *Reichstag* and has
> assured Prince von Bülow of his continued confidence'.

On the next occasion he had to make a speech, William ostentatiously took a text from Bülow's hand and returned it again after
reading it out. But two days later he had a nervous collapse, being
completely deflated and deprived of his usual self-confidence.
He was not even capable of making conversation to the adjutants
who, as a matter of routine, accompanied him on his morning
walk.[162] His host at Donaueschingen wrote that, 'If you met
Kaiser William, you would not know him', while one of his
fellow-guests recorded that, 'I had the feeling that in William the
Second I had before me a man who was looking with astonishment for the first time in his life on the world as it really is. Brutal
reality had swum into his ken and struck him as a horrible caricature.'[163] The illusions with which he usually surrounded himself
revealed themselves for once as illusions. After the first *Reichstag*
debate he had asked Valentini, the head of his Civil Secretariat,
'What is going on? What is the meaning of all this?'[164] Now he
talked of abdicating and sent for the Crown Prince. He could not
fail to be conscious of the universal criticism which was being
directed at him, criticism which extended to his whole reign and
way of life. He realized he was regarded as a failure and even a
menace but could not understand why. Convinced as he remained
that the article would fulfil its purpose of improving Anglo-
German relations, he could not realize that the objection of the
German public was not to the circumstances of its publication but
to the ability of their ruler to say such things, even in private. The
mood of dejection was, however, transient. Aided by time, Dona,
his entourage and his own vitality, he soon built up a picture

which made him into one of the greatest martyrs of all time. He wrote to the Austrian heir-apparent Franz Ferdinand:

'You will understand what agony it is for me to have to behave as though everything were normal, and to go on working with people whose cowardice and lack of responsibility has deprived me of the protection which anyone else would have accorded to the Head of the State as a matter of course. The German people is beginning to look into its soul and to realize the deed which has been done to it and the pass to which it has been brought.'[165]

Most of his enmity fell on Bülow whom he considered to have betrayed him. He had acted in accordance with the constitution by showing the text to his Chancellor before publication. Why then had Bülow not taken the blame and defended him more energetically? Had the whole business been staged as a deliberate humiliation? There is no doubt that the incident left a lasting scar. Henceforward something of the old self-assurance was lacking. His comments on documents showed no diminution in frequency or vigour but in public he increasingly consented to being bereaved of the sound of his own voice. He had been long in showing any development of character; the man of forty-nine had advanced little on the subaltern who came to the throne at twenty-nine. Now at last adversity began to leave some mark.

Critics such as Harden, Naumann and Weber demanded that Bülow should exploit the incident by taking the reins of government permanently out of the hands of the Emperor and putting them into the hands of the Chancellor and Ministers, as in their view the constitution required. Only thus would it become possible to get away from the zig-zag course imparted to German policy by perpetual imperial interference with Ministerial activities. The difficulty about this theory was that, so long as the Chancellor and Ministers were chosen by, and depended for their tenure of office on the good pleasure of the Emperor, he could not easily be denied a voice, and often a decisive voice, in their policy. If Ministers were not to be chosen by him, what other source was there except the *Reichstag*, which would inevitably have chosen party leaders? In other words, as Weber saw, the only effective guarantee against interference by the Emperor was interference by politicians.[166] Whether a majority could have been found for such a

change in 1908 is hard to say, while the question whether aristocracy, army and bureaucracy would have accepted such a change
without fighting is even harder to answer. What is certain is that
Bülow, no matter what he may have said later, never thought
of taking a step which conflicted with the whole theory on which
Germany was run. He did not believe that a parliamentary system
would work in a country where no single party would be strong
enough to form a government by itself and where so much
depended on co-operation between Federal and State machines.*
Before the history of Germany after 1918 is quoted as bearing
this out, it is necessary to consider what might have happened if
from a much earlier date some way had been found of allowing
the party leaders to gain practice in the art of government. In any
case, however, a dogma of the time held that Germany, threatened
as she was by enemies on two fronts, could not take the risk of such
an experiment. What is more interesting to consider is what would
have happened if the parties on their own initiative had refused to
support any Chancellor of whom they did not approve. But here
too there was nobody ready to contemplate the extremes which
might have been necessary before such a step could have been
made effective.

All this while the Bosnian crisis had been pursuing its course. To
the Russian demand for an international conference, Germany,
remembering Algeçiras, replied that such a meeting would do more
harm than good unless the main points in dispute had been settled
beforehand. When the Tsar asked the Kaiser to exercise a calming
influence in Vienna, William replied: 'Your views about Austria's
intentions are too pessimistic and . . . you are unnecessarily
anxious. We here at any rate have not the slightest doubt that
Austria is not going to *attack* Serbia.'[168] But in January 1909
Conrad von Hötzendorf, the Austrian Chief of Staff, asked von
Moltke where Germany intended to direct her major effort if an
Austrian occupation of Serbia produced a war with Russia in

* During the crisis the various German princes were to meet at Leipzig
to discuss what to do. The Minister President of Wurtemburg told his
rather weak King that they must force the Kaiser to withdraw from the
day-to-day affairs of government. The King was very doubtful. To keep
distracting influences away, the Minister drove the King to the station and
put him on his train. Just as it was starting the King let down the window
and said he could not do as the Minister wanted. When asked why not,
he replied: 'Because then Bavaria might get too powerful.'[167]

which France joined. Moltke's answer, approved before its despatch by both the Kaiser and Bülow, explained that the bulk of German forces would initially be thrown against France, irrespective (as it would seem) of the way in which France herself might act. Von Moltke, who in such circumstances would want Russia pinned down by an Austrian offensive, did not challenge the suggestion that Serbia might have to be invaded, merely saying that if Russia were then to attack, Germany would feel compelled under the 1879 Treaty to come to Austria's aid.[169]

Armed with this blank cheque, Austria called on Serbia to withdraw her demand for compensation, although at the same time Turkey was bought off by Austria and Bulgaria agreeing to pay her the value of the State property in the lands which she was losing. Izvolsky was by this stage in a very difficult position. He had to honour his promise to the Serbs that Russia would give diplomatic support to their demands for compensation. He had to avoid giving the impression that at Buchlau he had made Slav interests the subject of a barter agreement. He had to prove to the English and French that he had not betrayed their rights as signatories of the Berlin Treaty. It was preferable to avoid starting a war. He could offer no lasting opposition to the annexation in case Aehrenthal should then publish evidence showing exactly how far he had gone at Buchlau. Above all, after a considerable record of failure, he needed a success.[170] His first step was to advise the Serbs to place their claims in the hands of the Great Powers; this they did, while at the same time sending an intransigent reply to Austrian demands for unconditional recognition of all that had happened. The military party in Vienna was itching to stamp out the 'wasps nest' in Belgrade. The chances of peace seemed to depend on Russia, as Serbia's protector among the Great Powers, promising in advance of any conference that, when the Serb case was considered, she would treat the whole incident as closed (thereby leaving the Serbs without any satisfaction). Izvolsky, who was under some sort of personal pressure from Aehrenthal, privately asked the German Government to help him out of his predicament. The German reply was to assume the ostensible role of mediator and ask the Russians whether they would agree at a conference to regard the affair as being at an end. No immediate answer was given but the Ambassador in St. Petersburg reported that a Council of War had decided Russia to be incapable of intervening in an Austro-Serb conflict. On this William commented: 'Ha! Here is something definite! Now forwards and march in!'[171] Kiderlen-Wächter, who had been recalled from exile in the Bucarest Embassy to prop up the Foreign Office and who was seeking daily counsel from the dying Holstein,[172] repeated the German question but gave it a sharp edge by adding that, in the event of any answer other than 'Yes', Germany would give up her attempts at mediation and leave events to take their course. Upon this Izvolsky, without consulting either the French or British, gave an affirmative answer, thereby abandoning the Serbs. The German intervention had rescued him from his predicament, since he could now excuse his surrender by attributing it to a German ultimatum. This he proceeded to do, telling the British Ambassador that Germany had threatened, in default of a satisfactory Russian answer, to 'let Austria loose on Serbia'.[173] The Ambassador wrote to London (as was no doubt intended) that:

> 'The Franco-Russian Alliance has not borne the test. . . . The hegemony of the Central Powers will be established in Europe, and England will be isolated. . . . Our Entente, I much fear, will languish and possibly die [unless] it were possible to extend and strengthen it by bringing it nearer to the nature of an alliance.'[174]

Bülow for his part boasted that Germany had kept the peace of Europe and maintained towards Austria the 'faith of the Nibelungs', while William embarrassed Franz Joseph by saying he had stood beside his ally 'in shining armour'. But the success which the Germans and Austrians seemed at first sight to have scored proved in the end to be as damaging as a defeat. Serbian hatred for Austria was inflamed, the Russians developed a conscience-stricken grievance against Germany for apparently forcing them to abandon the Serbs, while the British and French realized that if they wanted to keep the friendship of Russia, they must be prepared to support her legitimate interests in the Balkans. The Annexation episode thus stands in the same relation to the Anglo-Russian Entente as the Morocco episode to the Anglo-French. In both, Germany's policy led (or was so represented as to lead) to a tightening of the coalition against her, and a further inroad was made on the stock of international willingness to compromise. Bülow subsequently claimed to have warned William never under any circumstances to repeat the Bosnian operation; the warning was not unfounded, whatever may be thought of the claim.[175]

* * *

In February 1909 King Edward had come on a State visit to Berlin although he knew that about the same time as the *Daily Telegraph* interview appeared, the German Foreign Office had only managed by a hair's breadth to stop the publication of a similar interview in the *New York World* containing 'things unfriendly to England and the King'. (William was rumoured to have said that in the event of an American-Japanese war, Germany would side with the United States against the Anglo-Japanese coalition and demand as her reward Egypt and Palestine!) 'I know the German Emperor hates me,' wrote the King to a friend, 'and never loses an opportunity of saying so behind my back, while I have always been kind and nice to him.'[176] The visit however proved a chapter of accidents rather than a clash of personalities. The Guard of Honour and the Germans attached *en suite* met the Royal train some way outside Berlin; the King had not been warned and took twelve minutes to change into uniform. All this while the band played 'God save the King' without interruption and the officials stood bare-headed on the icy platform. When the train did reach Berlin, the King emerged from the Queen's saloon and not from his own, five coaches down the platform, where William and the entourage were waiting.[177] He was given a bedroom without a lift although his asthma had got so acute as to make walking upstairs very difficult. Indeed, the asthma became so bad one day after lunch that he lost consciousness for several minutes. That evening the programme required him to arrive at a ball at 8.30 instead of 11 as in England. At the ball he asked for a glass of whisky—to be told there was none. He asked for a game of cards—to be told it was not the custom at the Prussian court. He demanded a cigar—to be told that smoking was forbidden in the Castle. So then he went to bed.[178] Next day, before he left, he and William talked political generalities for ten minutes;[179] then they parted, never to meet again. William gleefully reported to Franz Ferdinand that one of the Queen's ladies-in-waiting had expressed gratified surprise at finding bathrooms, dressing tables, soap and towels in the Castle, having been told (obviously by someone who remembered the early days of the Empress Frederick) that such things were not to be had there.[180]

Another memory of the Empress was revived when Edward asked to be introduced to a Dr. Renvers who had looked after his sister in her last illness. William said to Bülow, 'What nonsense! My mother never knew Renvers.' Bülow professed to have asked the doctor in due course how this flat disregard of the facts could be explained:

> 'If the Kaiser were an ordinary patient', said Renvers, 'I should diagnose *Pseudologia phantastica*—a tendency to live in phantasy or, putting it bluntly, to lie. Such tendencies are common enough in all neurasthenic patients and do not prevent their living to a ripe age, displaying great activity and real talent in certain fields, since such infirmities are entirely compatible with unusual, even brilliant gifts. Remedy? Bodily and mental quiet: composure: self-discipline. If you could persuade the Kaiser to read a serious book alone for two hours every day—the sort of book on which one had to concentrate—you would have done a great deal.'[181]

Bülow in his *Memoirs* seldom missed a chance of incriminating William if he could thereby present himself to advantage, and his stories must be accepted with reserve. But there is no doubt that all through this period the Kaiser was in a nervous overwrought state. In March Dona and her Chamberlain arranged a long interview between William and Bülow with a view to improving their relations; when in the course of this Bülow was going through the various indiscretions of his master which he had had to defend, William flatly denied ever having sent a telegram to the Bavarian Regent from Swinemünde in 1902![182]

During the winter of 1908–9 the British Government had become seriously perturbed at information reaching them to the effect that the German authorities were doing much as Fisher had done over the *Dreadnought* and collecting material for ships before the keels were laid down so as to accelerate the date at which they would be completed. If this evidence was valid it looked as though by 1912 Germany, instead of possessing thirteen

'Dreadnoughts' to Britain's eighteen, would in fact have seventeen or even twenty-one. Whether this was really the case or not is still uncertain. Tirpitz thought that British alarm was a political manœuvre to enable the Liberal Government to get fleet increases through Parliament. William said that the English figures of German building were incorrect, but at the same time refused to put all German future plans on the table or to allow mutual inspection. When Metternich asked for something to tell the British, the Kaiser wrote: 'The best thing for Metternich to do is to keep quiet. He is incorrigible.'[183] The expert view now is that Tirpitz was telling the truth when he denied that any acceleration had occurred—though what would have happened if the British had remained unsuspicious is another matter.[184] However that may be, the British saw no alternative but to announce in March 1909 a considerable increase in their own programme; to justify this to their reluctant supporters, they had to lay public emphasis upon German activities. The left wing pressed for an attempt to negotiate an agreement with Germany limiting building; the opposition criticized the Government for not going far enough and the British Navy League did what it could to rival in vigour its German counterpart. ('We want eight and we won't wait.') The consequent increase in the Naval Estimates was one of the factors leading to the Lloyd George budget of 1909 and so in due course to the Parliament Act. That the British were prepared to make radical changes in their constitution and social system rather than yield their superiority to Germany might have proved to the Germans that any attempt to compete would be hopeless. But for some time the Germans went on expecting a compromise which would save the constitution at the expense of the naval programme, and in any case reckoned that a serious constitutional crisis would damage Britain's fighting capacity.*   •

Britain, however, was not alone in finding the finance of naval building a strain. For a number of years, the effect of higher defence costs on the German national budget had been masked by meeting them from loans rather than taxation. But this resulted in growing debt charges, and the need to pay these put the national

* In the event, neither side maintained its building schedule and by 1912 Britain only had fifteen ships and Germany nine. But the building of eight ships in 1909-10 did mean that in 1915 the Grand Fleet, after allowing for other squadrons elsewhere, had nineteen ships to fight Germany's sixteen.[185]

finances more and more into the red. The deficit began to affect the prices of Government stocks and the business world became insistent that the position be remedied. A minor increase in taxes had been imposed in 1906 but during the next two years the national debt rose by nearly £500 million. In November 1908 a much larger increase in taxation was proposed, notably an inheritance tax and an increase in the amount which the states contributed to the Federal Government.[186] The Conservatives refused to vote for the inheritance tax, which they feared as the beginning of further taxation of land; the Liberals and Progressives refused to vote for the alternatives which the Conservatives proposed. Finally in July 1909 these substitutes were carried by the vote of the Conservatives, Centre and Poles. Germany's naval ambitions may not have caused such an obvious constitutional crisis as in Britain. But they spelt the end of Bülow's Block. The party which boasted most of its loyalty to the Emperor and laid most emphasis on German military traditions was not prepared, when it came to paying for William's beloved navy, to put their hands in their own pockets. Instead they preferred to break up an arrangement which in their view involved too many concessions to the Progressives; they pleaded in excuse that they were voting against a man who had lost their master's confidence. The Centre would probably have voted for the Bill in its original form if Bülow had held out any sort of olive branch to them, but their personal attacks on him had been so bitter that he refused to do so. As it was they gladly availed themselves of the opportunity to resume their role of government supporters, with the influence which this brought. But during their spell in opposition they had grown accustomed to working with the Social Democrats, and the need to maintain influence over the Catholic population was making the Centre more and more into a popular party. Thus Bülow's experiment only brought nearer the day when there might be a clear majority in the *Reichstag* ready to consider an alternative constitutional system.

The architect of the Block did not long outlast it. William had insisted on Bülow remaining until the Finance Reform had become law, but in spite of the March reconciliation, relations between them were highly uneasy. So Bülow availed himself of the excuse that he could not govern without the confidence of the *Reichstag* to conceal the fact that he was going because he had

lost the confidence of the Kaiser (who would have been only too
ready to back a Chancellor in whom he believed against the
'confounded *Reichstag*' which he described as 'a nice gang of
rascals' for their behaviour over the Finance Bill).[187] In July
1909 he was finally allowed to resign. The only question was, who
should be the successor? In the course of his spring voyage William
had practically offered the job to the Ambassador in Italy, Count
Monts, but found universal disapproval of the idea when he got
home.[188] Two Eulenburgs were approached but one thought he
was too old and the other thought the job too difficult. General
von Wedel, the Governor-General of Alsace-Lorraine, also
refused, though William in any case thought he would be too
obstinate. General von der Goltz was then suggested and, on it
being pointed out that he was reorganizing the Turkish army,
Valentini was told to get on the Orient Express that night. William,
however, decided that von der Goltz could not be spared from his
Turkish job and broke off a game of tennis to cancel Valentini's
trip. Bülow had from the start proposed Bethmann Hollweg, since
1907 Minister of the Interior, but William had been unenthu-
siastic. 'He always knows the answer and tries to instruct me. I
can't work with him.'[189] But after so many alternatives had come
to nothing, William began to weaken. Bülow pointed out that
Bethmann knew nothing of foreign affairs. 'Leave foreign affairs
to me,' replied the Kaiser, 'I have learnt a little about them from
you.' So Bethmann was given the job; the shipowner Ballin called
him 'Bülow's revenge'.[190]

Before he left office Bülow, on whom it was dawning that any
prospect of success in breaking up the Ententes depended on a
reduction in Anglo-German naval competition, made an attempt
to bring Tirpitz and the German Admiralty to reason. At a conference on 3 June he got Tirpitz to admit that, if war were to
break out there and then, Germany's chances would be slender.
Von Moltke said that as the navy saw no prospect of winning a
war against England, and as the Chancellor saw equally little
prospect of acquiring fresh allies, he himself would be strongly in
favour of an honourable agreement to slow down building on
both sides.[191] In face of this pressure and of Britain's clear indication that she would not let herself be outbuilt, Tirpitz agreed to
negotiate; indeed, he had already warned William of the dangers
of being too intransigent. The principal object of negotiation was to

be Britain's abandonment of the 'Two-Power Standard'. Tirpitz
had already written that:

> 'the only possible line for us to take is that we are perfectly
> prepared for negotiations on a basis which will leave the British
> our superiors at sea only not on the basis of a "Two-Power +
> 10% Standard" but on a basis that would at least offer us
> reasonable prospects in a defensive war against England.'[192]

William now echoed this view:

> '[England] can claim as big a superiority at sea as she likes
> and build on that basis without any objection from us. But it is
> absolutely beyond my power to agree to the Two-Power
> Standard especially when directed against us alone. Still less
> am I prepared to make such a ratio permanent by signing any
> kind of agreement.'[193]

As Britain had apparently been prepared to contemplate Germany
having thirteen 'Dreadnoughts' to her eighteen, the Two-Power
Standard had already become a dead letter in practice, if not in
theory. If William and Tirpitz had contented themselves with
demanding its abandonment, agreement might have been possible.
But they went further, insisting into the bargain that negotiations
must be begun by the British, that no modification of the Navy
Law should be involved, that Germany should acquire the right
to build three capital ships for every four built by Britain and that
Britain should in addition give assurances about her general
policy. The advisability of pitching German terms so high was
probably the key question of foreign policy, for which the Chancellor was responsible. Yet no matter what he might think on the
matter, he was powerless to override the head of the navy without
the Emperor's support, and that he had forfeited. Bülow claims
to have told William that a question of such importance could not
be decided by the students duelling code but the remark, even if
made, was more apt than effective.[194]

Bülow blandly maintained that the animosities with Britain
over the fleet constituted the only cloud on the horizon which he
left for his successor to tour.[195] In reality, however, the situation
was infinitely worse than the one which he had inherited. Both at
home and abroad forces were converging which could only be
resolved by drastic action and much slaughter of sacred cows. For

some of the deterioration Bülow was himself directly responsible. For much, he had to contend with deep-seated developments which it was beyond the power of any single man to deflect. But he cannot be said to have recognized their gravity, let alone begun to educate his countrymen about the choices and solutions which might lie ahead.

CHAPTER X

The Shadows Deepen

W HEN A LIEUTENANT, William had once been stationed near Bethmann Hollweg's family home. William I had known the grandfather and the parents were thought eligible for the Prince to visit.[1]

'I spent many happy hours with this sympathetic family. . . . As I had no civilian clothes with me, [the] long and lanky son lent me a shooting-jacket, which hung on me like a greatcoat, to everyone's amusement. [Bethmann was six inches taller than his master.] The loyal and deeply religious atmosphere which prevailed in that household gave me endless pleasure.'[2]

Bethmann senior was once frank enough to tell the Kaiser that: 'Your Majesty finds life impossible unless Prussia applauds you daily, Germany weekly and Europe once a fortnight.'[3] Bethmann junior had spent all his life as a Prussian official and knew little of the world outside Germany. He was a man of intelligence, learning and the utmost integrity, reminiscent in many ways of Caprivi. He spoke deliberately with a good choice of words but little sign of humour.[4] He kept a much tighter hold over the various departments than Bülow had done, and shouldered without complaint the enormous burden of work which resulted.[5] When a branch of the Pan-German League complained that the Foreign Office put the interests of other countries above that of Germany, they received, instead of the polite acknowledgement which Bülow would have sent, a blunt refusal to accept unsubstantiated accusations.[6] But one who loved him said he had a strong dash of 'the cautious bureaucrat' and he made on Haldane the impression of 'an honest man struggling somewhat with adversity'.[7] He was an administrator rather than a leader, too much inclined to endure

present evils and too little inspired with a vision of future possibilities.[8] His position was undoubtedly difficult. In home politics,
he had to steer between the *Reichstag* on the one hand and on the
other the élite, entrenched in the Prussian Parliament, court and
army. In external affairs he and the Foreign Office had continually
to compete with the direct access to the Emperor enjoyed by the
soldiers and sailors. Had he followed his own inclinations, he
would quickly have found himself replaced but in any case the
inherited outlook of a Prussian civil servant required him to
subordinate his own views to those of his King. His nobility of
character has distracted attention from the conservatism of his
opinions; the extent of the difference between his outlook and that
of Grey marks the ultimate gulf between Britain and Prussia.

In spite of William's initial misgivings, Bethmann's honesty of
purpose won him confidence and he was kept in office for eight
eventful years. He deserved the trust placed in him and developed
a technique of his own for handling his master. Whereas Caprivi
had resigned, Hohenlohe played for time and Bülow shrugged his
shoulders, Bethmann tried to anticipate the man whom Kiderlen
christened 'William the Sudden'.[9] In 1910 negotiations were in
progress about a greater measure of self-government in Alsace-
Lorraine. The soldiers thought it unsafe to give more freedom to a
population which was fundamentally disloyal; the civilians argued
that, as long as the population were treated as underlings, they
would remain disloyal. The Kaiser, on the eve of a visit to the
provinces, announced his intention of discussing the matter with
local notables. Foreseeing the toes that might impetuously be
trodden on, Bethmann wrote privately to Wedel and had the
programme so arranged as to cut opportunities for discussion to a
minimum. In 1911 William learnt from a Corps Commander that
French dragoons had been making provocative demonstrations
near the frontier and told Bethmann to have a protest made in
Paris; Bethmann took the precaution of getting a report from
Wedel which proved the story to be exaggerated. This he sent to
Valentini whom he asked to see that the imperial comments on it
stopped short of a formal order to protest. On another occasion
William decided to present medals to policemen who had suppressed a Socialist demonstration; Bethmann staged the ceremony
in the enclosed courtyard of the Castle and had the policemen
warned against repeating anything that the Kaiser might say.[10]

Such stories illustrate vividly the shifts to which William's servants were put and suggest that if the years after 1908 were marked by fewer 'rhetorical derailments', the sobering experience of the *Daily Telegraph* affair was not the only cause. The need to forestall tactlessness cannot, however, have eased the Chancellor's burdens.

Since October 1907 the Foreign Secretary had been von Schön and the new team as a whole provoked a comparison between Germany and a ship in which the captain was an actor, the first mate a professor and the second an Alpine climber.[11] Some reinforcement of the Foreign Office was clearly needed; Kiderlen-Wächter had more than once to be brought back for this purpose and in July 1910 Bethmann finally talked William into letting him become Secretary of State. This coarse but clever Swabian had stood high in the department during the early years of the reign and had often represented it on the Norwegian cruises, where his ability to absorb liquor and his fund of stories made him a boon companion.[12] But in 1895 letters written on such trips came to William's knowledge. There is some uncertainty as to whether their scurrilous witticisms were aimed at the All-Highest (as was generally supposed), at Dona (as William in later years declared) or at both (as one might expect); in any case they resulted in the author being sent to Bucarest as Ambassador for thirteen dreary years.[13] In agreeing reluctantly to the promotion William told Bethmann that he would soon find his ear had a flea in it, but if the remark came only too true, Bethmann was equally justified in saying that there was nobody else available with a comparable grasp of Germany's problems. All the same, the appointment proved unfortunate. It was not just that Kiderlen's yellow waistcoat and broad accent made the deputies laugh when he spoke in the *Reichstag*, or that his private life was unusually complicated—the Crown Prince, in seeking to repeat his feat over Eulenburg by passing on the story that the Foreign Secretary was living with his housekeeper, only touched the fringe of the problem.[14] One observer said that Kiderlen was apt to mistake roughness for energy, another that a careful analysis of his actions would reveal a strong percentage of alcohol. Bethmann's view was that Kiderlen's chief weakness consisted in cynicism.[15] Swabians are traditionally addicted to acts which combine courage and imagination with *naïveté*, and Kiderlen, in applying Balkan methods to his

dealings with Western Europe, showed more than the normal
German *'inconscience'* about the reactions of other people.[16]

When Bethmann took over, the officials of the Foreign Office
were quick to endorse Bülow's advice that Germany's relations
with England should be the first problem tackled. The warning
was reinforced by William's Jewish shipowner friend, Ballin, who
in the spring of 1910 wrote from London:

> 'Anti-German feeling is so strong that it is scarcely possible
> to discuss matters with one's oldest friends because the people
> over here have turned mad and talk of nothing but the next war
> and the protective tariffs of the future.'[17]

Ballin had joined with King Edward's Jewish banker friend, Sir
Ernest Cassel, in an attempt to get the two sides talking and
Bethmann, who knew little about the back-history, welcomed the
initiative. (Both in 1909 and 1912 the two mediators seemed to
have followed the bad example of Eckardstein and given each side
the impression that the initiative came from the other.) In his
anxiety not to offend British opinion, Bethmann had the draft for
a *Reichstag* speech sent to London for advance comment,[18]
but though this gesture improved the atmosphere, one man's good
will was not enough to remove the fundamental difficulties.
Bethmann secured authority to drop three ships in the German
programme before 1914 but in return asked Britain to accept the
3 : 4 ratio and so abandon the construction of several ships
authorized by Parliament. Moreover, he demanded that a naval
agreement be accompanied by a political one, whereas the British
wanted the naval agreement to come first. In any case the British
saw grave difficulty in entering into closer relations with Germany
than they had done with other Powers, whereas the Germans,
realizing that in order to help Austria they might have to attack
Russia or France, wanted at least a guarantee of the existing
territorial position. The British Ambassador summed up the
situation by saying that the naval proposal, based as it was on the
execution of the whole German programme, with only an off-
chance that if things went well it might possibly be reduced, did
not go quite far enough, and that the political proposal went
somewhat too far considering the present British arrangements.
But on one of the relatively few occasions on which the Kaiser
was consulted about these negotiations, he put very clearly the

considerations which made Germany insist on some political concession.

'England wants to obtain a political agreement of such a kind that the Powers with whom she has an Entente can be included in it—that is to say that she can immediately inform them of it to allay their suspicions. This is where we demand reciprocity. The Franco-Russian Alliance is a military agreement with detailed stipulations aimed against us (under the pretext of assumed threats of aggression). England by offering France military help on the continent [1904–5] has joined a coalition openly hostile to Germany. In spite of this England declares that her Ententes with the Anti-German Powers are not directed against us and that she has no hostile intentions. This is a piece of self-deception. The mere fact of England's accession to the Franco-Russian group is from the German standpoint an essentially unfriendly act in itself. Reservations in one direction or another do not affect this.'[19]

Grey certainly failed to disclose to the public that Britain could, by making political commitments, slow down the naval race. But not only was he afraid that the public's reaction to the idea would be hostile; Bethmann had pledged him to secrecy for fear of equally hostile reactions in Germany. Moreover, Tirpitz had a few months earlier prevented his Foreign Office from disclosing how far the British Government had gone in expressing its readiness to negotiate.[20] In such circumstances, there seemed little prospect of further talk producing results and the British used the imminence of the 1910 election as an excuse for letting things drop.

May 1910 saw William in England again when he came to stand by his uncle's grave. One of the main banes of his existence was gone, the source of continual frustration, but gone too was a link with many memories to which distance lent enchantment. So many of the figures which had dominated his early years were vanished now—his grandfather, the Queen, his parents, his uncle, Bismarck, Hohenlohe, Holstein, Salisbury. Yet the consequences of their loves and hates, their ambitions and fears and indifference lasted on. William seems to have been moved by very mixed emotions. 'My firm belief', wrote Lord Esher, 'is, that of all the royal visitors the only *mourner* was this extraordinary

Kaiser.'[21] William himself wrote to Bethmann that 'at such a moment one forgets a great deal'.

'I have been allotted as my quarters the very suite of my parents in which I often used to play as a little boy and which are famous for their wonderful view over the whole of Windsor Park. All sorts of memories flooded through me as I paced about the rooms where I played as a child, lived as a youth and first as grown-up man, then as ruler enjoyed the noble hospitality of the great Queen and all those distinguished men and women who have passed away. They kindle once again my old sense of belonging which binds me so firmly to this spot and which has made the political developments of the last few years so unbearable for me personally. I am proud to be able to call this place my second home, and to be a member of this royal house, for so everybody has treated me in the kindest way. It was very remarkable that when I left Windsor Castle in an open carriage in front of the very crowd which had stood there in silent grief, a sort of electric shock ran through the people as they recognized me. The words "the German Emperor" went on getting louder until suddenly someone shouted "Three cheers for the German Emperor", and thereupon a resounding threefold "hurrah" broke out from the densely-packed masses in all the streets. My eyes filled with tears and my neighbour, the King of Denmark, said, "Why are the people here so fond of you? It is quite extraordinary the way the people give you such an enthusiastic reception in spite of their deep grief for dear Bertie." I think one can regard this completely spontaneous demonstration as a good omen.'[22]

The practical conclusions which he drew from the change of monarchs were less emotional.

'English policy as a whole is unlikely to change much. But we should get fewer disturbing intrigues to make Europe hold its breath and prevent it from enjoying peace and quiet. The coalitions which owed so much to personal initiative will run down now their mainspring is gone since they were held together by personal magnetism and persuasive influence exerted over leaders of the various States. It is a bad blow for France. . . . And Isvolsky will feel very lonely without his guiding star. I expect on the whole European politics to become more peaceful; even if that is all, it will be a distinct advantage. As soon as there is no one fanning the flames, they will burn lower.'[23]

In September Izvolsky appointed himself to the key position of Russian ambassador in Paris and Sazonov, a less committed figure, became Foreign Minister in his place. The Tsar had been staying with his in-laws at Darmstadt where he could indulge in such simple pleasures as travelling incognito by train 2nd class, playing tennis or strolling in the park. On his way home, he was due to call at Berlin, and Sazonov expressed the hope that he would speak freely and openly to William on political matters. 'That', minuted the Kaiser, 'is what I have hoped for over many years but it has never happened.'[24] This time, there were discussions about a possible Russo-German Agreement to maintain the *status quo* in the Balkans and to stand aloof from any policies directed against one another. Germany was to recognize Russia's interests in North Persia in return for the withdrawal of Russian objections to the Baghdad Railway. The bargain caused eyebrows to rise sharply in London and Paris with the result that, when Nicky and his Ministers got home, their readiness to incorporate such terms in a formal treaty strangely evaporated; they suggested that verbal assurances exchanged between the monarchs were really much more reliable than any paper promises. Sazonov hinted that the real reason was fear of upsetting England; it is more likely to have been fear of interrupting the flow of French gold.[25]

* * *

There are signs that in these years William was beginning to tire of politics, where his efforts seemed to lead to so little and where so many people were reluctant to fall in with his views. One of his fondest preoccupations was his villa on Corfu where extensive excavations had been started under Dörpfeld's direction:

> 'The Kaiser who flung himself into the work with all his obstinacy and energy would have taken it very badly if his suite had not shown the same enthusiasm and this was especially true of the head of the Civil Secretariat in whose province learning belonged.'[26]

At Easter 1911 these efforts were rewarded by the discovery of a Gorgon's head dating from the seventh century B.C., apparently the centrepiece of a temple pediment. William, who must have wished that its traditional petrifying effects could have been brought into action against the Socialists and the Entente, was so excited that he sent streams of expensive telegrams to the Archaeological Society in Berlin. 'Frankly,' said Bethmann, 'it would be much worse if he showed the same interest in Morocco as he does in the Gorgon.'[27] But William had 'really had enough' of Morocco and 'did not wish to hear the word again'.

This wish, however, was not to be gratified. Since the Conference of Algeçiras both French and Germans had made considerable efforts to settle their differences in Morocco, although admittedly the Germans were hoping to see the French involved in another Mexico whereas the French were aiming to remove a weakness which might limit their freedom of action elsewhere. In August 1907, William wrote that he wanted the greatest possible reserve exercised both in diplomacy and in the press since there was no justification for provoking the French or making them nervous. After his November visit to Windsor, he said that the Moroccan question was to be so handled as to 'prevent the English from receiving the impression that we are again trying to deal cavalierly with the French, counting on our improved relations with England'.[28] In October 1908 he decided, on reading a report from his Consul in Fez, that Germany had no chance of maintaining her position in Morocco and that she would do well to cut her losses.

'In view of the Bosnian situation, the wretched Morocco business must be wound up as quickly as possible once and for all. There is nothing for us to do, it is bound to become French. . . . Our Moroccan policy hitherto has proved a failure.'[29]

Bülow commented that if Germany was to emerge from the affair with any credit, the first requisite was to conceal from the French her anxiety to do so. In the following month the French arrested the secretary of the German Consulate in Casablanca for harbouring German deserters from the Foreign Legion. The Pan-Germans clamoured for blood, London concluded that the matter had been engineered to distract attention from the *Daily Telegraph* article, and Europe was for a moment said to be on the verge of war. But William had no opinion of deserters on principle (one of them proved an Austrian anyhow, another a Swiss and a third a Pole) and the offending diplomat was reprimanded for exceeding his functions.[30] Thereafter, Schneider-Creusot made an arrangement with Krupp about access to Moroccan ore, and by a political agreement in February 1909 Germany recognized a special French position in the country while France promised to respect German economic interests. In the same autumn, the French Foreign Minister made an appreciative public reference to the accommodating spirit shown by the Germans, but when William wished to respond, Bethmann objected that a special mention of France might upset other countries. The Kaiser lost patience and put his foot down:

> 'This is the sort of advice which my Chancellors and Foreign Office have been giving me for twenty years and it has ended by our being completely isolated! The Moroccan Agreement is my very own personal doing which I have put through in spite of the procrastination and timidity of my officials and which has proved its value for both countries.'[31]

So incompetent were Morocco's own leaders and so incorrigibly given to intrigue that leaving the country independent meant letting it be mis-governed, to the detriment of all Europeans doing business there. As joint international intervention was impracticable, the effective choice lay between leaving the chaos to continue and allowing the French to reduce it, which would inevitably allow them increased advantages. Neither the logic of this situation nor the results following from it were appreciated by the Mannesmann family and other German trading interests, who were out to get control of valuable ore deposits. In the spring of 1911 the French began to make up their minds that nothing but force would shape the Moroccan administration to their desires and that to apply the force, a column must go to Fez. As no clear international authority existed for any such step and in order to forestall a repetition of 1905, feelers were put out to see how the Germans would react. Kiderlen decided to take the opportunity of salvaging something from the earlier wreck, and resuscitated von Kühlmann's policy of bartering German rights in Morocco for territorial concessions elsewhere in Africa. To this William, early in May, consented. The financier, Caillaux, one of the most controversial figures in French politics who in March 1911 became Minister of Finance, was ready to go further and use the 1909 agreement over Morocco as the starting point for a Franco-German reconciliation at the expense of Britain. (He was later to tell the British Ambassador that the Entente had worked against French interests.)[32] In secret negotiations carried on outside diplomatic channels, he led Kiderlen to expect generous compensation. But Kiderlen thought he knew better than to trust the word of a French politician. When in May the French without further consultation marched to Fez, he proposed to Bethmann that Germany should occupy Agadir, a port in South Morocco. Thus on the one hand he urged the French Ambassador (who, like most of the French Cabinet, knew nothing of Caillaux's overtures) to put forward proposals for a settlement, while on the other he prepared to stake out a claim which would compel the French to negotiate.

The Kaiser thought it would suit Germany well if the French got tied up in Morocco with troops and money; he had asked Bethmann in April to discourage any outcry there might be for sending ships. 'If the French break the Algeçiras Act, we can leave it to other Powers, particularly Spain, to protest.'[33] When leaving Victoria Station in May, after the unveiling of the Memorial to his grandmother, he agreed with King George that the French occupation of Morocco was a *fait accompli* about which little could be done. Among the various possible courses of action the despatch of a ship (to Mogador rather than Agadir) would seem to have been mentioned. He assured the King that Germany would in no circumstances go to war over Morocco but would try to maintain the open door for trade and might seek compensation elsewhere.[34]

On 19 June the Managing Director of the Hamburg-Morocco Company was asked by the German Foreign Office to collect from firms interested in Morocco signatures to a petition asking for official protection. Two days later such a petition was duly presented.[35] On 21 and 22 June Kiderlen had long conversations with the French Ambassador at Kissingen. On 23 June an aeroplane accident necessitated changes in the French Government and Caillaux became Prime Minister in a Cabinet with a nonentity as Foreign Minister and Delcassé as Minister of Marine. On 26 June, Bethmann and Kiderlen saw the Kaiser at Kiel and induced him, apparently with considerable reluctance,[36] to let the gunboat *Panther* and its crew of 125 men, on its way home from West Africa, be ordered to Agadir. (The Foreign Office had originally planned to send two cruisers to Agadir and two to Mogador but the ships could not be available in time. The object of the call was never explained to the German naval authorities.)[37] On 1 July the various governments concerned were told that the *Panther* had gone to Agadir to protect the lives and properties of 'certain Hamburg merchants living in the area'. Agadir was in fact a closed port inaccessible to European traders and it seemed highly unlikely that there were any German merchants south of the Atlas Mountains (though a young employee of a Hamburg firm is said to have been hastily despatched to give verisimilitude to the claim).[38] The reason given was so obviously a pretext that everyone speculated on what might lie behind it. The British Government (who knew nothing of Kiderlen's negotiations with the French) shared with the German public the belief that Germany wanted a slice of Morocco. The sailors were reluctant to see Germany obtain a harbour on the Atlantic; the politicians were afraid of arrangements being made about Morocco behind their backs. Grey regarded it as more important to prevent the second than the first; he was also determined to convince Britain's friends in France that they could count on support.[39]

Caillaux was in a quandary. While his appointment as Prime Minister had put him in a better position for pursuing his main policy of reconciliation with Germany, he knew well how widely and fiercely any such policy would be opposed in France, and indeed in his own Cabinet. The despatch of the *Panther* may have forced the French to make some concessions but it equally stopped them from making many. On 9 July, Kiderlen asked the French Ambassador what offers he brought from Paris, to be told that in the French view it was now for the Germans to make suggestions. This view coincided with that of the Kaiser who on 10 July told Bethmann that Germany should have formulated clear demands much earlier.[40] On 15 July, Kiderlen suggested that in return for the waiving of all their claims in Morocco, the Germans should receive the whole of the French Congo. He warned Bethmann that, to get so much, Germany would have to throw her weight about, words which when read by William on his Norwegian cruise, made him think about coming home.

'For I cannot allow my Government to take a line like this without being on the spot to supervise the consequences carefully and take a hand. In any case it would be unforgivable and make me look as if I was a mere constitutional monarch. *Le roi s'amuse!* And all the time we are heading for mobilization. That must not happen with me away.'

The diplomat in attendance reported that 'in any case you should reckon with the fact that it will be very difficult to get His Majesty's consent to any measures he considers likely to lead to war'. In the end it was a message rather than a monarch which came back and provoked Kiderlen into attempting resignation. His view was that 'we shall only secure a satisfactory outcome if we are prepared to go to all lengths and if other people feel and know as much. Anyone who starts off by declaring that he is not going to fight gets nowhere in politics.'[41] Kiderlen throughout the episode held close to his chest not only his cards but also a lady whose background is best described as nondescript since historians vary as to the precise way in which the Russian, Montenegrin and French elements were mixed in it. Besides enjoying her charms, he exploited her role as a double agent and the popular conviction that statements in love letters are more trustworthy than those in diplomatic despatches. In the middle of the affair, he took her on a holiday to Switzerland and even to Chamonix where the couple were embarrassed rather than honoured by finding at the railway station the Prefect sent on Caillaux's instructions to greet them. Through his statements to Madame Jonina and in all other ways, Kiderlen set out to make the world think Germany intended to fight and so intimidate the French into giving him the maximum compensation.[42] He had in fact got into a position where there was no other course open to him, since nobody was prepared for a return to the old state of affairs, and any attempt by Germany to stay at Agadir looked as though it would involve war with England.

For the English Cabinet had grown restive at the failure of the Germans to explain either their intentions or their desires. On 21 July, Mr. Lloyd George, having earned a name in home politics, suggested to Grey that he make his presence felt abroad by including a warning to Germany in a speech at the Mansion House. Grey and Asquith (the Prime Minister) saw advantages in getting the leader of the more pacific Ministers to commit himself in public to a firm line, and Lloyd George was allowed to say that:

'If a situation were to be forced upon us in which peace could only be preserved by the surrender of the great and beneficent position Britain has won by centuries of heroism and achievement, by allowing Britain to be treated as if she were of no account in the cabinet of nations, then I say emphatically that peace at that price would be a humiliation intolerable for a great country like ours to endure.'

This amateur intervention certainly created a great commotion; whether its long-term results were beneficial is more questionable. It encouraged the French to stiffen their resistance to the full German demands and enabled them to attribute their intransigence to British pressure. It created great popular anger in Germany where it was regarded as a threat of war, the first open statement by a British Minister that his country would if necessary fight with France. Four days later Grey told Churchill he had just received a communication from the German Ambassador so stiff that the fleet might be attacked at any moment. The fleet proved in no position for defence. The first division was in Ireland, the second at Portland, the third and fourth paying off reserve crews in home ports. The ships were short of coal, the colliers delayed in Cardiff because of a coal strike, the crews on four days' leave and the anti-torpedo precautions untaken. The German Fleet had been at sea for four days, and nobody seemed to know where it had got to. Emergency measures had hastily to be improvised.[43]

The Agadir crisis left behind it two firmly held beliefs, neither of which can really be substantiated. The Germans were convinced that the British fleet and army had been mobilized against them. It is true that the lack of water in Wiltshire, given as the reason for breaking off army manœuvres, was as much a pretext as the Hamburg merchants in South Morocco. It is also true that on 20 July General Wilson discussed with the French Chief of Staff the details of moving a British Expeditionary Force to France.[44] But these were precautionary steps to allow for help to be given quickly in case Germany attacked France. The naval moves were simply intended to enable the fleet to defend itself and were in no sense offensive, but their character could not be explained without disclosing the reasons for them and so for the time being Germany had to be left under a misapprehension. In any case, when Metternich in November hinted at the truth, William refused to believe him and asked 'What does a civilian know about it?'[45] More significant in the long run was the discovery by the Committee of Imperial Defence, when on 23 August it held its most important meeting prior to the 1930s, that whereas the army war plan was to send six divisions to France, the navy regarded the troops as a projectile for them to fire at whatever part of the European coastline might seem weakest at the moment. The divergence was resolved by the Prime Minister, the only person capable of doing so; he endorsed the army plan.[46]

The British for their part were convinced that the Germans had intended to attack France and that only Lloyd George's speech had stopped them. It is true that belief in an attack was what Kiderlen strove to create. It is equally true that some vocal members of the German public hoped for, and even more expected, something of the kind. It is true too that von Moltke wrote:

'If we once again crawl out of this affair with our tail between our legs, if we cannot pull ourselves together and take an energetic line which we are ready to back up with the sword, I despair of the future of the German Empire and shall quit.'[47]

But there is no firm evidence to show that those in authority ever began seriously to consider mobilization. Germany would have been insane to pick a quarrel with France over a matter in which Austria had no interest.

Negotiations with the French went quietly forward. The French succeeded in breaking the German cypher and thus discovered their own Prime Minister's clandestine negotiations. While this did not wholly assist his efforts, a Stock Exchange panic in Berlin, said to have been caused by the withdrawal of French and British funds, made the Germans more conciliatory. At one point the Germans were told that, unless they reduced their demands, a French gunboat would be sent to Agadir where it would be joined by an English one. This sent William into a fury:

'Scandalous! Insolence! Nobody has ever yet threatened me directly. [Did he forget Sir Edward Malet and Sir Charles Hardinge?] The ambassador must forthwith send his intermediary to the French and obtain within twenty-four hours an assurance that (a) they will withdraw the threat, (b) offer an apology, (c) promise to make us a firm offer without delay. If this does not happen within twenty-four hours, I shall break off negotiations since the tone in which they are being conducted is incompatible with the dignity of the German Empire and people.'[48]

Needless to say negotiations were not broken off and when a little later the question arose of making a fuss over some Frenchmen hoisting their flag at Agadir, the Kaiser refused to consider anything of the kind (partly because the fleet had gone into dock and Moltke on holiday).[49] Gradually the Germans came to see that they must drastically reduce their demands, the French that they must make possible a dignified retreat and in the autumn an agreement was signed by which France got a free hand in Morocco and Germany some sections of the French Congo; although these looked insignificant, they could have formed the core of a big Central African colony if the Belgian Congo and Angola had ever fallen into German hands. William sent Bethmann his 'best congratulations on the termination of this delicate affair'.

The reactions of William's subjects were different. They had originally assumed, in the absence of any guidance from their rulers, that Germany was to get a substantial slice of Morocco; they had then gradually transferred their expectations to the entire French Congo. When they learnt the meagre result of so much excitement, indignation ran high. 'Have we become a generation of women?' wrote *Der Post*. 'The Kaiser has become the strongest supporter of the English-French policy. What is the matter with the *Hohenzollerns*?' The French press did not improve matters by jeering at '*Guillaume le Timide*'.[50] The Conservative leader von Heydebrand was warmly applauded by the Crown Prince and many others for saying about Lloyd George in the *Reichstag*:

> 'When we hear a speech that we must consider as a threat, as a challenge, as a humiliating challenge, it is not so easy to pass it over as after-dinner speechifying. Such incidents like a flash in the dark show the German peoples where is the foe. The German people now knows, when it seeks foreign expansion and a place in the sun, such as is its right and destiny, where it has to look for permission. We Germans are not accustomed to that and cannot allow it and we shall know how to answer.'[51]

All the worst defeats in German history were paraded to provide a comparison. The Colonial Secretary, Lindequist, under the influence of Pan-German officials in his department, insisted on resigning, nominally on the ground that he had not been warned of the *Panther*'s visit but really, as he did not hesitate to explain, because he thought Germany had got the worst of the bargain. William's reaction once again illustrated the true position of a German Minister:

'I consider it unheard of for such a senior official to throw his portfolio at the feet of his Emperor at such a moment for absolutely trifling grounds. It is setting the Civil Service a very bad example of disaffection. It shows on the one hand that he sets far too high a value on his own personal importance (vanity), on the other a lack of tact which makes one's hair stand on end.'[52]

The whole Agadir episode provides an object-lesson in how diplomacy should not be conducted. Kiderlen forgot that those who suggest an intention to use force may turn their opponents into perverse animals who prepare forcible defence. Caillaux illustrated the predicament of a leader anxious to do the opposite of what his public wants without them noticing. Lloyd George showed how desirable it is for anyone putting down his foot to know the exact lie of the land he is going to tread on. The attitudes adopted and the actions taken showed up the accumulated mass of animosity and suspicion which had been aroused by repeated acts of arrogance, tactlessness and subterfuge. Each side, with no more than partial justification, placed the most sinister possible interpretation on all the moves of the other. Such was the difference of perspective that firmness was resented as provocation and readiness to negotiate was attributed to loss of nerve. Threats had their usual effect of making people angry rather than compliant. The total result was to increase the store of animosity and suspicion, and to reduce the future readiness of statesmen to compromise. In France, Caillaux was replaced by the anti-German Poincaré. In Britain, Grey in 1912 agreed to put his understanding with France into writing and so made it still more of a moral commitment. In Germany, as Haldane said afterwards, the diplomatic discomfiture drove the Kaiser away from Bethmann into the camp of Tirpitz and the soldiers;[53] certainly the redoubled taunts about his 'cowardice' struck home. Yet seen from a distance of fifty years, how petty and transient were the objects ostensibly in dispute!

*　　　　*　　　　*

On 27 August 1911 the Kaiser spoke at Hamburg of the need 'to strengthen our fleet further so as to make sure that nobody will dispute the place in the sun to which we are entitled'. Most of his audience made the mistake of interpreting this as a claim on Morocco but nobody could mistake the imminence of another Naval Bill.[54] Tirpitz' proposals reached Bethmann's desk three days later. Their starting point was the need to end the situation by which the German Fleet was put virtually out of action for several months every autumn by having to train a new intake of conscripts. To avoid this, a reserve fleet was to be created and used for training, which in turn involved the building of extra ships and a considerable increase in manpower. In addition more light craft and submarines were to be constructed. The project set off a brisk controversy in German government circles. To obtain *Reichstag* approval for extra taxation was clearly going to be difficult so that the probable result of the increased naval expenditure would be once again a big budget deficit, a prospect which led the Minister of Finance to resign rather than agree. Bethmann, supported by Valentini, could not believe that the benefits of the changes would outweigh the harm done to relations with Britain, and this view was naturally backed by Metternich from London. Bethmann was prepared to support the increase in manpower, with which von Holtzendorff, the Commander-in-Chief, would have rested content. But Tirpitz and other sailors insisted that the provision of extra material was an integral part of the plan for adding men, and the only concession which they were prepared to make was a slight cut in the number of ships.[55]

Tirpitz had the Kaiser behind him and indeed would have got nowhere without imperial support. But William's attitude to naval policy was changing. He wrote to Bethmann that:

'The Risk Theory has served its purpose and has been discarded. We now need a different, practicable and easily recognizable objective to steer the country towards and so meet the national desire to count for something at sea.'[56]

The immediate new objective was to be a ratio of 2 to 3 in capital ships which Britain was to accept in substitution for the obsolete Two-Power Standard. As Tirpitz put it:

'The purpose and aim of our naval policy is political independence from England—the greatest possible security against an English attack and a promising chance of defence if war should come. To accomplish this purpose, we must *diminish* the military distance between England and ourselves, not increase it. If we do not succeed, then our whole naval policy of the last fourteen years has been in vain.'

To the objection that Britain would never voluntarily accept such a ratio, William and his associates replied that limitations of money and men would in the long run leave her with no other choice.[57] But while there were some sailors, notably Widenmann, the Naval Attaché in London, who thought that war was inevitable and that the only course for Germany was to lose no time in argument but arm with speed,[58] for others, including the Kaiser, the real object of demanding the new ratio was to use the threat of an intensified naval race as a lever for extorting a change in British foreign policy. A memorandum by Admiral von Capelle explained clearly the reasoning behind this idea.

'Neither nation wants war. We do not because we are militarily the weaker. England does not because the military and political risk is already too great and the reason for fighting is not intelligible to the man in the street.

'England's insistence on the two keels standard puts her in a worse position than ourselves for maintaining a naval race. Moreover there are political reasons to prevent her keeping up indefinitely a race which involves a massing of all her forces in the North Sea. If war and a naval race are ruled out, the only alternative open to England is agreement. It is not we whose hand is being forced but England. . . . We have only got to wait patiently until our present Naval Law is passed. England must and will in the course of the next few years come out for us and against France because it is in England's clear interest to do so. An alliance with Germany would at one stroke give her back her position as a world power and complete security on water and land. . . . The Naval Policy is the masterpiece of the Imperial Government. If it is crowned by an alliance with England assuring us complete political and military equality of rights, it will have achieved its first great success. If on the contrary it leads to a cold war (*societas leonina*), the naval policy will have resulted in a fiasco and history will in due course pronounce appropriate judgement on it.'[59]

When Metternich suggested that it might be mistaken tactics to face Britain with the alternative between having to build still more ships in order to keep pace with Germany and abandoning her links with France, William refused to listen:

> 'Metternich's standpoint remains that of 1904 and 1908. If I had listened to him then, we should now have no fleet at all. His arguments imply that a foreign country is entitled to interfere in our naval policy which I as Supreme Commander and Emperor cannot allow to happen now or at any time.'[60]

What is not clear is how far Tirpitz really believed in using the fleet for political bargaining and how far he merely adopted the policy as a way round the opposition to further fleet increases.

Only with some difficulty had William been talked out of sending a personal letter to King George announcing the new Naval Bill. But rumours of expansion (which was, however, expected to be confined to capital ships) had reached London, where in turn they set up a brisk private discussion. Grey, supported by Eyre Crowe, Nicolson, Bertie and other diplomats as well as by Churchill, Fisher, and the Conservative opposition, thought (correctly) that any British overtures would be interpreted in Germany as a sign of weakness, and that nothing positive could result from them. There was another group, however, led by Haldane, Tyrrell of the Foreign Office and supported by the left-wing Liberals, which refused to believe that Tirpitz spoke for the whole of Germany or that where so much was at stake matters could be left to chance.[61] The conflict between the two attitudes was less heated in Britain than in Germany, but in Germany those who wished by arming to force a change in British policy were as anxious for negotiations as were those who thought that arming would only antagonize Britain further. Bethmann, the protagonist of the latter group, realized that his chances of persuading William to give up the Navy Bill depended on persuading the British to make political concessions and therefore told Metternich to start fresh soundings.[62]

These were the circumstances in which Cassel and Ballin made another attempt at mediation. Cassel began by suggesting to Churchill (apparently without any authority) that the Kaiser would be glad to see him in Berlin, but was told that it 'would not be wise for me at this juncture to parley with your august friend'.[63]

A memorandum was, however, drafted and approved 'by some influential members of the Cabinet' including Churchill, Lloyd George and Haldane, though it is not clear that Asquith or Grey knew of it: this Cassel took to Berlin at the end of January 1912.[64] He saw the Kaiser who regarded him as an official envoy and his document as the first sign of weakening resolution; he sent back a message in his own hand indicating that Grey or Churchill would be welcome if they cared to visit Berlin. Grey, however, thought that 'this would never do'[65] and the fact that he was involved in settling a coal strike provided a convenient reason for refusing. Accordingly it was agreed to send over Haldane for exploratory and confidential conversations rather than negotiations. On 7 February, the day before his arrival, William announced to the *Reichstag* the intention to bring in the Naval Bill, while two days later Churchill, disregarding the advice of Widenmann (who had been shown the text beforehand),[66] said in a speech that while a fleet was a necessity to Britain, to Germany it was 'from one point of view, more in the nature of a luxury'—no doubt without realizing that when translated into German the word 'luxury' acquires distinctly disreputable associations.

The most obvious result of the Haldane Mission was that each side thought the other had been trying to trick it into concessions; Bethmann got into trouble for being pro-English and Haldane for being pro-German. The talks, after a hopeful start, came to nothing, principally because the two parties started from different assumptions. Those Germans who did not regard the Mission merely as a British ruse to delay the introduction of the Naval Bill, took Cassel's memorandum as a sign that their previous policy was making Britain reconsider her position, and that before long she would be prepared to exchange a pledge of neutrality for a mere slowing down in the German programme. Those of the British who did not, like Fisher, deplore 'an English Cabinet Minister crawling up the back stairs of the German Foreign Office in carpet slippers'[67] took the Kaiser's invitation as a sign that Germany might at last be recognizing what a mutual waste of money was involved in an attempt to outbuild Britain. But the Germans were not in fact prepared to modify their original programme at all and only to make very limited concessions over their new one; the British were only prepared to promise neutrality in the event of Germany being attacked, and this, in view of what the Germans knew about their own strategic intentions, did not go far enough.

'Even if we for our part were to avoid "provocation" ', wrote the Kaiser, 'we would still be regarded as the "provokers". With experienced diplomats and a skilfully handled press, "provocation" can always be manufactured.'[68]

Each side felt that the other was asking too much and offering too little, thereby illustrating how differently each was assessing its relative physical strength.

In the last resort the Haldane Mission failed because British Ministers were not prepared to jeopardize the Ententes with France and Russia by giving Germany an unconditional promise of neutrality. William admitted that: 'We ask of Britain a reorientation of her whole policy.'[69] It can, of course, be argued that, since the Ententes were buoyed up by the unspoken hope of getting British support in war against Germany, a British withdrawal would have done much to keep the peace. If the object of those Ententes was to prevent war, they failed in their purpose. Could an alternative policy have produced worse results? Were not Grey and his immediate advisers taking up an unduly rigid attitude? But if the Ententes *had* broken down, France and Russia might have been expected to resume their practice of making difficulties for Britain wherever they could. British Ministers had to ask themselves whether, if that happened, they could automatically rely on German support or whether Germany would not take advantage of Britain's difficulties to demand a high price for that support. Moreover, the end of the Ententes would have vastly improved Germany's naval position and restored validity to the risk theory. Could she have been depended on to take no advantage of that fact? Neither the memory of conditions before 1904 nor experience since then could encourage an affirmative answer to these questions. The discrepancy of assessment which frustrated the Haldane Mission would at that time have made any fundamental negotiations between Britain and Germany still-born. What was required was not so much a reorientation of policy as of the appreciations on which policy is founded. When Metternich reported a conversation with Grey on the colonial question, William minuted:

'That is not the way in which the German Kaiser and his German people can and must expect to be approached by

England with a view to adopting a different political relationship and attitude. They dictate and we are to accept! There can be no question of this. *We must be approached and taken at our own worth* or things remain as they have been. In any case our shipbuilding programme must be pressed ahead. A very different tune has got to be played in London before I make any concessions.

'*In nuce* it is obvious that as long as Grey remains in office, a real political understanding is unobtainable. As long as the English Government does not feel any moral compulsion to come to terms with us, there is nothing to be done—except to arm.'[70]*

William had not always seen eye to eye with Tirpitz in the weeks preceding Haldane's arrival and at one stage in the talks had intervened to prevent them being halted by the Admiral's 'thickheadedness'. Haldane had the impression that the Kaiser genuinely wanted to reach an agreement (as indeed he did provided he could settle the terms). In the month following Haldane's departure, he found himself torn between the soldiers and the civilians. Tirpitz pressed for the Navy Bill to be published without further modification, and when in March Britain announced her intention of moving ships from the Mediterranean to strengthen the North Sea Fleet, William came down on his side. He not only told Bethmann to say that the transfer would be treated as an offensive act and answered by publication of the new Bill as well as by mobilization but sent direct instructions to the same effect. Bethmann, who was all the while making frantic efforts to extract some further political concession from Britain, took exception both to the message and to its method of communication. The British, while refusing to give him what he wanted, let it be known that they would regard his resignation with much regret. This touched William on a tender spot:

'I have never in my life heard of the conclusion of an agreement with one particular statesman without reference to the sovereign. . . . It is clear that Grey has no idea who really rules here and that *I* am the master. He dictates to me in advance who is to be my Minister if I conclude an agreement with England.'[71]

* Words in italics given as in original.

He also complained that Grey as a negotiator resembled Shylock. For some time it looked as though the Kaiser would have to part with either Bethmann or Tirpitz and many people urged him to replace the first by the second; he, however, remained determined to keep both his Bill and his Chancellor. The strain told on his nerves and prevented him from sleeping until finally Dona asked Bethmann to give in. How far her influence was decisive is uncertain, but William had his way, and went off to Rome and Corfu convinced that by his firmness he had saved the German people from dangerous concessions:

'Much valuable time, trouble, work and continual vexation have proved the result of Germany's ill-conceived diplomacy. I hope that my diplomats will draw from this the lesson that henceforward they should pay more attention to their rulers and to the orders and wishes of those rulers, particularly in questions concerning England. They don't understand how to handle these whereas I understand it well. Thank Heavens, nothing was dropped from the Bill; that could never have been put over to the German people. I saw through Haldane and his more prosaic colleagues in good time and put salt on their tails. I have preserved for the German people their right to count for something at sea and their freedom of decision in armament matters and shown the English that they bite on granite if they interfere with our arming and though I may perhaps have thereby made them hate us more, I have also won their respect which in due course will lead them to continue negotiations, let us hope in a more unassuming tone, to a favourable conclusion.'[72]

The failure of the talks put the last nail into Metternich's coffin as far as his master was concerned. One of the difficulties with which German Chancellors and envoys had to contend was the freedom enjoyed (despite Caprivi) by German military and naval attachés abroad of reporting direct to the Emperor through their chiefs in Berlin. Widenmann regarded it as his duty to warn his superiors about 'the danger from England' and sent back to Tirpitz regular reports which Kiderlen described as 'breathing hatred and mistrust'. His views frequently contradicted those of his Ambassador whom he described openly as 'a national misfortune'. At the time of the Haldane Mission he told Admiral

Jellicoe that Germany's aim was a 2 : 3 capital ship ratio with Britain. Bethmann complained to the Kaiser that such a statement was incorrect, unauthorized and likely to create false impressions. 'The unity of direction of German foreign policy must be most seriously jeopardized if Your Majesty's decisions are anticipated by the military agents assigned to foreign missions, without instructions from the agencies responsible for this policy.' He asked for authority to forbid such action in future. William refused. '[Widenmann] is an officer and can be disapproved only by the Supreme War Lord, not by his civilian superior. . . . I see in Widenmann's conversation absolutely no violation of his boundaries or his assigned functions.'[73] Tirpitz, of whom he was a favourite, considered that he was to be congratulated. Metternich was recalled and soon afterwards the attaché's tour of duty ended, but whereas the one came back to retirement, Widenmann was on his return invited to lunch at Potsdam where Dona told him that his excellent reports had been most helpful to her husband. At another lunch table several years later her husband was complaining of the situation in which Germany found herself. 'If only someone had told us beforehand that England would take up arms against us.' A voice was heard to murmur the name of Metternich, and the conversation had hastily to be changed.[74]

In the following year Churchill in private conversation with Widenmann's successor, Müller, suggested the possibility of a 'naval holiday'. Müller wrote asking Tirpitz whether this should be reported to the German Foreign Office. Tirpitz replied, through a subordinate, that 'in view of the universal desire for a permanent understanding with Britain', both Foreign Office and *Reichstag* might be receptive to the idea. Müller should therefore report the conversation as briefly as possible and state that the main impression made on him was Churchill's desire to delay or hinder the expansion of the German fleet for fear Britain could not maintain her superiority.[75] But when Müller in March 1914 sent reports which made William anxious to build still more ships, and even to send a battle squadron to the Pacific, Tirpitz began to draw back. The German bow was overstrung; any further increase in the German Navy would be 'a great political blunder'. And before fifteen more months had passed, Tirpitz was to be heard admitting that:

'The risk theory as so far presented, based exclusively on the battle fleet, has neither maintained peace nor as yet proved capable of bringing us victory in war. We shall never possess enough resources to challenge England's Two-Power Standard in big ships.'[76]

Apologists have argued that, misguided as Germany's naval policy may have been, it was not the cause of the war. Obviously it was not the reason why Austria attacked Serbia or Russia Austria. The naval rivalry did, however, ensure that when war broke out, Britain was on the side of Germany's enemies and that the struggle was in consequence extended from a European to a world-wide scale. The addition of British sea-power, not to mention the presence of Britain's 'contemptibly little' army at the Battle of the Marne and the later deployment of manpower and resources by the whole Commonwealth, may well have been the factor which decided the issue to Germany's disadvantage. What concessions would Germany have had to make in order to keep Britain out?

Once Germany had decided that an alliance with Britain was not to be had on acceptable terms, and assuming that the two countries could not simply ignore one another, there were four policies open to a Berlin government bent on winning a better 'place in the sun':

(1) They could try to outbuild Britain at sea. If one compares the figures for 1896 (Chapter VIII, p. 204) with those for 1912 (Chapter IX, p. 298), the extent to which the Germans had caught up is noteworthy. By 1912, however, it was clear to any hard-headed observer that Britain was determined at all costs to maintain a margin and that her relative economic resources were sufficient to make this possible. But two pardonable miscalculations encouraged German planners to take an unduly optimistic view of their chances in a naval war. One was that the British blockade would be instituted close to the German coast, thus giving frequent opportunities for isolated attacks on British ships (which were with some justification considered inferior in design).[77] It was, in fact, only a month before war broke out that the British Admiralty decided to substitute a distant blockade for a close one and so take advantage of what Fisher described as the peculiar fact

'that Providence has arranged England as a sort of huge break-water against German commerce which must all move either one side of the breakwater through the Straits of Dover or on the other side of the breakwater [round] the north of Scotland.'[78]

The second miscalculation was that the terms of the 1909 London Declaration regarding contraband would be observed and that Germany would remain able to import from overseas most food-stuffs and raw materials, if not directly, then through neutral countries like Holland. But though the British Government had sought to ratify the Declaration, an adverse vote in the House of Lords had prevented them from doing so, and Britain was there-fore free to make the blockade as tight as she could.

(2) They could try, as they did, to use the fleet as a bargaining weapon for securing a British Alliance on favourable terms. But such weapons are as likely to produce defiance as agreement.

(3) They could so manage their affairs as to reach alliance with other naval powers and thus restore reality to the 'Risk Theory'. But to conciliate France, Germany would have had to restore Alsace-Lorraine and to win Russia she would have had to abandon Austria; neither course was she prepared to consider. Italy was likely to side with France and Britain, and too much talk about a Yellow Peril was likely to deter Japan. Whether America could have been won is an interesting speculation.

(4) They could aim at knocking out their land enemies, France and Russia, by quick campaigns, and thus not only gain sources of supply immune to naval blockade but also a continent-wide base providing enough economic resources to outbuild the British fleet. This idea was popular at the beginning of the war and German military planning certainly assumed that victory would be quick. In 1911 William described it as 'ridiculous' to insinuate that Germany aimed at dominating Central Europe.

'We simply *are* Central Europe and it is quite natural that other and smaller nations tend towards us. To this the British object because it absolutely knocks to pieces their theory of the Balance of Power, i.e. their desire to play off one European Power against another at their own pleasure, and because it will lead to the establishment of a united Continent.'[79]

German historians then and since have argued that the so-called 'Balance of Power' was in fact the necessary condition of British domination, and that in transcending it Germany would be performing a service to all other countries since she would thereby increase their chances of genuine freedom.[80] But for fairly obvious reasons this argument never rallied many allies to Germany's cause and the experience of 1940–5 suggests that before Germany had had time to consolidate quick victories, she would have found a formidable coalition massed against her under British leadership. The gamble involved in this course was therefore as great as the prize at stake.*

All possible roads to world power involved uncertainties and none could have assured success. But instead of choosing one of the alternatives and sedulously pursuing it, Germany in practice oscillated between all four, thereby minimizing the chances of any succeeding. For in spite of a belief widely current in Britain, emotion played too large a part in the determination of German policy and rational calculation too small a one. The system of government allowed too many different individuals an intermittent say in deciding the course and turned it into a zig-zag. Ideas about Germany's rights were far too rigid. The atmosphere made a realistic appraisal of her position so difficult of achievement that it is not surprising if she precipitated a war which she stood little chance of winning. The only sure way for Germany to have avoided trouble would have been to remain content, as Bismarck had done, with her European position. But given the mood of those days, such passiveness would have been unthinkable. As the London correspondent of a German paper wrote in 1912: 'The English are accustomed to taking the lead in world affairs, while ever increasing numbers of Germans are becoming reluctant to go on playing second fiddle.'[81] Erzberger said in 1914:

'We cannot accept an understanding with England at the price of our sea armaments. National reasons preclude such an understanding. . . . A voluntary renunciation of the building of a navy according to our own judgement would be the end of Germany's policy of world power.'[82]

The conclusion may be that German aspirations were out of line with German capacities. But to suppose them reined in is to

---

* Some writers have suggested that Britain should have remained neutral in 1914 and intervened as arbiter after the first clashes. This, however, seems to assume that the clashes were bound to be indecisive.

suppose a different social order in Germany and therefore a different course for earlier German history.

*   *   *

In 1910, Bethmann endeavoured to carry out the promise which William had made two years earlier of giving the Prussian suffrage 'an organic development'. The relatively minor changes proposed were accepted by the Lower House which since the 1908 elections included seven Socialists and which would probably have supported an even more radical change. But the Upper House insisted on inserting reactionary amendments unacceptable to the Lower, and the only way to get the original proposals through would have been a creation of peers. Any such solution came to grief on the view that drastic measures might let loose uncontrollable forces and were therefore out of the question. Ministers were almost as convinced as the Kaiser that the three-tier suffrage was an essential bulwark against the conversion of the Empire into a parliamentary democracy, and that nothing which might endanger it was worth risking. The most that could be looked for was tinkering by agreement and, as soon as it became clear that such agreement was not forthcoming, the attempts to tinker were tacitly abandoned.

After the Bülow Block broke down, Bethmann set out 'to rule above the parties' which meant in practice getting a majority where he could find one. But a number of trends were combining to put his continued ability to do this in question. Among the Social Democrats a difference of view emerged with growing clarity between the revolutionary left which, under Karl Liebknecht and Rosa Luxemburg, pressed for a more active struggle against militarism and the revisionist right which, under Bebel, Scheidemann and Noske, argued that the road to power lay in persuading the lower middle classes that the party was neither revolutionary nor unpatriotic. Revisionism gained ground as living-standards improved; the better-paid workers became less and less interested in revolution (assuming that they had possessed a real revolutionary spirit to begin with). Moreover, the steady stream of social legislation, which had by now been flowing for thirty years, was beginning to have its delayed effect and make the proletariat feel that they had some stake in existing society. The Socialists also realized that to be effective they must become organized; when Ebert became party secretary in 1906, he found that the office was without telephones, typewriters or files.[83] But organization, though the key to democratic success, was also 'the spring from which conservative waters flow into the democratic stream'.[84] The party leaders, by becoming paid functionaries, tended to move into the lower middle class and thus compromise with the *status quo*. All these developments meant that the Socialists were ceasing to be political outcasts. A coalition between them and some of the bourgeois parties was becoming a practical possibility. Once it happened the ability of Ministers to get their way in the *Reichstag* must be expected to disappear and the whole constitution of the *Reich* to be called in question.

A natural link with the Liberals was provided for the Social Democrats by the Progressive Peoples Party founded in 1910 to reunite the three splinters into which the Progressives had split in the 90's. Indeed, as long as Liberals and Socialists remained seriously at variance, the new party's own cohesion was in jeopardy. But although a coalition between Liberals, Progressives and Socialists took over the government in Baden, it failed to materialize at the centre. The obstacle was not primarily the question of defence, on which Socialist views were by no means immutable. As early as 1907 Noske had said that 'it is our damned duty and responsibility to see that other nations do not push Germany around.'[85] The real difficulty was that though the Liberals were opposed to the farming interests (which divided them from the Conservatives) and stood for freedom of conscience (which divided them from the Centre), they were essentially the party of industry and, as such, hesitant about social reform. In particular, they were opposed to putting the workers on a footing of complete equality with employers as regards such matters as combinations, strikes and wage bargaining. But the grant of such equality was an essential plank in the Socialist platform. In the end therefore the alternative coalition was formed not with the Liberals but from that combination of Progressives, Centre and Socialists which as early as 1895 had prevented Bismarck from being officially congratulated on his 80th birthday. The fact that there were two alternatives looming up rather than one made the Government's life no easier. But any such coalition would have to be revisionist (since the bourgeois parties were not prepared to use violence). Yet without violence could the Conservatives ever be induced to surrender their position? And without middle-class support, would the workers ever be strong enough to revolt successfully?

The elections held in January 1912, just before Haldane's visit, seemed to bring the long-expected situation. The Socialists increased their seats from 43 to 110 to become the strongest party in the *Reichstag*; with the Liberals and Progressives, they could command 197 votes out of 391, with the Centre and Progressives 243. But during the election campaign, the willingness of the Progressives to work with the Socialists had proved limited, and when the *Reichstag* met to elect its officers, the Liberals voted in defiance of the conventions and so deprived Scheidemann of the position of President which by custom belonged to the nominee of the leading party.[86] In March 1912 the Liberals eliminated two left-wing leaders from their executive committee, broke up the youth organization, brought their members in the various state parliaments under firmer control and pledged themselves to a policy of 'positive collaboration with all bourgeois parties'. For the time being the Government remained able to get a majority for its measures. But reactionary legislation stood less chance than ever.

Legislation was, however, virtually confined to increases in the army and navy and to finance. The rising costs of defence, the unwillingness of the Socialists to increase indirect taxation, the unwillingness of the states to increase their contributions to the Empire, and the unwillingness of the right wing to increase taxes on property all combined to complicate Germany's financial problems. In 1912 the situation was saved by an expedient and in 1913 a capital gains tax on property was pushed through against opposition from the right and the states after all other proposals had broken down. Needless to say, the Socialists voted for it and even discussed taxing the princely houses, a suggestion which led the Kaiser to tell Bethmann in a telegram that 'German Parliamentarians and Politicians are steadily becoming utter cads'. Social legislation had come to a virtual stop; in January 1914 the Minister of the Interior openly admitted that the Government regarded it as a more or less closed chapter and said that employers must be allowed 'elbow room' to meet foreign competition.[87] In 1912 a violent strike broke out in the Ruhr mines, followed in 1913 by another in the Hamburg shipyards. In both the employers took strong action and for lack of working-class solidarity, both movements collapsed.[88]

At the end of 1913 great excitement was caused by a clash between soldiers and civilians at Zabern, in Alsace, where an officer was protected by his Colonel for egging on his men to beat up the townsfolk; civilians who demonstrated their disapproval were seized by soldiers and imprisoned in barracks. The Governor-General sympathized with the public, but found himself powerless to control the military. Both were directly responsible to the Kaiser, who took the soldiers' side and refused to give the Governor-General an audience. A threat of resignation by the latter and his chief officials was needed before William agreed to take action, and then he did little more than send the troops on manœuvres. The Alsatians were given the clear impression that the civil authorities were powerless to protect them against the army. The Chancellor had no authority in the matter and when it came up for debate in the *Reichstag*, gave a somewhat lame defence of the army's action; had he revealed the true state of affairs, he would certainly have been dismissed. The deputies, stung by an arrogant speech by von Falkenhayn, the Minister of War, passed by 293 votes to 54 a resolution that 'the handling of the incident by the Chancellor does not conform to the views of the *Reichstag*'. The attack on military high-handedness was led by a Centre deputy, and the Conservatives were isolated. But the vote had no result. The Government continued as before; the offending Colonel was acquitted by a court-martial.[89] Scheidemann proposed that, until the Government paid attention, the *Reichstag* should reject all appropriation bills. Erzberger, for the Centre, refused to listen to the idea, in view of Germany's external circumstances.[90]

The Zabern incident was the occasion of the Crown Prince's most notorious intrusion into politics, for he sent a telegram complaining of the 'shamelessness' of the local population, and expressing the hope that an example would be made 'to take the edge off their appetite for such activities'. A Berlin cartoonist pictured William asking, 'I'd like to know where the boy picked up that damned habit of telegraphing.' But in fact the Kaiser took his son to task, both then and on other occasions, in a way which showed that experience had not been altogether without effect.

'*Coups d'état* may have their place in the art of governing South American republics but in Germany I am thankful to say that they are neither customary nor desirable. People who take it upon themselves to talk in favour of such things are dangerous, more dangerous for the Monarchy and its survival than the wildest Social Democrats.'

'Don't always believe and accept as true everything you see in print. It is always easier to criticize than to improve. If you take my advice, you will in future be a little critical of the grumblers and critics, and always remember that the people in charge have to look at things from a rather broader standpoint than the heroes of the daily press.'[91]

The atmosphere in Imperial Germany during the years before the war cannot have been pleasant. The country was being run by an exclusive minority whose strength was waning and whose outlook was becoming increasingly repugnant to the general public. More and more people wanted change, change which the élite realized to be inevitable but were determined to resist as long as they could. On every side there was tension and disapproval. Yet the opposition shrank from drastic action, for much the same reasons as those advanced by the ruling minority for refusing to give way. The cement holding the society together was devotion to the cause of German national greatness, the product of the fervour with which during the nineteenth century the intellectual leaders had preached the national gospel. The German people might disapprove of their government but they remained faithful to their country. When they saw Germany surrounded by enemies, they hesitated to follow the example of the French in the Dreyfus case and give internal liberty priority over national security. The most reprehensible aspect of the Conservative attitude was that it took advantage of this patriotism and instead of recompensing devotion with trust, exploited it for sectional ends. But the historian has also to ask whether the sacrifice of liberal to national values was in the end justified, even in the interests of the German nation. The opposition failed to make any effective challenge to the pretence, the ostentation, the exaltation of force, the disregard for individual rights, the insensitiveness to the reactions of other people. These were precisely the qualities which caused Germany's downfall, by producing an overestimate of German strength, a disregard of the influence which could be exerted by world opinion and a false anticipation of the way other people would behave. That ambitions were out of line with capacities was, as has been said already, a natural result of the culture which had grown up. That culture was the end-product of the actions taken and views held by countless Germans in the past, and this is the reason why no people can escape responsibility for what happens to them. But perhaps the heaviest responsibility rests with the intellectuals, for forgetting Goethe's teaching that the real test of greatness lies in ability to maintain a sense of proportion.

The results of these various mistakes were to be even more obvious after the war than during it.

*   *   *   *   *

In the autumn of 1912 there were clear signs of trouble impending in the Balkans which might come to involve Austria-Hungary or Russia. A strong group in Austria was, as usual, pressing to settle the score with Serbia. Kiderlen could remember the early days of the Austro-German Alliance. Before his death at Christmas, he urged Bethmann to make clear in Vienna that Germany was only pledged to help against a direct attack by Russia and that if Austria chose to plunge without notice into Balkan 'adventures', Germany would stand aloof. This attitude disregarded the Austrian view that the so-called 'adventures' were in fact steps without which the Habsburg Empire might find itself in liquidation. Moreover, as Kiderlen himself made clear in the *Reichstag*, the exact way in which a war between Austria and Russia might arise was irrelevant to Germany's inability to remain a spectator while her only ally was being beaten. All the same Kiderlen's approach was sound, and it led him to suggest to the Entente that the Great Powers should take common action to localize any trouble. The Kaiser, for rather different reasons, sympathized with this view.

'The action of the Balkan states is described as an attempt to extort something from Turkey. Why? From the Austrian point of view was not the action taken by the young Frederick against Maria Theresa before the first Silesian War just the same thing? The Balkan states want and are compelled to extend their territory. They can satisfy their wants only at the expense of Turkey—probably a declining Power. They cannot do this without fighting and they are doing it together in order to make possible their own growth and extension. The Great Powers want to stop them. With what right? In whose interest? I will keep out of it. Just as we did not in '64, '66 or '70 allow any interference with our legitimate developments, so I have little ability and desire to hinder others or lecture them. . . . Let them get on with their war undisturbed. Then the Balkan states will show what they can do, and whether they can justify their existence. If they smash the Turks, then they will have right on their side and are entitled to some reward. If they are beaten, they will sing small: we shall have peace and quiet for a long time and the question of territorial changes will vanish. The Great Powers must keep the ring round the battlefield in which this fight will be conducted and to which it must be confined: we ourselves should keep cool and avoid overhasty action. Along with that and above all we must refrain from gratuitous lectures about the sacred importance of peace, since they will only have unpleasant consequences. Leave the people alone: they will either get a thrashing or give one and that will be the moment to start talking. The Eastern Question must be settled by blood and iron. But at a time favourable to us! That is now!'[92]

William blamed Turkey for not making concessions in good time and thought that the days of Turkish rule in Europe were over. His former sympathies had been largely effaced by his newly found interest in Greece, and in his consequent enthusiasm for the victories of Serbia, Bulgaria and Greece he turned a blind eye to the damage done to the military prestige of his own army by the defeat of the German-trained Turks. When the other Great Powers, at Turkish request, tried to get discussions going about peace terms, he refused to be a party to any action which impeded the Balkan states 'in their deservedly victorious course or proposed or imposed conditions unwelcome to them'. 'I am out to see *fair play: free fight and no favour*.'* He felt little enthusiasm over backing his Allies, and at one stage declared that he would only do so if the Russian attack was unprovoked.[93]

'Of course many of the changes which the war has brought about in the Balkans are inconvenient and unwelcome to Vienna but none of them so decisive as to justify us in exposing ourselves to the danger of any warlike development on their

* Words in italics in English in original.

account. I could never accept responsibility for that either before my people or before my own conscience.'[94]

'Russia seems anxious to support Serb aspirations and could in consequence get into a situation with Austria which made war inevitable. That would bring about the *casus foederis* for Germany—since Vienna would be attacked by Petersburg—according to the Treaty. This entails mobilization and war on two fronts for Germany, i.e. in order to march against Moscow, Paris must first be taken. Paris would undoubtedly be supported by London. That would mean Germany having to fight for her existence against three Great Powers with everything at stake and possibly in the end succumb. All of which would be the result of Austrian unwillingness to have the Serbs in Albania or Durazzo.'

'The obligations of the Triple Alliance Treaty apply if Austria is attacked by Russia but not if Austria has provoked Russia to attack her.'[95]

In the end the Russians persuaded the Serbs to make no demands affecting interests regarded by Austria as vital, and Germany exerted a moderating influence in Vienna. The result was that the Balkan Wars passed by without producing a general conflagration, although Russia, France and Austria all mobilized in November 1912. The Archduke Franz Ferdinand played no small part in preventing matters from going further, and in February 1913 when the crisis was over, William wrote to him as follows:

'Your kind letter has caused me immense pleasure. This is an occasion of which one can say "*Les beaux esprits se rencontrent*". Bravo, my friend! You have handled the matter and carried it through brilliantly. That hasn't been easy and getting your way has taken care, patience and endurance. But now comes the success which will compensate you for all outstanding debts. You have performed an immortal service since you have released Europe from the spell under which it lay. Millions of thankful hearts will remember you in their prayers. I think Tsar Nicholas will be glad too that he can demobilize his reserves. When that happens, we shall all breathe again.'[96]

Yet more and more people in Europe were coming to feel that rather than accept another compromise, they would prefer at the next crisis to stand and fight for their principles. Men were starting to consider not whether there was going to be a war but at what moment its outbreak would give them the greatest possible advantage. To make such a calculation is the business of soldiers and sailors and the fact that they do it is no proof that their country is contemplating aggression. As far back as July 1909 the German *Military Review* had written:

> 'If we do not decide for war, that war in which we shall have to engage at the latest in two or three years will be begun in far less propitious circumstances. At this moment the initiative rests with us: Russia is not ready, moral factors and right are on our side, as well as might. Since we have to accept the conflict some day, let us provoke it at once. Our prestige, our position as a Great Power, our honour are in question and yet more, for it would seem that our very existence is threatened.'[97]

Much attention was attracted in 1911 and 1912 by General von Bernhardi's book, *Germany and the Next War*, of which innumerable editions were sold. His main themes were the need to eliminate France, the foundation of a Central European Federation under German leadership and the need to become a world power through the acquisition of new colonies: Germany's choice was summed up as 'World Power or Decline'. Among those influenced by the book was Ludendorff but it did not represent the thinking of the General Staff, from which Bernhardi had been discharged by Schlieffen.

Military preparations were pressed ahead on all sides. In the first decade of the century the German Army had to its great indignation become something of a stepchild by comparison with the fleet, whose very guns exceeded in number and calibre those available to the soldiers. This was largely because only 52% of the available recruits were called to do military service (compared with 82% in France). Ludendorff on becoming head of the mobilization section of the War Office in 1911 discovered that there were not enough troops available to carry out fully the Schlieffen Plan.[98] Accordingly in both 1912 and 1913 increases were made in the Army's size* In 1913, France

---

* The 1913 increase involved extra expenditure both of a capital and a current nature. To meet the capital cost the special defence levy (p. 332 above) was imposed. This owed its form to the peculiar character of German finances; it did not necessarily imply, as some writers have made out, an intention to start a war before its course had expired.[99]

reverted from two to three years' military service. In February of that year the Poincaré Government balanced Isvolsky's appointment as Russian Ambassador in Paris by sending Delcassé to St. Petersburg with the explicit mission of securing an increase in the size and efficiency of the Russian forces; plans to this end were agreed in June. The fact that the French and Russian increases would need some time to take effect was no more lost on the Central Powers than the Entente failed to notice that the enlargement of the Kiel Canal would be complete in the summer of 1914.

About the beginning of 1913, the year of his Silver Jubilee, the feeling that a conflict was inevitable gained a grip on the Kaiser. In December 1912 he had spoken of the approaching war as 'the fight to the finish between the Slavs and Germans' which would find the Anglo-Saxons on the side of the Slavs and Gauls. He called for action to explain to the public the issues which would be at stake in a war started by an Austro-Serb conflict in the Balkans, so as to prevent such a war from taking them by surprise.[100] Bethmann said that: 'From the beginning of 1913 [the Kaiser] spoke to me of the coalition which was forming against us and would fall on us.'[101] In April and May he repeated his gloomy forecast of what might follow Austrian and Russian intransigence in the Balkans. In May he minuted a despatch from St. Petersburg: 'The fight between Slavs and Germans is no longer avoidable. It is bound to come. When? We shall soon see.'[102] In June an old English friend reported him as 'speaking with a note which was new—I felt he was under the influence of a great fear.'[103] He was undoubtedly affected by the widespread gossip that he had damaged German chances by losing his nerve and failing to stand firm in 1905 and 1911; an American politician at German manœuvres in 1912 heard senior officers announce their intention of seeing that this did not happen again.[104] Nobody likes to be called a coward, least of all a Supreme War Lord. When Sir John French came to German manœuvres in 1913, William said to him: 'You have seen how long my sword is: you may find it is just as sharp.'[105] In November Jules Cambon wrote:

'The Kaiser has ceased to be the friend of peace. His personal influence has been exerted on many crucial occasions but he has come to think that war with France is inevitable. As he advances in years, the reactionary tendencies of the court, and especially the impatience of the soldiers, obtain a greater hold over his mind. Perhaps he feels some slight jealousy of the popularity of his son who flatters the passions of the Pan-Germans.'[106]

In February 1914 William told the King of the Belgians that war between Germany and France was near at hand.[107]

This growing feeling of inevitability was probably responsible for a relaxation in his resolve to hold back Austria. When he visited Vienna in the autumn, William said to Conrad von Höt-zendorf: 'I go with you. The other Powers are not ready and will not attempt any counter-action.' (Conrad on the other hand, in the following spring, suggested to von Tschirschky, now German Ambassador in Vienna, an early war with Russia. Tschirschky replied that two important people were against it—the Kaiser and Archduke Franz Ferdinand.) To Berchtold, the Austrian Foreign Minister, William said that he would regard what the Austrian Foreign Office did as an order. 'You may rest assured that I stand behind you and am ready to draw the sword whenever the lead you take makes it necessary.'[108] In May 1914, Moltke, who had previously held that the time for the inevitable war had not yet arrived, expatiated to Conrad on the growing military power of Russia. 'Every delay means a lessening of our chances.'[109] About the same time a German paper which often drew on official sources published a statement that Russia was preparing for war with Germany in 1917. The Ambassador in St. Petersburg made some sarcastic remarks about the writer's ability to foresee the future. William minuted: 'This faculty exists. Often among sovereigns, seldom amongst statesmen, almost never among diplomats. As a soldier, I have no doubt on the basis of the information reaching me that Russia is systematically preparing for war against us and I frame my policy on that assumption.'[110]

In 1913 the Russians had attempted to pick a quarrel over the appointment of a German General not only as Instructor to the Turkish Army but as Commander of the Corps in the Constantinople area. William in the end disposed of the matter by promoting the General so that he could no longer be a corps commander, but at one stage minuted: 'Our reputation in the world is at stake, so heads high and hands on swords.'[111] In

February 1914 a conference is said to have been held in St. Petersburg at which Sazonov said that 'it would be a mistake to assume that Russia could undertake operations against the Bosphorus without causing a general European war.' The meeting then went on with the Tsar's approval to discuss plans for seizing the Straits 'in the near future'.[112] In June 1914 a Russian newspaper said that: 'Russia and France have no desire for a war but Russia is ready for one and France must be too.' This caused the Kaiser to comment, 'Now the Russians have put the cards on the table. Anyone in Germany who does not believe that the Russo-Gauls are working at high pressure for war with us at an early date deserves to be sent to an asylum.'[113] When the American, Colonel House, visited Berlin on a peace mission in 1914, he reported that: 'The whole of Germany is charged with electricity. Everybody's nerves are tense. It only needs a spark to set the thing off.'[114]

A situation such as this was one on which little influence could be exerted by steady work in London to remove the causes of Anglo-German tension other than the fleet. In the course of 1912 to '14, however, agreements were reached on both the Baghdad Railway and the Portuguese colonies. They were most unwelcome to the Naval Attaché and to the German Admiralty who regarded them as an insidious device invented by the diplomats to neutralize the effects of the Navy League and the Pan-Germans on public opinion at home and spread the idea that the best way of achieving results with England was to make concessions![115] William lent himself somewhat to this line of thought. He minuted:

'No! We have enough colonies! If I want to get any more, I will buy them or take them without England's help.'

'The idea is to dazzle us with the idea of a "Colonial Empire" in Africa, to be acquired along with the attendant complications at the expense of other people, and so to distract our attention from world politics, i.e. they want to settle the great Asiatic question with Japan and America but without us, who are to play no part. But if Asia is partitioned, lasting damage will be done to our exports, our industrial production and our trade, and we will have to force our way in with battleships and hand-grenades. My entire naval policy and my military concentration in Europe has been based upon the need for us to share in solving the Asiatic Question.'[116]

All the same, the efforts which the British Government made to be sympathetic and reasonable may have provided some slender foundation for those in Germany who wished to think that perhaps after all when the crunch came the British might stand aloof. Such hopes are likely to have received at least equal encouragement from the difficulties over Ulster.

Among all the gathering clouds there was one moment of relief. In June 1913 the Kaiser's only and much-loved daughter was married to the Duke of Cumberland's son whom William created Duke of Brunswick; the union buried the last of the dynastic hatchets forged by Prussia's acquisition of Hanover in 1866. After the young couple had met by chance and fallen in love, long family negotiations were necessary before they could become formally engaged. The success of these was largely due to the bridegroom's brother-in-law, Prince Max of Baden. Much of Europe's 'Beauty and Chivalry' came to Berlin for the wedding, including the Tsar and King George, who met William and one another for the last time. It was not quite a hundred years since a Duke of Brunswick had sat 'within a window'd niche' in Brussels to watch Youth and Pleasure 'chase the glowing hours with flying feet' at the Duchess of Richmond's ball on the eve of Waterloo.[117]

*   *   *

On Sunday, 28 June 1914, William was racing at Kiel in his yacht *Meteor* when the telegram announcing the Archduke's assassination at Sarajevo arrived. Admiral Müller, the Chief of the Naval Secretariat, put to sea in a launch and overhauled the *Meteor* sailing on a northerly course with a faint breeze. The Kaiser was standing with his guests in the stern and watched the launch with anxiety. The Admiral called out that he bore bad news and would throw the written message across. But William insisted on being given it at once by word of mouth; he took it calmly, merely asking whether to cancel the race.[118]

The offence once taken by Franz Ferdinand at William's boisterous sense of humour (see Chapter VI) had long ago been forgotten. The sympathy which the Kaiser displayed over the Archduke's morganatic marriage may have owed something to calculation, but its exercise did some credit all the same to so devout an upholder of King-hedging divinity. Only a month before, Franz Ferdinand had been showing off to William the rose-gardens of his Bohemian castle and discussing, in the light of his doubts as to what could be achieved by war with Serbia, whether a way could be found of satisfying Southern Slav ambitions within the Habsburg monarchy. So it was as a personal shock as well as an affront to monarchy that the news intruded on the Regatta.

The Kaiser's first impulse was to go to the funeral. But the German Consul at Sarajevo reported a Serb plot to assassinate him too if he appeared and Bethmann accordingly persuaded him to stay in Berlin. He therefore took no part in the petty revenge which the Austrian court took on the couple who had defied its starched conventions. The furtiveness with which their bodies were hustled off the stage was such as to create a suspicion that the Consul's story may have been an Austrian 'plant' designed to keep William from coming where he was not wanted. An important by-product was the removal of a chance for the European monarchs to meet and discuss the situation in personal terms. The Austro-Hungarian Government was left undisturbed in its task of reconciling divergent views about the vigour with which it should react. When von Tschirschky reported that he had counselled caution, William minuted: 'Who authorized him to do so? It is idiotic. . . . He should kindly stop such nonsense. The Serbs should be wiped out, and quickly at that! It is now or never.'[119]

Even those Austrians who were keenest to attack Serbia had little idea as to what they could gain by war. Conrad von Hötzendorf regarded the prospects of victory as small but felt that so old a kingdom and so famous an army could not be allowed to disappear without putting up a fight for themselves.[120] The Vienna Government, therefore, decided to make its own course depend on the backing it could get from its German ally. A special messenger was sent to Berlin on 4 July and the moment he arrived, his Ambassador, Szögyényi, nicknamed by William 'the gypsy', was summoned to lunch at Potsdam and to deliver the letters thus brought. One was a despatch which had been on the stocks before the murder, discussing, with more emphasis on problems than on solutions, the policy which should be adopted henceforward in the Balkans. The only mention of a show-down with Serbia came in a postscript which asserted that the impossibility of bridging over differences had been demonstrated. 'The monarchy must therefore firmly tear away the threads which its opponent is seeking to weave into a net over its head.' Along with this came a personal letter from Franz Joseph describing the assassination as the direct result of Serb and Russian Panslavism whose only object was the weakening of the Triple Alliance and the disintegration of the Habsburg monarchy.

'The investigations so far made indicate that the Sarajevo murder was not just the work of an individual but the result of a well-organized plot of which the strings extend to Belgrade. Even though it will probably be impossible to establish the complicity of the Serb Government, there can be no doubt that its policy of uniting all the Southern Slavs under the Serb flag encourages crimes of this kind, and the continuation of this situation constitutes a permanent danger for my dynasty and my lands.'[121]

This was a remarkably accurate assessment of the situation considering how little of the supporting evidence could have been available at the time it was made.* The Emperor's letter ended:

'To contain the Slav advance and assure peace to our laurels will only be possible if Serbia, which at present constitutes the focus of Pan-Slav policy, is eliminated as a political factor in the Balkans. After the recent tragedy in Bosnia, you too will have been convinced that there is no longer any hope of smoothing over the differences which separate us from Serbia and that the policy of peace which all European monarchs have pursued will be jeopardized as long as this gang of criminal agitators in Belgrade remains unpunished.'

The form of punishment was left vague; at the time the letter was written, the scheme finding most favour was invasion without notice.

After carefully reading both documents, the Kaiser told the Ambassador that he expected Austria-Hungary to recommend serious measures against Serbia but that, as he saw the possibility

* The chief instigator of the assassination was almost certainly the Serb Director of Military Intelligence, in his private capacity as head of the secret society 'The Black Hand'. The Russian Military Attaché at Belgrade equally certainly was in the secret. So was the Serb Prime Minister, Pasič who, although frightened of what war would mean for Serbia, was even more frightened of the 'Black Hand'. Pasič did send a warning to Vienna but by the time it had passed through several intermediaries, it became so muffled as to be disregarded.[122]

of grave European complications in what was proposed, he must consult the Chancellor before replying. But while they waited for Bethmann to arrive, Szögyényi maintained a tactful probing in the course of which William assured him that Franz Joseph could count on close German support. The Kaiser agreed that it would be a mistake to defer action against Serbia. Russia's attitude was bound to be hostile but that had long been foreseen and even if it did come to war between Russia and Austria-Hungary, Germany would stand by her ally. But Russia was not ready for war and would hesitate to plunge into it. William said he could well understand that Franz Joseph, with his well-known love of peace, would find it painful to invade Serbia but if the Austro-Hungarian Government decided that this was really necessary, the moment was favourable and should not be let slip. William was fond of urging other countries to strike while the iron was hot; at last he was to be taken at his word.

In due course Bethmann arrived and unhesitatingly endorsed his master's line. William said that, while there could be no doubt as to the gravity of the Pan-Slav challenge to the Monarchy, Austria must be left to make her own decisions since everything possible should be done to prevent the Austro-Serb controversy from developing into an international conflict! Franz Joseph must be assured, however, of German support in so grave an hour. Bethmann himself spoke in the same sense to the Ambassador next day, emphasizing in particular that the Kaiser could take no position in the questions between Serbia and Austria because they lay outside his competence.

Von Moltke was at Karlsbad trying to alleviate the kidney disease of which he was to die within two years; he had for some time been saying that such a good conjuncture for war was unlikely to recur.[123]* Tirpitz was on holiday in the Engadine. William, therefore, gave their deputies a brief summary of what had passed. The general view of the soldiers was that the sooner Austria moved against Serbia, the better: Russia was unlikely to intervene. To the sailor, William said that the Tsar was unlikely to protect regicides while Russia was militarily and financially incapable of

* By contrast President Poincaré, when asked on 29 July whether war could be avoided, is reported to have replied: 'It would be a great pity. We should never again find conditions better.' The anecdote, if true, illustrates the principle that wars usually break out when the two sides hold varying estimates of their respective chances.[124]

fighting. The French were also in a financial crisis and lacked heavy artillery so that they might be expected to restrain Russia. No military measures were taken as a result of these talks; so far as the army was concerned, there was nothing left to be done but mobilize and the plans for this had in 1914 as in previous years been thoroughly overhauled during the spring. Immediately afterwards, William left for his Norwegian cruise; he had suggested postponing it but Bethmann argued that to do so would cause unnecessary alarm. The Foreign Office later told the Bavarian Minister in Berlin that they proposed to use the absence of the Kaiser and von Moltke as evidence of the way in which Austria's action, then expected to occur within a few days, had taken them as much by surprise as everyone else.[125]

Allied propaganda later made much of a Crown Council having been held in Potsdam on 5 July at which the plans for war were decided. The allegation could scarcely be more misconceived; the real criticism of the German Government on that fateful day was that no full-dress discussion of the pros and cons of encouraging Austria ever occurred at all! On the other hand there can be little doubt that, had such a discussion taken place, the upshot would have been exactly the same; Germany's attitude had been decided by the experience of the preceding years. It has been plausibly argued that Germany should at least have insisted on being consulted about what Austria intended to do, instead of almost ostentatiously renouncing a say in the decision. But, in fact, for the rest of the month the drive for action seems to have come at least as much from Berlin as from Vienna. Bethmann, von Moltke and their immediate associates would appear to have made up their minds that, unless Austria-Hungary took resolute action against the Southern Slavs, Germany's chief ally might well become more of a liability than an asset. Austrians and Magyars must be stopped from looking before they leapt in case they thereby let slip the best opportunity for a show-down which was likely to present itself. The German leaders were by no means unaware of the danger that the war might spread, but considered it less likely to do so in 1914 than later, and less likely to do so when Austria was punishing a shocking crime than under any other circumstances.

How far the Kaiser shared in the calculations of his subordinates is not wholly clear. There can be little doubt that he had a shrewd idea of what was in the wind and as usual, acted up to the role

expected of him. There are on the other hand signs of nervousness
lest he should draw back at the last minute; certain despatches,
including most of those from London, were not sent to him, and
the encouragement given to his cruise may partly have been
prompted by a desire to have him out of the way. Certainly the
exclusive company of his court entourage kept him on the boil. A
despatch from Vienna made clear that the Austrians would insist
on establishing in Belgrade their own machinery for controlling
Southern Slav agitation and would leave very little time for their
ultimatum to be answered. On the margin William wrote impatient
comments about the time which the Austrians were taking to
make up their minds, and quoted Frederick the Great:

> 'I am averse to councils and deliberations in which the more
> timorous party is wont to gain the upper hand.'[126]

On the report that the Austrians were wondering how to ensure
that their demands were refused, he suggested asking for a vital
piece of territory. He poured scorn on Tisza, the Hungarian
Prime Minister, for trying to exercise restraint, and on learning
that the attempt had been abandoned (largely as a result of
German pressure) remarked: 'Now he is a man again.'[127] The
news that the Austrian note was to be held back until the French
President and Prime Minister ended their State visit to St. Petersburg was greeted with the comment: 'What a pity!' When Sir
Edward Grey expressed confidence that Germany would give no
support to demands intended to precipitate war, William called it
a gross piece of British impertinence and demanded that Grey be
spoken to firmly and shown that the German Emperor was not to
be trifled with.

> 'The Serbs are a gang of criminals and should be treated as
> such. I will not interfere in matters which are the [Austrian]
> Emperor's business and his alone. This is the typical British
> attitude of condescending authority and I want my repudiation
> of it put on record.'[128]

To a further British suggestion of mediation, he replied: 'One does
not confer with others on a vital question of honour.' On 19 July
he had a confidential warning given to the two big German
shipping companies that, once the Austrian ultimatum was
delivered, events might move fast, and on the following day
started to bring the fleet back to Kiel. When Bethmann objected

on the ground that the English might thereby be alarmed, he
received short shrift.

*   *   *

The Austrian note to Serbia was delivered at 6 p.m. on 23 July
and an answer demanded within forty-eight hours. William learnt
of the text through ordinary news channels and decided it was
time to hurry home.[129] When Bethmann objected on the ground
that this might lead to demonstrations, the Kaiser remarked:
'Things get madder every minute! Now the man writes that I
must not show myself to my own subjects.'[130] He reached Potsdam
about midday on 27 July and that afternoon held a Council at
which he approved the Chancellor's action in rejecting the British
proposal for a conference without waiting for his own return. But
something must have been agreed about the need for care in
handling Britain because when Bethmann that evening reported
having transmitted to Vienna at Grey's request a plea for moderation, he represented himself as having acted in accordance with
William's instructions. He did not mention that he had accompanied the English plea with a message calculated to prevent any
attention being paid to it.

Early next morning William read the text of the Serb reply
which the Foreign Office had obtained some twenty hours previously from the Serbs themselves.[131] His immediate reaction was:

> 'A brilliant achievement at forty-eight hours notice. More
> than anyone could have expected. A great moral victory for
> Vienna but it removes any reason for war. . . . I would never
> have ordered mobilization on such a pretext as this.'[132]

He suggested that the Austrian forces should agree to halt once
they had captured Belgrade (a concession all the easier for them to
make since Conrad declared that he would not be ready to cross
the frontier at all for another seventeen days!). This would provide
a breathing-space in which William could mediate; Bethmann was
instructed to put the suggestion to Vienna but took the whole day
over doing so. By the time he did, Austria, in response to earlier
pressure from Germany, had burnt some additional boats by
declaring war on Serbia. But at a Council held the following
afternoon (29 July), the situation still seemed encouraging.
Austria was considering the 'Halt in Belgrade'; William and

the Tsar were exchanging telegrams about mediation and a conversation between Prince Henry and King George was misinterpreted to mean that Britain would stay neutral.

Austria, however, followed up her declaration of war by bombarding Belgrade. News of this caused the Russians to lose patience and decide on mobilization, though principally as a means of inducing a more pliable attitude in Vienna. Before the telegrams could go out, a message from William led the Tsar to restrict the order to the four military districts adjacent to the Austrian frontier and leave out the three on the German frontier. Yet even this involved the mobilization of more than double the number of Austrian divisions left after the main army had been despatched against Serbia. In any case the reversal came too late. On the morning of 30 July, William received news of Russia's partial mobilization and wrote on the margin: 'Then I must mobilize too.'[133] Trusty observers were not lacking to convey this conclusion to the General Staff, who had hitherto shown considerable understanding of Bethmann's objectives but now decided to take the bull by the horns. The whole German plan of campaign was based on winning a quick victory in the West before the Russian steam-roller could get under way. Germany's ability to complete her mobilization was therefore a factor of crucial importance and one which depended on both mobilizations beginning simultaneously. Once Russia started, Germany could not afford to wait.

By this time, however, despatches from London had made the Chancellor see a red light; Grey had stressed the unlikelihood of Britain remaining aloof once France was at war. Bethmann, therefore, began at last to urge caution on Vienna. But his attempts to do so had first to contend with the backstairs hints he had given earlier that such attempts were only designed to dress the stage for England and as such not to be taken seriously. By this time too the Austrians had made up their minds to act and were reluctant to draw back. Moreover, Bethmann was faced by the demand of his generals for mobilization. They sent a message to Vienna telling the Austrian staff to mobilize within the next twenty-four hours against Russia (which had not yet been done) so as to bear the brunt of the attack in the East while Germany dealt with France and promising that, if this were done, Germany would regard herself as bound by the terms of the Alliance. From this moment onwards German pressure on Vienna was to take the form of persuading the Austrians to direct their efforts against Russia rather than against Serbia. Moltke also told Conrad, in contradiction to Bethmann though perhaps in ignorance of the latter's changed views, that English attempts at mediation were to be resisted. Late on the evening of the 30th Bethmann finally gave way, first cancelling his efforts in Vienna and then despatching a warning to St. Petersburg that, unless Russian mobilization was cancelled within twelve hours, Germany would be forced to mobilize as well. And whereas in Austria and Russia mobilization could be completed without any frontiers being crossed, the character of German plans was such that mobilization inevitably led straight on to war.

These were the circumstances in which, on the night of 30–31 July, William read a report from St. Petersburg that, according to Sazonov, Russian mobilization could not be reversed. He was quick to see that, if the statement was correct, war was inevitable and in the excitement of the moment poured out his feelings without reserve in a note that must have needed a big margin to contain it. Tension had broken down his last reticences and the result illustrates so vividly how he behaved in one of his nervous crises that it deserves to be quoted in full:

'If [Russian] mobilization cannot any longer be reversed—*which is not true*—why did the Tsar ever invoke my mediation three days ago without saying a word about issuing the mobilization order? That shows clearly that he himself considers that order to have been overhasty and he took this step afterwards as a matter of form to quiet his uneasy conscience although knowing that it would be no good, since he did not feel strong enough to *stop* the mobilizing. Frivolity and weakness are going to plunge the world in the most frightful war of which the ultimate object is the overthrow of Germany. For I no longer have any doubt that England, Russia and France have *agreed* among themselves—knowing that our treaty obligations compel us to support Austria—to use the Austro-Serb conflict as a *pretext* for waging a war of *annihilation* against us. That is the explanation of Grey's cynical remark to Lichnowsky that "as long as the war is *confined* to Russia and Austria, England will sit still, and only when we and France get ourselves *mixed up* with it will he be forced to take active steps against us". That means we are either basely to betray our ally and *leave her to the mercy of Russia*—thereby breaking up the Triple Alliance, or as a reward for keeping our *pledges* get set upon and *beaten* by the Triple Entente in a body, so that their longing to *ruin* us completely can be finally satisfied. That is in a nutshell the bare bones of the situation, slowly but surely brought about by Edward VII; carried forward systematically by the secret conversations in Paris and St. Petersburg, the occurrence of which England has always denied; finally completed and put into operation by George V. In this way the stupidity and clumsiness of our ally is turned into a noose. So the celebrated *encirclement* of Germany has finally become an accomplished fact, in spite of all efforts by our politicians to prevent it. The net has suddenly been closed over our head, and the purely *anti-German policy* which England has been scornfully pursuing all over the world has won the most spectacular victory which we have proved powerless to prevent while they, having got us despite our struggles *all alone* into the net through our loyalty to Austria, proceed to throttle our political and economic exist-ence. A magnificent achievement which even those for whom it means disaster are bound to admire. Even after his death Edward VII is stronger than I, though I am still alive! And yet there were people who thought we could win England over or quiet her down with this or that little measure. Relentlessly, inexorably she has pursued her goal, with notes, proposals for naval holidays, scares, Haldane, etc., until we have come to this. And we fell into the net and started to build only one capital ship a year in the pious hope that we would thereby reassure England!!! All requests and warnings on my part went un-regarded. Now we get what the English consider to be gratitude. Our dilemma over keeping faith with the old and honourable Emperor has been exploited to create a situation which gives England the excuse she has been seeking to annihilate us with a spurious appearance of justice on the pretext that she is helping France and maintaining the well-known Balance of Power in Europe, i.e. playing off all European States for her own benefit against us. Now our job is to show up the whole business ruth-lessly and tear away the mask of Christian peaceseeking and put the pharisaical hypocrisy about peace in the pillory!!! And our consuls in Turkey and India, agents, etc., must get a conflagration going throughout the whole Mohammedan world against this hated, unscrupulous, dishonest nation of shopkeepers— since if we are going to bleed to death, England must at least lose India.'[134]

Not even the expedient of putting the blame on others could conceal the fact that the German gamble was going wrong. Chances of keeping the war localized were vanishing; William took Britain's participation for granted. The sailors and soldiers never seem to have entertained any illusions on that score, but with ninety-five divisions to be thrown against a distinctly smaller number of French ones,[135] and the war in the West to be decided within six weeks, they did not much concern themselves as to whether six British divisions reinforced the French or not. William realized more clearly what British intervention might mean, as Bethmann certainly did; in their anxiety to secure British neutrality, they clutched at arguments suggesting it might happen and the keenness of their resentment when they saw their hopes vanishing suggests that their original state was one of nervousness rather than of confident expectation. This is probably why Bethmann described the Treaty guaranteeing Belgian neutrality as 'a scrap of paper'. They would have done better to devote more time in preceding years to considering the political consequences of German strategic planning. For at this point a factor which could and should have been foreseen emerged to secure for Germany the most unfavourable of all openings. If Bethmann's first objective had been to confine the war to the Balkans, his second had been to place clearly on the shoulders of Russia the responsibility for widening it. Russia had certainly been the first to mobilize— but mobilization was not equivalent to aggression. It was the inexorable demands of the German military timetable which forced Bethmann to call on St. Petersburg to halt Russian mobilization, to declare a 'state of imminent danger of war' and when the time limit had passed without any Russian reply, to place in front of William an order for general German mobilization, signed at 5 p.m. on 1 August on a table made from timbers of Nelson's *Victory*.[136] A short time later the German Ambassador in St. Petersburg handed over a declaration of war, thereby

bringing into operation the Franco-Russian Alliance, and relieving the Italians of any obligation to support the two other members
of the Triple Alliance. The desire of the soldiers to make sure that
the Austrians shouldered the Russian attack had overridden the
aims of the politicians.

Nor was this all. The German strategy of attacking first in the
West assumed that either France would declare war on Germany
as soon as Russia was at war with her or that it would not matter
if Germany were openly the aggressor. To complete the predicament, the Schlieffen Plan for a wide encircling sweep by the right
wing involved marching through Belgium, which was to be invited
to give passage to German troops and in the event of a refusal,
overrun. Although Hohenlohe, Bülow and Bethmann Hollweg
had all known of this when Chancellors, nobody had ever challenged it.[137] The only modification made had been to omit the
original intention of marching through Holland as well, principally in order that Germany might exploit Dutch neutrality for
drawing in supplies. In 1913, Jagow, Kiderlen's successor as
Foreign Secretary, had pointed out to Moltke that an invasion of
Belgium would undoubtedly bring in Britain. Moltke promised to
think the point over with the General Staff, but seems to have
decided that, in the absence of any satisfactory alternative, the
strategic gains involved in violating Belgian neutrality outweighed
any political or psychological disadvantages.[138] By contrast, when
the French and British General Staffs had considered entering
Belgium themselves in order to forestall the German plans (of
which they had a shrewd idea), they were refused consent by their
political masters. Moreover, although the French mobilized on 1
August, the Minister of War, with his eye on British opinion,
ordered all his troops to keep ten kilometres back from the
frontier. Since the Germans could not afford to wait, they were left
only the choice between declaring war on France and attacking
her without a declaration.

No sooner had German mobilization been ordered, however,
than a telegram arrived from the German Ambassador in London
which, by misinterpreting a remark by Tyrrell, led the German
leaders to think for a short space of time that Britain would after
all remain neutral if Germany did not attack France. William
called for champagne; a war on two fronts could after all be
avoided. Summoning Moltke, he gave orders for the German

troops to be halted at the French frontier and for the main attack
to be switched against Russia. The General was aghast. Not only
would chaos ensue if mobilization plans were stopped in mid-
execution but Germany (like Britain but with less excuse) had
planned for only one strategic contingency. Once there had also
been a plan for an offensive eastwards but during the annual
revision in 1913 this had been discarded as superfluous![139] The
Kaiser has often been laughed at for telling Moltke 'Your uncle
would have given me a different answer', but the implied criticism
was a perfectly valid one. That does not, however, dispose of the
matter. Under the German Constitution responsibility for ensuring
that the military and civilian spheres of government were co-
ordinated rested with the Emperor. William had never realized
what the job implied, let alone started to tackle it. Moreover, by
brusquely rebuffing any attempt by civilian Ministers to express
opinions on military matters, he had stacked the cards against their
raising objections about the political implications of the soldiers'
plans. It is fascinating to consider how events might have developed
if an alternative plan *had* existed, if Germany had stood on the
defensive in the west without crossing her frontiers, and had flung
heavy forces eastwards as soon as Russia attacked Austria.

Although Moltke never really regained his nerve after the
Kaiser's intervention, his embarrassment (which extended to the
question of using the Luxemburg railways)[140] was of short duration, for an hour or so later the Kaiser received a telegram from
King George which showed the previous report to have been
misleading. Next day he heard that Grey had called on Germany
and France to respect the neutrality of Belgium. But although he
minuted: 'This is what English intervention against us will be
decided by'; although in the past he had assured the Belgians that
their suspicions of Germany were groundless,[141] he offered no
protest when on 2 August the Ambassador in Brussels was told to
open the sealed envelope sent to him four days earlier and present
to the Belgian Government the ultimatum which it contained. In
later years William used to say that he was swept away by the
military timetable and up to a point the excuse is valid.[142] But
he had only himself to thank if the implications of that timetable
took him unawares or if, having actively assisted in pushing the
Austrians over the brink, he found himself unable to pull them
back. When at a meeting of Prussian Ministers on 3 August

Bethmann announced that British participation in the war must be regarded as inevitable, Tirpitz is said to have cried 'All is then lost' and Moltke about the same time to have exclaimed 'Thank God! I would rather have the English army in front of me so that I can defeat it, than have England observe malevolent neutrality out of my reach.'[143]

Thus it came about that on 4 August, Kaiser William called members of the *Reichstag* to the White Hall of Berlin's castle and told them that, despite all efforts for peace, Germany was at war. Austria had been compelled to attack Serbia; Russia had interposed; treaty obligations and interest caused Germany to stand by her ally. Nobody, he said, should be surprised that France, which had so often rebuffed German overtures, should support Russia. (Britain, whose attitude was still undefined, passed without mention.) The situation did not result from temporary conflict of interest or diplomatic manœuvres but from long-standing jealousy of German strength and growth. Germany was inspired by no lust of conquest but, for the sake of holding what she had, seized her sword with a clean hand and a clear conscience. From the balcony, he had already told the cheering crowds that henceforward he knew no parties, he knew only Germans.

A few anecdotes may serve to round off the story. Twenty years before, von Köller, then Prussian Minister of the Interior, had said: 'Let us hope that we never have a war while William II is on the throne. For he would lose his nerve, he is a coward.'[144]

On the day war broke out, the financier Rathenau said to a friend: 'The Kaiser is never going to ride on a white horse with his paladins through the Brandenburg Gate as conqueror of the world. On the day he did so, history would have lost its meaning.'[145]

In a final interview with the German Ambassador on 5 August, Grey said that Britain would always be prepared to mediate when Germany wished to end the war. 'We do not want to crush Germany but to restore peace as soon as possible.' On this being reported the Kaiser commented: 'Canting liar, slippery as an eel.'[146]

About the same time Jules Cambon remarked to his British colleague: 'There are three people in Berlin tonight who regret that war has broken out; you, me and Kaiser William.'

William on the other hand is reported to have said: 'To think that George and Nicky should have played me false! If my grandmother had been alive, she would never have allowed it.'[147]

CHAPTER XI

A Whirlwind to be Reaped

AT CHRISTMAS the *Frankfurter Zeitung* published an
article discussing the saying of Clausewitz that war is the
continuation of policy by other means. It ended by claiming
that the military standpoint must be subordinate to the political;
for the reverse to occur would make nonsense. This article angered
the Kaiser; he took it as a veiled criticism of his Chief of Staff
and himself. His view was that during war 'idiotic civilians' must
keep their mouths shut until the soldiers authorized them to
talk.[1] William did not, of course, go so far as to keep his own
mouth shut, but he regarded his function as a military rather than
as a political one. He was after all Supreme Commander of all
the armed forces. He kept more out of the public eye than he had
done in peacetime, thereby losing contact with his civilian subjects;
his principal utterances consisted of speeches to troops. He only
visited Berlin at intervals and throughout the next four years
spent most of his time at or near headquarters, which moved with
the emphasis of the fighting from Coblenz to Luxemburg, on to
Charleville, away eastwards to Posen and Pless, back again to
Kreuznach and ultimately to Spa. At times he lived in the royal
train, which assumed a service livery of green.

This arrangement was not on the whole fortunate. The Kaiser's
performance during peacetime manœuvres did not encourage the
soldiers to allow him much say in what went on. In the secondary
sphere of politics, he might behave as he chose, but when it came
to Prussia's national activity, he had to act as a constitutional
generalissimo. The staff at headquarters were usually too busy
to spare time for him and nobody was prepared to take the
responsibility of letting him get near the front line. This meant
that he had not very much to do and that little of what he did

really mattered. Before the war had been going on three months, he told Max of Baden that

'If people in Germany think I am the Supreme Commander, they are grossly mistaken. The General Staff tells me nothing and never asks my advice. I drink tea, go for walks and saw wood, which pleases my suite. The only one who is a bit kind to me is the Chief of the Railway Department [General Gröner] who tells me all he does and intends to do.'[2]

Meanwhile, the job of co-ordinating the military and naval high commands with one another and with the home and diplomatic fronts, so vital to any country at war, went largely by default. William became more than ever thrown back upon the narrow circle of his suite, the Adjutant-General von Plessen, in 1914 an old gentleman of seventy-three, the Military Secretary von Lyncker (sixty-three), the Naval Secretary Admiral von Müller (sixty-two) and the Civil Secretary Valentini (fifty-nine). The Chancellor, after spending the first four months at headquarters, found it essential to go back to Berlin, leaving a liaison officer behind him. The 'Hydra', as the entourage were known by their opponents, were conscientious and faithful servants and all but von Plessen were in due course displaced for their refusal to swallow the conservative outlook in its crudity. But their background was limited and they like their master suffered from being cut off from the fighting troops, from political circles in Berlin and from the common people. Instead of acting as a rallying-point for the entire nation, a function which the Kaiser alone was capable of performing, William managed to convey the impression that he lived a life apart, bearing neither the hardships of the rank-and-file nor those of workers and housewives.

For such a view there was considerable justification. Descriptions of court diet differ. While some writers recall pea soup, sausage and cheese, others mention banquets and the frequent consumption of champagne in celebration of victories, real or supposed. There is certainly nothing to show that William himself insisted on luxurious living. If he was capable of saying, while in the act of consuming buttered rusks and pastries, that he always observed the same rationing regulations as his subjects, the explanation for the apparent hypocrisy is likely to have been unawareness of what his subjects were actually eating. In any case a number of influential guests from abroad had not only to be entertained but given the best possible impression of Germany in wartime. Messing officers are apt to think they will be judged by the quality of their table and use the name of their chief to secure, by hook if not by crook, the best available; 'fair shares' is not an idea which comes naturally to court officials. Dona had in this as in many other things an unfortunate influence; she thought it part of her duty to cherish her husband and keep him capable of filling the role which everyone made out to be so important.

For most of the time, his physical and nervous health was far from good. The views which he expressed before war broke out make plain that he did not enter it with any unshakeable confidence in victory. An old and intimate friend who had much to do with him during the first days of August professed never to have seen so tragic and disturbed a face.[3] Someone who saw him leaving an intercession service a day or two later said that his face had completely changed, having stiffened as though the life had gone out of it. 'Here was a man whose world had collapsed and who had some premonition of impending disaster.'[4] He was soon rumoured to be found in tears in corners of churches all over the Rhineland, praying for hours together.[5] By March 1916 he was saying privately that 'One must never utter it nor shall I admit it to Falkenhayn but this war will not end in a great victory.'[6] His staff felt it their task to convince him that 'all setbacks left the way open for a happy ending'; General von Plessen said he must be kept in good spirits 'at all costs'.[7] But even without such help, his volatile nature would never have allowed permanent pessimism, and when good news arrived, he would quickly change to a 'hurrah mood', much more akin to that of the German people as a whole. Moreover, the most obvious prerogative of leadership left to the Kaiser was the inspiring of confidence, and this duty he faithfully discharged in his public appearances till the end. He thereby misled not only the pessimists who deplored what they took to be his ignorance of the true situation but also those who felt obliged to think as their ruler did. But the strain of keeping up appearances, combined with the strain of fluctuating from one extreme to the other, took its toll of his nerves. In 1915, Tirpitz, furious at the lack of vigour with which he thought the war was being prosecuted, seems to have instigated a move to get the Kaiser declared temporarily incapable of ruling and though the Chief Staff

Physician refused to be a party to any such scheme, there were clearly enough symptoms visible to make the proposal plausible. Two years later the same doctor was talking about the probability of breakdown for 'this highly nervous man of whom before the war we all entertained such an entirely false impression'.[8]

His attitude to warfare displayed the same alternating inconsistency. Ballin in 1918 considered William to have been worn out by the war which was 'completely uncongenial to his character'.[9] He himself once said that were he the captain of a submarine, he would never torpedo a ship if he knew that women and children were on board. On another occasion he claimed to have spent the night a prey to the thought that he might be responsible for involving the unhappy German nation, which had already made such huge sacrifices, in a new war with America. After resisting air-raids on London, he agreed to them on the understanding that only targets of real military importance would be bombed. Yet in the early days of the war he revelled in repeating stories of piles of corpses six feet high and the sergeant-major who killed twenty-seven Frenchmen with forty-five shots. Phrases like 'Take no prisoners' or 'Kill as many of the swine as you can' were often on his lips. He once said that 'When it comes to throat-cutting, Wilson should have his throat cut first'.[10] Within five months of the Armistice he was still saying, 'We know our goal, our rifles cocked and traitors to the wall'. For him to be the strong man may have involved playing a part but it was one into which he threw himself with energy. And his outward appearances were what gave Allied propaganda its ammunition.

The Kaiser's disregard of civilian affairs was rendered easier by the decision of the parties at the outbreak of war to establish 'Peace within the fortress' (*Burgfrieden*). The Social Democrats gave the lie to all the fears which had for so long bedevilled internal German politics by deciding to vote in the *Reichstag* for the war credits, on the principle that Germany must be defended from the invading troops of the autocratic Tsar; even the fourteen deputies who opposed this in the party meeting accepted the whip in the chamber. Instead of taking to task the leadership which had brought Germany with only one moribund ally into a war against three major powers, six million against ten million fighting men, the population greeted the outbreak with enthusiasm and the *Reichstag* allowed itself to be put into cold storage. Nor was it only about the past that the *Burgfrieden* fostered misconceptions. Right and left continued to differ about what should happen once the war was over almost as widely as they had done before it began. To prevent a head-on collision about war aims, Bethmann decided to boycott all official discussion of the subject.

There was, however, one sphere in which the Kaiser's influence proved decisive. The Commander of the North Sea Fleet was responsible to the Chief of the Naval Staff (at General Headquarters) who was responsible to the Kaiser through the Chief of the Naval Secretariat. Tirpitz, as Secretary of State for the Navy, was thus side-tracked; in any case William seems to have been losing faith in his judgement. The Kaiser had on his own authority recalled the fleet to its bases before war broke out and thereafter ordered it to remain at them. The strategic intention was to wait until the British fleet came close to the German coast and then attack it, principally with light craft, in the hope of whittling down its superiority sufficiently to enable a general action to be undertaken on terms not too unfavourable. But the British decision to substitute a 'distant' for a 'close' blockade knocked the bottom out of this plan; instead of having the British fleet as a convenient target at the mouth of the Elbe, the Germans found that they could only get at it by themselves making a risky journey across the North Sea. The High Command was convinced that sooner or later British public opinion would force an offensive and this was indeed one of the considerations which brought light forces into the Heligoland Bight on 28 August; the German reconaissance system failed and by the time the High Seas Fleet got on the scene, the raiders were gone. The absence of other results led to exaggerated propaganda being made out of the sinking by a submarine of three old British cruisers patrolling off the Dutch coast on 22 September.[11] The refusal of the British to play the part expected of them led some German commanders, especially Tirpitz, to urge that the fleet should be sent out on sweeps into the North Sea. But William would not agree. 'The fleet must keep close to the German coast and avoid any action which might lead to heavier losses.'

Behind this fateful decision lay more than a fear for the safety of the instrument which had been so laboriously built up. The war was to be a short one which would end in a decisive victory by German land forces. Had not William promised his departing troops that they would return home 'before the leaves fall from the trees'?[12] When peace negotiations followed, an intact fleet would be a bargaining counter of importance. Moreover, its offensive use might, in Bethmann's view, make the English less willing to accept the verdict of the land battle. William thought to profit by the lessons of history, forgetting that the chief of those lessons is the smallness of variation needed to make two similar situations different. In his view, more than one 'Punic War' would be required to destroy Britain, and the decisive struggle for which the navy would be required had not yet arrived. But this conception, and the policy which it entailed, remained effective long after the hypothesis originally justifying it had ceased to be valid.

For not many weeks of campaigning in France were needed to show that the German strategic plan had miscarried; the odds against it were such that the surprising thing would have been its success.[13] On 14 September, after the Battle of the Marne, the Kaiser on his own authority relieved von Moltke of a command for which he was palpably unfit and without much consultation appointed the debonair and chauvinist General von Falkenhayn, the Prussian Minister of War, who forthwith substituted a policy of holding gains by limited offensives in place of the original war of movement. This was the last time on which William acted on his own initiative in a major military matter. Moltke later criticized the choice and von Falkenhayn was probably the wrong man for the job.[14] But although there were better generals in the German Army, they had hardly had time to prove themselves; at that very juncture Ludendorff, the most notable, was making his name, under the nominal generalship of Hindenburg, by repelling the initial Russian onset at the battles of Tannenberg and the Masurian Lakes. But as Russian manpower became fully deployed, its weight lay heavily on the Eastern front while in the West the determined attempts of William and Falkenhayn to break through at Ypres had by the end of the autumn failed to bring any adequate return for the casualties involved. The war was going to be a longer affair than anticipated, and for a long war Germany was by no means prepared; to take only one example, her stock of nitrates, which had mostly to be imported, would only last six months. Indeed if the General Staff had been asked in peacetime to contemplate prolonged resistance in the situation which had arisen, they would have held up their hands in horror.

How was the war to be won? How even was Germany to escape disaster? One obvious solution would have been a compromise peace on the terms of the *status quo*. But such a peace would have been regarded by the Allies as tantamount to defeat, since it would have been an open acknowledgement that their combined resources were inadequate to bring down the Central Powers.[15] Nor had the Allies any intention of playing into enemy hands by winding up one war and thereby giving the Germans time to prepare for the next. On the other hand the German élite had staked their reputation on the war, which but for their attitudes might never have come about. For them to return empty-handed and weakened by their casualties on the battlefield would involve a confession of strategic and political failure and therefore, given the state of German politics, the surrender of their privileges. The only hope which they could see of reconciling the under-privileged to continued exclusion from political power lay in a rapid rise in living standards such as vast annexations alone would make possible. Two further factors added to this fundamental difficulty. First, Helfferich, the Finance Minister, had placed all German military expenditure in a special budget covered not by taxes but by loans and Treasury bills, on the theory that the cost of the war was to be paid after victory by the defeated. If, there-fore, Germany were to accept any outcome short of victory, the first problem of peace would be footing the bill, which by 1918 amounted to over £7 billion.[16] If the mind of the hierarchy had been amenable to reason, this factor alone would have been a considerable bar to its exercise.

But in the second place the overestimate of their own strength, which had done so much to involve the Germans in the war, continued to delude them while fighting it. William, as has been seen, felt it his duty to exude confidence, and anyone who openly failed to follow his example would have been regarded as a traitor. Many leaders of the intellectual world had mobilized their pens in what they imagined to be the service of their country and the minority (like Solf and Troeltsch) who preferred to show their patriotism by hanging on to their objectivity were rewarded by being ignored. It was the irresponsible, and those who talked loudest, who paid least attention to the *Burgfrieden*. The majority of people, even in responsible positions, had little idea of the real situation. Such communiqués as were issued breathed optimism;

the German public, for example, were never given any idea of what had happened in the Battle of the Marne. The belief that Germany would gain by the war, which was to bring her 'break-through to world power', was general. The outbreak unbridled many ambitious tongues and imaginations which had till then been reined in for fear of frightening Germany's neighbours. A week after William had told the *Reichstag* that 'we are not led on by lust of conquest', he told his Guards that he would never sheathe the sword till he could dictate the terms of peace.[17] Germany might merely be fighting in self-defence but as a compensation for having to do so once and as security against having to do so twice, she considered herself entitled to 'guarantees'. What these guarantees should be was decided on the advice of the soldiers and the industrialists, two groups which seldom underestimate their needs. Germany's exact war-aims showed minor variations from time to time, but most or all of Belgium, the Longwy-Briey basin with its valuable ores, Poland and the Baltic States figured regularly. The readiness with which William adopted these aims was only equalled by the regularity with which he endorsed them. Even those like Bethmann who realized them to be unattainable in their totality found it politically expedient to pay them lip-service. In the background hovered the more grandiose conception of 'Mitteleuropa'. This was popularized in 1915 by Naumann who foresaw that the Habsburg Empire in its existing form was doomed; the war, however it ended, would finally free the Slavs and Balkan nationalities from the Austrian Germans and Magyars. Imperial Germany must therefore expect to see a region of great political and economic importance to her become fragmented and hostile. Naumann's remedy was to organize it as a customs union or loose federation run from Berlin. In this form the idea was sensible, if visionary. It was, however, taken up by the strategists who saw in it their only chance of creating an area large enough to sustain a series of wars and believed that only by such a series could the Anglo-American monopoly of world power be broken. In the long run this attempt to exploit the proposal for the benefit of Germany proved its undoing; in the short run the arguments were too plausible and the prospects too attractive for resistance. Thus the bones of Pomeranian grenadiers came to be scattered in Macedonia and the Dobrudja, while the Czechs, Serbs, Roumanians, Poles and Greeks were driven into the arms of the Allies.[18]

If a general compromise peace was ruled out, the next alternative was by the offer of favourable peace terms to detach one of the Allies from the rest and then concentrate all resources on achieving victory over the others. This policy involved giving up, at any rate temporarily, Germany's aims in one direction but was explored with some vigour during the winter of 1914–15. The object of the policy was, however, somewhat transparent and in September 1914 the Allies had forestalled it by agreeing not to make peace separately. The German leaders therefore came to think that to pursue it successfully, they must first make one of the Allies amenable to argument by a resounding defeat. The only question was which to tackle first. The war had let loose a flood of vituperation against England, exemplified by the phrase '*Gott strafe England*' and Lissauer's 'Hymn of Hate'; these attacks, which were reciprocated on the other side of the North Sea, pointed to an awareness of Britain being the chief obstacle to German ambitions and the mainspring of the coalition against her. This led Falkenhayn and Tirpitz to argue that only by a victory in the West could the war be ended. In opposition Hindenburg and Ludendorff, flushed with success, argued that Russia was the weak link in the coalition and the only enemy against whom the Austrians would show even an appearance of enthusiasm. They regarded the Western Front as too confined a space in which to manœuvre with effect the masses of men who had been concentrated there and maintained that the 'limited offensives' proposed by Falkenhayn would achieve nothing but loss of life. Yet he again had history behind—and in front of—him when he pointed to the difficulty of securing a decision in the vast spaces of Russia. Each alternative had its difficulties, but the difficulty which proved insuperable was making a choice between the two.

*   *   *

At the beginning of 1915, the clash between 'Easterners' and 'Westerners' led to open defiance. Von Hötzendorf, planning an Austrian offensive in Galicia, appealed for German divisions. Falkenhayn refused them on the ground that they would be needed in the West. Ludendorff, with an assurance possible to the only German general yet victorious, sent them all the same. William, called on to intervene as mediator, yielded to the wishes of the Easterners in everything except the dismissal of Falkenhayn who was kept in post for another eighteen months but denied the full means of carrying out his policy. Through the campaign of 1915 Germany stood on the defensive in the West, resisting with success the onslaught of British and French. In the East two major offensives were launched, the first of which made considerable progress. Falkenhayn conducted the second himself and had another sharp clash with Hindenburg and Ludendorff over its handling, in the course of which one of his aides exclaimed: 'These people only want to attack where there is nobody to oppose them.'[19] William was again called in to adjudicate and his backing for his chosen Chief of Staff was said by the opposition to have led to the last chance being lost of decisively defeating the Russians, who won considerable victories against the Austrians. Bulgaria joined the Central Powers and the defeat of Serbia reopened communications with Turkey, but on the other hand Italy joined the Entente. By the end of the year, a victory in the field looked as far off as ever.

The search for alternative solutions intensified. One of these was subversion, by which at one time the Kaiser hoped to achieve great things in the British and Russian Empires. But Germany's gospel was not one to strike sparks in men's minds. The attempt to rally Britain's Moslems to a Holy War under Turkish leadership proved a sad disappointment, and Ireland was little better. In due course war weariness was to make Russia and France more fruitful ground, but the crop had not yet ripened.

The second alternative was economic war for which Germany was badly prepared and ill-situated. The British were treating as contraband all goods destined for Germany, instead of only munitions of war, and rationed neutral countries to prevent them being used as channels of supply. The effects of this policy were accumulating and a time could be foreseen when, unless the blockade could be broken, the people and cannon of Germany would be starved into submission. Britain might be even more dependent on imports than Germany but the German surface fleet was not capable of interrupting her supplies. In December 1914, William had agreed to his ships being used for quick raids on seaside towns, but a month later one such raid was caught by British battlecruisers on the Dogger Bank. In the ensuing fight the Germans did more damage than they sustained, but a battle-cruiser was sunk and heavier losses only avoided as a result of

British tactical faults. William was so scared by the episode that he decided not to risk his big ships any more. Attention was in consequence focused on what a British admiral described as the 'underhand, unfair and damned unEnglish' practice of submarine warfare.[20]

Tirpitz had despised submarines with the result that on the outbreak of war Germany possessed only 29: even after eighteen months the figure was no more than 54, of which only about a third could be on patrol at the same time.[21] Moreover, submarines were vulnerable when they surfaced, yet unless they did so could not identify victims or rescue the people on board. On 4 February 1915 the German Government announced that any merchant ship found off British coasts would be sunk; no assurance was given about the safety of the crews. On 15 February William asked Admiral Bachmann, the new Chief of the Naval Staff, whether he could promise that unrestricted submarine warfare of this kind would compel England to surrender within six weeks. Bachmann, like his patron Tirpitz, believed that impossible questions deserved irresponsible answers, and gave the required assurance.[22] But in fact the German forces at this time were not nearly strong enough to make a submarine campaign effective, and as the weeks slipped by, the only obvious result of the new policy was a series of protests by neutrals, notably America, over the number of their ships and citizens which perished. Nothing the Germans could say could persuade the Americans that their submarine tactics were a fair reply to British methods of blockade. A dreadful and much resented choice began to loom between risking loss of the war by failure to press home a submarine blockade of Britain, and making such an attack effective at the risk of provoking American intervention and so losing the war. For the moment Bethmann preferred the first risk and got the Kaiser's consent to an order preventing U-boat commanders from torpedoing large liners and when this proved inadequate, to another which in effect suspended the whole campaign. Tirpitz thereupon resigned and though William refused to let him go, Bachmann was replaced by Admiral von Holtzendorff who was more alive to political considerations and more congenial to his master. Six months later, however, the sailors demanded authority to restart the campaign; William hedged whereupon Tirpitz refused to stay any longer.

To dispense with the submarine campaign was, however, one thing; to find an alternative means of shaking the British blockade was quite another. William had already discovered that his order confining the surface ships to their bases was not being carried out. Bachmann had denied receiving any such instructions.

'At this the Kaiser gave me a quite indescribable look for several seconds on end. I felt I should either go through the roof the next minute or else get my way. Suddenly His Majesty's expression changed and with a kind of laugh he said: "Well then, if it isn't all that dangerous in the North Sea, the fleet can go on operating there—only of course all precautions must be taken." '[23]

But the resumed freedom of movement did not radically alter the situation. The Commander of the High Seas Fleet was required to find 'a balance between intelligent boldness and ordered caution'.[24] Consequently the Germans dared not venture far enough from their bases to make a major battle inevitable, and the British were thereby enabled to achieve their object without fighting. The case for caution was well illustrated when gradually increasing German boldness led in May 1916 to the Skagerrak encounter (Jutland). The British losses in the opening stages did credit to the way Tirpitz had designed his ships and led an excited William to proclaim that 'the first mighty hammer-stroke has been delivered, the spell of Trafalgar has been broken'. But the result might have been very different if the main British fleet had arrived earlier in the day, had been trained in night fighting, or had had a more decentralized command system. The British needed only to learn their lessons for German prospects to become grim and after the battle William agreed with the Commander-in-Chief that:

'Even if further operations by the High Seas Fleet take a favourable course and we are able to inflict serious damage on the enemy, nevertheless there can be no doubt that even the most successful outcome of a fleet action will not *force* England to make peace.'[25]

During the rest of the war the German fleet made at least three major sorties and a few successful raids on merchantmen, but it never fought the major sea battle for which it had been professedly built. The existence of a German 'fleet in being' compelled the British to keep their own fleet in the North Sea and use destroyers for protecting it instead of escorting convoys. But the British could achieve their objectives without forcing a battle whereas the Germans could not.

On land, Falkenhayn, rejecting calls for action in the East, proposed and secured William's approval for an attack on Verdun, since this town was too near lateral communications for Germany's comfort and too important for France to be let go. But though holding the town cost over a quarter of a million French casualties, the Germans lost almost as many and in the end gained little ground. Moreover, the attack in the West was answered by Russian onslaughts in the East, which drew off a high proportion of the available German resources and in June 1916 produced a demoralizing Austrian collapse. All the combatants were tiring themselves out without getting any nearer victory. The demand grew in Germany for new men such as Hindenburg and for new methods such as an unrestricted submarine campaign. Although William continued to give Falkenhayn faithful support, Bethmann turned against him and the star of the Easterners was increasingly in the ascendant. The crisis came at the end of July. The British launched a successful offensive on the Somme, the French regained ground at Verdun and the Austrians were heavily defeated in Galicia. The policy of concentrating effort in the West became more impracticable than ever when Roumania joined the Entente. Though Falkenhayn had foreseen this, he had misjudged its timing; William was severely shaken by the arrival of the news a few minutes after he had confidently predicted that it would not occur.[26] Falkenhayn was sent to dispose of the new enemy, which he did in a brilliant campaign, and Hindenburg became Chief of the General Staff with Ludendorff to do the thinking for him as First Quartermaster-General.

William disliked Hindenburg because of his 'dry, solid simplicity' while he rightly thought Ludendorff brusque and humourless.[27] The newcomers owed their appointment to their own successes in the field and to the national reputation which these had given them. So far from being chosen by the Kaiser, they had forced themselves upon him and despised him for his indecision. As long as they remained successful, they could do anything on which they insisted. The resignation of Tirpitz had already provoked right-wing criticism; for William to have dismissed his new commanders would have meant an outcry which might have cost his throne. Henceforward he was faced by two determined men—or rather by one man too stolid to lose his nerve and by another in whom the lust for having his own way came to acquire pathological dimensions. The Supreme War Lord from now on had less say than ever in the military field and though he was often called in to mediate between the soldiers and the civilians, the former had only to put their feet down for mediation to turn into submission. Gradually the baneful pair swept internal opposition aside until all the vital posts, civilian as well as military, had been filled by people who could be relied on to make no trouble. What Hindenburg and Ludendorff undertook was in fact nothing less than a Titanic struggle to impose on the world an outcome to the war acceptable to the German élite and for that purpose to extract from all Germans a concentrated effort corresponding to the ideals of that élite. But since the political ideas of that élite, external no less than internal, were more appropriate to the Stone Age than to the twentieth century, the unlimited power secured by the two generals proved in the long run even more disastrous to the monarchy than interference with them would have been. As Bethmann put it, 'with Falkenhayn we lose the war strategically, with Ludendorff politically'.[28]

The new brooms first made themselves felt by demanding the introduction of compulsory national service, either in the armed forces or in essential home occupations, for all men between seventeen and sixty. The ordinary German, faced by this demand for sacrifice at the beginning of what was to be known as the 'Turnip Winter', showed signs of losing confidence in his leaders. Drastic action to force a decision was going to become inevitable before long and the most obvious form for such action to take was unrestricted submarine warfare. Even the *Reichstag* in October 1916 pledged its support for such a course. Bethmann, realizing that the sands were running out, sought through the second half of 1916 to bring about peace negotiations or else to place on other people the onus for not bringing them about; Germany could then argue that since she was being forced to go on fighting, she could not be blamed for using submarines. William warmly backed this attempt to avoid choosing between starvation as a result of failing to break the blockade, and American intervention as a result of using submarines to break it. The best chance of negotiating peace seemed to be through American mediation. But the Kaiser was afraid of appearing anxious for this and thereby suggesting that Germany's position was desperate. Yet with the armed forces and the Pan-Germans growing restive, the civilians could not afford to wait long.[29]

At the end of the autumn the German military position improved and Bethmann with William's support decided that the chance of negotiating from strength must be seized. On 12 December 1916 the Central Powers announced their readiness to start negotiations. But fear of provoking internal dissensions ruled out any mention in their offer of the terms which they would accept and while Bethmann had merely wished to represent Germany as unconquerable, William and the High Command insisted on portraying her as already in effect victorious. William declared to his American dentist that:

'We've got the English and French Governments in a nice predicament, trying to explain to their people why they don't make peace. They're wild with rage at us for surprising them in this way.'[30]

But in fact the Entente treated the German move 'less as an offer of peace than as a manœuvre of war',[31] while Wilson called for detailed suggestions about terms. The Kaiser was convinced that the President's reply had been concerted with the Entente Powers and was designed to rescue them from almost certain defeat.

'The Powers that, like a band of robbers, have made a surprise attack on Germany and the Central Powers, with the avowed intention of its destruction, have been failed [*sic*], beaten off, and crippled. They began the war, they have been beaten all along the line, they must state their intentions first. We the party attacked, being on our defensive purely, will state our proposals afterwards as victors'. [In English in original.]

'If the President wants to end the war all he need do is make good a threat of denying the English pirates any more munitions, close the loan market in their face and institute reprisals against letter-snatching and black lists. That would quickly end the war without any notes, conferences, etc.'[32]

Moreover, the Germans thought that Wilson's aim was to preside over a conference attended by all the belligerents and the principal neutrals; fearing to be put at a disadvantage by such a gathering, they proposed to negotiate with their enemies one by one. 'I go to no conference,' said William. 'Certainly not to one presided over by him.' Not only were the difficulties of separate negotiations disregarded but the chances of beginning the process with Russia had been wrecked (when talks were already under way) because the High Command insisted that, to get Polish recruits, Poland must be proclaimed an independent Grand Duchy.

A brusque answer to Wilson was rushed through for fear that the Entente, in replying to the German offer, would call for German terms to be stated and so gain a bargaining advantage; the tone enabled the Entente to reject the offer out of hand without estranging American opinion. The rejection disappointed and angered the Kaiser:

'After their note and its flagrant cynicism I must insist on our previous peace terms being modified. No concessions in France, King Albert not to be allowed to stay in Belgium, the Flemish coast to be ours.'[33]

But indignation could not remedy the failure to manœuvre into a favourable position for restarting submarine warfare, the pressure for which was worrying William into a state of acute nervous tension. Von Holtzendorff's reluctance to embarrass the Chancellor was overcome by accusations from the fleet that it was without leadership, while late in December Hindenburg and Ludendorff decided that they could no longer take responsibility for military operations if unrestricted submarine warfare was not introduced at the end of January. For Bethmann to have resisted further would have been to precipitate a conflict which could only have ended in his resignation, and so weakened the confidence of moderate opinion throughout Germany and Austria in the régime; he sacrificed personal consistency to his sense of duty to his master. For this he has been criticized. But had he been the kind of man to insist on all the issues being thoroughly debated or on final efforts to conciliate America, he might never have been appointed to his post and would certainly never have remained at it so long. The decision was taken on 9 January 1917 without comprehensive consideration being given to the relevant factors; William, having made up his mind the previous evening, listened with obvious impatience to what little the Chancellor did have to say.[34] The decision was warmly welcomed in Germany; even the Stock Exchange sent the Kaiser a telegram of congratulation.[35] The sailors promised that England would be forced to her knees within six months and that war would be over before a single American soldier could land in Europe. The reply of the United States was to break off relations on 3 February and declare war on 6 April 1917. The first American troops landed early in July.

*　　　　*　　　　*

Winston Churchill has suggested that if the decision on submarine warfare had been put off for two months, it might never have been taken.[36] The United States would never have entered the war, France would have collapsed before the year was out and a compromise peace would have been in sight (though whether on terms acceptable to the German leaders is another matter). For in March the Cossacks mingled with the demonstrators in front of Petrograd's Winter Palace instead of riding them down; revolution broke out and the Tsar abdicated. The exact attitude of the Provisional Government to the continuation of hostilities and the correct policy for Germany to follow were for some time in doubt. Unofficial negotiations for an armistice were opened in Stockholm and Lenin was assisted to return from Switzerland. The German Foreign Office seems to have fancied that the Kaiser might not see the point of supping with the devil for he was left to learn of the possibility from the newspapers and only informed of the fact when it was an accomplished one.[37] The German objective was to cause as much dissension in Russia as possible without making any promises, counting on war-weariness to ensure that before long in one way or another she would cease to be a serious enemy. Not only would this mean that troops from the East could be turned against the West; a prospect was opened of escaping from the stranglehold of the blockade, provided only that means could be found of tapping Russian wheat, oil and ores.

But if the revolution afforded hope, it also brought danger. The overthrow of autocratic rulers might prove as infectious as influenza among war-wearied peoples. The left wing of the German

Socialists had been restive for some time and towards the end of March broke away to form the Independent Socialist Party. The Chancellor was quick to see that some dramatic gesture was needed if the loyalty of the masses was to be retained. On 5 April (three days after President Wilson had said that 'the world must be made safe for democracy') Bethmann, as Prussian Prime Minister, proposed to his colleagues the immediate introduction of universal suffrage. Three other Ministers supported him but the opposition of the remainder was so strong that the proposal had to be watered down. When on 8 April the Kaiser issued an 'Easter Message' to his people, it merely said that 'after the massive contributions of the entire nation in this terrible war, I am sure there is no room left for Prussia's class suffrage'. Such vague phrases were totally inadequate to avert a wave of strikes in the munitions industry. The constitutional issue was spelling the end of the *Burgfrieden*.

It was not the only issue on which fundamental differences of opinion were becoming palpable. On 27 March the Petrograd council of Workers and Soldiers had proclaimed their object to be 'a peace without annexations or reparations'. On 19 April the German Socialists adopted this as their official policy. If Bethmann were to have his way, these were the people likely to come to power in Prussia. The question of Prussian constitutional reform was bound up with that of German war aims; both involved the future political and social position of the German élite, and for that reason every inch of the way was bound to be hotly contested. The *Reichstag* set up a committee to consider changes in the constitution which in May decided that the Chancellor ought to be made responsible to Parliament. But meanwhile on 28 April the Conservatives had introduced a protest against the Easter Message; they followed it five days later with another against the attitude of the S.P.D. Their demand that 'Germany's immense sacrifices during the war should receive due compensation after a victorious peace in order to rebuild her economic, social and cultural future' was supported by twenty-two organizations, among them the Agrarian League, the German Peasants Union, the Central Union of German Industrialists, the Army League, the Navy League, the Pan-German League and the confessional Trade Unions:

'Only a peace with compensations, with increase of strength

and acquisition of territory can provide our people with lasting
security for their national existence, their place in the world
and their freedom of economic development.'[38]

Meanwhile, trouble was blowing up from another quarter. The
previous November had seen the death at the age of eighty-six of
the Emperor Franz Joseph (whom William had once described, at a
moment when he wanted sympathy, as 'my sole surviving friend
in the world'). He was succeeded by his great-nephew, Karl, much
under the influence of his Bourbon wife, Zita. William made the
mistake of patronizing the newcomer. 'Who,' he once asked,
'does this young man think he is?'[39] The Austrians left no doubt
of their anxiety to get out of the war quickly and as a preparation
for a thoroughgoing discussion with them, a Council was held at
Bad Kreuznach on 23 April. Four days previously William had put
down on paper his own ideas about the form which peace should
take. He thought that Germany should demand Malta, the
Azores, Madeira, the Cape Verde Islands, the Belgian Congo and
Longwy-Briey: while Poland, Courland and Lithuania should be
annexed indirectly if not directly. The Ukraine, Latvia and
Estonia should become independent, America and England
should pay 30 billion dollars in reparations, France 40 billion and
Italy 10 billion![40]

If the Council in fact stopped short of adopting all these terms,
the principal reason was that its discussions were confined to
ending the war on land. There was to be no question of suspending
the war at sea, including the submarine campaign, and accordingly
colonial and economic terms were left to be settled later. Ludendorff insisted on extreme demands being adopted under threat of
resignation; Liège, the Flanders coast, Luxemburg, Longwy-
Briey, Courland, Lithuania and parts of Poland were to be
annexed and the whole of Belgium kept under military control.
Even the Chief of the Naval Secretariat was shocked by the
'complete lack of restraint in East as well as West'.[41] Bethmann, in
a complete minority, was reduced to circulating a document to his
staff in which he absolved himself from any obligation to continue
the war until all these aims were attained. Yet his disappointment
with the decisions of the Council was largely a matter of presenta-
tion and in public he was bound by them.

There had, however, already arrived in Berlin a memorandum

from the Austrian Foreign Minister, Count Czernin, with a cover-
ing letter from Karl to William. The contents were very different
from those which William had read over lunch on that July day in
1914. According to Czernin, Austria was at the end of her resources
and could not face another winter. The effect of the Russian
example on the Slavs inside the Habsburg monarchy was even
more demoralizing than in Germany, though Czernin's appreciation of the outlook in that country was none too bright. Peace
must be sought immediately on the basis of the *status quo*.

'If the monarchs of the Central Powers are not able to conclude
peace during the next few months, the peoples will go over their
heads and the waves of the revolutionary flood will sweep away
everything for which our brothers and sons are still fighting and
dying.'

Karl implored William to heed the warning:

'We are fighting against a new enemy which is more dangerous
than the Entente—against international revolution which
finds its strongest ally in general starvation. I beseech you not
to overlook this portentous aspect of the matter and to reflect
that a quick finish to the war—even at the cost of heavy sacrifice
—gives us a chance of confronting the oncoming upheaval with
success.'[42]

But William and the High Command thought that they knew
better and in so far as the Communist revolution never submerged
Germany, they did. In the first instance it was the dynasties which
were to suffer; for the Prussian homelands the reckoning, though
terrible, was to be delayed and to arrive by a complex route. But
at end-April 1917 the submarine war was going well. The English
attack at Amiens, after causing Ludendorff a crisis of confidence,
had petered out. The trade unions had collaborated to overcome
the German strikes. Lenin had just reached the city which now
bears his name and Russia seemed in the throes of dissolution. So
far from being afraid of revolution, the High Command thought
they could exploit it to achieve their aims in Russia and then turn
to complete the victory in the West. The war, it was thought,
would be over by August. 'Time', as Bethmann told the Austrians,
'is our latest ally.'[43] Moreover, the state of opinion in Germany was
such that the quickest way to have produced a revolution—

though in this case from the right—would have been to make peace on a *status quo* basis. William was convinced that the submarine campaign would produce a peace offer from England and had every intention of making her pay heavily. On 13 May he repeated his previous suggestions about terms, throwing in for good measure the cession of Gibraltar to Spain, of Cyprus, Egypt and Mesopotamia to Turkey, the return of all German colonies, the acquisition of the French as well as the Belgian Congo, and the subjugation of Belgium (split between Flemings and Walloons)! China, Japan, Brazil, Bolivia, Cuba and Portugal were to contribute to the toll of reparations which were to be exacted mainly in kind. When Czernin reached Kreuznach on 17 May, he found himself confronted by an inflexible and, as he thought, visionary opposition on which he could make no impression. He returned disillusioned and empty-handed to Vienna. Karl sent another letter urging moderation towards Russia, but when William came to the sentence, 'Peace with Russia will enable the war to be brought to a quick and favourable end', he commented: 'On condition we give way.'[44]

*   *   *

The Austrians, however, were in touch with others in Germany besides the Government. Among those who knew the terms of the Emperor's letters was Erzberger, now more than ever the dominating personality of the Centre.[45] Erzberger had proved a loyal subject, even if a discerning one, and as such had been of considerable assistance to the Government and the High Command, particularly over propaganda abroad. He it was who had recently negotiated a draft armistice with a Russian emissary in Stockholm. But the Russians insisted on the 1914 frontiers being re-established, though they did not exclude the possibility of minor modifications. Erzberger believed that the wisest course was to accept this principle for the sake of getting Russia out of the war while seeing to it that the term 'modifications' was later stretched to give the Germans all they wanted. The Kaiser and the High Command did not believe in accepting any principles whatever at this stage, preferring to keep their hands free and see what happened. When Erzberger's draft reached Bad Kreuznach it produced 'heavy storms over the whole district with intermittent thunder'. 'Militarily and politically impossible and hair-raising', was how William described the proposals.[46] Any negotiations must keep to the terms agreed at the Council, which as things then stood doomed them from the start.

Erzberger, however, had had a depressing conversation earlier in the year with General Hoffmann, the brains of the Eastern Headquarters. In June he was sought out by Colonel Bauer on behalf of the High Command. The atmosphere at Kreuznach had taken one of those sudden turns as characteristic of Ludendorff as of his master. The submarine campaign was no longer producing the expected results. So far from the war being over by August, another winter of fighting was seen to be inevitable. The Americans were about to arrive: by 1918 the fourfold Allied superiority in munitions would become sixfold. Home morale and the production figures must be raised at all costs. Defeatism must be countered wherever it appeared. Prominent among the defeatists in the view of the High Command was the Chancellor, who must be replaced. The candidates for the succession were Prince Bülow and Prince Hatzfeldt.

The strategic picture revealed to Erzberger by Hoffmann and Bauer, when added to the confidences of the Austrians, made him almost as doubtful of victory as Bethmann himself. But his experience over the armistice negotiations had convinced him that, if anything was to be saved, greater adroitness must be shown and that a subtler tactician than Bethmann was in consequence needed; he therefore lent himself to the generals' game. The Conservatives had marked the Chancellor down for overthrow ever since the Easter Message, although William still refused to listen to their complaints. But while these groups were preparing Bethmann's downfall, he received an ultimatum from the opposite side. Three years to the day after the murder of Franz Ferdinand, the Socialist leaders told him the concessions which, in their view were essential to keep the masses from transferring their loyalty to revolutionary parties: official disavowal of Pan-German war aims, acceptance of the principle of peace without annexations, prompt introduction of universal suffrage in Prussia. What was more, they intimated that, unless their party got a satisfactory answer, it would refuse to vote for the war credits which were about to be presented to the *Reichstag*. Discussions failed to remedy the situation. On 3 July, Ebert launched in the main *Reichstag* committee a strong attack on the Government and repeated in public the demands already made privately. On 6 July, Erzberger followed with a speech which for the first time gave the German people some idea of the true war situation and suggested into the bargain that the *Reichstag* take the initiative by setting up a committee to draft the terms of a compromise peace. The speech created a sensation and in the excitement which followed, it became clear that the Centre, the Progressives and the Socialists, who between them possessed a majority, were agreed in favouring a compromise peace and a reform of the Prussian suffrage.

An observer unversed in German conditions might have expected that this development would have strengthened the hand of the Chancellor in the somewhat half-hearted fight which he was making to retain the loyalty of the workers by increasing their political power and offering some hope of peace, and for a time this result appeared likely William, though fundamentally averse to diminishing his own prerogatives, could never close his mind completely to rational arguments, especially when he was nervous. On 9 July he held a Council in Berlin at which Bethmann proposed that the Socialist demands be accepted; if the war was to be won the workers must be given reason for putting their backs into it. The Prussian Minister of the Interior retorted that to have Prussia dominated by Socialists and Poles would be worse than losing the war. The chairman not unfairly summed up the discussion by saying: 'One side thinks that by proclaiming universal suffrage we shall ruin Prussia, the other thinks that by failing to proclaim it we may very well lose the war and thereby ruin both Prussia and Germany.'[47] He himself thought that the Crown Prince and the Prussian Parliament should be consulted, and postponed his decision. Stresemann, as the leader of the National Liberals, accused Bethmann of defeatism and called openly in the *Reichstag* for his replacement. But when the Chancellor asked leave to resign, it was refused. The Crown Prince then came down in favour of granting the suffrage and a proclamation to this effect was issued on 11 July. The majority in the *Reichstag* were busy drafting a 'Peace Resolution' which, after recalling William's claim in August 1914 that 'Germany had no lust of conquest', called for a negotiated peace and international conciliation. Bethmann's position seemed secure.

But the politicians reckoned without the soldiers. Already on 7 July Ludendorff had pressed on William the need to replace

Bethmann by Bülow; he was told to return to the front and mind his own business. Now he and Hindenburg redoubled their arguments through the mouth of the Crown Prince, whose adherence to the other side had been reluctantly given and was only too readily withdrawn. On 12 July the leaders of the six main parties were summoned before the heir to the throne and while they stood respectfully to attention in sweltering heat, cross-questioned about their political views. Only the Progressive and Socialist spoke in support of Bethmann and the Socialist made his support conditional on a new policy being followed; both Stresemann and Erzberger said that a change of Chancellor was essential. The Crown Prince reported this result to his father, who was indignant that his magnanimous concession over the suffrage should not have ended the crisis. Bethmann arrived at the palace to discuss the *Reichstag*'s Peace Resolution (which William found innocuous) at the very moment when the High Command delivered the *coup de grace*. A telephone message announced that Hindenburg, Ludendorff and the entire staff found themselves incapable of working any longer with Bethmann and offered their resignations. The Kaiser commented that if Bethmann was to go, he might as well abdicate himself, but for once he refrained from ordering the resigners to stay in office.[48] Bethmann saw clearly that obstinacy on his part could only result in an open clash with the military, and that it was still too early for a change in command to be possible; next day he offered his resignation in terms which made no mention of the soldiers' interference and this time he was allowed to go.

But who should be put in his place? This was the moment for the *Reichstag* to insist on establishing the responsible government which it had been demanding for several months, and refuse to support any Chancellor except one of its own choice. But the Centre were not ready for such a break with German tradition and the parties were not sufficiently united to agree on a common candidate. Moreover, only the Socialists had so far gone to the length of threatening to vote against the war credits unless their wishes were met, and without the demand being backed by a sanction of this kind, to which patriots do not easily bring themselves in wartime, there was no way of enforcing it. Indeed, it is questionable what effect a denial of credits would have had upon the haughty and determined men at Bad Kreuznach. As William told members of the *Reichstag* after the crisis was over: 'Where my Guards appear, there is no room for democracy.' The truth was that nothing short of revolution or defeat in battle could take the control of events out of the hands of the military dictators, so that the politicians were deluding themselves in a world of make-believe. But those who refuse concessions except to superior force are asking to have superior force concentrated against them. The Centre and National Liberals had certainly not helped the cause of sanity by deserting Bethmann at the crucial moment. But they imagined that in doing so they would obtain a substitute who paid more and not less attention to their opinions.

They were soon undeceived. William flatly refused to consider Bülow who had never been forgiven for his behaviour in 1908–9. Hatzfeldt had been discarded for fear he would pay too little attention to the High Command. The Crown Prince wanted Tirpitz (who had always been Dona's hero), but his appointment would have constituted too obvious a challenge to the *Reichstag*. Bethmann himself recommended the Bavarian Prime Minister, Count Hertling, who had long been a member of the *Reichstag*, but Hertling refused partly on the ground that he was seventy-four, and partly because he disagreed with the High Command about war aims. Count von Bernstorff, the former Ambassador in America, was proposed but vetoed by Hindenburg. The Kaiser then commissioned Valentini to find a Chancellor whom Hindenburg would accept. Valentini, being on bad terms with Hindenburg, went to ask von Lyncker to carry the message. They scoured the Gotha Almanack and the Official Directory in vain for a suitable candidate. Von Plessen arrived and suggested a certain Michaelis, the Prussian Food Controller. Nobody knew much about Michaelis—the Kaiser proved never to have met him—but his brusque manner was said to have made a good impression on staff officers during occasional visits to headquarters. Hindenburg declared that he would do and William was by this time in no mood to boggle over a candidate acceptable to the Field Marshal; when Ludendorff later claimed that Michaelis was his candidate, William replied: 'Why didn't you say so earlier then we could have had a closer look at the fellow!'[49]* Valentini was sent to

---

* In fact Michaelis's name seems to have occurred first to Baron von Braun, the secretary of Helfferich (the State Secretary for the Interior).[50] Fifteen years later von Braun was to be Minister of Supply in von Papen's Cabinet.

interview the dumbfounded Michaelis and bring him back to dinner with William.[51] The truth was that anyone more radical than Bethmann would have been unacceptable to the High Command as Chancellor, while anyone more reactionary would have been unacceptable to the *Reichstag*; the only way out was to choose a nonentity. As the historian Meinecke put it, Bethmann's departure left moderate opinion in Germany 'homeless'.[52] Von Kühlmann, Chargé d'Affaires at Tangier in 1905 and the moving spirit behind Anglo-German negotiations in 1912–14, was made Foreign Minister.

Michaelis made clear to the *Reichstag* his intention of working hand-in-glove with the High Command. In their name he accepted the Peace Resolution, since the deputies had brushed aside suggestions that it would be better dropped and the Socialists had let the cat out of the bag by publishing the text so as to ensure it being voted on. The price of this acceptance was the insertion of modifications to placate the High Command, and agreement to vote the war credits. More or less impromptu, Michaelis let fall the sinister comment that what he accepted was his own interpretation of the Resolution's fairly general phrases; he told the Crown Prince that 'one can make any peace one likes and still be in accord with the Resolution'.[53] Erzberger, its main author, himself said that, 'in this way I can get the Longwy-Briey line by means of negotiation'.[54] But he had only imperfectly achieved his original object of getting Germany out of a situation in which she seemed to have nothing but demands for annexation to set against the high-sounding principles offered by the enemy. In any case the *Reichstag* soon found that its achievements were nil. The Peace Resolution for all practical purposes remained a dead letter. No steps were taken to change the Prussian suffrage. Ludendorff wrote: 'I continually hope that [it] falls through. If I didn't have that hope, I would favour the conclusion of any kind of peace. With this franchise, we cannot live.'[55] There was no middle way between leaving the High Command to run Germany and taking power out of their hands by force. Unfortunately for Germany, the force had to be provided by her enemies.

*   *   *

But the question of war aims was not so easily disposed of. The Pope had already hinted at a readiness to mediate and though

William gave his Nuncio (later Pius XII) little encouragement,[56] the Austrians warmly welcomed a move which might provide a way out of their difficulties. Accordingly, in mid-August the Vatican offered to both sides its mediation in achieving a compromise peace. The British so handled the offer that the Germans were called on to state their intentions over Belgium, and the Pope urged the need for answering categorically. This was embarrassing for two reasons. Not only were German intentions ambitious; the soldiers wanted as a minimum to annex Liège, and the sailors to hold the entire coastline. In addition the civilians believed that Britain was about to make a peace offer herself and did not want either to offend neutral opinion by asking too much or weaken their bargaining position by asking too little. 'Who told you', said Kühlmann, 'that I am prepared to sell the horse Belgium? It is for me to decide that. At present the horse is not for sale.' He induced the Kaiser to abandon the naval claims which William had been talked into supporting but a decision over the military ones was shelved and the Pope got an evasive reply. Germany lost an opportunity of reassuring the world—and after all no British peace offer ever materialized.[57]

Inside Germany the writing was beginning to appear on the wall. At the end of July a movement among naval ratings in favour of an early peace was turned into a mutiny by the harshness of their officers and then drastically suppressed. When this came to be debated in the *Reichstag*, Michaelis put the blame on the Independent Socialists. The majority parties, already dissatisfied by the lack of action over the Prussian suffrage, took this as a proof of Michaelis's subservience to the élite and demanded his immediate dismissal. They still had no successor of their own to propose (largely because the Socialists would not support Bülow) but they did insist on the next Chancellor discussing his programme with them before announcing it and even went so far as to draw up a list of points which he was to be made to include. The Kaiser was by no means pleased at another change being forced on him so soon. He said to Kühlmann: 'I didn't know Michaelis at all but the Field Marshal assured me he was a good conscientious chap and I took him in the common interest.'[58]

Count Hertling was now persuaded to accept the post of Chancellor. He was only a year younger than Hohenlohe had been on appointment and so nearly blind that he had to have most documents read to him. He belonged to an older generation in the Centre Party, and his appointment reduced the influence of Erzberger so that for the next few months the extent to which the party would support left against right was always doubtful. The best comment on his appointment came from his own lips when he asked a friend if it was not absurd for an old, exhausted Professor of Philosophy to be given the job of Chancellor when problems of life and death had to be decided. The party leaders insisted on von Payer (a Progressive deputy) and von Friedberg (a Liberal one) being appointed Vice-Chancellors; their ages were such as to earn for the new team the nickname of 'grandfathers' government'. Hertling acquiesced in the innovation though regarding the *Reichstag*'s interference as unwarranted, a view echoed by Dona who answered Valentini's hint that a few concessions to the national representatives might perhaps be timely by saying that she was prepared to suffer the worst rather than see the rights of the Crown infringed by one jot or tittle. The Constitution required both deputies to resign their seats in the *Reichstag* on becoming Ministers and in practice the effect of the change was small.[59]

Hardly had Hertling taken office than one of the decisive events of the century occurred. Under the leadership of Lenin, the Bolsheviks overthrew the Provisional Government and from their headquarters in an academy for young ladies set out to organize world revolution. One of their first actions was to publish a decree proposing to all warring peoples the immediate conclusion of a peace without annexations and without indemnities. The 'Workers and Peasants Government' announced its intention of seeking forthwith a three-months armistice to permit the conduct of peace negotiations. In addition, it called for 'open diplomacy' and proceeded to publish all the secret treaties concluded between the Allies and the Tsarist Government. The German High Command did not hear of this decree for several weeks and even then failed to grasp its implications. Hitherto, peace terms had been discussed on a theoretical basis; now the moment had come to start turning them into practice. This was bound to demonstrate clearly to the world what kind of peace it was that Germany sought. The Allies in their propaganda accused Germany of world conquest and had thereby done much to secure the sympathy of independent opinion. The Germans maintained that a war of defence had been forced on them against their will. The way in which they now treated Russia would show which version was correct.

There were, of course, inside Germany all varieties of opinion from the Socialists who genuinely accepted the principle of no annexations and no indemnities to the Fatherland Party, founded in September 1917 by Tirpitz and Dietrich Schäfer as a rallying point for nationalists.[60] But within the ruling élite it can fairly be said that broad agreement as to ends was masked by bitter disagreement as to means. Germany must be compensated for having had to fight the war; this compensation must principally take the form of territorial security against future attacks *by* others which in the nature of things must simultaneously confer advantage in future attacks *on* others. On a famous occasion Hindenburg, when asked by Kühlmann why he must annex so much of the Baltic states, replied: 'For the manœuvring of my left wing in the next war.'[61] As soon as Germany achieved any military success, and thereby made the Allies more inclined to consider peace, the German leaders put up the amount of territory which they proposed to demand, so that 'The more we win, the further off does peace get.'[62] But while the soldiers saw no objection to barefacedly stating—or taking—what they wanted, the civilians sought to make annexation look respectable under the cover of a formula. The most convenient one for this purpose was 'self-determination', it being tacitly assumed that Germany would control the conditions under which determination took place. Yet since this refinement could hardly be explained in public, the nationalists bitterly attacked acceptance of the formula as a betrayal of Germany's interests.

On 18 December 1917 a Council was held at Kreuznach to discuss the conditions which should be imposed on the Bolsheviks in the forthcoming peace negotiations at Brest-Litovsk. On 3 March 1918 a Treaty was finally signed at that town. The Kaiser was not involved in, or even informed of, all the complex details of the intervening negotiations. On balance his influence was thrown in support of the civilians and at one point Kühlmann called him 'the only sensible person in the whole of Germany'.[63] The wrangling among his subordinates, however, pained him and in the final resort he gave way to the High Command. On New Year's Day 1918, during an interval in which the negotiators had come to Berlin for briefing, he received General Hoffmann, who

three years before had made his name by devising the plan underlying Hindenburg's victory at Tannenberg. Hoffmann, however,
had remained in the East when Hindenburg and Ludendorff
had taken over the High Command, and when he was now asked
for his opinion as to what should be done, he begged to be excused.
For his first-hand knowledge of the situation led him to be content
with less than the objectives which the High Command, some
seven hundred miles distant from the scene of operations, had
decided to be essential. 'When Your All-Highest War Lord wishes
to hear your views on any subject it is your duty to give them to
him, irrespective of whether they coincide with those of the
High Command or not.'[64] Hoffmann, thus admonished, suggested
that, since Poles had proved notoriously difficult to manage, as few
extra ones as possible should be incorporated in Germany.
William listened, thought this reasonable and had Hoffmann
illustrate his proposals on a map. Kühlmann begged his master in
using the map not to disclose where he had got it from for fear
of Ludendorff's jealousy. William brushed the objection aside:
'With you diplomats each is jealous of the other—but that sort of
thing doesn't happen among soldiers.'[65] At a Council next day he
produced the map as Hoffmann's, saying it represented his own
decision as to where the frontier should be drawn. After a
moment's stunned silence, Ludendorff shouted that the Kaiser had
no right to invite the opinion of subordinate officers over the heads
of his chief military advisers; the imperial decision could not be
accepted until the High Command had had time to reflect. The
matter of the remark was more justified than its manner; in face
of the outburst, William temporized and said he would await the
reflection's outcome.

This was duly conveyed by Hindenburg in a letter of Ludendorff's drafting; it confrónted William with a choice between
accepting their advice and their resignations. While hedging on the
immediate issue, the Kaiser backed Hertling in insisting that the
handling of the peace negotiations must be left to the civilians,
with the soldiers acting as technical advisers. He further sent
Hindenburg a friendly but firm letter (drafted by Kühlmann)
explaining that his frequent disagreement with the views of his
generals did not imply any lack of confidence:

'It is wholly natural that in the biggest coalition war in history, soldiers and statesmen should have different views as to what the aims of the war should be and how best they can be achieved. This is an old and familiar phenomenon which does not surprise me now. It is your right and duty to put forward your views with energy, just as it is the duty of the responsible statesman to place in front of me his rather different approach. . . . I have shown your letter to the Chancellor and enclose a memorandum giving his views on it. With these I agree and confidently expect that you and General Ludendorff will feel that these views put an end to your doubts and enable you to devote yourselves wholeheartedly to the tasks of the actual conduct of operations. . . . I can promise, my dear Field Marshal, that you will always find in me a ready listener and that the last thing I would wish to do is to dispense with your valuable advice.'[66]

For the time being the demi-gods (as the generals were nicknamed) had to knuckle under, but they did so with a bad grace. Baulked of their demand for Kühlmann's dismissal, they consoled themselves by insisting on that of Valentini, the Kaiser's faithful Civil Secretary, whom they alleged to be 'entirely to blame for the swing to the left in the government'. William was infuriated by the demand, and slammed the door in Hindenburg's face saying: 'I don't want your paternal advice.' He called Ludendorff a 'Malefactor with whom he would never shake hands again'.[67] But Valentini insisted on sacrificing himself to ease his master's position. He was replaced by von Berg, a dyed-in-the-wool reactionary whose influence in the succeeding months was almost wholly unfavourable; under his prompting William's marginal comment came to consist of 'continuous sabre-rattling, contempt for the diplomats and anti-Semitism'.[68] As an observer remarked, Germany had reached the point where the Kaiser had the members of his personal entourage dictated to him just as much as the Ministers of his Government.[69]

Later in the Brest-Litovsk negotiations William, incensed by a Bolshevik threat to his life and moved by an appeal from Estonian landowners, ordered Kühlmann to give the Russians twenty-four hours to abandon all claims to the Baltic provinces. But when Kühlmann tactfully protested against having his elbow jogged, William did not insist. Equally, however, when Trotsky confronted the Germans with his celebrated paradox 'No war, no peace', the Kaiser fell in with the High Command and ordered hostilities to be resumed. As Kühlmann said to him, he could not defy their views on such a subject unless he was ready to take personal responsibility for the outcome of the war. But this did not justify the enthusiasm with which those views were embraced. He called the Brest-Litovsk peace 'one of the greatest victories of history the significance of which will only properly be appreciated by our grandchildren', though almost simultaneously placing 'the blame for the blood now being shed in the East' on 'the slipshod behaviour of our negotiators at Brest-Litovsk'.[70]

The High Command were of course defeated by a new species of adversary and experienced the fate described by the Psalmist: 'he gave them their desires and sent leanness withal into their soul'. Though they occupied the entire Ukraine and penetrated to Finland, Sevastopol and Baku, they only obtained from the area 42,000 truck-loads of corn and in the process of extracting it tied up a million men. The openness of Bolshevik diplomacy and the final refusal to argue about the German terms before accepting them left the world in no doubt that peace was being dictated at the point of the bayonet. Trotsky's tactics forced Kühlmann to reveal that the term 'no annexations' was being interpreted to admit 'assisted' self-determination. The Bolshevik principles which the Germans so scornfully rejected would, in fact, have brought them a more favourable peace than the one to which they found submission inevitable. But their chance of getting peace would all along have improved if they had been prepared to consider a compromise. As long as they were set on victory, they had not merely to conquer in the West but also to break the blockade, and only supplies from Russia would enable them to do that. They had to gamble for high stakes because their political requirements could not be met with lower ones.

Even before they knew of the October Revolution the twin dictators had committed themselves. In a conference on 11 November 1917 Ludendorff decided to stake Germany's all on breaking the Allies in France the following spring before America was fully deployed. 'It will be an immense struggle,' said Ludendorff to the Kaiser, 'which will begin at one point, continue to another and take a long time; it is difficult, but it will be successful.'[71] William, who had not been invited to the conference, decided with apparent misgiving to accept its conclusions. After all, no better way of winning on the battlefield was in sight. The only alternative to a military victory was a compromise peace and even supposng that the Allied leaders had been ready to compromise (which is far from certain) the forces whose prestige depended on victory were still dominant in Germany. The insistence on a peace with annexations did not come merely from the generals and the Fatherland Party. Erzberger, under attack in his own party for his share in the Peace Resolution, said in September 1917 that: 'We renounce nothing which is necessary for German greatness, for German development and for German freedom in the world.' The Central Committee of the Liberals, in criticizing the Resolution, resolved that:

> 'Germany's future security cannot rest on international treaties alone but must be based on German might and strength. Without accessions of strength in East and West, assurance of our position as a world power overseas and adequate reparations, we shall have no security against future threats to our existence; we shall experience a political and economic setback for decades.'[72]

A Liberal leader speaking in the *Reichstag* in January 1918 said that:

> 'The statesman who returns from the war without Longwy-Briey, without Belgium in his hand, without the Flanders coast-line freed from England's power, without the line of the Meuse in our control, will go down to history as the grave-digger of German prestige.'[73]

It is extremely doubtful whether a majority could have been obtained in the *Reichstag* at any time between July 1917 and July 1918 for a peace genuinely free from annexations or reparations.

Like the majority of men at most periods, William was the prisoner of the culture in which destiny had placed him and to which he had conscientiously tried to conform. He might have inner doubts about the destination for which the train was heading but his was not the kind of character which could have been expected to pull the communication cord. Kühlmann, in the spring of 1918, attacked the High Command in anonymous newspaper articles. In one he wrote that 'there comes again and again a cry from the German people for a statesman to lead them. Conditions, however, are not such as to allow any statesman to become great.' William, on reading this, minuted: 'Very true, either he is unpopular with the *Reichstag* or with Kreuznach or both.' A few lines lower Kühlmann wrote that 'the relations between the soldiers and civilians leave much to be desired'. William's comment was: 'Naturally: the Kaiser is ignored by both sides.' When Field Marshal Mackensen submitted a gloomy report on the situation in Austria and the Balkans, William expressed his complete agreement. 'Unfortunately I have been unable to get a hearing for these views from the General Staff.'[74] He forgot how he had himself treated the Emperor Karl's approaches a year earlier. Inconsistency of this kind was the explanation of his relegation to the side-lines. Had his views about the right course for Germany been both clear and steady, he would have stood more chance of putting them across. But people paid less and less attention to a ruler whose ideas changed with the seasons, no matter how sensible they might sometimes be. Unfortunately for William, though not wholly unjustly, Allied opinion failed to realize that his boasts about who settled German policy had lost even the limited validity which they once possessed, and on the other hand took the views of the Socialists to represent the genuine though impotent voice of the German people. As President Wilson put it in answering the Pope's offer of mediation:

> 'The object of this war is to deliver the free peoples of the world from the menace and the actual power of a vast military establishment, controlled by an irresponsible Government. . . . This power is not the German people. It is the ruthless master of the German people. . . . We cannot take the word of the present ruler of Germany as a guarantee of anything that is to endure unless explicitly supported by such conclusive evidence of the will and purpose of the German people as the other peoples of the world would be justified in accepting.'[75]

*　　　　*　　　　*

On 15 March, to prepare for the offensive, the High Command moved to Spa where headquarters were paradoxically situated in the Hotel Britannique. Nearby a chateau was prepared for the Kaiser. The attack opened on 21 March and made quick progress. Although casualties were ghastly, optimism was widespread. William, who had been up near the front, shouted to the stationmaster as his return train pulled in: 'The battle is won, the

English have been utterly defeated.'[76] He also said that if an English M.P. came to ask for peace, he would first of all have to kneel in front of the Imperial standards since what was happening was a victory of monarchy over democracy.[77] William was only upset when a German newspaper christened the operation 'The Kaiser's Battle' since he thought this might suggest that he had never been involved in any of the earlier ones. Hindenburg received a decoration which had previously been given only to Blücher after Waterloo. But after a fortnight the advance ground to a halt without quite breaking the British line. The same experience was repeated further north in April and further south against the French in May.

Throughout the succeeding months the ambivalence of William's attitude to the war became more marked than ever, and was buttressed by a refusal to consider the East and West fronts together. Thus on the one hand he talked and planned confidently about his future policy towards Russia:

> 'Peace between the Slavs and Germans is completely impossible. . . . Only fear of us will maintain peace with Russia. The Slavs will always hate us and remain enemies. . . . We must dominate the Germanic lands in order to keep Russia away from our eastern frontier.'[78]

On 7 June he 'emphatically endorsed' proposals for incorporating Georgia in the *Reich*, and stressed the importance of Transcaucasia as a bridge to Central Asia and a threat to the British position in India.[79] In August he was still discussing how best to arrange the annexation of Courland, and scorning the idea that the Americans should have any say in the matter.[80] As late as 10 September he received Skoropadski, the leader of the dissident Ukrainians, as a prelude to the signature of alliance with his régime.[81] Yet it was in these same months that a court official said Ballin must be told not to talk pessimistically in front of his master. 'The Kaiser must not hear such remarks. They make him lose his nerve.'[82] On 15 June, the thirtieth anniversary of his accession, he issued a message describing the war as

> 'a conflict between two approaches to the world. Either the Prussian-German-Germanic approach—Right, Freedom, Honour, Morality—is to remain respected or the Anglo-Saxon, which would mean enthroning the worship of gold.'[83]

But it was with more piety than conviction that he went on: 'Victory will go to the German approach.' And it is said to have been with William's approval that at the end of June, Kühlmann, thinking to prepare opinion for the course which he believed to be inevitable, dropped hints in the *Reichstag* about the possibility of an approach becoming necessary to the Allies for peace negotiations. The Conservative leader Westarp at once declared that 'just as our good sword has won us peace in the East, so it will in the West'. A spokesman for the Centre seconded this view and Stresemann for the Liberals claimed that there had never been less reason to doubt a German victory.[84] The High Command, to whom Kühlmann's lack of assurance had for some time been anathema, once again pronounced the verdict that further co-operation was impossible. At a Council held at Spa at the beginning of July, Hertling had to apologize for his subordinate, 'like a teacher excusing a pupil's bad essay to a school inspector'.[85] Kühlmann was replaced by von Hintze who had worked his passage into diplomacy from the navy and, although looking in uniform like the Kaiser's head coachman, was regarded as sound on the fundamentals. The Council confirmed German annexationist aims without modifications; on 14 July the Kaiser rejected a suggestion that he send President Wilson his terms for peace and on the previous day all parties in the *Reichstag* except the Independent Socialists voted for a fresh instalment of war credits.

But the offensive launched on 15 July proved a failure and three days later the Allied counter-offensive was only with difficulty halted. On 22 July Hindenburg admitted to a hitch and advised the Kaiser to return to Spa. William was much cast down. He described himself as a defeated War Lord and asked his staff to treat him gently. Next day he told them how in sleepless hours mocking visions of his English and Russian relatives and all the Ministers and Generals of his own reign (doubtless led by Bismarck) had filed before him; only the little Queen of Norway had been kind.[86] He was particularly worried about the sector between Albert and Montdidier and it was there on 8 August that the British broke through. For the first time the fighting morale of the German troops failed, particularly in face of the tanks, which caused Ludendorff in his *Memoirs* to call the date 'the Black Day of the German Army'. During the next two days William behaved with considerable dignity. He avoided recriminations, said that too much had been expected of his troops, and encouraged Ludendorff who talked of resigning. But he also said: 'Things can't go on like this indefinitely and we must find a way to end it all.'[87] When Hintze arrived on 13 August, Ludendorff admitted that, as he saw no prospect of breaking the resolution of the enemy by an offensive, the only hope now lay of wearing it down by a strategic defence. But at a Council next day he left the job of repeating this to Hintze and contented himself with leading a chorus of condemnation against defeatism on the home front. Hindenburg considered that it would remain possible to keep German troops on French territory and so in the end force a peace on German terms. William consoled himself with stories of the other side's troubles and hopes of what could be achieved at home by propaganda. Peace would have to be reached by negotiation but the opening of negotiations was best postponed until after there was a lull in the fighting. Capitulation was as yet undreamt of. A week later Hintze saw fit to assure the *Reichstag* that 'there is no ground for doubting our victory. The moment we doubt whether we are going to win, we shall have been defeated.'[88] By that time William had moved to Kassel to be near Dona whose heart had been affected by the mounting troubles. One night as they were sitting on the terrace, someone brought out a picture and asked William if he had painted it. He identified it as the work of someone else, and added: 'You know, if I had that man's talent, I should have been a painter instead of an Emperor and I shouldn't be in such a horrifying position today.'[89]

Early in September Ballin tried to bring home to William the realities of the situation but was obstructed by Berg who insisted on attending the interview and prevented it from getting down to brass tacks.[90] On 10 September, as an experiment in home front propaganda, the Kaiser visited Krupps and spoke to the workmen; the occasion was not a success. A fresh British break-through at Arras and Cambrai brought on an attack of neuralgia which by William's own admission bordered on a nervous breakdown; he went to bed for twenty-four hours and declared himself a new man again.[91] Unfortunately a similar cure was not available to Ludendorff who by his unremitting efforts over four years had driven himself as well as the German army and the German people to a virtual standstill. For some months past he had been subject to attacks of blinding rage; now all of a sudden he collapsed. On the

27 of September, Bulgaria capitulated thereby putting at risk German supplies of Roumanian oil. On 28 September, Ludendorff told Hindenburg that the only way of insuring against a collapse in the field was to ask forthwith for an armistice on the basis of President Wilson's Fourteen Points (which it later became patent that he had not taken in). Together on the following day they went to their master and, in contrast to the boastful predictions which they had so often made, admitted that they had lost the war. An armistice must be concluded immediately. Treating them with more consideration than he had often received at their hands, he listened to them without surprise and without excitement. Thirteen years before he had advised the Tsar how to behave in a similar situation:

'National honour is a very good thing in itself but only in the case that the whole of the Nation is determined to uphold it with all the means possible. But when a nation's ways show that it has had enough and that *"tout est perdu fors l'honneur"* is its way of thinking, is it not reasonable that its Ruler should then—no doubt with a heavy heart—draw the consequences and conclude peace?'[92]

Now Nicky was dead on the far side of the Urals and Willy had his own crisis to meet. He told his staff that he would have preferred to have had the facts faced earlier. The army was obviously worn out. Bavarian and even Saxon divisions were surrendering wholesale. The war was over but in a very different manner from the one expected. Hintze was told to take the necessary steps. William admitted in reply to a question that the German people had behaved most gallantly. But their politicians had failed them badly.

The failure, of course, lay not so much in politicians or even in soldiers so much as in a system, a way of looking at the world. So often had the German people seen their enthusiasms frustrated for lack of blood and iron that they had fallen into an uncritical admiration of force. The getting of what they thought themselves entitled to have was seen as a matter of being sufficiently determined. The virtues of manliness, self-reliance, courage and discipline were exaggerated to the point of distortion, like cancerous cells. As a result, the nation largely lost the capacity for objective appraisal either of themselves or of other peoples. They allowed their phenomenal progress to go to their heads. Many of the defects which have been noticed in this story—the excessive qualities required of an Emperor, the predominance of the soldiers over the civilians, the false estimates of German strength, the illusions of grandeur about war aims—were all symptoms of this basic cultural malady. In fact the judgement of the despised civilians—and particularly of the slandered Socialists—was usually better than that of the élite. But so convinced were the élite of their superior wisdom that many of their bodies had to be literally dead and the remainder discredited before an alternative point of view could become politically effective. The consequence was that responsible government started on its German career with all the associations of unhappiness and failure; from such associations many subsequent evils flowed.

Now, however, the fateful moment had arrived; the old system could go on no longer. For one thing, the victorious Entente had made its abolition one of their main aims. In the same breath as he told William that an armistice must be asked for, Ludendorff told Hertling that 'an alteration in the Government or its reconstitution on a broader basis' had become necessary. The majority parties in the *Reichstag* had been pressing with growing impatience for the introduction of the changes promised fourteen months before and Hintze declared that a revolution from above was the only way of forestalling a revolution from below. On the day on which William gave orders for an armistice to be sought, he announced his wish that the German people should be enabled to co-operate more effectively than hitherto in the control of their destinies. Accordingly, he had decided that men who possessed the public confidence should take a larger part in the rights and duties of the Government. But polite phrases could not conceal the fact that internal defeat went hand-in-hand with external. William was overcome by a bad attack of sciatica and had to walk with a stick; he seemed a broken and suddenly aged man. Hertling was unwilling to have any part in the new development; he foresaw that a parliamentary government would be a centralizing one and was not prepared to help in humbling Bavaria. A new Chancellor had to be found, a process which was not assisted by Ludendorff who, in his anxiety to fend off a break-through by negotiating an armistice, was behaving like a cat on hot bricks. Bursting into the room where the Kaiser was consulting with Hertling, he asked whether the new government was ready yet, to which William replied, 'I'm not a conjurer'.[93] Berg on the other hand attempted bluster about who might or might not be appointed, and as a result found himself among the discards.

The first democratic Chancellor of Germany proved to be Prince Max, heir to the Grand Duchy of Baden which had for some time been governed by a coalition of Liberals and Social Democrats. A few weeks earlier, the Prince had been induced to offer his services to William with a programme which involved peace negotiations as soon as the Western front was stabilized but stopped short of a full parliamentary system. The offer had at the time of its making been refused; by the time of its acceptance, its achievement had become impossible. Now Max stepped into the breach with reluctance: 'I thought I should have arrived five minutes before the hour but I arrived five minutes after it.'[94] He still hoped for a free hand in choosing his team and argued strongly against a precipitate appeal to the Allies. But before he had effectively taken over, the party leaders were called to hear from a representative of the High Command a statement similar to the one made by Hindenburg to his master. 'We can no longer win. To avoid further sacrifices, His Majesty has been advised to break off the battle. Each day that goes by makes the position worse and increases the danger of the enemy realizing how weak we are.' None of the deputies had realized the pass to which things had come and the result was consternation. Even the Socialist, Ebert, went white as a sheet and was unable to utter; Stresemann looked as though someone had struck him; the Conservative, von Waldow, walked up and down saying that the only course left was to put a bullet through one's head (which he did not, however, proceed to do). Heydebrand—the man who had reacted so violently to Lloyd George in 1911—summed up the situation in a phrase destined to echo down the years, 'We have been deceived and betrayed' (*Wir sind belogen und betrogen*). The Independent Socialist, Haase, on the other hand rushed up to a colleague and shouted, 'Now we've got them!'[95] There was, therefore, no arguing when the parties insisted on most of the Cabinet being chosen from their ranks, while the Socialists made their entry conditional on the Constitution being amended to make office compatible with a seat in the *Reichstag*. The Chancellor was made responsible to the *Reichstag*, and authority over the armed forces transferred from the

Kaiser to Ministers.[96] Parliamentary government thus came to Germany as an expedient conceded by a bankrupt régime rather than as a right insisted on by the people. Yet the sneer implied in the judgement is hardly fair. To have insisted on such government being introduced earlier would have required ability to mobilize superior force. That the state of public opinion precluded this from being done is one of the fundamentals of German history. What the democrats lacked was not so much readiness to fight as ability to convince.

*   *   *

Prince Max had equally little luck in getting the High Command to allow time for preparing the ground before an armistice was openly sought. Hindenburg had been briefed by Ludendorff to deny that the army could wait as long as forty-eight hours. A fresh enemy offensive might at any moment produce disaster. William backed him up. 'The High Command consider an armistice necessary and you have not been brought here to make difficulties for the High Command.'[97] But when Prince Max asked the generals whether they were prepared to lose Alsace-Lorraine and the parts of Prussia inhabited by Poles (as laid down in Wilson's Points 8 and 10), Ludendorff replied that, while they were ready to cede the French-speaking parts of Lorraine, any surrender of territory on the east was out of the question! Hindenburg even said that, if the terms of the Allies proved too humiliating, he would be in favour of fighting to the last man, which, as the Finance Minister tried to explain to him, is not a practicable proposition where 65 million people are concerned.[98] But Ludendorff was still in a panic and the appeal for an armistice was sent to Washington. Whether anything would have been gained by waiting is doubtful. The Allies were by this time confident of victory and determined that once hostilities stopped there should be no chance of a resumption. They were therefore set on imposing armistice terms which would put Germany at their mercy; there was to be no question of negotiation.

The first American reaction was to ask for further information. Did the German Government accept the Fourteen Points completely? Was it prepared to evacuate all occupied territory? Did it speak in the name of the whole German people? These points raised no difficulty. But the second American note contained unmistakable signs that birds of ill omen were coming home to roost. For one thing the torpedoing by a U-boat of the *Leinster* between Dublin and Holyhead, effected after the appeal for an armistice had been launched, naturally produced a warning that, unless such things stopped forthwith, there would be no further discussions. But in addition the note reminded Germany that one of the terms she had accepted was 'the destruction of every arbitrary power anywhere that can separately, secretly and of its single choice, disturb the peace of the world'. The power which had hitherto guided the destinies of the German people was now named as being one of those thus described. It was within the choice of the German people to change this and there could be no peace until such a change was made. Indeed the execution of peace would largely depend on the preciseness and adequacy of the assurances given on this fundamental point. The third note spoke even more plainly. The only form of armistice acceptable to the Allies would be one which put out of question any renewal of hostilities. And while it might be true, as the Germans now claimed, that a far-reaching change had been made in their system of government, what guarantee was there that the change would be permanent and the authority of the new government effective?

'It is evident that the German people have no means of commanding the acquiescence of the military authorities of the Empire to the popular will; that the power of the King of Prussia to control the policy of the Empire is still unimpaired; that the determining initiative remains with those who have been masters of Germany. . . . The nations of the world do not and cannot trust the word of those who have hitherto been the masters of German policy. . . . If the Government of the United States must deal with the military masters and the monarchical autocrats of Germany now, or if it is likely to have to deal with them later . . . it must demand not peace negotiations but surrender.'[99]

At about this time Prince Ernst zu Hohenlohe wrote from Switzerland to Prince Max that 'William is regarded as the embodiment of all the real and invented atrocities of this war and as the most determined opponent of any limits being placed on the Imperial authority.'[100] The picture though incorrect was hardly unfair. 'There is only one person who is master in this Empire and I am not going to tolerate any other.' 'I am the Balance of Power in Europe since the German constitution leaves decisions about foreign policy to me.' 'It is clear that Grey has no idea who really rules here and that *I* am the master.' However much William may during the war have disagreed with the soldiers and the extreme right, he had never made his disagreement obvious. The *Reichstag* had for over a year seemed ready for constitutional reform and a compromise peace but had equally seemed powerless; William had shown it no support. Others might in fact be more to blame than he for the position in which Germany found herself—but rank has its responsibilities as well as its privileges. The Allied preoccupation with the Imperial symbol made sense, since an Emperor (and still more a King of Prussia) was such an integral part of the German Establishment that his disappearance would be a clear sign that the power of the old ruling class was broken.

Nor were the Allies without cause in suspecting the genuineness of the German conversion. In fact, Max of Baden during these weeks played the part of an honest and public-spirited man; but his birth and such evidence as could be found about his views did not immediately identify him as a tireless fighter for popular freedom. Indeed at this very moment a French paper published a letter in which ten months earlier Max had spoken slightingly of pale parliamentarianism and the democratic slogans and had described the 1917 Peace Resolution as 'the hideous offspring of fear and the Berlin dog days'. The Vice-Presidents were still the same as under Hertling; the Minister of War was still a general. The attempts made by people like Erzberger (a Minister in Max's Cabinet) to reconcile the Peace Resolution with a settlement like Brest-Litovsk recoiled heavily on the German reputation for good faith. And in suspecting that the request for an armistice might be just an attempt to secure a military breathing-space, the Allies came inconveniently close to the mentality of the High Command.

Immediately he read the second American note, William realized what it implied. 'The hypocritical Wilson has at last thrown off the mask. The object of this is to bring down my House, to set the Monarchy aside.' Dona raged at 'the audacity of the parvenu across the sea who thus dares to humiliate a princely house which can look back on centuries of service to people and country'.[101] Her husband told the Bavarian Ambassador that he knew many people wanted him to go 'but a descendant of Frederick the Great does not abdicate'.[102] He had spoken contemptuously of the Tsar for being willing to give up his throne. Though more and more responsible people in Germany were coming to think that abdication would prove inevitable, the groups which had made it inevitable still refused to contemplate it. A Conservative newspaper said that the Allies must think a people capable of the depths of treason when they expected it 'to abandon a dynasty that had been the architect of its greatness through the course of a glorious history'.[103] It was freely asserted that, if the Kaiser went, the army would break up. Ludendorff by this time had recovered his nerve, lost his fear of a sudden catastrophe and was talking of renewed offensives in the spring. The inwardness of what he had brought on his monarch and his army was beginning to dawn on him and he recoiled from the prospect of surrender in horror. The third American note provoked the High Command to deny ever having insisted upon an immediate armistice, although Max had taken the precaution of getting that insistence put in writing. Not content with such a demonstrable untruth, they sent to all Army Commanders a telegram describing the proposed conditions as 'impossible for us soldiers to accept', and ordering 'resistance with every means in our command'. Before the telegram could be suppressed, an Independent Socialist who happened to be a military wireless operator succeeded in transmitting the text to his leaders in Berlin.

The constitutional law bringing the armed forces under Ministerial control was at that moment being discussed by the *Reichstag*, so that the High Command's action was an open defiance of the new system and the very thing which, if allowed to pass unchallenged, would convince the Allies that the new government did not possess the authority it claimed. Prince Max went straight to the Kaiser and warned him that, unless Ludendorff were dismissed, the Cabinet would resign. The weapon which the High Command had used to bring down Bethmann, Valentini and Kühlmann was now turned against them—for it was they who, since their open admission of failure, were becoming expendable.

'For weeks', said William, 'I have been working with all my might to weld all sections of the people into an united front. Now the whole structure threatens to collapse. Still, it *is* an impossible state of affairs that such a manifesto can come out without my consent and the Chancellor's. I see nothing for it but to comply with the Chancellor's request.'[104]

On 26 October Hindenburg and Ludendorff were called before him in Berlin and he spoke to Ludendorff in such terms that the latter offered his resignation, which was at once accepted. That of Hindenburg was however refused, Max fearing that his departure might prove the final blow to the army's morale. 'The operation is over', said the Kaiser. 'I have separated the Siamese twins.'[105] The new First Quartermaster-General was Gröner who had once pleased William by keeping him in the picture about field railways and had since shown administrative genius in organizing munitions production and exploiting the Ukraine.

On 27 October the Emperor Karl wrote to tell William that Austria had decided to stop fighting forthwith and make peace. The news led Max's Cabinet to decide that the American requirements must be complied with, and the Kaiser had no alternative but to agree. Conditions were developing inside Germany which undermined the assumptions on which the Chancellor's policy had been framed. The German people had held out with amazing tenacity against adverse conditions for four long years. But it was the hope of making their country great which had kept them going. Once the prospect of success was almost without warning removed they not unreasonably asked why they should go on enduring cold and illness and hunger. The Socialist, Scheidemann (now a Minister), put their thoughts into words (which were to become even more familiar twenty-seven years later): 'Better an end accompanied by terror than a terror without end.' As in Russia, the one thing which the majority of people wanted was peace; the left-wing parties, aided and abetted by the Russian Embassy, had no hesitation in promising to secure peace as a means of securing power. A fight to the death, as an alternative to capitulation, had little attraction for anyone. And with the question of peace went that of abdication. For though the Allies did not make any more precise the principles which had been stated in the American notes (the Kaiser's name did not occur in the text of the armistice), the word began to be passed round that 'if the Kaiser goes, we shall get a decent peace'. Ministers, who had begun to consider abdication as early as 6 October, were rapidly coming to the same conclusion. The only hope for the throne was felt to lie in the abdication of Kaiser and Crown Prince in favour of one of the latter's sons. If this had been done, there was good prospect of wide support (including the majority Socialists) for a constitutional monarchy with a regent. But the independent Socialists were hard at work for a Republic and if people once came to believe that this was the quick way to peace, they would be likely to take it.

The problem was how to bell the cat. Max as a Prince and a relative seems to have felt a delicacy in broaching the subject even if he had not been overcome by influenza at the crucial moment. While he seems to have been remiss in keeping William informed about the general situation, he sent on the letters which he received from abroad and used various intermediaries to urge that the longer abdication was delayed, the smaller the chance of saving the monarchy. William was quicker to take the hint than to draw the intended conclusion. He had been bitterly offended by the Cabinet's refusal to publish a letter and a decree which he sent them on 28 October promising his full support for them and for the constitutional changes. On the night of 29 October, he yielded to the arguments of Dona and von Berg (who was still lurking on the backstairs) and slipped away from Potsdam-for ever as it proved—back to Spa.[106] His entourage supposed that at Head-quarters he would be safe against pressure to abdicate, since Hindenburg would never agree to it. 'Prince Max's Government', he said on arrival, 'is trying to throw me out. At Berlin I should be less able to oppose them than in the midst of my generals.'[107] So far from serving the monarchy, this flight may well have proved fatal to it, since if William had remained at Berlin, subject to the arguments of his civilian Ministers and under the influence of developments in the capital, he might have abdicated in time to forestall the proclamation of the Republic. On the other hand, he might have fallen into the hands of the revolutionaries, have failed to escape from Germany and so had inadequate security against Allied demands for his surrender.

*   *   *

Scheidemann had already asked Max to submit the question of abdication to the Cabinet but had agreed to hold his hand while fresh efforts were made to secure a voluntary withdrawal. The search for emissaries continued but all with one consent contrived to make excuses. On 31 October the question did come before the Cabinet. Four members thought abdication desirable and inevitable. Two others (one being Erzberger) thought that the Allies should be left to impose it. The War Minister feared the effect on army morale. Finally, the Prussian Minister of the Interior, Dr. Drews, agreed to go to Spa where on 1 November he told William of the mounting demand for his departure and pointed out the possible consequences of delay. William himself described the interview two days later in a letter to a friend:

'I said, "How comes it that you, a Prussian official, one of my subjects who have taken an oath of allegiance to me, have the insolence and effrontery to appear before me with a request like this?" You should just have seen how that took the wind out of his sails. It was the last thing he expected, he made a deep bow on the spot. "Very well then, supposing I did," I said. "What do you suppose would happen next, you, an administrative official? My sons have assured me that none of them will take my place. So the whole house of H would go along with me." You should have seen the fright that gave him, it again was the last thing he'd expected. He and the whole of that smart govt in Berlin. "And who would then take on the regency for a twelve-year-old child? My grandson? the Imperial Chancellor perhaps? I gather from Munich that they haven't the least intention of recognizing him down there. So what would happen?" "Chaos," he said, making another bow. You see, you only have to question such muddle-heads, and go on questioning them for all their confusion and empty-headedness to become obvious. "All right then," I said, "let me tell you the form chaos would take. I abdicate. All the dynasties fall along with me, the army is left leaderless, the front-line troops disband and stream over the Rhine. The disaffected gang up together, hang, murder and plunder—assisted by the enemy. That is why I have no intention of abdicating. The King of Prussia cannot betray Germany, etc. I have no intention of quitting the throne because of a few hundred Jews and a thousand workmen. Tell that to your masters in Berlin!" When he was going, I called the Field Marshal and First Quartermaster-General. Hindenburg told him the same thing bluntly and then Gröner who is a Swabian, in other words a South German, a jolly little chap,

he went for Drews like a wild-cat, he fairly gave it to him. . . .
Now I may have ruled well or badly, that's not the point at the
moment, most of it was of course bad! But I have lived for sixty
years and spent thirty of them on the throne. There is one thing
you must allow me, experience! Who is to take my place? The
famous Max of Baden?'[108]

Next day the Kaiser saw Hintze who, on leaving office with
Hertling, had become Foreign Office representative at Spa, and
talked to him about plans for leading an army back into Germany.
'We shall soon see whether England will lend a hand in crushing
Bolshevism.' Hintze cautiously explained the desirability of
the Supreme War Lord showing himself among fighting troops.
Hintze was away for the next three days but when they next met
William expanded on the enthusiasm with which he had been
received at 'the front'—although in fact he had been allowed to do
no more than visit depots on the lines of communication. But one
evening some bombs had fallen near the royal train and started a
conversation in the dining-car about death. William spoke
slightly of people who feared death and then, leaning back,
with an apparent effort of memory, began to quote:

> *'Cowards die many times before their deaths:*
> *The valiant never taste of death but once.*
> *Of all the wonders that I yet have heard,*
> *It seems to me most strange that men should fear;*
> *Seeing that death, a necessary end,*
> *Will come when it will come.'*[109]

When he got back to Spa, the news was bad.[110] Not only had the
British broken through again on 4 November; Gröner told the
Chancellor, 'We shall have to cross the lines with a white flag.'
But on 30 October an attempt to send the navy to sea (under-
taken without the Government's knowledge) was met by refusal
to obey orders, and the ensuing courts-martial by a revolution in
which on 4 November the mutinous sailors took over the town of
Kiel. The revolt spread quickly to other ports and thence through
Germany: on 7 November, for example, Kurt Eisner proclaimed a
Workers Republic in Munich. As later events showed, the number
of people who wanted a radical recasting of society was infinites-
imal. But as long as they could promise peace and as long as the
Government failed to secure it, war-weary workers, soldiers and

peasants flocked to them. Those officers who talked of preferring death to dishonourable capitulation were asking for trouble from their rank-and-file. Indeed the Headquarters' view could not have been more wrong; it was the Kaiser's continued presence, not his abdication, which threatened the army's morale. Accordingly, on 7 November Prince Max's Socialist Ministers told him that unless within twenty-four hours William had gone, they would go instead. In communicating this to Spa, Max, who offered his resignation, suggested as a compromise that William announce his intention of abdicating immediately after the signing of an armistice, for which negotiations were at that moment beginning. But William refused and announced his intention of remaining with his troops; he ordered a plan to be prepared for marching back with them into Germany and restoring order.

The world which he knew was dissolving round him, the world of discipline and deference, the outer signs of a loyalty and unselfishness on which the German Empire had been built up and on which its rulers had come to count. One of the gravest charges against the culture which was collapsing was that it had taken too much for granted the willingness of humbler people to subordinate their own interests to the common good and had betrayed those people by exploiting their loyalty for mistaken purposes. Certainly William was alive to his responsibility for the welfare of his subjects; his unpublished proclamation of 28 October had ended with the words: 'The function of the Emperor is to serve his people' (*Das Kaiseramt ist Dienst am Volke*). But, like many people in authority, he had expected them to accept his own interpretation of what was good for them. He had allowed himself to live in an imaginary world in which things that were conditional were assumed to be permanent. The harsh hammer of reality was shattering the illusions but the process was far from complete. For the civil population to turn against him only confirmed his views about Socialists. But he had yet to realize that in the last resort an army is only composed of human beings in uniform and that the bonds of discipline are psychological rather than material. By 8 November this ugly fact had dawned on almost all the headquarters staff. Only the Field Marshal, the one man whose word would be decisive, still remained to be convinced.

The man who effected Hindenburg's conversion was the jolly Swabian, Gröner. Since the interview with Drews, the General (who had only arrived back from Russia at the end of October) had been both to the front and to Berlin. What he saw in both places convinced him that the situation was untenable. The troops inside Germany were not prepared to fight the revolution; the troops at the front were not prepared to fight the enemy. Soldiers and Workers Councils were rapidly being formed on all sides and had the lines of communication in their hands. There were only supplies for a few days longer. The Austrian collapse had left the whole south-eastern frontier defenceless. An armistice was under negotiation, though the full severity of its terms was as yet unknown. The possibilities of resistance had been exhausted. Gröner himself even before his trips had advised that the Kaiser should go to the front line and there if possible get killed. But the entourage had been horrified at the idea and Hindenburg had disapproved of the risks involved; of these capture by the enemy or by mutinous troops was probably more serious and more likely than death. It would probably have been too late for such an exit anyhow; fighting was practically over. The idea of marching the army back into Germany and restoring order was out of the question; apart from the military and logistic difficulties of the operation, the troops would not march. Slowly Hindenburg came to see that William must be made to abdicate and go into retirement; above all, he must be saved from the fate of the Tsar. Yet the repeated telephone messages from Berlin which with mounting stridency urged the need for abdication were still meeting uncompromising refusals. The Kaiser had to be convinced that his army could no longer be counted on, that army of which he had begun his reign by saying, 'We belong to each other . . . will cleave indissolubly to each other, whether it be the will of God to send us calm or storm.' That night calls went out from Spa to selected commanders of units all along the front, ordering them to report at headquarters next morning. On the same night, a Dutch general visited Spa.

*   *   *

The 9th of November was a raw and damp autumn day. A thick mist hung round the villa which the Kaiser had been using since his return from Berlin. Water dripped from the trees and the last leaves of the year fell gently down. William rose early and went through the papers which had come in during the night.

They included a telegram from Prince Max to the effect that, failing abdication, the Empire would find itself 'without a Chancellor, without a government, without any compact Parliamentary majority, utterly incapable of negotiating'. On reading this the Kaiser wrote against it: 'This is what has happened already.'[111] It was the last marginal note of his reign.

After breakfast he went as usual for a walk with his adjutant to whom he talked of the danger of revolution. 'It is to be hoped that the enemy will ultimately see the danger to the whole of European civilization if Germany is delivered over to Bolshevism.' He already saw himself leading a white crusade. 'We will overcome the immediate difficulties by swift military action.' He was called back by the news that Hindenburg and Gröner had arrived. They were received in a room overlooking the garden, heated inadequately by a wood-fire. Leaning against the mantelpiece and shivering from the combination of cold and anxiety, William asked the Field Marshal for a report. But for once emotion had got the better of that rocklike character. He asked leave to resign; he could not find it compatible with his oath as a Prussian officer to say what his King had to be told. Gröner stepped into the thankless breach and set out the facts in some detail. They added up to the impossibility of relying any longer on the army, which was not prepared to go on fighting. Looking round in perplexity, the Kaiser saw obvious signs of disagreement on the face of General von der Schulenburg, the Crown Prince's Chief of Staff, and one of those called to Spa from forward units.[112] Told to give his views, von der Schulenburg contested Gröner's opinion of the forward troops. Plenty of them were reliable, many others would respond to firm leadership. It would not take many days to collect a reliable force with which the lines of communication could be brought under control. Then the white-haired von Plessen, William's Adjutant-General, broke in:

'His Majesty cannot simply and quietly capitulate to the Revolution. The expedition against Aachen and Verviers must be put in hand at once.'

Gröner explained that it was too late for such measures. The army was so unreliable that the order 'Fight against the home front' would provoke bloodshed inside its own ranks.

At that William drew back. He did not want to be responsible for civil war. He would wait till the armistice and then lead his troops back into Germany.

Now it was for Gröner to shatter the final illusion. 'The Army will march home in good order under its generals, but not under Your Majesty.'

The Kaiser's eyes blazed. He moved towards Gröner and said incisively, 'I require that statement in writing. I want all the commanding generals to state in black and white that the army no longer stands behind its Supreme War Lord. Has it not taken an oath?'

The question which had silenced Drews now got a realistic answer. 'In such a situation oaths are meaningless.'

Schulenburg again broke in protesting but Gröner, asked to account for the discrepancy, merely said: 'I have other information.'

At this moment Prince Max came on the telephone from Berlin (which was indeed in almost ceaseless use during the whole morning). Revolution had broken out there. The workers had left the factories and were marching to the centre. The troops were fraternizing with them. Only an instant announcement of abdication could save the situation. But William was not prepared to accept a report which sounded to him the product of panic. He insisted on hearing the views of the military governor. Then he went out into the garden with his generals. They stood talking in groups among the beds of withered flowers.

Grünau of the Foreign Office came up. The previous night the Chancellor had instructed him to represent to William that, if civil war were to break out on the eve of an armistice, the blame would be laid at the door of the man who had clung so obstinately to his throne whereas, by withdrawing at once, he would earn the gratitude of his people. This was the first opportunity of delivering the message. William in answer affirmed his desire to avoid civil war. But he was convinced that abdication would lead to the proclamation of a republic and that this would leave Germany powerless before its foes. The democratic government had in the last month done nothing to counteract the currents of thought directed against monarch and monarchy. Yet he had willingly agreed to all the schemes of reform and to all the consequent changes of personnel. But the government thus created had allowed itself to be dragged at the chariot-wheels of the Socialists whose watchword was 'absolute power'. He was ready to abdicate if such was the will of the German people. He had reigned long enough to see how thankless was a monarch's task. He had no intention of clinging to power. He had done his duty in not leaving his post and refusing to desert his people and army. It was now up to others to show whether they could do better.

The Crown Prince arrived after a long and cold drive. He found his father passionately excited, his features distraught, his emaciated and sallow face trembling. Messages from Berlin arrived continually, each gloomier than the last. Von Plessen suggested that William might abdicate as Emperor but not as King of Prussia. The fact that such a step might make constitutional nonsense and inflame rather than alleviate the situation did not prevent its being eagerly taken up. Other Germans might do what they liked; Prussian soldiers would stay faithful to their King. Then Colonel Heye arrived, called away prematurely from cross-examining the officers brought to headquarters. They had been first asked whether the Emperor had any hopes of regaining control of Germany by force at the head of his troops. To this only one had answered 'Yes' and twenty-three 'No', with fifteen uncertain. The second question had been whether the troops would march against the Bolsheviks in Germany, to which eight had replied 'Yes', nineteen 'No' with twelve uncertain. The sample has been condemned as unrepresentative and the questions as weighted, but, given the circumstances, it was not an unreasonable way of obtaining a reliable verdict quickly. Heye summed up:

'At the present moment the troops will not march against the enemy, even with Your Majesty at their head. They will not march against Bolshevism. They want one thing only, an armistice at the earliest possible moment. It is only under the command of their generals that the army will return to the Fatherland. If Your Majesty wishes to march with them, the troops will ask nothing better. But the army will fight no more.'

A long silence followed. Hintze came out of the house to report that the situation in Berlin was now so alarming as to make it impossible to preserve the throne unless the Kaiser decided upon instant abdication. William, his lips compressed and colourless, his face livid, gave a brief nod and sought the eyes of Hindenburg. But the Field Marshal could offer no comfort. Hintze was instructed to tell the Chancellor that William was prepared to renounce the Imperial throne if in this way alone civil war could be avoided, but that he remained King of Prussia and would not leave his army. Von der Schulenburg urged that the wording of such a momentous statement should not depend upon memory; a drafting committee was appointed and the others went in to an improvised lunch 'in a bright white room whose tables were decked with flowers but surrounded only by bitter anguish and despairing grief'.

Hintze brought the draft announcement to be signed. He then went to the telephone and started to read it to Berlin, only to be told that so limited a document was futile. He insisted on finishing but was no sooner done than another document began to be read to him. Prince Max, believing on the strength of the answers to his earlier messages that abdication was only a matter of minutes and convinced of the need to save time, had at 11.30 on his own authority issued to the German News Agency a message announcing the abdication of both Kaiser and Crown Prince. Hardly had he done so when the Socialists arrived at the Chancellery and demanded that the Chancellorship be handed over to Ebert.

William's fury knew no bounds; he never forgave Prince Max. 'Treason, gentlemen! Barefaced, outrageous treason! I am King of Prussia and I will remain King. As such I will stay with my troops.' With feverish haste he filled telegraph form after telegraph form with messages of protest. Hintze, Plessen and Schulenburg were instructed to go to Hindenburg (who was back in his own quarters) and tell him of Max's announcement and of William's reaction. The Crown Prince went off to his headquarters in the conviction that his father was going to stay at Spa. On the steps of the *Reichstag* building, Scheidemann had just proclaimed a republic.

But when the delegation came to review the situation with Hindenburg, they decided that the Berlin declaration would have to be accepted, at any rate for the time being. Certainly a protest against the way in which it had been reached ought to be placed on record, but any attempt at publication would be injudicious. And William must be advised to place himself out of the reach of untrustworthy troops by leaving the country, preferably for Holland. At five o'clock Hindenburg reluctantly returned to the villa to break these decisions to his master. Just about the same time Karl Liebknecht went out on to the balcony of the Berlin Castle and waved from it a red flag, thereby fulfilling the prophecy which Posadowsky had once made to Bülow. (See above, p. 270.)

William was still seething with rage at the way his hand had been forced. The returning delegation was greeted with the words, 'My God, are you back again already?' To Gröner he refused to speak —'You are only a Wurtemburg General.'[113] But Hindenburg could not be brushed aside. 'I cannot accept the responsibility of seeing Your Majesty haled to Berlin by mutinous troops and handed over as a prisoner to the revolutionary government. I must advise Your Majesty to abdicate and to proceed to Holland.' Hintze asked leave to put in hand negotiations with the Dutch. The Kaiser turned on him in fury. 'Was he thought to be incapable of remaining with his troops?' But this was the side-kick of a passionate temperament accustoming itself to the inevitable and a few minutes later the necessary permission was given.

The next visitors were Admiral Scheer, as Chief of the Naval Staff, and two other sailors. To them Hindenburg was ordered to repeat his remarks. When he had done so, Scheer announced his agreement, saying it was no longer possible to rely on the navy. 'I no longer have a navy, Admiral. The fleet has let me down completely.' He went into his study and shut the door. Presumably it was at this point that he wrote to the Crown Prince:

My dear Boy,

As the Field Marshal cannot guarantee my safety here and will not pledge himself for the reliability of the troops, I have decided, after a severe inward struggle, to leave the disorganized army. Berlin is totally lost; it is in the hands of the Socialists, and two governments have been formed there—one with Ebert as Chancellor and one by the Independents. Till the troops start their march home, I recommend your remaining at your post and keeping the troops together! God willing, I trust we shall meet again.[114]

Your sorely-stricken father,
William.

There followed some five hours of indecision. After telling his A.D.C.s that he would stay at Spa, William sent von Plessen to warn Hindenburg of his decision to leave for Holland next day. He then left his villa to dine, as usual, on the royal train and on reaching it was given a message from his son, Eitel Friedrich, in Berlin that, despite all the events of the day, Dona was well and in good heart. 'You see,' he said, 'my wife stays where she is, yet people are talking me into going to Holland. I will do nothing of the kind, it would be like a captain leaving a sinking ship.' A few minutes later von Plessen told the staff that the orders for leaving stood. Yet at dinner the decision seemed to have been taken to stay. About 10 p.m., however, Grünau rang up on behalf of Hindenburg and Hintze to report a rapidly deteriorating situation. Risings at Aachen and Eupen threatened to spread to Spa, on which mutinous troops were said to be marching. The way to the front and the way back into Germany were both blocked. The only road still open was northwards into Holland and that might not be available much longer. The Kaiser paused for a moment before deciding. 'Very well then if it has to be. But not until tomorrow morning.' And with that he went to bed.

There is some obscurity about the journey, probably created deliberately to reduce the risk of interference. The start had been fixed for 5 a.m., but the train slipped away at 4.30. The direct distance to the Dutch frontier was only some twenty miles, but the railway route was roundabout. At 2 a.m. the Kaiser's chauffeur had been woken in Spa and told to get the royal motor, stripped of insignia, ready for a long trip. A convoy of ten cars left Spa at about the same time as the train, but after going for some distance met another car coming in the opposite direction. In it were William and three officers. They all transferred to the main party which reached Eÿsden, south of Maastricht, at ten minutes past seven on a cheerless Sunday morning. His staff had drawn back and throughout the journey left him to his thoughts.[115]

Twenty-seven years earlier the Kaiser had risen in the White Hall of Berlin Castle to speak at a large military dinner. Someone had given him alarmist information about Russian troop movements and he felt a firm tone to be necessary. He is unlikely to have remembered what he had then said as he kicked his heels at the Dutch frontier in that November dawn, but the contrast between the two occasions provides as good a clue as any to the thoughts which must have been running through his mind when his moment of truth arrived.

'The soldier and the army, not parliamentary majorities and decisions, have welded together the German Empire. These are serious times in which we live and evil times may await us in the next few years. . . . But whatever may come, let us hold high our flag and our traditions, mindful of the words and deeds of Albrecht Achilles who said: "I know no more reputable place to die than in the midst of my enemies." This is also my innermost thought, upon which rests my unshakeable confidence in the fidelity, courage and devotion of my army.'[116]

*   *   *

During the weeks preceding the armistice the tables had been turned and the German élite found themselves in the position so familiar to German democrats of being unable to carry the nation with them. The unaccustomed experience filled them with frustrated fury. Both at the time and later they were inclined to say that if only more people had kept their heads and shown determined leadership, the collapse could have been avoided and a 'decent' peace secured. They could not have been more wrong. By the autumn of 1918 Germany was militarily defeated. If internal order had been maintained, she might have been able to go on fighting until the spring but the example of 1945 suggests that she would then have been overborne, especially after her oil supplies had been cut off. Once the Central Powers began to crack, the Allies were going to insist on armistice terms which amounted to complete surrender. There might have been advantages in a course of events which demonstrated clearly that the German army had been defeated in the field and perhaps involved an Allied invasion of Germany. But the view that the civilians let the army down, like the view that the army gave up before it was beaten, are two more symptoms of the distorted outlook which has already been pointed to as the ultimate cause of the catastrophe.

CHAPTER XII

Out to Grass

Among the Dead
Were Cousin Mary, Little Fred,
The Footmen (both of them), the Groom,
The man that cleaned the Billiard-Room,
The Chaplain, and the Still-Room Maid.
And I am dreadfully afraid
That Monsieur Champignon, the Chef,
Will now be permanently deaf—
And both his aides are much the same;
While George, who was in part to blame,
Received, you will regret to hear,
A nasty lump behind the ear.

HILAIRE BELLOC

THE ARRIVAL OF the little group at the frontier post cannot have come as a complete surprise to the Dutch Government since overtures of some sort had been on foot for several days. All the same, it caught them unprepared; William and his suite had to spend six hours in the bare waiting room.[1] At the end of that time his special train arrived and in this they were all accommodated while the search went on for more permanent quarters. Next day a party arrived from The Hague. This included the German Ambassador, to whom William said: 'I am a broken man. How can I begin life again? My prospects are hopeless. I have nothing left to believe in.' It was then announced that Count Bentinck, who like William was a knight of St. John, had agreed to receive him at the castle of Amerongen. 'Who is this Bentinck? I don't think I know him.' The arrival of so large a party in such circumstances was not without its embarrassments but William's training at putting people at their ease did not desert him. As the car came through the gateway in the pouring rain he turned to his host and said: 'Now give me a cup of real good English tea.'[2] (He got it, with Scotch scones added!)

On 28 November, Dona arrived after an anxious journey from Berlin and on the same day William regulated the situation by signing a formal act of abdication releasing all his servants, whether military or civilian, from their oaths of allegiance. The Crown Prince, who had reached Holland on 12 November, similarly renounced his rights.

In Article 27 of the Treaty of Versailles, the German Emperor was arraigned 'for a supreme offence against international morality and the sanctity of treaties'. On 4 June 1919 the Supreme Council at Paris agreed that he should be brought to trial. In January 1920 they invited the Dutch Government to extradite the accused but this that Government stoutly and repeatedly refused to do, merely extracting a promise, willingly given and faithfully kept, to refrain from political activity. The exiles in consequence suffered nothing more alarming than an irruption in the worst Wild West tradition by a couple of unauthorized American officers. The Dutch decision removed a considerable load of anxiety; Dona used to start from sleep crying, 'They are coming for him.' It also made possible thought for the future. The party clearly could not remain indefinitely at Amerongen and in the spring of 1920 William acquired the castle of Doorn, four miles to the west, a fourteenth-century house radically rebuilt at the end of the eighteenth century; a new gate house was put up at the entrance to hold the retinue. Here he settled down, bringing furniture, books and pictures of his ancestors from Germany and here he was to spend the remaining twenty-one years of his life as a retired country gentleman.

Dona, however, was not to be with him for long. She had taken the outcome of the war badly. As early as the summer of 1918 her heart had begun to give trouble, and when she met William on his last return to Potsdam, she was described as 'a completely broken woman'.[3] Private griefs were added to public misfortunes. She had been much upset in 1913 when the wife of Prince Eitel Fritz had run away with someone else,[4] and in 1920 her son Joachim committed suicide. 'Yes,' she would say, 'it is beautiful here, but it is not my Potsdam, the New Palace, my little rose-garden, our home.'[5] In February 1921 she and William celebrated the fortieth anniversary of their wedding; on 11 April she died. One of her last acts was to tell Countess Brockdorff, for all the forty years her Mistress of the Robes, that William must quickly marry again. Her husband with his five sons in full uniform saw her coffin put on the train for burial in Germany but the Dutch Government refused permission for William to go with it to the frontier. He is said to have been near collapse when the train drew out.[6]

William meanwhile had started on a process of self-justification. His first production was an elaborate 'Comparative Historical Tables', designed to show that neither he nor his Government had been guilty of bringing about the war. He sent a copy to Hindenburg who replied:

> 'I know that the best of all the efforts of Your Majesty throughout Your reign were towards the maintenance of peace. I can realize how immeasurably hard it is for Your Majesty to be eliminated from active co-operation for the Fatherland.'
>
> 'Yes,' replied William, 'such an elimination causes me burning anguish in my soul. . . . As you know I forced myself to the difficult and terrible decision to go into exile only upon the urgent declaration of yourself.'[7]

Hindenburg took a year to answer but then wrote back formally accepting responsibility for the decision that William must go into exile. He quite correctly gave as his reason the danger of his master being captured by mutinous troops and surrendered to the enemy at home or abroad, whereas William maintained that the object had been to avoid civil war and secure better terms of peace. He only delayed his reply for two months, but made it none too gracious. He had had to wait a long time before the persons responsible had been willing to admit publicly that they had forced departure on an unwilling master.

> 'Convinced that you were loyally discharging a difficult task, you gave to Your Kaiser and King the counsel which you thought it your duty to give as a result of your considered view of the situation. Whether that view was correct cannot be finally decided until all the facts of those unhappy days are known.'[8]

In the course of 1922 William received in his mail a letter of respect and sympathy from a young child—though the pen may well have been put in its hands. He answered by inviting his admirer to visit Doorn. In escort came the mother Hermine, a widow of thirty-five who had been born a Reuss and married a Prince Schönaich-Carolath. She commended herself to the widower and on 3 November they were married. By this time his youngest child, the Duchess of Brunswick, was herself thirty and the arrival of younger step-children, along with the visits of grand-children, added interest and gaiety to his life. He treated them more genially than he had done his sons, even if he could still be stern when cause arose, and in return won a considerable measure of affection.

With the journalist Rosen as 'ghost', he proceeded to write the memoirs of his reign, which appeared in 1922. The book appeared before a number of other memoirs came out and well before the large-scale publication of official documents began. It was there-by able to skate over a number of episodes without facing up to the real points at issue. But even so it was not as good a book as it might have been. It relied too largely on its author's memory which was no more trustworthy than most people's and as a result the account which it gave of its author's actions was neither detailed, accurate nor convincing. *My Early Life* which followed in 1923 was less concerned to prove a case and consequently a more interesting book. In 1924, *Memories of Corfu* appeared, with a dedication to Dona; it gives the impression that though the happy days were out of reach, their recollection was not as great a grief as Dante suggested.

In 1928, Sir Frederick Ponsonby, a godson of the Empress Frederick, published in England her letters to Queen Victoria which on the Empress's instructions he had smuggled out of Germany just before her death in 1901, having gone to visit her in attendance on King Edward. The copyright undoubtedly belonged not to the editor but to William, who at first thought of obtaining an in-junction and having the book withdrawn. (Under the Act of Settlement he could have sued as a British subject!) Wiser counsels however prevailed and when the German edition appeared it opened with an essay in which William sketched his side of the case; he achieved a creditable degree of understanding and restraint.[9]

In 1929, William published a set of short essays about his ancestors containing pleasant anecdotes rather than serious critic-ism. Thereafter his studies became more eclectic. In 1933 he founded the Doorn Research Community which held a conference once a year at which lectures were read by persons claiming to do so with authority. The subject for 1934 was 'The Significance of Symbols in Ancient Civilizations', to which William contributed a paper on 'The History and Meaning of the Chinese Monad' (an appropriate sub-title would have been 'Sidelights on the History of the Swastika'). In 1936, there followed 'Studies about the Gorgon', dedicated to the Emperor Frederick, which took off from the statue found on Corfu in 1911 and pursued its subject through a welter of archaeological theories to a conclusion in which the swastika again figured. Wealthy men with a bent for intellectual hobbies and not quite enough to do are apt to become cranks, and the ex-Kaiser was no exception. But his occupations were innocent enough and the fact that they led nowhere was almost an advantage.

Meanwhile, life as a squire passed pleasantly enough. A beard softened his face and white hair gave him a venerable appearance. The man who had travelled so constantly now seldom left his estate and never went far. The days passed to a regular routine. He sawed wood (a habit acquired during the war), dealt with his correspondence, supervised his property, developed a rose-garden which has since vanished and an arboretum which still remains. He even had a chance to spend that hour a day concentrating on a serious book which Dr. Renvers had recommended. There were often visitors calling from Germany or from other countries (though he refused to receive British subjects until after our army of occupation had left the Rhineland in 1929). There was, as always, plenty to talk about. As he sat after tea on the terrace or looked out from his study window over the lawns and the beeches, the moat with its swans, the deer feeding in the park beyond the ha-ha, the gravestones of his favourite dogs, he must have felt that he had come, if not home, at least to the Home Counties. The effect must have been enhanced when on his seventieth birthday his family and friends gave him a stable clock which chimed the quarters. He had once said he would rather be an English country gentleman than anything else; now he almost had his desire. The tension between his German and his English instincts was relaxed and he had come to rest, psychologically as well as geographically, at a middle point. The feverish energy, the pressure of business was gone and he no longer had either cause or opportunity to open his mouth in public. It was a life without real purpose but one to which he was well fitted.

He had, of course, a grievance against the world which had sadly misjudged him. His inveterate belief that it was he rather than others who had been right was assisted by the fact that most of the charges made against him in those days were crudely enough formulated for retorts to be easily devised. He was able to denounce the injustice of Versailles and the Allied reparations policy, to deplore the Bolsheviks and the Weimar Republic, to scorn the parvenu Hitler without any apparent realization that he had helped to bring about the conditions in which these phenomena could occur. This is the charge which has to be set against the quiet dignity with which he accepted his lot, the only ground for wondering whether flight was after all the most appropriate solution in 1918. He once wrote to an English friend: 'When Britain was on the verge of losing the unjust war which she had for many years engineered against me and my country, she led America into the fight and *bought* the subversive part of my people with money to rise against their ruler.'[10] Isolated to the end in a world of his own, he never quite achieved contact with reality. In this he again proved typical of many of his former subjects.

In 1931 his grandson Louis Ferdinand asked him for advice about political trends in Germany. He replied that Hitler was the leader of a strong movement which embodied the energy of the German nation. He could not tell what would come of it nor did he find the movement pleasing in all its aspects, but he was convinced that only national forces would lead the Germans forward again. Accordingly he allowed his sons, Oscar and August Wilhelm, to join in the Nazi activities. On the other hand he refused to allow the Crown Prince to stand as a candidate for the Presidency of the Republic in opposition to Hindenburg in 1932. His wife, Hermine, regarded Hitler as Germany's saviour and trusted him completely. After 1933 William and his sons certainly refrained from any public criticism of the Third Reich, which may not have been unconnected with the fact that they depended on the good-will of the Prussian government under Göring if they were to continue drawing the allowances which since 1926 they had been allowed to obtain from the former royal estates there. But once well into the saddle the Nazis turned against their predecessors. In January 1935 a public celebration in favour of William was broken up by the police and when a month later the Crown Prince asked Hitler to allow his father to return to Germany, he was met by a firm refusal. The Jewish persecutions of 1938 horrified the exile. 'For the first time I am ashamed to be a German.'[11]

In 1938 he once again made an incursion into English history. At the beginning of October, Queen Mary was surprised to receive a letter written in indelible pencil:

'May I with a grateful heart relieved from a sickening anxiety by the intercession of Heaven unite my warmest sincerest thanks to the Lord with yours and those of the German and British people that He saved us from a most fearful catastrophe by helping the responsible statesmen to preserve peace! I have not the slightest doubt that Mr. N. Chamberlain was inspired by Heaven and guided by God who took pity on his children on Earth by crowning his mission with such relieving success. God bless him. I kiss your hand in respectful devotion as ever.'[12]

The document was wonderfully in character; his unsureness of judgement did not desert him, even at the end! The letter was acknowledged and followed four months later by royal telegrams of congratulation on his eightieth birthday. This was also the occasion of Crown Prince Rupprecht's only visit to Doorn. With him came Mackensen, now eighty-nine (the man who had initiated the habit of kissing the Kaiser's hand, who had shared with Hindenburg, Ludendorff and Hoffmann the laurels of Tannenberg and with Falkenhayn the rout of Roumania). The two were the last survivors of William's Marshals. The officers and reserve officers of the German armed forces were, however, forbidden to send greetings.

In November 1939 the British Government found time to consider what would happen to its former *bête noir* in the event of a German invasion of Holland, and the Ambassador in The Hague was urged to get William moved beforehand to Sweden or Denmark. Nothing, however, came of this and on 10 May 1940 Mr. Churchill asked Lord Halifax whether the ex-Kaiser should be told that he would be received 'with consideration and dignity' if he cared to seek refuge in England. King George agreed and an offer was sent privately but politely declined.[13] So was the idea of returning to Germany. 'Old trees', he said, 'cannot be transplanted.'[14] Next month, however, he sent congratulations to Hitler on the capture of Paris. The success of the Third *Reich* where the Second had failed prompted a final 'undergraduate impetuosity', conveyed as of old by telegram.

He was indeed growing old and for some time had had trouble with his stomach. On 3 June 1941 a clot of blood developed on his lung and he fell into a coma from which he never emerged, dying at 11.30 the following morning in the presence of his wife, daughter and three grandsons. Hitler offered a State funeral in Berlin but William had left directions that, unless he returned to Germany during his lifetime, he was to be buried in a mausoleum in the Doorn grounds. The service was taken by a Pastor of Berlin Cathedral who had visited Doorn annually to preach a birthday sermon. Mackensen returned again to lead the representatives of the old order, who included Admiral Canaris, head of the *Abwehr* and a ringleader in the 1944 plot. One of Mackensen's former A.D.C.s commanded a battalion of honour drawn from all three sections of the *Wehrmacht*. The Führer was represented by Seyss-Inquart, the Nazi Commissioner in Holland.[15] In accordance with instructions laid down by Goebbels in 1933 the German papers gave the news of William's death 'with single column headlines on the lower half of the front page'. 'William II is the representative of a system which failed. One may concede to him that he desired the best. But in this world it isn't a question of intention but of success.'[16]

Six years later William's widow died in Russian internment.

CHAPTER XIII

The Frontiers of Morality

THE CARNAGE WHICH occurred between 1914 and 1918 is sometimes now referred to as 'The Kaiser's War'. The term fairly, even if unintentionally, sums up the view taken of William by his Anglo-Saxon contemporaries; he was a wicked man who had deliberately instigated a crime against humanity. Previous chapters have shown this to be exaggerated and based on an oversimplified version of the facts. But the question of the 'war guilt' of Germany, if not of William, is fundamental to any study of the period and demands unimpassioned analysis.

The spectacle of 13 million people[1] being killed stirred to the depth the emotions and conscience of the world and made it inevitable for historians to ask and be asked: 'What went wrong? Who was at fault?' Yet such are the 'complexities of mire and blood' that questions like these admit of no straightforward reply. The only answer which is both short and true is that the system had gone wrong and human thinking been at fault. The war of 1914–18 showed up the hollowness of the assumption made during previous centuries about the possibility of divorcing economic from political development. As contact between distant points grew easier, as techniques of production improved, international exchange of goods turned from a luxury into an indispensable condition of efficiency. An internationally interdependent society was brought into being without the political institutions necessary to give it law and order. Men had excused themselves from the exceedingly difficult task of developing these institutions by the convenient fiction that politics and economics were distinct things.

As developing technology gradually disclosed to man possibilities of profit and welfare hitherto unimagined, the temptation

to pursue them was bound to prove beyond the capacity of human
nature to resist. It is futile to suppose that men could have reined
themselves in and said 'We will not develop the resources available
to us until we can do so in peace'—even assuming them gifted with
the insight needed to discern the choice involved! It is not as
though the transcendance of State sovereignties involved in
achieving international order was a simple step to take, even after
the need for it had been recognized. Equally futile is any expectation that men could have rigidly observed a division between the
political and economic spheres. Even if the social repercussions of
economics are disregarded, those who found themselves unable to
secure their desired ends by economic action alone were bound to
seek help from every possible source, including that most potent
of all, the agreed organization for the achievement of common
purposes which we call Government. As struggle between
members of autonomous political units became the normal state
of things, the temptation increased for the governors of those units
to deploy force whenever the purposes of their citizens appeared
otherwise to be in danger of frustration.

In the resulting clashes, victory seemed to go to the side which
was most successful in concentrating the resources of the entire
community on the contest. In an age where progress owed so
much to improvements in organization, it was natural for war to
become steadily more total. In an age which was increasing its
efficiency by the devising of machines, it was inevitable for war to
become mechanized. Before long a practical demonstration was
bound to be given of what happened in a world of interdependent
sovereign States once machine-guns and high explosive had been
invented; the result outraged human susceptibilities. Man came
within sight of conquering his immemorial problems of hunger
and pestilence, only to be faced with the spectre of mass mutual
destruction. To maintain the standards which had come to be
regarded as 'civilized', the creation of an international authority
became imperative.

But we should hesitate before we judge past generations by
criteria which we are ourselves struggling to establish. For many
centuries, war was taken for granted. It was the ultimate means of
adjustment to the inevitable and perpetual changes in the relative
strength of States. To Luther, it was divinely ordained and as
necessary as eating and drinking. 'Peace,' said Clausewitz, 'is the

snowy mantle of winter under which the forces of development sleep and slowly gain strength: war is the fiery heat of summer which brings them out and carries them quickly to fruition.'[2] Hegel and Ranke regarded war as the task in which nations demonstrated the moral justification for their existence.[3] Treitschke said that 'whoever believes in the infinite growth, in the external youth of our race, must acknowledge the unalterable necessity of war'.[4] The elder Moltke thought perpetual peace a not very pleasant dream. Waldersee once wrote when war was expected, 'A good many men will be killed. However, . . . I am not inclined to regard death for the individual as a misfortune.'[5] Weber, in 1914, wrote that: 'We had to let this war occur in order to have our say in deciding the future of the earth.'[6] The Kaiser, in 1918, described war as 'a disciplinary action by God to educate mankind' (although he added that 'God has not always been successful with these measures', much as the Irish preacher, telling how God surveyed the world on the seventh day of creation and found it good, added, 'And he was partly right!').[7] All these quotations come from Germans. But there is little reason to suppose that, until recently, people elsewhere thought otherwise.

Nor is there reason to suppose that the passions which give rise to war have altered their character in recent years. What evidence exists to show that men's urge to violence is greater than in the past? It is the opportunities for exerting that urge which have changed, as have the technical tools which can be deployed in the process. But such enlargements do not necessarily also enlarge the moral reprehensibility of wishing to use violence. For in what sense is it 'worse' to want to kill two hundred men with a machine-gun than to want to strangle a single man with one's hands? If we now judge it worse, may that not be because greater insight and wider experience have altered our thinking about what is 'moral'?

For our views on morality, and particularly on the morality of a State's actions, are obviously affected by our circumstances and consequently liable to change. The realization of the consequences which can follow in the modern world from claiming unlimited sovereignty for individual States has made us reconsider the role of morality in international affairs. For one thing, the spectacle of the First World War made painfully acute as never before the problem of the relationship between men's sense of duty to the

State or national community, and their sense of duty to humanity. In so far as men had hitherto looked beyond their own country, they had mostly taken the coincidence of these two duties for granted. Such an assumption is bound to be encouraged by the sovereign State, an institution which is insatiably greedy of loyalty. For the success of its leaders depends so much on the degree of ready co-operation which is forthcoming from their citizens that they cannot be expected to encourage the idea of there being other and possibly conflicting purposes with claims on the allegiance of those citizens. To suspect that the ends of one's national community are at variance with the good of mankind is productive of so much indignation to the average individual and of so much agony to the sensitive one as to make it infinitely tempting to assume that the two objectives coincide and that, in serving the nation to one's best ability, one is also serving humanity. If the Anglo-Saxons have seemed particularly good at both holding and propagating this belief, their antagonists have not been conspicuous for resisting the temptation. So upright and Christian a man as Naumann declared that 'our faith in nationalism and our faith in humanity are for us two sides of the same question'.[8] German historians in the 1900's have been described as thinking that 'Germany represented a great ideal of justice for all nations— the ideal that civilization should develop only through the diversity of free nations all over the world'.[9] But this diversity could only develop freely when the supremacy of Britain had been broken and the balance of power in Europe extended on to a world-wide scale 'Only then,' wrote Meinecke in 1916, 'will every nation have the free breathing-space which it requires.'[10] Thus Germany, in seeking to break the predominance of Britain, claimed to be performing a supranational service to humanity. One of the most curious and pathetic spectacles of the war was the genuine conviction of honest men on both sides that a God whom all admitted to be universal was more in favour of them than of their opponents.

'History', said Eyre Crowe, 'is apt to justify the action of States by its general results, with often but faint regard to the ethical character of the means involved.'[11] How far is it possible to stand apart from communal judgements and say that there are absolute standards of morality by which men's conduct must be judged in their collective actions as well as in their personal ones? An honest answer to this question must take into account what is perhaps the biggest of all the factors conditioning our views on international morality, namely the difference between the standards of an expanding country, or challenger, and those of a satisfied country, or possessor.

A contemporary German historian, Ludwig Dehio, has said that 'it is inherent in the nature of the younger and more ambitious State, sometimes instinctively, sometimes deliberately, to try to win territory from the *beati possidentes*'[12] (thus incidentally begging the important question why expansion should always be thought of in terms of territory). But the possessors are naturally inclined to regard any attempt to disturb the existing order as nefarious; whatever is, seems to them right. Few people can be expected to achieve the open-mindedness of Winston Churchill who in 1914 wrote that:

> 'We have got all we want in territory, and our claim to be left in the unmolested enjoyment of vast and splendid possessions, mainly acquired by violence, largely maintained by force, often seems less reasonable to others than to us.'[13]

The advantage of getting moral indignation on one's side explains only too well the emotional overtones which have become associated with the word 'aggressor'. The character of modern war has made it more natural than ever for those who are attacked to feel that the side which started all the killing is 'wicked'. To Fafner, Siegfried must have seemed guilty of a wanton act of unprovoked aggression.

To many, the essential step in establishing an international order is to secure acceptance for the rule of law. The justification for accusing William of a 'supreme offence against international morality' was that the invasion of Belgium involved the unprovoked breach of a treaty which Germany had promised (more than fifty years previously) to observe and that relations between States become impossible if the promises of Governments cannot be trusted. But this is the approach of the possessor. For to establish the rule of law is not by itself sufficient, since we know by experience inside States that law cannot hope to endure unless it is capable of being adapted to changing conditions and is dominated by a sense of fairness. Treaties maintain the *status quo* and can only be amended with the consent of all concerned, which is unlikely to be forthcoming from those who will lose by the change. Expanding nations are bound to claim that the sovereign State shall not be regarded as limited by the rule of law nor war be regarded as a crime unless at the same time an effective means is found of solving the problem of peaceful change. The law-abiding society must not be a stagnant society; room must be allowed for growth.

Was Germany then entitled to invade Belgium?

The answer must be that, on the rules of the game as played up to that time, there was nothing very different between her action and those of countless predecessors. How was Germany to expand except by war? Britain could hardly expect the map of the world to be frozen at the moment of her apogee! If Germany had won, little would have been heard thereafter about her 'crime'. Much of the indignation expressed against her was the unreflecting reaction to something which was inconvenient and even repulsive rather than the considered verdict of history. Yet in so far as men like Edward Grey, Robert Cecil and Woodrow Wilson protested against her action as immoral, they must be given the credit for having reached a stage of insight into the problems of human relationships in advance of anyone on the other side. Theodore Roosevelt put it well when he wrote in 1911 that:

> 'Germany has the arrogance of a very strong power as yet almost untouched by that feeble aspiration towards inter-national equity which one or two other strong powers, notably England and America, do at least begin to feel.'[14]

Admittedly it was easier for Englishmen and Americans, as citizens of satisfied Powers, to achieve such insight and in so far as their picture of the world allowed inadequate machinery for change, they were disregarding a vital side of the problem (though the colonial agreements negotiated in 1914 may be regarded as a step in this direction). But by contrast men on the German side like Gustav Stresemann and Max Weber had not managed to transcend the nineteenth-century outlook in which the sovereign national State in a world of similar States still represented a perfectly adequate solution to the problem of human organization. The views of the Kaiser and the élite on the subject have been abundantly illustrated in this book, particularly in their approach to The Hague Peace Conferences. Bismarck may have regarded Germany after 1870 as a 'satisfied' State, but the following generation was still far too deeply involved in the effort to establish the world position of their own nation-state to realize the objections to accepting such States as the last word. They made no contribution to the extremely difficult process of evolving something in the nature of a world-wide public opinion which can be mobilized both to uphold the law and to see that it is changed; instead, they disregarded the whole problem. They were not so much wicked as lacking in vision, blinkered by their environment.

Certainly this insensitiveness of the German leaders to the consequences of insisting on the unlimited freedom of the nation-state recoiled upon their own heads. For the invasion of Belgium provided Germany's opponents with a powerful appeal to the emotions of the public in their own countries and the neutral ones. This was the cause which put the consciences of the Anglo-Saxon world into uniform. The atrocities which the German troops undeniably committed in Belgium and elsewhere (though no doubt exaggerated by rumour) had the same effect, outweighing the military advantages expected of them.[15] If the war had broken out by Germany intervening in the East to help Austro-Hungary against a Russian attack, the ardour of the British public would have been less and the chances of pro-German sympathies among the uncommitted greater; the outcome of the fighting might well have been affected. But to argue that the German 'crime' was at any rate a mistake involves a shift of position; the invasion of Belgium is no longer being condemned as wrong but criticized as injudicious. If the charge of wickedness cannot be indisputably established against the leaders of Wilhelminian Germany, what about the charge of incompetence?

*   *   *

However much we may argue about the rights and wrongs of the war's origins, nobody can dispute the fact that Germany lost it. Was this because promising chances of victory were thrown away by bad generalship, or did the leaders, political as well as military, involve their country in a struggle which she had no prospect of winning?

The three main turning-points during the war were the battle of the Marne, the adoption of submarine warfare in 1917 and the Peace of Brest-Litovsk, with its repercussions on the 1918 offensive in the West. Of the first, Professor Ritter has said:

'The great Schlieffen Plan was never a sound formula for victory. It was a daring, indeed an over-daring, gamble whose success depended on many lucky accidents. A formula for victory needs a surplus of reasonable chances of success if it is to inspire confidence—a surplus which tends quickly to be used up by "frictions" in the day-to-day conduct of the war. The Schlieffen Plan showed an obvious deficit of these; it was in Schlieffen's own words, "an enterprise for which we are too weak". '[16]

In somewhat the same way the attack which Tirpitz wanted to make on the British fleet might conceivably have won the war 'in an afternoon', but would have been an enormous gamble against the probabilities, with heavy penalties in the event of loss. In any case, the experience of 1940 makes it doubtful whether a German victory in France in 1914—or in 1918—would have ended the war. For Germany to have left Russia unoccupied in the latter year might have released more divisions for the West but would have involved accepting the likelihood of starvation.

There can be no dispute that a wiser disposition of resources and greater moderation at the right moments might have produced results much more favourable to Germany. But it is hard to see how any achievement short of the conquest of Britain by invasion or starvation (and some people might add, the conquest of America as well) could have brought Germany outright victory. The result would at best have been a stalemate and though a compromise peace which proved lasting might have had more satisfactory consequences than outright victory by either side, such a peace is more likely to have turned out a temporary truce broken after a few uneasy years by fresh fighting—the series of Punic Wars which at one stage the Kaiser envisaged. In any case, as has been shown in Chapter XI, neither side could have accepted a compromise peace without profound internal dislocation. The attitudes which led Germany into the war committed her to a choice between victory and social upheaval. The roots of those attitudes go so deep that, once one starts assuming her élite to have been capable of compromise, one might as well assume them capable of other actions which would have avoided the war altogether. Germany did not lose by accident or bad luck.

The main charge against her is then that she allowed her

ambitions to outrun her capacities. The consequences in social and material destruction were as enormous as the losses in human lives and the diversion of resources which could otherwise have been put to more constructive ends. Not only was Germany weakened as a result but the whole of Western and Central Europe. When Hitler had completed the work which William began, the balance of power in Europe had indeed been destroyed but the effect, at any rate immediately, was to create a vacuum of power. Although Britain was among the victors, her position as a first-rate nation was weakened sooner than might otherwise have been the case, and the net effect was to accelerate the decline of European influence over the remaining continents. The dominance of America and China which William foresaw was assisted in no small degree by the actions of his own government. Even if moral considerations are excluded, this is a grave indictment. What led Germany astray?

The first answer must be that the German leaders overestimated their own resources and underestimated those of other people. Bethmann Hollweg said as much to the *Reichstag* in 1916:

'Since the war began we have not been free from the mistake of underestimating the strength of our enemies. The astonishing development of our nation during the last twenty years has led broad groups of the population to succumb to the temptation of overestimating our undeniably great resources in comparison with those of the rest of the world.'[17]

But this mistake was also connected with that disregard of the practical effect of moral factors which has already been mentioned. This *inconscience* is in turn connected with the exaltation of force which has been pointed to as a characteristic of German and particularly of Prussian society. The frustrations and other factors which gave rise to it lie deep in history and need no further analysis now.

The second answer—bad organization—is one which at first sight may cause surprise. Surely this is the last thing of which to accuse Germans! Did not Houston Stewart Chamberlain, in telling William that political freedom for the masses had proved a failure, point to good organization as the virtue by which Germany could achieve 'everything, absolutely everything'?[18] But the truth was that, though all minor aspects of life were studied with diligent care and organized with much thoroughness if perhaps inadequate elasticity, the position at the top was unorganized and haphazard in the extreme. This was due to excessive respect for out-of-date views about monarchy and to the fact that the German Empire's constitutional arrangements had been devised by an arbitrary genius to suit himself. The consequence was utter inadequacy in the procedures for identifying and analysing problems, for ensuring their discussion in the light of all the relevant facts, and for securing clear decisions in good time. The arrangements for linking military to political policy were particularly unsatisfactory, being vitiated by an exaggerated respect for the military caste.

Thirdly, the German élite displayed a marked lack of empathy, an inability to appreciate and so to anticipate the reactions of other people. It was not so much that they thought public opinion unimportant; the official machinery for manipulating the press, for example, was probably more highly developed than in Britain. But public opinion was something to be manipulated, not desirable as a critical force. The ruling classes were excessively preoccupied with their own interests and lacked imaginative sympathy. Emotions like pity, mercy and charity were too often suspected of being likely to reduce the effectiveness of the strong man. This applied to internal as much as to external affairs. As a Berlin deputy said when a sentry had shot a drunken worker, 'The people who draw up regulations seem totally unfamiliar with the theory of practical Christianity.'[19] The rulers of Germany were too seldom able to enter into the minds of the people whom they ruled, or understand their interests and motives, the things which they could be expected to do and endure, the limits of their loyalties and self-control. The élite were so intent on inculcating what their inferiors ought to think, so indignant over any evidence about the real thought being different, that they insensibly came to base their own course of action on theories rather than facts. Dogmas survived because they corresponded to the prejudices and fulfilled the wishes of their authors, not because they embodied realities.

Closely linked with this was the determination of a possessing class to hold on at all cost to out-of-date privileges, without realizing that positions can only be held if there is constant adaptation to change. Fundamentally there was a confusion, not confined to Germany, between 'democracy' and the social implications of industrialization. Too many people expected to enjoy at one and the same time the personal relationships of feudalism and the material wealth of the industrial age. They thought that provided they could prevent the introduction of the political forms associated with quantity production, all social adjustments could be avoided. The net result of this refusal to abandon a position which was not in the long run defensible was to distort Germany's internal development and feed the flames of class war. It also encouraged external adventures as a means of distracting attention and providing a decisive reason why Germany could not 'afford' political reform.

All these weaknesses add up to a charge of bad political judgement and a distorted sense of values. No single cause is adequate to explain this situation. For one thing, the likeliest place to find political judgement is among politicians; to draw Ministers from officials not only brings to power people distinguished for other qualities but denies party leaders the sobering experience of putting their policies into practice. Again, three of the institutions which in many countries generate a healthy criticism of official policy failed to function properly in Germany; the press tended to be financially dependent on the government, the Lutheran Church traditionally kept clear of politics, and the professors competed to extol the virtues of the established order. But these are all aspects of the failure of the German middle classes, on reaching economic and social maturity, to seize political power as well and take their fate and that of their country into their own hands. Instead they were faced by an unyielding ruler-caste, hypnotized by the success of anti-Liberal forces in uniting the nation, fascinated by the gigantic personality of Bismarck and obsessed with an anxiety-complex about the proletariat. All these factors led them to accept ready-made the ideals of the Prussian aristocracy as those ideals were ceasing to have a valid economic basis; they allowed themselves to be assimilated to the existing culture instead of imposing new and realistic values on it. The Prussian ideals made heavy demands on human nature and the fear of being unable to live up to them resulted in their exaggeration. To say that people exaggerate is another way of saying that their values are distorted.

The truth is that the economic changes caused by the technological break-through have presented each country experiencing them with immense problems of internal social adjustment, while at the same time presenting countries collectively with problems of international relationship. Naturally these problems have inter-acted. To solve them successfully requires imagination and breadth of mind; 'where there is no vision, the people perish'. To com-plicate the matter, the pace of change is now such that the picture of the world which individuals acquire in their teens is growing out-of-date by the time they reach their fifties. Yet the effectiveness of any society largely depends on the extent to which its intellectual tools are up-to-date and correspond with reality. This places on the members of modern societies, and particularly on their élites, a duty to remain accessible to new ideas and to be capable of taking a view of the contemporary scene which is not distorted by emotion, self-interest and fear. Preference for the familiar can easily blind us to the fact that no effective resistance is possible to the forces which are sweeping away loved surroundings and arrangements advantageous to us (we are quicker to recognize the need for changes which increase our advantages!). Many élites have failed to display the qualities of mind needed to make the adjustments without convulsion. Prominent among these were the ruling classes of the Romanov, Habsburg and Hohenzollern Em-pires. The varying reasons for their failures are deeply embedded in history and it is not for those whose history has been different lightly to condemn. The consequences, however, constitute much of the background to our daily life.

*   *   *

The final question is, how far should William be blamed for the mistakes made under his rule?

The popular picture, which he himself did so much to foster, is here largely misleading. The discussion of the main episodes in earlier pages has shown that William played a smaller part in the formation of policy than was permitted by the constitution or supposed by the public. Bismarck's departure was undoubtedly his doing, but in the controversies leading to it there was much to be said on the side of the Kaiser, who was in any case only anticipat-ing by a few years the action of natural causes. As regards the failure to renew the Reinsurance Treaty, the Morocco crisis of 1905–6 and the Agadir episode, William was a somewhat unwilling accessory to the acts of other people. This may even be true of the Krüger telegram. In the negotiations over the Anglo-German

Alliance, the Bosnian crisis of 1908–9, the steps leading to war, the decision to adopt unrestricted submarine warfare and Brest-Litovsk, his co-operation was more willingly given but the responsibility for initiating the policy still rested in other hands. The only major German policy for which prime responsibility must be laid at the Kaiser's door is that regarding the fleet. This is certainly a heavy burden. But, even so, some movement in this direction was probably inherent in German development. For Germany to become a Great Power was considered to involve freeing herself from dependence on the attitude of others. Her chief weakness was vulnerability to sea blockade and the most obvious way of remedying this was possession of a strong fleet. In building such a fleet, William was only carrying to their logical consequence the aspirations of many of his subjects. Both he and they failed adequately to consider how far one country can be independent of others without dominating over them, how far any attempt at such domination is bound to provoke resistance and how far accordingly they stood any chance of realizing their aims. Their desires outran their sense of realities.

This major error points to the main judgement which history must pass on William II. He was a distracting rather than a steadying influence who, instead of helping his Ministers to identify and pursue the ends which really mattered, impeded the cool, objective study of Germany's problems. He contributed materially by his example and influence to that false assessment of values and to that unsoundness of judgement which we have identified as Germany's basic weakness. Holding a position in which he could have done much to counteract the tendencies around him, he instead gave them added emphasis. While claiming to be a leader, he in fact followed others and allowed himself to be moulded by his environment instead of impressing his personality upon it. Though he would have hated to be told so, he was a bourgeois monarch in terms of the German bourgeoisie. He embodied the faults of Germany's middle classes, taking over uncritically the traditions of Prussian landowners, and seeking to apply them in a situation for which they were no longer appropriate. Frightened that he might not achieve the standards expected of him, he resorted to over-emphasis.

William's story demonstrates clearly that good intentions and intelligence are not enough in a ruler. Energy unaccompanied by

steadying qualities is a menace rather than an advantage. The effect
of charm is apt to be misleading since it does not last. The statesman needs in addition the ability to distinguish the things which
matter from the things which seem to matter and the pertinacity
to pursue a steady course undistracted by transient excitements.
He needs that cool commonsense which, when it is ripened by
experience, men call wisdom. But these are the marks of an
integrated personality and that, as we know, was emphatically
something which William did not possess. His nervousness and
impetuosity doomed him to be a lightweight, jostled along by the
forces among which he found himself. The simple truth about
the Kaiser is that, for all his undoubted gifts, he was not up to the
outsize job which destiny had assigned to him. He had had a
Carabosse at his christening and lacked a Lilac Fairy to put things
right.

Yet how far can he be blamed? He was, as the Alsatian deputy
said (see above, p. 86) 'the product of his milieu' and the character
of that milieu was shaped by the past course of German history.
The more one examines his heredity and environment, the greater
the inclination to exclaim with Amonasro (see above, p. 109).

'O! Tu non sei colpevole, era voler del fato.'

Is it reasonable to expect William to have been other than he was?
Should not one blame instead the system which could assign so
onerous a post to someone who had so little chance of filling it
with credit?

The reader of this book may have noticed two themes recurring
through it. One is the deep-seated character of the forces which
were determining the collective actions of the German people and
of their rulers. There are a number of things which one cannot
imagine happening in a significantly different way unless one presupposes so many other alterations in the world as to turn the
exercise into idle speculation. But on a number of other occasions
attention has been deliberately called to the altered consequences
which might have followed from a comparatively minor change in
behaviour, even on the part of inanimate objects. To concentrate
on the one aspect without remembering the other leads to a false
reading of history.

Nobody today would deny the influence of heredity and environment, and the effect of recent scientific discovery has been to

emphasize aspects of their influence which had previously passed unnoticed. But to regard these two forces as completely decisive makes nonsense of our awareness of choice and of all ideas about moral responsibility.[20] For how can a man be praised or blamed for what he does if the way in which he acts is decided by genes, isotherms and culture-patterns? Our genes and our culture patterns are themselves the accumulated outcome of innumerable past choices and decisions by our parents and our forebears, our pastors and our masters and those set in authority over us today and throughout the years that are no more. We cannot escape the consequences of all those choices and decisions: 'what's done cannot be undone'. Our own freedom of choice is vastly circumscribed by this fact. But to admit that we are largely determined does not deny us any freedom to choose. Bismarck called himself the 'helpless child of time' but went on to say 'for that very reason we must do our duty faithfully in the state of life to which it has pleased God to call us'.[21] We must always remember that it is *our* choices and decisions which will go to circumscribe the freedom of succeeding generations. Taken individually they may seem trivial, but taken together and along with other people's, they add up to destiny. The fact that we can understand why someone has chosen in a particular way does not make his choice wise or prove that he had no alternative. We shall, if we are sensible, reflect that we should have been lucky to do better ourselves, but the compassion called for by our common humanity must not make us shrink from passing judgement, since only thus can we profit by experience.

When therefore we consider how far we may reasonably blame Kaiser William in view of all the influences which went to make him the man he was, the last word would seem to rest with the Russian courtier on the Berlin station platform (see above, p. 113).

'*Ça explique mais ça n'excuse pas.*'

FAMILY TREE OF THE KAISER

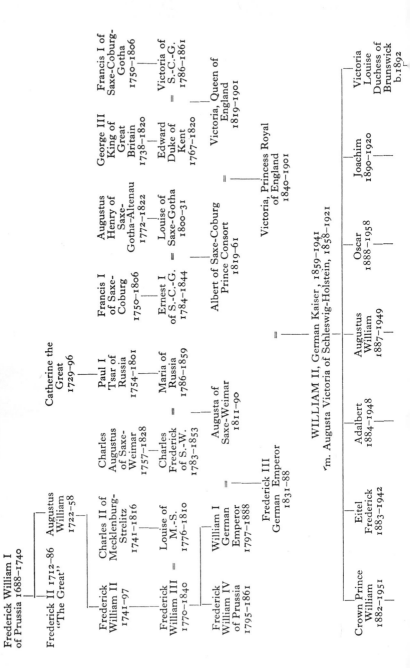

Appendix I

A Statistical Comparison between the Economies of the United Kingdom and Germany, 1870–1914

(NOTE: The last thing which the author would claim to be is a statistician, and only the apparent absence of a more expert alternative would have induced him to embark on the following compilation. The precision of the figures varies considerably and some of the tables are best regarded as approximations.)

I *AREA*

U.K. 119,654 sq. miles   GERMANY (1871) 208,780 sq. miles of which

England and Wales	58,020 sq. miles
Scotland	29,795 sq. miles

AREA UNDER CULTIVATION

1893 U.K. 13,987,000 acres   Germany 42,175,000 acres

1914 U.K. 12,797,000 ,,   Germany 45,414,000 ,,

Source: Accounts and Papers No. 218 of 1914.

II *POPULATION*

a. *Total population* (millions)

Date	U.K.	England and Wales	Germany
1871	31·8	22·7	41
1880	35·2	26	45·2
1891	38·1	29	49·4
1901	41·9	32·5	56·3 (1900)
1911	45·3	36	64·9
1913	46·0	n.a.	66·8

b. *Percentage of population living in towns*

1871	54·5	61·8	36·1
1881	60·7	67·9	41·4 (1880)
1891	65·6	72	47 (1890)
1901	71·3	77	54·3 (1900)
1911	73·4	78·2	60 (1910)

c. *Population density per square mile*

Date	U.K.	England and Wales	Germany
1871	265	391	196
1881	294	446	216
1891	318	500	236
1901	350	560	270
1911	373	618	310

Sources: Clapham: *Economic Development of France and Germany.*
Cmd. 4954 of 1909.

Note: British and German definitions of town do not exactly correspond.

III HOURS OF WORK OF WORKER PER YEAR

Date	U.K.	Germany
1877	2746	3300
1883	2738	3300
1890	2727	3250
1900	2715	3150
1905	2699	3075
1910	2734	3000
1912	2731	2970

Source: Colin Clark: *Conditions of Economic Progress* (3rd edition),
pp. 132–41.

IV TRANSPORT

a. *Railway development* (route miles)

Date	U.K.	Germany (1871 frontiers)
1850	10,500	6,000
1870	24,500	19,500
1890	33,000	43,000
1910	38,000	61,000

Source: Clapham, p. 339.

b. *Shipping.* Mercantile Tonnage: sail and steam ('000 tons)

Date	U.K.	Germany
1870	5681	982
1900	9304	1942
1910–12	11,700	3000

Source: E. J. Passant: *A Short History of Germany*, pp. 75 and 114.

V PRODUCTION

a. *Coal* ('ooo tons)

Date	U.K.	Germany (including lignite)
1871	118,000	37,900
1880	149,000	59,100
1890	184000	89,100
1900	228,000	149,300
1910	268,700	192,300
1913	292,000	279,000

b. *Steel* ('ooo tons)

Date	U.K.	Germany
1880	982 (1878)	1548
1890	3579	2195
1900	4901	6260
1908	5300	10,900
1913	6903	18,654

c. *Index of Manufacturing Activity* (1913 = 100)

Date	U.K.	% increase	Germany	% increase	World	% increase
1871–5	49		20·5		22·4	
		2		7·3		9·8
1876–80	50		22		24·6	
		14·6		21·8		23·6
1881–5	57·3		26·8		30·4	
		7·0		25		20·4
1886–90	61·3		33·5		36·8	
		5·4		20		15·8
1891–5	64·6		40·2		42·6	
		15·0		40·3		25·8
1896–1900	74·3		56·4		53·6	
		4·1		21·6		25
1901–5	77·3		68·8		67·0	
		7·5		17·4		19·2
1906–10	83·1		80·8		79·9	
		12·0		20·5		18·0
1911–13	93·1		97·4		94·3	

Source: *Industrialisation and Foreign Trade*, (League of Nations, 1945).

d. *Index of Total Production* (1913 = 100)

Date	U.K.	% increase	Germany	% increase	World
1860	38·6		14·1		14·1
		32		24	
1870	52		17·4		19·0
		23		43	
1880	64		24.·8		25·6
		16		64	
1890	74·2		40·5		43
		22		60	
1900	91·7		64·5		60·3
		10		37	
1910	100·5		88·4		87·6

Sources: For U.K., W. G. Hoffman: *British Industry* 1700–1950,
Table 54.
For Germany and the World, P. Jostock, *Income and Wealth*,
Series V, p. 103.

Notes: The U.K. reached 14·1% of its 1913 production in 1829!
The two indices are not necessarily on an identical basis. That
for the U.K. includes building.

e. *Real Product per person in work per year* (International Units)

Date	U.K.	Germany
1876	684	580
1877–85	829	673
1885–93	877	776
1894–1903	842	820
1904–10	1001	847
1911–13	1017	881
1913	1019	930

Source: Colin Clark: *Conditions of Economic Progress* (2nd edition),
pp. 63, 101.

VI NATIONAL INCOME (*yearly averages*)

	Total (millions of marks)		Per head of population (marks)	
Date	U.K.	Germany	U.K.	Germany
1871–75	23,374	15,171	701	364
1876–80	23,065	16,280	639	369

	Total		Per head of population	
	(millions of marks)		(marks)	
Date	*U.K.*	*Germany*	*U.K.*	*Germany*
1880–85	24,151	17,557	672	381
1886–90	26,605	20,104	712	417
1891–95	28,978	22,638	742	445
1896–1900	33,701	27,028	823	497
1901–05	36,912	31,548	863	538
1906–10	41,595	39,919	936	635
1911–13	50,491	47,374	1107	716

Sources: For U.K.: W. Ashworth: *An Economic History of England, 1870–1939*, p. 188.

For Germany: W. G. Hoffmann and J. H. Müller: *Das deutsche Volkseinkommen 1851–1957*, p. 30.

Notes: 1. All the above figures are on the basis of current prices. The U.K. price index (1871 = 100) rose to 119 in 1873, thereafter declined more or less steadily till it reached 70 in 1896, after which it began to rise again. The German price index (1913 = 100) rose to 103.4 1871–75, thereafter fell more or less steadily to 79.4 in 1896–1900, after which it began to rise again.

2. Converted at £ = 20.45 marks.

VII *TOTAL NATIONAL WEALTH* (£m)

Date	*U.K.*	*Germany*
1865	6114	—
1875	8548	—
1885	10,037	—
1895	11,393	10,000
1908	—	16–17,000
1914	14,300	15,000

Sources: For U.K.: Giffen's figures as quoted in R. C. K. Ensor, *England 1870–1914*.

For Germany: Helfferich: *Germany's Economic Progress and National Wealth 1888–1913* (for 1895 and 1914).

The Times, 14 September 1908 (for 1908).

VIII *OVERSEAS TRADE*

a. *Imports and Exports.* Averages over 5-year periods.
(£m. Current prices.)

Date	Imports		Exports	
	U.K.	Germany	U.K.	Germany
1870–4	290·6	—	234·8	113·7 (1872–4)
1875–9	319·5	—	201·5	132·3
1880–4	343·6	151·8	234·3	152·8
1885–9	318·8	159·9	226·2	151·0
1890–4	357·1	198·9	234·4	152·5
1895–9	392·7	232·8	237·8	181·3
1900–4	466·1	287	282·7	235·6
1905–8	519·3	387·9	368·5	311·5
1913	659·4	525·9	525·5	495·6

b. *Imports and Exports*   *Per head of population*

	£	s.	d.	£	s.	d.	£	s.	d.	£	s.	d.
1870–4	9	2	4	—			7	7	4	2	15	0
1875–9	9	10	4	—			6	0	0	3	1	5
1880–4	9	15	3	3	7	2	6	13	2	3	7	8
1885–9	8	14	2	3	7	7	6	3	8	3	3	10
1890–4	9	7	1	3	18	10	6	2	10	3	0	5
1895–9	9	16	5	4	6	6	5	18	11	3	7	5
1900–4	11	2	2	4	19	0	6	14	9	4	1	3
1905–8	11	16	8	6	5	5	8	7	11	5	0	8
1913	14	6	5	7	17	5	11	8	3	7	2	2

c. *Exports as % of National Income*

1870–9	20·6	18·4	Source: Cmd. 4954 of 1909.
1875–84	20·7	17·1	Accounts and Papers No. 218 of 1914.
1880–9	19·7	16	
1885–94	17·8	13·6	
1890–9	16·3	13	National Income statistics in Table VI.
1895–1904	16·2	14·3	
1900–8	18	15·8	
1905–14	20	19·1	

d. *Share in World Trade*

Date	Exports of manufactured articles. $ m. Annual averages			% of World Trade in Manufactures		Increase in Exports of own Manufactures (1881–5 = 100)	
	World	U.K.	Germany	U.K.	Germany	U.K.	Germany
1881–5	2600	993	464	38·2	17·2	100	100
1886–90	2700	996	509	36·7	18·5	100	110
1891–5	2720	937	496	34·5	18·2	94	107
1896–1900	3230	1018	627	31·4	19·4	103	135
1901–5	3990	1172	800	29·4	20	118	172
1906–10	5400	1554	1110	28·8	20·6	157	237
1911–13	6920	1902	1478	27·3	21·5	192	318
1913	7450	2029	1615	27·2	21·7	204	349

Source: *Industrialization and Foreign Trade*, League of Nations, 1945, pp. 157–8.

Notes: 1. Figures are for actual values. The fall in prices between 1880 and 1896 means that the expansion in volume of trade between those years is understated, and thereafter exaggerated.

2. By 1880 Germany was already the second largest exporter of manufactured goods in the world.

e. *Exports of certain Commodities* (£'000. Current prices.)

U.K.	1885	1890	1895	1900	1905	1910
Chemicals	6975	8948	8295	9272	14,535	18,572
Metals and metal wares	31,726	45,251	28,907	45,423	45,800*	59,700
Textiles	98,325	108,441	97,897	101,046	127,578	155,739
Machinery	11,074	16,413	15,215	19,622	23,268	29,297
Coal	10,632	19,019	15,443	38,606	26,061	37,812
Germany						
Chemicals	11,313	13,734	16,947	19,881	27,117	34,829
Metals and metal wares	17,813	21,535	24,083	39,164	49,644	61,481*
Textiles	43,932	53,606	49,953	54,937	68,629	66,785
Machinery	5791	8219	10,090	17,214	22,089	40,716
Fuel	4758	7325	7453	14,310	15,325	n.a.

Source: *Statesman's Year Book.*

Notes: 1. German customs rules as to the goods classified under a particular heading will not have corresponded exactly with British ones so that the figures should only be regarded as broad indications and not as fully comparable.

2. * indicates a change in the basis on which the figures in the series are calculated.

3. German figures prior to 1885 do not seem to be available.

4. Marks converted at 20 = £1.

f. *Comparative Exports to Particular areas (£m. Current prices).*

Date	W. Europe (excluding U.K. and Germany)		Russia and E. Europe		Central and South America		Canada Australia S. Africa Malaya		Main Empire Markets	
	U.K.	Ger-many	U.K.	Ger-many	U.K.	Ger-many	U.K.	Ger-many	U.K.	Ger-many
1880	85	64								
1883					29	3				
1890	96	69	14	15	36	8				
1896							43	4·3		
1900	113	105	19	28	27	10				
1902										
1910	136	187	20	58						
1912					60	36				
1913							107·4	11·3	228	21·7

Source: R. J. S. Hoffmann: *Great Britain and the German Trade Rivalry 1875–1914*, pp. 115–35 and 199–201.

g. % of trade of U.K. (including Ireland) with Empire Countries

Dates	Imports	Exports	Re-exports
1854–7	32·2	47·1	58·7
1877–9	44·7	45·4	53·9
1899–1901	56·4	48·8	50·1
1909–13	54·6	50·1	71·9

Source: W. Schlote: *British Overseas Trade from 1700's to 1930's.*

IX INVESTMENT

a. Total Investment
Ratio of Net National Capital Formation to Net National Product.

Dates		U.K.		Germany	
		Current Prices	Constant Prices	Current Prices	Constant Prices
U.K.	Germany				
	1851–60			8.6	7.9
1860–9		10.0	11.5		
	1861–70			9.7	10.6
1870–9		11.8	10.9		
	1871–80			13.5	13.0
1880–9		10.9	8.1		
	1881–90			14.0	14.5

1890–9		10.1	6.0		
	1891–1900			15.4	15.9
1895–1904		10.5	6.7		
1900–9		11.7	7.8		
	1901–13			16.5	15.9
1905–14		13.0	8.0		

Source: S. Kuznets: Quantitative Aspects of the Economic Growth of Nations VI Long-Term Trends in Capital Formation Proportions. *Economic Development and Cultural Change* IX 4 Part II (July 1961) 58, 59, 64.

b. *Overseas Investment, Cumulative totals* (billion marks)

Date	U.K.	Germany
1883	—	5
1885	27 +	—
1893	—	10–13
1895	33 +	—
1905	41 +	15–18
1909	47 + (60)	—
1914	80	22–25

Source: H. Feis: *Europe, The World's Banker*, pp. 14 and 71.

The British figures are based on C. K. Hobson, *The Export of Capital*, described by Feis as much too low. The alternative figure for Britain in 1909 was given in the *Economist* for 20-ii-09 and seems much closer to the truth.

Notes: 1. In 1913 (according to a report of the New York Bureau of Economic Research on *Capital Formation and Economic Growth*) overseas investment represented 27% of U.K. total national wealth and 10% of German. On the basis of the figures for total national wealth given in Table VII above, this would indicate a total overseas investment of around 80 billion marks for the U.K. and 30 billion for Germany.

2. According to Feis (pp. 16 and 72) only about 4% of U.K. annual national income was drawn from abroad in the 80's; by 1903 it had risen to 7% and by 1914 did not fall

far short of 10%. In Germany, income from foreign investment contributed 3–4% of national income up to 1900; thereafter it tended to fall to about 3%. Between 1911 and 1914 it was no more than 2%.

c. *Foreign Investment as % of Total Net Capital Formation at current prices*

Date	U.K.	Date	Germany
1855–64	29.1	1851/5–61/5	2.2
1865–74	40.1	1861/5–71/5	12.9
1875–84	28.9	1871/5–81/5	14.1
1885–94	51.2	1881/5–91/5	19.9
1895–1904	20.7	1891/5–1901/5	9.7
1905–14	52.9	1901/5–1911/13	5.7

Source: D. Landes: *The Unbound Prometheus*, p. 331.

X DEFENCE EFFORT

a. *Proportion of the population in the armed forces*

	U.K.				Germany			
Date	Size of Army	Size of Navy	Total	% of population	Size of Army	Size of Navy	Total	% of population
1872	196,600	60,000	256,600	0·81	403,600	6500	410,100	1
1880	198,200	59,000	257,200	0·73	401,650	7350	409,000	0·9
1891	209,000	97,600	306,600	0·8	511,650	17,000	528,650	1·07
1901	773,500	114,900	888,400	2·1	604,100	31,200	635,300	1·16
1911	247,000	128,000	375,000	0·83	622,500	33,500	656,000	1·01
1914	247,000	146,000	393,000	0·85	791,000	73,000	864,000	1·3

Source: *Statesman's Year Book*.

Notes: 1. The table has sought to include U.K. and German soldiers serving abroad but not natives of other countries in U.K. or German service.

2. Reservists have only been included when there was reason to think that they were serving full time (in S. Africa in 1901).

b. *Percentage of National Income devoted to Defence*

	U.K.		Germany	
Date	Total defence expenditure, yearly average, millions of marks	% of National income	Total defence expenditure, yearly average, millions of marks	% of National Income
1870–9	515	2·38	355	2·6
1875–84	536	1·97	408	2·55
1880–9	572	2·18	419	2·3
1885–94	628	2·39	487	2·14
1890–9	724	2·43	672	2·57
1895–1904	1335	3·98	770	2·59
1900–9	1568	4·4	939	2·65
1905–14	1385	3·26	1243	2·88

Source: *Statesman's Year Book*, combined with Table VI. So far as possible, figures are those of total actual expenditure falling on the domestic economy. German figures do not begin until 1872.

Appendix II

Strength of Parties in the *Reichstag*

	Number of seats obtained at election in					
Name of Party	*1890*	'*93*	'*98*	*1903*	'*07*	'*12*
Conservatives and Free Conservatives	93	100	79	75	84	57
National Liberals	42	53	46	51	54	45
Progressives	76	48	49	36	49	42
Centre	106	96	102	100	105	91
Social Democrats	35	44	56	81	43	110
Poles, Danes, Alsace-Lorrainers and Hanoverians	38	35	34	32	29	33
Others	7	21	41	22	33	19
TOTAL SEATS	397	397	397	397	397	397

Source: E. J. Passant, *A Short History of Germany 1815–1945*, p. 132. adapted from Mommsen u. Franz: *Die deutsche Parteiprogramme*.

Appendix III

Notes on Sources

I have tried to set out below the main evidence on whicn this book is based and occasionally to discuss points of interpretation. But I have been reading about this period for over thirty years, usually without keeping detailed page references. Hence there are a number of books not mentioned below, such as Meinecke's *Weltbürgertum und National-staat* and Langer's books on diplomatic history to which I am considerably indebted without being able to point out the precise location of my debts.

ABBREVIATIONS

GP = *Die Grosse Politik der Europäischen Kabinetten*, quoted by document number.

BD = *British Documents on the Origins of the War 1898–1914*, quoted by page number.

DD = *Die Deutsche Dokumente zum Kriegsausbruch 1914*, quoted by page number.

DDF = *Documents Diplomatiques Français 1871–1914*, quoted by page number.

OU Aussenpolitik = *Oesterreich-Ungarns Aussenpolitik von der Bosnische Krise bis zum Kriegsausbruch 1914*.

GW = Bismarck's *Gesammelte Werke*.

GuE = Bismarck's *Gedanken und Erinnerungen*, quoted by page from the Cotta one-volume edition.

HZ = Historische Zeitschrift.

AHR = American Historical Review.

EHR = English Historical Review.

Letters of QV = *Letters of Queen Victoria*, 3rd Series (unless an earlier series is expressly cited).

The volumes of Prince von Bülow's Memoirs, quoted from the English edition, are distinguished by the dates '*49–97*', '*97–03*' and '*03–09*'.

HP = Holstein Papers.

Z-T = Count Zedlitz-Trützschler: *Twelve Years at the Kaiser's Court*.

Preface: 1 GW XII, 237.
Facing page 1: Z-T 290.

Chapter I

In addition to books mentioned in individual notes, considerable use has been made in writing this chapter of F. L. Carsten: *The Origins of Prussia*, of Golo Mann: *Deutsche Geschichte des 19 u. 20 Jahrhunderts* and of K. E. Born: *Staat u. Sozialpolitik seit Bismarck's Sturz*.

1 G. Barraclough: *Factors in Modern German History* 17.
2 Speech at Aachen 19.vi.02.
3 J. A. Hawgood: *The Evolution of Germany* 149.
4 W. M. Becker: *Aktenstücke zur Gründungsgeschichte d. Universität Giessen* 85; E. Troeltsch: *The Social Teaching of the Christian Churches* 697–8.
5 A. J. P. Taylor: *The Course of German History* (Capricorn edn 1961) 18 (cited as 'Taylor: *Course*')
6 W. Hofer: 'Towards a Revision of the German Concept of History' in H. Kohn: *German History, Some New Views*; Bülow: *97–03*, 57.
7 Gordon A. Craig: *The Politics of the Prussian Army 1640–1945* (cited as 'Craig: *Prussian Army*') 16.
8 Speech at Bertha Krupp's wedding 15-x-06.
9 Speech at Erfurt 14-ix-91.
10 G. Ritter: *Staatskunst u. Kriegshandwerk* I 71.
11 See Troeltsch: 'The Idea of Natural Law and Humanity in World Politics'. Appendix to Sir E. Barker's translation of Gierke: *Natural Law and the Theory of Society*.
12 Ritter I 266.
13 T. Heuss: *Friedrich Naumann* 360.
14 R. J. Sontag: *Germany and England, Background of Conflict 1848–94*, 40.
15 Quoted in A. Dorpalen: *Heinrich v. Treitschke* 74.
16 Ritter I 157.
17 Taylor: *Course* 95. Text slightly altered for brevity.
18 K. W. Epstein: *Matthias Erzberger and the Dilemma of German Democracy* 40.
19 See W. W. Rostow: *The Stages of Economic Growth*.
20 Bülow: *03–09*, 96.
21 GW XIII 329.
22 Craig: *Prussian Army* 143–4.
23 GW XIII 390.

24 E. Eyck: *Bismarck and the German Question* 273. (Cited as 'Eyck: Question').

25 Sir Lewis Namier: *Avenues of History* 50; H. Heffter: *Die deutsche Selbstverwaltung im 19 Jahrhundert* 469.

26 A. v. Hohenlohe: *Aus meinem Leben* 271–2; R. Vierhaus (ed): *Das Tagebuch der Baronin Spitzemberg* 239 (cited as '*Spitzemberg*').

27 Sontag 108.

28 Eyck: *Question* 34.

29 Craig: *Prussian Army* 233.

30 P. R. Anderson: *The Background of Anti-English Feeling in Germany 1890–1902*, 75.

31 Eyck: *Question* 240. Bismarck later denied having made the remark.

32 See H. V. Dicks: *German Personality Traits and Nazi Ideology* in Daniel Lerner: *Propaganda in War and Crisis* 100–161.

33 Eyck: *Question* 274.

Chapter II

1 Rostow (*Stages of Economic Growth* 32) suggests that the British 'take-off' occurred during 1783–1802 and the German during 1850–70. But see Appendix I, Table Ve, which (by the risky process of combining two separate Indices) suggests that Germany reached in 1860 the level of production relative to 1914 which Britain had reached in 1829. This points to a somewhat earlier date for the start of the German process.

2 Rostow 31.

3 L. T. C. Rolt: *George and Robert Stephenson* 235.

4 A. Cairncross: *Home and Foreign Investment 1870–1914*, 1.

5 W. O. Henderson: *The Zollverein* 143.

6 ibid. 98–99.

7 Sontag 33.

8 U. F. J. Eyck: *The Prince Consort, a political biography* 66.

9 Dorpalen 228.

10 R. Barkeley: *The Empress Frederick* 81; Letters of QV, 1st Series III 588.

11 R. J. S. Hoffman: *Great Britain and the German Trade Rivalry 1875–1914*, 115, 127, 131.

12 A. J. Imlah: *Economic Elements in the Pax Britannica*.

13 Hoffman 45–50, 90–92.

14 Consular reports quoted in Hoffman 82–87.

15 Memorandum by James Bryce on p. 15 of *Correspondence with the Association of Chambers of Commerce 1884*.

16 Sontag 217.
17 Hawgood 181.
18 M. E. Townsend: *The Rise and Fall of Germany's Colonial Empire* 40–41.
19 ibid. 34.
20 Sontag 331.
21 A. J. P. Taylor: *Germany's First Bid for Colonies 1884–5.*
22 Eyck: *Question* 275.
23 Townsend 91.
24 Sontag 193–200.
25 Townsend 107.
26 Sir James Rennell Rodd: *Social and Diplomatic Memories* I 63–6.
27 Sontag 94.
28 Townsend 115.

Chapter III

(Use has also been made of W. Richter: *Kaiser Friedrich III* and R. Fulford: *The Prince Consort.*)

1 Bülow: *97–03*, 17.
2 H. Eulenburg: *The Hohenzollerns* 225; Veit Valentin: *Geschichte der Deutschen Revolution vom 1848 bis 1849* I 28–37.
3 U. F. J. Eyck 72.
4 Craig: *Prussian Army* 88.
5 H. Eulenburg 234.
6 A. v. Hohenlohe 348–9; Bülow: *97–03*, 529.
7 H. Kohn: *Wege u. Irrwege* 204.
8 H. v. Reischach: *Under Three Emperors* 68.
9 E. Eyck: *Bismarck* III 502.
10 Ex-Kaiser William: *Meine Vorfahren* 210.
11 E. Ludwig: *Kaiser William II* 18.
12 Egon Cesar, Count Corti: *The English Empress, a Study in the Relations between Queen Victoria and her Eldest Daughter* 163 (cited as 'Corti: *Empress*').
13 ibid. 54.
14 *Letters of the Prince Consort 1831–61* (ed. Jägow) 242.
15 Letter of Prince Consort to King William, 1.v.61, quoted U. F. J. Eyck 248.
16 Letter of Prince Consort to King Leopold of Belgium, 4.vii.61, quoted U. F. J. Eyck, 249.
17 Letters of QV, 1st Series III 462.

18 Quoted in an exhibition about the Prince Consort at the British Museum, Dec. 1961.

19 Sir H. Ponsonby (ed): *Letters of the Empress Frederick* 250 (cited as 'Ponsonby: *Letters*').

20 Letters of QV I 417.

21 Hon. Sir H. Nicolson: *George the Fifth* 40.

22 Speech on 25.i.02: Reischach 144.

23 Barkeley 12.

24 Ponsonby: *Letters* 7.

25 Barkeley 46.

26 Sir S. Lee: *King Edward VII* I 40.

27 Ponsonby: *Letters* 86.

28 Corti: *Empress* 212. The envoy sent to Marx was Sir M. Grant-Duff.

29 Bülow: *97–03*, 533.

30 Ponsonby: *Letters* 426.

31 Rennell Rodd I 49.

32 ibid. I 169; Bülow: *03–09*, 83.

33 F. Holstein: *Lebensbekenntnisse in Briefen an eine Frau* 308.

34 Ex-Kaiser William: Introduction to German edition of Ponsonby *Letters*, x.

35 L. V. Ballhausen: *Bismarck's Erinnerungen* 396.

36 A. Maurois: *King Edward and His Times* 62.

37 Bülow: *97–03*, 317.

38 A. F. Whyte: *A Field Marshal's Memoirs from the Diary, Correspondence and Papers of Alfred Count v. Waldersee* xvii (cited as 'Waldersee: *Memoirs*').

39 Ponsonby: *Letters* 26.

40 Corti: *Empress* 126. Letter dates from 1864.

41 Ponsonby: *Letters* 48.

42 Eyck: *Question* 99.

43 Corti: *Empress* 147–8.

44 Letters of QV, 2nd Series I 274.

45 Corti: *Empress* 130.

46 Ponsonby: *Letters* 426.

47 Speech at Aachen 18-x-11.

48 HP II 40.

49 *War Diary of Crown Prince Frederick* 241.

50 Waldersee: *Memoirs* 95.

51 E. F. Benson: *The Kaiser and his English Relations* 10.

52 Ponsonby: *Letters* 191, 368.

53 ibid. 151–3.

54 ibid. 160 and 190.

55 Monypenny and Buckle: *Life of Disraeli* II 1089–90.
56 GP XXI, 7125.
57 Graf J. Stürgkh: *Im Deutschen Grossen Hauptquartier* 232.
58 GW XIV I, 465.

Chapter IV

1 The main source for the Kaiser's ancestors is Wilhelm Karl, Prinz von Isenburg: *Die Ahnen der deutschen Kaisern, Könige u. ihrer Gemahlinnen.* See also *Stammtafeln zur Geschichte der Europäischen Staaten* by the same author. Analysis at almost any other generation would, of course, result in the inclusion of at least one person counting as English. The seventh generation has been deliberately taken to raise the question how far the Kaiser can be said to have had English blood in his veins.

2 Sir John Wheeler-Bennett: *Three Episodes in the Life of Kaiser William II*, 2–4; Henry W. Fischer: *The Private Lives of William II and his Consort: A Secret History of the Court of Berlin* 1–10; E. F. Benson: *Queen Victoria's Daughters* 50. According to one version, the damage was done by the midwife in getting the baby to breathe.

3 *Princess Daisy of Pless* by Herself 260.

4 R. v. Kühlmann: *Lebenserinnerungen* 227; John Gore: *King George V, A Personal Memoir* 29; Countess Keller: *40 Jahre in Dienst der Kaiserin* 34; Bülow: *03–09*, 141.

5 *New York Times* 5-vi-41.

6 Ponsonby: *Letters* 20–24.

7 W. P. Frith (ed. N. Wallis): *A Victorian Canvas* 8-xi-63.

8 GP XXVIII 10389.

9 Ex-Kaiser William: *Meine Vorfahren* 188.

10 Ponsonby: *Letters* 123.

11 Corti: *Empress* 139 (letter of 27-i-65).

12 Mrs. Rosslyn Weymss: *Memoirs and Letters of Sir Robert Morier* II 97; W. Richter: *Kaiser Friedrich III* 296 says that Hinzpeter was an anti-Liberal who did not hide his preference for absolutism. Alson J. Smith: *A View of the Spree* 76 says that 'Old Hinz' was a political Liberal who openly predicted the ultimate triumph of the Social Democrats. Neither author gives any indication of his evidence.

13 Article on Hinzpeter in *Biographisches Jahrbuch u. Deutscher Nekrolog* XII 1907.

14 H. S. Chamberlain: *Briefe* II 141.

15 Poulteney Bigelow: *Seventy Summers* I 70.

16 G. v. Müller: *The Kaiser and His Court* (For full title, see X, 118,) 19-vi-18; speech at wedding of Prince Augustus William 22-x-08.

17 Karl F. Nowak: *Kaiser and Chancellor. The opening Years of the Reign of the Emperor William II*, 13.

18 Z-T xii; Bülow: *97–03*, 101.

19 Speech at Stargard 30-viii-11.

20 *Denkwurdigkeiten des Botschafters General v. Schweinitz* I 305 (cited as '*Schweinitz*').

21 J. v. Kürenberg: *The Kaiser, A Life of William II, Last Emperor of Germany* 335.

22 Corti: *Empress* 194.

23 Ludwig 8; J. Hohlfeld: *Dokumente der deutschen Politik u Geschichte: Das Zeitalter Wilhelms II* 10.

24 Lee I 474 quoting Jowett's letters.

25 E. Eyck: *Bismarck* III 557 quoting French diplomatic documents.

26 Ponsonby: *Letters* 179.

27 Ludwig 10.

28 Kürenberg 32.

29 E. F. Benson: *The Kaiser and His English Relations* 34 (all future references to Benson are to this book); GP XXXI 11435.

30 Corti: *Empress* 159.

31 Ponsonby: *Letters* 119

32 ibid. 133.

33 A. Dorpalen: 'Empress Augusta Viktoria and the Fall of the German Monarchy' in AHR (Oct. 1952) Vol. LVIII 20 (cited as 'Dorpalen: AHR').

34 Corti: *Empress* 213.

35 W. Helfritz: *Wilhelm II als Kaiser u. König* 333.

36 A. N. Davis: *The Kaiser I Knew* 333.

37 R. Fulford: *Royal Dukes* 159.

38 BD III 435.

39 Helfritz: loc. cit.

40 Princess M. Radziwill: *This Was Germany* 109–11.

41 GP XII 3228.

42 Bülow: *97–03*, 145; Z-T 41; A. Topham: *Memories of the Kaiser's Court* 80.

43 Bülow: *97–03*, 53, 80 and 185; HP III 280.

44 W. Schröder (ed.): *Das persönliche Regiment: Reden u. sonstige öffentliche Aeusserungen Wilhelm II* 149.

45 Letters of QV I 485.

46 Letters of T. Roosevelt (ed. Morison) VII, 396.

47 *Daisy of Pless*, 263.

48 ibid. 256.

49 V. Chirol: *50 Years in a Changing World* 276.

50 *Daisy of Pless*: loc. cit.

51 A. v. Hohenlohe 344.

52 Alson J. Smith, op. cit. 63, says that the match was suggested to William by Countess v. Waldersee after a visit to herself and her husband at Hanover 'in or about the year 1880', when the Prince 'had just turned 21'. There are, however, a number of difficulties about this story of which Mr. Smith seems unaware: (*a*) No hint of such a suggestion is made by anyone else; (*b*) The Waldersees seem to have been given to extravagant claims so that their evidence (which Mr. Smith does not reproduce in detail) must be accepted with caution; (*c*) the story seems to be contradicted by Ponsonby: *Letters* 411; (*d*) General v. Waldersee not only made no reference in his Diaries to any visit to him by William at Hanover but speaks on 6-xii-82 as though he had only recently come to know the Prince; (*e*) The timing, on Mr. Smith's account, is awkward. William was 21 on 27-i-80; his engagement took place on 14-ii-80. On 21-ii-80 the General does, however, refer to it, saying that nobody realized it to be almost a year old. This suggests that the visit to Hanover, if it occurred, was prior to 1880 and that the Waldersees had some inside knowledge about the engagement.

53 Ponsonby: *Letters* 174–83.

54 Radziwill 16.

55 *Daisy of Pless* 160.

56 Waldersee: *Memoirs* 127.

57 Eyck: *Bismarck* III 506.

58 Dorpalen: loc. cit.; Bülow: *97–03*, 244.

59 Bülow: ibid.

60 Dorpalen: ibid.

61 GuE 672; *Daisy of Pless* 225, 265 and 369.

62 Radziwill 30; Z-T 236.

63 Keller 151.

64 Holstein: *Lebensbekenntnisse* 216; Kürenberg 176.

65 Keller 22; Alson Smith 67.

66 Princess Marie Louise: *My Memoirs of Six Reigns* (Penguin edn.) 54.

67 Kürenberg 44.

68 Spitzemberg 484.

69 Nowak 50.

70 Craig: *Prussian Army* 226–30.

71 Alson Smith 82 states that 'the lurid stories and insinuations that appeared in the magazines' to the effect that Countess v. Waldersee was William's mistress 'had, on the evidence, a basis in fact'. This is undoubtedly a matter on which adequate evidence must be hard to come by. But Mr. Smith's assertion would be a good deal more acceptable if he had added at least some illustration of what it is based on. As most of the other evidence (or lack of evidence) points the other way and as the Waldersees are known to have used American correspondents in Berlin to advance themselves, it must be regarded for the present as 'not proven'. Reluctance to accept Mr. Smith's judgement would be less if his detailed knowledge of the period were greater. But he thinks, for example, that Bismarck was at Friedrichsruh when dismissed and is unaware of the letter which Queen Victoria wrote to the Kaiser after the Krüger telegram.

72 Waldersee: *Memoirs* 117, 124; HP III 352.

73 HP I 137.

74 Rennell Rodd I 110.

75 *Schweinitz* II 132.

76 Ponsonby: *Letters* 214–15.

77 HP II 95.

78 Corti: *Empress* 220; Waldersee: *Memoirs* 120–3; HP II 34, 165.

79 HP II 214–15.

80 Bülow: *97–03*, 467.

81 Prince P. zu Eulenburg: *Aus 50 Jahren* 176.

82 Corti: *Empress* 50.

83 Lee II 117.

84 Ponsonby: *Letters* 101; HP III 291.

85 *Economist* 30-vi-62; Alson Smith 70.

86 Fulford: *Royal Dukes* 183.

87 Lee II 237, 544.

88 Benson 40.

89 Lee I 478.

90 Ex-Kaiser William: *My Early Life* 323.

91 Lee I 485–6, quoting Krasny Archiv.

92 Egon Cesar, Count Corti: *Alexander of Battenberg* 129–31 (cited as 'Corti: *Battenberg*').

93 Corti: *Empress* 226–7.

94 HP II 254; Corti: *Empress* 229.

95 Corti: *Battenberg* 122.

96 Eyck: *Bismarck* III 447; HP II 298.

97 HP II 225; Corti: *Battenberg* 126.

98 Corti: *Battenberg* 236, quoting 'exactly as in the original' gives 'your barbaric semi-Asiatic tyrannical cousin'. Ponsonby: *Letters* 209 gives 'the barbaric Asiatic tyrannical Tsar'.

99 Corti: *Battenberg* 222-3; GP v 982.

Chapter V

1 Quoted in Gordon A. Craig: *From Bismarck to Adenauer* 27.

2 Eyck: *Bismarck* III 464.

3 GP VI, 1163.

4 Bülow: *97–03*, 394; Craig: op. cit. 13-15.

5 J. Haller: *Philip zu Eulenburg the Kaiser's Friend* I 64.

6 Sontag 218.

7 HP III 219.

7a The sources for the Crown Prince's illness are collected and discussed in R. S. Stevenson: *Morell Mackenzie* and H. J. Wolf: *Die Krankheit Friedrichs III u. ihre Wirkung auf die deutsche u. englische Oeffentlichkeit*. When stories of syphilis appeared in the French press, the Crown Prince authorized Mackenzie to deny them. But Mackenzie's subsequent statement to a friend makes clear that he himself was far from convinced by the denial.

8 'No, it is not you who are to blame, it was the will of fate'. *Aida* Act II. *Aida*, though commissioned in connection with the opening of the Suez Canal, was not finished until two years later.

9 Ex-Kaiser William: 'Introduction' to German edn. of Ponsonby: *Letters* xvi.

10 Ponsonby: *Letters* 256-7.

11 This story was much circulated at the time by enemies of the Empress and might be suspect were it not confirmed on good authority in HP III 228.

12 P. zu Eulenburg 147.

13 GP IV, 926.

14 Rennell Rodd I 123.

15 A. Ponsonby: *Henry Ponsonby, Queen Victoria's Private Secretary, his life from his Letters* 291-2 (cited as '*Henry Ponsonby*').

16 GuE 584.

17 W. Frank: *Hofprediger Adolf Stöcker* 167.

18 Ponsonby: *Letters* 271.

19 Born 57.

20 HP II 87.

21 ibid. 363.

22 For the correspondence, see GuE 586–99.

23 Schröder 111; C. zu Hohenlohe: *Denkwürdigkeiten* III 236.

24 J. Bühler: *Vom Bismarckreich zum geteilten Deutschland* (Vol. VI of *Deutsche Geschichte*) 136.

25 P. zu Eulenburg 146. There are a number of varying versions of what the Emperor said about Russia. See GuE 551; Corti: *Battenberg* 275.

26 Lady G. Cecil: *Life of Lord Salisbury* IV 96.

27 For message to Queen Victoria, see Letters I 390.

28 Eyck: *Bismarck* III 530.

29 Ponsonby: *Letters* 293–302.

30 Eyck: *Bismarck* III 520.

31 Corti: *Battenberg* 288.

32 Ponsonby: loc. cit.

33 H. Bolitho: *Further Letters of Queen Victoria* 268.

34 Ponsonby: *Letters* 321.

35 ibid. 311.

36 Esmé Howard: *Theatre of Life* I 332–3.

37 Ponsonby: *Letters* Introduction.

38 Ludwig 57.

39 Z-T 104.

40 Barkeley 280.

41 L. Bamberger: *Bismarcks Grosses Spiel* 416.

42 Henry Ponsonby 110–11.

43 Ponsonby: *Letters* 337.

44 Henry Ponsonby: loc. cit.

45 Ponsonby: *Letters* 324.

46 Letters of QV I 145. See also Benson 71.

47 Letters of QV I 429.

48 A. L. Kennedy: *Salisbury 1830–1903* 336.

49 Letters of QV I 440.

50 Kennedy 389.

51 Letters of QV I 443.

52 ibid. 467

53 Lee I 654–8.

54 H. O. Meissner (ed.): *Aus dem Briefwechsel des General Feld-marschalls Alfred Grafen von Waldersee 1886–91*, 207, 219 (cited as 'Waldersee: *Briefwechsel*')

55 Cecil IV 367.

56 Ludwig 77.

57 Bülow: *97–03*, 246.

58 Waldersee: *Briefwechsel* 224; Waldersee: *Memoirs* 156.

59 W. Schüssler: *Kaiser Wilhelm II. Schicksal u. Schuld* 84.

60 Ponsonby: *Letters* 363.
61 Waldersee: *Memoirs* 154.
62 GuE 612.
63 E. Schiffer: *Ein Leben für den Liberalismus* 146.
64 Cecil IV 124.
65 Nowak 182.
66 Eyck: *Question* 39.
67 G. P. Gooch: *Studies in Diplomacy* 88.
68 GP IV, 943–5.
69 There are a number of detailed chronological accounts of Bismarck's Fall, among the most recent being J. Alden Nichols: *Germany after Bismarck*; Eyck: *Bismarck* III and A. J. P. Taylor: *Bismarck*. Bismarck's own account is in GuE 615–69, William's in *Deutsche Rundschau* (Jan. 1919) LVIII, 100–07. See also Born: *Staat u. Sozialpolitik*.
70 There seems to be some doubt as to whether Bismarck actually used these words in the Council or merely claimed to have done so afterwards. In either case, they sum up his line of argument.
71 See account in Kürenberg 79–80 which would seem based on what the Kaiser told the author at Doorn.
72 GW XII 329.
73 GP VI, 1360n.
74 Letters of QV I 591.
75 Five sources for this story are noted in Eyck: *Bismarck* III 587. See also Princess Marie Louise 75 who claims to have heard it direct from the Empress Frederick.
76 Haller II 140.
77 Schröder 92.
78 Spitzemberg 407; E. Ludwig: *Bismarck* 485, 595.
79 Holstein: *Lebensbekenntnisse* 223.
80 Waldersee: *Briefwechsel* 335.
81 HP II 349.
82 A. v. Tirpitz: *My Memoirs* I 44–45.
83 GuE 600.
84 Helfritz 141.
85 Craig: *From Bismarck to Adenauer* 102.
86 *Schweinitz* II 404–5.
87 ibid. 405–7.
88 Lord Crewe: *Lord Rosebery* II 673.
89 Ludwig 130.

Chapter VI

1 Kühlmann 229; Schröder 191.

2 C. zu Hohenlohe: *Memoirs* II 406.

3 A. v. Hohenlohe 359; Schiffer 9.

4 A. Topham: *Memories of the Fatherland* 149.

5 Topham 150; *Diaries of Theodor Herzl* 267. Herzl's deductions as to William's character were so overdone that his excitement over William's eyes is best taken with a grain of salt.

6 Davis 205.

7 J. Pope-Hennessy: *Queen Mary* 288.

8 Davis 24.

9 Maurois 268.

10 HP III 280; Davis 48.

11 Princess Marie Louise 73.

12 H. v. Treschkow: *Von Fürsten u. anderen Sterblichen* 146; Davis 55.

13 Sir John Wheeler-Bennett, personal communication; Schröder 19–21.

14 J. Amory: *Life of Joseph Chamberlain* IV 198; W. v. Rathenau: *Der Kaiser, eine Betrachtung* 27; C. zu Hohenlohe II 411; Wheeler-Bennett, personal communication.

15 Z-T 222; Princess Marie Louise 68.

16 *Daisy of Pless* 262.

17 P. Radziwill 30.

18 Fulford: *Prince Consort* 17.

19 Sir B. Pares: *History of Russia* 278.

20 Z-T 60.

21 Craig: *Prussian Army* 239; *Daisy of Pless* 259.

22 Holstein: *Lebensbekenntnisse* 258.

23 HP III 251.

24 Pope-Hennessy 288–9.

25 HP III 659.

26 L. De Hegermann-Lindencrone: *The Sunny Side of Diplomatic Life 1875–1912*, 315.

27 Bülow: *97–03*, 3.

28 Topham 129.

29 Gore 61.

30 Holstein: *Lebensbekenntnisse* 236.

31 Topham 129–35.

32 Hegermann-Lindencrone 315.

33 Z-T 246.

34 *Daisy of Pless* 199.

35 BD III 433.

36 Z-T 174–5.

37 Hegermann-Lindencrone 299.

38 Schiffer 41.

39 Müller, 20-ix-15.

40 Kühlmann 497–8.

41 Müller 20-viii-18.

42 Z-T 199.

43 Kühlmann 233, 279.

44 N. F. Grant (ed.): *The Kaiser's Letters to the Tsar* (cited as '*Kaiser's Letters*') 87.

45 D. S. McDiarmid: *Life of Lieut-General Sir John Grierson*, 123 and 129.

46 Schröder 173; Herodotus, *Histories* VI, 129.

47 Müller, 29-ix-17.

48 *New York Herald Tribune* 5-vi-41.

49 Helfritz 357.

50 Bülow: *97–03*, 543.

51 Schröder 193.

52 R. v. Valentini (ed. Schwertfeger): *Kaiser u. Kabinettschef* 117.

53 Topham 168.

54 HP IV 8, III 383.

55 Lerchenfeld in Rassow u. Born: *Akten zur staatlichen Sozialpolitik in Deutschland 1890–1914* (cited as 'Rassow u. Born') 138–41.

56 Bülow: *97–03*, 3.

57 Bülow: *03–09*, 32: Tirpitz I 157.

58 Maj-Gen. Sir Frederick Maurice: *Haldane 1856–1915*, 193.

59 Topham 167.

60 Rassow u. Born, loc. cit.

61 Lee II 152.

62 Nichols 118.

63 ibid. 315.

64 Bülow: *97–03*, 450.

65 Kühlmann 553.

66 Sir E. Goschen in BD VI, 437.

67 A. v. Hohenlohe 342.

68 ibid. 337.

69 HP III 612–13.

70 BD III 434; HP IV 10.

71 Quoted repeatedly in Spitzemberg.

72 HP III 16; IV 10.

73 Ponsonby: *Letters* 328.

74 BD III 391; Müller 24-v-15; Schiffer 117

75 Bülow: *97–03*, 237.

76 Müller 14-vi-17; Robert A. Kann AHR June 1952, 330; BD III 391.

77 Bülow: *03–09*, 470.

78 Haller I 39.

79 Kürenberg 115: HP IV 11.

80 Nowak 110; Spitzemberg 362.

81 HP III 577.

82 BD III 436.

83 E. Eyck: *Das Persönliche Regiment Wilhelms II* (cited henceforward as 'Eyck') 84.

84 GP XXVI 9533.

85 Topham: loc. cit.; Rennell Rodd I 50.

86 Bülow: *97–03*, 397.

87 Ludwig: *Kaiser William II* 144.

88 Z-T 172.

89 Sir John Wheeler-Bennett: *Hindenburg, The Wooden Titan* 103.

90 GP XXIII 7877.

91 Bülow: *03–09*, 166; also *97–03*, 161.

92 Waldersee: *Memoirs* 167-8.

93 Wheeler-Bennett 5.

94 Bülow: *97–03*, 3.

95 Speech of 12-xi-06.

96 Topham: *Memories of the Kaiser's Court* 174.

97 Reischach 238.

98 Tirpitz I 292.

99 HP III 352–3.

100 Haller I 183.

101 Haller II 53–54; HP I 176; W. Hubatsch: *Die Aera Tirpitz* 69; HP III 593; C. zu Hohenlohe III 289.

102 Epstein 125.

103 O. Czernin: *In the World War* 62.

104 Tirpitz I 73.

105 Schiffer 108.

106 Z-T 196.

107 Bülow: *97–03*, 537.

108 E. v. Vietsch: *Wilhelm Solf, Botschafter Zwischen den Zeiten* 145.

109 Waldersee: *Briefwechsel* 319.

110 Craig: *Prussian Army* 240; Valentini 48–55.

111 Tirpitz I 158.

112 Z-T xvi.

113 Ludwig 79; Z-T 261–72.

114 A. v. Hohenlohe 317; Treschkow 148.
115 Z-T 114; H. G. Zmarzlik: *Bethmann Hollweg als Reichskanzler 1909–14*, 91.
116 Z-T 190.
117 GP XXIV 8448, XXXII 11383, XXXIII 12154.
118 Z-T 208.
119 ibid. 47.
120 *Boston Transcript* 1882, quoted in Smith 73.
121 Schröder 188.
122 Bülow: *03–09*, 72–73.
123 Bülow: *97–03*, 264.
124 Müller, 13-viii-17.
125 *Kaiser's Letters* 152.
126 Speech to the Brandenburg Assembly, 24-ii-92.
127 Speech to Deputies, 6-v-98.
128 Ex-Kaiser William: *My Memoirs* 214; also Schüssler 136.
129 BD III 435.
130 Attempts were made to explain away this entry on the ground that there were two visitor's books, that the wrong one was presented and signed first, that the Prince Regent tried to prevent the city authorities from bothering the Kaiser with the second and that, in solving the dilemma by writing as he did, William was using the words to refer to the Regent. But not only was the Regent not a Rex; William had made the same remark to *Reichstag* deputy von Rauchhaupt a fortnight earlier. See Schröder 189.
131 Speech at Düsseldorf 4-v-91.
132 Bülow: *97–03*, 314.
133 Speech at Königsberg 25-viii-10.
134 Telegram to Hinzpeter 11-vi-99.
135 Müller 25-vi-15.
136 *Kaiser's Letters* 254.
137 Z-T 201.
138 T. Roosevelt to Sir G. O. Trevelyan, 1-x-11 in *Letters of T.R.* (ed. Morison) VII 397.
139 Winston Churchill: Article on 'The Ex-Kaiser' in *Great Contemporaries*.
140 Speech 18-iv-91.
141 Speech 23-xi-91. This speech was doctored before publication and three disparate texts exist.
142 Schröder 18-19; Z-T 75.
143 GP XIX 6104; *Kaiser's Letters* 132.
144 Speech at launching of battleship *Wittelsbach* 3-vii-1900.
145 Speech on 18-x-99.

146 Davis 144.

147 Speech to Brandenburg Assembly 24-ii-92.

148 Speeches on 14-v-89 and 2-ix-95.

149 Speech on 26-ii-97. The words 'rooted out to the very last stump' were cut out of the version circulated by the Wolf Telegraph Bureau.

150 HP III 658.

151 H. S. Chamberlain: *Briefe* II 188.

152 GP XIX 6280, XXXII 11675 and 11690.

153 T. Fontane: *Briefe an Friedländer* 5-iv-97, p. 309.

154 Davis 50; P. Green: *Life of K. Grahame* 291; R. H. Bruce-Lockhart: *Retreat from Glory* 344; Schröder 159.

155 Born 135.

156 Gärtringen: *Fürst Bülows Denkwürdigkeiten* (for full title, see IX 161) 179.

157 Radziwill 25.

158 Kürenberg 176.

159 C. zu Hohenlohe III 24; Kühlmann 509.

160 Speech on 18-xii-01.

161 Speech on opening of Pergamon Museum 18-xii-01.

162 Ernest Newman in *Sunday Times* 1-xi-36.

163 Davis 45.

164 H. S. Chamberlain II 200.

165 Schüssler 138.

166 Speech on 12-iii-06.

167 H. S. Chamberlain II 142.

168 Helfritz 264.

169 Speech at Bremen 22-iii-05.

170 Speech in Berlin 5-iii-90.

171 Schröder 197.

172 Tirpitz I 160.

173 Rassow u. Born 138–41.

174 GP XX 6376.

175 GP XXXI 11424.

176 GP XXVI 9569.

177 GP XXXII 11704.

178 Rassow u. Born: loc. cit.

179 Müller 14-xii-15.

180 Remark to Prince Radolin, German Ambassador in Paris, quoted in BD III 438.

181 Remark to Sir E. Goschen BD VI 437.

182 Gooch 113.

Chapter VII

1 Born 92.
2 Waldersee: *Briefwechsel* 262–8.
3 Holstein: *Lebensbekenntnisse* 207.
4 Waldersee: *Memoirs* 174.
5 Nichols 357.
6 See articles by W. Hallgarten in HZ (1954) 177 and N. Rich in HZ (1958) 186.
7 Bülow: *49–97*, 394.
8 It has often been suggested that Holstein had a special hold over Bülow based on the possession of some inconvenient knowledge. This appears to rest mainly on a statement by Raschdau in the *Süddeutsche Monatshefte* for March 1931. 'In the early stages of our acquaintance Holstein told me about matters of a very serious character which could put Bülow at the mercy of a ruthless opponent.' The fear that Holstein would prove such an opponent may have influenced Bülow's conduct towards him, but that conduct can equally well be explained by the value to Bülow of Holstein's unrivalled knowledge of German diplomacy. The Holstein Papers, by providing no evidence to support the first explanation, have the effect of supporting the second. See also Haller II 308 and HP IV 130.
9 Haller I and C. zu Hohenlohe III 309; also HP III generally.
10 D. R. Gillard: *Salisbury's African Policy and the Heligoland Offer of 1890* in EHR (Oct. 1960) 75.
11 GP XIII 3399.
12 M. S. Wertheimer: *The Pan-German League 1890–1914*.
13 Nichols 305.
14 Speech of 6-ix-94.
15 Nichols 276.
16 Born 107.
17 Nichols 89; also Born.
18 Craig: *Prussian Army* 236.
19 Nichols 192.
20 Z-T 39.
21 Ritter I 182–3.
22 Holstein *Lebensbekenntnisse* 164n.
23 Speech on 21-ii-91.
24 Hohlfeld 25–26.
25 Nichols 301.
26 Müller xxi.
27 Tirpitz I 102.

28 Schüssler 28.

29 H. Rogge: *Die Kladderadatsch Affäre* in HZ (1962) 195, pp. 90–130.

30 HP III 469.

31 ibid. 432n.

32 Eyck 84; Ludwig 136–8.

33 Spitzemberg 386.

34 Letters of QV II 125.

35 Benson 91.

36 Nichols 315; Eckardstein I 207.

37 Princess Marie Louise 118.

38 Henry Ponsonby 297.

39 Nichols 280–82; Haller I 146.

40 T. Bayer: *England u. der Neue Kurs 1890–1914*, 15.

41 Nichols 278.

42 Bayer 55.

43 Rosebery to Sir E. Malet 11-i-93 quoted in Bayer 114.

44 Sontag 288.

45 Nichols 323.

46 GP IX 2152.

47 Ex-Kaiser William: *My Memoirs* 305.

48 Nichols 329.

49 ibid. 351.

50 Haller I 260–70.

51 HP III 480; H. Rogge: *Holstein und Hohenlohe* 411.

52 Spitzemberg 382.

53 Bühler 197.

Chapter VIII

1 Stephen Gwynn (ed.) *Letters and Friendships of Sir C. Spring-Rice* I 182.

2 Spitzemberg 477.

3 Waldersee: *Memoirs* 194.

4 C. zu Hohenlohe III 21; A. v. Hohenlohe 352–4.

5 C. zu Hohenlohe III 231.

6 C. zu Hohenlohe III 48.

7 ibid. 63.

8 ibid. 321; HP III 477.

9 Bülow: *03–09*, 84.

10 *Kaiser's Letters* 24.

11 GP IX 2318.

12 GP IX 2251; Eyck 118.

13 GP X 2385, 2391; Letters of QV II 547; HP III 536; Benson 123.

14 Letters of QV II 586.

15 W. Hallgarten: '*L'Essor et L'Echec de la Politique Boer de l'Alle-magne*' in *Revue Historique* 1936, 512–29; Anderson 248–50.

16 GP XI 2578.

17 *Kaiser's Letters* 22; R. Rodd I 162.

18 GP XI 2580.

19 ibid. 2572.

20 Holstein: *Lebensbekenntnisse* 175–7.

21 Craig: *Prussian Army* 246–51.

22 The evidence on the Krüger Telegram was set out by F. Thimme: 'Die Krüger Depesche' in *Europäische Gespräche* 1924, 200–41, supplemented by K. Lehmann: 'Die Vorgeschichte der Krüger-depesche' in *Archiv für Politik u. Geschichte* (1925) V 159–177. and 'Zu Kaiser Wilhelms England Politik' in HZ (1933) CXLVII 553–8. The third volume of Prince Hohenlohe's *Memoirs* (pp. 151 and 613) and HP I 163 throw little fresh light on the matter. But the entry for 5 Jan. 1896 in Baroness Spitzemberg's *Tagebuch*, contains the phrase 'the Kaiser was induced to send the telegram though not without difficulty because of his English sympathies'. This seems particularly significant because the Baroness (*a*) was usually well-informed and went out of her way on this occasion to say that her statements were derived from influential circles so that she could vouch for their authenticity, (*b*) shows herself in general a discriminating judge of character and of the value of evidence, (*c*) was as a rule highly critical of the Kaiser, (*d*) wrote within two days of the event, (*e*) kept her diary for herself with no idea of early publication. Her statement lends weight to the other-wise suspect reports by Eckardstein (I 272 and 277) that v. Hollmann (one of the Admirals present) and Holstein both attrib-uted responsibility to v. Marschall (who may well have been her informant).

23 Benson 113; Kürenberg 101.

24 Lee I 724; Letters of QV III 7.

25 Belgian Documents on the Origins of the War 109.

26 Thimme 223.

27 Letters of QV III 8–9, 17.

28 Mary Lutyens (ed.) *Lady Lytton's Court Diary* 80.

29 E. Pakenham: *Jameson's Raid* 99.

30 Richter 130.

31 Helfritz 239; Hallgarten: op. cit.; GP X 2513, 2520, 2522.

32 W. Hubatsch: *Der Admiralstab* 82.

33 C. zu Hohenlohe III 323; HP III 589n.

34 C. zu Hohenlohe III 327.

35 Ritter II 157.

36 ibid. 165n.

37 Born 133.

38 Born 140; HP III 652n.; C. zu Hohenlohe III 287.

39 Letters of QV III 138, 162, 198.

40 C. zu Hohenlohe III 306; Eyck 170; GP XI 3169–70.

41 *Diaries of Theodor Herzl* 238.

42 Spitzemberg 372.

43 BD VI 198; HP IV 245.

44 Rassow u. Born 141–3.

45 Born 143; Rassow u. Born 143.

46 W. Churchill: *World Crisis* I 114.

47 Eyre-Crowe Memorandum BD III 407.

48 Admiral Knorr, quoted in W.·Hubatsch: 'Die Kulminations-punkt der deutsche Marinepolitik in 1912' in HZ (1953) CCXXVII 293. See also Kühlmann 292 and Ludwig 246.

49 Eckardstein II 168. The literal translation of Hatzfeldt's remark is 'baked pigeons would fly into our mouths'.

50 A. J. Marder: *Correspondence of Lord Fisher 1904–14*, 169.

51 W. Hubatsch: *Die Aera Tirpitz* 74.

52 McDiarmid 133.

53 Helfritz 247.

54 Tirpitz I 112–3.

55 Anderson 165.

56 Speeches of 17-vi-97 and 23-ix-98.

57 Speech of 26-ii-97.

58 Ritter II 127.

59 Inaugural lecture at Freiburg 1895. Heuss 141.

60 Eyck 219.

61 Letters of QV III 126–7.

62 Eyck 195.

63 Hoffman 287.

64 GP XIII 3413.

65 GP XIV 3690.

66 Speech of 15-xii-97.

67 GP XIV 3739.

68 J. L. Garvin: *Life of Joseph Chamberlain* III 95.

69 Garvin III Ch. 59. 'You will see that in every case the interviews were sought by the Germans and the initiative was taken by them'.

70 For the German version of 1898 negotiations, see GP XIV 3782–3804; HP IV 64–88.

71 Blanche E. Dugdale: *Arthur James Balfour* I 258.

72 GP XIV 3789.

73 ibid. 3803.

74 *Kaiser's Letters* 51; GP XIII 3396.

75 A. Moorhead: *The White Nile* 337.

76 ibid. 340.

77 *Kaiser's Letters* 64–78; GP XIII 3554, XIV 3926.

78 GP XIV 4216, 4320.

79 ibid. 4351.

80 ibid. 4320.

81 *Kaiser's Letters* 64–78.

82 *Diaries of Herzl* 282.

83 According to J. Alson Smith (*A View of the Spree* 134): 'William rode on horseback from Jerusalem to Damascus . . . but he took the train back from Damascus to Jerusalem'. As there is not and never has been a railway from Damascus to Jerusalem and as even the Hedjaz Railway east of the Jordan was not built in 1898, it is difficult to see how he accomplished this feat, or how he was expected to get from Jerusalem to Damascus. Where he took the train was, of course, from Damascus to Beirut.

84 Hohlfeld 102.

85 Dugdale I 260.

86 GP XIV 3806.

87 Dugdale I 292.

88 GP XIV 3867.

89 Kennedy 318.

90 Bülow: *97–03*, 271.

91 Letters of QV III 358–9.

92 Lee I 740.

93 Letters of QV III 340, 358–9.

94 Lee I 742.

95 Letters of QV III 375–9.

96 ibid. 379–80.

97 ibid. 381–2.

98 Eckardstein II 29.

99 Townsend 200.

100 Eyck 237.

101 Bülow: *97–03*, 219.

102 GP XV 4195.

103 Bülow: *97–03*, 395.

104 Hallgarten: loc. cit.

105 Garvin III 521.

106 Dugdale I 291.

107 Bülow: *97–03*, 332.

108 Lee I 759.

109 GP XV 4969; BD III 437.

110 Letters of QV III 508.

111 Lee I 770.

112 GP XV 4394.

113 Eyck 259; Tirpitz I 121.

114 Bülow; *97–03*, 357; the text here given combines the version given by the *Nordwestdeutscher Zeitung*, which omitted the words in brackets but included those in italics, with that given by the official *Reichsanzeiger* which did the reverse. See Schröder 41–43.

115 Schulthess: *Geschichtskalendar* 1900, 212.

116 H. McAleavy in *History Today*, May 1957.

117 HP IV 209.

118 C. zu Hohenlohe III 582.

119 Eyck 275.

120 Jostock, *Income and Wealth*, Series V 95.

121 Appendix I.

122 Kürenberg 149.

123 Lord Newton: *Lord Lansdowne, A Biography* 197.

124 Hon. Sir H. Nicolson: *King George V* 182; M. V. Brett (ed.) *Journals and Letters of Reginald, Viscount Esher* I 281 (cited as '*Esher*'); information from Sir John Wheeler-Bennett.

125 W. A. Wilcox and Charles E. Lee: 'Queen Victoria's Funeral Journey' in *Railway Magazine*, March 1940, 136–40. For the German royal train, see Topham: *Memories of the Kaiser's Court*.

126 Bülow: *97–03*, 50.

127 199; HP IV 211.

128 DDF 2nd Series I 86.

129 GP XVI 4784.

130 Eckardstein II 298.

131 For 1901 negotiations generally, see GP XVII 4982–5029; BD II 82–96; Garvin III Chs. 57–59; Eckardstein II 279; HP IV 217–47.

132 GP XVII 5023.

133 Newton 204.

134 GP XVII 5020.

134 GP XVII 5020.

135 Dugdale I 260.

136 Eckardstein II 282.

137 BD II 91.

138 GP XIV 3785; HP IV 244.

139 GP XVII 4985.

140 Bülow: *97–03*, 506.

141 GP XIV 3790, 3799.

142 GP IX 2161, XVII 4980, 5373; HP III 599.

143 K. Garvin: *J. L. Garvin* 8.

144 GuE III 696.

145 He does not appear to have seen GP XVII 4994, 4997, 5005, 5006 or 5010.

146 GP XVI 4793.

147 R. Niebuhr: *The Irony of American History* 98.

Chapter IX

1 BD III 435.

2 Nicolson 77–78, 42.

3 T. Roosevelt VII 397.

4 Lee II 147–9.

5 Newton 330, 351. Newton attributes this to a proposed visit in 1904 but there was no official occasion in that year when the question of representation would have arisen. Cowles, *Gay Monarch* p. 239, states without any supporting evidence that slippers were not the only things taken off.

6 Newton 249.

7 Spitzemberg 416.

8 BD VI 7.

9 Bülow: *97–03*, 574.

10 GP XVII 5140.

11 Newton 257.

12 Spitzemberg 464.

13 Newton 277.

14 Eckardstein II 377.

15 GP XVII 5369–79.

16 BD II 370.

17 GP XVIII 5912.

18 Maurois 158.

19 *Kaiser's Letters* 99.

20 Holstein: *Lebensbekenntnisse* 226.

21 GP XX 6383.

22 BD III Appendix A.

23 A.J.Marder: *From the Dreadnought to Scapa Flow, the Royal Navy in the Fisher Era* I 107.

24 See Marder, op. cit., Esher *Journals* and J. P. Mackintosh: 'The Role of the Committee of Imperial Defence before 1914' (EHR July 1962).

25 GP XX 6146.
26 Speech of 28-iv-04.
27 GP XX 6513.
28 GP XX 6375.
29 GP XXI 6953, 7034; HP IV 339.
30 Eyck 383.
31 Z-T 80; Maurois 161; Winston Churchill, article on Kaiser in *Great Contemporaries*.
32 Spitzemberg, 437.
33 GP XIX 5937.
34 GP XIX 5972; BD II 232.
35 *Kaiser's Letters*, 131–2.
36 ibid. 147. For the use made of this despatch by the Tsar in November 1908, see Nicolson: *Lord Carnock* 289.
37 *Kaiser's Letters* 154.
38 GP XIX 6146.
39 J. A. Spender: *Journalism and Politics* II 67–68.
40 GP XIX 6149.
41 Lee II 327.
42 Lee II 329.
43 Sir E. L. Woodward: *Great Britain and the German Navy* 94–96.
44 BD VI 118.
45 Hubatsch: *Admiralstab* 117.
46 Told to the author by the man to whom it happened (in 1911).
47 GP XIX 6157.
48 Charles W. Porter: *The Career of Théophile Delcassé* 178, 221–3; BD II 274–5.
49 This was what William said to Haldane in 1906. See Maurice: *Haldane* 197. See also BD III 421.
50 *Rheinische-Westfälische Ztg.* 11-iv-04, quoted in Townsend 312.
51 GP XVII 5035 XX 6599.
52 W. Goetz: *Kaiser Wilhelm II u. die deutsche Geschichtschreibung* HZ 179 (1955) 29; Kühlmann 225.
53 P. Rassow: *Holstein u. Schlieffen* HZ 173 (1952); Ritter: *The Schlieffen Plan—Critique of a Myth*, p. 100; Craig, *From Bismarck to Adenauer*, 43–44; Holstein: *Lebensbekenntnisse* 239.
54 Ritter 107; GP XXI 7252.
55 Speech at Bremen 22-iii-05.
56 GP XX 6564–89; Kühlmann 228–30.
57 GP XIX 6237.
58 GP XX 6589.
59 Valentini 81.
60 Z-T 147.

61 Lee II 339–40.
62 GP XX 6573; BD III 76.
63 Marder: *Correspondence* 55.
64 Newton 342; Porter 200–2.
65 GP XX Chapter CXLVIII.
66 *Kaiser's Letters* 179–80; F. N. Cornford, *Microcosmographia Academica.*
67 GP XIX 6193.
68 Haller II 278.
69 GP XIX 6220.
70 GP XIX 6229.
71 GP XIX 6237.
72 GP XX 6378.
73 GP XIX 6093.
74 GP XIX 6047.
75 See GP XXXII 11801 and 12026 (1912) and GP XXXII, 11704 (1910).
76 GP XXI 6953, 7034.
77 Kühlmann 246–50.
78 GP XXI 7252 XXIV 8282.
79 Esher III 61.
80 GP XX 6881, 6887; Rassow u. Born, *Akten* 245.
81 v. Einem: *Erinnerungen* 114; Z-T 200; Kühlmann 251–3.
82 GP XXV 8503.
83 Nicolson, *Carnock*, 189–94
84 BD III 436; Holstein, *Lebensbekenntnisse* 246; H. Rogge: *Holstein u. Harden* 64.
85 GP XXI 7139, 7154.
86 Rogge 70.
87 H. J. L. v. Moltke: *Erinnerungen, Briefe, Dokunente 1887–1916,* 304–8.
88 GP XXI 7064.
89 GP XXI 7082.
90 Kaiser's *Letters* 193.
91 Newton 330.
92 Lee II 336, 528.
93 T. Roosevelt *Letters* VII 397.
94 Eckardstein I, 209; Z-T 150, 178; *Kaiser's Letters* 198; GP XXI 7180; XXV 8821; Bülow: *03–09* 182; Maurois 202.
95 Maurice 199–200; D. Sommer: *Haldane of Cloan* 180.
96 Fritz Fischer: *Griff nach der Weltmacht* 32.
97 Esher II 180, 186.
98 Marder: *Dreadnought to Scapa* I 109.

99 Esher II 249.

100 Marder: *Dreadnought to Scapa* I 114.

101 Hoffman 98–101; R. C. K. Ensor: *England 1870–1914*, 500–5.

102 Newton 254; GP XXI 7223; Maurice 215.

103 Carl E. Schorske: *German Social Democracy, the Development of the Great Schism*, 12, 32; Born 53–54.

104 Schorske 130 quoting Pachnicke: *Liberalismus als Kulturpolitik.*

105 Naumann.

106 Born 64.

107 Bülow: *03–09*, 117; HP IV 439.

108 Epstein 54–59.

109 Born 206; W. Frank; *Bernard v. Bülow* HZ (1933) 147, 365.

110 Epstein 56–57; Bühler 297; Woodward 152.

111 Schorske 150.

112 Speech at opening of Prussian Landtag 20-x-08.

113 Harry F. Young: *Maximilian Harden, Censor Germaniae;* Rogge HZ (1962) 120; Rogge: *Holstein u. Harden* 385.

114 Rogge: *H u. Harden* 59.

115 ibid. 72.

116 H. v. Treschkow: *Von Fürsten u. anderen Sterblichen, Erinnerungen eines Kriminalkommissars* 115, 164.

117 Helfritz 122.

118 Rogge: *H u. Harden* 12; Holstein: *Lebensbekenntnisse* 208; Treschkow 190.

119 BD VI 62.

120 Rogge: *H u. Harden* 234–7.

121 Bülow: *03–09*, 296.

122 H. S. Chamberlain *Briefe* II 226–7.

123 Lee II 548; Bülow: *97–03*, 337.

124 Lee II 546; Keller 253.

125 Esher, II 255.

126 Esher II 255; Trevelyan: *Grey of Fallodon*, 151.

127 Lee II 525.

128 Esher, II 259.

129 H. S. Chamberlain, loc. cit.

130 GP XXIII 7815.

131 GP XXIV 8179.

132 Woodward 100–120; Hubatsch, *Admiralstab*, 115.

133 Marder: *Correspondence* 215.

134 Esher II 144.

135 Hubatsch: *Admiralstab* 122.

136 Holstein: *Lebensbekenntnisse* 292.

137 GP XXI 7024; XXIV 8228.

138 The story that German naval officers regularly drank to 'Der Tag' when they would attack England seems to have originated in articles published by Blatchford in *Clarion* in 1910. It was denied by Prince Henry of Prussia, GP XXVIII 10371n. Ludwig 410 quotes a command of the Kaiser at the beginning of the war that the naval commanders were to await 'the Day' against the English in patience, but I have not been able to identify the source of this statement.

139 GP XXIV 8181.

140 v. Schoen: *Memoirs of an Ambassador* 101; Princess Radziwill 22–24.

141 Esher: II 286; Newton 367.

142 GP XXIV 8187.

143 GP XXIV 8193.

144 Esher, II 286, 289.

145 Lee II 606.

146 ibid. 604.

147 GP XXIV 8193.

148 Fisher: *Memories* 234. Mrs. Tuchman *August 1914* 19 has reproduced this episode inaccurately.

149 Nicolson: *Carnock* 273.

150 Prince Gottfried Hohenlohe to Princess Daisy of Pless 159.

151 GP XXIV 8217.

152 GP XXIV 8219.

153 GP XXIV 8226; BD VI 124, VII 179–200; Bülow: *03–09*, 313.

154 Esher, II 343.

155 H. Rothfels: *Studien zu Annexionskrisis 1908*, HZ (1933) 147 p. 326.

156 H. Uebersberger: *Oesterreich zwischen Russland u. Serbien: Zur südslawischen Frage und der Entstehung des Ersten Weltkrieges*, pp. 20–21. Nicolson: *Carnock* 279n.

157 Lee II 632.

158 GP XXVI 8939.

159 O–U. Aussenpolitik I 345.

160 Rothfels 337.

161 For the *Daily Telegraph* article, see F. Frhr Hiller v. Gaertringen: *Fürst Bülows Denkwürdigkeiten. Untersuchungen zu ihrer Entstehungsgeschichte u. zu ihrer Kritik* and W. Schüssler: *Die Daily Telegraph Affäre. Fürst Bülow, Kaiser Wilhelm u. die Krise des Zweiten Reiches 1908*. The solution here suggested to the problem 'Did Bülow look at the article or did he not?' is hypothetical, as all solutions must be, but besides accounting for all known facts, has the merit of being the one to which the two people best acquainted with Bülow's ways, namely Holstein (HP I 172) and William himself

(Schoen's *Memoirs*, 108) both inclined. The still-extant newspaper which Bülow on the morning of publication sent to Stemrich with the query, 'Is this in accord with the draft checked in the office at the time?' (GP 8254n.) is almost conclusive evidence that Bülow did *not* actually read the draft. That this was due to mere pressure of business is very hard to believe. Schüssler claims that Bülow would have been incapable of the duplicity here imputed to him but his conduct over Holstein's dismissal and in the Harden case makes this hard to believe.

162 Topham: *Memories of the Fatherland* 146.

163 Schüssler 62 quoting Fürstenberg; O. Czernin, *Im Weltkriege* 72.

164 Hiller v. Gärtringen 173.

165 Robert A. Kann: *Kaiser William and Archduke Franz Ferdinand in their correspondence*, AHR (Jan. '52) LVII p. 324; v. Gärtringen 182.

166 Wolfgang C. Mommsen: *Max Weber u. die deutsche Politik 1890–1920* 167.

167 Told to the author by someone who heard it from von Weizsäcker, the M.P. concerned.

168 *Kaiser's Letters*, 245.

169 Craig: *Prussian Army* 290.

170 Uebersberger 38, quoting Aehrental's despatch in OU Aussen-politik II 1270.

171 GP XXVI 9460.

172 Holstein, *Lebensbekenntnisse* 335.

173 Nicolson, *Carnock* 301.

174 ibid. 305. Was the German action an ultimatum or the intervention of a friend? The Tsar in his letter to the Kaiser of 22nd March declared himself as 'very happy about it' which is hardly the way one speaks of an ultimatum, while Isvolsky admitted later that year to the British Ambassador in Vienna that it had not been one (BD V 809). On the other hand Kiderlen boasted that it had been (Jäckh, *Kiderlen-Wächter* II 26). The answer is that the Germans thought they were being very clever in devising an ultimatum which could be excused as a friendly intervention. What they did not notice was that they were thereby playing into Isvolsky's hands.

175 Bülow: *03–09*, 502.

176 Lee II 622.

177 Z–T 256.

178 Princess Radziwill 72. Countess Hegermann-Lindencrone, how-ever, (*Sunny Side of Diplomatic Life* 319) says that the arrival of the train at the wrong spot took place during the Danish Royal visit in 1908, and that in the evening King Edward and Queen

Alexandra retired to their rooms immediately after supper which they took at the Kaiser's table.

179 GP XXVIII 10620.
180 Kann 332.
181 Bülow: *03–09* 410. I am indebted to Dr. H. V. Dicks for the following note on *Pseudologia fantastica*: 'It is a well-known symptom (*a*) in small children, and (*b*) in hysterical character-types—who are in some sense small children unconsciously. It is in a way more like "tall story telling" or "line shooting" than deliberate lying; it is histrionic in motive, but often with a dash of getting one's own back for being thought small or silly and thus misinformed or fobbed off with half-truths by one's elders. Hence it can be part of an over-compensation for infantile inferiority feelings and lack of adult self-esteem. The story-teller is apt half to believe what he tells at the time, as ready identification with one's fantasied rôle in the tall story is part of hysterical personality disorder.'
182 Spitzemberg 503.
183 GP XXXI 11411.
184 Marder: *Dreadnought to Scapa* I 177. See also Woodward Ch. X.
185 Marder: *Correspondence* 208.
186 Schorske 147; Epstein 80–82.
187 Kann, 338.
188 Theodor Wolff: *Through Two Decades* 47–49.
189 Valentine, 121–2; v. Gärtringen 220.
190 Bülow: *03–09*, 501; Hans Leip: *Der Kaiser's Reeder*, 251.
191 Tirpitz: *Politische Dokumente. Der Aufbau der deutschen Weltmacht*, I 157.
192 Hubatsch: *Aera Tirpitz*, 86.
193 GP XXVIII 10294.
194 Bülow: *03–09*, 501.
195 Tirpitz, *Dokumente*, loc. cit.

Chapter X

1 Mrs. Tuchman, *August 1914*, p. 124, revives the story that Bethmann Hollweg and v. Jagow were both in the Borussia Korps at Bonn, as the Kaiser had been, and received their appointments partly at any rate in consequence. F. Hartung, *Deutsches Biographisches Jahrbuch 1921*. p. 21, denied this story categorically, and according to the article on him in the *Neue Deutsche Biographie*, Bethmann was at Strassburg, Leipzig and Berlin universities, never at Bonn. Jagow *had* belonged to the Korps but the Kaiser, so far from advocating his appointment, opposed it (Bülow: *09–19*, 336).

2 Kürenberg, 205.

3 Spitzemberg 414.

4 Schiffer: 187–90.

5 H. G. Zmarzlik: *Bethmann Hollweg als Reichskanzler 1909–14*, 7.

6 Spitzemberg 518.

7 ibid. 535; Haldane, *Before the War* 59.

8 Heuss, 371, 511.

9 Woodward 275.

10 Zmarzlik, 26.

11 Haller II 275.

12 Gooch: 'Kiderlen-Wächter, the Man of Agadir', in '*Studies in Diplomacy* 129–61.

13 Kürenberg 137.

14 Bülow: *03–09*, 403.

15 Spitzemberg, 527, 529; Gooch, quoting v. Rosen, 160.

16 Epstein 6.

17 Hoffman 292.

18 Bühler 323.

19 GP XXVIII 10401.

20 Hubatsch: *Aera Tirpitz* 87; Woodward 285.

21 Esher *Journals* III 4.

22 GP XXVIII 10389.

23 ibid.

24 GP XXVII 10152.

25 GP XXVII 10152, 10171, 10173; Nicolson, *Carnock* 356.

26 Valentini 117.

27 Spitzemberg 527–8; I. C. Barlow: *The Agadir Crisis* 226.

28 GP XXIV 8282; Townsend 320.

29 GP XXIV 8457.

30 Bülow: *03–09*, 398–401; GP XXIV 3871; Esher II 359.

31 GP XXIX 10485.

32 BD VII, 317.

33 Gooch 50.

34 These sentences are an attempt to reconcile the Kaiser's account of the interview (*My Memoirs*, p. 141) with that given by King George (Nicolson: *George V*, 185–6). See also GP XXIX 10562.

35 Gooch 146.

36 The Kaiser appears to have seen no papers between 11 June and 10 July except for a short reassuring telegram from Bethmann on 3 July (GP XXIX 10587). See also Spitzemberg 529.

37 Hubatsch: *Admiralstab*, 147.

38 F. Rosen: *Aus einem diplomatischen Wanderleben* 338–50.

39 Marder: *Dreadnought to Scapa* I 115; GP XXXI 11435.

40 GP XXIX 10600.

41 GP XXIX 10607-9.

42 A number of Kiderlen's letters to Mme Jonina were acquired by the French and are reproduced in Caillaux, *Agadir*.

43 Marder: *Dreadnought to Scapa* I 242-3.

44 Mackintosh, EHR July '62.

45 GP XXXI 11316.

46 Marder: *Dreadnought to Scapa* I 244; *Correspondence* II 143; Lord Hankey: *The Supreme Command*. I 78.

47 H.J.L. v. Moltke 362.

48 GP XXIX 10694.

49 ibid. 10750.

50 Townsend 325-7.

51 T. Bethmann Hollweg (tr. Young): *Reflections on the World War*, I 37.

52 GP XXIX 10699, 10702; Zmarzlik, 135; Spitzemberg, 536.

53 Sommer 255.

54 GP XXI 11307.

55 Hubatsch HZ (1953) 176, p. 291; *Aera Tirpitz* 96-102; GP XXIX 10659.

56 Hubatsch: *Aera Tirpitz* 91; Marder: *Dreadnought to Scapa* I 274.

57 Hubatsch: *Aera Tirpitz*, 91.

58 W. Widenmann: *Marine Attaché an der Kaiserlichen deutschen Botschaft in London*; GP XXX, 11396.

59 Hubatsch: *Aera Tirpitz* 92.

60 GP XXXI 11323.

61 Sir Lewis Namier, in the *Quarterly Review* for July 1950, criticized the exaggerated picture of the situation in London given by von Kühlmann in his *Erinnerungen* (pp. 339-40). But for evidence that Tyrrell did not see wholly eye to eye with Nicolson and Eyre Crowe, see Nicolson, *Carnock* 329.

62 GP XXXI 11321.

63 BD VI 492.

64 Maurice 291; Sommer 257.

65 BD VI 499.

66 Widenmann 234. This speech is only mentioned by Woodward in a footnote forty pages removed from the description of Haldane's arrival in Berlin.

67 F. Fischer: *Griff nach der Weltmacht* 55; Marder: *Correspondence* I 436.

68 GP XXXIX 15560.

69 Tirpitz: *Dokumente* I 301.

70 GP XXXI 11344.

71 GP XXXI 11403, 11410.

72 Tirpitz: *Dokumente* I 324; Ritter: *Staatskunst* II 234; *Süddeutsche Zeitung* 24-i-59; GP XXXI 11422.

73 GP XXXI 11314; Tirpitz: *Dokumente* I 322.

74 Widenmann 278; B. Huldermann: *Albert Ballin* 212.

75 Craig: *Prussian Army* 298.

76 Tirpitz: *Dokumente* I 423; Hubatsch: *Aera Tirpitz* 117.

77 Marder: *Dreadnought to Scapa* I Ch. XII; Heuss 452.

78 Marder: *Correspondence* II 72.

79 Huldermann: 164.

80 See L. Dehio: *Germany and World Politics in the Twentieth Century*.

81 Hubatsch: HZ 303.

82 Epstein: 75.

83 Schorske 124.

84 Robert Michels, quoted in Schorske 118.

85 Bühler 319.

86 Schorske 228–40.

87 Born 245–6.

88 Schorske 257–61.

89 A. Rosenberg: *The Birth of the German Republic* 56–58; Zmarzlik 114–130.

90 Epstein 89.

91 Zmarzlik 37–40.

92 GP XXXIII 12225.

93 GP XXXIII 12405.

94 GP XXXIII 12339.

95 GP XXXIII 12349.

96 Schüssler: *Kaiser Wilhelm* 96.

97 Quoted in *Annual Register* for 1914, 305.

98 Ritter: *Staatskunst* II 270–80.

99 Epstein 78.

100 Fischer 46–7.

101 Gooch 55.

102 GP XXXIX 15612.

103 Gooch, loc. cit.

104 Craig: *Prussian Army* 291.

105 J. Terraine: *Mons* 33.

106 Gooch: loc. cit.

107 The Kaiser and Moltke denied the Belgian story after war had broken out but it is too well authenticated to have been invented, though the actual words attributed to the Germans may be inaccurate.

108 L. Albertini: *The Origins of the War* II 122; GP XXXVI 14161; OU Aussenpolitik VII 512–15.

109 C. v. Hötzendorf: *Aus meiner Dienstzeit* III 670.
110 GP XXXIX 15844.
111 GP XXXVIII 15483.
112 Bethmann Hollweg I 83.
113 DD I. 2.
114 Gooch 56.
115 Tirpitz: *Dokumente* I 403.
116 GP XXXI 11345, 11346.
117 Byron, *Childe Harold's Pilgrimage*, Canto III.
118 G. A. v. Müller (ed. Goerlitz): *The Kaiser and His Court, the Diaries, Note Books and Letters of Admiral G. v. M., Chief of the Naval Secretariat 1914–18*, 28-vi-14. It is instructive to compare this first-hand account with that given by E. Ludwig p. 382.
119 DD I 7.
120 G. R. Ritter: *Der Anteil der Militärs an der Kriegskatastrophe von 1914.* HZ (1962) 193 p. 72.
121 DD I 13.
122 See L. Albertini: *The Origins of the War of 1914*; Ritter: *Staatskunst* II and Uebersberger. The account given here of developments down to 4 August is in general based on the first two books.
123 DD IV Appendix IV. No. 27.
124 Albertini III 82.
125 *My Memoirs* 240–2; DD IV App. IV No. 2.
126 DD I 50.
127 DD I 75.
128 ibid. I 43.
129 He himself recorded in his memoirs that he read the text in a Norwegian newspaper but Müller is probably right in saying that it came through the Norddeich morse wireless news service.
130 Müller 8.
131 The copy given to the Austrian Minister in Belgrade at 5 p.m. on 25th did not reach Vienna till the afternoon of the 26th and had then to be translated and copied; the Austrians certainly did not hurry over its onward transmission to Berlin but the suggestion that the delay was deliberate and mischievous seems uncalled for.
132 DD I 264.
133 DD II 128.
134 DD II 132.
135 Numbers taken from Edmonds: *Military Operations in France and Belgium 1914.* I Appendices 3 and 6.
136 The story that after signing William said, 'Gentlemen, you will live to regret this' appears to rest on A. C. Gardner: *The War Lords* (1915) where 'high authority' is quoted as the source, and Admiral

Mark Kerr: *Land, Sea and Air* (1927) where Princess v. Bülow is quoted. Both sources seem suspect and Falkenhayn, who was present, made no record of any such remark in his diary (Hans v. Zwehl: *Erich von Falkenhayn* 58).

137 Ritter: *Schlieffen Plan* 91–96.
138 Ritter: *Staatskunst* II 271.
139 Ritter: *Staatskunst* II 251. See also Tuchman 85.
140 Albertini III 176–8.
141 DD III 584; Albertini III 425.
142 Wheeler-Bennett: *Three Episodes* 24.
143 Wheeler-Bennett: *Wooden Titan* 35; Bülow: *97–03*, 423.
144 A. v. Hohenlohe 338.
145 Rathenau: *Der Kaiser* 28.
146 Albertini III 479.
147 Princess Blücher: *An Englishwoman in Berlin* 14.

Chapter XI

1 O. Hamman: *Bilder aus der letzten Kaiserzeit*, 129.
2 Müller 6-xi-14.
3 Tirpitz I 279–80.
4 Paul Fechter quoted in Schiffer 134.
5 Princess Radziwill 331.
6 Müller 10-iii-16.
7 ibid. 6-viii-14 and 6-vii-16.
8 ibid. 30-iv-17.
9 Huldermann 285.
10 Davis 161. All the other quotations in the paragraph come from Müller.
11 For the naval war, see S. W. Roskill: *The Strategy of Sea Power, its Development and Application*, 99–142.
12 Princess Blücher 137.
13 Ritter: *Schlieffen Plan* 66.
14 Wheeler-Bennett: *Wooden Titan* 34; H. J. L. v. Moltke: *Erinnerungen* 413; Craig: *Prussian Army* 287.
15 Epstein 180.
16 ibid. 331–2.
17 Fisher: *Griff nach der Weltmacht* 102.
18 Heuss: *Naumann*; Taylor: *Aspects* 164.
19 Wheeler-Bennett 58.
20 Sir Arthur Wilson quoted in Marder: *Dreadnought to Scapa Flow* I 332.

21 The figure of twenty-nine is taken from *Krieg zur See* I 158–62. Woodward 453 says that in 1914 Germany had twenty-three submarines not more than six years old with an additional fourteen and an uncertain number of others building; Bühler p. 421 says that only twenty-one 'were available'. Marder gives a figure of forty-six. Epstein (156–40) says there were fifty in the winter of 1915–16.

22 Hubatsch: *Aera Tirpitz* 130.

23 ibid. 125.

24 Müller 6-viii-15.

25 Bühler 427. See also Roskill.

26 Wheeler-Bennett 71.

27 Dorpalen: AHR Oct. '52 p. 26.

28 Schüssler: *Kaiser Wilhelm* II 106.

29 Karl E. Birnbaum: *Peace Moves and U-Boat Warfare*.

30 Davis 152.

31 Birnbaum 248.

32 ibid. 368–9.

33 ibid. 290.

34 Birnbaum 322; Valentini 145.

35 Müller 16-i-17.

36 Churchill, *World Crisis* III 213.

37 Fischer 475.

38 ibid. 437.

39 Müller 16-i-18.

40 Fischer 448; Epstein 176–7.

41 Müller 23-iv-17.

42 Fischer 454.

43 ibid. 455.

44 ibid. 467.

45 Erzberger seems to have been shown the text of the letters by the German Foreign Office, not as has been generally supposed by Karl or the Austrian Foreign Office. See Fischer 484.

46 Fischer 488–9.

47 Fischer 515.

48 Schüssler 106.

49 Müller 16-vii-17.

50 See Fischer 519n.; Müller 286n.

51 Valentini 164–70.

52 Quoted in Vietsch: *Solf* 173.

53 Fischer 523.

54 Wheeler-Bennett 112.

55 Craig: *Prussian Army* 339.

56 So Müller 29-vi-17. Kühlmann 476 says that 'the Kaiser always an ardent friend of peace, seemed to have spoken so warmly that the Vatican was encouraged to make open proposals'.

57 Wheeler-Bennett 112–14.

58 Kühlmann 502.

59 Epstein 225–30; Valentini 211; Heuss 528; Kühlmann 577.

60 Fischer 560. The basic proclamation of the party is in Hohlfeld: *Dokumente* 357.

61 Wheeler-Bennett: *Brest-Litovsk, the Forgotten Peace* 109.

62 Vietsch 181.

63 Czernin II 228.

64 Wheeler-Bennett 128.

65 Kühlmann 528–9.

66 Kühlmann 538; Hohlfeld II 372.

67 Müller 16-i-18.

68 ibid. 27-ii-18.

69 Craig: *Prussian Army*, 336.

70 Fischer 665; Müller 25-ii-18.

71 Wheeler-Bennett: *Wooden Titan* 137.

72 Fischer 556, 558.

73 Wheeler-Bennett: *Brest-Litovsk* 198.

74 Wheeler-Bennett: *Wooden Titan* 140–1.

75 *Messages and Papers of Woodrow Wilson* I 421.

76 Müller 10-iii-16.

77 Fischer 831.

78 ibid. 775.

79 ibid. 746.

80 ibid. 811.

81 ibid 852.

82 P. F. Stubmann: *Mein Feld ist Die Welt. Albert Ballin* 257.

83 Fischer 832.

84 Wheeler-Bennett 153–5; Fischer 835.

85 Rosenberg 228.

86 Müller: 23-vii-18.

87 Müller 11-viii-18; A. Niemann: *Kaiser und Revolution. Die entscheidenden Ereignisse in Grossen Hauptquartier* 43.

88 Fischer 777.

89 Müller 24-viii-18.

90 Huldermann 282–4.

91 Müller 6-ix-18.

92 *Kaiser's Letters* 186.

93 Karl Graf v. Hertling: *Ein Jahr in der Reichskanzlei* 183.

94 Wheeler-Bennett 164.

95 Bühler 471.

96 Epstein 260–2.

97 Wheeler-Bennett 165.

98 Rosenberg 246.

99 W. Wilson I 538.

100 Bühler: 478.

101 M. Baumont: *The Fall of the Kaiser* 3–4.

102 Bühler 477.

103 Baumont 5.

104 Niemann 113–15.

105 Vietsch 378–9.

106 Dorpalen AHR Oct. '52, 35–36.

107 Baumont 22, quoting von Hintze.

108 Schiffer 135–7.

109 Niemann 128.

110 The following paragraphs are based principally on Niemann, Baumont and Wheeler-Bennett.

111 Baumont 82, quoting von Hintze.

112 Von der Schulenberg was called to Spa by a Major von Stülpnagel. This is, however, likely to have been Joachim v. S. who in Sept. 1918 was appointed an Abteilungschef in OHL. It was not Heinrich v. Stülpnagel, the German G.O.C. in France in July 1944, since he was not promoted Major till 1925.

113 *Süddeutsche Zeitung* 24-i-59.

114 *Memoirs of the Crown Prince of Germany* 258.

115 Information from Sir John Wheeler-Bennett.

116 Speech on 18-iv-91; Nichols 119.

Chapter XII

1 It is generally said that the Kaiser gave up his sword to the Dutch sentry on crossing the frontier but this is denied by Schiffer, 78, on the authority of the German Ambassador at The Hague who, however, does not mention the question in his own account of the proceedings (Rosen: *Aus Einem Diplomatischen Wanderleben* III 220). It was suggested by Scheidemann (*Memoirs of a Social Democrat* II 538) that King George V asked the Queen of Holland to give the Kaiser asylum but I am told by Sir Harold Nicolson that he found nothing in the papers or diaries of King George to indicate such an initiative.

2 Rosen: loc. cit.; Lady Norah Bentinck: *The Ex-Kaiser in Exile* 14–16, 22–25.
3 Müller 400.
4 Princess Radziwill 279.
5 Crown Prince 231.
6 *New York Herald Tribune* 5-vi-41.
7 Wheeler-Bennett: *Wooden Titan* 241–2.
8 ibid. 243.
9 Sir R. H. Bruce-Lockhart: *Retreat from Glory* 339.
10 W. H. H. Waters: *Potsdam and Doorn* 97.
11 Klaus W. Jonas: *The Life of Crown Prince William* 175, 190; B.B.C. broadcast 15-vi-59.
12 Pope-Hennessy: *Queen Mary* 592.
13 Sir E. L. Woodward: *British Foreign Policy in the Second World War* 44.
14 *New York Herald Tribune* 4-vi-41.
15 *New York Times* 5-vi-41.
16 Jonas 285.

Chapter XIII

1 The figure of casualties is taken from C.R.M.F. Cruttwell: *History of the World War* 630.
2 Quoted in Ritter: *Staatskunst* I 69.
3 ibid. 129.
4 A. Dorpalen: *Heinrich v. Treitschke* 149.
5 Craig: *Prussian Army* 268.
6 Mommsen 209.
7 Müller 10-ii-18.
8 Dehio: *Germany and World Politics in the 20th Century* 72.
9 ibid. 87.
10 ibid. 59.
11 Eyre-Crowe Memo, BD III 405.
12 Dehio 75.
13 Quoted in Marder: *Dreadnought to Scapa* I 322 from the original Admiralty document. The words 'mainly acquired by violence, largely maintained by force' are omitted from *The World Crisis* I 175.
14 T. Roosevelt: *Letters* VII 396.
15 For a recent account of German atrocities in Belgium, see Tuchman.

16 Ritter: *Schlieffen Plan* 66.
17 Quoted in Fischer 99.
18 H. S. Chamberlain: *Briefe* II 140.
19 Schröder 18.
20 See esp. Sir Isaiah Berlin: *Historical Inevitability*.
21 Spitzemberg 524.

Appendix IV

Biographical Index of Persons Mentioned

ABRAHAM. 156, 164

ADAMS, CHARLES FRANCIS, 1807–86.
American diplomat and author, U.S. Ambassador in London, 1861–8. 118

AEHRENTHAL, ALOIS LEXA, COUNT VON, 1854–1912.
Austro-Hungarian Ambassador, Bucarest, 1895; St. Petersburg, 1899; Foreign Minister, 1906–11. 286–8, 294

ALBERT I, KING OF THE BELGIANS, 1875–1934.
Succeeded 1909; m. Elisabeth of Bavaria. 340, 371, 480

ALBERT THE BEAR, 1100?–70.
1st Margrave of Brandenburg, founder of the ruling House of Anhalt. 5

ALBERT PRINCE CONSORT, 1819–61.
2nd Son of Ernst, Duke of Saxe-Coburg-Gotha; m. Queen Victoria, 1840. 57–64, 66–8, 75, 79, 96, 114, 138, 219

ALBRECHT ACHILLES OF HOHENZOLLERN, ELECTOR OF BRANDENBURG, 1414–86. 6, 412

ALEXANDER III, TSAR OF RUSSIA, 1845–94.
Succeeded 1881; m. Marie, daughter of King Christian IX of Denmark. 99, 103–4, 113–14, 122, 126, 128, 135–6, 172, 182, 188

ALEXANDER OF BATTENBERG, PRINCE, 1857–93.
Son of Prince Alexander of Hesse, grandson of Grand Duke Ludwig II, Prince of Bulgaria 1879–86; m. Johanna Loisinger 1889 and became Count von Hartenau. 99–104, 112–13, 116–20

ALEXANDER OF MACEDON, 352–323 B.C.
Emperor 336 B.C. 255

ALEXANDRA, QUEEN, 1844–1925.
Daughter of King Christian IX of Denmark; m. Prince of Wales, 1863. 68, 98, 139–40, 242, 284, 296

ALVENSLEBEN, FRIEDRICH JOHANN, COUNT VON, 1836–1913.
German Ambassador, Brussels, 1886–1901; St. Petersburg, 1901–5.
134

ANDRÁSSY, JULIUS, COUNT, 1823–90.
Hungarian Minister-President, 1867; Austro-Hungarian Foreign
Minister, 1871–9. 30

D'ARCOURT, MADEMOISELLE.
French governess to Kaiser. 77

ARMINIUS. 2

ASQUITH, HERBERT HENRY, 1852–1928.
Liberal politician; Home Secretary, 1892–5; Chancellor of the
Exchequer, 1906–8; Prime Minister, 1908–16; 1st Earl of Oxford
and A., 1925. 148, 261, 314, 316, 322

AUGUSTA, EMPRESS, 1811–90.
Daughter of Grand Duke of Saxe-Weimar, granddaughter of Tsar
Paul; m. William I of Prussia, 1829. 58–9, 62, 78

AUGUSTA VICTORIA (DONA), KAISERIN, 1858–1921.
Daughter of Duke Frederick of Schleswig-Holstein-Sonderburg-
Augustenburg; m. William II, 1881. 86–9, 91, 99, 101, 108, 114,
125–6, 140, 143, 216, 221, 242, 245, 277, 291, 297, 305, 325–6, 358,
381, 383, 392, 398, 401, 410, 414–15, 416

AUGUSTENBURG, FREDERICK, DUKE OF, 1829–80.
Father of Kaiserin; claimant to Duchies of Schleswig-Holstein,
1863. 68, 86, 99

AUGUST WILHELM, PRINCE, (Auwi), 1887–1949.
4th son of William II; m. Alexandra Victoria of Schleswig-
Holstein. 418

BACHMANN, GUSTAV, ADMIRAL, 1860–1943.
Chief of Naval Staff, 1915–16. 366–7

BADEN, see Frederick, Grand Duke of, Louise, Grand Duchess of and
Max, Prince of.

BAGEHOT, WALTER, 1826–77.
Editor, *National Review* 1855, *Economist* 1860. 27

BALFOUR, ARTHUR JAMES, 1848–1930.
Nephew of 3rd Lord Salisbury; First Lord of Treasury, 1895–1902;
Prime Minister, 1902–5; First Lord of Admiralty, 1915; Foreign
Secretary, 1916–18; 1st Earl, 1922. 140, 210–11, 217–18, 223, 237

BALLIN, ALBERT, 1857–1918.
Chairman of Hamburg-America Steamship Company. 150, 300, 306,
321, 359, 390, 392

BAUER, MAX HERMANN, COLONEL, 1869–1929.
In Operations section of General Staff, 1914; artillery officer at General Headquarters, 1917; tried to induce Crown Prince to supplant his father, 1918; took part in Kapp rising, 1920. 377

BEATRICE, PRINCESS, 1857–1944.
Youngest daughter of Queen Victoria; m. Prince Henry of Battenberg, 1885. 101–2

BEBEL, AUGUST, 1840–1913.
Deputy (Social Democrat) in *Reichstag* from 1871; Party leader; editor of *Vorwärts*. 25–6, 330

BENTINCK, GODARD JOHN GEORGE CHARLES, COUNT, 1857–1940.
Host of ex-Kaiser at Amerongen, 1918–20. 413

BERCHTOLD, LEOPOLD, COUNT VON, 1863–1942.
Austro-Hungarian Ambassador at St. Petersburg, 1906–12; Foreign Minister, 1912–15. 340

BERG, FRIEDRICH WILHELM VON, 1866–1939.
Prussian civil servant, Head of Kaiser's Civil Secretariat, February–October, 1918. 164, 386, 392, 396, 401

BERGSON, HENRI, 1859–1941.
French philosopher, author of *L'Evolution Créatrice*. 73

BERLEPSCH, HANS HERMANN, BARON VON, 1843–1926.
Prussian Minister of Trade, 1890–6. 172, 199

BERNHARDI, FRIEDRICH VON, MAJOR-GENERAL, 1849–1930.
Author of *Germany and the Next War*, 1911. 338

BERNHARDT, SARAH, 1845–1923.
French actress. 85

BERNSTEIN, EDUARD, 1850–1932.
German Social Democratic writer and politician. 48

BERNSTORFF, JOHANN HEINRICH, COUNT VON, 1862–1939.
German Ambassador in U.S., 1908–17. 380

BERTIE, SIR FRANCIS LEVERSON, 1844–1919.
British Ambassador in Rome, 1903–4; in Paris, 1905–18; 1st Viscount, 1918. 237–8, 321

BETHMANN HOLLWEG, THEOBALD VON, 1856–1921.
State Secretary for the Interior, 1907–9; Chancellor, 1909–17. 203, 273, 300, 303–6, 310–13, 317–19, 321–2, 325–6, 330, 332–3, 335, 339, 343, 345–50, 352–3, 355, 361, 363, 366, 368–9, 370–1, 373–5, 377–81, 399, 429, 477

BISMARCK, HERBERT, COUNT VON, 1849–1904.
Elder son of following, State Secretary for Foreign Affairs, 1886–90; m. Marguerite, Countess Hoyos, 1892. 52, 54, 92, 96, 102, 120-1, 124, 127, 133–5, 177

BISMARCK, OTTO, PRINCE VON, 1815–98.
Prussian representative at Frankfurt Diet, 1851–9; Prussian Minister in St. Petersburg, 1859–62; in Paris, 1862; Minister-President and Foreign Minister, 1862–90; Chancellor of North German Confederation, 1866–71; Chancellor of German Empire, 1871–90; m. Johanna von Puttkamer. 20–25, 27–34, 36–7, 52–4, 59, 65–71, 81, 85–7, 92–4, 96, 99, 100, 102–10, 112–18, 120–37, 154, 158–9, 161, 167–9, 173–4, 177–9, 184, 188, 195, 198–9, 201, 211, 215, 220, 222, 237, 245, 265, 273–4, 284–5, 288, 307, 329, 331, 426, 432, 459. Dismissed 128–37, 459. Quoted v, 24, 72, 106, 107, 113, 126, 131, 132, 146, 178, 239, 435

BLÜCHER, GERHARD LEBERECHT VON, FIELD MARSHAL, 1742–1819.
Prussian general at Battles of Leipzig and Waterloo. 390

BÖTTICHER, KARL HEINRICH VON, 1833–1907.
State Secretary for the Interior, 1880–97. 199–201

BOULANGER, GEORGES ERNEST JEAN MARIE, GENERAL, 1837–91.
Leader of French nationalist anti-German movement; Minister of War, 1886–7. 104

BRAUN, MAGNUS BARON VON, born 1878.
Secretary to Helferich 1917; Minister in Von Papen's cabinet 1932. 380

BRENTANO, LUDWIG, 1844–1931.
German writer on economics. 80

BROCKDORFF, THERESE, COUNTESS VON, 1846–1924.
Mistress of the Robes to Kaiserin, 1881–1921. 415

BRUNSWICK, ERNST AUGUST, DUKE OF, 1887–1953.
Son of Duke of Cumberland, created Duke of Brunswick, 1913. 342

BRUNSWICK, VICTORIA LOUISE, DUCHESS OF, born 1892.
Only daughter of Kaiser, m. Duke of Brunswick, 1913. 88, 164, 342 416, 420

BÜLOW, BERNHARD, PRINCE VON, 1849–1929.
German Ambassador in Rome, 1893–7 and 1914–15; State Secretary for Foreign Affairs, 1897–1900; Chancellor, 1900–9; m. Maria, Princess di Camporeale. 136, 143, 149, 152–3, 160, 166, 201–2, 206, 211–12, 215–16, 218, 221–3, 228, 232–5, 237–40, 242–3, 245, 247–50, 252, 254–60, 262–3, 269–77, 279–80, 283, 288–97, 299, 302–5, 310, 330, 353, 377, 379–80, 382, 410, 465, 475

BYRON, GEORGE GORDON, LORD, 1788–1824. 77

CAILLAUX, JOSEPH, 1863–1944.
French Minister of Finance, 1894, 1906–11, 1913–14, 1925, 1926–7; President of Council, June 1911–January 1912. 311–14, 316, 318

CAMBON, JULES, 1845–1935.
French Ambassador, Washington, 1897–1902; Madrid, 1902–7; Berlin, 1907–14. 82, 232, 312–13, 339, 355

CAMBON, PAUL, 1843–1924.
Brother of above; French Ambassador, Madrid, 1886–90; Constantinople, 1890–8; London, 1898–1920. 232, 245, 247

CANARIS, WILHELM VON, ADMIRAL, 1887–1945.
Head of German Counter-intelligence in Second World War; ringleader of attempted *coup d'état* 20 July 1944. 420

CAPELLE, EDUARD VON, ADMIRAL, 1855–1931.
Succeeded Tirpitz as State Secretary for Navy, 1916–18. 320

CAPRIVI, GEORG LEO VON, GENERAL, 1831–99.
Head of Naval Section of General Staff, 1883–8; Divisional Commander in Hanover, 1888–90; Chancellor, 1890–4; Count, 1891. 51, 133–7, 145, 167–80, 183–6, 188, 201, 204, 269, 303–4, 325

CASSEL, SIR ERNEST, 1852–1921.
Banker, friend of King Edward VII. 306, 321–2

CECIL, LORD ROBERT, 1864–1958.
Son of 3rd Lord Salisbury; Minister of Blockade, 1916–18; Assistant Foreign Secretary, 1918, helped to draft League of Nations Covenant; 1st Viscount Cecil of Chelwood. 426

CHAMBERLAIN, HOUSTON STEWART, 1855–1927.
English writer living in Germany, author of *Foundations of the Nineteenth Century*, etc.; m. daughter of Richard Wagner. 161, 164, 276, 429

CHAMBERLAIN, JOSEPH, 1836–1914.
Colonial Secretary, 1895–1903. 193, 209–13, 215, 222–3, 232, 235–7, 239, 242, 245

CHAMBERLAIN, NEVILLE, 1869–1940.
Son of above; Prime Minister, 1937–40. 419

CHARLEMAGNE, 742–814. 2, 3, 156

CHILDERS, ROBERT ERSKINE, 1870–1922.
Writer; executed by Free State authorities as a member of Irish Republican Army. 266

CHIROL, SIR IGNATIUS VALENTINE, 1852–1929.
The Times correspondent in Berlin, 1892–7; Foreign editor, 1897–1912. 234–5

CHRISTIAN, PRINCE OF SCHLESWIG-HOLSTEIN, 1831–1917.
Uncle of Kaiserin, m. Helena, daughter of Queen Victoria, 1866. 86

CHURCHILL, SIR WINSTON SPENCER, 1874–1965.
Present at battle of Omdurman, 1898; President of the Board of Trade, 1908–10; Home Secretary, 1910–11; First Lord of the Admiralty, 1911–15. 157, 202, 315, 321–2, 326, 372, 419, 425

CLARENCE, DUKE OF, 1864–92.
Eldest son of King Edward VII. 181

CLARENDON, GEORGE WILLIAM FREDERICK VILLIERS, 4TH EARL OF, 1800–70.
Foreign Secretary, 1853–8, 1865–6, 1868–70. 60, 65

CLAUSEWITZ, KARL VON, 1780–1831.
Prussian military writer. 14, 356, 422

CLEMENCEAU, GEORGES, 1844–1929.
French President of the Council, 1906–9, 1917–19. 73

CLEVELAND, STEPHEN GROVER, 1837–1908.
(Democrat) President of U.S.A., 1885–9 and 1893–7. 195

COLIGNY, GASPARD DE, ADMIRAL, 1517–72.
Huguenot leader, killed in Massacre of St. Bartholomew. 161

CONNAUGHT, ARTHUR, DUKE OF, 1850–1942.
Youngest son of Queen Victoria; m. Louise Margaret of Prussia, 1879. 218, 276

CONRAD II, DUKE OF FRANCONIA, EMPEROR, 990–1039. 3

CONRAD III, EMPEROR, 1138–52. 5

CONSTANTINE, 288–331.
Recognized as Emperor, 306. 156

CONSTANTINE I, KING OF GREECE, 1868–1923.
Reigned, 1913–22, m. Sophie, sister of Kaiser, 1889. By birth a Prince of Denmark. 125, 200, 256

COOK, THOMAS, 1808–92. 147

COOPER, JAMES FENIMORE, 1789–1851. 77

CROWE, SIR EYRE, 1864–1925.
Assistant Under-Secretary, Foreign Office, 1912; Permanent Under-Secretary, 1920. Had a German mother. 267, 321, 424, 479

CUMBERLAND, ERNST AUGUST, DUKE OF C. AND BRUNSWICK-LÜNEBURG, 1848–1923.
Son of George V, last King of Hanover; m. Thyra of Denmark. 131, 342

CURZON, GEORGE NATHANIEL, 1859–1925.
Viceroy of India, 1898–1905; President, Air Board, 1916; Foreign Secretary, 1919–23; 1st Marquess, 1911. 80

CZERNIN, OTTOKAR, COUNT VON, 1872–1932.
Austro-Hungarian Foreign Minister from August 1916 till April 1918. 152, 291, 375–6

DAIMLER, GOTTLIEB, 1834–1900.
Pioneer of internal-combustion engines. 46

DANTE ALIGHIERI, 1265–1321. 416

DEALTRY, MR.
English tutor of Kaiser. 77

DEEPING, GEORGE WARWICK, 1877–1950.
English novelist. 161

DEHIO, LUDWIG, 1888–1963.
Professor of History at Marburg. 425

DEHMEL, RICHARD, 1863–1920.
German poet. 161

DELANE, JOHN T., 1817–79.
Editor of *The Times*, 1841–77. 62

DELCASSÉ, THÉOPHILE, 1852–1923.
French Foreign Minister, 1898–1905 and 1914–15; Minister of Marine, 1911–12; Ambassador in St. Petersburg, 1913–14. 214–15, 253, 256–7, 265, 312, 339

DENMARK, FREDERICK VIII, KING OF, 1843–1912.
m. Princess Louise of Sweden; succeeded, 1906. 308

DERNBURG, BERNHARD, 1865–1937.
German banker; Head of Colonial Department in Foreign Office 1906; State Secretary for Colonies, 1907–10. 272

DEROULÈDE, PAUL, 1846–1914.
French nationalist writer and politician, supported Boulanger. 214

DEVONSHIRE, SPENCER COMPTON CAVENDISH, 8TH DUKE OF, 1833–1908.
Secretary of State for India, 1880–2; for War, 1882–5; Lord President of the Council, 1895–1903. 237

DICKENS, CHARLES, 1812–70. 77, 161

DIESEL, RUDOLF, 1858–1913.
Pioneer of the heavy oil engine. 46

DISRAELI, BENJAMIN, 1ST EARL OF BEACONSFIELD, 1804–81.
Prime Minister, 1868 and 1874–80. 34, 71, 104, 128

DOBERNECK, FRÄULEIN VON
Governess to Kaiser. 75

DÖRPFELD, WILHELM, 1853–1940.
Architect and archaeologist, especially at Olympia. 309

DREWS, DR. WILHELM, 1870–1938.
Prussian civil servant, Minister of Interior in Max of Baden's
Cabinet, 1918. 402–4, 407

DREYFUS, ALFRED, 1859–1935.
French army officer convicted as a German spy, 1894; conviction
set aside, 1906. 214, 334

DROYSEN, JOHANN GUSTAV, 1808–84.
Professor of History at Berlin. 16, 64

DRYDEN, JOHN, 1631–1700. 85

EBERT, FRIEDRICH, 1871–1925.
Deputy (Social Democrat) in *Reichstag*; Secretary of Party, 1907;
Chancellor, 9 November 1918; President of German Republic,
1919–25. 330, 377, 395, 409–10

ECKARDSTEIN, HERMANN, BARON VON, 1864–1933.
Worked in German Embassy, London, as First Secretary and
Counsellor, 1891–1902. 210, 221, 232–3, 236–7, 306

EDINBURGH, ALFRED ERNEST ALBERT, DUKE OF, 1844–1900.
2nd son of Queen Victoria; Duke of Saxe-Coburg-Gotha, 1893;
m. Marie Alexandrovna, daughter of Tsar Alexander II. 182

EDWARD VII, KING, 1841–1910.
m. Alexandra of Denmark, 1863, succeeded January, 1901. 63–4,
68–9, 75–6, 79, 81, 84, 96–9, 100–1, 114, 120–4, 126, 143–4, 148,
151, 162, 180–2, 190, 195–6, 208, 221, 223–4, 231, 233–4, 242, 244–5,
247–8, 250, 256–7, 260, 264–5, 277–8, 283–4, 286, 296–7, 306–8, 351,
416

EISNER, KURT, 1867–1919.
Editor *Vorwärts*, 1899, *Fränkische Tagespost*, 1907–10; Minister-
President Bavarian Republic, 1918; assassinated. 403

EITEL FRIEDRICH (FRITZ), PRINCE, 1883–1942.
2nd son of Kaiser; m. Sophie Charlotte of Oldenburg. 410, 414

Biographical Index

ELISABETH, EMPRESS OF AUSTRIA, 1837–1898.
b. princess of Bavaria; m. 1854; assassinated in Geneva. 256, 284

EMIN PASHA (EDUARD SCHNITZER), 1840–92.
Entered Egyptian service, 1878; explored Central Africa; murdered by natives. 54

ERDMANN, OTTO LINNE, 1805–92.
German philosopher. 47

ERNST GÜNTHER, PRINCE OF SCHLESWIG-HOLSTEIN, 1863–1921.
3rd son of Duke Frederick of Augustenburg and brother of Kaiserin. 93

ERZBERGER, MATTHIAS, 1875–1921.
Deputy (Centre) in *Reichstag* from 1903; Minister without portfolio in Max of Baden's Cabinet, 1918; Chairman of Armistice delegation, November 1918; Minister of Finance; assassinated. 151, 271–2, 329, 333, 376, 378–9, 381, 383, 398, 402, 483

ESHER, REGINALD BALIOL BRETT, 1ST VISCOUNT, 1852–1930.
Secretary of Office of Works, 1895–1902; Chairman, War Office Reconstruction Committee, 1902–4; member of Committee of Imperial Defence, 1904–14. 266–7, 277, 280, 282–3, 307

ETZEL, KING OF THE HUNS (Attila), 406?–453. 226

EUGEN, PRINCE OF SAVOY, 1663–1736.
Austrian general. 6

EULENBURG, BOTHO, COUNT ZU, 1831–1912.
Prussian Minister of Interior, 1878–81; Minister-President, 1892–4. 175, 184–5

EULENBURG, PHILIP, COUNT ZU E. AND HERTEFELD, 1847–1921.
Prussian envoy in Oldenburg, Stuttgart and Munich, 1881–94; German Ambassador in Vienna, 1894–1902; made a Prince, 1900. 84, 88–90, 112, 143, 146, 149–51, 168–9, 175, 179, 182, 185, 188, 192, 200–1, 216, 253, 257, 262, 265, 274–7, 288, 305

FALKENHAYN, ERICH VON, GENERAL, 1861–1922.
Prussian Minister of War, 1913–15; Chief of General Staff; 1914–16; Commander in Roumania and Caucasus, 1916–18. 333, 358, 361, 364–5, 368, 419

FEODORA, PRINCESS OF SCHLESWIG-HOLSTEIN, 1874–1910.
Sister of Kaiserin, unmarried. 150

FERDINAND, KING OF BULGARIA, 1861–1948.
b. Prince of Saxe-Coburg-Gotha; Prince of Bulgaria, 1887; raised to King, 1908; abdicated, 1918. 82, 112, 146, 148

FERRY, JULES FRANÇOIS CAMILLE, 1832–93.
French President of the Council, 1880–1 and 1883–5. 52

FISHER, SIR JOHN ARBUTHNOT, ADMIRAL, 1841–1920.
First Sea Lord, 1904–10 and 1914–18. 1st Baron 1909. 205, 250–1, 256, 267, 279–80, 282, 284, 297, 321–2, 327

FOCH, FERDINAND, 1851–1929.
French general, Allied Commander-in-Chief, 1918. 73

FONTANE, THEODOR, 1819–98.
German poet and novelist. 160

FRANZ FERDINAND, ARCHDUKE, 1863–1914.
Son of Archduke Charles, nephew and (after 1889) heir to Emperor Franz Joseph; married morganatically to Sophie Chotek Duchess of Hohenberg, 1900; assassinated. 148, 292, 296, 337, 340, 342–3, 377

FRANZ JOSEPH, EMPEROR OF AUSTRIA-HUNGARY, 1830–1916.
Succeeded 1848; m. Elisabeth of Bavaria, 1854. 152, 177, 230, 262–3, 284, 286–7, 344–5

FREDERICK BARBAROSSA, EMPEROR, 1123?–90. 4, 7, 69

FREDERICK OF HOHENZOLLERN, 1371–1440.
Made Elector of Brandenburg by Emperor Sigismund, 1415. 6

FREDERICK I, KING IN PRUSSIA, 1657–1713.
Elector of Brandenburg, 1688; took royal title, 1701; m. Sophia Charlotte of Hanover. 11

FREDERICK II, EMPEROR, 1194–1250.
Recognized as King of Germany, 1196; as Emperor, 1212. 256

FREDERICK II (THE GREAT), KING OF PRUSSIA, 1712–86.
Succeeded, 1740; m. Elisabeth Christine of Brunswick-Bevern. 11, 14, 57, 85, 127, 148, 158, 159, 164, 285, 335, 347, 398

FREDERICK III, GERMAN EMPEROR (Fritz), 1831–88.
Succeeded 1888; m. Victoria, Princess Royal of Britain. 53, 62–3, 66–70, 75, 81, 92–5, 99–100, 102–4, 106, 109–12, 115, 116–20, 122–3, 125, 128, 132, 138, 142, 307, 417, 457

FREDERICK WILLIAM (THE GREAT ELECTOR), 1620–1688.
Succeeded as Elector of Brandenburg, 1640; m. (1) Louise Henrietta of Orange-Nassau. (2) Dorothea of Holstein-Glücksburg. 11, 53, 148

FREDERICK WILLIAM I, KING OF PRUSSIA, 1688–1740.
Succeeded 1713; m. Sophia of Hanover. 146

FREDERICK WILLIAM III, KING OF PRUSSIA, 1770–1840.
Succeeded, 1797. 66

FREDERICK WILLIAM IV, KING OF PRUSSIA, 1795–1861.
Succeeded, 1840; m. Elisabeth of Bavaria. 52, 56–8, 62, 66–7, 75, 85, 118, 131

FREDERICK, GRAND DUKE OF BADEN, 1826–1907.
  Regent, 1852; succeeded, 1856; m. Louise, d. of Emperor William I.
  69, 127, 134

FRENCH, SIR JOHN, FIELD MARSHAL, 1852–1925.
  Chief of Imperial General Staff, 1911–14; Commander-in-Chief,
  British Expeditionary Force, 1914–15; 1st Viscount, 1916. 284, 339

FREUD, SIGMUND, 1856–1939. 72

FRIEDBERG, ROBERT VON, 1851–1920.
  Deputy (Liberal) in *Reichstag*, Vice-Chancellor, 1917–18. 383

FRITH, WILLIAM POWELL, R.A., 1819–1909. 75

FÜRSTENBERG, MAXIMILIAN EGON, PRINCE ZU, 1863–1941.
  Landowner in Baden; host to Kaiser at Donaueschingen. 147, 152,
  290–1

GALBA. Roman general, Emperor, A.D. 69. 201

GALSTER, KARL, VICE-ADMIRAL, 1851–?
  Wrote (after retirement) on naval strategy, 1908. 280

GAMBETTA, LÉON, 1838–92.
  French Minister of Interior, War and Finance, 1870–1; President
  of the Council, 1881–2. 25, 214

GEFFCKEN, HEINRICH, 1830–96.
  German lawyer, friend of Crown Prince Frederick. 123–4, 133

GEORGE III, KING, 1738–1820.
  Succeeded, 1760; m. Charlotte of Mecklenburg-Strelitz, 1761. 85

GEORGE V, KING, 1865–1936.
  Succeeded, 1910; m. Mary of Teck, 1893. 63, 73–4, 84, 140, 231, 242,
  312, 321, 342, 349, 350, 354–5, 478, 485

GEORGE VI, KING, 1893–52.
  Succeeded, 1936; m. Lady Elizabeth Bowes-Lyon, 1923. 419

GEORGE, PRINCE OF SAXONY, 1869–1938. 147

GIERS, NICHOLAS KARLOVITCH DE, 1820–95.
  Russian Foreign Minister, 1882–95. 100, 117

GLADSTONE, WILLIAM EWART, 1809–98.
  Prime Minister, 1868–74, 1880–5 and 1892–4. 37, 53–4, 127, 220

GLUCK, CHRISTOPH WILLIAM, 1714–87. 89

GNEIST, RUDOLF, 1816–95.
  Professor of Constitutional Law, Berlin; expert on British Law. 80

GOEBBELS, JOSEPH, 1897–1945.
  Nazi Propaganda Minister, 1933–45. 420

GOERTZ, FRIEDRICH WILHELM, COUNT VON, 1851–1914.
  Friend of the Kaiser. 148

GOETHE, JOHANN WOLFGANG VON, 1749–1832. 14, 58, 156, 266, 335

GOLTZ, COLMAR, BARON VON DER, GENERAL, 1843–1916.
Reorganized Turkish Army, 1883–96; head of German Military Mission to Turkey, 1909–11. 300

GORDON, CHARLES GEORGE, GENERAL, 1833–85.
Served in China, 1860–5, and Sudan, 1870–80; besieged for 317 days in Khartoum and killed there. 53, 210

GÖRING, HERMANN, 1893–1945.
Nazi leader; Prussian Minister of the Interior, 1933; Field Marshal, 1938. 418

GRAHAME, KENNETH, 1859–1932.
English novelist. 161

GRANVILLE, GRANVILLE GEORGE LEVESON-GOWER, 2ND EARL, 1815–91.
Foreign Secretary, 1851–2, 1870–4 and 1880–5; Secretary for Colonies, 1868–70 and 1886. 53, 60, 65

GREEN, T. H., 1836–82.
Professor of Philosophy at Oxford. 80

GREY, SIR EDWARD, 1862–1933.
Foreign Secretary, 1906–16; 1st Viscount, 1916. 266, 277–8, 283, 304, 307, 313–15, 318, 321–5, 347–50, 354–5, 398, 426

GRIERSON, SIR JAMES MONCRIEFF, 1859–1914.
Military Attaché, Berlin, 1896–1900; led staff talks with the French, 1906; commanded corps of B.E.F. in 1914. 205, 219, 220, 261

GRÖNER, WILHELM, GENERAL, 1867–1939.
Head of Railway Section, General Staff, 1914–16; head of War Section, War Ministry, 1916–18; Chief of Staff, Kiev Army Group, 1918; First Quartermaster-General, October–November, 1918. 357, 400, 402–7, 410

GRÜNAU, WERNER, BARON VON, 1874–1957.
Liaison officer of German Foreign Office with Kaiser, November 1918. 407, 411

GUIZOT, FRANÇOIS PIERRE GUILLAUME, 1787–1874.
French President of the Council, 1840–8; historian. 27

HAASE, HUGO, 1867–1919.
Deputy (Social Democrat) in *Reichstag*, organized and led Independent Socialist party, 1917; assassinated. 395

HABY. Court barber. 138

HALDANE, RICHARD BURDON, 1856–1928.
Secretary of State for War, 1905; Lord Chancellor, 1912–15 and 1923–4; 1st Viscount, 1912. 144, 203, 261, 266, 269, 278, 303, 318, 322–4, 325, 332, 351

HALIFAX, EDWARD FREDERICK LINDLEY WOOD, 3RD VISCOUNT, 1881–1959.
Viceroy of India, 1926–35; Foreign Secretary, 1938–40; Ambassador to U.S., 1940–5; 1st Earl, 1944. 74, 419

HAMMURABI. *c.* 1700 B.C. Babylonian lawgiver. 156

HANOTAUX, ALBERT AUGUSTE GABRIEL, 1853–1944.
French Foreign Secretary, 1894–8; historian. 214

HARDEN, MAXIMILIAN (real name Witkowski), 1861–1927.
German journalist; founded *Die Zukunft*, 1892. 164, 274–6, 292

HARDINGE, SIR CHARLES, 1858–1944.
In Foreign Office, 1880–1910; Viceroy of India, 1910–16; 1st Viscount. 286–7, 289, 316

HARMSWORTH, ALFRED, LORD NORTHCLIFFE, 1865–1922.
Newspaper magnate; pioneer of the popular press; owner of *The Times* from 1908. 208

HARNACK, ADOLF VON, 1851–1930.
German theologian. 142

HARTE, BRET, 1839–1902.
American humorist. 89

HATZFELDT TRACHENBERG, HERMANN, PRINCE ZU, 1848–1933.
Prussian landowner; Deputy (Conservative) in *Reichstag*. 377, 380

HATZFELDT-WILDENBURG, PAUL, COUNT VON, 1831–1901.
German ambassador in Madrid, 1874; Constantinople, 1878; State Secretary for Foreign Affairs, 1881–5; Ambassador in London, 1885–1901. 54, 190, 195, 210–12, 217, 233–4, 237–9

HAUPTMANN, GERHARD, 1862–1922.
German poet and dramatist. 161

HEBER, REGINALD, 1783–1826.
Bishop of Calcutta, 1822; author of 'From Greenland's icy mountains'. 77

HEGEL, GEORG WILHELM FRIEDRICH, 1770–1831.
Professor of Philosophy at Berlin, 1818–31. 13, 15, 47, 48, 423

HELFFERICH, KARL, 1872–1924.
Financier; State Secretary for Finance, 1915–16; for the Interior, 1916–18. 362, 380

HENRY IV, EMPEROR, 1056–1106. 4

HENRY, PRINCE, 1862–1929.
Brother of the Kaiser; naval officer from 1878. 79, 198, 210, 242, 349

HENRY, PRINCE OF BATTENBERG, 1858–96.
3rd Son of Prince Alexander of Hesse; m. Beatrice, youngest daughter of Queen Victoria, 1886; died on Ashanti Expedition. 101, 102

HERTLING, GEORG, COUNT VON, 1843–1919.
Minister-President of Bavaria, 1912; German Chancellor, 1917–18.
380, 382–3, 385–6, 391, 394, 398, 403

HERZL, THEODOR, 1860–1904.
Journalist in Vienna and Zionist leader. 216, 460

HEYDEBRAND UND DER LASE, ERNST VON, 1851–1924.
Deputy (Conservative) in *Reichstag;* Party leader from 1903. 317, 395

HEYE, WILHELM, COLONEL, 1869–1946.
Chief of Staff of an Army, 1914; Chief of General Staff, 1926–30. 408

HILDEBRAND (Pope Gregory VII from 1073), 1020–85. 4

HINDENBURG UND BENCKENDORFF, PAUL VON, FIELD MARSHAL, 1847–
1934.
Recalled from retirement in September 1914 to take command on
Eastern front; Chief of the General Staff, 1916–18; President of the
Republic, 1925–34. 150, 361, 364–5, 368–9, 371, 379–80, 382, 384–6,
390–3, 395–6, 400, 402, 404–6, 408–11, 415, 418, 419

HINTZE, PAUL VON, ADMIRAL, 1864–1941.
Military plenipotentiary at Russian court, 1908–11; German Ambassador in Norway, 1917–18; Foreign Secretary June–October
1918; Foreign Office representative with High Command, October–
November 1918. 391–4, 403, 408–11

HINZPETER, GEORG ERNST, 1827–1907.
Son of teacher at Bielefeld; tutor to Kaiser, 1866–79. 76–9, 81, 87,
115, 127, 132, 453

HITLER, ADOLF, 1889–1945. 418–20, 429

HOFFMANN, MAX, GENERAL, 1869–1927.
On Staff at Eastern Headquarters, 1914–18. 377, 384–5, 419

HOFMANNSTHAL, HUGO VON, 1874–1929.
Austrian poet and dramatist. 95

HOHENLOHE-LANGENBURG, ERNST, PRINCE ZU, 1863–1950.
Regent of Saxe-Coburg-Gotha, 1900–5; Head of Colonial Department
in Foreign Office, spring-autumn 1906. 271–2, 397

HOHENLOHE-SCHILLINGSFÜRST, CHLODWIG, PRINCE ZU, 1819–1901.
Bavarian Minister-President, 1866–70; German Ambassador in
Paris, 1874; Governor of Alsace-Lorraine, 1885; Chancellor, 1894–
1900. 87, 138, 186–8, 192–4, 198, 200–2, 205, 222, 228, 304, 307,
353, 382

HOLLMANN, FRITZ   AIRAL, 1842–1913.
Secretary for the   }90–7. 198, 201, 205

HOLSTEIN, FRIEDRICH, BARON VON, 1837–1909.
1878–1906 Senior Counsellor in German Foreign Office. 127, 133, 136, 140, 145–7, 167–9, 172, 178, 183, 186, 189, 190, 192, 194, 202, 211, 215, 220, 228, 234, 237–40, 247, 252, 254, 257, 261–3, 274–6, 288, 295, 307, 465

HOLTZENDORFF, HENNING VON, ADMIRAL, 1853–1919.
Chief of Naval Staff, 1916–18. 319, 366, 371

HÖTZENDORF, FRANZ, COUNT CONRAD, 1852–1925.
Chief of Austro-Hungarian General Staff, 1906–11 and 1914–17. 293, 340, 343, 348, 350, 364

HOUSE, E. M., COLONEL, 1858–1938.
Adviser to President Wilson, sent on peace mission to Europe, 1914. 341

HÜLSEN-HÄSELER, DIETRICH, COUNT VON, 1852–1908.
Chief of Kaiser's Military Secretariat, 1901–8. 290

HUMBOLDT, WILLIAM, BARON VON, 1767–1835.
Prussian Minister, Rome, 1801–8, Vienna, 1810, London, 1817; founder of University of Berlin; Philologist and Historian. 15, 58

IZVOLSKY, ALEXANDER, 1856–1919.
Russian Foreign Minister, 1906–10; Ambassador in Paris, 1910–17. 284, 286–7, 294–5, 308–9, 339

JAGOW, GOTTLIEB VON, 1863–1935.
German State Secretary for Foreign Affairs, 1913–16. 353, 477

JAMESON, DR. LEANDER STARR, 1853–1917.
Leader of raid on Transvaal, 1896; Prime Minister, Cape Colony, 1904–8. 193, 195–6, 210

JELLICOE, SIR JOHN RUSHWORTH, ADMIRAL, 1859–1935.
Commander-in-Chief, Grand Fleet, 1914–16; First Sea Lord, 1916–18. 1st Earl, 1925. 326

JOACHIM, PRINCE, 1890–1920.
6th son of Kaiser; committed suicide. 155, 414

JOWETT, BENJAMIN, 1817–93.
Master of Balliol College, Oxford, from 1870. 47, 80

KANDINSKY, VASSILY, 1866–1944.
Russian painter working in Munich. 161

KANITZ-PODANGEN, HANS WILHELM, COUNT VON, 1841–1913.
Deputy (Conservative) in *Reichstag*, 1889–1913. Introduced motion in 1894 calling for government monopoly on grain imports, the grain to be resold at a fixed minimum price 60 per cent. above prices then current (*Antrag Kanitz*). 171

KANT, IMMANUEL, 1724–1804.
Professor of Philosophy at Königsberg from 1770. 12, 132, 156

KARDORFF, WILHELM VON, 1828–1907.
Industrialist and Deputy (Free Conservative) in *Reichstag*. 32

KARL, EMPEROR OF AUSTRIA-HUNGARY, 1887–1922.
Nephew of Franz Ferdinand and great-nephew of Franz Joseph; m. Zita of Bourbon-Parma, 1911; succeeded, 1916; abdicated, 1918. 164, 374–5, 389, 400

KENT, EDWARD AUGUSTUS, DUKE OF, 1767–1820.
4th son of George III, father of Queen Victoria, great-grandfather of Kaiser. 83, 97

KENT, VICTORIA MARIA LOUISE, DUCHESS OF, 1786–1861.
Princess of Saxe-Coburg-Gotha; m. firstly Prince Emile of Leiningen; secondly Duke of Kent, 1818. 86

KEPPEL, MRS., 1869–1947.
Daughter of Sir William Edmondstone; m. Hon. George Keppel, 1891; friend of King Edward VII. 265

KIDERLEN-WÄCHTER, ALFRED VON, 1852–1912.
Worked in German Foreign Office till 1895; Ambassador in Bucarest, 1895–1908; State Secretary for Foreign Affairs, 1910–12. 148, 168, 179, 295, 305, 311–14, 316, 318, 325, 335, 353

KIPLING, RUDYARD, 1865–1936. 161, 244

KITCHENER, SIR HERBERT, 1850–1916.
Served in Sudan and Egypt, 1883–96; led expedition to recover Sudan, 1896–8; Chief of Staff and later C.-in-C., South Africa, 1900–2; C.-in-C. India, 1902–9; Secretary of State for War, 1914–16; drowned on way to Russia; 1st Baron, 1898; Earl, 1914. 210, 213

KLEE, PAUL, 1879–1940.
German painter. 161

KOCH, ROBERT, 1843–1910.
German bacteriologist, discoverer of tubercle bacillus. 142

KÖLLER, ERNST MATTHIAS VON, 1841–1928.
Prussian Minister of the Interior, 1894–5. 193, 355

KOTZE, LEBERECHT VON, 1850–1920.
Court Chamberlain till 1894. 179

KRÜGER, PAULUS (OOM PAUL), 1825–1904.
President of Boer Republic of Transvaal, 1883–1900. 194–5, 198, 208, 211, 217, 221–3, 236, 467

KRUPP, FRIEDRICH ALFRED, 1854–1904.
Essen industrialist, grandson of Friedrich K. who founded firm at beginning of nineteenth century; committed suicide after accusations of immorality. 197, 206, 252, 276, 311, 392

KÜHLMANN, RICHARD VON, 1873–1948.
German Chargé d'Affaires, Tangier, 1905–6; Counsellor, London, 1909–14; State Secretary for Foreign Affairs, July 1917–June 1918. 253–5, 311, 381–2, 384–9, 391, 399, 479

LANSDOWNE, HENRY CHARLES KEITH PETTY-FITZMAURICE, 5TH MARQUIS, 1845–1927.
Governor-General, Canada, 1885–8; Viceroy of India, 1888–94; Secretary of State for War, 1895–1900; for Foreign Affairs, 1900–6; Leader of Opposition in House of Lords, 1906–16. Had a French mother. 222, 232–5, 256, 268

LASCELLES, SIR FRANK CAVENDISH, 1841–1920.
British Ambassador in Berlin, 1892–1907. 200, 219, 241–2, 249, 251, 279, 283

LASKER, EDUARD, 1829–84.
Deputy (Social Democrat) in *Reichstag*, 1871–83. 48

LASSALLE, FERDINAND, 1825–1864.
German socialist thinker; friend of Bismarck. 38

LENIN, VLADIMIR ILYITCH ULYANOV, 1870–1924.
Lived in exile in Switzerland, 1900–17; Chairman of Council of People's Commissars, 1917–24. 21, 73, 372, 375, 383

LEOPOLD I, KING OF THE BELGIANS, 1790–1865.
m., 1816, Princess Charlotte, d. of George IV; she died, 1817; m., 1832, Louise, d. of Louis Philippe; made King of Belgium, 1831; uncle of Queen Victoria. 123

LEOPOLD II, KING OF THE BELGIANS, 1835–1909.
m. Marie Henriette of Austria; succeeded 1865. 155

LEOPOLD, PRINCE, DUKE OF ALBANY, 1853–84.
Fourth son of Queen Victoria. 75

LERCHENFELD-KOEFERING, HUGO, COUNT VON AND ZU, 1843–1925.
Bavarian envoy in Berlin, 1880–1919. 165

LESSEPS, FERDINAND, COUNT DE, 1805–94.
French constructor of Suez Canal. 109

LICHNOWSKY, KARL MAX, PRINCE VON, 1860–1928.
Secretary in German Embassy, Vienna, 1894–9; in Foreign Office, 1899–1904; Ambassador, London, 1912–14. 350, 355

LIEBERMANN, MAX, 1847–1935.
German painter. 161

LIEBKNECHT, KARL, 1871–1919.
Son of following; Deputy (Social Democrat) in *Reichstag*; leader of left-wing 'Spartacist' group; voted for war credits August and against them December 1914; imprisoned 1916–18; hoisted red flag on Berlin Palace 9 November 1918; refused to join Ebert's government; founded German Communist Party 1 January 1919; shot in trying to escape imprisonment 15 January. 330, 409

LIEBKNECHT, WILHELM, 1826–1900.
Deputy (Social Democrat) in *Reichstag* from 1874; editor, *Vorwärts*. 23, 25

LILIENCRON, DETLEV, BARON VON, 1844–1909.
German poet. 161

LINDEQUIST, FRIEDRICH VON, 1862–1945.
State Secretary for Colonies, 1910; resigned over Agadir Agreement, 1911. 318

LIPTON, SIR THOMAS, 1850–1931.
Head of firm of tea merchants; friend of King Edward VII; raced for America Cup with yacht *Shamrock* from 1899. 248

LISSAUER, ERNST, 1882–1937.
Author of German 'Hymn of Hate' against Britain, 1914. 364

LIST, FRIEDRICH, 1789–1846.
German economist. 48, 52

LLOYD GEORGE, DAVID, 1863–1945.
President, Board of Trade, 1905–8; Chancellor of Exchequer, 1908–15; Minister of Munitions, 1915–16; Prime Minister, 1916–22; 1st Earl, 1945. 72, 298, 314, 316, 318, 322, 395

LONGFELLOW, HENRY WADSWORTH, 1807–82.
American poet. 161

LONSDALE, HUGH CECIL LOWTHER, 5TH EARL OF, 1857–1944.
English landowner and sportsman. 180

LORTZING, GUSTAV ALBERT, 1801–51.
German composer, especially of operas. 161

LOUBET, EMILE, 1838–1929.
President of France, 1899–1906. 244

LOUIS I, KING OF FRANCE AND EMPEROR OF GERMANY, 778–840. 3

LOUIS PHILIPPE, KING OF FRANCE, 1773–1850.
Reigned 1830–48. 27

LOUIS FERDINAND, PRINCE, born 1907.
Son of Crown Prince William. 418

LOUISE, GRAND DUCHESS OF BADEN, 1838–1923.
Daughter of Emperor William I of Germany. 62

LOUISE, QUEEN OF PRUSSIA, 1776–1810.
Princess of Mecklenburg-Strelitz; m. King Frederick William III of Prussia; mother of Kings Frederick William IV and William I. 56, 258

LUCANUS, HERMANN FRIEDRICH VON, 1831–1908.
Head of Kaiser's Civil Secretariat, 1888–1908. 151, 153

LUDENDORFF, ERICH FRIEDRICH WILHELM, 1865–1937.
Head of mobilization section, General Staff, 1911–14; responsible for capture of Liège, 1914; Chief of Staff to Hindenburg for victories of Tannenberg and Masurian Lakes, 1914; Chief Quartermaster-General, 1916; planned Caporetto offensive on Italian front, 1917, offensive in West, 1918; resigned, October 1918; took part in attempted risings by Kapp (1920) and Hitler (1923). 338, 361, 364–5, 368–9, 371, 374, 377–81, 385–7, 391–4, 396, 399–400, 419

LUDWIG II, KING OF BAVARIA, 1845–86.
Patron of Wagner; deposed as mad 1886. 163

LUDWIG, PRINCE OF BAVARIA, 1845–1921.
Eldest son of following; succeeded father as Regent, 1912; claimed throne, 1913; abdicated 1918. 115, 147

LUITPOLD, PRINCE REGENT OF BAVARIA, 1821–1912.
Acted for his mad nephews, Kings Ludwig II and Otto. 147, 243, 297

LUTHER, MARTIN, 1483–1546. 7, 11, 114, 156, 422

LUXEMBURG, ROSA, 1870–1919.
German socialist, leader of left-wing 'Spartacist' group; assassinated. 330

LYNCKER, MORITZ, BARON VON, 1845–1923.
Head of Kaiser's Military Secretariat, 1908–18. xii, 357, 380

MACAULAY, THOMAS BABINGTON, 1ST BARON, 1800–59. 77

MACDONALD, CAPTAIN.
British officer travelling in Germany, 1860. 48

MACHIAVELLI, NICOLO, 1469–1527. 202

MACKENSEN, AUGUST VON, GENERAL, 1849–1945.
Commanded in Poland, 1914–15, in Balkans, 1916–18; Field Marshal, 1915. 152, 389, 419–20

MACKENZIE, SIR MORELL, 1837–92.
British doctor called in by Germans to advise on Crown Prince Frederick, 1887; knighted by Queen Victoria at Crown Prince's request. 109–10, 117–18, 457

MAHAN, ALFRED THAYER, ADMIRAL, 1840–1914.
American sailor and writer on naval strategy, author of *The Influence of Sea-Power on History*, etc. 197, 204, 214

MALET, SIR EDWARD, 1837–1908.
British Ambassador in Berlin, 1884–95; friend of Bismarck. 84, 191–2, 215, 316

MANN, THOMAS, 1875–1955.
German novelist. 161

MANNESMANN, REINHARD, 1856–1900.
Eldest of six brothers who founded concern for making seamless metal tubes in Remscheid, later moved to Düsseldorf; interested in Moroccan ore from 1906. 311

MANTEUFFEL, EDWIN, BARON VON, 1809–85.
Chief of Military Secretariat to William I, 1857; led Army of Main, 1866; 1st Governor of Alsace-Lorraine; Field-Marshal, 1873. 31

MARCHAND, JEAN BAPTISTE, CAPTAIN, 1863–1934.
French colonial officer and explorer. 213

MARCUS AURELIUS ANTONINUS, 121–180.
Recognized as Emperor of Rome, 161. 64

MARIE LOUISE, PRINCESS, 1872–1956.
Daughter of Prince Christian and Princess Helena. 139

MARIUS, CAIUS, 157–86 B.C.
Roman general. 1

MARRYAT, CAPTAIN, 1792–1848.
Writer of novels about sea life. 77, 161

MARSCHALL VON BIEBERSTEIN, ADOLF, BARON, 1842–1912.
Baden envoy in Berlin, 1883–90; State Secretary for Foreign Affairs, 1890–7; Ambassador in Constantinople, 1897–1912; in London, 1912. 127, 134–6, 177, 183, 187, 191, 193–4, 196, 199, 200, 201

MARX, KARL, 1818–83. 19, 25, 38, 64, 73

MARY, QUEEN, 1867–1953.
Daughter of Duke of Teck; engaged to Duke of Clarence; married George, Duke of York (George V), 1893. 140, 242, 419

MAX, PRINCE OF BADEN, 1867–1929.
Nephew of Grand Duke Frederick; Chancellor, October-November, 1918. 342, 357, 395–401, 403–4, 406–7

MAXSE, LEOPOLD JAMES, 1864–1932.
Editor of *National Review* from 1893. 266

MEINECKE, FRIEDRICH, 1862–1954.
German historian; Professor at Strasbourg, Freiburg and Berlin; 1st Rektor of Free University of Berlin, 1948. 381, 424

MELBOURNE, WILLIAM LAMB, 1ST VISCOUNT, 1779–1848.
Prime Minister, 1834 and 1835–41. 59

MENDELSSOHN–BARTHOLDY, FELIX, 1809–47. 75

METTERNICH, PAUL, COUNT VON WOLFF– 1853–1934.
German Ambassador in London, 1901–12. 232, 234–5, 247, 262–3, 265, 283–4, 298, 315, 319, 321, 323, 325–6

MEYERBEER, GIACOMO (really Jakob Liebmann Beer), 1791–1864.
Composer, German-born, living in Paris. 161

MICHAELIS, GEORG, 1857–1936.
Prussian civil servant; Food Controller, 1915–17; Chancellor, July–October, 1917. 165, 380–2

MILNER, ALFRED, 1854–1925.
High Commissioner for South Africa, 1897–1905; member of the War Cabinet, 1916–19; 1st Viscount, 1902. Father was German. 80

MIQUEL, JOHANNES VON, 1828–1901.
Friend in youth of Karl Marx; Deputy (National Liberal) in *Reichstag*, 1871–77 and 1887–90; State Secretary for Finance, 1890; Vice-president of Prussia, 1897–1901. 127, 174–5, 186

MOLTKE, HELMUTH, COUNT VON, FIELD MARSHAL, 1800–91.
Chief of General Staff, 1857–88. 20, 43, 62, 90, 134, 263, 354, 423

MOLTKE, HELMUTH J. L., COUNT VON, GENERAL, 1848–1916.
Nephew of foregoing; Chief of General Staff, 1906–14. 141, 150, 263, 293–4, 300, 316–17, 340, 345–6, 350, 353–5, 361, 480

MOLTKE, KUNO, COUNT VON, LIEUTENANT GENERAL, 1847–1923.
City Commandant of Berlin. 275

MOMMSEN, THEODOR, 1817–1903.
German historian of Rome; Professor at Berlin, 1858. 58, 142

MONTS, ANTON, COUNT VON, 1852–1930.
Prussian Ambassador in München, 1895–1902; German Ambassador in Rome, 1902–9. 270, 300

MORIER, SIR ROBERT BURNETT DAVID, 1826–93.
British representative at various German courts, 1873–6; Minister at Lisbon, 1876–81; Madrid 1881–4; Ambassador at St. Petersburg, 1884–93; friend of Crown Prince Frederick and of Jowett. 76, 80

MORLEY, JOHN, 1838–1923.
Chief Secretary, Ireland, 1885 and 1892–5; Secretary of State for India, 1905–10; Lord President of the Council, 1910–14; resigned August 1914; biographer of Gladstone; 1st Viscount, 1908. 277

MOROCCO, SULTAN OF, ABDUL AZIZ, 1881–?
Succeeded, 1894; overthrown by his half-brother, Mulay Hafid, 1908. 255

MOSES. 156

MOTLEY, JOHN, 1814–77.
American historian, author of *History of the Dutch Republic.* 23

MOZART, WOLFGANG AMADEUS, 27 January 1756–91. 73

MÜLLER, GEORG ALEXANDER VON, ADMIRAL, 1854–1940.
Head of Kaiser's Naval Secretariat, 1909–18. 342, 357, 374, 481

MÜLLER, ERICH VON, born 1877.
German Naval Attaché in London, 1912–14. 326, 341

MÜNSTER-LEDENBURG, GEORG, COUNT ZU, 1820–1902.
German Ambassador in London, 1873–85; in Paris, 1885–1900. 53,
54, 239

NAPOLEON BONAPARTE I, EMPEROR, 1769–1821. 14, 15, 16, 30, 57, 116,
207, 230, 245, 255

NATZMER, CAPTAIN VON.
German infantry officer in 1893. 145

NAUMANN, FRIEDRICH, 1860–1919.
Lutheran pastor; founder and president National Socialist Party,
1896; German Democratic Party, 1918. 207, 229, 292, 363, 424

NELSON, HORATIO, LORD, ADMIRAL, 1758–1805. 124, 182, 352

NESSELRODE, KARL ROBERT, COUNT, 1780–1862.
Russian Foreign Minister and Prime Minister, 1816–56. 168

NICHOLAS I, TSAR OF RUSSIA, 1796–1855.
m. Charlotte, d. of Frederick William III of Prussia, 1817; succeeded,
1825. 258

NICHOLAS II, TSAR OF RUSSIA, 1868–1918.
m. Alix (Alexandra Fedorovna) of Hesse; succeeded, 1894. 99, 143,
146–7, 149, 155, 158, 171, 188–9, 196, 209, 212–15, 219, 226, 232, 237,
245, 248–50, 257–60, 264–5, 284, 293, 309, 337, 341–2, 346, 349–50,
359, 372, 393, 398, 405

NICOLSON, SIR ARTHUR, 1849–1928.
British Minister in Morocco, 1895–1905; Ambassador in Madrid,
1905–6; representative at Algeciras Conference, 1906; Ambassador in
St. Petersburg, 1906–10; Permanent Under-Secretary in Foreign
Office, 1910–16; 1st Lord Carnock, 1916. 321, 479

NIEBUHR, BARTOLD GEORG, 1776–1831.
German historian of Rome. 58

NIEMANN, AUGUST, 1839–before 1928.
Retired officer, novelist. 266

NORWAY, QUEEN MAUD OF, 1869–1938.
Daughter of King Edward VII; m. 1896 Charles, Prince of Denmark,
who became King Haakon of Norway, 1905. 391

NOSKE, GUSTAV, 1868–1946.
Deputy (Social Democrat) in *Reichstag*; first Minister of Defence in Republic. 330, 331

OLGA, GRAND DUCHESS, 1882–1952.
d. of Tsar Alexander III, m. Duke Peter of Oldenburg 1901. 284

OSCAR, PRINCE, 1888–1958.
5th son of Kaiser; m. Countess Ina von Bassewitz (renounced rights). 418

OTTO I, KING OF THE GERMANS AND EMPEROR 912–73. 4

PALMERSTON, JOHN HENRY TEMPLE, 3RD VISCOUNT, 1784–1865.
Secretary of State for Foreign Affairs, 1830–41, 1846–51; for Home Affairs, 1852, 1853–8; Prime Minister, 1856–8 and 1859–65. 47, 61

PAPEN, FRANZ, VON, 1879–1969.
Chancellor, 1932; Vice-Chancellor to Hitler, 1933–4; Ambassador in Vienna, 1934–8; to Turkey, 1939–44; acquitted at Nuremberg, 1946. 381

PARETO, VILFREDO, 1848–1923.
Italian sociologist. vi

PAŠIĆ, NIKOLA, 1845–1926.
Prime Minister of Serbia, 1906–26. 344

PAUL I, TSAR OF RUSSIA, 1754–1801.
Son of Catherine the Great; succeeded, 1796. 58, 85, 140

PAXTON, SIR JOSEPH, 1801–65.
Gardener at Chatsworth 1826; designed Crystal Palace for 1851 Exhibition. 62

PAYER, FRIEDRICH VON, 1847–1931.
Deputy (Progressive) in *Reichstag*; Vice-Chancellor, 1917–18. 383

PEEL, SIR ROBERT, 1788–1850.
Prime Minister, 1834–5 and 1841–6. 41

PHILIP AUGUSTUS, KING OF FRANCE, 1165–1223. 4

PITT, WILLIAM, 1759–1806.
2nd son of 1st Earl of Chatham; Prime Minister, 1783–1801 and 1804–6. 284

PIUS XII (EUGENIO PACELLI), 1876–1958.
Papal nuncio in Germany, 1917–20; elected Pope, 1939. 382

PLESS, DAISY, PRINCESS OF, 1873–1943.
b. Daisy Cornwallis-West; m. Hans Heinrich, 15th Prince of Pless, 1891. 85–6

PLESSEN, HANS, COUNT VON, 1841–1929.
Chief A.D.C. to Kaiser, 1888–1918; Adjutant-General, 1914. 151–2, 179, 198, 357–8, 380, 406, 408–11

POINCARÉ, RAYMOND, 1860–1934.
French President of the Council, 1912–13; of the Republic, 1913–20.
318, 339, 345, 347

PONSONBY, SIR FREDERICK, 1867–1935.
Son of Sir H. Ponsonby; godson of Empress Frederick; published letters of Empress Frederick to Queen Victoria, 1928; Treasurer to King George V; 1st Baron Sysonby, 1935. 119, 416

PONSONBY, SIR HENRY, 1825–95.
Private Secretary to Queen Victoria, 1870–95. 64, 117

POPE BENEDICT XV, 1854–1922.
Giacomo della Chiesa; elected 1914. 381–2

POSADOWSKY-WEHNER, ARTHUR, COUNT VON, 1845–1922.
State Secretary for the Interior, 1897–1907. 201, 269–70, 273, 276, 410

QUEUX, WILLIAM LE, 1864–1927.
English writer. 266

QUIDDE, LUDWIG, 1858–1941.
German journalist. 180

RADOLIN, HUGO, PRINCE VON (RADOLINSKI), 1847–1917.
Chamberlain to Crown Princess Frederick; German Ambassador in Constantinople, 1892–5, St. Petersburg, 1895–1901, Paris, 1901–10. 111, 239

RADZIWILL, PRINCESS ELISA , 1803–34.
Youthful love of Kaiser William I. 58

RADZIWILL, PRINCESS MARIE, 1861–1915.
d. of Marquis de Castellane. 86

RANKE, LEOPOLD VON, 1795–1886.
German historian; Professor in Berlin, 1834–71. 15, 58, 423

RATHENAU, WALTHER , 1867–1922.
Industrial financier and politician; Minister of Reconstruction, 1921; assassinated. 355

REISCHACH, HUGO, BARON VON, 1854–1934.
Master of the Horse to the Kaiser. 150

RENAN, ERNEST, 1823–92.
Wrote *Origines du Christianisme*, 1863–81. 70

RENVERS, DR. RUDOLF, 1854–1906. 297, 417

REUSS, HERMINE, PRINCESS . See Schönaich-Carolath.

RHODES, CECIL, 1853–1902.
South African Industrialist; Prime Minister of Cape Colony, 1890–1896. 196

RICHTER, EUGEN, 1838–1906.
Lawyer; Deputy (Progressive) and Party Leader in *Reichstag*, 1871–1906. 199, 225

RICHTHOFEN, OSWALD, BARON VON, 1847–1906.
Deputy State–Secretary for Foreign Affairs, 1897–1900; Secretary, 1900–6. 238, 259

RITTER, GERHARD, 1888–1969.
Professor of History at Freiburg. 427

ROBERTS, SIR FREDERICK SLEIGH, 1832–1914.
C.-in-C. India, 1885–93, Ireland, 1895, South Africa, 1899; 1st Earl, 1901. 223, 267

RÖNTGEN, WILHELM CONRAD, 1845–1923.
German scientist; discoverer of X-rays. 142

ROON, ALBRECHT, COUNT VON, 1803–79.
Prussian War Minister, 1859–73; Minister-President, 1873. 20, 25

ROOSEVELT, THEODORE, 1858–1919.
President (Republican) of U.S.A., 1901–9. 84, 157, 242, 244, 265

ROSEBERY, ARCHIBALD PHILIP PRIMROSE, 5TH EARL, 1847–1929.
Secretary of State for Foreign Affairs, 1885–6 and 1892–4; Prime Minister, 1894–5. 54, 137, 181, 183

ROSEN.
German journalist, ghosted the Kaiser's memoirs. 416

ROUVIER, PIERRE MAURICE, 1842–1911.
French Minister of Finance, 1887, 1889–92, 1902–5; President of the Council, 1887 and 1905–6. 256–7, 261

RUDOLPH, CROWN PRINCE OF AUSTRIA, 1858–89.
m. Stephanie of Belgium; committed suicide at Mayerling. 123, 126

RUPPRECHT, CROWN PRINCE OF BAVARIA, 1869–1956.
Son of Prince Ludwig; commanded Army/Army Group on Western Front, 1914–18. 419

RUSSELL, MISS. English heiress with whom Bismarck was in love, 1837. 128.

RUSSELL, LORD JOHN, 1792–1878.
3rd son of 6th Duke of Bedford; Prime Minister, 1846–52; 1st Earl, 1861. 54

SAI-CHIN-HUA, 1874–1936.
A wife of Hung-Wen-Ch'ing, Chinese Envoy in Berlin, 1888–90. 227

SAINT-VINCENT, ADMIRAL SIR JOHN JERVIS, 1ST EARL OF, 1735–1823.
Defeated Spanish fleet off Cape St. Vincent, 1797. 124

SALADIN (SALA-UD-DIN), 1138–1193.
Arab leader in Crusades; Sultan, 1175. 217

SALISBURY, ROBERT ARTHUR TALBOT GASCOYNE-CECIL, 3RD MARQUIS, 1830–1903.
Secretary of State for India, 1874–8, for Foreign Affairs, 1878–80; Prime Minister and Foreign Secretary 1885–6, 1887–92, 1895–1900; Prime Minister alone, 1886–7 and 1900–2. 54, 60, 108, 112–13, 116–17, 122–4, 127–8, 132, 161, 169, 183, 190, 192–3, 196, 210–11, 213, 216, 218–20, 233, 235, 237–8, 242, 307

SAZONOV, SERGEI DIMITREIVITCH, 1886–1927.
Russian Foreign Minister, 1910–16. 309, 341, 350

SCHÄFER, DIETRICH, 1842–1929.
Professor of History, Berlin; co-founder of Fatherland Party, 1917. 384

SCHEER, REINHARD, ADMIRAL, 1863–1928.
Commanded High Sea Fleet, 1916–18. 410

SCHEIDEMANN, PHILIPP, 1865–1939.
Deputy (Progressive) in *Reichstag;* Party leader. 330, 332–3, 440–1, 409, 485

SCHILLER, JOHANN CHRISTOPH FRIEDRICH, 1759–1805. 64

SCHINKEL, MAX VON.
German banker. 266

SCHLIEFFEN, ALFRED, COUNT VON, GENERAL, 1833–1913.
Chief of General Staff, 1891–1906. 150, 252, 254, 261, 263, 288, 338, 353, 428

SCHMOLLER, GUSTAV, 1838–1917.
Economist, Professor in Berlin from 1882. 80

SCHOEN, WILHELM, BARON VON, 1851–1933.
German Ambassador in St. Petersburg, 1905; State Secretary for Foreign Affairs, 1907–10; Ambassador in Paris, 1910–14. 255, 263, 283, 305

SCHÖNAICH-CAROLATH, PRINCESS HERMINE VON, 1887–1947.
born Reuss; widow of Prince S.-C.; m. ex-Kaiser as second wife, 1922; died in Russian internment. 416, 418, 420

SCHULENBURG, FRIEDRICH, BARON VON DER, GENERAL, 1865–1939.
Chief of Staff to Crown Prince, 1918. 406–7, 409, 485

SCHWENINGER, ERNST, 1850–1924.
Bismarck's doctor. 133

SCOTT, SIR WALTER, 1771–1832. 77, 161

SELBORNE, WILLIAM WALDEGRAVE PALMER, 2ND EARL, 1859–1942.
Secretary of State for Colonies, 1895–1900; First Lord of Admiralty, 1900–5; High Commissioner South Africa, 1905–10. 246, 248, 252

SENDEN-BIBRAN, GUSTAV VON, ADMIRAL, 1847–1909.
Head of Kaiser's Naval Secretariat, 1890–1909. 151

SEYSS-INQUART, ARTHUR, 1892–1946.
As Minister of Interior in Schuschnigg Cabinet, helped to arrange Nazi annexation of Austria, 1938; German Commissioner in Holland, 1940–5; executed as war criminal. 420

SHAKESPEARE, WILLIAM, 1564–1616. 156, 403

SHAW, GEORGE BERNARD, 1856–1950. 161

SHUVALOV, PAVEL ANDREIVITCH, COUNT, 1830–1908.
Russian Ambassador in Berlin, 1885–94. 135

SIEMENS, GEORG, 1839–1901.
Banker. 36

SIEMENS, WERNER, 1816–92.
Pioneer of electric dynamo. 46

SIGISMUND, EMPEROR (elected 1411), 1368–1437. 6

SIGISMUND, PRINCE, 1864–6.
3rd son of Frederick III; died in infancy. 75

SKOROPADSKY, PAVEL, 1873–1945.
Officer in Russian Army, made Hetman of Ukraine by Germans April–December 1918, later lived in Berlin. 390

SMITH, ADAM, 1723–90. 48

SOLF, WILHELM, 1862–1936.
Governor of Samoa, 1900; State Secretary for Colonies, 1911–18; for Foreign Affairs, October–November 1918. 362

SOPHIE, PRINCESS, 1870–1923.
Sister of Kaiser; m. Duke of Sparta (later King Constantine), 1889. 125, 200

SOVERAL, MARQUIS DE, 1853–1922.
Portuguese Ambassador in London, 1890–1910. 152

STÖCKER, DR. ADOLPH, 1835–1909.
Court Chaplain; founder of Berlin Mission. 91–2, 114, 115, 127, 133, 207

STOCKMAR, CHRISTIAN FRIEDRICH, BARON VON, 1787–1862.
Secretary to King Leopold I of Belgium, 1816–34, and to Queen Victoria from 1837 to his death. 66

STOCKMAR, ERNST ALFRED CHRISTIAN, BARON VON, 1823–86.
Son of above; Secretary to Crown Princess Frederick from 1859 till 'soon after 1863' when he resigned from ill-health. 76

STRAUSS, RICHARD, 1864–1949.
German composer. 88, 162

STRESEMANN, GUSTAV, 1878–1929.
Deputy (National Liberal) in *Reichstag*, 1907–12, 1914–29; Party leader, 1917; Chancellor of Republic, 1923; Foreign Minister, 1923–9. 378, 391, 395, 426

STUART-WORTLEY, EDWARD JAMES MONTAGU, MAJOR-GENERAL, 1857–1934.
Host to the Kaiser at Highcliffe Castle, Hampshire, 1907; guest of the Kaiser at German manœuvres, 1908; drafted *Daily Telegraph* article. 278, 289

STUMM-HALBERG, KARL, BARON VON, 1836–1901.
Industrialist; Deputy (Free Conservative) in *Reichstag*. 32, 92, 115, 184, 206

SWAINE, LEOPOLD, COLONEL, 1840–1931.
British Military Attaché in Berlin, 1882–4, 1885–9, 1892–6; knighted 1909. 113, 119, 122, 182, 192

SYBEL, HEINRICH, 1817–95.
German historian, director of Prussian State archives. 18

SZÖGYÉNYI-MARICH, LADISLAUS, COUNT, 1841–1916.
Austro-Hungarian Ambassador in Berlin, 1892–1914. 343–5

TACITUS, CORNELIUS, *circa* A.D. 50–120. 2, 201

TALLEYRAND-PERIGORD, CHARLES MAURICE, MARQUIS DE, 1754–1838. 58, 120

TAYLOR, DR. ALAN J. P., born 1906. 52

TENNYSON, ALFRED, 1809–92. 77

THUCYDIDES. 284

TIRPITZ, ALFRED VON, ADMIRAL, 1849–1930.
State Secretary for Navy, 1897–March 1916; co-founder of Fatherland Party, 1917. 150, 152, 165, 178, 201–6, 221, 225, 251–2, 280–1, 298, 300–1, 307, 318–19, 321, 324–6, 345, 355, 358, 360, 364, 366–8, 381, 384, 428

TISZA, ISTVAN, COUNT, 1861–1918.
Hungarian Prime Minister, 1903–5 and 1913–17; assassinated. 347

TOYNBEE, ARNOLD, 1852–83.
English historian. 80

TREITSCHKE, HEINRICH VON, 1834–96.
German historian; professor in Berlin from 1874. 10, 16, 48, 52, 56

TROELTSCH, ERNST, 1865–1923.
German historian and sociologist. 362

TROTSKY, LEON (LEV DAVIDOVICH BRONSTEIN). 1877–1940.
Russian Communist leader; expelled from Russia after the death of Lenin. 386–7

TSCHIRSCHKY UND BÖGENDORFF, HEINRICH VON, 1858–1916.
State Secretary for Foreign Affairs, 1906–7; Ambassador in Vienna, 1907–16. 243, 263, 276, 340, 343

TURKEY, SULTAN OF, ABDUL HAMID II, 1842–1918.
Succeeded, 1876; deposed, 1909. 103, 126, 216–17

TWAIN, MARK (SAMUEL CLEMENS), 1835–1910.
American humorist. 89

TWEEDMOUTH, EDWARD MARJORIBANKS, 2ND BARON, 1849–1909.
1st Lord of the Admiralty, 1905–8. 282–4

TYRRELL, SIR WILLIAM GEORGE, 1860–1947.
Worked in Foreign Office till 1928; Ambassador to France, 1928–1934; 1st Baron, 1929. 321, 353, 479

VALENTINI, RUDOLF VON, 1855–1925.
Head of Kaiser's Civil Secretariat, 1908–18. 143, 151, 291, 300, 304, 309, 319, 357, 380, 383, 386, 399

VARUS. 2

VELAZQUEZ, 1599–1660.
Spanish painter. 138

VERDI, GIUSEPPE FORTUNIO FRANCESCO, 1813–1901. 109

VERSEN, MAX VON, GENERAL, 1833–93.
Sent by Bismarck and Moltke on a mission to Spain, April 1870; Adjutant to Kaiser after 1888. 89

VICTOR EMMANUEL III, KING OF ITALY, 1869–1947.
m. daughter of King of Montenegro; reigned 1900–46. 146, 149, 155

VICTORIA, QUEEN OF GREAT BRITAIN, 1819–1901.
Succeeded, June 1837; m. Albert of Saxe-Coburg, 1840. 48, 58-60, 63–4, 66, 68, 70–1, 74–6, 78–80, 83–4, 86, 96, 100–2, 108, 111, 114, 117–8, 122–4, 132, 150, 164, 180–1, 190, 195–6, 208, 218–20, 222, 224, 238, 244, 289, 307–8, 355, 416. Death 230–1

VICTORIA, PRINCESS ROYAL OF GREAT BRITAIN AND GERMAN EMPRESS, 1840–1901.
Eldest child of foregoing; m. Frederick of Prussia, 1858. 59–60, 62–71, 74–6, 80–1, 83, 86–7, 92–6, 101–2, 109–12, 116–24, 132, 233, 297, 307, 416

VICTORIA, PRINCESS OF PRUSSIA, 1860–1929.
Daughter of foregoing; wished to marry Alexander of Battenberg; m. (1) Adolf of Schaumburg-Lippe (2) Alexander Zoubkoff. 102, 116, 118, 119

WAGNER, ADOLF, 1835–1917.
Professor of Social Economics at Berlin, advocate of State action in social field. 80

WAGNER, RICHARD, 1813–83.
German composer. 58, 64, 83, 115, 128, 140, 425

WALDERSEE, ALFRED LUDWIG HEINRICH KARL, COUNT VON, GENERAL, 1832–1904.
Quartermaster-General, 1882–8; Chief of General Staff, 1888–91; G.-O.-C. Hamburg District, 1891–1900; Field Marshal and commander of European forces in China, 1900–1. 89, 90–2, 113–14, 127, 133, 150, 165, 167, 185, 198, 226–8, 423, 455

WALDERSEE, MARY, COUNTESS VON, 1838–1914.
Daughter of Daniel Lee of New York; m. (1) Prince Friedrich of Schleswig-Holstein, 1864 (he died 1865), (2) Count von Waldersee, 1874. 91, 127, 133, 455, 456

WALDOW, WILHELM VON, 1856–1931.
Prussian Minister, 1918. 395

WEBER, LUDWIG, 1846–1922.
Founder of Christian trade unions. 92

WEBER, MAX, 1864–1920.
Sociologist; Professor in Freiburg and Heidelberg. 161, 207, 292, 423, 426

WEDEL, KARL, COUNT VON, GENERAL, 1842–1919.
Military Attaché, Vienna, 1877–87; Ambassador in Rome, 1899, Vienna, 1902; Governor of Alsace-Lorraine, 1907–14. 300, 304, 333

WESTARP, KUNO, COUNT VON, 1864–1945.
Deputy (Conservative) in *Reichstag*. 391

WIDENMANN, WILHELM, CAPTAIN, 1871–195?.
German Naval Attaché, London, 1907–12. 320, 322, 325–6

WILAMOWITZ-MOELLENDORFF, ULRICH VON, 1848–1931.
German classical scholar. 142

WILLIAM I, KING OF PRUSSIA AND (from 1871) GERMAN EMPEROR 1797–1888.
m. Augusta of Saxe-Weimar, 1829; fled to London, 1848; acted as Regent, 1858; succeeded, 1861. 20, 28–30, 53, 56–8, 61–2, 67–70, 73–4, 79, 92, 104, 106, 111, 112, 116, 120, 125, 155–6, 175–6, 197–9, 258, 307

WILLIAM II, 'THE KAISER', 1859–1941.
For character: 74, 82–6, 96–9, 138–66, 175, 291–2, 297 and note, 358, 433–5. For relations with individuals see entries under their names. For other aspects, see Subject Index especially entries under Abdication, Ancestry, Art, Cruises, *Gedankensplitter*, Health, 'Noodles', Religion, Speeches, Telegrams, Visits to England.

WILLIAM, CROWN PRINCE, 1882–1951.
Eldest son of William II; m. Cecilie of Mecklenburg-Schwerin, 1906; commanded Army/Army Group, 1914–18. 231, 242, 248, 275, 291, 305, 317, 333, 378–81, 401, 408–10, 414, 418, 471

WILSON, SIR HENRY HUGHES, GENERAL, 1864–1922.
Planned mobilization of B.E.F., 1911–14; Deputy Chief of General Staff, 1914; assassinated. 315

WILSON, WOODROW, 1856–1924.
President of Princeton University 1902–10; President (Democratic) of U.S.A., 1912–20. 73, 359, 370–1, 373, 389, 391, 393, 396, 398, 426

WINDTHORST, LUDWIG, 1812–91.
Minister of Justice in Hanover, 1851–3 and 1862–5; Leader of Centre Party in *Reichstag* from its foundation in 1871. 130

WINTERFELDT, HUGO VON, GENERAL, 1836–98.
Commanded Guards cavalry Division in 1880's; A.D.C. to Emperors Frederick III and William II; chosen to convey formal announcement of Kaiser's accession to Queen Victoria. 122

WODEHOUSE, PELHAM GRENVILLE, born 1881.
English humorist. 161

WRANGEL, FRIEDRICH, COUNT VON, FIELD MARSHAL, 1784–1877.
Prussian leader in war of 1864. 73

WURTEMBURG, WILLIAM II, KING OF, 1848–1921.
Reigned 1891–1918. 184, 188, 293

ZEDLITS-TRÜTZSCHLER, ROBERT, COUNT VON, 1837–1914.
Prussian Minister of Education, 1891–2; Father of Robert, Count Von Z-T (1863–1942; Controller of the Kaiser's Household, 1903–10.) 174–5

ZEPPELIN, FERDINAND, COUNT VON, 1838–1917.
Airship pioneer. 290

ZITA, EMPRESS OF AUSTRIA-HUNGARY, born 1892.
Daughter of Duke Robert of Bourbon-Parma; m. Archduke (later Emperor) Karl, 1911. 374

Subject Index

Abdication, Kaiser's, 399, 400, 401, 402, 405–9, 414

Africa, Central, 1, 214, 317; East, 54, 169 (see also Zanzibar); North, 171 (see also Egypt and Morocco); South, 52, 191–6, 210, 218, 221, 225, 235 (see also Boer Republic and Transvaal); South-West, 52, 53, 54, 55, 164, 268, 271–2; West, 52, 54, 210, 246 (see also Cameroons)

Agadir, 312, 313, 315–18, 432

Agrarians, German, 29, 32, 36, 171, 173, 184, 187, 199, 222, 225, 269, 273, 331, 373 (see also Conservatives, Junkers)

Algeçiras Conference, 261–4, 272, 293, 310, 312

Alsace-Lorraine, 25, 52, 69, 86, 107, 121, 140, 186, 214, 300, 304, 328, 333, 396, 434

America, see United States

Ancestors, Kaiser's, 56–66, 73, 82, 139, 434, 453

Anglo-French Entente, 215, 245–7, 251, 254, 261–4, 288, 295, 310, 312, 323, 335, 351, 375, 392; Military conversations, 261, 307, 315, 353; Relations, 181, 183, 210, 212–15, 238, 240, 253, 257, 313

Anglo-German Relations, 43, 47–8, 65, 68, 83–4, 96–9, 114, 121, 128, 137, 180–3, 191–6, 210–13, 217–25, 228, 232–40, 248, 264–9, 289–90, 296–7, 306–7, 314–18, 325, 351, 432, 468 (see also Colonies, Naval Affairs, Trade Competition)

Anglo-Japanese Alliance, 241, 249, 251

Anglo-Russian Entente, 239, 288, 295, 323; Relations, 213, 240, 284

Archaeology, 142, 309–10, 417

Armenia, 190

Armistice, 359, 393, 394, 396, 397, 398, 400, 403, 404, 405

Army Laws, German (1874) 23, 105, (1880) 105, (1886) 105–6, (1887) 113, (1890) 130, 172, (1892) 176, 184, (1912) 338, (1913) 338; Prussian (1862) 20, 23, 67

Army, relation to Emperor/King, 25, 90, 119, 144, 150, 154, 173, 304, 354, 357, 385–6, 396, 397, 404, 406–12

Art, changes in world of, 162–3; Kaisers views on, 161–2

Atlantic, Blue Riband of, 208, 267

Attachés, position of German Naval and Military, 167, 325–6

Austria-Hungary (see also Habsburg Empire), vi, 17, 20, 21, 44, 103, 104, 107, 112, 190, 192, 200, 262, 269, 286–9, 294–5, 306, 316, 327, 363, 374–6, 389, 400, 405, 427

Austro-German Alliance 1879, 30, 70, 99, 106, 113, 128, 288, 294, 335–7, 350; Relations, 18, 26, 27, 29, 68, 69, 108, 113, 170, 288–9, 328, 340, 343–52

Baden, 58, 269, 331, 395

Baghdad Railway, 183, 268–9, 277, 309, 341

Balance of Power, 328–9, 351, 424–5

Balkans, 2, 29, 30, 107, 108, 142, 165, 286, 288, 295, 305, 339, 343, 344, 363, 389; Wars (1912–13), 335–7

Balmoral, 62, 81, 196

Baltic, 5, 122, 243, 257, 280, 363, 374, 384, 386

Bangkok, 181

Banks, 40, 46, 47

Bavaria, 2, 16, 17, 21, 22, 90, 187, 193, 207, 230, 243, 269, 275, 293, 346, 380, 393, 394, 398

Belgium, 44, 134, 170, 261, 340, 352, 353, 354, 363, 371, 374, 376, 382, 388, 425–7

Belgrade, 294, 344, 347, 348, 349

Berlin, 5, 15, 18, 53, 54, 57, 58, 65, 70, 73, 87, 96, 111, 113, 114, 116, 118, 119, 120, 122, 126, 131, 134, 135, 140, 143, 147, 151, 161, 163, 168, 178, 181, 182, 199, 227, 230, 237, 242, 244, 245, 251, 257, 265, 267, 275, 296, 309, 310, 322, 325, 327, 341, 342, 343, 346, 355, 357, 363, 375, 378, 384, 398, 399, 400, 401, 405, 407–10, 414, 420, 430, 435; Royal Castle (*Schloss*) in, 66, 88, 200, 270, 296, 304, 355, 402, 409, 411; Congress of, 1878, 29, 70, 81, 287, 294
Björkoe, 257, 258, 260, 264
Black Day of German Army (8 August 1918), 142, 391
Blockade, 43, 279, 327, 328, 360, 365, 366, 367, 369, 372, 387
Boer Republic, 191, 193, 218, 232, 242; War, 144, 221–4, 240, 247, 268, 289
Bonn, 48, 80, 81, 89
Bosnia-Herzegovina, 286–9, 290, 293–6, 310, 344, 433, 476
Bosphorus, 104, 107, 217, 284, 286, 287, 341
Boxer Rebellion, 225–8
Brandenburg, 5, 11, 17, 75, 89; Gate, 78, 88, 91, 355
Brest-Litovsk, Treaty of, 384–7, 398, 427, 433
Britain, Great, 4, 8–9, 10, 24, 28, 35, 36, 39, 44–51, 70, 104, 109, 112, 140, 142, 165, 170, 200, 217, 279
Buchlau, 287, 294
Buckingham Palace, 75, 102
Bulgaria, 99, 100, 101, 102, 103, 104, 107, 112, 117, 145, 287, 294, 336, 365, 393
Bundesrat, 21–3, 175, 209
Burgfrieden, 359–60, 362, 373

Cameroons, 52, 54, 145
Catholics, 7, 10, 16, 21, 27, 28, 37, 106, 107, 147, 161, 164, 176, 187, 216, 230, 271, 272, 299
Centre Party, 27, 37, 106, 114, 130, 151, 174, 176, 198, 206, 225, 230, 271, 272, 274, 299, 331–3, 378–80, 383, 391
China, 152, 160, 189, 190, 209–10,

213, 225–8, 238, 261, 290, 376, 429
Coburg, Saxe-, 61, 75, 84, 112, 218
Cologne, 31, 67, 80, 143
Colonies, 51–5, 184, 197, 204, 217, 271–2, 317, 338, 376; Portuguese, 217, 218, 238, 341; Spanish, 217
Committee of Imperial Defence, 247, 280, 316
Congo, Belgian, 183, 317, 374, 376; French, 313, 317
Conservative Party, German, 28, 31–2, 37, 70, 92, 106, 130, 171, 173, 176, 230, 270, 272–4, 290, 299, 331, 373, 391, 395, 399
Constantinople, 71, 104, 126, 183, 192, 200, 216
Constitution of German Empire, 1, 21–5, 61, 69, 70, 137, 154, 157, 175, 184, 185,·198, 199, 229, 273, 292–3, 301, 331, 333, 334, 354, 373, 383, 394, 395, 397, 430
Contemptibly Little Army, 327
Corfu, 256, 284, 309, 416–17
Councils, Crown, 5 July 1914 (supposed), 346; 29 July 1914, 348; 23 April 1917, 374; 9 July 1917, 378; 18 December 1917, 384; 2 July 1918, 391; 14 August 1918, 392
Courts Martial, 193, 198, 229, 403
Cowes, 81, 180, 181, 190, 195, 196, 197, 220–1
Crete, 199, 200, 210
Cronberg, 286, 289
Cruises, 122, 145, 147, 177, 243, 247, 254, 300, 305, 313, 346
Czechs, 26, 363

Daily Express, 251
Daily Mail, 209
Daily Telegraph, 227, 289–93, 296, 305, 310, 475
Damascus, 216–17, 469
Darmstadt, 181, 309
Delagoa Bay, 191, 193, 194, 217–18
Denmark, 1, 121, 125, 182, 197, 419
Dobrudja, 145, 363
Döberitz, 284–5
Dogger Bank, 158, 248, 365
Donaueschingen, 147, 290, 291
Doorn, 278, 414–20, 459

Dreadnought, 267, 279–81, 297–8, 301
Dual Alliance, see Franco-Russian Alliance

Easter Message 1917, 373, 377
Eastern Front, 361, 364, 368, 383–7, 390
Education, German, 15, 41, 76–7, 79, 174, 176, 184, 206
Egypt (and Sudan), 52, 53, 70, 71, 104, 183, 210, 213, 245, 251, 296, 376
Elbe, River, 2, 3, 5, 7, 17, 28, 29, 32, 171, 360
Elections, German, 447; (1860) 20, (1878) 29, (1884) 104, (1887) 105, (1890) 130, 132, (1893) 176, (1898) 269, (1903) 269, (1907) (Hottentot) 272, (1912) 332
Electors, 4, 6, 11
Elite, German, vi, 9, 17, 19, 20, 26, 33, 42, 160, 173, 186, 207, 228, 229, 273, 304, 362, 369, 373, 384, 394, 412, 426, 430, 432
Employers Associations, German, 32, 269, 373
Exports, 46, 48–9, 51, 204, 209, 228, 267, 442–4
Eÿsden, 411, 485

Fashoda, 213–16, 245
Fatherland Party, 384, 388
Federal Council, see *Bundesrat*
Fez, 310, 311, 312
Finance Bills, German, (1909) 298–300, (1912) 332, (1913) 332, 338
Foreign Office, German, 94, 127, 135, 142, 153, 154, 234, 289, 295, 296, 303, 304, 305, 306, 307, 312, 322, 326, 346, 348, 372, 403, 407, 483
Fourteen Points, 393, 396
France, 2, 4, 8, 9, 10, 11, 14, 15, 16, 18, 21, 25, 26, 27, 29, 30, 44, 47, 52, 54, 68, 70, 104, 106, 107, 108, 121, 128, 142, 160, 172, 182, 187, 214, 217, 218, 226, 288, 294, 306, 308, 339, 374
Franco-German relations, 232, 254, 261–3, 274, 304, 310–18, 328
Franco-Russian Alliance, 137, 172, 176, 183, 199, 215, 218, 236, 238–9, 241, 247, 249–50, 258, 260, 295, 307, 341, 353; relations, 136, 189, 309
Frankfurt, 18, 57, 121, 143
Frankfürter Zeitung, 356
Free Conservative Party, 32–3, 34

Galicia, 364, 368
Garter, Order of the, 80, 140, 231
Gedankensplitter, Kaiser's on Boer War, 223, 289
General Staff, German, 15, 90, 91, 127, 133, 134, 150, 153, 172, 223, 252, 269, 289, 338, 349, 353, 361, 389
Gibraltar, 53, 183, 255, 376
Greece, 125–6, 199, 200, 336, 363

Habsburg Empire, 6, 17, 288, 335, 343, 344, 363, 375, 432; family, 6, 10, 16, 17, 26, 152, 288
Hague Peace Conferences, 215–16, 277, 278–9, 426; Tribunal, 158
Hamburg, 152, 177, 199, 269, 312, 313, 319
Hanover, 16, 27, 69, 121, 134, 167, 213, 245, 342
Health (Kaiser's), 74, 104, 192, 245, 276, 297, 325, 358–9, 392, 394, 420
Heligoland, 53, 169, 360
Highcliffe, 278, 289
Holland, 10, 49, 261, 353, 405, 409, 410, 411, 413–15, 419, 420, 485
Hungary (see also Austria-Hungary and Habsburg Empire), 26, 107, 346–7, 363
Huns, 226–7

'*Inconscience*', 147, 306, 429
Independent Socialist Party, 330, 373, 382, 391, 395, 399, 401, 410
India, 259, 268–9, 281, 352, 390
Industrial Revolution, 8–9, 17, 23, 28, 33, 39–47, 91, 430
Insurance law, 33, 129
Investment, 8, 28, 39–40, 44–7, 52, 55, 444–6
Italy, 2, 4, 9, 10, 19, 44, 106, 108, 112, 118, 145, 155, 170, 171, 190, 262–3, 300, 328, 365, 374

Japan, 160, 189, 190, 228, 232, 233, 239, 246, 248, 249, 251, 260, 261, 266, 288, 290, 296, 328, 341, 376
Jerusalem, 56, 216, 469
Jews, 115, 156, 164, 216, 218, 274, 276, 277, 402; Anti-Semitism, 115, 164, 386, 419
Junkers, 11, 16, 20, 32, 61, 83, 106, 171, 187

Kassel, 79, 147, 277, 392
Kiao-Chou, 190, 209
Kiel, 87, 171, 197, 267, 312, 342, 347, 403; Canal, 77, 256, 280, 339; Regatta, 147, 152, 247
Kissingen, Bad, 312
Kladderadatsch, 179, 274
Köpenick, 270
Kreuznach, Bad, 356, 374, 376, 377, 379, 389
Kreuzzeitung, Die, 127
Kulturkampf, 27, 31, 70, 106

Landwehr, 15, 16, 20
Leipzig, 57, 140, 293
Liberalism, 18, 19, 21, 28, 33–6, 37, 42, 57, 61, 62, 67, 69, 91, 128, 187, 431
Liebenberg, 90, 262, 274
Lippe-Detmold, 147
Lombardverbot, 113, 133
Longwy-Briey, 363, 374, 381, 388

Madrid Convention 1880, 253
Manchuria, 233, 248
Marne, Battle of the, 327, 361, 363, 427
Mediterranean, 4, 10, 106, 108, 124, 145, 147, 182, 183, 247, 254, 256, 264, 284, 324
Merchandise Marks Act 1887, 50
Meteor (Yacht), 180, 182, 221, 342
Mexico, 52, 151, 310
Middle classes, 8–9, 10, 11, 17, 18, 35, 40, 70, 207, 229, 332, 431, 433
Mitteleuropa, 338, 363
Mobilization, 337, 349–53
Montenegro, 146, 314
Morocco, 232, 238, 245, 246, 249, 253, 254, 256–7, 261–3, 274, 275, 295, 310–18, 319, 432 (see also Agadir, Algeçiras, Fez and Tangier)

Munich, 157, 178, 275, 402, 403
Mutinies, 382, 403, 410, 415

National Liberal Party, 28, 33–6, 48, 92, 106, 127, 130, 174, 184, 230, 272, 299, 331–2, 378, 380, 383, 388, 391, 395
National Review, 266
Naval Affairs, 34, 43, 124, 134, 151, 182, 192, 197–8, 203–9, 224–5, 246, 250–2, 256, 267, 279–84, 285–6, 290, 297–8, 300–1, 306–7, 315, 319–30, 433, 475 (see also *Dreadnought*, Risk Theory, Two-Power Standard)
Naval War, 360–1, 365–8, 403, 428 (see also Submarine Warfare)
Navy Bills, (1897) 206, 208; (1900) 224–5, 301; (1904) 252; (1907) 279; (1911) 319–25
Navy Leagues, British, 298; German, 206, 224, 252, 272, 279, 281, 341, 373
New Course, 132, 169, 173, 186
New York Herald, 118
New York World, 296
Nibelungs, 143, 295
'Noodles', 233, 241
Norddeutsche Rundschau, 115
Norway, 147, 177, 243, 305, 313, 346, 391

Osborne, 77n, 81, 124, 180, 190, 230

Pan-Germans, 165, 169, 206, 218, 303, 310, 340, 341, 370, 373, 377
Pan-Slavs, 103, 288, 339, 344, 345
Paris, 80, 97–8, 113, 140, 144–5, 163, 171, 244, 256, 287, 304, 309, 313, 337, 339, 351, 414, 419
Patents, 268
Peace Offers, (1916) 370–1; (1917) 381–2
Peace Resolution of *Reichstag*, 378–9, 381, 388, 398
Persia, 250, 259, 309
Poles, 16, 26, 27, 32, 173, 184, 272, 299, 311, 363, 371, 374, 378, 385, 396
Politics, German View of, 13, 15–16, 34–5, 48
Pope, see Vatican

Port Arthur, 210

Portugal, 102, 217–18, 220, 238, 376 (see also Colonies)

Post, Der, 317

Potsdam, 14, 58, 75, 82, 89, 140, 326, 343, 346, 348, 414

Press Relations, 27, 115, 150, 167, 186, 199, 213, 226, 234, 235, 251, 264, 274–5, 430

Prices, 28, 29, 45, 69, 268, 441, 443

Progressive Party, 34, 36–7, 70, 106, 159, 184, 199, 272–4, 299, 331–2, 378, 379, 383

Protestants, 9, 21, 27, 79, 91, 114, 125, 216–17, 274, 431

Prussia, characteristics, 12, 35, 76, 82, 393–4, 429, 431; constitution, 22, 24, 29, 34, 67, 193, 373; decree of 1852, 131; franchise, 22, 29, 176, 273, 330, 373, 377, 378, 381, 382; history, 5, 11–22; Minister President, 22, 24, 175, 185, 373; Parliament, 269, 273, 304, 330, 378

Reichstag, 21–5, 28, 37, 38, 53, 88, 90, 91, 104, 105, 106, 113, 130, 132, 151, 159, 171, 174, 175, 176, 177, 184, 185, 186, 188, 193, 197, 198, 199, 200, 201, 205, 206, 219, 225, 228, 229, 230, 235, 247, 251, 263, 269, 271, 272, 273, 276, 280, 281, 286, 290, 291, 299, 300, 304, 305, 306, 317, 319, 322, 326, 331, 332, 333, 335, 355, 359, 363, 369, 373, 377, 378, 379, 381, 382, 383, 388, 389, 391, 392, 394, 395, 398, 399, 409, 429

Reinsurance Treaty, 107–8, 131, 135–7, 171, 178, 237, 432

Religion, Kaiser's Views on, 164, 258

Resignations, Ministerial, 175, 183–4, 259–60, 290, 300, 319, 399

Reval, 243, 284, 286

Rhine, Rhineland, 2, 3, 16, 37, 358, 402, 417

'Risk Theory', 205, 251, 319, 327, 328

Rome, 2, 125, 195, 244, 264, 279 (see also Vatican)

Russia, 16, 28, 29, 30, 44, 47, 70, 71, 99, 100, 103, 104, 107, 108, 112, 113, 142, 158, 160, 165, 170, 172, 197, 215, 217, 218, 232, 233, 241, 268, 286–9, 306, 327, 328, 335, 376, 427

Russian Revolution, (1905) 270; (1917) 372, 375, 383, 387

Russo-German Relations, 30, 99, 107, 116, 117, 126, 127, 131, 135–6, 182, 189, 192, 210, 212, 224, 248, 257–60, 264, 293–6, 309, 340–1, 345. Proposed Treaty 1904–5, 249–50, 257–60, (see also Brest-Litovsk, Reinsurance Treaty, Three Emperors' League, Ukraine)

Russo-Japanese War, 233, 239, 246, 248, 253, 257, 279

Saint Petersburg (from 1914 Petrograd), 30, 103, 122, 125, 133, 135, 136, 192, 194, 210, 215, 224, 249, 294, 337, 339, 341, 347, 350, 351, 352, 372, 373, 375, 383

Samoa, 52, 217, 219–21

Sandringham, 98, 101, 152

San Remo, 109, 111, 114, 116, 119

Sarajevo, 342–4

Saturday Review, 208

Saxony, 2, 16, 21, 22, 188, 207, 269, 393

Schleswig-Holstein, 68, 69, 86, 256

'Scrap of Paper', 352

Secretariats, Imperial (*Kabinette*), 151; Civil, 151, 152, 153, 291, 309, 357; Military, 90, 153, 154, 193, 198, 290, 357; Naval, 153, 197, 342, 357, 360, 374

Serbia, 26, 103, 288–9, 293–5, 327, 335–7, 339, 343–50, 363, 365

Shimonoseki, Treaty of, 189

Silesia, 5, 17, 37, 335

Skagerrak (Jutland), Battle of, 367

Social Affairs, German, 26, 32–3, 41–2, 92, 114, 128–30, 172–3, 202, 229, 269–71, 273, 331–2, 334–5

Social Democratic Party (SPD), Socialists, 28, 34, 37, 38, 48, 130, 159, 171, 176, 198, 199, 227, 230, 269–70, 272, 276, 299, 304, 310, 330–32, 334, 359, 373, 377, 378, 379, 382, 384, 389, 394, 395, 400, 401, 404, 407, 409, 410

Spa, 356, 389, 391, 402–6, 409–11
Spain, 2, 10, 53, 183, 221, 262, 376
  (see also Colonies)
Speeches, Kaiser's, 80, 114, 154,
  155, 156, 157, 158, 159, 162, 164–
  5, 177, 185, 206, 210, 217, 225,
  226, 254, 285, 290, 380, 464, 470
State-Secretaries, 22, 153, 197, 198
Stock Exchanges, 145, 152, 191,
  267, 273, 316, 372
Straits, 104, 192, 287, 341 (see also
  Bosphorus)
Strikes, German, (1889) 129, (1905)
  269, (1912) 332, (1913) 333,
  (1917) 373, 375, (1918) 407
Submarine Warfare, 280, 360, 366,
  369–72, 375, 376, 397, 427, 483
Suez Canal, 28, 79, 109
Swabians, 2, 15, 271, 305, 402, 404
Sweden, 49, 125, 372, 376, 419
Swinemünde, 147, 243, 297

Tangier, 253–5, 381
Tannenberg, Battle of, 361, 385,
  419
Tariffs, 28–9, 34, 81, 170, 187, 209
Telegrams, 132, 145, 147, 194–5,
  198, 200, 208, 211, 221, 243, 297,
  332, 333, 399, 409, 420, 467
Three Emperors' League, 99, 107,
  171
Times, The, 47, 48, 61, 209, 234,
  236, 281, 283, 290
Trade Competition (Anglo–Ger-
  man), 45, 47, 48–51, 208, 267,
  442–4
Trade Treaties, 170, 208–9, 269
Trade Unions, German, 92, 269,
  373, 375
Trafalgar, 182, 223, 352, 367
Train, Imperial, 125, 231, 356
Transvaal, 191, 193–4 (see also
  Boer Republic)
Triple Alliance, 106, 171, 183, 190,
  192, 218, 233, 234, 236, 238, 337,
  344, 351, 353
Tshushima, Battle of, 257
Turkey, 103, 113, 126, 190, 199,
  200, 217, 251, 268, 286, 287, 294,
  300, 335–6, 340, 352, 365
Two-Power Standard, 205, 279,
  301, 319, 320, 327

Ukraine, 374, 387, 390, 400
United States, 51, 52, 151, 160,
  165, 193, 216, 219, 221, 232, 244,
  257, 260, 265, 279, 296, 328, 339,
  341, 359, 366, 369–72, 374, 377,
  390, 397, 399, 400, 414, 418, 426,
  428, 429

Vatican, 4, 27, 88, 106, 164, 187,
  244, 382, 389
Venezuela, 193, 196, 244
Verdun, 3, 368
Vienna, 16, 121, 124, 125, 177, 178,
  216, 274, 287, 288, 293, 294, 335,
  336, 337, 340, 343, 344, 346, 347,
  348, 349, 350, 376
Visits to Britain, Kaiser's, (1861)
  75; (1863) 75; (1877) 81; (1880)
  86, 98; (1887) 108; (1889) 124,
  180; (1890) 180; (1891) 180;
  (1892) 181; (1893) 181–2; (1895)
  190; (1899) 221–2; (1901) 140,
  230–2; (1907) 269, 276, 310;
  (1910) 276, 307–8; (1911) 312

Waterloo, 25, 245, 342, 390
Western Front, 361, 364, 368, 375,
  387–8, 389–93, 395
White Hall of Berlin Castle, 88,
  355, 411
Windsor, 88, 101, 119, 222, 269,
  276, 277, 278, 308, 310
Wurtemburg, (*Württemberg*), 16,
  21, 207, 293, 410 (see also
  Swabians)

Yellow Peril, 143, 165, 189, 226,
  241, 248, 260, 328

Zabern incident, 333
Zanzibar, 52, 54, 169, 183
Zionism, 90, 216
Zollverein, 17, 47, 208
Zukunft, Die, 274–5

Afterword

Fortunate is the historical writer who does not begin to think of omissions and to discover mistakes from the moment that his final proofs are gone beyond recall. Fortunate too the writer who does not, by the mere act of publication, appear to release an avalanche of fresh material which would have made his own humble production into a far far better thing! As I have not been immune from either occupational hazard, I must console myself with the reflection that nothing has led me to revise substantially any of the major judgements which I reached ten years ago.

I have however taken the opportunity of the present edition to remove a number of factual mistakes, misprints and infelicities of expression. I have also found better figures for some of the tables in Appendix I.

If I were writing the book afresh today, on the basis of such reading as I have managed to do since it first came out, I think my main changes would be as follows:

1. In Chapter I I would make more of the economic aspects of German unification, as emphasized by Professor H. Boehme in his *Deutschlands Weg zur Grossmacht* (1966). I did not sufficiently bring out Prussia's role as a granary of Europe and hence the interest of the Prussian landowners in free trade up to that moment in the 1870's when cheap grain from overseas took away their markets in Europe and threatened those at home. In alliance with the commercial interests, they committed Prussia to a low-tariff policy connected with Western rather than Central Europe. It was only after that policy had helped to produce a German Empire from which Austria was excluded that they turned to protection, and to an alliance with the industrialists who had

wanted it all along. This has caused the year 1879 to be described as "Bismarck's Second Founding of the Reich". For the remaining thirty-nine years of its existence, it was based not on blood and iron nor on coal and iron so much as on rye and iron.

2. I would considerably extend Chapter II, which I all along felt to be inadequate, in the light of the extensive discussion of Imperialism which in recent years has been one of the growth industries of the historical world. I would particularly bring out the effects of the 'Great Depression', as described by Professor H.U. Wehler in his book *Bismarck und der Imperialismus* (1969)—though I wonder whether German economic historians may not be tending to overemphasize the Depression just at the moment when British ones are beginning to play it down. There is however no doubt that, rightily or wrongly, German businessmen (and to some extent German statesmen) were led to think that they must seek abroad the growth which was at home failing to sustain the phenomenal rate of the years 1850–73. I would also be bolder in suggesting that, by comparison with Germany, Britain was probably investing too little altogether and certainly placing too much of that investment abroad.

3. In Chapter III I would have been happy to draw on the correspondence between Queen Victoria and the Crown Princess Frederick which Mr. Roger Fulford has given us in *Dearest Child* (1964), *Dearest Mama* (1968) and *Your Dear Letter* (1971). There is also material which I would have liked to use in Mrs. Daphne Bennett's biography *Vicky, Princess Royal of England and German Empress* (1971), particularly with regard to the Kaiser's birth.

4. Although I was criticised by one reviewer for failing to heed Ranke's view that Germany's internal polity and policies were dictated by her external position, I was in this only moving with the tide of German historical thought, as exemplified by the republication in 1965 of Eckart Kehr's pre-1933 essays *Das Primat der Innenpolitik*. I would now lay even greater emphasis on the deliberate adoption of a chauvinist foreign policy, as a means of winning popular support for the

regime and so reducing pressure for a redistribution of political power (somewhat as Bismarck had done in 1863–6).

5. I would considerably amend Chapter VII in the light of Dr. J.C.G. Röhl's *Germany Without Bismarck* (1967) so as to bring out more strongly the significance of the Ministerial changes in 1897. Since Bismarck's resignation, politics had been dominated by the question whether the final power of decision in the Reich was to be put as it were into commission and exercised by a group of which the Emperor was only a member, or whether the Emperor was entitled to choose Ministers who could be relied on to act as his tools. For seven years the first method was tried without much success; in 1897 it was replaced by the second. For the next twelve years the Kaiser and Bülow sought to maintain the rye-and-iron status quo and collect a majority prepared to back it in the *Reichstag*, distracting attention by an active foreign policy which seemed to suggest that Germany was at risk in the world and could not afford the luxury of a government responsible to the electorate rather than to the Kaiser. Even after the Daily Telegraph incident and the replacement of Bülow by Bethmann, there was no real change of policy though rather more deference was paid to public opinion.

But, as I indicated in the *Historical Journal* (1969 No 1), I do not see how under the Constitution devised by Bismarck, Ministers could prevent the Kaiser from having his way when he wanted to do so, at any rate without precipitating a major constitutional crisis. Nor do I consider that the Kaiser really did run the country. He was much too inconstant, both in his aims and in his efforts to reach them, to do anything of the sort. The system could work with a determined, competent and assiduous ruler directing pliable Ministers or with an unassertive ruler who gave a free hand to a determined, competent and assiduous Chancellor. In the hands of an inconstant but assertive ruler and pliable Ministers, it led to disaster.

6. Working on scanty evidence, I strongly suspected that Tirpitz had from the outset been scheming to challenge

Britain but could not see how he managed to persuade himself that such a scheme stood any chance of success. Now, in the light of Dr. Jonathan Steinberg's *Yesterday's Deterrent* (1965) and Dr. Volker Berghahn's *Der Tirpitz Plan* (1971), I would be much more definite. Dr. Berghahn in particular has shown that Tirpitz saw Britain's Achilles heel in lack of trained manpower even more than in lack of finance. But he has also shown that the naval policy was all of a piece with the internal policy described in previous paragraphs. In the long term Tirpitz planned to leave to the *Reichstag* as little influence over naval policy as it already possessed over military and foreign policy. In the short term, however, since there seemed little chance of succeeding in an open challenge, he had to devise a programme which the *Reichstag* would be willing to finance. The obsequiousness of the deputies found its limit when taxes began to make real holes in their pockets. Thus it was the coming of the much more expensive all-big gun ship (of which Britain's 'Dreadnought' was the first) which played havoc with the programme by raising its cost to a level for which there was little chance of finance being forthcoming.

7. At a number of points, I would adjust my account of Anglo-German and Anglo-French negotiations to take account of such books as Dr. G.W. Monger's *The End of Isolation* (1963), Professor J.W. Grenville's *Lord Salisbury and Foreign Policy* (1964), Dr. C. Andrew's *Theophile Delcassé and the Making of the Entente Cordiale* (1968), Dr. S.R. Williamson's *The Politics of Grand Strategy* (1969) and Dr. Z.S. Steiner's *The Foreign Office and Foreign Policy* (1970). I would want to bring out more strongly the deep suspicion of Germany's intentions which from about 1902 onwards filled a number of Englishmen in high places (though not King Edward to the extent popularly supposed), their fear that some French Ministers might make a deal with Germany at Britain's expense, and their anxiety to prevent any British action which might provide an excuse for such a deal. Skilful French diplomacy may have lured Britain into a position which her public failed to suspect but there were plenty of people in the country who knew quite well what

was going on and did all they could to help. The propriety of their conduct would be open to serious question were it not for what has come to light about the aims of Tirpitz.

8. The study of many books and articles about the outbreak of war, and in particular of Professor Fritz Fischer's *Der Krieg der Illusionen* (1969; American edition *The War of Illusions*, 1973, Norton) make me anxious to enlarge in the following respects the account given in Chapters X and XIII.

(a) Ideas about what happened in 1914 must not be influenced by knowledge of what happened afterwards. The German military and civilian leaders were not thinking in terms of 1918 and 1940 so much as of 1866 and 1870; the last thing which most of them reckoned with was a long war. They were in fact gambling on being able to secure a quick and relatively bloodless victory over France. (In my book on *West Germany* (1968) I described the 1914–18 struggle as 'The War of the Three Gambles'.)

(b) In this calculation, the behaviour of Britain would not be of decisive importance.

(c) Motivating the gamble was a belief that war—at any rate with France and Russia—was inevitable sooner or later. The German leaders considered—almost certainly correctly—that their chances of victory would be better in 1914 than later. This made it in their interest to force the issue in that year, which almost inevitably meant taking the offensive.

(d) To have let slip the opportunity for war offered by the Sarajevo murders would, as they thought, have meant accepting a choice between being compelled to offer forcible resistance to the actions of the Triple Entente at a later date with smaller chances of success or alternatively of acquiescing in those policies in all circumstances. To do the latter would, in their view, have been equivalent to allowing Germany to cease to count as a Great Power, and this they were determined to avoid.

(e) Other countries as well as Germany could have averted the outbreak of war in 1914 by adopting different courses of action. But they in turn considered that they might as a result be deserted by their allies and thereafter face a choice between resisting Germany on their own and accepting German policies. Their position was thus the converse of the German one.

(f) What was at issue in the years leading up to 1914 was a difference of view about the relative position in the world to which Germany was entitled (or, in other words, would be able to secure if she resorted to force). The German leaders—and many of the German people—assumed that the resources which they had come to command in the course of the nineteenth century entitled them to a larger say in world affairs than other countries were willing to allow them. Some of these countries not merely believed that Germany could only secure that larger say at their expense but judged that, provided they acted together, their chances of resisting such an attempt to diminish their influence were good. In other words, they disputed the German estimate of relative power—and events proved them right.

(g) This analysis is not altered by saying that Germany was not claiming predominance but only equality of status. For whatever she was claiming, it was something which she had not got and therefore something which appeared to involve a loss on the part of other countries. And since status is not capable of exact definition or measurement, a position which a claimant considers to be equality may in the eyes of possessors amount to predominance.

(h) It is hard to see—certainly in terms of 19th century political concepts—how this difference of view could have been resolved except by the test of physical force.

(i) Seen from this angle, the question of what national aims were adopted by which German leaders at what date seems relatively unimportant. Such aims were merely a form of expressing the fundamental belief that Germany was entitled to more influence, or else were a means towards securing such influence. The existence of the belief itself cannot be seriously denied.

(j) A major task of historians is to establish how such an erroneous judgement about relative strength came to be adopted and used as a basis for national policy. Here the Kaiser's personality was clearly of great importance.

9. I have recently gone over the story of the Kaiser's abdication and tried to clear up minor problems of chronology and topography. The result was published by Messrs. Purnell in Volume 7 Number 16 of their "History of the First World War."

10. I would have liked to enlarge slightly my account of the Kaiser's later years by drawing on the recently published diaries of his last adjutant Captain von Ilseman (*Der Kaiser in Holland* 1967 and 1969). The chief conclusion to be drawn is that he remained the same intelligent, impetuous and inconstant evader of reality down to the end.

M. L. G. B.